SERVICE OPERATIONS
MANAGEMENT

Fourth Edition

SERVICE OPERATIONS MANAGEMENT

Improving Service Delivery

Robert Johnston
Graham Clark and
Michael Shulver

PEARSON

Harlow, England • London • New York • Boston • San Francisco • Toronto • Sydney • Auckland • Singapore • Hong Kong
Tokyo • Seoul • Taipei • New Delhi • Cape Town • São Paulo • Mexico City • Madrid • Amsterdam • Munich • Paris • Milan

Pearson Education Limited
Edinburgh Gate
Harlow
Essex CM20 2JE
England

and Associated Companies throughout the world

Visit us on the World Wide Web at:
www.pearson.com/uk

First published 2001
Fourth edition published 2012

© Pearson Education Limited 2012

ISBN 978-0-273-74048-3

British Library Cataloguing-in-Publication Data
A catalogue record for this book is available from the British Library

Library of Congress Cataloguing-in-Publication Data
A catalog record for this book is available from the Library of Congress

ARP impression 98

Typeset in 10/12pt Minion by 73
Printed and bound by Ashford Colour Press Ltd

Contents

Part 4   Deliver   161

Part 5   Improve   319

Part 6   Implement   387

Supporting resources for lecturers

Please visit **www.servops.net** to find valuable online resources. These include:

- A downloadable Instructor's Manual
- PowerPoint and Keynote slides that can be downloaded and used for classroom presentations
- Instructional video screencasts by the author team showing you how we approach the subjects in our own teaching
- Lesson plans
- Opportunities to network, share ideas and provide feedback
- …and much, much more.

Preface

Introduction

This book is about how to manage and improve the operations in service organisations. Service operations are *important*. They are the parts of the organisation that create and deliver service to customers. The service could be that delivered to customers inside an organisation, such as staff in other functions, or the service provided by public sector organisations, voluntary organisations, mass transport services, professional services, business-to-business services, retailers, internet services, tourism and hospitality, for example. In this book we do not focus on any particular type of service but seek to cover the many decisions faced by operations managers in all these organisations. To illustrate this diversity we have provided examples from many different organisations and from many countries, including Australia, Denmark, France, Hong Kong, India, Japan, Malaysia, the Maldives, New Zealand, Singapore, Sweden, Thailand, the United Arab Emirates, the UK and the USA.

Service operations management is important. Operations managers are usually responsible for most of the costs in an organisation, and for most of the revenues, and they manage most of the people and physical assets. Operations managers deliver the 'profit'. In this book we refer to many aspects of 'business performance', not simply profit. Although many organisations are motivated by profit, most operations are also assessed on criteria such as costs, revenues, adherence to budgets, customer loyalty and technological leadership.

Service operations management is also very *challenging*. We have captured many of the challenges that operations managers face every day and the book is structured around how to deal with those challenges. Managing operations is also *exciting*. Operations deal with customers, often in real time, so part of the excitement comes from the immediacy of operations; dealing with the needs of a stream of customers, managing the staff and making operational decisions to ensure the delivery of an appropriate quality of service at an appropriate cost.

The aim of this book

The aim of this book is to provide a clear, authoritative, well-structured, easy to read and interesting treatment of service operations management. Our objective in writing this book is to help students and managers understand how service performance can be improved by studying service delivery and associated management issues. Service delivery is the focus of this book, yet we recognise that success depends not only on the obvious territory of operations in managing processes and resources, but also in understanding how operations managers must be involved in aspects of the organisation's strategy, organisational culture, and the way employees and customers are motivated and managed. How well a service is delivered reflects the ability of the organisation to pull all these strands together. The result should be a service which meets the demands of its various stakeholders, including an appropriate and achievable level of service for customers, delivery of the required operational and financial targets and implementation of the organisation's strategy.

Who should read this book?

This book is intended as a textbook for those who want to build on knowledge of the basic principles of operations management. It will also serve as a handbook for operations managers in service organisations as they seek to develop and implement operations strategies. Specifically it is intended for:

- *Undergraduates* on business studies or joint studies degrees or those specialising in hospitality, tourism or the public sector, for example, who wish to enhance their understanding of service operations management.

- *MBA students* who are managing service organisations and want to stretch their understanding of the area and assess and improve their operations.

- *Executives* who want to focus on certain aspects of service delivery, such as the customer experience, process design, capacity management, improvement, creating high-performance teams, performance measurement, world-class service or service strategy development, for example, in order to challenge and change their own organisations.

Distinctive features

- *Operations focused.* This text has a clear operations focus and is concerned with managing operations. It explores operational issues, problems and decisions. It exposes undergraduates to the problems faced by service operations managers and helps practising managers deal with those issues. Each of the main chapters addresses how to deal with a particular problem or challenge.

- *Frameworks and tools.* Each chapter provides tools, frameworks and techniques that will help students and managers not only analyse existing operations but also understand better how they can deal with the issues that operations managers face. The frameworks, approaches and techniques will vary from topic to topic and will include, for example:
  - a list of key points to bear in mind when making decisions in a particular area
  - a diagram or chart showing the relationship between two variables or sets of variables to help position an operation or help identify the nature of the relationships
  - a list of questions, checks or tests that can be applied to a situation
  - ways of quantifying or assessing qualitative variables
  - the key stages in undertaking a particular activity.

- *Real world illustrations.* Operations management is an applied subject so each chapter includes a number of short illustrations, case examples, from around the world that show how organisations have either identified or dealt with the particular issues being discussed.

- *International.* The real world illustrations – examples in the text, case examples and case exercises – are drawn from many countries to show the diversity and international nature of operations issues and activities. The Case Examples are listed on pages xvii−xviii.

- *Underpinned by theory.* Appropriate theoretical underpinning and developments are included and we have tried to explain them in an unobtrusive and accessible way. References, web links and suggestions for further reading are provided for anyone wishing to undertake more work in a particular area.

- *Managing people.* A key task for operations managers is managing people and so this book contains a significant 'managing people' element. This includes not only employees but also customers, as well as managing and changing the culture of the organisation as a whole.

- *E-service.* Information technology, e-service and virtual operations are integrated into the book and their operational implications explored.

- *State of the art.* The book contains some of the most recent ideas and information, covering in particular world-class service, performance management, service concept, the customer experience and service processes.

- *Summaries.* Each chapter includes a bullet-point checklist summarising key points, structured using the questions at the start of the chapter.

- *Web links.* We have provided some web links at the end of each chapter which will provide further information about the subject material or suggest some service organisations that are demonstrating interesting service operations approaches.

- *Questions for managers.* At the end of each chapter there are some questions aimed at practising managers, which they can ask of their/an operation. We hope that these questions will encourage you to apply the material in the chapter to your situation and allow you to understand better, challenge and improve your service operations.

- *Discussion questions and further reading.* We have also provided some general discussion questions, aimed at undergraduates, to help them both assess and apply the material to a variety of situations. There are also some suggestions for further reading.

- *Case exercises.* Each chapter, with the exception of the first chapter, concludes with a case exercise suitable for class discussion. The cases are short but focused on the topic and are a rich source of material for debate and development.

- *Instructor's manual.* An instructor's manual is available to lecturers adopting this textbook. It can be downloaded from www.servops.net and provides detailed questions to go with the cases and bullet-point answers to the questions.

- *Servops.net* is the instructor's companion website for our textbook. Besides the instructor's manual it provides a range of presentations in PowerPoint and Keynote formats to suit a range of teaching styles, experience and time constraints. The site also makes available a series of video screencasts in which the authors explain their approach to teaching each topic. Servops.net also gives instructors a series of lesson plans and handout designs.

Feedback and ideas

We would welcome feedback and suggestions to help us develop our textbook. In particular we would like to know how you use the book, and if you have any suggestions for web links, readings or case examples, for example. Please do not hesitate to contact bob.johnston@wbs.ac.uk.

New features for this edition

We are delighted to welcome Dr Michael Shulver to the author team for this fourth edition of the book. Michael brings a wealth of teaching experience and has been instrumental in developing some of the chapters. More importantly Michael has taken the lead in developing the teaching materials which we know will be greatly appreciated by the lecturers.

The first edition of this textbook was published in 2001 and the subject of service operations management and service management has advanced in that time. As a result we have made quite a few changes to this edition. In particular we have taken the bold step of changing the chapter structure – our apologies in advance for those classes who are using the third edition at the same time. This has allowed us to expand the first chapter about service and services, providing some important and recently developed concepts and definitions. Importantly we have split the process chapter into two with one whole chapter now focusing on the customer experience. We have also provided a much clearer explanation of the structure in Chapter 2, which covers the challenges for operations managers. There are more things we want to do in future editions and we always appreciate and welcome feedback. Indeed, your suggestions have led to many of the changes we have made. In summary the changes have included:

- A new 17-chapter structure
- A practical focus on how to deal with the key issues and challenges facing service operations managers
- A new more helpful structure diagram summarising the 'how tos'
- Sharpened definitions of key terms and concepts
- A new chapter on the customer experience
- A new chapter on driving continuous improvement
- A new chapter on learning from other operations
- A new chapter on world-class service
- Several new case examples; others have been updated
- Six new end-of-chapter Case Exercises
- Updated web links
- Full colour pictures to illustrate the case examples
- A new look and format.

Case Examples

Authors' acknowledgements

Many people have helped us in the writing of this book. Academic colleagues from around the world have provided stimulation, encouragement and/or contributions, including important ideas and material, useful feedback, illustrations and case examples. We would like to express our gratitude to all of them. Practising managers from around the world have also been kind enough to provide some rich material about their activities and organisations; our grateful thanks to them.

We are particularly grateful to the book's reviewers over the various editions whose considerable efforts and expertise provided us with comments, ideas and suggestions, all of which have had a significant influence on the text. The reviewers included Par Ahlstrom, Chalmers University of Technology; Thomas Christiansen, Technical University of Denmark; Steven Disney, University of Cardiff; John Flanagan, University of Wollongong; Andrew Greasley, Aston University; Lesley Kimber, Southampton Business School; Geoffrey Plumb, Staffordshire University; Graham K. Rand, University of Lancaster; Frank Rowbotham, De Monfort University; Rhian Silvestro, Warwick Business School; Martin Spring, UMIST; Remko Van Hoek, Erasmus and Cranfield Universities; and Jan de Vries, the University of Groningen.

Our colleagues at Warwick and Cranfield have helped us greatly by not only providing ideas and encouragement but also creating the stimulating environment in which we work. We are particularly grateful to our secretaries, Mary Walton and Lyn Selby, whose efforts have kept us focused on the task and as organised as is possible.

We have greatly benefited from the guidance, encouragement and support of Rufus Curnow and the highly polished and professional team at Pearson Education.

It is appropriate also for us to thank all our students, both past and present. They have, over many years, been a source of great stimulation and development. Each one of them has had an influence on this book.

Finally we would like to thank our partners, Shirley, Dawn and Helen for allowing us to dedicate a significant amount of our time to this project. They have been our major source of encouragement; without their support, and also their direct involvement in the book, we would never have completed this task.

Bob Johnston, Graham Clark and Michael Shulver

Publisher's acknowledgements

We are grateful to the following for permission to reproduce copyright material:

Figures

Figure 4.5 from SHAPE International, www.shape-international.com; Figure 4.6 adapted from *Relationship Marketing for Competitive Advantage*, Butterworth Heinemann (Payne, A., Christopher, M., Clark, M., Peck, H. 2000); Figure 6.4 adapted from *Customer Service and Support*, Pearson Education (Armistead, C.G., Clark, G.R. 1992); Figure 6.7 from *Strategic Global Manufacturing Management: A Study of the Process and Current Practices*, Cranfield School of Management Report (Sweeney, M.T. and Dr M.Q. Szwejczewski 2002); Figure 15.5 adapted from *Operations Management*, 6 ed, FT Prentice Hall (Slack, N., Chambers, S., Johnston R. 2010); Figure 16.1 adapted from *Organisational Culture and Leadership*, 3 ed, John Wiley & Sons, Inc (Schein, E.H. 2004)

Tables

Table 15.1 adapted from *Operations Management*, 6 ed, Pearson Education (Slack, N., Chambers, S., Johnston, R. 2010); Table 15.2 adapted from *Operations Management*, 6ed, Pearson (Chambers, N.S., Johnston, R. 2010)

Text

Case Example 4.1 adapted from Sara Sheppard, ITSMA, Europe

Photographs

Alamy Images: Chuck Pefley 139, David Bagnall 163, David Levenson 353, Portus Imaging 335; **Andy Maluche/Photographers Direct:** 57; **Aspectra/Maurine Traffic:** 93; **BT Image Library:** 213; **Cathay Pacific:** 27; **Graham Clark:** 202, 269, xxi; **Corbis:** Chris Gasgoigne 361, Jonathan Drake / epa 9; **First Direct:** 271, 420; **Fotolia.com:** Wingnut Designs 322; **Helen Jones:** 33; **Image courtesy of The Advertising Archives:** 236, 448; **Getty Images:** 374, AFP 181, 409; **iStockphoto:** Eimantas Buzas 394, istrejman 85, Sheryl Griffin 138; **James Davies:** 309, 349; **Bob Johnston:** 13, 47, 55, 135, 168, 284, 401, 438, xxi; **National Grid:** 88; **Natural History Museum Picture Library:** 59; **Northwards Housing:** 146; **Pearson Education Ltd:** Andy Myatt / Alamy 73, Corbis 426, Corbis / BrandX 298, David R. Frazier Photolibrary, Inc. Alamy 333, Image State / John Foxx Collection 359, Imagestate / John Foxx Collection 170, Imagestate / John Foxx Collections 10, Jon Barlow 133, Jules Selmes 24, 251, Naki Kouyioumtzis 60, Photodisc / David Buffington 210, Studio 8 260, Thinkstock / Alamy 71; **RAC:** 233; **Michael Shulver:** 287, xxii; **Shutterstock.com:** Adriano Castelli 81, Laurence Gough 380, Stuart Jenner 327; **Singapore Airlines:** 002 442, 121; **Soumik Kar:** 144; **Southwest airlines:** 23; © 2010 TNT N.V.: 436; **TNT Dubai:** 118; **Zane's Cycles:** 355

In some instances we have been unable to trace the owners of copyright material, and we would appreciate any information that would enable us to do so.

About the authors

Robert (Bob) Johnston is Professor of Operations Management at Warwick Business School. He has a management degree from the University of Aston and a PhD from the University of Warwick. Before moving to academia Bob held several line management and senior management posts in a number of service organisations in both the public and private sectors. He continues to maintain close and active links with many large and small organisations through his research, management training and consultancy activities. Bob teaches both undergraduate and postgraduate courses and has global experience in executive education with leading companies. Bob's research interests include service transformation, service excellence and leadership, service recovery, complaint management, performance management, service design and service strategy. He has published around 150 papers, books and chapters, and has written over 100 case studies. Bob has served as Deputy Dean of the Business School, the Academic Director of the Warwick MBA and Head of the Operations Management Group. He serves on the editorial boards of ten leading journals. He is a member of several international advisory boards, an Honorary Fellow of the European Operations Management Association and a Vice President of the Institute of Customer Service.

Graham Clark is Senior Lecturer in Operations Management at Cranfield School of Management and Director of the Executive MBA Programme. He has a degree in mechanical engineering from Leeds University and a master's degree in management from Imperial College, London University. Prior to moving to Cranfield in 1986, Graham managed both manufacturing and customer support operations for companies in the engineering sector. His focus is on the development and implementation of operations strategies, with a specific interest in the leadership of service employees through operational transitions. Graham teaches across Cranfield's MBA and executive education programmes, and is engaged in management development and consultancy activities with organisations from all sectors. He also leads the 'Implementing Change' theme on the MBA programme and tutors' personal development programmes. He is a non-executive director of the Institute of Customer Service and a member of the leadership team of the UK chapter of the Association for Service Management.

Michael Shulver is a Senior Teaching Fellow in the Operations Management Group at Warwick Business School where he is the Academic Director of the School's BSc in Management. Michael has an astrophysics degree from the University of London, and MBA and PhD degrees from the University of Warwick. Before his time in academia Michael was an aircraft engineer, and he actively retains his Chartered Engineer status. Michael also took a two-year sabbatical as a consultant in performance management in 2005/6. In this role Michael worked with the UN, Syngenta and BP. Michael's teaching portfolio covers mainstream Operations Management, Service Management, Performance Management and Service Sector Innovation / Design Management. Michael has delivered lectures and workshops in these fields at Executive, MBA and undergraduate levels at Warwick Business School and has taught as a visiting lecturer for Stockholm School of Economics, Vlerick Gent Management School, Templeton College, Oxford and the UBS Business University. Michael is an innovator in games and simulations for management education and research, and in pedagogy as it relates to operations management teaching.

Part 1 Introduction

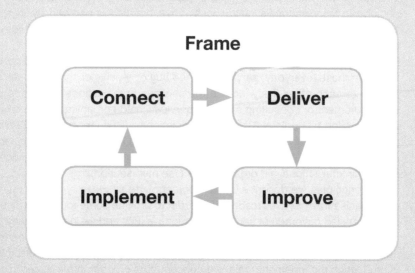

Chapter 1
Introducing service operations management

Chapter objectives

This chapter is about how to understand the role of service operations management and its contribution to organiational success.

- What are services?
- What is 'service'?
- What is service operations management?
- Why is service operations management important?

1.1 Introduction

We all come into contact with service operations and experience their services every single day. We are customers or users of a wide range of commercial and public services, such as childcare services, hospitals, shops, schools, holiday firms, restaurants, television and the internet. Furthermore, many of us are responsible for providing services not only as part of our jobs, in organisations such as those above, but also as part of daily life for our friends and families; providing cooking, cleaning and 'taxi' services, organising holidays and providing emotional support services for example.

It is important to note at the start of this book that service operations covers a far broader field than these 'everyday' services that we buy or receive or the 'personal' services that we provide to each other. They include the services organisations provide to each other such as procurement or consulting services; services inside organisations (internal services) such as information technology (IT) or human relations (HR) support; public services provided by governments (social services, police services or fire and rescue services); and the many and diverse services provided by not-for-profit and voluntary organisations such as faith organisations or international aid organisations (see next section).

The principles we describe in this book apply to all these types of organisations, indeed any organisation that uses resources in order to provide some form of service. In this book we give a detailed coverage of service operations issues and we provide many tools and frameworks that managers can use to understand, assess and improve the performance of their operations. While the development of operations management as a discipline has its roots in production management,[1] this text concentrates on operations issues in service organisations. However, many of the concepts are equally relevant to manufacturing organisations because all manufacturing companies provide services, such as after-sales service and customer training, and internal services such as HR or IT support.

Every single organisation is involved in service and so a knowledge and understanding of service operations management can make a real difference to their success. In this introductory chapter we want to explain its role in delivering organisational success. But first we will introduce some key concepts, starting with what we mean by services.

1.2 What are services?

Services come in many shapes and forms provided by a variety of types of organisations, including business-to-consumer (B2C) services, business-to-business (B2B) services, internal services, public services and not-for-profit and voluntary services.

Business-to-consumer services are services provided by organisations to individuals, examples being financial services (from banks and insurance providers), retail services (from supermarkets and clothes shops), travel services (airlines and bus companies), leisure services (cinemas and gyms), and hospitality services (restaurants and hotels). A subset of B2C services are those organisations which facilitate communication and service provision between customers (sometimes described as customer-to-customer or C2C services); examples are social networks such as Facebook, business networks such as LinkedIn, video-sharing sites such as YouTube, peer-to-peer games such as Farmville and Cafe World, and buying and selling sites such as eBay.

Business-to-business services are services provided between businesses and include consulting, office equipment provision and support, communications, corporate travel services, business insurance, finance and legal services.

Internal services are the many sorts of formal and informal services that people inside organisations provide to each other. The formal ones include internal services such as personnel, IT, HR, payroll or security services. Sometimes organisations subcontract or outsource such services so they become B2B services. Furthermore, almost everyone working in an organisation provides some form of service to other people in the organisation, such as writing reports, arranging meetings, taking part in discussions or providing information. These are informal internal services.

Public services (sometimes referred to as G2C – government-to-consumer) cover the wide range of services provided by local, regional and central governments to their citizens and communities. These include social housing, police, education, welfare and health services.

Not-for-profit and voluntary services include the services provided by non-governmental organisations (NGOs) such as aid organisations like Oxfam, Red Crescent and Médecins sans Frontières. Other not-for-profit and voluntary organisations include faith organisations, charities, trusts, the Scouting Association and the many small voluntary clubs and societies such as sports clubs and photographic societies.

Finally we cannot ignore the wide range of services that customers and users provide for themselves and each other. This includes the personal services we provide to each other, friendship and support services, catering and taxi services.

1.2.1 Customers

It is important to note that all these different organisations often use different terms for their customers. Public services provide services to citizens, the police service has victims and criminals, IT service providers talk about users, hotels have guests and radio stations have listeners. We use the word 'customer' to cover all of these individuals and communities to which organisations deliver service. We also use the word 'customer' to cover all the individuals and departments within organisations who provide each other service (internal customers) and also the external organisations with which they provide services. For example, the police work with social services and the courts to look after vulnerable children. While the child is the recipient, the other organisations need to provide service to each other to help the child.

We will develop the concept of customers further in Chapter 4.

What is 'service'?

It follows then that 'service' will mean different things depending on the type of service that is being provided. The service provided by your local bar or gym will be quite different to that provided by IBM to its business customers. When we talk to managers it is clear that the word 'service' conjures up many different images. For some it is synonymous with complaints or customer care, for others it is the equivalent of the logistics function, or internal services such as accounting or personnel. For others it means the 10,000-mile check-up to their car. The word 'service' is used to describe around 80 per cent of economic activity in developed nations; it includes the activities of all those organisations listed in the previous section. It is therefore perhaps not surprising that there is, as yet, no single, agreed and comprehensive definition of what a 'service' is.[2]

However, there are the beginnings of an emerging consensus.[3] While a product is a thing, a service is an activity – a process or a set of steps – which involves the treatment of a customer (or user) or something belonging to them, where the customer is also involved, and performs some role in the service process (also referred to as the service delivery process).[4] Defined as such, 'service' is much more than the point of staff–customer interaction – the service encounter, sometimes referred to as customer contact or the moment of truth.

We also find it helpful to consider service from two perspectives, the service provided from the operation's point of view and the service received from the customer's point of view (we will expand this idea into the 'service concept' in Chapter 3). Let us use the example of a hospital to illustrate this (see also Case Example 1.1).

1.3.1 Service – the operation's perspective

A hospital is a very complex service organisation that employs large numbers of staff (or employees – we use the terms interchangeably), from cleaners and porters to highly skilled surgeons. It will care for hundreds of patients each day, through many different specialist departments, each providing a range of treatments. Managing this type of service operation is extremely challenging, not only because they are dealing with life and death situations every hour, but also because of the complexity of the operation. The complexity is in part due to the volumes of patients and the wide range of treatments available, but also due to the fact that, like many service organisations, hospitals comprise many different service operations that must be coordinated and linked together in order to deliver healthcare to their customers. For the hospital, these include reception services, diagnostics, pharmacy, theatres (where operations *on* people are carried out), catering, portering, physiotherapy and so forth. In addition, there are the internal services such as information systems support, human resource services, training and finance.

Each of these service operations uses and manages many input resources, such as nurses, surgeons, drugs, equipment such as defibrillators, scanning and X-ray machines, and facilities such as wards, beds and theatres. One important input is also the customer – the patient who is getting the treatment or the internal member of staff who requires IT support or training services for example. Thus the hospital has many operations that 'process' customers whether they are patients or members of staff. These processes (activities) are the services they provide, such as reception services, diagnostic services, heart transplant surgery, intensive care

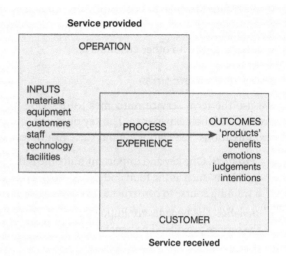

Figure 1.1 Service provided and received

treatment, or staff catering, IT support and training. The outputs of these processes are, hopefully, cured patients, fed staff and more knowledgeable operators, for example.

So from the operation's point of view, **the service provided** is the service process and its outputs which have been designed, created and enacted by the operation using its many input resources, including the customer, where the customer also takes some part in the service process. This involvement may be limited, in the case of pharmacy services for example, or significant, for diagnostic and surgical services for example. Services are therefore 'co-created' or 'co-produced' along with the customer (see Section 1.3.4). Thus the **service provided** occurs, or is enacted, where the operation and the customer meet as represented by the overlap in Figure 1.1.

1.3.2 Service – the customer's perspective

So while a service is the process or activity, from the customer's perspective, sometimes referred to as the customer-dominant logic perspective,[5] the **service received** is their *experience* of the service provided which results in *outcomes* such as 'products', benefits, emotions, judgements and intentions.

The customer experience

The customer experience is the customer's direct and personal interpretation of, and response to, their interaction with and participation in the service process, and its outputs, involving their journey through a series of touch points/steps. An experience is perceived purely from the point of view of an individual customer and is inherently personal, existing only in the customer's mind. Thus, no two people can have the same experience.[6]

Aspects of the customer experience include:

- the degree of personal interaction
- the responsiveness of the service organisation
- the flexibility of customer-facing staff
- customer intimacy
- the ease of access to service personnel or information systems

- the extent to which the customer feels valued by the organisation
- the courtesy and competence of customer-facing staff
- interactions with other customers.

The service outcomes

We use the term service outcomes to describe the results for the customer of the service process and their experience. The key outcomes are 'products', benefits, emotions, judgements and intentions (see Figure 1.1 and Case Example 1.1).

- *'Products'.* One key and important outcome is the 'functional' output of the service provided, 'products' such as the food and drink provided by a restaurant, or the ability of a delegate on a training course to construct a spreadsheet, or the new heart for the heart operation patient.
- *Benefits.* The benefits are important to the customer. This is why they have chosen or used the service provider. The benefits of a service are how the customer perceives they have 'profited' or gained from the service provided, their experience of it and the 'products' provided, i.e. how well their requirements and needs have been met. The patient who has undergone the heart operation will benefit from a longer and more active life. The benefits for students will be better job prospects or higher salaries and/or new capabilities and skills. The benefit of using a firm of consultants may be reduced costs and/or greater commercial success.
- *Emotions.* Experiencing a service results in the customer feeling emotions, of which there are many hundreds, including joy, surprise, love, fear, anger, shame and sadness (see Chapter 7). In a hospital the patient hopefully experiences a well-managed stay, where they feel at ease and assured throughout with minimal pain and inconvenience. A student at a university may have an enjoyable and challenging experience with some memorable lectures and seminars and exciting extra-curricular activities. A senior manager employing a firm of consultants will hopefully feel assured with increased confidence to pursue a particular strategy.[7]
- *Judgements.* Another outcome of the service from a customer's point of view will be their conscious or unconscious assessment of the service provided, their experience and the perceived benefits gained. This results in judgements about fairness (or equity), and, importantly, their perceived value of the service received. (Value (see Chapter 3) is the customer's assessment of the service provided, their experience and the benefits derived weighed against all the costs involved.) These assessments and feelings, conscious or unconscious, will then be rationalised into a feeling of satisfaction or dissatisfaction (an emotion) about the overall service (as well as individual elements of it) (see Chapter 5).[8]
- *Intentions.* These judgements, good, bad or indifferent, will result in intentions, such as the intention to repurchase or not (see Chapter 4), the intention to recommend to others, or the intention to complain or not. These intentions may or may not result in action.

It is important to note that in some cases some of these outcomes may be related and a customer's evaluation of one component may influence their perception of another. A superb learning experience may help the student better understand the material and thus benefit from greater knowledge and confidence. Sometimes they can be contradictory, for example a patient may feel annoyed or disappointed that the outcome of the operation was not a success (i.e. of no benefit for them) but be delighted (highly satisfied) with the way they were treated during their hospital stay (the experience).

The outcomes outlined above are from a customer perspective. There are also important outcomes from the organisation's perspective. Organisational outcomes will be concerned with meeting targets and objectives. A hospital may have clinical targets such as waiting times, number of operations carried out and recovery rates; operational targets such as theatre usage; and financial targets such as adherence to budgets (see Section 1.5). To be successful an operation has to meet both its desired customer outcomes and organisational outcomes. Service operations management plays a vital role in both of these.

Case Example 1.1	Singapore General Hospital

Singapore General Hospital (SGH) is the country's largest acute care tertiary hospital and national referral centre for specialities like haematology, orthopaedic surgery, plastic surgery, renal medicine, nuclear medicine and pathology. With almost 7,000 staff, from clinical and research directors to hospital attendants, covering over 30 clinical specialities the hospital has nearly a million patient encounters a year. Dedicated to providing multidisciplinary medical care and backed by state-of-the-art facilities, SGH offers team-based quality patient care widely acknowledged to be the best in the world. SGH is structured as a private limited company for flexibility of operations, but is a not-for-profit organisation owned by the Government of Singapore.

Source: Corbis/Jonathan Drake/epa

The hospital's mission is to deliver quality care to every patient through comprehensive integrated clinical practice, medical innovation and lifelong learning. It has three pillars supporting the mission statement. The first pillar is service – their number one priority – taking care of patients. The second pillar is education and nurturing the next generations of care-givers, doctors, nurses, physiotherapists, etc. The third pillar is undertaking clinical research to expand its knowledge and skills in medical science.

The hospital has defined its quality commitment as 'best outcome, best experience' for its patients. Best experience is about the way it serves its patients and their families by providing quality healthcare with compassion, respect and integrity. Best outcome is about treating the patient's medical condition as well as they can to achieve the best health benefits for the patient. Lawrence Lim was the Chief Executive who introduced this commitment. He explained:

We want to provide the best outcome by providing the best clinical care. I know people do not wish to come to a hospital, but if they have to, we want to provide them with the best experience possible. This idea was derived and drawn up by the doctors and administrators together and provides a common purpose, mindset and language that permeate the whole hospital. There are three key principles underlying this:

- *assure best outcomes and benefit for the patient (i.e. clinical quality)*
- *create seamless service (i.e. operational quality)*
- *delight with personalised care (i.e. service quality).*

We created a Quality Council comprising doctors and administrators that came together to chart the strategies and programmes for quality in the hospital. They discussed clinical quality, which has to do with getting doctors, nurses, physiotherapists, etc. to produce the best outcome and health benefits for the patient. We also talked about operational quality; that is how we moved a patient around and how we could organise our services around the patient. These activities mainly concerned operational processes, which we then 'engineered' to create a seamless service for the patient. We were also concerned with what we called service quality, which was about the patient's experience; building a relationship with the patients and showing that we cared. From the patients' perspective all these three types of quality, i.e. clinical, operational and service, are intertwined, but we needed to ensure that our staff were focused on all of them too.

We worked with all the different people in the hospital to try to get everybody to think how they could improve the service. We got them to think about communication skills, even grooming, dress and body language. SGH is a government hospital and people's concept of government hospitals was that they are bureaucratic, officious and slow to respond. I told my staff, let's surprise the patient!

1.3.3 Products, services and value

Most, if not all, organisations provide a combination of products (things) and services (activities). A manufacturer of washing machines or cars not only makes the machine – they also provide sales services, and after-sales services such as servicing and repairs. Service organisations such as restaurants 'manufacture' food and the restaurant would be of little value without it. Consultants provide tangible reports, but their main value is their diagnostic and advice services.

Many product-based organisations recognise the value provided by their 'add-on' services. Indeed IBM (see Case Example 1.2) has capitalised on its service provision to create its Global Services division, recognising that only a small part of its value was in hardware and software. Indeed, many product-based organisations see 'service' as a means of differentiating themselves from the competition. Amazon, initially a bookseller and now a global retailer, gained an advantage over traditional booksellers by allowing customers to buy online, store their delivery address and credit card details to allow one-click future purchases, receive suggestions and read reviews, all from their laptop or phone, wherever they might be.

The movement towards thinking in terms of the complete product-service offering, and changing product-based organisations' business models to market and deliver this, is often referred to as servitisation.

One could argue that 'product' versus 'service' is now an old fashioned distinction and the boundaries between them are blurred. What is more important to customers, the product or the service? What is a 'product'? Is Amazon a product or a service organisation? The critical point is not the relative amount of product versus service that an organisation delivers, or whether it sees itself as a product producer or service provider, but where the value is for the customer. Take the example of a car. From a car manufacturer's point of view a vast amount of value (cost) is tied up in the product and paid for by the customer (value-in-exchange).[9] But from most customers' point of view, its value is in its use (value-in-use).[10] Having a car allows us to go where we want, when we want, in relative comfort, listening to what we want to listen to.

Value is created in the experience and the outcomes (in particular the benefits) at the point(s) of consumption.[11] Importantly, the customer is the ultimate judge of value. Value is perceived by the customer over the time we keep the car and we hope that its value-in-use is at least as good as the price we had to pay for it; though we may often not realise this until the car breaks down. We will return to the notion of value in Section 1.5 and Chapter 3.

One important corollary to this is that the customer has a significant role in value creation in services. How we use and maintain the car has an impact on how we value it. How well the staff co-operate with the firm of consultants may well affect their ability to do their job. How well we explain our symptoms to our doctor will not only help them but aid our recovery. The role the customer plays in service delivery is referred to as co-production.

Case Example 1.2	IBM Global Services

IBM is widely regarded as a successful global service company providing its business customers with solutions to their problems. In 2010 IBM had a turnover of over $99bn with a gross profit of over $46bn. While sales of systems, technology and software accounted for around 40 per cent of revenue, its service division, IBM Global Services, generated 57 per cent of its revenue, accounting for 33 per cent of the organisation's gross profit. IBM's Global Services has expanded rapidly (see Figure 1.2) establishing IBM as a leading global IT service company. In 2007 Global Services was split into two reporting

Source: Pearson Education Ltd/Imagestate/John Foxx Collections

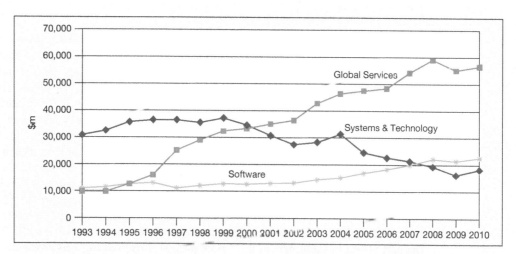

Figure 1.2 IBM Turnover ($ millions) 1993–2010: Global Services, Systems & Technology and Software

divisions: Global Business Services (GBS) and Global Technology Services (GTS). GBS provides professional services (consulting) and application outsourcing services whereas GTS focuses on infrastructure services (computer installation and maintenance services) and business process services.

Brian Sellwood was the general manager of IBM Global Services responsible for delivery, operations and applications management services across Europe, Africa and the Middle East. He described the importance of services:

> In today's computing industry it is very difficult to differentiate one supplier from another in terms of their hardware and software. The product itself is no longer, or very rarely, a differentiator. It's what you can offer the customer around that product, and that's invariably service, services such as project management, application implementation, fixing a fault with a machine, how you manage and perform that service. It's about what you do with that product, how you manage that relationship, how you treat the customer, how you respond to their problems and the solutions you can offer your customers to make their businesses stronger and better.

This approach is considerably different to that 15 years ago when IBM was renowned as a product-based company specialising in developing and selling computer hardware and software. It was also making a loss. IBM then set about creating an organisation that was focused on its services and the needs of its customers and not on the company's products. Brian Sellwood explained:

> We were not into services; we were a hardware/software product company. The first step was to start understanding what the customer wanted; what they wanted to buy and how they wanted to see it packaged. Having undertaken some market analysis we decided to start very simply with what we had, and package it better, rather than build a whole new set of new services. Over time we realised that what we had was not quite what the customers wanted to buy; they wanted value-add. That meant we had to change and redefine our portfolio. We had to listen to what our customers were asking for and at the same time observe what the competition were doing and try to see where there were gaps in their portfolios and opportunities for us. And this has been a continuous process ever since. This continual refinement of what we are offering to the customer has played a key role in stimulating our growth over the last ten years.
>
> In the early stages we found that customers were looking for help but had not always been able to express that need because there was not always someone willing to listen. In fact there was no shortage of opportunities for us to go and advise customers on how to make better use of their installed equipment. We found customers wanted almost anything and our challenge was to respond appropriately. No two customers were the same and so the challenge was to be able to offer the customers solutions to their specific problems rather than saying we have this solution and that will fit your business. From that beginning we were able, slowly, to add more services, eventually developing a business consulting capability where we could advise on how to use and manage applications more effectively, how to install and help customers install applications, and advise customers on process engineering, supply chain development and business transformation.

1.3.4 Co-production

One of the most important, intriguing and challenging aspects of managing service operations (certainly when compared to manufacturing operations) is that many, though not all, service operations 'process' customers. (Other service operations process things belonging to the customer.) These are sometimes referred to as customer processing operations. The theme park cannot physically give you the rides unless you turn up, the doctor cannot give you an injection unless you are physically in the same place. This means that the customer's experience is an intrinsic part of the operation's process (see Figure 1.1). As a result, the customer sees much of the process and, in many cases, plays a key role in the process itself as well as receiving the service – thus service is a two-way flow. We will develop this idea in Chapter 4.

It is important to note that customers may not see and/or experience the whole of the process; they will only be involved in the 'front office' (the overlapping section in Figure 1.1). The 'back office' contains tasks that are carried out usually unseen by the customers, such as cooking the food in restaurants, or baggage handling at an airport (see Chapter 7).

The part played by customers in the service process is referred to as co-production (or co-creation). (This was an idea that emerged over 40 years ago describing the way citizens could get more involved in public sector services.[12]) We all play a part in many services. We take ourselves around the supermarket shelves, pick the items, take them to the checkout, sometimes scan them ourselves, then pack them and transport them to the car. (Alternatively we could reduce our input and go for home delivery and let the supermarket pick, pack and deliver our goods, though we still have to get involved in ticking the boxes on the order form.) When we visit the doctor with an ailment we are needed to describe the symptoms to them and discuss alternative treatments.

In a restaurant or on a train, for example, we also provide services to other customers. In the restaurant we help provide the ambiance, the gentle buzz of conversation around the room, and our adherence to a formal or informal dress code which helps set the scene (the servicescape). In a train, we keep other seats free of our luggage so that others can sit down, and we refrain from noisy or unruly behaviour. So, besides managing materials, technology, people and processes, service operations managers also have to manage the customer as a resource too (see Chapter 11).[13]

This overlap of the process and the customer's experience, together with the direct involvement of the customer in many services, makes the job of a service operations manager particularly challenging, exciting and, at times, frustrating (see Chapter 2).

1.4   What is service operations management?

Service operations management is the term that is used to cover the activities, decisions and responsibilities of operations managers in service organisations. It is concerned with providing services, and value, to customers or users, ensuring they get the right experiences and the desired outcomes. It involves understanding the needs of the customers, managing the service processes, ensuring the organisation's objectives are met, while also paying attention to the continual improvement of the services. Operations managers are responsible for most of an organisation's assets, for managing most costs and staff and for generating the organisation's revenues. As such, operations management is a central organisational function and one that is critical to organisational success.

Service operations managers are often called operations managers but many other titles are used, such as managing partners in consultancy firms, nursing managers in hospitals, headteachers in schools, fleet managers in transport companies, call centre managers, customer service managers, restaurant managers . . . They may be responsible for managing 'front office' operations – the parts of the process that a customer might see, or the 'back office' operations invisible to the customer, or indeed both. The back office operation on the exotic island of Baros in the Maldives (see Case Example 1.3) involves a wide range of activities such as water treatment plants, laundry, catering etc., all hidden from the guests' view. The front office operations include restaurants, accommodation and watersports. Ahmed Jihad is the operations manager with overall responsibility for both the back and front office operations.

All operations managers have a number of things in common:

- They are responsible for the service operation – the configuration of resources and processes that provide service for the customer (see Figure 1.1).

- They are responsible for some of the organisation's resources (we refer to these as inputs – see Figure 1.1), including materials, equipment, staff, technology and facilities. These resources often account for a very large proportion of an organisation's total assets, so service operations managers are responsible for much of an organisation's cost base.

- They are responsible for the organisation's customers (sometimes referred to as clients, users, patients or students, for example) and/or the things belonging to their customers, such as their parcels or orders.

- They are responsible for 'processing' their customers or their parcels or orders. For the managing partner in a consultancy firm this might involve overseeing meetings with clients, data gathering, analysis and report writing. For the nursing manager it might involve overseeing patient admissions, tests, treatment and discharge. (The service process is the set of activities or steps in the provision of the service.)

- They are also responsible for the outputs; the 'products' provided to their customers. The nursing manager delivers (discharges) recovering patients together with their prescriptions for medicines and outpatient appointments. The managing partner delivers the final report and the solution to a problem to the client.

- They are responsible for designing, creating and providing the right experience and outcomes for their customers. The nursing manager will be concerned to ensure the patient feels well cared for and leaves in a better condition than how they came in. The managing partner will want their clients to feel informed, assured and valued, and provide them with some real business benefits.

- They are responsible for delivering value to their customers and also to the organisation. Value to the customers comes from their experiences and the benefits gained. Value for the organisation comes from operations managers keeping to budgets, delivering revenue, reducing costs and delivering the organisation's strategy, for example.

- Service operations managers are responsible for generating most, if not all, of an organisation's revenue/income and managing most of its assets and staff.

Case Example 1.3   Baros, the Maldives

The Republic of the Maldives is a small country lying 700 kilometres south-west of Sri Lanka in the Indian Ocean. It consists of over 1,000 small islands grouped together in atolls. Spread over an area of about 90,000 square kilometres, this country stretches from the equator to 1,000 kilometres north, yet it has a total land mass of less than 470 square kilometres. With its coral reefs, white sandy beaches and a climate of between 28 and 32 degrees it is a holiday paradise and a destination for the affluent traveller.

The tiny island of Baros is a five-star de luxe resort, owned and operated by Universal Resorts

which run eight secluded island resorts in the Maldives, Seychelles and Sri Lanka. Baros is just a 25-minute speedboat ride from the island airport which is close to the main island containing the capital Malé. Guests are met in the airport and escorted to the resort's awaiting boat.

There are just 75 luxury villas on the island. Some are beach villas, sheltered and secluded in lush tropical vegetation, with direct access to the beach. Other villas are water villas, built above the water, each with their own private balcony and sea view. All the villas are spacious and air-conditioned. The resort has its own spa, diving and snorkelling centre, gym, bars and three restaurants, including the famous Lighthouse Restaurant.

In charge of all back office and front office operations is Ahmed Jihad, a Maldivian with international experience in hotel management. From the point of view of the guests the place is stunning, peaceful and quiet and their expectations are well met, if not exceeded. Although Baros looks the perfect posting for an operations manager, Mr Jihad explained that there was a lot of hard work behind the scenes.

We have to manage around 275 staff looking after our 100–150 guests. The operation never stops; it is 24 hours a day, 7 days a week. We have to make sure everyone has the energy and the motivation to keep our high standards, every hour, every day. We have to keep the place, all the wooden decks, furniture, the thatched roofs, looking in pristine condition. We also have a significant logistical operation as all our supplies are brought in by air then by boat. There is also a considerable back office operation which our guests don't see, or even think about.

Most of the back office operations are hidden away in the centre of the island overseen by the resort manager and the chief engineer. As there are no utilities to the island the resort has to generate its own electricity, run a desalination water treatment plant, an electricity generating plant and a sewerage treatment plant. It also has to provide all the facilities, including accommodation, for its staff.

Mr Jihad explained:

Baros is the real essence of the Maldives. It has a natural beauty, white sands, reefs, the lagoon, and a high customer profile – people with very high expectations. My main responsibility is the front office operations – to make sure the guests are happy; from airport receiving through their stay here to their departure at the airport. I usually greet the guests and talk to them during their stay. I make sure we have all the right SOPs (standard operating procedures) to create the high standards of this resort and I make sure they are all implemented correctly, from check-in to catering to cleaning. I also oversee the food and beverage operations and the sales and marketing; I check all their materials and provide my ideas. I conduct daily and weekly meetings and briefings with the staff, and with contractors, and oversee the training of staff.

There is no typical day, but if we take yesterday, Monday, for example, I started at 7.30 in the morning. This is one of our very busy days so my key objective was to make sure all the rooms were ready for our incoming guests, make sure reception goes smoothly for them, and that all the facilities they booked are ready for them. I also like to know who the returning guests are. The first thing I did was to check my emails, then I had a breakfast meeting with our chef. I held a meeting with all my departmental managers where we deal with any issues and brief them about the day's activities. This was followed by the general staff meeting at 10.00. I then spent some time talking to guests around the site, followed by a meeting with the Spa Manager at 11.30; we discussed how we can increase utilisation of this facility. This was followed with a similar meeting with the Diving Centre Manager. I then went off to my room, had a shower and freshened up. I had lunch at 1.30. I usually have it with one of my managers; yesterday it was with the HR Manager. We are in the middle of developing our fire and safety training programme so I was checking how it was going and also the new SOPs we had recently put in place. These meetings are important, it gives me time to check things and discuss issues. I then went to my office and signed all the cocktail party invitations for all our guests and the personal welcome letters for our arriving guests; I also checked the special arrangements for the honeymoon guests. Throughout the afternoon I then met the boats bringing in the arriving guests. At 5.30 I went back to my room and had a shower and watched the BBC and CNN for a while. At 7.30 I went back to the office and checked the emails again. I then went over to the Lighthouse to talk to guests, and checked over one of the other restaurants; it's important for the staff to see managers around. I then went to reception to talk about today's (Tuesday's) departures. I had dinner around 9.30 with my chief engineer and the HR manager, again about the fire and safety training. This is quite a big project for us at the moment. I then went back to the office, checked the emails and went to bed at 10.30.

No two days are the same, but every one of them is enjoyable.

Why is service operations management important?

We hope by now it is becoming clear that service operations managers have an important and responsible role. In essence, service operations managers

- are responsible for managing the design and delivery of services to organisations' customers,
- are responsible for managing most of organisation's resources,
- have a significant impact on the success of an organisation.

The success of service operations managers is not simply about performing a good technical task, such as educating a student, delivering a project on time, or providing a holiday. Good service operations management should lead to better (or more appropriate) services and experiences that are better for the customer, better for the staff and also better for the organisation – the 'triple bottom line'.

1.5.1 Better for the customer

Customers will be satisfied, even delighted if they are provided with the right service, a good experience and the desired outcomes. This delivers value for the customer (for more discussion on value see Chapter 3).

A problem for service managers is that the customer's idea of what represents value may well vary from customer to customer and shift through time, and even from day to day. At the most basic level, the economising customers will think of value as getting more for their money. Other customers may be prepared to pay more in order to receive a higher service specification. Still others will value the psychological value in being able to say that they are able to afford to be customers of high-status services (even though the specification may be no better than a lower priced service). The service operations manager must be aware of the full range of influences on the customer's assessment of value. A key element in this understanding is the relationship between the service brand values as communicated to the customer and the potential mismatch in terms of customer experience.

1.5.2 Better for the staff

Good service operations management and the provision of the right services, experiences and outcomes for the customer will also mean a better experience for the staff:

- Customers will be easier to deal with because they are satisfied and the service and experience meet their needs.
- Because the operation works well and generates the right outcomes there will be fewer problems and therefore less hassle for the staff and fewer (unpleasant) complaints to deal with.
- Customers who are satisfied tend to be more tolerant, so when things go wrong they are much more accepting than they might otherwise have been, again making life easier for the staff.
- A smooth operation and contented customers means things are going well, thus staff are more likely to have pride in both the job they do and the organisation they work for.

1.5.3 Better for the organisation

Delivering the right service and experience through good operations management delivers many organisational benefits:

- Satisfied customers who perceive value from the service are more likely to return and also more likely to provide positive word-of-mouth and recommend the organisation and its services to others, thus generating more revenue (assuming it's a revenue-generating organisation).

- Better service operations management means improved processes which should be cheaper and more efficient, reducing the organisation's costs.

- Increased revenue and/or reduced costs will improve the profitability and/or viability of the organisation.

- Better services may also provide the organisation with a source of competitive advantage.

- Better and more efficient services will enhance the organisation's reputation and brand.

- Delivering the right services and experiences should also enable the organisation to achieve its goals/objectives/mission, supporting the organisation's strategic intent.

- Good service operations management which thinks both reactively and proactively should be able to help shape and develop the organisation's future intent and develop skills and competencies that will support the development of the organisation.

1.5.4 Economic contribution

A final and important contribution, but at a macro level, is the contribution that services, in general, make towards a nation's economy. Service activities are a vital and significant part of most developing and developed economies. In most developed countries services account for in excess of 80 per cent of gross domestic product (GDP), and for over 50 per cent of GDP in developing economies. They also provide employment for a significant number of people. The challenges facing service operations managers throughout the whole range of service organisations – such as financial institutions, government bodies, retailers, wholesalers and personal service providers – need to be taken seriously and managed well to support economic success and development.

We can see that from the standpoint of economic value alone we should pay attention to the service sector, and to service operations in particular as this is where the service, and therefore wealth and value, are created. Services also have an important economic role in non-service organisations. Many manufacturing companies have significant revenue-earning service activities, such as customer support, and also many service activities internal to the organisation, such as payroll, catering, information and IT services etc. Indeed it has been estimated that around 75 per cent of non-service organisations' activities may be directly or indirectly associated with the provision of services.[14]

Service organisations provide employment for the vast majority of the working population in most developed and developing countries. In many economies the service sector is the only area where new jobs are being created, notably in tourism and leisure. Many service organisations, such as hospitality and transportation, are people-intensive, requiring different mixes of skilled and unskilled labour. Other organisations, such as banking and many financial services, are more technology-based.

Finally, we cannot ignore the vast numbers of people employed in the public and voluntary sectors. Managing services such as education, health, fire, police, social services, famine relief organisations, faith organisations and charities requires as much expertise as their private sector counterparts. Governments are increasingly subcontracting many services to the voluntary sector that were previously provided directly by the state. In so doing, governments are applying commercial approaches to supplier assessment, and there is therefore a growing pressure on the voluntary sector to apply improvement methodologies (see Chapter 12). Whatever the type of service organisation, there is no doubt that there is ever-increasing pressure to provide higher levels of 'value for money' with the same or reducing resources.

1.6   Summary

What are services?

- Services are provided by a variety of types of organisations, including business-to-consumer services (B2C), business-to-business services (B2B), internal services, public services and not-for-profit and voluntary services.

What is 'service'?

- A service is an activity – a process or set of steps (unlike a product which is a thing) – which involves the treatment of a customer (or user) or something belonging to them, where the customer is also involved, and performs some role (co-production), in the service process.
- From the operation's point of view, the service provided is the service process and its outputs which have been designed, created and enacted by the operation using its many input resources, including the customer, where the customer also takes some part in the service process.
- From the customer's perspective, the service received is the customer's experience of the service provided and their interaction with it, perceptions of it, and response to it, which results in outcomes such as 'products', benefits, emotions, judgements and intentions.

What is service operations management?

- Service operations management is concerned with the activities, decisions and responsibilities of operations managers in service organisations. It entails providing services, and value, to customers or users, ensuring they get the right experiences and the desired outcomes. It involves understanding the needs of the customers, managing the service processes, ensuring the organisation's objectives are met, while also paying attention to the continual improvement of the services.

Why is service operations management important?

- Service operations managers
  - are responsible for a large proportion of the organisation's assets
  - are responsible for delivering service to the organisation's customers
  - have a significant impact on the success of an organisation.
- Good service operations management, resulting in good services and experiences, will deliver the 'triple bottom line', i.e.
  - better for the customer
  - better for the staff
  - better for the organisation.
- At a macro level services are a critical part of most economies, accounting for a significant proportion of GDP and employment.

1.7 Discussion questions

1 Describe the customer experience and outcomes for a fast-food restaurant, a doctor's surgery and an internet-based fashion clothing retailer. Compare and contrast the services of these three organisations.

2 How do students assess the value of a university course? How does this differ from the organisation's view of value?

3 Think of a time when you recently received poor service. If service operations are so important, why do you think they sometimes deliver poor service?

1.8 Questions for managers

1 Describe your service from both an operational and customer perspective. Assess the mismatches between these perspectives.

2 How is the success of your operation assessed? Is this approach appropriate?

3 How well is the contribution of the operation understood in your organisation and what are the implications?

Suggested further reading

Johnston, Robert (2005), 'Service Operations Management: From the Roots Up', *International Journal of Operations and Production Management* 25 (12) 1298–1308

Johnston, Robert and Xiangyu Kong (2011), 'The Customer Experience: A Road Map for Improvement', *Managing Service Quality* 21 (1) 5–24

Lusch, Robert F., Stephen L. Vargo and Matthew O'Brien (2007), 'Competing through Service: Insights from Service Dominant Logic', *Journal of Retailing* 83 (1) 2–18

Neu, Wayne A. and Stephen W. Brown (2005), 'Forming Successful Business-to-Business Services in Goods-Dominant Firms', *Journal of Service Research* 8 (1) 3–17

Sampson, Scott E. and Craig M. Froehle (2006), 'Foundations and Implications of a Proposed Unified Services Theory', *Production and Operations Management* 15 (2) 329–343

Shaw, Colin, Qaalfa Dibeehi and Steven Walden (2010), *Customer Experience: Future Trends and Insights*, Palgrave Macmillan

Slack, Nigel, Stuart Chambers and Robert Johnston (2010), *Operations Management*, 6th edition, FT Prentice Hall, Harlow

Vargo, Stephen L. and Robert F. Lusch (2004), 'Evolving to a New Dominant Logic of Marketing', *Journal of Marketing* 68 (January) 1–17.

Wong, Amy (2004) 'The Role of Emotions in Service Encounters', *Managing Service Quality* 14 (5) 365–376

Useful web links

A list of many service operations management texts, practitioner books, service journals, videos and links to a site with practitioner papers can be found at:
http://group.wbs.ac.uk/om/teaching/service/materials/

IBM is leading a Service Science, Management, and Engineering (SSME) initiative. Their website provides articles, case studies, materials and references to what some organisations and universities are doing in this emerging discipline:
http://www.ibm.com/university/ssme

The Customer Service Network is an independent UK forum for customer service professionals:
http://www.customernet.com/

The Institute of Customer Service is the UK's professional body for customer service:
http://www.instituteofcustomerservice.com/

Notes

1 For a discussion see Johnston, Robert (2005), 'Service Operations Management: From the Roots Up', *International Journal of Operations and Production Management* 25 (12) 1298–1308 and Johnston, Robert (1994), 'Operations: From Factory to Service Management', *International Journal of Service Industry Management* 5 (1) 49–63

2 See Haywood-Farmer, John, and Jean Nollet (1991), *Services Plus: Effective Service Management*, Morin, Boucherville, Quebec; Sampson, Scott E. and Craig M. Froehle (2006), 'Foundations and Implications of a Proposed Unified Services Theory', *Production and Operations Management* 15 (2) 329–343

3 Johnston, Robert and Xiangyu Kong (2011), 'The Customer Experience: A Road Map for Improvement', *Managing Service Quality* 21 (1) 5–24

4 Sampson, Scott (2005), *Understanding Service Businesses*, 2nd edition, Wiley; Sampson, Scott E. and Craig M. Froehle (2006), 'Foundations and Implications of a Proposed Unified Services Theory', *Production and Operations Management* 15 (2) 329–343

5 Lusch, Robert F., Stephen L. Vargo and Matthew O'Brien (2007), 'Competing through Service: Insights from Service Dominant Logic', *Journal of Retailing* 83 (1) 2–18

6 Pine, II, B. Joseph and James H. Gilmore (1998), 'Welcome to the Experience Economy', *Harvard Business Review* 76 (4) 97–105

7 For more information on the customer experience see Shaw, Colin (2005), *Revolutionize Your Customer Experience*, Palgrave Macmillan, Basingstoke; Pullman, Madeleine E. and Michael A. Gross (2004), 'Ability of Experience Design Elements to Elicit Emotions and Loyalty Behaviors', *Decision Sciences* 35 (3) 551–578; Csikszentmihalyi, Mihaly (2000), 'The Costs and Benefits of Consuming', *Journal of Consumer Research* 27 (2) 267–272; Ding, David Xin, Paul Jen-Hwa Hu, Rohit Verma and Don G. Wardell (2010), 'The Impact of Service System Design and Flow Experience on Customer Satisfaction in Online Financial Services', *Journal of Service Research* 13 (1) 96–110

8 Zomerdijk, Leonieke G. and Christopher A. Voss (2010), 'Service Design for Experience-Centric Services', *Journal of Service Research* 13 (1) 67–82 and Carbone, Lewis P. (2004), *Clued In*, FT Prentice Hall, New Jersey

9 Lusch, Robert F., Stephen L. Vargo and Matthew O'Brien (2007), 'Competing through Service: Insights from Service Dominant Logic', *Journal of Retailing* 83 (1) 2–18

10 Lusch, Robert F., Stephen L. Vargo and Matthew O'Brien (2007), 'Competing through Service: Insights from Service Dominant Logic', *Journal of Retailing* 83 (1) 2–18 and Edvardsson, Bo, Bo Enquist and Robert Johnston (2005), 'Co-creating Customer Value through Hyperreality in the Prepurchase Service Experience', *Journal of Service Research* 8 (2) 149–161

11 Vargo, Stephen. L. and Robert F Lusch (2004), 'The Four Service Marketing Myths – Remnants of a Goods-Based, Manufacturing Model', *Journal of Service Research* 6 (4) 324–335 and Edvardsson, Bo and Jan Olsson (1996), 'Key Concepts for New Service Development', *The Service Industries Journal* 16 (2) 140–164

12 See for example *Brudney, Jeffrey L. and Robert E. England (1983),* 'Toward a Definition of the Coproduction Concept', *Public Administration Review* 43 (1), 59

13 Johnston, Robert (1989), 'The Customer as Employee', *International Journal of Operations and Production Management* 9 (5) 15–23

14 Quinn, Joseph B. and Christopher E. Gagnon (1986), 'Will Services Follow Manufacturing into Decline?', *Harvard Business Review* 64 (6) 95–103

Chapter 2
Understanding the challenges for operations managers

Chapter objectives

This chapter is about how to understand the key challenges facing service operations managers.

- What are the key strategic challenges faced by service operations managers?
- What are the key tactical challenges faced by service operations managers?
- What are the challenges for different types of services?
- What are the challenges for different types of processes?
- What are the challenges in working with other management functions?
- How can this book help?

2.1 Introduction

From Chapter 1 it should be clear that the key decision areas for operations managers include managing their inputs – materials, staff/employees, technology and their customers and designing, creating and enacting service processes which provide a range of services. They also have to create the right experience for their customers whilst generating the right outcomes for the customer ('products', benefits and emotions) and also creating the right outcomes for the organisation (revenue, cost management, achievement of strategic aims etc.).

In this chapter we want to share with you the main problems and challenges facing service operations managers and introduce the structure of this book to show how to deal with these challenges. While each operation has its own particular demands, there are a number of key challenges faced by most if not all service operations and service operations managers. In the first part of this chapter we want to outline the nature of those challenges; the strategic and the tactical challenges. We will then look at the particular challenges faced by specific types of service operations and the various types of processes found within them. We will also discuss the issues faced by operations managers in working with other management functions such as strategy, marketing and HR. As we describe all these challenges we will point you to the parts of this book that provide ideas and tools to help deal with them. We will conclude with an overview of the structure of the book.

<table>
<tr><td>2.2</td><td>

What are the key strategic challenges faced by service operations managers?

</td></tr>
</table>

The key strategic challenges faced by most service operations managers include

- Managing tactically and strategically
- Making operations a contributor to strategy as well as an implementer
- Making the business case for service
- Understanding the service concept.

2.2.1 Managing tactically and strategically

Operations managers need to manage both tactically and strategically. Being tactical is about being focused on the short-term, day-to-day activities. Strategy is concerned with the long-term and with the operation's wider contribution to the organisation (see Chapter 1, Section 1.5). You may have noticed that Ahmed Jihad in Case Example 1.3 was bogged down with day-to-day activities and seemed to have little time to deal with the future and with important medium- and longer-term operational issues such as:

- How will the resort need to change to compete with the opening of new high-quality resorts in the Maldives?
- How can it reduce costs to deal with economic slowdown?
- As sustainable tourism is becoming increasingly important what changes will the operation need to make?
- How can the resort deal with rising sea levels over the next twenty years? The highest point in the Maldives is just 2.4 metres (8 feet) above sea level.

The problem for operations managers is that a significant part of the excitement of managing operations is its immediacy. By this we mean the constant challenge of dealing with the needs of a stream of customers, managing the staff and making operational decisions to ensure the delivery of an appropriate quality of service at an appropriate cost. The danger of this immediacy is that it can lead to a short-term focus. Many service operations managers concentrate their time and effort on managing the day-to-day operations for the following reasons:

- The pressure on the operation to deliver its day-to-day services may leave little time for medium-term operational improvement activities or longer-term strategic planning. For example, it is difficult for a headteacher to put time into dealing with solving major underlying problems, such as poor facilities, inadequate funding, high levels of absenteeism etc., when they are heavily involved in trying to find part-time staff to cover for sudden absences, recruiting new staff to vacant posts, processing the many forms and requests that land on the desk each day and also dealing with a constant stream of student behavioural problems.
- Operations managers, because of the nature of the job and often their background, tend to feel more comfortable with the unambiguous and rational nature of many short-term tactical decisions. The more intuitive processes required for strategic thinking are quite different and excuses found to put them to one side. The headteacher is likely to have been promoted through the profession and they may get a 'buzz' and feel more comfortable in dealing with students and the curriculum. They may be less inclined to put time into the 'less exciting' and 'less pressing' tasks of data collection, analysis, report writing and high-level debate and discussion with various parties to try to resolve underlying and longer-term issues.

As a result, the development and strategic aspects of operations management are frequently neglected and a disproportionate amount of time is spent on managing the day-to-day operations. In some organisations this problem is built in by not giving senior operations managers a seat at the boardroom table (or its equivalent). Given they are responsible for most of the organisation's assets, people, costs and revenue, this would seem very short-sighted.

Good operations managers are those who can pay attention to, and create time in their day for, both strategic issues and also managing the day-to-day operations in order to create and sustain a successful organisation (see Chapters 7–14 for managing the day-to-day, tactical issues and Chapters 15–17 for the strategic issues).

2.2.2 Making operations a contributor to strategy as well as an implementer

Operations managers are involved in the 'doing' part of the business. It is the operation and its staff that deliver the service, not its marketers or financial managers, though in a small organisation these roles may be undertaken by the same people. As such operations managers are responsible for the implementation of strategy. As an implementer of strategy operations managers must first of all understand the organisation's strategy. This may be market dominance for a large retailer, or the speedy provision of water and food for an aid agency, or a high level of childcare with strong links into the community for a nursery. This then defines what the operation has to be good at (or how it has to compete for competitive organisations). This might involve delivering service at a low cost with dependability (see Case Example 2.1) or providing a wide range of services or a pleasurable customer experience, for example. This then defines the key decision areas and tasks for the operation, such as minimising costs and implementing lean initiatives, or focusing on speed of delivery and developing supply networks, or continually improving quality and innovating new services (we will develop this further in Chapter 15).

Case Example 2.1	SouthWest Airlines

SouthWest Airlines is a US organisation that many budget airlines have copied in recent years. There are a number of reasons for its continued success but first and foremost SouthWest delivers the concept of low-cost, dependable transportation incredibly well. They understand that what passengers want is not airport to airport transport but rather door to door. They also understand that competition comes in the form of buses and cars rather than other airlines.

In order to deliver this proposition, SouthWest Airlines have focused on cost and dependability as the heart of their operations strategy. Key decision areas were

Source: Southwest airlines

- Using secondary airports (lower cost and less congestion delivering dependability)
- Using short haul flights with no interconnections (dependability)
- Use of one type of plane (lower maintenance and crewing costs)
- Direct booking only (low cost – and greater visibility of demand)
- Choice of routes with potential to grow volume (cost and dependability).

The additional stroke of genius with SouthWest Airlines is that even though this is a high-volume, stand-ardised service, they have managed to create a customer-focused culture with some life to it! As the CEO of SouthWest Airlines, Gary Kelly, stated, 'Our people are our single greatest strength and most enduring long-term competitive advantage'. You only have to go on to YouTube to see some of the antics of cabin crew which go towards creating a friendly service and an incredibly loyal customer base. SouthWest concentrates on building relationships, both internal and external, and this is their leadership focus. It is perhaps no sur-prise that other low-cost airlines can copy the product but not the experience!

As we can see from Case Example 2.1 operations also have an important proactive role as a major contributor to strategy. For example service operations managers might be able to provide the platform for future competitive advantage. Rather than taking a service concept (see Chapter 3) and designing and running an operation to deliver it, it may be that there are a set of competences in the operation that can be turned to create a strategic advantage. The webcam installed by the nursery (see Case Example 2.2) might provide it with a competitive advantage that may be difficult for less technologically advanced nurseries to provide by, for example, extending it to provide a daily or weekly webcast by the children to their parents.

Thus service operations managers can have a significant contribution into developing strategy (Chapter 15) by knowing what they can, or could, deliver (Chapters 7–11) and by driving change and improvement through the organisation to provide it (Chapters 12–17).

Case Example 2.2   Cybernurseries

The very first webcam was set up by a group of Cambridge University students from the School of Computer Science. They focused it on the faculty coffee machine so that members of staff could see on their desk computer a 'live' picture of the machine, up-dated every few minutes. This allowed them to check whether or not the coffee jug was empty before they went to use the machine.

Webcams are now everywhere. Anyone with an internet connection can now see some breathtaking and bizarre sights, includ-ing the conditions at 3,880 metres on Mount Everest, the view of the top of the ski run at

Source: Pearson Education Ltd/Jules Selmes

Lake Tahoe, sights in the African bush, views from the Palazzo Senatorio in Rome, weddings at Las Vegas' Little White Chapel, the view from the Trans-Siberian Railway during its 5,700-mile journey from Moscow to Vladivostok, even the contents of a Swedish family's fridge!

One application has been the use of webcams in nurseries so that anxious parents can use their computer at work or home to 'look in' on their children. Security is tight, with pictures being encrypted and passwords required for access. The pictures parents receive are single frames, updated every minute, but the quality is good enough for parents to check if their child is relaxed, happy and well cared for – and to remind them what life is about!

While parents and grandparents are revelling in this innovation, others are queuing up to condemn it. Some psychologists are concerned that it becomes an on-screen substitute for involvement in a child's up-bringing that simply assuages the guilt of working mothers. Other people worry about it fuelling the current paranoia about child safety. However, at a time when childcare is needing an injection of trust and with more and more working parents, cybernurseries could soon be commonplace.

2.2.3 Making the business case for service

Many of the service operations managers we speak to tell us that they totally understand how important service is. At the end of Chapter 1, we summarised why good service, and good operations management, mean making things better for the customer, better for the staff and better for the organisation. (Better for the organisation may mean retaining customers, attracting new customers, entering new markets, increasing revenues, reducing costs, making greater profit or simply meeting budget targets.) Yet when asked to make the case to demonstrate that better service does indeed make things better for the organisation they often fall back on belief and intuition. The nursery manager (see Case Example 2.2) will intuitively know that spending more money on improving the facilities will bring in more customers, thereby increasing revenue, but they may have difficulty persuading the owner to invest without some hard evidence. Making a business case to the financial director, or the equivalent, in order to obtain the resources required to provide a better operation and deliver a better service requires a clear argument providing evidence of the relationship between service and costs and revenues. Such knowledge will also enable the operations manager to understand the impact of any decisions they make on both the service provided and organisational success. We will explain how this can be done in Chapter 17.

2.2.4 Understanding the service concept

Strategically it is important that there is a shared and defined view about the nature of the service that the organisation provides. The service concept defines what the organisation does, what marketing have to sell and what the operations have to deliver. In a product-based organisation this is usually straightforward; the product can be seen and touched. But a service is an activity or process and it is easy for various people inside the organisation to have quite different views about what that process is. Likewise there may also be differing views about what an organisation is 'selling' and what the customer is 'buying'. Some parents may see the nursery as simply a babysitting service; others may see it as a critical educational experience for their offspring. Articulating and communicating the service concept (Chapter 3) is critical for clarifying the organisation's product to all its customers, internal and external, and for ensuring that it can be, and is, delivered (Chapters 7–11).

2.3 What are the key tactical challenges faced by service operations managers?

The key tactical, day-to-day, challenges faced by most service operations managers include:

- Understanding the customer perspective
- Managing multiple customers
- Managing the customer
- Managing in real time
- Co-ordinating different parts of the organisation
- Encouraging improvement and innovation.

2.3.1 Understanding the customer perspective

A key challenge (and sometimes a difficulty) for many managers in service operations is that they see things from an internal, organisational viewpoint, often referred to as

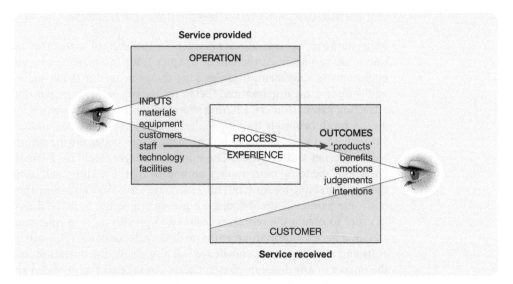

Figure 2.1 Inside-out versus outside-in

'inside-out'.[1] The operation's perspective understands the *service provided*. It focuses on the inputs that have to be managed (including the customer – often seeing them as an 'input' to be processed rather than as a person) and making sure that all the processes are working well. Managers, quite naturally, spend their time worrying about managing their resources and processes, managing capacity, scheduling people, meeting performance targets and financial goals (see Chapters 8–11).

However, the customers will see (the same) things from a very different perspective, 'outside-in' (see Figure 2.1). They are interested in the *service received*, their experience and the outcomes such as how they feel, the 'products' they receive and how they benefit from the service. Customers of the service are less concerned with the management of resources, processes and targets; they want a good experience, they want to have a good outcome and to benefit from the service. The nursery staff may see their key activities as child development and education, whereas the parent (as customer) may see it as an expensive babysitting service while they are at work. These different views may cause some conflicts. For example, when the parent is held up at work they may expect a babysitting service to wait a while for them, whereas a teacher will expect the parent to be on time and make alternative arrangements should they be late. Managing the relationship with the customer (see Chapter 4), managing customer expectations and perceptions (see Chapter 5) and delivering the customer experience (see Chapter 7) are key challenges in managing service operations.

Seeing things from a customer point of view is, surprisingly, unusual in service organisations. Table 2.1 illustrates these two perspectives for three different services, hip replacement surgery, education and consultancy.

Recognising both of these perspectives is important. Operations managers need to manage their operations to create their services; they need to manage their suppliers, people, facilities, process and technology (see Chapters 6 and 8–11), but at the same time they need to recognise how their efforts create value for the customer which in turn creates value for the organisation (see Chapter 1). Indeed some people argue that the customer is the ultimate arbiter of the value an organisation creates and delivers.[2] While value is delivered through the process and the service, it is located in the customer's experience and the outcomes for the customer (see Chapters 1 and 3).[3]

Table 2.1 The operation's and customer's perspectives

Service	The operation's (inside-out) perspective		
	Inputs	Processes	Outputs
Surgery	GP, nurses, surgeon, bed, operating theatre	Diagnosis, operation, aftercare	Hip replacement
Education	Lectures, library, computers, seminar rooms	Timetabling, lectures, exams, marking	Information, slide packs, degrees
Consultancy	Consultants, information, skills, knowledge	Data collection and analysis	Presentations, reports

Service	The customer's (outside-in) perspective		
	Experience	'Products'	Benefits
Surgery	Empathetic and pain-free treatment	A working hip	Greater mobility
Education	Memorable and useful lecturers/seminars	Knowledge, confidence and skills	Better job prospects/ capability
Consultancy	Helpful and timely discussions and advice	Solutions	Reduced costs and greater commercial success

We find many organisations today talk about developing a 'customer focus' or becoming 'customer orientated'. A better understanding of the outside-in perspective is a good way to start this process. Cathay Pacific is one organisation that takes an outside-in perspective, focusing on the customer's experience and the emotions they should feel (see Case Example 2.3). In Chapters 4, 7 and 15–17 we explain how this outside-in perspective can be developed.

Case Example 2.3   Cathay Pacific Airways

Cathay Pacific Airways is an international airline based in Hong Kong, offering scheduled passenger and cargo services to over 100 destinations around the world. The airline owns Dragonair and is also a major shareholder in Air Hong Kong, an all-cargo carrier operating in the Asian region. Cathay Pacific and its subsidiaries and associates employ over 25,000 people worldwide, with around 18,600 staff in Hong Kong, making it one of Hong Kong's biggest employers. The airline is a founder member of the **one**world global alliance, whose combined network serves almost 700 destinations in 150 countries worldwide.

Source: Cathay Pacific

The company's vision is to make Cathay Pacific the most admired airline in the world by:

- Ensuring safety comes first
- Providing 'Service Straight from the Heart'
- Encouraging product leadership
- Providing rewarding career opportunities.

Angelique Tam was Cathay Pacific's Head of Customer Relations. She explained what was meant by 'Service Straight from the Heart':

Service Straight from the Heart means that our staff have to be resourceful, and be able to find sensible on the spot solutions. They need to be dynamic and be proactive and find opportunities to excel and serve our customers well. We also expect them to show the highest standards of care and professionalism so they need to be fully committed. We want to create an experience that makes our customers feel welcome, comfortable, appreciated and above all, reassured. This is not as easy as it sounds. We need to be friendly but not overly intimate, caring but not over-attentive, efficient but not mechanical, consistent but with a willingness to be flexible, anticipating but not presumptuous and professional but very approachable.

Not surprisingly Cathay Pacific has been the recipient of many awards for its service. It was named as Airline of the Year 2009 by Skytrax, and most admired company in Hong Kong by Wall Street Journal Asia in 2010.

2.3.2 Managing multiple customers

Many service organisations do not serve a homogeneous group of customers; they often serve, in different ways, different types of customers. The nursery's customers (see Case Example 2.2) include both the child for whom it is providing an education and social experience, and also the parents for whom it is providing a 'parental substitute' service. There are other customers, sometimes termed stakeholders, such as education authorities and health and safety officials, for whom the nursery provides information and related services. There are also internal customers – the staff – whose welfare and training needs, for example, need to be provided for. Understanding who are the various customers (Chapter 4), understanding their needs and expectations (Chapter 5), developing relationships with them (Chapter 4) and managing the various customers (Chapters 7–9) are key tasks for service operations managers.

2.3.3 Managing the customer

The nature of service means that the operation's process is the customer's experience. In product-based organisations these two are usually distinct. A car manufacturer's processes for building a car are quite separate from their customer's experience of buying and then driving the car. This is not the case in service organisations. In universities, for example, the process of education is inseparable from the educational experience. Likewise the childcare and the childcare experience are inseparable. This provides several particular challenges for service operations managers.

Firstly customers are an input into some of the service operation's processes and they take some part, active or passive, in that process. As a consequence service operations managers not only have to manage their usual inputs and processes, they have to manage the customer as well. In universities we don't only have to deliver the material in a lecture, for example; we also need to manage the student's learning experience by trying to enthuse them and create a passion for our subject and learning (see Chapters 7 and 8).

Secondly the customer's mood, attitude and actions may affect not only their own experience but that of other customers, thereby having a direct bearing on the quality of other people's experiences. The behaviour of students in a lecture (such as talking, coming in late, taking phone calls) or the behaviour of diners in a restaurant (such as talking loudly, swearing or throwing bread rolls) will impact the other customers and affect the quality of their experience.

Thirdly, the experiential nature of services provides particular problems for both specification and indeed control. Some contact centres, for example, use scripts to ensure conformance and clarity, but such scripts lose out on flexibility, development of rapport and maybe also opportunities for cross-selling. The nursery needs clear guidelines and protocols about how to deal with particular issues but each situation may be different; the staff will need to apply some degree of judgement. This requires clarity about the service concept (see Chapter 3), how to deal with and learn from problems (see Chapter 13) and how to set up appropriate measurement and control systems to make sure that staff respond in the 'right' way (see Chapter 9).

So, service operations managers, unlike their manufacturing counterparts, have to manage, so far as is possible, the customer during the service process. This requires careful design of not only the back office processes but those front office processes that handle the customer. The design of these processes must manage the customer through the process with an awareness of the impact on the customer's experience and other customers' experiences. A good design will also take account of how the processes impact on the employees' feelings, as their attitudes will have a significant bearing on service performance (see Chapters 7–11). A key task for the nursery workers is managing the children in their care and recognising that tears or tantrums can easily affect the other children in the group.

The presence of the customer also means that the operation is visible to the customer. In the nursery the facilities and activities are visible not only to the child but also to the parents when dropping off and picking up the child and during the day as they 'drop in' via the web. So the service environment, sometimes referred to as the 'servicescape', needs to be designed to create the right atmosphere for the service to fit with the service concept (Chapter 3). A high-class restaurant, for example, should not have peeling wallpaper and dirty floors. The nursery should smell fresh and look clean with tidy and colourful pictures around the room.

2.3.4 Managing in real time

Because the customer is an input to, and involved in, the process, i.e. the process is their experience, many services happen in real time – they cannot be delayed or put off. A passenger wanting to purchase a ticket for immediate travel may not be willing to return if the agent is busy. Streams of aircraft coming into land cannot easily be put on hold while equipment is serviced or controllers take a break. Children screaming for attention or in danger of hurting themselves in the nursery likewise cannot be ignored. Furthermore, during a service encounter it is not possible to undo what is done or said – things said in the heat of the moment or promises made that cannot be kept. Unlike in manufacturing organisations where it is possible to scrap defective products and remake them, in service there is no 'undo' or 'rewind' button. Smacking a child in the nursery is inexcusable and will not go unnoticed with webcam 'spies' in the room. Managing resources (Chapter 11), managing staff/employees (Chapter 10) and creating an appropriate culture (Chapter 16) are key tasks in managing real time services.

2.3.5 Co-ordinating different parts of the organisation

The service operations manager is responsible for co-ordinating the various parts of the organisation in the delivery of the service; this includes not only understanding the needs of customers (see Chapter 5) but also overseeing the logistics of the supply chain to ensure that all materials and equipment are in the right place at the right time (see Chapter 6) and working closely with the other functions in the organisation (see Section 1.5). A nursery without the right staff and the right materials will not only provide a poor experience for the child but could be potentially dangerous.

2.3.6 Encouraging improvement and innovation

A challenge faced by all service operations managers is how continually to improve and develop their processes and their customers' experiences (Chapters 12–14), ensure that the outcomes are real improvements (Chapter 9) and that there is a culture that is supportive of service and change (Chapters 15 and 16). The challenge for some organisations is how to create a world-class service organisation (Chapter 17).

Improving the operation is about taking what exists and developing it. Innovation, on the other hand, looks for what is not there, i.e. what is new. Innovation therefore usually requires an element of risk; financial risk because innovations require time and money, and often personal risk as the 'champion' for change puts their reputation on the line. Introducing the webcam to the nursery was an innovation that required some expense and no doubt attracted some detractors. Whether it is a success only time will tell. A critical role for service operations managers is to be alert to, and seek out, new ideas but also to have the will, and support, to assess them carefully and follow through if appropriate (see Chapters 12, 13, 14 and 17).

2.4 What are the challenges for different types of services?

Although much of the general theory and practice described in this book applies to all operations, each sector of the service economy (such as financial services, tourism, leisure, charities, government, hospitals, business-to-business services) has its own set of specific challenges. Managing a for-profit consultancy with a small number of high-value clients poses rather different problems to managing an aid agency in a disaster-struck, heavily populated region of a developing country. This section describes some of the differences between the various types of services and outlines some of the particular challenges faced by each sector. In reading this section, it is necessary to be aware that each of these services will also have issues relating to aspects such as:

- The volume of transactions in a given time period. The hypermarket has very different operation challenges from the local grocery store, not least in simply managing the flow of hundreds of customers in the store.
- The mode of service delivery. The retail sector provides a good example of this diversity, with face-to-face service in traditional stores, remote service through mail order, telephone shopping or web-based services.

We will deal with these 'process' differences in the next section. Here we explore some of the key differences in service provision between five broad sectors of the service economy (see Table 2.2):

- business-to-business (B2B) services
- business-to-consumer (B2C) services
- internal services
- public (G2C) services
- not-for-profit services.

It is important to remember that we use the term 'customer' as an all-embracing term that covers users, consumers, internal customers, etc.

Table 2.2 Types of service and their key challenges

	Business-to-business (B2B) services	Business-to-consumer (B2C) services	Internal services	Public services (G2C)	Not-for-profit services
Description	Services provided for businesses	Services provided for individuals	Services provided by internal functions within organisations	Services provided by central or local government	Services provided by non-government organisations (NGOs) or charities
Examples	Maintenance Consultancy Training Catering	Shops Hotels Banks Food	Finance Purchasing IT Personnel	Prisons Hospitals Schools Leisure	Hospices Counselling Faith organisations Aid agencies
Customers	Professionals, who are not necessarily the end users	Individual consumers	Users who have little or no choice of provider; frequently funded by central budget	Citizens who may have little day-to-day choice; funded through taxation with the allocation of resources influenced by political processes	Beneficiaries are self-selecting or chosen recipients; funded through individual and organisational giving
Key challenges	Providing high-quality services to business customers who frequently have high purchasing power	Providing consistent service to a wide variety and high volume of customers	Demonstrating value for money against possible external alternatives	Balancing the various political pressures and providing acceptable public services	Dealing with differences between volunteers, donors and beneficiaries; dealing with emotional and sometimes overwhelming needs

2.4.1 Business-to-business (B2B) services

B2B services are provided by businesses for other businesses or organisations. IBM Global Services, for example (see Chapter 1), provides a range of services to its business customers, including computer installation and maintenance and a range of management consulting services. Other B2B services include outsourced catering services, buildings' maintenance or leasing and supporting equipment, financial services and market research. Some of the challenges for B2B services include:

● Dealing with multiple contacts in the organisation. Consultants may have to work with a wide range of employees in their client organisations and so maintain relationships at different levels in the organisation (Chapter 4).

● Working with a complex set of relationships. The users or recipients of a service will frequently not be the purchasers, and this purchasing group may in turn be different from those who commission or specify the service standards (see Chapter 4).

● B2B relationships may last for a long time. The challenge here is for the relationship not to become too 'cosy', with the customer or supplier being taken for granted (see Chapters 4 and 6).

2.4.2 Business-to-consumer (B2C) services

B2C services are those that individuals purchase for themselves or on behalf of another individual. They range through leisure services such as hotels, restaurants and sports provision, retail services such as shops and supermarkets, financial services such as banks and insurance providers, through to professional services such as lawyers and accountants. The challenges faced by most B2C services include:

- The organisation may deal with many different customers each day. Each has their own special needs and expectations of the service provided and, to make matters more difficult, these may change for the same individual from day to day (see Chapters 4 and 5).

- Because the operation serves so many customers, it faces a major challenge in keeping the experience fresh for the next new customer. It may be the first and only time the customer experiences this service, although the customer may be just one out of hundreds that an individual member of staff sees in a day (see Chapters 7 and 8).

- Many B2C service operations have the added complication of the need for consistency across many points of contact with customers, frequently spread nationally if not globally (see Chapter 9).

2.4.3 Internal services

Most managers are involved in providing and receiving internal service, not just internal services such as personnel, finance, purchasing and IT support, but also the day-to-day service they provide to each other, such as information and support. Indeed the Internal Service Rule highlights the importance of internal service provision: the level of external customer service will never exceed the level of internal customer service. The challenges posed by internal service provision include:

- Getting people within an organisation to recognise the service and the importance of the service they provide to each other, and treat it, assess it, measure it and improve it in just the same way as they deal with external service (see Chapters 3 to 11).

- Demonstrating that the internal services, such as IT and finance, provide at least as good 'value for money' as an external alternative. This is a challenge faced by many IT departments, for example, whose users often feel that they could obtain cheaper equipment more rapidly from the local computer store or via the internet (see Chapters 3 and 6).

- Adapting the service to business needs. If the service provision is effectively a commodity, it can be outsourced (see Chapter 6). Internal service providers must demonstrate their ability to tailor their offerings to the changing business needs in a way that external providers cannot (see Chapter 15).

- Gaining acceptance from their internal customers. Centrally funded services are frequently viewed with suspicion by local operating units and may not receive the co-operation required to carry out their tasks effectively (Chapter 6).

2.4.4 Public services (G2C)

These services are provided by central or local government for the community at large. Funding comes through the various forms of business and individual taxation, which is then largely allocated by policies set by government. Examples include police, prisons, hospitals and education. Specific challenges for public sector services include:

- The provision of 'best-value' services. Public services are under continual scrutiny. As a result, aspects of service operations that might be taken for granted by their private sector colleagues must be carefully justified in these organisations (see Chapter 9).

- Rationing supply of service. Public sector organisations cannot use the pricing mechanism to regulate demand. With essential services, this can be a very sensitive issue. The health service must make policy decisions as to how much resource can be devoted to heart operations, to maternity services, and so on. Expenditure on intensive care units, accident and emergency provision and very expensive drugs is particularly sensitive since lives are at stake, but inevitably there will be times when demand outstrips supply or costs exceed budgets (see Chapter 11).

- Multiple stakeholders. Public services suffer from having many 'customers'. With B2C services it is reasonably clear who the customers are, and if this group is satisfied, generally speaking the organisation should be successful. This is not the case with the public sector, where the recipients of the service, as individuals, have little power to influence. Politicians and service managers themselves may have far more power to decide current priorities (see Chapter 4).

- A confused service concept. The service concept provides direction for the organisation (we devote Chapter 3 to the discussion of the role of the service concept). Some public services are provided for the good of society at large and are not necessarily loved by those who have to deal with them. Prisons, police services and tax collectors may fall into this category.

2.4.5 Not-for-profit services

Charities of various types form the majority of these services. Most engage in a mixture of fund raising, providing information about the cause or issue that concerns them, and some form of social action. An organisation such as Oxfam must gather funds for famine relief and then organise to supply and distribute aid as required (see Case Example 2.4). Challenges for these services include:

- Managing a workforce of volunteers who, though highly motivated, may not always follow the organisation's procedures (see Chapter 10).

- Managing the allocation of resources to ensure that maximum funds flow to the beneficiaries of the organisation, while developing effective processes and people (see Chapters 7 to 11).

- Dealing with differences between the activities that might influence and impress donors, but which might conflict with the requirements of their 'customers' (see Chapter 3).

- Working in a highly emotional area, sometimes being overwhelmed by demand for service (see Chapter 11).

Case Example 2.4	Oxfam International

Oxfam is a major international development, relief and campaigning organisation dedicated to finding lasting solutions to poverty and suffering around the world. It is a confederation of 15 international organisations (country-based Oxfams) working with over 3,000 local partner organisations and alongside communities in 98 countries. It has three main activates: firstly, responding quickly to emergencies providing life-saving assistance to people affected by disasters; secondly, helping people living in poverty take control of their lives. Third, as a part of global movement for change, Oxfam spends time raising public awareness about the causes of poverty and pressing decision makers to change policies and practices to reduce poverty and injustice.

Source: Helen Jones

Each year Oxfam International launches emergency responses when lives, health, and livelihoods are threatened by disasters; natural disasters, such as earthquakes and storms, or political conflicts, such as riots and wars. In 2008–09 it worked on over ten major disaster areas where over 1,500,000 people were affected. The emergency programmes are usually run by Oxfam's regional and country offices. The organisation's headquarters provides advice, materials and staff, deploying emergency support personnel (ESP) on short-term assignments when and where their skills are required. Shelters, blankets and clothing can be flown out at short notice from the emergency warehouses. Engineers and sanitation equipment can also be provided, including water tanks, latrines, hygiene kits and containers such as the 'Oxfam bucket', which is light, easy to carry and transport, and has a sealable lid.

Every emergency is different, with differing security situations, aid needs, logistical problems and access issues. The responses of other agencies, such as governments or other relief agencies, will also be different, depending on the nature and location of the disaster. Oxfam relies on its local team, with support from headquarters as necessary, to assess each situation and decide whether and how the organisation can make a difference. Furthermore, local teams and partners are sometimes able to provide warnings of impending disasters, giving more time to assess need and enable a multi-agency response.

Importantly, when an emergency is over, Oxfam often continues to work with the affected communities through its local offices and partner organisations, to help people rebuild their lives and livelihoods.

With more than one billion people living in poverty across the world, Oxfam, like other aid and development organisations, has no shortage of 'non-emergency' work. Oxfam is recognised as a global expert in water and sanitation. Around 80 per cent of diseases and over one-third of deaths in the developing world are caused by contaminated water, and this can escalate in crises. Oxfam also puts pressure on governments to invest in agriculture and develop policies to help poor people benefit from international trade. It also promotes education and works with communities to provide education opportunities and with governments to train new teachers for poor countries.

All this work comes at a cost. The organisation's total expenditure on programmes in 2009–10 was €596.3 million which has to be raised through its affiliate organisations. Oxfam GB, for example, raised a total of £318 million, from legacies, gifts and donations and through events such as the Trailtrekker team endurance event and a Bookfest. The organisation also sells items donated by the public as well as Fair Trade products – food and handicrafts from around the world, giving small-scale producers fair prices, training, advice and funding support. Orders for items can be made by mail or over the internet through Oxfam GB's online shop, or through its network of 250 charity shops staffed by over 20,000 volunteers.

2.4.6 Different services within a sector

Just as each particular sector has its own set of challenges, there can be significant differences between service operations within sectors. This may relate to the way the organisation has chosen to compete or which customer segments are to be served. Table 2.3 outlines some key

Table 2.3 Comparing airline operations

	Low-cost airline	Full-service airline
Business model	High volume, low cost	Global network, profit made on business travel
Network	Short haul, with no connections to other carriers	Long haul, with connections to global partner airlines
Cabin service	Basic, no food, no frills	Range from economy to first class
Locations	Secondary, low-cost airports	Primary airports to allow interconnections
Volume	Multiple flights per route each day	Range from three flights per day to one flight per week for less popular destinations
Booking system	Direct through own website, and/or own contact centre	Usually through intermediaries (travel agents) or websites

differences between two B2C organisations operating in the same sector: a 'low-cost' airline and a 'full-service' airline.

One of the challenges for service operations managers is to match the style of operations, decisions about processes, people and technology to the overall strategy of the organisation (Chapter 15). To do this, the operations manager must have a clear understanding of how the operations function contributes to the overall success of the organisation (see Chapter 1).

2.4.7   A merging of distinctions

Over the last few years the distinctions between different types of organisations that we have outlined above are starting to disappear: 'Old borderlines are evaporating, old categories are merging. The divisions between commercial, public-sector and non-profit organisations are becoming blurred. All organisations now act on the same stage, and need to justify their place on that stage.'[4] Some non-commercial organisations, public sector organisations and charities, for example, emulate the private sector; they have chief executives, strategic plans, marketing departments and talk about 'customers'. Public organisations, although they do not have competitors, recognise that their customers judge their service against for-profit organisations. Charities and government bodies have money-making arms. The British Council, for example, which promotes British culture around the world, also runs for-profit language schools. Universities, charities and faith organisations talk openly about market share.

On the other hand, some commercial organisations commit themselves to adhere to the principles of corporate social responsibility (CSR). Some appoint board members to check that company decisions support human rights, environmental goals and conservation projects, for example, to demonstrate that the organisation stands for something beyond the usual commercial goals. Sir Richard Branson, who heads up the Virgin group of companies, supports a wide range of non-commercial activities, including supporting AIDS work and wildlife and habitat conservation in Africa. Finding himself in a position of power and influence after working hard to establish a profitable set of companies, he is keen to fulfil his lifelong ambition of 'trying to change the world'. He explains: 'I'd always thought that Virgin should be more than just a money-making machine, and that, as Virgin has the wealth of a small nation, we should use that wealth to tackle social issues . . . Companies do have a responsibility to tackle them.'[5]

2.5   What are the challenges for different types of processes?

From an operations perspective we tend to be less concerned with the type of organisation or the sector in which we are working and more concerned with the types of processes we are managing.

Different processes provide us with different benefits and also different challenges. Extremely flexible processes may be excellent for responding to a wide range of special customer requirements but may be quite costly to maintain. On the other hand, processes suited to delivering high-volume low-cost services are usually not very flexible. A simple example drawn from the hotel industry illustrates the differences:

- A five-star hotel prides itself on providing a wide range of services for its guests. Staff at the reception desk are prepared to spend time dealing with each customer's request and endeavour to answer every question. As a result, each transaction is quite lengthy and the hotel employs extra staff to ensure that the highest levels of service are achieved at all times for guests, who are paying premium prices.

- A budget hotel provides basic, reasonably comfortable accommodation for travellers normally staying for one or two nights. In this case, reception processes are designed to carry out only the basic check-in and payment activities as quickly as possible. Guests are not encouraged to request extra services and the number of receptionists is maintained at the minimum level to keep costs low.

Operational process design is influenced by two key parameters: the volume of transactions to be performed per period per unit, and the variety of tasks to be carried out by a given set of people and processes (we will discuss these in more detail in Chapter 8).

Commodity (high volume and low variety)

The budget hotel reception process is close to the 'commodity' position (high volume and low process variety) in Figure 2.2. Processes here are clearly defined, leaving little room for individual customisation. Many consumer services employ these types of processes, having benefits of consistency as well as economy. Other examples include many contact centre processes and retail activities. We have termed these commodity processes because there is little differentiation between services. They, however, have the benefit of delivering a clear service concept. A customer knows exactly what product and service to expect when purchasing a Big Mac from McDonald's.

Capability (low volume and high variety)

At the other end of the spectrum, we find 'capability' processes. Processes here have much less definition, with each task potentially significantly different from its predecessor. The reception activity in the five-star hotel is probably closer to this position rather than the commodity position of the budget hotel. The service concept is likely to be far less defined than the Big Mac and the 'have-a-nice-day' service that goes with it. In fact, many customers will be buying the ability of the service organisation to work with them to clarify the need or problem to be solved and then to develop a customised solution. Some professional service providers, such as consultants, will work in this way, although larger,

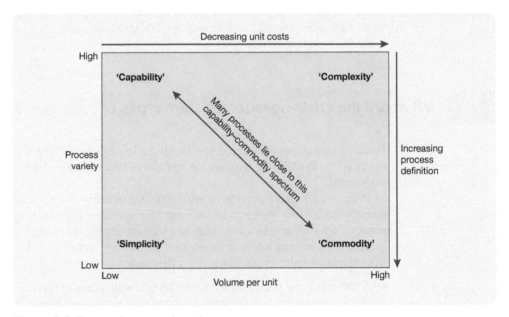

Figure 2.2 Four main types of service processes

Table 2.4 Capability versus commodity processes

	Capability	Commodity
Examples	Luxury hotel	Budget hotel chain
	Management guru	Software package training provider
	Corporate lawyer	House conveyancer
	Builder of architect-designed luxury homes	Garden shed erector
	Aviation insurance broker	Motor insurance provider
Process style	Flexible processes allowing for wide range of experiences and outcomes	Relatively rigid processes focused on narrow range of experiences and outcomes
Service offer	Ability to diagnose customer needs and to develop a customised solution	Ability to provide an economical and consistent service to meet the needs of many customers
What do they do well?	Flexible, innovative and responsive to individual customer needs	Low cost, with consistent quality and often rapid response
Major challenges	Co-ordinating the response of individual employees	Delivering consistently across multi-sites and many providers
	Maintaining differentiated competencies to justify premium prices	Employee morale and ownership of process and customer
	Managing productivity	Managing innovation
	Making best use of highly skilled and knowledgeable individuals	Managing large numbers of staff and customers

global professional service firms often adopt a relatively standardised way of working, implementing pre-packaged solutions, which places them closer to the bottom right corner of Figure 2.2. Table 2.4 summarises some of the key differences between capability and commodity processes. We have provided examples at each end of the capability–commodity spectrum from similar sectors to demonstrate that not all services within a broad sector will employ the same processes. In Chapter 8 we will return to the challenge faced by many services, which is that they must operate in more than one position on this volume–variety matrix.

There are two 'off-diagonal' positions also identified in Figure 2.2: simplicity and complexity.

Simplicity (low volume and low variety)

These include small operations such as microbreweries, and small and specialist consultancies. Some larger organisations may also develop 'simple' operations as start-up services, which then may grow in terms of volume or variety or both (we refer to this as an incubator in Chapter 8).

Complexity (high volume and high variety)

At first sight, this position might seem to be the ideal, providing maximum flexibility for as many customers as possible. In reality, however, providing flexibility for large numbers of customers is invariably expensive, achieved by employing large numbers of highly skilled people and/or high-tech equipment.

One of the challenges for service operations managers is to ensure that the type of process is appropriate to deliver the service concept (see Chapter 3). As service concepts change and evolve, existing processes may become less appropriate for the task in hand. Effective managers will recognise this issue and proactively develop new process designs to meet the future requirements.

2.6 What are the challenges in working with other management functions?

The management of service operations, as we hope is becoming clear, is extremely demanding. However, operations managers cannot do their job in isolation; they require a close working relationship with other internal functions, such as marketing (to ensure what is sold can be delivered), IT (to ensure the equipment and software used by the operation is appropriate and available when needed), HR (to ensure the right people with the right skills are in place) and so on. However, working closely with other management functions poses some particular challenges; indeed for some organisations these internal challenges are some of the most difficult that they face!

- *Too much focus on the day-to-day.* We mentioned earlier that the excitement of managing operations is its immediacy, dealing with the needs of a stream of customers, managing the staff and making the many tactical decisions that are needed to ensure the delivery of an appropriate quality of service at an appropriate cost. As a result operations managers tend to focus on the day-to-day issues. Indeed, this is what many of them are good at; sorting out the day-to-day problems. The perspective of other functions may be concerned with more long-term issues; the board may be focused on strategic decision-making, IT may be investigating new technological opportunities and HR trying to evaluate how changes in regulations may affect pensions. Of course many of these functions are running day-to-day activities as well. IT is keeping the hardware and software going, HR is dealing with staff grievances. These are their 'operational' activities – as all managers are operations managers and deliver service in the short or long term to their internal customers. The point is that operations' focus on the here-and-now can cause tensions with other functions where managers are trying to plan for the longer term. Operations managers are often too tied up to be able to spare the time to become involved.

- *Lack of strategic influence.* Because of the short-term focus of the job, operations tend to attract and recruit people who are good at being reactive and fire-fighting problems as they arise. As a result they tend to lack strategic focus and are naturally less good at dealing with the higher-level and more intuitive processes required for contributing to strategic decision-making. As a result operations managers' influence in the boardroom is sometimes limited and therefore the organisation's understanding of the present and future capability of the operation is not always taken into account.

- *Limited focus on innovation.* Operations managers tend to be rooted in the present, dealing with the day-to-day issues. They tend to be reactionary and conservative, though we prefer to call it being 'rooted in reality'. As a result operations managers are not always willing to open themselves to new ideas and opportunities. Any change usually has often unwelcome and significant operational consequences (see the Case Exercise on Sky Airways at the end of this chapter). Such tensions and differing points of view, however, are ideal ingredients for innovation, so operations managers need to be better at managing the conversations with other functions.

- *Difficulty of making the business case.* Any changes tend to have to be justified in financial terms. Operations managers usually know the cost of any change they want to make, whether it's the purchase of new equipment or the recruitment of new staff; they also intuitively understand the positive impact this will have on customers, staff and sales for example, but these things can be very difficult to demonstrate in concrete enough terms to convince a financial director. This is an important area and in Chapter 17 we will explain how operations managers can make the business case to support their requirements.

2.7   How can this book help?

One of the key purposes of this book is to help you deal with the many challenges that service operations managers face which we have outlined in this chapter. The book is structured into five main parts: Frame, Connect, Deliver, Improve and Implement. The chapters in these parts are focused on how to deal with the various challenges. The single chapter in the Frame part deals with a critical and central issue: how to develop and use the service concept to define and communicate the nature of the business, create organisational alignment, drive innovation and strategic advantage, and design the service. The following parts, Connect, Deliver, Improve and Implement, each contain several chapters with their associated 'how tos', as shown in Figure 2.3.

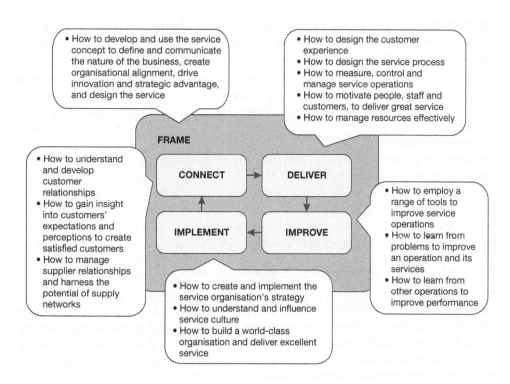

Figure 2.3 The structure of the book

2.8   Summary

What are the key strategic challenges faced by service operations managers?

- Managing tactically and strategically
- Making operations a contributor to strategy as well as an implementer
- Making the business case for service
- Understanding the service concept.

What are the key tactical challenges faced by service operations managers?

- Understanding the customer perspective
- Managing multiple customers
- Managing the customer
- Managing in real time
- Co-ordinating different parts of the organisation
- Encouraging improvement and innovation.

What are the challenges for different types of services?

- There are five broad sectors of the service economy: business-to-business services, business-to-consumer services, internal services, public services and not-for-profit services.
- The key challenges are:
  - B2B – providing high-quality services to business customers who frequently have high purchasing power
  - B2C – providing consistent service to a wide variety and high volume of customers
  - internal services – demonstrating value for money against possible external alternatives
  - public services (G2C) – balancing the various political pressures and providing acceptable public services
  - not-for-profit services – dealing with differences between volunteers, donors and beneficiaries.

What are the challenges for different types of process?

- There are four main types of service processes: capability, commodity, simplicity and complexity. A key challenge for service operations managers is to ensure that the type of process is appropriate to deliver the service concept.

What are the challenges in working with other management functions?

- Too much focus on the day-to-day
- Lack of strategic influence
- Limited focus on innovation
- Difficulty of making the business case.

2.9 Discussion questions

1 What are the similarities and differences in terms of the operational challenges faced by global service organisations such as FedEx, Accenture, Amnesty International and Red Crescent? Use their websites for more information about what the organisations do.

2 Consider your university/college. What do you think are the challenges their course delivery operations face in providing you with good service?

3 What do you think are the challenges faced by multi-site operations (organisations that have many outlets)?

2.10 Questions for managers

1 What are the key tactical and strategic challenges your service operation faces?

2 How would you categorise your service operation? What are the implications?

3 What are the key relationships operations has with other parts of the organisation and how well are they managed?

Case Exercise   Sky Airways

Robert Johnston and Bridgette Sullivan-Taylor, Warwick Business School

Sky Airways is a major European airline with routes predominantly in Europe but offering daily flights to New York, Johannesburg, Mumbai and St Petersburg. At the last meeting of the board of directors the airline's chief executive, Bernie Williamson, expressed concern at the growing number of complaints his airline was receiving. His analysis of the increasing trend revealed a strong link between number of complaints and minutes' delay. This did not surprise him. What did surprise him was the large number of underlying complaints that were, in the main (around 72 per cent), about the on-board catering.

Given his desire to increase RPK (revenue passenger kilometre), which had declined by 5 per cent over the past three years, he was keen to hear ideas from his team as to how they could deal with the problem. This was an opportunity seized upon by Angela Carter-Smith, Sky's recently appointed marketing director. She suggested that the airline should consider moving away from pre-packed and reheated meals in tourist class to the business-class style of service, whereby food is pre-cooked but heated, assembled and served in front of the customers. She explained: 'Many international airlines are attempting to enhance their competitive edge by differentiating their in-flight service offering across their global network.' The food costs, she suggested, would be little different but simply require more time by cabin attendants, which they have on the longer flights. If this proved to be successful on the long hauls, it could then be considered on the short hauls. When Bernie reminded her that they needed to provide an upgraded service for the premium-fare passengers, she added that the answer here was to provide 'culturally sensitive' meals: flying to and from Mumbai, the food should be Indian, while to Johannesburg it should have a distinct African flavour. All eyes then turned to Peter Greenwood, the operations director, who had his head in his hands and was groaning. He promised to 'look into it' and report back at the next meeting.

The next day Peter made time to talk about the rising trend in complaints to Christina Towers, the catering subcontract manager, Justin Maude, a senior cabin attendant, and David Goh, senior gate manager.

Christina Towers explained:

The problem we have, like all other catering companies, is consistency. Although we can specify menus, portions and costs there are inevitably wide variations in quantity and quality loaded at various airports around the world. We have the biggest problems at the furthest destinations. You also put us under pressure to reduce costs, so we only try to load the precise number of meals required in order to reduce wastage and space required. It is not easy making pre-flight predictions about both numbers and choices, and you cannot expect it to be right 100 per cent of the time without substantially increasing the number of meals loaded over and above passenger predictions. It is not cost effective and it is weight prohibitive to load two of every meal option, even for a business-class passenger who would expect, more than anyone else, to receive their first choice. I think we would get fewer complaints if we reduced choice of menus.

Justin Maude added:

You would not believe the difficulties we face in providing something as simple as meals to passengers. We frequently have to explain to passengers, in all the cabins, why they can't have their first choice of meal. This creates a great deal of stress for the crew. There is just no room for more meals on board; the galleys are really tight for space. The biggest problem we have is over passengers who order special meals for religious, dietary or health reasons. I reckon one in five is not loaded on to the aircraft. Sometimes we have passengers on board who ask whether the food contains nuts and we have no idea. We can only offer them water and bread rolls to be safe. I think we should ensure the caterers let us know the contents of every meal and always provide extra vegetarian and kosher meals because passengers don't always remember to pre-book them. Another problem is caused by the last-minute passengers whom you want us to take to fill seats, so we often have to ask for more meals shortly before take-off. I know this causes problems but, unlike a restaurant, during flight there is nowhere to find additional supplies. I think it would help if we could have meals that needed less preparation time and take less space, so we can load more meals in anticipation of an increase in passengers and also load additional special meals, just in case.

David Goh then added his views:

The main problem I have is ten minutes before take-off when we find that the incorrect quantity, quality and meal type are loaded and the crew request extra meals. We often end up delaying a plane and missing a slot while the caterers rush over half a dozen extra meals. We should let the plane go. I am sure not everyone actually wants a meal. They only eat because they are bored. I think we should stop providing meals altogether, certainly on the short hauls. Tourist-class passengers often eat at the airport anyway and we already provide food for business class in the executive lounges.

Peter had not dared raise the idea of changing the methods of service in tourist class and increasing the range and type of meals to business-class passengers. His thoughts turned to how he could explain to the board the difference between what might be desirable and what is deliverable and appropriate.

Questions

1 What problems does Peter Greenwood face?

2 If you were Peter Greenwood, what would you say to the board?

Suggested further reading

Johnston, Robert (2005), 'Service Operations Management: From the Roots Up', *International Journal of Operations and Production Management* 25 (12) 1298–1308

Neu, Wayne A. and Stephen W. Brown (2005), 'Forming Successful Business-to-Business Services in Goods-Dominant Firms', *Journal of Service Research* 8 (1) 3–17

Shaw, Colin, Qaalfa Dibeehi and Steven Walden (2010), *Customer Experience: Future Trends and Insights*, Palgrave Macmillan

Slack, Nigel, Stuart Chambers and Robert Johnston (2010), *Operations Management*, 6th edition, FT Prentice Hall, Harlow

Useful web links

A short paper by Robert Hayes outlining his view of operations challenges:
http://findarticles.com/p/articles/mi_qa3796/is_200204/ai_n9067667/

An interesting piece by Carina Paine Schofield of the Ashridge Public Leadership Centre on key challenges facing public sector leaders:
www.ashridge.org.uk—KeyChallengesFacingPublicSectorLeaders.pdf

A piece on topical service management challenges from CTMA consulting in New Zealand:
www.ctmaworld.com/Challenges.htm

An article on the challenges faced by female service managers at the Diversity in Leadership blog:
www.robturknett.com/diversityinleadership

Currently a topical issue: third sector management challenges discussed at The Australian Review of Public Affairs:
www.australianreview.net—cutcher.html

Notes

1   Shaw, Colin and John Ivens (2002), *Building Great Customer Experiences*, Palgrave, London; Price, Reg and Roderick J. Brodie (2001), 'Transforming a Public Service Organization from Inside Out to Outside In', *Journal of Service Research* 4 (1) 50–59

2   Carbone, Lewis P. (2004), *Clued In*, FT Prentice Hall, New Jersey

3   Edvardsson, Bo and Jan Olsson (1996), 'Key Concepts for New Service Development', *The Service Industries Journal* 16 (2) 140–164

4   Jones, Robert (2001), *The Big Idea*, Harper Collins Business, London

5   Branson, Richard (2003), *Losing My Virginity: The Autobiography*, Virgin Books, London, p. 529

Part 2 Frame

Chapter 3 Developing and using the service concept   46

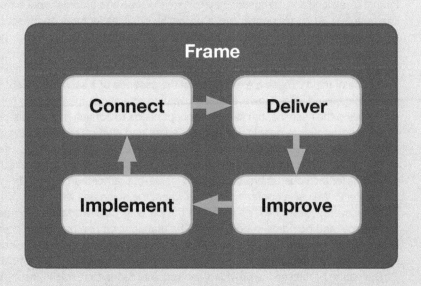

Chapter 3
Developing and using the service concept

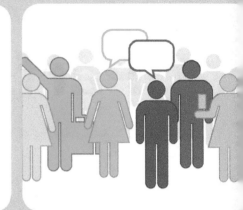

Chapter objectives

This chapter is about how to develop and use the service concept to define and communicate the nature of the business, create organisational alignment, drive innovation and strategic advantage, and design the service.

- What is a service concept?
- How can managers use the service concept?

3.1 Introduction

It is important to recognise that when buying (or using) services customers tend not to be simply buying the elements of a service but something much greater and usually more intangible. Looked at simply, in terms of its elements, a hotel provides a bed, bathroom and food. Looked at as a concept a hotel can provide anything from a low-cost, comfortable night's sleep, through a relaxing and pampered stay, to a truly unique and unforgettable experience (see Case Example 3.1). At an elemental level a university provides lectures, food, accommodation and books, but what its customers are looking to acquire is something much greater and more intangible – an 'educational experience' or 'improved job prospects'. Likewise, we go to Disney for a 'magical experience' or to a restaurant for a 'great evening out' or to a firm of consultants for 'peace of mind'. These are examples of the **essence** of a service concept, what we refer to as the 'organising idea'. However, to be useful to operations managers to help design, deliver and develop their service, the service concept needs to contain much more detail.

An important issue here is that the managers and staff of just about every service organisation can easily lose sight of what customers or users want. Service providers tend to focus on their processes and the output of those activities rather than the desired experience and outcomes for their customers, i.e. thinking inside-out rather than outside-in – as we discussed in Chapter 2. We use a conference centre where the delegates want a quick and simple buffet lunch or even sandwiches, so they can get on with their workshop and get their 'learning experience' and go home in good time. The manager, whose background was in fine dining, believes the centre should provide a three-course lunch, with several choices, and service at table. These different yet firmly held views often cause tensions and complaints.

The nature of the service provided and required tends to reside in the minds of managers, staff and customers and is seldom captured and clearly articulated. Importantly these mental pictures and assumptions about the organisation's services may be different in the minds of those managers, staff and customers.[1] The service concept is an attempt to create a clear, agreed, shared and articulated definition of the nature of the service provided and received, in order to ensure that the essence of the service is delivered. Note that when we use the word 'service' in this book we are using it as a shortened version of the term 'service concept'.

It should also be noted that marketers may use terminology similar to the service concept to describe the service promise or service proposition, i.e. the service provided. We use the term 'service concept' to pull together the provider's view (service provided) and the customer's view (service received or required) to help provide a shared and agreed base for the design, delivery and development of a service.

In this chapter we will explain how the service concept can be articulated and show how it can be used to drive understanding and also innovate new services.

3.2　What is a service concept?

When asked his secret of success, Ingvar Kamprad, the founder of the IKEA chain of furniture stores, replied 'We are a concept company.' He went on to share his vision and explain the concept: 'Our vision is to contribute to a better everyday life for the majority of people. We do this by offering a wide range of home furnishing items of good design and function, at prices so low that the majority of people can afford to buy them.' This concept has captured the imaginations of both IKEA's employees and customers. People buy IKEA products because they are well made, stylish and inexpensive. They also buy into the idea of self-selection, self-service, self-delivery and self-build.

The service concept is an important way of capturing the nature of a service so that customers know what they are getting and staff understand what they are providing. The service concept can also be used to help develop new services. For example, Yngve Bergqvist, president of Icehotel, created a new concept in hotels. Having few visitors in the very cold winter months he got the idea of creating a hotel made out of ice, as described in Case Example 3.1. Some years ago, First Direct implemented a new concept in banking. At a time when banks were (unwelcoming) places with lavish banking halls, long queues and a 'you-should-be-grateful' style of service, First Direct created a bank to suit the customer. It is open 24 hours a day and accessible by phone or the internet. The phone service is not staffed by traditional bank clerks but by people who are interested in helping people. First Direct is a bank with personality. Its staff are witty and warm, straightforward, informed and informing, and certainly not ordinary. (We will develop the use of the service concept to create new services in Section 3.3.)

Case Example 3.1　The Icehotel

Jukkas AB is a company offering a wide range of activities, such as white-water rafting, fishing, reindeer and dog-sledding tours, cross-country skiing, snowmobile safaris and guided tours. It is based in Jukkasjärvi, a small village in Swedish Lapland, which lies 200 kilometres north of the Arctic Circle by the River Torne.

The problem was that visitors were few and far between in the long, dark winter months when the temperature drops to −40 °C. Manager, Yngve Bergqvist, now president of Icehotel, saw this as an opportunity. In the winter of 1989 he invited a group of Japanese ice artists to come to Jukkasjärvi to carve sculptures from

the crystal clear ice that forms from the pure waters of the River Torne. He then built a 60-square-metre cylinder-shaped igloo, made out of clear ice blocks, to protect the sculptures. Visitors flocked to see the exhibits in his 'ice gallery'. One day when his hotel was full he was pressed by a good friend to find accommodation for ten colleagues. Yngve could only offer them space in his 'ice gallery' with sleeping bags on reindeer skins. In the morning the guests enthused about the 'warm and intense experience'. The Icehotel was born.

In winter the Icehotel covers approximately 5,000 square metres and is built out of 30,000 tonnes of snow and 4,000 tonnes of ice. The hotel has a reception, around 40 rooms and 25 suites. It has its own Iceart exhibition, Icebar and Icechurch. Since the hotel melts every spring the number of rooms, as well as the exhibits, varies from year to year!

The temperature in the bedrooms is a relatively warm −5 °C. Guests sleep on a bed of warm insulating reindeer hides in an ultra-warm sleeping bag. In the morning they can enjoy an early morning sauna followed by breakfast. Toilets are located in a small heated building adjacent to the Icehotel. In the evening the guests drink in the Icebar from Iceglasses sculpted from the pure ice of the River Torne. During the day guests eat in the restaurant 100 metres away and take part in the adventure activities such as dog sledding and snowmobile safaris.

Each year a new Icehotel is constructed by around 30 local artists and builders before the arrival of the first guests in mid December. Snow cannon are used to blast snow on to a frame of arched steel sections, and ice pillars are added for extra support. The walls are made from huge, clear blocks of ice, weighing almost two tonnes, cut from the frozen river with special saws and moved by front-loading tractors. Work on the interior starts in early December, when sculptors cut and work the ice to create windows, doors, pillars, beds, lamps and ice sculptures. Guest ice artists are invited each year to design the ice décor in some of the rooms.

When April comes the roof of the Icehotel begins to drip. The hotel is closed and it slowly melts back into the river from where it came.

Source: This illustration is based on material on the Icehotel website, www.icehotel.com, and discussions with managers.

The service concept is something very important to service organisations, but is often not articulated, shared or understood. It is something that is more emotional than a business model, deeper than a brand, more complex than a good idea and more solid than a vision. It is also something that can unite employees and customers and create a business advantage.

A service concept is a **shared** and **articulated** understanding of the nature of the service provided and received, which should capture information about:

- *The organising idea* – the essence of the service bought, or used, by the customer.
- *The service provided* – the service process and its outputs which have been designed, created and enacted by the operation using its many input resources, including the customer.
- *The service received:*
  - *The customer experience* – the customer's direct and personal interpretation of, and response to, their interaction with and participation in the service process, and its outputs, involving their journey through a series of touch points/steps.
  - *The service outcomes* – the results for the customer of the service process and their experience including 'products', benefits, emotions, judgements and intentions (see Chapter 1).

The detailed service concept may be based upon an explicit statement made by the organisation or it may be inferred from marketing information – either direct marketing by the organisation or indirect marketing through experience and word-of-mouth. In Figure 3.1 we provide an example of a service concept and some of its key elements for a UK theme park (see Chapter 11 for more details of this organisation) and Figure 3.2 provides one for an internal IT support provider.

Organisation	**Alton Towers**	
Organising idea	**A great day out at a theme park**	
Service concept (summary)	A great day out with friends or family at a UK theme park that provides an inclusive package of over 100 rides and attractions to suit all ages and tastes with thrills, fun, fantasy, fast food and magnificent gardens.	
Service provided	• Car parking • Transport to entrance • Ticketing • Security • Clean and tidy park • Uniformed and helpful staff • Fair queuing systems	• White knuckle rides • Shows and attractions • Children's rides • Well-kept gardens • Food outlets • Toilets • Street entertainers
Service received	**Customer experience:** • Easy parking • Good signage • Exhilarating rides • Enjoyable attractions • Full day out • Fun time • Never a dull moment • Lots of rides • Lots of food available • Helpful staff • Clean toilets	**Outcomes:** • Good food • 18 rides used • 3 attractions experienced • Fun day out with the family • Thrills • Terrifying rides • Exhausting • Car parking is extra • Good value for money • Want to go again • Will recommend to friends

Figure 3.1 Alton Towers' service concept

Organisation	**IT Infrastructure Support Group**	
Organising idea	**Helpful and dependable IT support for internal users**	
Service concept (summary)	Helpful and dependable helpdesk service, professionally managed, and reliable IT infrastructure (storage, servers, network, internet) and expert advice to end users and business leaders at low total cost in accordance with set standards and policies.	
Service provided	**End users** • Hardware and software support • Training services • Helpdesk available 8x7 • Phone/email support for non-critical problems 8.00 to 6.00 • Walk-in facility from 9.00 to 5.30 • At desk service available 9.00 to 5.30	• On call support by phone/email for critical problems 24x7 • Reliable infrastructure • Responsive and effective call resolution **Business leaders** • Monthly management meetings • Monthly utilisation and satisfaction metrics • Services within budget and value for money
Service received	**Customer experience:** **End users** • Personalised, capable helpdesk • Informed about issues • Fast recovery from failures • Good communications during failures • Confident, assured and professional **Business leaders** • No surprises • Professional technical advice • Genuine concern and understanding of business needs	**Outcomes:** **End users** • IT problems sorted • No service disruptions • All critical services available > 99.995% • Highly satisfied users and high perceived user value **Business leaders** • Planned infrastructure availability and expansion • Low cost of infrastructure and within budget • Effective advice on increasing employee productivity • Low cost of service • Efficient resource utilisation • High employee productivity • IT standards and policies implemented

Figure 3.2 IT Infrastructure Support Group's service concept

A service concept should provide sufficient detail to make it clear what the organisation is selling/providing and what the customer is buying/receiving. Thus the service concept represents the nature of the service offering, which guides operations staff and managers to know what to deliver and how to deliver it and helps marketing know what to offer to the customers or users.

3.2.1 The organising idea

The 'organising idea' provides a powerful way of reminding the service provider what the customer is really buying, and therefore provides focus for resource allocation and service design. It acts as a 'magnifying glass' helping the organisation focus on what is important. For example, a store selling paint, tools and other items for home improvements may be organised around 'providing the cheapest hardware in town' or 'enabling the customer to carry out high-quality home improvements'. The first idea would require an operation focused on 'no frills', efficiency and economy, whereas the second idea might require investment in skilled sales staff to provide guidance for customers as to how best to carry out their do-it-yourself (DIY) projects.

There may be more than one 'organising idea' for a service provider. We worked with a house builder and identified that although the output for each customer was a completed house, the outcome could be very different from the customer's viewpoint. Here are the two examples:

- **The investor:** This customer is interested in a property that they can rent out for the short or medium term and sell in the longer term. The property needs to be of acceptable quality in a good location. This customer is not emotionally involved in the construction process.
- **Building the dream:** This customer sees the house as part of their identity. It clearly needs to be of good quality in the right location and this customer is emotionally involved in the process and wants to be present at key stages in the construction process. The customer also wants to be involved in the decision-making as the project progresses.

Understanding the differences between customer groups is key to success. Not surprisingly, the builder saw the second customer group as interfering and made no accommodation for them. We will return to this theme later in the chapter but it is important to understand that the organisation's culture is at the heart of the issue here. If an organisation has been successful (survived) for any length of time the mindsets become quite rigid. So the builder believed that customers should not be involved in the construction. Getting the builder to accept a different 'organising idea' was a significant challenge in organisational culture terms. We will return to this in Chapter 16, but it is important to note that however much we accept a change in theory, there has to be an emotional commitment for this to work.

3.2.2 The customer experience

Service academics and service practitioners are focusing more attention on the customer experience. We have devoted Chapter 7 to discussing this in more detail. We know that customers will often judge the quality of the outcome by the quality of the experience they receive, not least because they may have limited or no understanding of the processes involved in delivering the service. The patient will normally have no understanding of the detail of hip surgery, but they will certainly be able to evaluate the quality of care and attention they receive in the process. Many patients report frustration with the lack of information they receive in the course of treatment. This may not be that medical staff don't care, but more likely that they don't understand that information which they require to do their job (manage their internal process) is also of interest to the patient. They see a 'body in a bed' that needs treatment, not a human being with fears and anxieties that a little information would ease.

3.2.3 The service outcomes

The key point here is to recognise the subtle difference between outcomes for customers versus outputs from the service process. Using examples from Chapter 2, the output from surgery is the replaced hip, whereas the desired outcome for the patient will be a working hip providing the benefit of greater mobility. The output from an educational process may be a student who has satisfied the requirements of the examiners but the desired outcome for that student will be greater employability.

This may seem obvious, but as we hinted earlier there is a tendency to continue what some academics refer to as 'provider push'. Providers keep delivering what has worked in the past, and what they are good at! The conference centre we mentioned earlier started losing business to its competitors who provided simpler meals. Their costs were lower and so they could compete at marginally lower prices which were enough to get the business in this highly competitive market. If this company had been able to respond more rapidly, it would have been much more successful, focusing its resources and processes in different areas. There may be significant competitive advantage in recognising how customer needs are shifting, frequently in quite subtle ways.

3.2.4 Service value

In Chapter 1 we provided some information about the customer experience and service outcomes. The main service outcomes are 'products', benefits, emotions, judgements, including value, and intentions. It is appropriate here to provide a little more detail about value.

An important element of the marketing mix is price. Price is the value placed on the service. This could be its monetary value, the financial price, or its comparative value if the service is bartered. The price of a service may be referred to in many different ways: the price of money is called interest; the price of poor motoring may be, in financial terms, a fine; while the price for use of equipment is rent.

The cost of a service to a customer is a combination of the financial price together with the cost, or inconvenience, of making the purchase – sometimes called the sacrifice. For example, the cost of buying the weekly groceries involves not only the monetary value of the goods but also the cost of going to the shops to make their purchase – this is not only the cost of travelling by car but also the sacrifice of effort and time involved, which could have been put to other uses. The cost of poor driving is not only the fine, but also loss of a no-claims bonus, higher insurance premiums and possibly injury or even death, with the mental 'cost' that follows.

To understand value, these costs to the consumer have to be weighed against the benefits consumers perceive in the service. The benefits are not just the tangible benefits but also the intangible feelings and emotions resulting from the experience, such as a feeling of well-being or being recognised in a restaurant. Value, therefore, does not necessarily mean low price. Value is the customer's assessment of the benefits of the service weighed against all the costs involved.

A key role of marketers is to try to assess these issues to understand what customers value in order to help the organisation make pricing decisions. Operations management, on the other hand, is the art of creating and delivering value. The task for operations is to find the balance between maximising the value for customers and minimising the cost to the organisation; that is, striking a profitable or in-budget balance between

- maximising the benefits to the consumer,
- minimising the financial and sacrificial costs to the customer, and
- minimising the cost to the organisation.

The service concept is therefore a key tool that can communicate the set of benefits (tangible 'products' and psychological experiences) to the customer in order to demonstrate the potential value of the service.

An operation delivers and creates value by playing a part in the supply chain (see Chapter 6): adding value to the supply chain to create its services and value to its customers. Some organisations go further – indeed the more successful organisations do not just *add* value, they *reinvent* it.[2] Many services have been reinvented over the last few years. For example, internet banking has challenged and radically changed the value delivered by banks and received by their customers. From a customer's point of view, new approaches to banking, such as those pioneered by First Direct, have provided 'a new kind of value. In particular, it eliminated traditional constraints of time and space'.[3] Now customers can manage their accounts and move funds at any time of day or night, almost anywhere. Internet banking, and many other internet services, have not only reinvented value for customers but also changed the nature of value creation by the operation. Bank managers are now concerned with the design and maintenance of customer-interaction technology (websites, plastic cards and computer networks to support the machines), and in dealing with the inevitable disadvantages of automation, such as trying to maintain a relationship with customers they rarely see.

It is important to emphasise that the ultimate judge of value is the customer. More important still is that the real test is perceived value – whether the customers feel that they are receiving value, based on criteria that are their own, and frequently intangible and intuitive. Here again, the service concept is central to understanding customer requirements: facilitating marketing in presenting the service offer in the most effective manner, and focusing the operation's performance measures on those areas that have most impact on the customers' perceptions.

In Chapter 12 we will return to the issue of value, in particular the difference between customer perceived value and organisational value. In Chapter 15 we will show how delivering perceived value is central to creating competitive advantage.

3.2.5 The emotional dimension

A key element of the 'service received' is the emotional dimension. The service designer and operations manager must understand what emotions are likely to be evoked during the customer experience and also resulting from the service outcomes.

Home Depot is an American home improvement store. Its customer statement used to be 'We sell you the opportunity to improve your home and therefore your self esteem'. Home Depot understood that this emotional connection was central to their success. The customer experience was designed around building confidence in the mind of the customer that they could carry out the necessary home improvement tasks, and they recognised that a better home would mean better 'self esteem' as an outcome. Home Depot was the first store of this kind to invest more heavily in employing older, more experienced staff who could advise inexperienced customers, and also to provide customer demonstrations to build confidence to tackle home improvement projects.

In a similar vein, a UK mobile phone provider has employed 'gurus' in their stores to solve customer problems. Their role is not to sell products but to ensure that customers and potential customers are happy with their purchases and understand how to get the best out of their phones.

3.2.6 What the service concept is not

In this section defining what a service concept is, it will be helpful to clarify what it is not.

- **The service promise.** The promise defines what the organisation will do for the customer – which may not be what the customer wants. The service concept is an agreed view of the service provided and received.
- **The business proposition.** The business proposition defines the way in which the organisation would like to have its services perceived by all its stakeholders – customers, employees, shareholders and lenders. This view, however, may not be shared by customers, who may perceive the nature of the service in a different way.
- **The 4 Ps.** Services and products are sometimes described in terms of their constituent parts. The marketing literature often refers to the 4 Ps of marketing (Product, Price, Promotion

and Place), sometimes expanded to the 8 Ps, which encompass some of the elements of the service concept – Product, Process, Place, Physical evidence, People, and Productivity and quality – plus additional marketing elements: Price and Promotion.[4] Deconstructing a service in this way is helpful in that it allows us to identify the various elements of a concept, check them against customers' needs (see Chapter 4), design and deliver those elements and measure performance against them (Chapters 7–11). However, this 'bits and pieces' approach belies the complexity of many services and also ignores the fact that customers' perceptions of service are more intangible. For example, a day out at Disney's Magic Kingdom is more likely to be defined by its designers and its visitors as a 'magical experience' rather than six rides and a burger in a clean park.[5]

- **Business model.** A business model describes how an organisation achieves its financial goal. A 'no-frills' airline's model is based on low cost: minimising airport charges, fuel costs, employee costs, food costs etc., providing very limited service, using a point-to-point operation and appealing to large volumes of cost-conscious passengers. This certainly helps describe the value part of the service concept and some of the operations too, but it misses out on the more emotional level of the customer experience.

- **Vision.** An organisation's vision is usually concerned with where the organisation hopes to be at some time in the future. The service concept is usually concerned with the present; what the organisation does now and what its customers think it does today. However, the service concept can be used to provide some details about a vision to help managers bring it about by developing new services.

- **Mission.** The service concept is not usually the same as a mission statement. Organisations' mission statements cover many notions from 'vision statements' to 'company philosophy'. Like vision statements, mission statements may be concerned with the future rather than today's reality. On the other hand, if they define the organisation's philosophy it is possible that they tend to be more concerned with organisational values rather than the detail of the service that is provided and received.

- **An idea.** An idea is an initial, often unformed, notion of a service. A service concept is a more complete picture, which includes details about the service provided and the experience and outcomes for the customer.

- **Brand.** The service concept is more closely related to the notion of brand. However, brand has many meanings, including: brand name – the name, design symbol or any other feature that identifies a service (or a product);[6] presented brand – how the organisation presents itself and its promise through its marketing efforts; external brand – how the organisation is presented through word-of-mouth communication and the media, for example; and brand meaning – the customers' perception of the organisation and its services. While these four perspectives may be different, a service concept is a shared view and is articulated in much more detail (sufficient for both marketers to know what they are selling and operations to know what they have to deliver and how it has to be delivered). Thus the service concept is usually more detailed and concrete than a brand.

3.3 How can managers use the service concept?

At a strategic level the service concept can be used to define and communicate the nature of the business, to create organisational alignment and to develop new service concepts to drive innovation and strategic advantage. The concept is also the starting point for the development of an operations strategy. We will discuss this last point in more detail in Chapter 15. The service concept can be used operationally to help design and specify the service and assess the operational implications of those design changes.

3.3.1 Defining and communicating the nature of the business

We believe there is an opportunity for many service organisations to take control of their service concept and make it explicit. When we ask groups of individuals, managers, staff and/or customers to define the service concept of a particular organisation, we invariably find a range of views. Even managers working in the same department often have differing views about what their department does for the rest of the organisation (their internal service concept). The problem is that 'what we do around here' and 'what our customers expect' are seldom discussed, articulated or compared. Differing and unspoken perspectives and assumptions result in inconsistent service provision and confused and annoyed customers, internal and external. Managers need to take responsibility for making the nature of their service explicit by ensuring a clear and appropriate 'marketing' message to both employees and customers about the nature of the service concept. Only in this way will they help ensure appropriate, and consistent, service delivery.

3.3.2 Creating organisational alignment

We would argue that the service concept can therefore act as an alignment tool that links together different organisational functions with a common purpose and 'standard' against which their actions can be checked. 'In this respect the service concept acts as a lens and filter through which internal functions may see each other's roles and contributions to the service delivered to the customer.'[7] The articulation and agreement of a service concept is a means not only of identifying the nature of the business but also of providing it with a sense of purpose and common direction. It also provides a means of assessing the contributions and interrelationships among the various functional groups.

We would therefore suggest that in order to share, communicate and evaluate a concept, it needs to be written down, discussed and indeed agreed. This requires staff and managers to reach agreement about what is being provided and why. It also provides explicit signals to customers, existing and potential, about what the service will be like and the benefits they should expect. One problem is that even when written down, the service concept does not have an objective reality in the same way that a manufactured product has. However, it is still an important means of articulating what an organisation does and what its customers should expect, thus aligning its internal and external customers to the nature of its service.

3.3.3 Developing new service concepts to drive innovation and provide strategic advantage

Developing new service concepts can drive innovation and provide strategic advantage by, for example, opening up new markets (see Case Examples 3.1 and 3.2) or differentiating the organisation from the competition (see Case Example 3.3). As such the service concept provides an ideal vehicle for challenging the status quo. The mere process of writing down the key elements of each concept for the main customer groups will encourage service managers to look at some of the key assumptions that may be implicit in current service provision. Moving beyond a potential new 'organising idea' to identify changes to processes, outcomes and experiences allows the service operations manager to assess the viability/desirability of new services. This can not only help managers understand their business but also challenge them to view their business in ways that can make it stand apart from other organisations. Lord Marshall, a past chairman of British Airways, made the point:

> There are different ways to think about how to compete in a . . . service business such as ours. One is to think that the business is merely performing a function – in our case, transporting people from A to B, on time and at the lowest possible price. That's the commodity mind-set, thinking of an airline as the bus of the skies. Another way to compete is to go beyond the function and compete on the basis of providing an experience. In our case,

we want to make the process of flying from A to B as effortless and pleasant as possible. Anyone can fly airplanes but few organisations can excel in serving people. Because it's a competence that's hard to build, it's also hard for our competitors to match.[8]

By thinking carefully about the market, the different customer segments and the needs of the customers in those segments, while also having an in-depth understanding of the core competencies of the operation, managers may be able to develop totally new and innovative concepts that have great appeal to customers and give the organisation a significant competitive edge.

Case Example 3.2 describes the development of an innovative new concept at Singapore Zoo, which could be difficult for other organisations to follow. This development springs from an understanding of current operational competencies together with a realisation of why the zoo did not attract foreign visitors – a very large and lucrative market.

Case Example 3.2   Singapore Zoo

Singapore Zoo is no stranger to innovation. In 1982 the zoo started offering a new service, breakfast with an orang-utan called Ah Meng. This has now developed into the Jungle Breakfast with Wildlife. This morning attraction (held daily from 9.00 to 10.30) begins with watching the elephants' morning bathing routine followed by the chance to feed them with a selection of fruits. Guests then go to the Ah Meng Restaurant (named after Ah Meng who died in 2008 at the old age of 48) for breakfast and some close encounters with tamarinds, pythons and orang-utans in the adjacent 'forest clearing'.

Wildlife Reserves Singapore (WRS) is a public limited company owned by the Government of Singapore. It is the parent company of three award-winning attractions: Singapore Zoo, Jurong Bird Park and the world-famous Night Safari. Fanny Lai is the Chief Executive Officer of WRS and she explained what they are trying to achieve:

We try to create a memorable wildlife experience for our visitors with a focus on wildlife conservation and education. While our vision is to be the foremost wildlife institution in the world, our mission is to inspire an appreciation of nature through exciting and meaningful wildlife experiences. We also help to protect wildlife in their natural habitat, especially endangered species facing extinction. Our visitors are not just looking for a great experience with their friends and family, and value for money, many of them also want to contribute to wildlife conservation. So we try to educate our visitors through interactivity; interpretation boards, our rangers talking to them, the narrators on the trams . . . We even train our non-zoological staff, such as our food and beverage staff, so they are able to have interesting discussions with our visitors about the animals and conservation.

Singapore Zoo was one of the pioneers of the open zoo concept. Here the animals are kept in spacious, landscaped enclosures which try to re-create their natural habitat. They are separated from the visitors using psychological restraint techniques based on the animals' natural instincts for defining a territory as their own, or by a natural fear of some elements such as water. The water moats, for example, are concealed with vegetation or dropped below the line of vision. The result is a feeling of openness. Oppressive cages, which typify traditional zoos, are not used.

The use of psychological restraints requires a sound knowledge of the behaviour of the animals concerned. By providing the right habitat, privacy, stimulation, food and social structure zoo management enables the animals to turn the spaces into their homes and, even though some could escape, they don't. Stimulation is provided by trying to re-create the natural stresses of the wild and bring out the animals' natural instincts and reflexes. For example, instead of throwing neatly chopped chunks of meat to the big cats, the keepers will hang a large hunk of meat in a gunnysack packed with hay and smeared with blood in a tree. The cats have to compete with each other to get the bag and to tear it apart before getting their reward. Other animals are stimulated in other ways: polar bears and fishing cats, for example, have to go fishing for their food.

One major innovation has been the Night Safari. Despite having a successful world-class zoo the managers know that it has limited appeal, in that the majority of the zoo's visitors are local residents. For the large numbers of tourists on short stopovers, visiting a zoo, which they could easily do at home, was not a high priority, especially as the weather is hot during the day and many animals sleep then. For these potential visitors the zoo offered little excitement compared to Singapore's famous shopping malls and superb food. The zoo needed a new concept.

Following a rapturous response to a few night tours conducted at the zoo in the late 1980s and after four years of planning and three years of construction, Singapore's Night Safari was opened in May 1994 at a cost of S$63 million. The Night Safari is the world's first night-time wildlife park. The Night Safari, adjacent to the zoo, has its own entrance and facilities, and attracts over a million visitors a year.

The Night Safari is nothing like an ordinary zoo. Visitors are 'transported' into a real safari experience. To give visitors this feeling of stepping into a very different place from modern Singapore, Bornean tribal performers perform attention-grabbing tribal dances (from 6.30 p.m. to 8.30 p.m.). They also provide blowpipe demonstrations and fire-eating displays. Fanny Lai added:

We have recently redesigned the Night Safari so that you suddenly walk into the Village of the Rainforest. You immediately feel that you are entering into a different world. We have music, dancing, performers, aimed at all of your senses; you hear the music, you see the performers, you smell the rainforest and the food. You can have a nice dinner by candlelight in a jungle setting then you go into the Night Safari to experience the wilderness and the animals in their 'natural' settings. We also provide the opportunity to have close encounters with some of the tamer animals in our Creatures of the Night Show where we can explain about them, their habitat and the need for conservation. Memorable experiences often come from the small things, these small personal experiences.

All the facilities are consistent with the safari theme. The walkways from the car parks to the tram station are constructed from wooden boards with wooden handrails. The Ulu Ulu Safari Restaurant, where you can eat a wide selection of local favourites, such as the famous chilli crab, maintains the jungle feel with its beamed ceilings with their rustic rattan fans. The restaurant also has an alfresco eating area where you can dine with the sounds of cicadas, frogs and other night creatures while a herd of Ankole cattle grazes nearby. The alternative Bongo Burger Bar provides high-quality burgers and alfresco dining close to the tribal dancers. Even the toilets have a safari feel: they are open to the sky with sinks set in stone outcrops surrounded by jungle.

Quiet electric trams provide guided safaris for visitors around a 3.2-kilometre trail, which takes about 45 minutes to complete. The narrators on the trams educate and inform the visitors as they enjoy the ride, just as safari guides would do. During the ride the landscape changes through eight geographical zones to provide appropriate settings for its animals, from the rocky outcrops of the Himalayan foothills to the grassy plains of Equatorial Africa and ending with the forests of South-east Asia. Three walking trails, totalling 2.8 kilometres, are well marked and provide opportunities to see all of the animals at close range.

The 'open concept' is used to tremendous effect. Indeed, under the cover of darkness, the moats can be very effectively camouflaged using netting and shade. Other less dangerous animals, such as deer, are roaming freely in large areas bounded by cattle grids. Occasionally the tram has to stop and wait for animals to move out of its way.

The right sort of lighting was a key element in the design of the Night Safari. There was a need to provide sufficient light so the guests could see the animals but without detracting from the ambiance or disturbing them. The result is lighting that resembles soft moonlight using a combination of mercury and incandescent lights, mounted on tall poles. Only selected areas are 'moonlit' as the dark background adds to the atmosphere and lighting the foreground would spoil the effect of the appearance of freedom. Flash photography is forbidden to ensure the animals are not disturbed.

Source: This illustration is based on visits to Singapore Zoo, and discussions with staff and material from the zoo's website, www.zoo.com.sg.

3.3.4 Designing and specifying the service

The role of service operations managers is to understand the organisation's business model and to construct a service concept based upon the organisation's vision, mission, brand and any new organising idea. Having agreed and articulated the service concept, operations managers then need to design and acquire the resources (inputs) and design and develop the processes and experiences required to deliver that concept to the organisation's customers (we will cover the design of experiences and process in more detail in Chapters 7 and 8). Case Example 3.3 explains how a Japanese businessman designed a chain of hairdressing shops in Japan to deliver a new service concept.

| Case Example 3.3 | Designing a new hairdressing concept in Japan |

Takao Kondo, Graduate School of Global Business, Meiji University, Japan

Traditional men's hairdressers (barbers) in Japan provide a haircut, a shampoo, a shave and a head and shoulder massage. This service usually takes about 40 minutes to one hour and the charge is usually around 4,000 to 5,000 yen (about £35). One day Mr Kuniyoshi Konishi, a senior manager in one of the big commercial firms in Japan, while having a haircut in one of the top hotels in Tokyo, realised that the core value of this service was the haircut which only takes about 10 minutes. He thought by just providing the core service (the haircut), a lot cheaper and a lot quicker, one might be able to open up a new market and attract a large number of customers. He said 'Busy people seek shorter service if the quality of the outcome (haircut) is the same.' He added 'You can collect the money today which you lost yesterday but you can't collect the time you lost yesterday.'

As a result he left his well-paid job and launched QBNET (Q for quick and B for barber). His service concept was, at maybe no surprise to us but quite a shock for the Japanese, a quick and inexpensive haircut (about 1,000 yen, £10), no shampoo, no shaving and no massage. He focused on mak-ing things as simple, cheap and efficient as possible. He

Source: Andy Maluche/Photographers Direct

provided small vacuum cleaners to quickly remove hair around the neck after the cut. Disposable paper towels were used around the neck and disposable paper combs were also provided. The interior of the shop was simple; there was no cash register, no telephone and no toilet. There were no chairs for people waiting but a small bar where customers could lean.

On the first day of opening the shop had over 100 customers. He quickly expanded to a second and then a third shop, developing efficient processes as he went along. For example, when the customer arrives he has to buy a fixed-price ticket from a vending machine, and the time when the customer arrived is noted. When the employee starts working on the customer he registers the number of the customer's ticket so that the difference between the time when the customer bought the ticket and the time started is recorded. This is used to provide potential customers with the waiting time using lights on the outside of the shop. A green light means there will be no waiting, a yellow light means a wait of five to ten minutes, and red means over ten minutes. The door of the shop also has a sensor to count the number of people passing through. All this information is transmitted via the internet to the head office.

To help expand his business and deal with the problem that the barber's job was now quite routine and standardised, he paid higher salaries than traditional barbers. He also started a Business-Partner Scheme, whereby an employee who had worked for three years could take over the franchise for the shop paying 10% of turnover plus a shop rental charge.

In 2006, nine years after opening the first shop in Kanda in Tokyo, Mr Konishi had 291 shops with a total turnover of about 3.8 billion yen (about £29m). He then sold the business. By 2010 QBNET was running nearly 400 shops including premises in Singapore, Hong Kong and Thailand.

Part of the task of service design is also to create specifications for the service inputs and processes, and operating procedures to try to ensure that staff deliver the service consistently. A specification takes the elements of the concept and identifies the quality factors associated with each, details the standards to be achieved in each and the organisation's procedure (often referred to as standard operating procedures – SOPs) to ensure conformance to the standard (operational control). Where the organisation delivers multiple concepts, several specifications and control mechanisms need to be developed. We will develop these ideas in Chapters 5, 9 and 11.

3.3.5 Assessing the implications of design changes

The service concept can be used as a driver for long-term service development. By defining the concept, service designers can compare it to alternatives, proposed or already provided by other service suppliers, to help operations managers identify the implications of change. Whether the changes are deliberate changes to the concept or an evolutionary approach with modifications to process or procedures, changes to service concepts have implications for all parts of the organisation. Our research has found that 'there is substantial evidence to suggest that significant changes to service concepts expose the weaknesses in the organisation, its ability to co-ordinate all the various constituencies and its capacity to communicate effectively both internally and externally'.[9]

Such a 'concept audit' can be achieved by using a simple profiling tool. Case Example 3.4 describes a change of concept in the Natural History Museum in London, which is profiled in Figure 3.3.

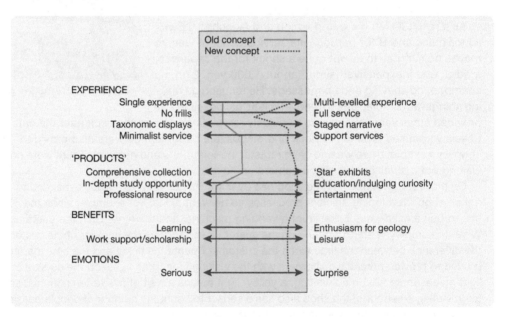

Figure 3.3 Changing the service concept of a museum of geology

Source: Adapted from Clark, Graham, Robert Johnston and Michael Shulver (2000), 'Exploiting the Service Concept for Service Design and Development' in Fitzsimmons, James and Mona Fitzsimmons (eds), *New Service Design*, Sage Publications, Thousand Oaks, California.

Case Example 3.4   The Earth Galleries at the Natural History Museum, London

From the mid 1930s to the early 1990s the Geological Museum, in Cromwell Road, London, consisted largely of taxonomic displays of rocks, gems and minerals and was a place for quiet study of 'rocks in boxes' by specialist geologists. This contrasted sharply with the noisy, lively and enthusiastic atmosphere of its neighbour, the Natural History Museum. In the 1970s the Natural History Museum had begun a programme of exhibition renewal, using advanced and innovative methods of display to interest and entertain visitors, to support its mission 'to maintain and develop its collections and use them to promote the discovery, understanding, responsible use and enjoyment of the natural world'. The resultant Life Galleries are very popular and have won awards for excellence in design. In 1985 the Geological Museum merged with the Natural History Museum and took a new name, the Earth Galleries, with a duty to communicate the natural world to the general public in a way that it could understand.

Putting that mission into operation was not going to be easy. A survey of museum-goers found that they were less than enthusiastic about geology as a subject. It was perceived as dry, dull and having little to do with everyday life – in short, it was just about rocks. The perception was that the only reason you would visit something called the Geological Museum was because you had to pass an exam in geology.

Source: Natural History Museum Picture Library

The museum took up this challenge, as Dr Giles Clarke, Head of Department of Exhibitions and Education, explains:

Surely volcanoes are interesting, fascinating things, and earthquakes are really significant, fascinating and important. Gems are beautiful, especially in jewellery, and fossils, they are interesting too. So, there is a whole range of topics there that don't immediately come to mind when people say geology, but nevertheless are perceived as being fascinating. What we can then do is take the breadth of the subject that we want to display and talk about in the galleries, and to shuffle it around so that the high-profile ones come early, and so they will be an attraction to visitors to come in to the subject, and we can use those as a leader to collect people and move them around the exhibitions.

Value, hitherto defined as access to a superlative reference collection of gems and minerals, was now to be reflected more in the degree to which the museum educated, enthused and entertained the public in the earth sciences. The target consumer was now a 15-year-old intellect who would already have had significant exposure to television and film of volcanoes, earthquakes, mining and so on. If the museum was to 'promote the discovery, understanding, responsible use and enjoyment of the natural world' to this consumer group, then it could not rely on the collection alone. Such consumers would need to be helped by staging devices that moved them from the world they knew into the unfamiliar world of geology and inspire engagement with the subject. The exhibits would also have to educate consumers gradually, and gently guide them through the museum's narrative.

The museum would also have to cater for groups, in particular children, who would be more inclined to sample 'chunks' of galleries rather than the whole, so the galleries had to be structured to accommodate short attention spans. Mini-exhibits or galleries, each with a complete story, were created, but the logic of the story was integrated with the overall museum theme. Some displays became interactive, encouraging visitors to experiment with geological processes through hands-on engagement with both hard and soft exhibits, such as minerals, molten surfaces and water, for example. To support the social and family groups in which the public visited the museum, facilities such as restaurants, shops and restrooms had to be developed to be at least as good as those at a theme park.

When the Earth Galleries had been transformed geologists still had access to a world-class reference collection, although in very different surroundings. However, the material was now used to enthuse and educate a much wider audience about the secrets of the earth.

A key point here is that of alignment. It is rare that a change to the customer experience or service outcomes can be made in isolation. Changes in one element will have consequences in others. Sometimes these represent opportunity, sometimes the potential for conflict. The use of the service concept and a profiling tool allows the people involved in the design or redesign of a service to understand what is required and to assess and therefore manage the implications of change.

Capability mapping

One enhancement of the profiling tool is the identification not only of the old concept and the new requirement, as in Figure 3.3, but also the capability of the existing service (see Figure 3.4), i.e. its current potential. This capability envelope can be used by organisations that perhaps do not have a specific new or revised service in mind but can use capability mapping to explore what opportunities there might be for using operational potential.

Case Example 3.5 explains how one organisation used the capability envelope to identify the areas where the company could develop new opportunities.

Case Example 3.5	TECLAN Translation Agency

TECLAN provided a one-stop shop for language translation. The company used 35 in-house translators for most European languages, Japanese and Chinese. Translation to and from other languages was subcontracted to a network of some 3,000 translators. Though the company would handle just about any translation work, over time it had developed a distinctive competence in translating technical documentation, particularly computer software. The majority of software translation was the 'localisation' of software written in English – the conversion of hypertextual help-files. However, TECLAN often encountered help-files that lacked

Source: Pearson Education Ltd/Naki Kouyioumtzis

sufficient flexibility, and in localising they had to resort to developing completely new help-file structures. Thus it developed a new competence in help-file authoring and rudimentary programming.

By themselves these new competencies were not particularly distinctive, but coupled with the company's translation capability they provided the potential for a highly competitive resource-set. TECLAN's service

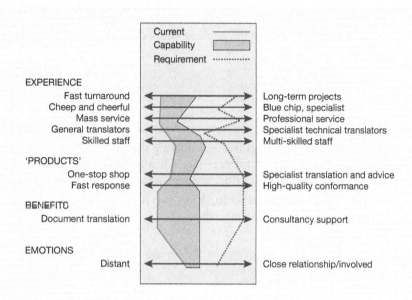

Figure 3.4 Capability mapping at TECLAN

concept profile is mapped in Figure 3.4. The profile shows where the company started from and the shaded portion represents the new operations potential that TECLAN developed. The dotted line indicates an idealised service concept for a new service that exploits the newly developed potential. This also highlights the gaps between current capability and that required for the new service concept. The main areas requiring attention and development were in quality performance and the company's ability to manage relationships with its new class of customers. Although translators had developed the ability to manage relationships with clients' own technicians, TECLAN's account managers lacked the technical knowledge to market and sell the new capabilities.

Source: This illustration is taken from Clark, Graham, Robert Johnston and Michael Shulver (2000), 'Exploiting the Service Concept for Service Design and Development' in Fitzsimmons, James and Mona Fitzsimmons (eds), *New Service Design*, Sage Publications, Thousand Oaks, California.

3.4 Summary

What is a service concept?

- A service concept is a shared and articulated understanding of the nature of the service provided and received, which should capture information about the organising idea, the service provided and the service received – the experience and outcomes.
- A service concept is more emotional than a business model, deeper than a brand, more complex than a good idea and more solid than a vision.

How can managers use the service concept?

- It can be used to help define and communicate the nature of the business.
- It can be used to create organisational alignment by developing a shared understanding and making it explicit.

- It can be used to develop new service concepts and drive innovation and strategic advantage.
- It can be used operationally to help design and specify a service.
- It can be used to assess the implications of design changes using capability mapping.

3.5 Discussion questions

1 Construct the service concept as in Figures 3.1 and 3.2 for an organisation of your choice.

2 Select two service organisations offering similar but different services (a fast-food and a high-class restaurant, for example). Identify the key elements of the service concept and compare their profiles using the mapping tool illustrated in Figure 3.3.

3 The chief executive of Singapore Zoo is keen to continue developing the zoo. Can you develop a new service concept?

3.6 Questions for managers

1 How well is your organisation's service concept articulated and shared? You may like to ask some of your colleagues to describe what the organisation is providing to its customers, internal or external, and ask some customers what the organisation provides. Capture the details as set out in Figures 3.1 and 3.2.

2 Does your organisation provide a range of service concepts? Are some of these delivered more effectively than others and if so, why?

3 Profile your process and assess areas of weakness (non-alignment) and any opportunities to use it to drive strategic advantage.

Case Exercise   The Sunningtree Golf Club

Joe Tidsdale was confused. As General Manager and head golf professional at the Sunningtree Golf Club he was no longer sure what kind of business he was running. He came into golf course management because he was passionate about the game but he feels like he has become an events organiser.

The golf course opened in 1990 and at that time there was a small group of members whose prime interest was in playing golf and improving their handicap. Apart from the course itself, there were few facilities apart from some basic changing rooms and a makeshift bar/clubroom in a temporary building. Over twenty years later, the business has grown in size and complexity. There are several hundred members, about 500 having an official golf handicap and who take part in competitions on a fairly regular basis. The majority of members are men but there is a strong Ladies section and a growing Juniors section. The club has a reputation for being a friendly place and positively encourages people to play with people they don't know rather than solely with a narrow group of friends.

The social side of the club is a significant revenue earner. The temporary clubhouse has been replaced with a building that not only provides a place for people to relax after a game but also has a function area which can be hired out for parties and wedding receptions. This area is on the first floor of the clubhouse, with balconies overlooking the course. It is an excellent space for parties, though having excited children running around the balconies can disturb golfers making that all important putt on the eighteenth green! The catering staff enjoy functions because they provide an opportunity to deliver a different style of food than the normal light snacks served up to golfers. They have also experimented with special 'gourmet' nights, using the club membership to advertise these events and to bring their friends. These have been a mixed success. The food has been of a reasonable standard but the ambience and service probably does not justify the 'gourmet' prices that the club would like to charge.

Another source of revenue is what is termed society golf. In this case, perhaps twenty or thirty visitors will come to play the course, setting up an internal competition amongst themselves. Although this provides revenue for the club, it can be a source of irritation to members as they may take tee times (playing slots) at popular times and, because they are less familiar with the course, they may be rather slow, delaying people behind them. Society golfers contribute a substantial amount to the bar takings and often want a meal after they have finished playing – as part of the social activity.

There are over 700 full club members, paying £750 annual subscriptions. This allows them to play at any time, seven days a week. There are just under 300 seniors and others who pay just £400 per annum, but they are restricted to Monday to Friday playing times. This is the club's core income and supports the day-to-day running of the club, paying the salaries of the golf professional, shop staff, catering and bar staff, and the greenkeepers who maintain the course. The average member is worth another £300 per annum to the club in food and drink revenue. A 'golf society' booking with 20 people playing the course and meals after may be worth in excess of £1,000 per booking. There are about two of these per week from May to September though some of these are on Saturdays, restricting playing slots for members. The wedding business is growing with about one big event per month, again often on Saturdays during the summer period. Each event brings in around £2,000.

Joe explained the problem:

The challenge is to provide excellent golf facilities and appropriate service for my core membership while at the same time developing and maintaining other revenue streams that ensure that the club is viable. I am not sure how to strike the right balance between maintaining the core revenue from members with the undeniably profitable marginal revenue provided by golf societies and weddings. To make things more difficult many members really resent the society golfers and don't see the need for gourmet nights and other events. I have here a few quotes from some of our customers that give some insight into the problems I face.

I used to enjoy a drink in the bar with my friends after a long round of golf. Now there seem to be all kinds of people I don't recognise here and they get in the way!

(Member)

There's a good group of couples playing here now and we like the friendly atmosphere in the club and in the competitions provided for us. We sometimes annoy a handful of very good golfers because we may not play as quickly as they do.

(Husband and wife members)

The facilities here are very good, and there's a lovely view over the golf course from the main function room. Our only comment is that although the staff try hard, they don't really provide a very sophisticated service.

(Wedding customer)

We really enjoy coming here. The course is great and it's a convenient place to meet up though the food isn't up to much. Some of the other golfers seem to resent our being here and make it quite clear!

(Society golfer)

Questions

1 What are the service concepts for the members, the society golfer and the wedding function guests? What are the potential conflicts?

2 What advice can you give to Joe Tidsdale as to how to manage his business in the future?

Suggested further reading

Anderson, Shannon, Lisa Klein Pearo and Sally K. Widener (2008), 'Drivers of Service Satisfaction: Linking Customer Satisfaction to the Service Concept and Customer Characteristics', *Journal of Service Research* 10 (4) 365–381

Clark, Graham, Robert Johnston and Michael Shulver (2000), 'Exploiting the Service Concept for Service Design and Development' in Fitzsimmons, James and Mona Fitzsimmons (eds), *New Service Design*, Sage Publications, Thousand Oaks, California, pp. 71–91

De Chernatony, Lesley, Susan Cottam and Susan Segal-Horn (2006), 'Communicating Service Brands' Values Internally and Externally', *The Service Industries Journal* 26 (8) 819–836

Goldstein, Susan Meyer, Robert Johnston, JoAnn Duffy and Jay Rao (2002), 'The Service Concept: The Missing Link in Service Design Research?', *Journal of Operations Management* 20 (2) 121–134

Kwortnik, Robert J. and Gary M. Thompson (2009), 'Unifying Service Marketing and Operations with Service Experience Management', *Journal of Service Research* 11 (4) 389–406

Prahalad, C.K. and Venkatram Ramaswamy (2004), *The Future of Competition – Co-Creating Unique Value with Customers*, Harvard Business School Press, Boston

Useful web links

A good example of an organisation that has a clear service concept, linked to appropriate service offers:
www.homedepot.com

For a view on service branding and propositions from a marketing perspective, visit the knowledge hub of the Chartered Institute of Marketing:
www.cim.co.uk

In this website an American company called letsgototurkey outline their service concept:
http://www.letsgototurkey.com/servicepack.html

Notes

1   Clark, Graham, Robert Johnston and Michael Shulver (2000), 'Exploiting the Service Concept for Service Design and Development' in Fitzsimmons, James and Mona Fitzsimmons (eds), *New Service Design*, Sage Publications, Thousand Oaks, California, pp. 71–91

2   Normann, Richard and Rafael Ramirez (1993), 'From Value Chain to Value Constellation: Designing Interactive Strategy', *Harvard Business Review* 71 (4) 65–77

3   Normann, Richard and Rafael Ramirez (1993), 'From Value Chain to Value Constellation: Designing Interactive Strategy', *Harvard Business Review* 71 (4) 65–77

4   See for example Lovelock, Christopher H. and Jochen Wirtz (2010), *Services Marketing: People, Technology, Strategy*, 7th edition, Pearson/Prentice Hall, New Jersey; the 8 Ps were

developed from the 4 Ps suggested by McCarthy, Edmund Jerome (1960), *Basic Marketing: A Managerial Approach*, Irwin, Homewood, Illinois

5 Clark, Graham, Robert Johnston and Michael Shulver (2000), 'Exploiting the Service Concept for Service Design and Development' in Fitzsimmons, James and Mona Fitzsimmons (eds), *New Service Design*, Sage Publications, Thousand Oaks, California, pp. 71–91

6 Dibb, Sally, Lyndon Simkin, William M. Pride and O.C. Ferrel (2005), *Marketing Concepts and Strategies*, 5th European edition, Houghton Mifflin, Boston

7 Clark, Graham, Robert Johnston and Michael Shulver (2000), 'Exploiting the Service Concept for Service Design and Development' in Fitzsimmons, James and Mona Fitzsimmons (eds), *New Service Design*, Sage Publications, Thousand Oaks, California, pp. 71–91

8 Prokesch, Steven E. (1995), 'Competing on Customer Service: An Interview with British Airways' Sir Colin Marshall', *Harvard Business Review* 73 (6) 100–112

9 Clark, Graham, Robert Johnston and Michael Shulver (2000), 'Exploiting the Service Concept for Service Design and Development' in Fitzsimmons, James and Mona Fitzsimmons (eds), *New Service Design*, Sage Publications, Thousand Oaks, California, pp. 71–91

Part 3 Connect

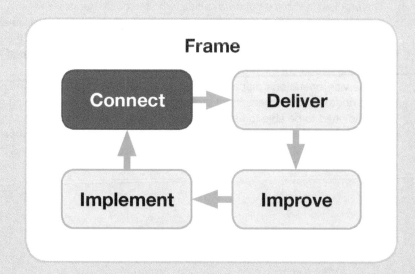

Chapter 4
Understanding customers and relationships

Chapter objectives

This chapter is about how to understand and develop 'customer' relationships.

- Customers, who are they?
- What are the benefits of retaining good customers?
- How can managers develop good customer relationships?
- How can managers develop good business relationships?

4.1 Introduction

It should perhaps be self-evident that a text on service operations should include an examination of customers and customer relationships. Indeed, as we saw in Chapter 1, a 'service' is synonymous with the 'customer'; service is an activity (a process) which involves the treatment of a customer (or user) or something belonging to them and, where the customer is involved, and performs some role, in the service process.

The problem is that it's not always clear who the customer is! As we saw in Chapter 2, the customer of the nursery is not just the child but also the parent. There are also stakeholders such as education authorities and health and safety officials, for whom the nursery provides information and related services, as well as internal customers – the staff – whose welfare and training needs, for example, need to be provided for.

So service operations managers need to know who all their customers are. They also need to understand the benefits of providing a good service and retaining good customers. They also need to be able to manage those multiple customers, i.e., know the services they provide each of them with and how to do it well. One key element in managing customers in many organisations, particularly business-to-business, is developing and maintaining good relationships with them.

4.2 Customers, who are they?

A 'customer' is the recipient and often also a provider (co-producer) in a service process. Thus we use the word 'customer' to refer to all the individuals, units or even organisations to whom, and often with whom, an individual, unit or organisation provides service.

Take the seemingly simple example of booking a holiday. Let's imagine you are booking a holiday for your friends or family using a travel agent. You are the customer of the travel agent and they provide you with a service (see Figure 4.1). Both parties are involved in this service (the activity of discussing options). Things flows both ways as you explain what you want and later make a payment; they provide ideas and later provide the tickets. Your friends or family are also your 'customers' – you are providing a service to them by arranging the holiday for them. They discuss the options the travel agent provides, take your opinions and provide you with their decisions or preferences (again service is a two-way flow with customers receiving and providing service). The tour operator is also the customer of the hotel and the airline. They make the booking with the hotel and the airline, providing them with your details and dates of travel and preferences, and the hotel and airline give them the booking (an agreement) which they then pass on to you. At the start of the holiday the airline provides you and your friends or family with service. They process you by gathering (batching) you up with other passengers to get onto the aircraft and transport you to your destination. You and your friends or family do your bit by turning up on time and reporting to the gate for the flight and getting on and off the plane in an orderly fashion. The airline is supported by many internal services such as HR, IT and training. They also require the services of many other organisations to do all this, such as the airport, ground handling services, the aviation authority, catering service etc. The hotel provides your party with a range of services involving many internal service providers, such as their restaurant and bar services, housekeeping and laundry services

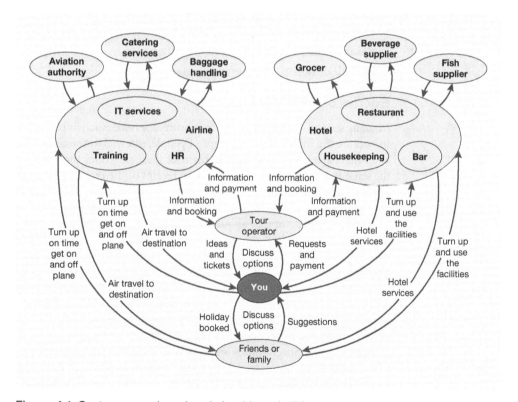

Figure 4.1 Customers and services in booking a holiday

and external services such as grocers, fish suppliers, beverage suppliers etc. You all turn up at the hotel, provide information, and use the restaurant and bar etc.

There are a few important things to take away from this example:

- Everyone in the diagram is a customer of somebody. You (in the diagram) are of course the 'customer', but you are also a supplier, providing service to others, the service providers and your friends/family; they are your customers.
- Some customers are individuals, some are units and some are organisations.
- Service is usually a two-way process; i.e., things flow both ways. You provide information to the tour operator and the tour operator gives you a booking; in essence both parties are 'customers' of each other as they are both recipients and providers.
- Services are delivered through networks, like Figure 4.1, and we will return to how we manage these networks in Chapter 6. It is important to note that service is provided (to you) by many organisations working together and providing each other with services.
- There are internal service providers, such as the restaurant in the hotel, and also external service providers such as their beverage supplier. Thus there are both external and internal customers.
- Different organisations use different names for their customers; to the airline you are a passenger, to the tour operator you are a client, to the hotel you are a guest.

Thus, to reiterate, the word 'customer' refers to all the individuals, units or organisations to whom, and often with whom, an individual, unit or organisation provides service.

4.2.1 Classifying customers

We can classify our customers into several broad and overlapping types:

- external or internal customers
- intermediaries or end users or consumers
- stakeholders: payers, beneficiaries or participants
- valuable or not-so-valuable customers.

External or internal customers

In many service sectors, particularly consumer services such as banks and restaurants, the customers are the individuals or groups of people, external to the organisation, who are receiving and often paying for the service. In many of these situations there is a clear time connection in the sense that service will be provided on receipt of the required price, as in a fast-food restaurant or a retail store. These customers are sometimes referred to as users, end users, or consumers; they tend to be the people in mind when managers and employees talk about customers.

However, when we talk about customers, we are referring to both external and internal customers, and much of the material in this book can be applied to both internal and external customers. Internal customers are individuals or groups of individuals who are a part of the same organisation but from a different unit or operation. For example, the accountancy department, the personnel department and the IT department all in their own way provide services to the other parts of the organisation, just as they also require services from the rest of the organisation. The recognition of internal customers, and the need to provide them with services and good experiences, is one of the key elements of many quality improvement programmes. These programmes are based on the important premise that the quality and cost of service provided to external customers depends upon the quality of the service provided to and by the network of internal customers. Or put simply, the level of external customer service will never exceed the level of internal customer service; this is referred to as the Internal Service Rule.

Many organisations recognise the value in refocusing their 'putting customer first' philosophies to 'putting employees first', realising that the level of external service is constrained by the level of internal service. While many organisations see their quality improvement activities (see Chapters 5 and 12) being about improving the quality for external customers, we believe that organisations should start by improving their levels of internal customer service. We often find that it is management's internal policies, procedures and practices that constrain the service providers' ability, and interest, in delivering good service to external customers.[1]

Intermediaries or end users or consumers

One of the design issues under debate for many service supply chains (see also Chapter 6) is the question of whether or not to use intermediaries – the 'middlemen' who sell a product or service to an end customer on behalf of one or more suppliers. Some financial services, for example, have recently removed the intermediary stage of an independent insurance broker to set up their own direct operations. They have done this largely to reduce the transaction costs for commodity-type services such as car insurance, but also to gain ownership of the end customer. This has been possible to achieve as increasing customer knowledge about industry prices has forced companies and customers alike to re-evaluate the worth of the broker network.

The situation that many organisations face is the need to manage their direct customers, such as brokers or retailers, while at the same time being aware of the needs of the end consumer or user; therefore they have to encourage the intermediaries to give the desired service to their customers. In theory this should make perfect sense though, as GSV Software found, this is not always straightforward (see Case Example 4.1).

Case Example 4.1   **GSV Software**

Sara Sheppard, ITSMA, Europe

As a global software vendor with a well-established range of software products for desktops and laptops, GSV Software had developed a largely channel-centric model to meet its broad range of customer technical services requirements. Service and support were allied to specific software products and were delivered by third parties. GSV put most of its service and support efforts into selecting the right intermediaries to deal directly with its user base, and also into providing any product training required to ensure that the intermediaries were effective. The advantage of this approach was

Source: Pearson Education Ltd/Thinkstock/Alamy

that GSV had a limited number of support relationships to deal with.

This strategy to develop and support the channels to customers was supplemented by the provision of a limited range of direct technical services targeted at large accounts or provided to those few customers who wanted to come directly to the GSV for 'paid for' support at premium rates. Individual customers normally dealt with GSV's accredited agents or other partners such as value-added retailers (VARs) for service and support.

This model worked well: the software applications were relatively simple and there was very little customisation or integration with other software products. However, as GSV's target market was moving towards 'enterprise class software', its service and support model needed to be revisited. Its software offerings were moving from largely standalone products to being part of a business solution, and enterprise class software implied significant amounts of customisation for each client. As a consequence, the ultimate support accountability for the performance of the solution, and type of technical support required, was becoming less clear.

In some cases a client would be acquired by one of GSV's agents and not unreasonably would expect a share of revenue. However, the support requirements for these 'enterprise' or bespoke systems could not be fully anticipated at point of sale, though it was recognised that some elements would be beyond the capability of GSV's agent. This was not an issue that could be just fixed behind the scenes as the possibility of 'flip flop accountability' (or nobody taking full responsibility) was becoming a major purchasing concern for major customers. It needed to be clearly articulated where responsibility lay, not least because these customers represented a significant part of GSV's business.

Customers were asking GSV to take 'more skin in the game'. This is an American term that means taking more business exposure themselves or shared risk – particularly in innovative business solutions that were using leading-edge technology. At the same time GSV knew that its own business model, with a high commitment to continuing a channel-centric services model, would not support a heavy investment in a direct services business. There needed to be a hybrid model between a pure channel-based service and a direct-to-vendor model. It needed to be a way that improved customer confidence in the more complex solutions world: allowing GSV to encourage a healthy channel-orientated services business, and at the same time offering a way of improving customer satisfaction, with the level of responsibility being taken by GSV.

One of the solutions has been with 'leading-edge solutions' (which are seen to be breaking into new markets): the software vendor will commit to either taking the lead in the solution development or playing a significant role, alongside other channel partners. The role of the vendor is to transfer its superior knowledge of its software product into the solution being developed, and to pass this intellectual property on to the partners (which could also be the IT development group within a customer). This defined role then changes once the solution moves from the development and build stage to roll-out and management. The software vendor then plays a more 'behind the scenes' role, providing a back-up and escalation support route to the chosen third-party IT service provider, with contractually agreed service level agreements.

The customer sees GSV software playing a key role in the solution development, and therefore ensuring that the long-term supportability of the ultimate business solution is built into the design. Once the solution moves into roll-out stage, an IT service provider is selected with the appropriate competencies, but with a clear route back to the software vendor if required.

Source: This illustration is used with permission from ITSMA Europe.

Stakeholders: payers, beneficiaries or participants

This categorisation explores the customers' extent of involvement with the service. In many services the customer participating in the service expects benefit from the service and also is required to pay for it. In the case of a restaurant, if there is a problem with the food or the service, customers are aware of it because they participate in the service, and care about the outcome because they are beneficiaries. Because they are also paying for the service, they are able to take appropriate action.

In many service situations, for example prisons, public health services and voluntary services, there may be a clear distinction between and indeed conflicts among payer, beneficiary and participant. This is not only the case in not-for-profit organisations. In business-to-business services, such as photocopier leasing, it is possible that the purchasing department may have cost reduction targets for its overall spend which may conflict with the need for high copy quality in the user functions.

However, the links between purchaser and beneficiary can become extremely difficult when we consider public services. These are funded by taxpayers, but the budget is determined by politicians who (supposedly) represent the views and interests of their constituents. In the case of the police service, the beneficiary is again society at large, although the participants (criminals and offenders) may not see the actions of the police as a benefit! Even the most law-abiding citizens may be annoyed when stopped by the police for what seems to them to be a trivial matter.

As another example, the UK Benefits Agency is responsible for distributing money to the unemployed, those receiving disability benefit, etc. The Agency has invested heavily in improving its service standards for those who are out of work. This stems from a belief that all members of society deserve to be treated as human beings and also that better service will elicit a less aggressive response from individuals who may be under stress from their difficult circumstances.

This approach can be expanded. We can identify all the stakeholders of a service and understand their different perspectives. Case Example 4.2 describes the stakeholders for a prison service, and recognises that not all stakeholders will be willing participants. The value of this type of analysis is that it then allows the operations manager to identify the varying (and sometimes conflicting) requirements of each stakeholder group.

Case Example 4.2   The Prison Service

The prison service provides an excellent example of the complexity of stakeholder requirements, to some extent reflecting the mixed task it faces. Society requires the service to carry out potentially conflicting activities:

- to ensure that 'dangerous criminals' are locked up for the safety of society

- to provide a regime that will punish wrongdoers as a means of payment for their crimes

- to support inmates, providing counselling and training to rehabilitate and reform them, to reduce the likelihood of re-offending.

Source: Pearson Education Ltd/Andy Myatt/Alamy

The principal stakeholders and their requirements are as follows:

- *Government ministers* with responsibility for the prison service will be concerned to fulfil manifesto promises while meeting spending targets. At the same time they will be concerned about stories of prisoner escapes or drug abuse that may be damaging to their personal reputation, possibly forcing their resignation.

- *Prison governors* will seek to provide an appropriate environment for inmates, while keeping to strict operating budgets.

- *Prison officers* will be concerned to strike a balance between building a rapport with inmates and enforcing discipline.

- *Offenders* will have a wide range of requirements depending on the nature of the offence, length of term, desire to change, and so on.

- *Families of offenders* may wish to maintain contact with inmates.

- *Members of society* want to feel safe from criminals, but will also believe that some help should be provided for those who wish to reform.

The relationships between these stakeholder groups are often complex. Clearly, politicians ultimately report to those who elect them, including prison officers and families of offenders. Prison governors, with hopes of career advancement, may feel that they must satisfy the demands of the current party in power, which may be at odds with the requirements of other groups.

Valuable or not-so-valuable customers

The service marketing literature proposes that organisations prioritise service towards customers who can create the most value for the organisation.[2] Given that any operation has finite resources, it would seem sensible to ensure that any prioritisation safeguards long-term business interests. The problem is that what is meant by value is not always clear.

We define a valuable customer as one that is either of high value and/or valued. Note that we use the term valuable rather than loyal. While some customers are loyal, in the sense that they frequently use the organisation, they may also have other loyalties and may also not be very profitable or helpful to the organisation.[3]

- *High value* means that the financial value of the customer, over the long term, is of value to the organisation. This view links with the idea of assessing the lifetime value of a customer (see Section 4.3). For organisations that deal with many relatively small (in value) transactions it has been found useful to calculate the lifetime value (the historic value plus extrapolated value of a customer over time). For example, a customer with a weekly supermarket spend of £100 represents annual revenues of £5,000 and lifetime revenue in excess of £250,000. Some service organisations claim that this understanding helps motivate managers and front-line employees to treat customers with respect – it certainly may help justify investment in customer service. Equipment-related services have been used to this approach for some years, since their customers understand the difference between lifetime cost of ownership as against the cost of acquisition. Indeed it is common in some industries for companies to make a loss on the sale of original equipment, knowing that 25 years of spares and service contracts would ensure long-term profitability.

  The difficulty with this approach is that it is not always obvious who are the high-value and low-value customers. Again, business-to-business services may have a reasonable idea about customer value, perhaps represented by size of contracts; indeed, in some cases these organisations may have only one customer. Consumer services may have more difficulty. Financial services, for example, may be able to classify customers according to social economic groups, credit ratings or spending habits and make judgements accordingly. However, just because an individual is, for example, earning a relatively small sum today, it does not mean they will not be a millionaire in a few years' time, or indeed vice versa.

  High-value customers are also those that tend to spend more per transaction than other customers (incremental value) and purchase additional services (strategic value); and, importantly, they may also act as an advocate for the organisation encouraging or recommending others, by word-of-mouth for example, to use the service (social network value). They may also be prepared to pay premium prices for the service.

- *Valued* customers are those individuals who are positively disposed to the organisation and are thus relatively easy to deal with (see the discussion of Allies and Champions below). They appear to appreciate the service and interact helpfully and pleasantly with employees.

  Valued customers are not only a pleasure to deal with, they can also create financial value for the organisation. They could be involved in cost reduction by taking time to help the organisation and its staff by, for example, clearing tables after use, or reporting incorrectly functioning equipment. They are also usually cheaper to service since it can be costly to recruit new customers into an organisation. Valued customers can be involved in revenue generation by providing positive word-of-mouth advertising and by encouraging others to use or support the service.[4]

  Valued customers are also supporters of the organisation and are ready and willing to help the organisation and to maintain and improve its service, for example by completing questionnaires and providing suggestions. Valued customers also do not place undue demands on the service. For public sector organisations, such as a hospital, this might mean not using the service more than is necessary. For all organisations it might mean not asking for, or expecting, more than the service can provide.

4.2.2 Customer segmentation – an operation's view

Marketing has long devoted attention to segmenting its customers. Market segmentation is traditionally based on customer characteristics. Thus organisations will focus on particular economic groups or target a geographic region. Other marketing approaches will consider lifestyles, family circumstances (for example single parents, empty-nesters or economising customers) or the reasons why customers buy a service (for example for its benefits or utility or in response to promotion).

Clearly, service operations managers must be aware of the emphasis behind the marketing approach adopted by the organisation. Not only does it make sense to target marketing effort on people most likely to buy the service, but market segmentation also helps operations managers design their facilities appropriately and provide the right service, experience and outcomes.

A restaurant provides a simple example. If the restaurant is targeting couples for romantic dinners for two, the design of seating and ambience will be rather different from a restaurant that considers families as its prime source of revenue. The type of food served and the way in which it is served – for example speed, manner and information provided – will be different. In the case of a family restaurant, easy-to-clean facilities with flexible seating will be required, together with value-for-money meals served efficiently. The romantic restaurant will require different furnishings, lighting, music, staff competencies and food. Clearly, a wide range of other decisions flows from this initial identification of the customer group to be served. Some restaurants manage to adapt to changing needs, providing classical music and reasonably bright lighting for early evening family groups and more elderly diners, moving to more upbeat music and dimmer lighting for younger couples as the evening progresses.

Thus decisions about market segmentation may define the target customers, such as families or romantic diners, and drive key decisions such as process and resource management (see Chapters 8 and 11) and staff competencies (see Chapter 10). However, once the operation is up and running, customers can be reclassified to allow the operations manager to identify issues critical to service delivery.

Customer types

We believe that operations managers and their staff need to develop an understanding of the nature of individual customers and their resultant behaviour, particularly when these customers are the direct recipient of the service delivery process, and may in fact be an integral part of it. The nature of the customer could significantly influence the type of service provided, how they need to be dealt with by staff, and their potential impact on other customers in the operation. Possible categories of customers classified by behaviour or attitude (see Figure 4.2) could include:

- *The Ally*. These valued customers usually arrive in a positive frame of mind, willing to help and give positive feedback to facilitate the service. The most helpful Ally is the customer whose opinion is respected by others. If the Ally is happy, then other customers will infer that the service must be good.

- *The Hostage*. These customers require service, but may be 'locked in' to a particular service provider contractually. An example is customers who must have their car serviced by the dealer appointed by the manufacturer. The service may cost rather more, but if an approved dealer is not used, their warranty will be invalid. These customers may not be in the most positive moods and will become very difficult whenever service performance deteriorates.

- *The Anarchist*. These customers dislike rules and systems. Indeed, notices suggesting what should and should not be done present a challenge. It is tempting to let the customer 'get away' with not following the system, but this may set up problems with other customers who feel that they have not been treated fairly.

- *The Patient*. These customers are very similar to the Hostage in that they are locked into the service; examples are hospital patients or students at school or university. These customers

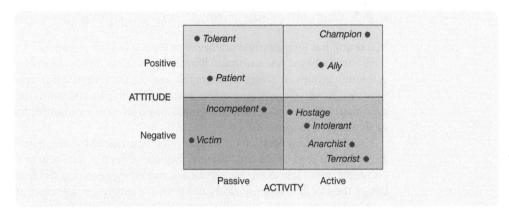

Figure 4.2 Customer types

may be positively or unequivocally oriented towards the organisation and are willing to submit themselves to rules and regulations. However, unnecessary restrictions may turn them into a Hostage or Anarchist.

- **The Tolerant.** These customers may be passive, always waiting patiently for service providers to acknowledge their presence and deliver service. In fact they may be so patient that they become invisible to service staff and get ignored as a result. It may be dangerous to trade on their apparent goodwill.

- **The Intolerant.** These customers are seldom passive or patient, and often cause stress and problems within the service for themselves, the service providers and other customers. Although initially they may be positively disposed to the organisation, without careful handling these people can easily turn into Terrorists.

- **The Victim.** When something goes wrong in service organisations, some customers appear to attract bad luck. Some jobs seem to be dogged by ill fortune. Victims may react in a number of ways, perhaps blowing incidents up out of all proportion or alternatively becoming resigned to their inevitable fate.

- **The Terrorist.** The Terrorist is the customer who mounts a damaging attack when you least expect it. An example might be the customer who declares their dissatisfaction loudly in the middle of a crowded restaurant, having said earlier how good the food was.

- **The Incompetent.** Front-line staff should pay particular attention to these customers. It is possible that new customers may be confused by the organisation's procedures and, if not 'trained' by staff, may find the experience threatening, with the result that they do not return. It is possible, of course, that some customers are incapable of being trained.

- **The Champion.** What all organisations want – valued customers who are not only supportive of their staff and its service and helpfully participate in the process, but who also make a point of providing positive word-of-mouth about the organisation, its services and staff.

Creating Allies

Converting customers from the top left quadrant of Figure 4.2 into Allies is the easiest of the tasks. Allies are already positively disposed to the organisation but require engaging in the service process. Providing information, good communication and explanations and involving them in process development through soliciting feedback may easily convert these customers.

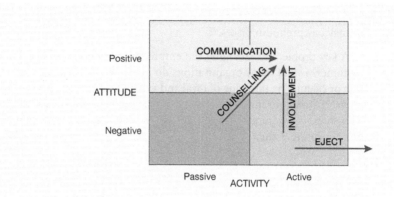

Figure 4.3 Creating Allies

The negatively disposed victims in the bottom left quadrant may require counselling and support to turn them into Allies. The risk here is that even after considerable effort Victims can easily turn into Hostages or Anarchists.

Anarchists and Terrorists are the most difficult, yet most important, group of customers for the operation to deal with. De-selection (removal from the organisation) may be the best way out (see Chapter 10). On the other hand, if these activists can be employed to the good of the organisation by harnessing their negative energy through personal involvement in the organisation and its processes, they can make powerful Allies, or even Champions, for the organisation and its cause (see Figure 4.3).

| 4.3 | |

What are the benefits of retaining good customers?

A key task for some operations managers is retaining their valuable customers. It should be noted that retention may be of limited concern to some service organisations, such as local government services, housing associations, police, charities and health services, who may not be able to choose their customers, or whose customers have no or little choice. These organisations have to accept and deal with whoever 'comes through the door'. However, they still have to have relationships with them (see later) and manage those customers as well as they can (see Chapter 10).

Retaining valuable customers, for those organisations that wish to retain their customers, provides significant benefits, as we saw in Section 4.2.1. In summary, valuable customers:

- are easy to deal with
- act as advocates and provide positive word-of-mouth advertising
- assist in service provision
- reduce operating costs
- increase revenues
- help the organisation maintain and improve its services
- do not place undue demands on the service
- generate long-term revenue streams (high lifetime values)
- spend more than other customers

- increase spending over time
- may pay premium prices.

A key problem in changing the emphasis to retention and/or building relationships with customers is that many organisations do not have adequate means of either measuring retention or calculating the value of loyal and valuable customers. Few companies know the value of a loyal customer or the true cost of a lost customer, or even worse the cost of an upset customer who stays. If organisations could calculate these values they might be in a position to make more accurate evaluations of investments designed to develop relationships with customers.[5]

4.3.1 Measuring customer retention

There are some simple measures of customer retention to put alongside sales or revenue figures. Retention, for example, may be assessed on an annual basis, for instance by tracking the number of customer accounts still 'active' during the year. In practice, of course, this is not always so straightforward. Retail customers frequently shop at more than one store, continuing to make regular purchases in each. Some customers hold several 'loyalty' cards – undermining the very concept! Indeed studies into the behaviour of supermarket customers[6] have identified large segments of 'promiscuous customers' who switch loyalty to whichever provider is currently offering the best deal. In this case the issue is more 'share of the wallet' than customer loyalty. Information systems linked to loyalty cards enable retailers to track trends in spending patterns to assess the 'loyalty' of various customer segments.

For some business-to-business services, customer retention is easy to measure because the organisation may have only one or two major accounts. Loss of a customer in these cases will mean that the business will probably not survive. This is not the case for many mid-range businesses. One company that supplied chemicals to a wide range of business customers appeared, superficially, to be healthy with reasonable annual sales growth. This hid the fact that of a nominal customer base of over a hundred business accounts, more than 20 per cent had not placed an order in the last twelve months and a further 15 per cent had reduced their order value in the last six months. This analysis prompted the organisation to re-examine the nature of its customer relationships in order to reverse what had become a trend that threatened the business's future profitability.

The Net Promoter Score™

One useful measure, though not without its detractors,[7] is the Net Promoter Score™.[8] This suggests that organisations measure their customers' willingness to recommend the organisation and/or its services. The usual question asked is 'How likely is it that you would recommend us to a friend or colleague?' This question is clearly aimed at those organisations for which retention is important. We would suggest that a good question to ask for customers of organisations where retention is not an issue (such as monopoly services) or where customer retention is not desirable (such as fire and rescue services) is 'How likely is it that you would speak highly of us?' By measuring the answers on a 0 (not at all likely) to 10 (extremely likely) scale, organisations can calculate and track, and compare with other organisations, their net promoter score (NPS). NPS is calculated at the percentage of 'promoters' (those scoring the organisation 9 or 10) minus the percentage of 'detractors' (those scoring the organisation from 0 to 6 inclusive).

Calculating the lifetime value of a customer

Lifetime value of a customer is of particular interest to high-volume consumer services, for two reasons:

- It provides a degree of motivation for personnel who may deal with high numbers of short customer transactions each day. The customer who makes a regular £4 purchase may not seem that important in the grand scheme of things, but this viewpoint might be changed if this equates to £1,000 annual spend multiplied by the expected loyalty lifetime in years.

- Calculating the lifetime value gives focus to marketing activities.

As indicated above, there are a number of issues to be resolved when examining lifetime value. The first is to understand what 'lifetime' really means, and to what extent this can really help in marketing and providing service. If the argument about lifetime value is followed to its logical conclusion, would this lead service providers to ignore all customers over a certain age? Clearly not, because the direct revenue gained is still valuable, and the value of word-of-mouth advertising and referrals (social network value) is impossible to calculate.

For the purposes of employee motivation, it may be useful to calculate a value such as annual spend. This makes the point that this £4 transaction customer is someone worth looking after; at the same time it does not make potentially exaggerated claims about worth.

Equipment-based service providers have for a long time calculated lifetime revenues based on the economic life of the piece of capital equipment, its original sales price plus expected service, maintenance and repair revenues. This has enabled them to create competitive original equipment-pricing strategies, and to understand that significant resources must be made available to support these revenue streams.

More recently, mobile phone service providers had to use customer value information more defensively. In the rapid growth of the mobile phone market, providers supplied handsets free or at a fraction of their manufacturing cost in a bid to gain a significant market share. They discovered that many customers were not paying line rentals for a sufficiently long period to enable the promotional equipment discount costs to be recouped. As a result, a wider range of tariffs and contracts was introduced to reduce this deficit.

When thinking about the value of the customer it is therefore useful to generate estimates of the following:

- Current and potential annual spend of customer segments, recognising that customers may use more than one service provider.
- The duration and durability of customer relationships. How long do customers remain loyal and is there potential for this to be extended?
- The number of points of contact with customers. How many different services do they buy? Is there potential for cross-selling of service?
- What is the current profitability of the customer? Is it costing more to keep this customer than we are likely to recoup?

Financial services providers are particularly sensitive to this type of analysis. Although the company may offer a number of products from loans and mortgages through to pensions and insurance products, many find that a typical customer only takes one product from the range. They find, though, that once a customer buys two or three products, they tend to stay loyal for rather longer than the single-product customer.

4.4 How can managers develop good customer relationships?

It is important to note that there is a difference between customer loyalty and having a relationship with the customer; it is easy to confuse the two, particularly in high-volume services delivered to the mass consumer market. For organisations such as train companies, mass transit systems and even financial service providers, customers may be extremely loyal (and use them every day) but not have a 'relationship' with the organisation (indeed they may despise the company!).

Managing customer relationships (sometimes referred to as relationship marketing) is about establishing, maintaining and enhancing relationships with customers for mutual benefit. The emphasis in relationship marketing is on the requirement to develop relationships with individual customers – one-to-one marketing – and with groups of like-minded people – affinity groups – rather than see any and every service as a one-off transaction.

While the notion of relationship marketing appears to be very attractive, it is not appropriate in all situations. For example, in high-volume or commodity-based services, such as retail operations or mass transit systems, many customers may be more influenced by value for money than by a concept as intangible as a relationship. Indeed, many customers do not wish for a relationship with some organisations and their staff. Despite this, there is no doubt that people often make decisions based on emotional or unconscious factors, even when they think that they have been driven totally by logic. Indeed some marketing professionals believe that brands and brand values far outweigh any other factor in customer decision-making.

Three types of customer relationships

There are essentially three main types of customer relationships. Firstly, there is a relationship based on a portfolio of services or products frequently found in higher-volume operations. Secondly, there is a personal relationship created between an individual customer and an employee, particularly prevalent in low-volume professional organisations. Thirdly, we also cover here temporary customer relationships, recognising the transactional, one-off nature of many services. We will also cover the risk in a customer relationship and the means of managing customer relationships in high-volume consumer services – customer relationship management (CRM).

4.4.1 Portfolio relationships

Portfolio relationships involve the 'capture' of the customer using a variety of products or services. Banks, for example, work hard to establish a relationship with their customers by selling (and in order to sell) multiple 'products', such as current accounts, loans, house loans, insurance and executor services. This provides the customer with benefits such as a single point of contact for their service/product portfolio, discounts for new services/products bought, loyalty bonuses etc. The downside for customers who wish to switch is often the difficulty in untying themselves from the set of services/products. The benefits for the organisation are that portfolio relationships provide higher-value customers, a longer-term revenue stream, opportunities to cross-sell other services or products to customers who are already engaged with the organisation, and also valuable information from and about that customer base.

Many service providers, such as retailers, airlines and restaurant chains, actively promote portfolio relationships and loyalty on existing services and products through loyalty schemes such as frequent-flyer programmes or 'club' cards for supermarkets. Most of these are in essence discount schemes encouraging the customer to earn points by spending more money with a particular provider rather than the competition. Such providers are 'buying loyalty' rather than building relationships. However, the relationship can be developed by holding information about a customer's needs: for example, some hotels store information about their card-holding customers so that these customers are provided with a room that meets their requirements. Customers may also gain certain privileges: airline loyalty customers may be provided with access to executive lounges, free seat reservations, cheque-cashing facilities, company newsletters, opportunities to participate in special events and opportunities to provide information to the organisation.

The Harley Owners Group (Case Example 4.3) demonstrates that there is more than one way to build loyalty with customers who have some affinity with the company, its products and services, and with each other. This case demonstrates that Harley-Davidson has clearly understood the breadth of the service concept, recognising that customers are buying rather more than a manufactured product. With this knowledge, Harley-Davidson has been able to capitalise on what has become virtually a cult of owners, each fiercely loyal to the brand, some even having the name of the company tattooed on their bodies.

Case Example 4.3	Harley Owners Group (HOG)

Harley-Davidson does not just make world-famous motorbikes – it sells a dream. From its start more than 100 years ago, Harley-Davidson has had a profound impact on the sport of motorcycling and the people who ride motorbikes.

From its humble beginnings in a small shed in Milwaukee where three friends turned out their first bike, the company now produces over 300,000 bikes a year. The company's turnover for the year ending 2010 was around $4 billion, generating a gross profit of around $1.4 billion. Besides making its famous bikes, such as the Ultra Classic Electra Glide touring bike weighing over 370 kilograms with a twin-cam 1500 cc

Source: Shutterstock.com/Adriano Castelli

engine, the company also produces parts and accessories and a range of branded clothes and collectables. It is a global company, selling bikes all over the world; the fastest growth area in bike sales is currently in Asia.

Not content with simply owning a bike, Harley owners wanted to have an organised way to share their passion and show pride in their bikes so, in 1983, Harley-Davidson established the Harley Owners Group (HOG). By 1985, 49 local chapters had sprouted around the USA, with a total membership of 60,000. By 2010 HOG had over 1 million members worldwide, making HOG the largest factory-sponsored motorcycle organisation in the world.

HOG has a simple intent: 'To ride and have fun'. The organisation is split into local chapters where people who share the Harley passion come together. Each chapter is sponsored by a local dealership with events organised by the members. Membership (which costs around $45/£50 a year) provides a range of benefits, including *HOG* Magazine, the official publication of the Harley Owners Group. A HOG handbook provides maps, dealer locations, climate information and riding laws for members planning long-distance trips. The local chapters organise member events, including national and international rallies, touring rallies, open houses and pit stops. There is also a members' website with details, dates and information about all HOG activities and events.

Source: This illustration is based on information from www.harley-davidson.com and www.hog.com.

4.4.2 Personal relationships

Personal relationships exist in many professional and low-volume, high-margin services, where there is time and value in developing one-on-one relationships with clients or customers. These relationships, often using key account managers (see later), create multilayered or deep personal relationships with customers.

The objective on the service provider's part is to create a situation where the customer thinks of them when the customer next needs the service, or when planning to place more orders. For personal relationships in B2B organisations there are advantages on both sides.

The provider gets to know the customer's business well and this leads to a more effective service with a faster response, because providers do not have to go through another development phase. Many B2B services take place over weeks, months and in some cases years. Management consultants may work alongside the client's employees and it is frequently critical that effective relationships are built in order to carry out the assignment. Technical expertise is clearly only part of the requirement for an effective consultant; the ability to build personal relationships with clients and clients' employees is also essential.

There are four key elements to a personal relationship between service provider and customer:[9]

- *Communication.* The extent to which there is two-way communication; the ability to deliver clear messages and the ability to listen carefully.
- *Trust.* The degree to which one partner depends on the work or recommendation of the other, without seeking extra justification or collaboration. In some cases, the partner may commit the other to work without prior consultation.
- *Intimacy.* The extent to which each partner shares their plans, strategies, profits, etc.
- *Rules.* A mutual acceptance of how this particular relationship operates: what is acceptable and desirable, and what is not.

Developing personal relationships often has significant operational implications. In Table 4.1 we compare two organisations, one a professional service (business-to-business), the other a high-volume consumer service (business-to-customer), and identify the issues that must be dealt with by operations managers. As we can see from Table 4.1, there may be

Table 4.1 Developing personal relationships

	Professional service: management consultant	Consumer service: restaurant chain
Communication	Two-way Free flowing Transfer of knowledge Relates to business possibilities as well as current contracts A significant amount of time is devoted to communication	Largely one-way – from provider to customer, apart from order-giving and paying Formal communication Relates to formal service offer No budget for significant informal communication
Trust	Built between individuals (clients and consultants) in the course of the involvement May involve significant amounts of confidential and sensitive information	Built between customer and organisation largely by reliability (delivery to promise) Scope strictly limited to providing value-for-money meals in safe surroundings
Intimacy	Consultants become completely involved with the life of the client's organisation and are often regarded as semi-permanent employees Part of the team	Involvement between employees and customers may be limited to order-taking and basic service Customer intimacy is often linked to fortuitous discovery of common interests
Rules	May be developed as part of the initial relationship-forming process Negotiation as to who does what is often part of initial evaluation, but the brief may change as the relationship develops	Largely set by the organisation or service sector Based on established 'scripts', expected behaviour and assumed knowledge

considerable resource implications in adopting an approach based on broadening the relationship between customer and provider. Some of these implications are:

- Processes and activities become less well defined and harder to predict.
- Capacity management is less precise and efficiency goals become harder to achieve.
- Processes must be more flexible in order to meet requirements that are ill-defined at the start of the relationship.
- Staff will require a different set of competencies.

4.4.3 Temporary customer relationships

High-volume consumer services often require the formation of temporary relationships, where customer connections are made quickly. Many sales processes depend on the ability of the salesperson to establish common ground with the prospective customer. When the customer is buying something that cannot be readily assessed, part of the purchasing process may include a conscious or unconscious assessment of the competence and honesty of the organisation's representative.

A combination of perceived risk and lack of knowledge on the customer's part will mean that the possibility for a relationship will increase, given the need for reassurance on the customer's part. Examples might include purchasing a used car or a personal pension, where the customer is often incapable of making a totally informed decision.

These relationships might, at face value, appear relatively shallow, but there are clear implications for the service operation that recognises their value. The development of information systems to give customer history, training of customer contact staff and allocated time for each customer transaction (performance targets) are examples of areas that can be addressed. Some contact centres have intentionally relaxed their 'talk time' targets to allow more space for these temporary relationships and have found that although each agent may talk to fewer customers, orders of higher value are being taken as a result of the effectiveness of the temporary relationship.

4.4.4 Risk and relationships

There is often a link between customers' perceived risk in purchasing or using the service and their desire for a personal relationship with the provider (see Table 4.2). Where the customer does not feel that there is much risk, either in making the purchase or in receiving the service, there may be limited opportunity for relationship building. The majority of supermarket customers probably do not have any depth of relationship with Tesco or Walmart, though they may have preferences as to which store they shop in. This reluctance on the part of supermarket customers to build a meaningful relationship with Tesco or Walmart only applies, of course, when things are going well. If there is a significant service failure, customers may move quickly from low to high perceived risk. We will discuss this in more depth in the section on learning from problems in Chapter 13. Where there is high customer perceived risk, but as yet a weak, transaction-based relationship, there is an opportunity for the organisation to build stronger links.

Table 4.2 Links between customer relationship and customer perceived risk

	Weak relationship (transaction-based)	Strong relationship (partnership-based)
High customer perceived risk	Opportunity	Protected
Low customer perceived risk	Buy loyalty	Familiarity

Where there are strong personal relationships in situations where the customer feels there is significant risk, the emotional switching costs for customers are high. It is likely that these customers will not move unless the relationship is significantly damaged in some way. An example of services of this type is a consultant who may have both a particular expertise and intimate knowledge of the client's company and markets. These relationships are most common in professional services and/or B2B services.

Of course, strong personal relationships may exist where there is low perceived risk, though they are probably rare in commodity services. In many cases these may be one-sided relationships where the customer has a stronger emotional bond to the company than is possible for any one employee to reciprocate. Again, we will return to these customers in our discussion of service recovery in Chapter 13, but it is sufficient to say that if there is service failure, these customers may feel let down, rather than merely angry that something has gone wrong.

It is important to recognise that in many cases the relationship is formed at the deepest level between individuals rather than with the organisation as a whole. This is particularly true with professional services. When a senior partner leaves to join another firm, their clients may follow them. The risk for the client in forming a relationship with an unknown quantity, even from the same organisation, may be too great.

In this instance, risk may also have an explicit or implicit cost dimension. The time spent on the client's behalf so that the professional can understand the issues fully in order to make informed judgements will represent a personal investment that will not be undertaken lightly. Cost is clearly not the only issue. If the process demands that client and professional work together for significant periods of time, personal chemistry may well be a significant factor.

4.4.5 Customer relationship management (CRM)

Customer relationship management (CRM) is a term given to the management of customer relationships in high-volume consumer services, with the objective of growing a more profitable business and trying to form some closer understanding of the needs of individual customers. The essential difference between CRM and other approaches to customer retention is that the identification and enhancement of customer relationships is facilitated by technology. CRM attempts to integrate the many communication channels between an organisation's units and its customers, for example recording information about customer preferences and then using the information to develop and strengthen the relationship and the profitability of the customer.

The aim of CRM is to collect data from all parts of the organisation to enable tracking and analysis of a single customer relationship, as well as the identification of more general trends. For example, until recently it was possible that a customer of a financial services company would have a number of the products – a mortgage (house loan), savings accounts and insurance. Each of these products would be handled by separate parts of the business, with no knowledge of the others. As a result, customers rarely felt that they had a relationship with 'the company'.

To redress this, many financial service organisations are turning to data warehousing. A data warehouse is an integrated source of data that collects, cleans and stores information about customers. This is sometimes referred to as 'information-based continuous relationship marketing'.[10] Data warehousing allows the organisation to view relationships and profitability across the organisation.

Companies are now moving to integrated CRM solutions with the advent of e-commerce. Internet-enabled activity allows companies to give information to their customers and collect data from them in a much more structured manner than previously. A smaller version of the data warehouse is the data mart. This serves a division or department of the organisation and should ideally be integrated with the enterprise's data warehouse. Such integration avoids repetition of the original problem of invisibility of customer relationships across the company.

Finally, these data marts and warehouses are linked to the various forms of technology at the customer interface. Telephone contact centres are rapidly being replaced by multimedia contact centres. Customers have a choice of routes into the organisation, whether by letter, phone or internet. Paper-based transactions have virtually disappeared from most organisations, though companies must guard against devaluing such transactions to the extent that insufficient attention is paid to them. An increasing number of transactions are carried out electronically. Computer telephony integration (CTI) allows the customer to browse the company website and to make contact with a human agent only if required.

CRM is therefore aimed at both customer retention and relationship growth approaches. CRM is defined as 'the management process that uses individual customer data to enable a tailored and mutually trusting and valuable proposition. In all but the smallest of organisations, CRM is characterised by the IT enabled integration of customer data from multiple sources.[11] Case Example 4.4 demonstrates that CRM demands much more than the introduction of an IT system, but also demands significant changes in the way the company operates. Not least, CRM requires the commitment of customer-facing staff to think behind the raw data from IT systems to apply insight to each customer transaction.

Case Example 4.4	Travelco Ltd

Moira Clark, Director of the Henley Centre
for Customer Management

Travelco is a large UK package holiday company that has experienced difficult times since September 11th, SARS, the Iraq War and the economic recession. Travelco's customer retention rate was around 20 per cent annually and its market was declining by 10 per cent annually. As a result of this the company had focused predominantly on a sales-led strategy and very little attention had been devoted to customer relationship management (CRM). However, this changed with the implementation of a comprehensive CRM strategy.

The company began with a thorough audit of its state of readiness for CRM. This included an assessment of its marketing strategy conditions, its culture and climate conditions and its IT system conditions (see Figure 4.4). These conditions are defined as follows:

Source: iStockphoto/istrejman

- *Marketing strategy.* This is the set of management decisions concerning the definition and selection of target customers and the value propositions made for them. CRM will only work in situations where the target markets are homogeneous, distinct segments and the propositions are segment-specific.

- *Culture and climate.* The values of organisational culture must be aligned to the marketplace and be commonly held throughout the company, yet still remain flexible. Without these attributes, culture will hinder CRM progress. Similarly, the best CRM systems will fail if the organisational climate, that is the practices, procedures and rewards of the company, are not aligned to the organisation culture. In these circumstances tension will occur and a negative climate will lead to failures in CRM.

- *IT systems.* In effective CRM companies these include not just the software and hardware systems but also all data and information processes connected to customer contact and proposition delivery. They also include organisational structures and systems that support the IT process, such as internal intranets.

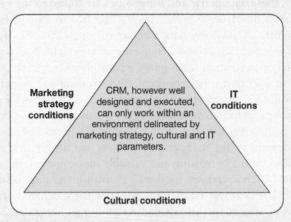

Figure 4.4 Readiness for CRM

By applying these conditions to the company, Travelco identified that

- Its customer retention was weak and that while customer data from across the organisation was gathered and organised centrally, it was not analysed in such a way as to identify customer segments and value propositions. This analysis has since led to the development of meaningful customer segments and tailored value propositions for each of these segments in order to gain a single view of the customer.

- Its culture and climate were not designed for developing customer retention strategies. The marketing strategy had traditionally focused on rewarding sales, leading to behaviour that did not support a customer-centric approach. As a result of this the company improved customer retention by adopting a complete cultural realignment. Training programmes were introduced and staff are now rewarded not only for acquiring customers but also for improvements in customer retention, cross-selling and customer satisfaction.

In summary, while there is no such thing as the 'perfect' CRM company, Travelco has gone a long way towards developing and maintaining long-term mutually trusting and profitable relationships with customers. It is now more focused in terms of selecting the right customers and developing tailored propositions for those customers. This has led to increases in customer satisfaction, and its retention rate has now significantly improved.

4.5   How can managers develop good business relationships?

The work of the Industrial Marketing and Purchasing (IMP) Group over the last fifty years has demonstrated that building business relationships is different to building 'customer' relationships, though business relationships will involve many personal relationships.[12] In essence business markets are often made up of a small number of powerful customers who are seeking solutions to problems. Many business relationships are close, complex and long-term, and each relationship is part of a network of relationships; others are short-term and adversarial in nature. The drivers for improving B2B relationships include

- gain in market share
- acquisition of intellectual property rights (IPR) or technology
- portfolio re-balancing
- reduced cost base
- improved productivity
- margin growth

and the most frequently cited benefits arising from improved business relationships are

- improved bottom line
- long-term differentiation
- growth
- shifts in behaviour
- increased trust
- fruitful co-operation
- improved working patterns
- enhanced capacity for problem solution.

4.5.1 Forms of business relationships

Business relationships exist in many forms.[13] Some are complex and long-term often forming part of a wider network of relationships. Others are short-term. Some are close and collaborative while others can be contract-driven and quite adversarial in nature. Some of the most frequently encountered business relationships include the following:[14]

- *Contracts* are often non-equity agreements 'specifying the cooperative contributions and powers of each partner'[15], where greater power usually lies with the purchasing 'partner'.
- *Partnerships*, sometimes also referred to as alliances, may be contractual or informal, and tend to imply parity-type relationships built on equal input of both partners with shared goals and for mutual benefit. Some partnerships are focused on short-term activities; others might be a prelude to a full merger of two or more companies.[16]
- *Strategic alliances*, sometimes also referred to as global alliances, are 'voluntary arrangements between firms involving exchange, sharing, or co-development of products, technologies or services',[17] though they tend to exist as asymmetric relationships since they often involve one party acquiring a partial stake in the other.[18]
- *Partnering* is concerned with developing closer relationships between the partners in an environment of openness and trust.
- *Joint ventures* (JVs) are one form of alliance and involve the partners creating a new, separate body or subsidiary, jointly owned, to exploit a particular opportunity.
- *Networks* are structures of interconnecting partnerships, alliances or JVs, which can take many different forms.

Importantly, all inter-organisational relationships are created, developed and influenced by the mindset and behaviours of a small number of individuals who form and hold the relationships by their words and actions. Typically, as these players change, so can the nature of the relationship.

4.5.2 Transactional and strategic relationships

Research and consultancy work has shown that though inter-organisational relationships exist in many forms there are only two types of relationship – transactional and strategic – each with their own distinct set of characteristics.[19] Both types are valid though the differences are commonly misunderstood. The important point to remember is that the two types need to be managed and measured quite differently. The key characteristics of these two types are summarised in Figure 4.5.[20]

Typically any one organisation is likely to have only a very small number of truly strategic relationships, so for many managers the challenge is how to become the best they can at the transactional type. As Case Example 4.5, illustrates, it is no simple task moving from a transactional to a strategic relationship. The decision is likely to involve a change of strategic direction – a move usually seen as the prerogative of the CEO.

Transactional type	Strategic type
• Arm's length • Value specified • Contract-led • Asymmetric • One of many • Shorter-term • Tightly defined	• Arms linked • Value created • Spirit-driven • Parity • Selective • Longer-term • Continually developing

Figure 4.5 Transactional versus strategic business relationships

Source: Developed by SHAPE International.

Case Example 4.5 — National Grid Transco Group

Roy Staughton, SHAPE International
(www.shape-international.com)

Peter Roberts was the head of assets for National Transmissions and Trading within Transco, which is part of the National Grid Transco Group. Transco is a major player in the regulated industry and manages multi-million-pound projects that create the infrastructure used to transport energy across the UK. Peter was responsible for the planning and construction, maintenance and ultimately decommissioning of the high-pressure gas pipelines and pumping stations within the UK.

Source: National Grid

Peter had some experience in developing strategic relationships:

A number of organisations want to move to having strategic relationships but they are struggling with how to do it. Strategic relationships call for a change in culture from an adversarial to a collaborative style. And that takes time – because it's a trust issue and trust is earned, not switched on overnight, and it quickly unpicks when things go wrong. People default back to type when under pressure, and that's a problem.

In a strategic relationship each party knows what turns the other party on, what is important to them and what they are trying to deliver. And they come together to agree how they can combine to meet each other's aspirations. There's a realisation that each party should provide added value and each party has a right to make a decent return. Such relationships can be quite hard for some clients because they are used to dictating to the supply chain exactly what they want. Part of a collaborative relationship is accepting that you've got to stop dictating and actually come together and look at what is best for the whole chain.

We did it by identifying which of our project managers had the mindset to move towards a collaborative way of working. We started to think about how we could bring the supply chain together in a spirit of trust and understanding. We had to stop dictating and start involving our contractors in important issues. We brought project managers and contractors together, outside a project context, to start to work collaboratively on things like policy and procedures for, say, health and safety and environmental issues. In that way both parties learned what collaborating involved, while working on issues that were important to the industry.

Peter believes that developing strategic relationships is not easy. He added:

There isn't a hard and fast rulebook that works for everyone. It requires a leap of faith. If you think it's the right thing to do you should go with it and, if you've got any sense, you'll put some key performance indicators in place to help you and your partners.

Using a process designed and facilitated by SHAPE International, Transco and one key partner agreed a jointly developed set of performance indicators, or metrics, to assess and develop their relationship. The process involved the key players from each party in identifying the things that make a difference to their relationship. These included a range of issues, from the attitude of key players, to document quality and the nature of communications. Once this was agreed, Transco and each partner shared their two sets of independently developed characteristics to agree a joint set. Using descriptive anchored scales for each agreed characteristic, the two parties were then able to agree on their existing and desired current position.

Peter Roberts concluded:

This process provided us with a jointly constructed set of weighted metrics that defined the relationship, together with agreement on the current and required performance for each one and a shared action plan to move things forward.

While some of the issues and approaches contained in the previous section on customer relationships apply also to business relationships, there are three additional aspects to managing business relationships: measuring business relationships, using key account managers, and additional ways of developing personal relationships.

4.5.3 Measuring business relationships

Among the questions frequently considered by managers involved in inter-organisational relationships are:

- Where is the relationship currently?
- Why is it like that?
- What is the best the relationship might be?
- What might need to change to get there?
- How should we monitor progress?

These questions highlight an area that is of key concern to operations managers: how to assess and measure relationships. 'Regular assessment of a customer relationship is a prerequisite for conscious, purposeful intervention in it. Assessment is particularly valuable when any major change in the relationship is being considered, such as developing or adapting an offering or investing in operational capability for the relationship.'[21] Yet, surprisingly given its importance, measurement of relationships is poorly understood. From an operational perspective, managers need to assess and measure relationships to understand where the deficiencies are, in order to work on them with their suppliers or partners. Measurement of existing relationships will also influence decisions about which partners to use in the future.

It is vital to recognise that the two types of relationships call for completely different approaches to measurement.

Assessing transactional relationships

Managing highly contractual, transactional relationships is often fraught with difficulty. This is particularly true where an aspect of the customer's business has been outsourced to a

Table 4.3 Examples of service-level agreement measures

Help desk support	
Telephone response	95% within 3 rings
Problem resolution	65% through first-line support within 8 hours
	35% through second-line support within 24 hours
Complaint escalation	To first-line manager after 8 working hours
	To senior manager after 16 working hours
Request for software fix	Initial response within 5 working days
	Outline proposal within 15 working days
Equipment maintenance	
Response to non-critical fault	2 working days
Response to critical fault	2 hours
First-time fix rate	95%
Schedule adherence	95% within 2 working days
Spares availability	95% within 48 hours
	100% within 5 working days

specialist provider. Examples of this lie in the area of facilities management or information technology support.

Measurement of transactional relationships tends to be concerned almost entirely with financial and hard measures of operational performance, such as price and on-time completion or delivery quality, and is frequently defined by service-level agreements (SLAs) which are often imposed on the supplier by the purchaser.

It is important to be aware that relationships by definition are 'owned' by both parties. They are fundamentally two-way and shared, so this approach, whilst perfectly valid in a transactional context, cannot be seen as genuinely measuring the relationship. What is actually being monitored is the performance of the supplier against the contract – something which in itself is entirely proper but it should not be confused with measurement of the relationship which is something that is and can only, properly, be measured jointly. Table 4.3 gives examples of key measures included in typical SLAs.

The advantage of SLAs is that the measures provide a basis for review of how well the contract is working. The disadvantage is that it is impossible to describe all facets of service provision through an SLA. If the working relationship deteriorates to a 'nit-picking' review of performance against an increasing list of measures, it is likely that it will not continue. Worse still, SLAs are sometimes used to exert undue pressure on suppliers. For example, if a supplier has performed very well against the agreed measures, instead of providing thanks and an extended contract the purchaser may try to reduce the price on the assumption that the supplier had more resources than necessary to meet the performance targets. (We will cover more about SLAs in Chapter 6.)

Assessing strategic relationships

As part of a strategic relationship, partner organisations trying to work closely together in a long-term relationship, and with mutual benefits in mind, will wish to assess the nature or strength of that relationship and how they might together develop it. Though many operations managers would claim that it is difficult, if not impossible, to measure some of

Table 4.4 The seven dimensions of business relationships

Dimension	Definition
Partner selection	Who you choose to work with
Nature of contract	Impact of the contract on the relationship and vice versa
Understanding each other	Understanding each other's expectations and perceptions
Interpersonal relationships	One-on-one relationships at work and socially
Way of working	Relationships at an organisational level
Dealing with problems	Dealing with and learning from problems
Performance management	Using measures to drive action and improvement

Source: Developed from Johnston, Robert and Roy Staughton (2009), 'Establishing and Developing Strategic Relationships – The Role for Operations Managers', *International Journal of Production and Operations Management* 20 (6) 504–590.

the softer, often more personal characteristics of a relationship, such as attitude, behaviour and trust, it is usually these softer characteristics that are essential for the success of the relationship.[22] We believe it is only possible to understand and manage a relationship from both parties' points of view rather than simply carrying out supplier assessments or customer satisfaction exercises.[23]

This calls for a radically different approach, one which reflects the mindset and aspirations of the parties to the relationship. This is almost always based on the joint development of a process for capturing and monitoring an agreed set of hard and soft metrics. One extremely successful way of doing this has been perfected by SHAPE International, a firm that specialises in the facilitation of business relationships. It involves facilitated agreement of the important characteristics of the relationship – typically a selection of elements of the seven dimensions of business relationships shown in Table 4.4 – which are then jointly assessed, using semantic anchored scales (numerical scales with descriptive anchors for the two extremes).[24]

The jointly agreed scores then form the basis for discussion and agreement of action plans for improvement.[25] Case Example 4.5 demonstrates how a progressive organisation is addressing the development of strategic relationships and the process for jointly developing metrics of their key strategic relationships.

4.5.4 Key account management (KAM)

An approach appropriate for those situations where organisations have a relatively small number of strategic customers is key account management (KAM). KAM recognises that these relationships are complex, with more than one channel of contact between provider and customer. Figure 4.6 illustrates the transition from a traditional ('bow tie') approach to buyer–supplier relationships, to the KAM approach represented by the diamond.

In the traditional approach, transactions are channelled through one point of contact, a sales or contract manager. As Figure 4.6 indicates, the weakness of this approach is that the relationship is only as strong as the link between a single buyer and the sales or contract manager. This relationship is vulnerable to changes in personnel, so some organisations regularly change their buyers in order to maintain 'arm's length' trading conditions. The danger for the supplier is that a change in a buyer might lead to a less favourable environment. The key point to note is that the relationship may be easily broken by competitors who manage to forge a strong contact with other influencers in the customer organisation.

The aim of KAM is to turn the traditional 'bow tie' relationship into a much stronger 'diamond'. In this format, links are encouraged across the boundary between the two organisations. The role of the key account manager is now not to act as a conduit through which all communication must flow, but rather to act as an enabler for the relationship. If the customer has a particular need, KAM is focused on setting up the dialogue between the appropriate

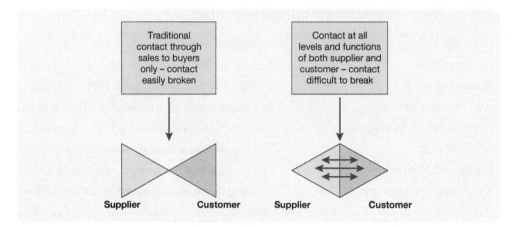

Figure 4.6 'Bow tie' and diamond relationships

Source: Adapted from Payne, Adrian, Martin Christopher, Moira Clark and Helen Peck (1995), *Relationship Marketing for Competitive Advantage*, Butterworth Heinemann, Oxford.

parties. Of course, the key account manager must monitor the effectiveness of these relationships to avoid the occurrence of problems that will damage the long-term business.

This approach is particularly useful for professional service firms that contain individuals or groups that are encouraged to be entrepreneurial in business development. It is not uncommon for customers to be approached by numbers of these, all from the same organisation, effectively in competition with each other for the same business, thus giving the customer the impression that the firm does not know what it is doing.

For B2B customers, the customer retention approach is so vital that it is almost a 'blinding flash of the obvious' to say that the organisation should focus on customer loyalty. A loss of a customer can threaten the existence of many of these services. The relationship growth approach has to be the main emphasis here, looking to build more links and broadening the base of business connection.

4.5.5 Building interpersonal relationships in business

Enhancing business relationships can easily be overlooked by organisations that are operationally focused and busy delivering services, and also by organisations at the other extreme, which are market focused and intent on increasing their customer base.

Interpersonal business relationships can be established and enhanced in four key ways:[26]

- *Going the extra mile*. Providing higher than expected levels of service on a current project, such as providing enhanced documentation, analyses, explanations or even presentations, and/or greater accessibility to staff.

- *Increasing the amount of client contact*. Making frequent visits or telephone calls, creating contacts at different levels in the organisation, scheduling meetings and feedback/development sessions.

- *Building the business relationship*. Putting on special seminars for the client, helping them make other contacts, assisting with benchmarking, sending useful articles, even referring business to the client.

- *Building a social relationship*. Providing social activities and tickets for events, remembering personal anniversaries, etc.

In Case Example 4.6 the head of a global trading and shipping conglomerate explains how he tries to strengthen relationships with his suppliers and customers.

Case Example 4.6   GP Group (Bangkok)

The GP Group is a global trading and shipping company based in Bangkok. It is a family firm, which was established 125 years ago in Burma. It now has a turnover in excess of US$2 billion and comprises over 20 companies worldwide, specialising in commodity trading, ship chartering, ship management, rice production, seed research and production, manufacturing and exporting rubber products, chemicals, pharmaceuticals, jewellery and soya bean. It provides services such as property development, tour operations, plastic security cards, port management and project management.

Source: Aspectra/Maurine Traffic

Kirit Shah is the chairman and owner of the Group, and he explained his role in the diversified business.

I am no longer personally involved in running any of my companies directly. All the companies have managing directors and they run the business on their own. I have good people. For the past 25 years I have been recruiting graduates from business schools. My typical day would involve meeting some of the directors and talking about what they are doing or working on a problem that they might have. I would meet a lot of their customers, their suppliers and their buyers, and I would typically host a lunch or dinner and meet them face-to-face to help them in their work.

The way I try to strengthen our business relationships is to have face-to-face meetings with people. I know this is very much against the trend, which is about global communications, mobile telephones and instant communication. But just think about it: if I can sit face-to-face with someone I can see their reaction, which on a fax or e-mail I cannot. As a buyer today you have a choice, the whole world wants to sell to you. So why me? Because you know me, because we had a meeting, had a drink, maybe our families know each other. It is the personal touch that I think is important in today's faceless world. We are all trying to get to a faceless situation but I don't think there is an effective substitute for personal interaction. And it's surprisingly easy to do, it's like an illusion. If you were in London and I was in London and I asked you for a meeting, chances are you would tell me, 'OK, let's meet next month', or you might not even accept my call. On the other hand, if I call you from Bangkok, chances are you will take my call as a priority over something else that you were doing. So if I said I was coming from Bangkok and I can meet you the day after tomorrow, chances are that you will see me faster than you would see a guy who is next door or in the next street. It's the perception that he is always there but the guy from Bangkok is not, so I must see him at a time convenient to him, not at a time convenient to me.

The downside is that we have to travel a lot more than we ever did. Now it's more intense than ever. Before, when I went on a trip it was for one week; now, because of frequency of flights, I go somewhere for one day. Even when I go to London I land at 6.00 in the morning and I take a flight back at 10.00 in the evening, having spent the day there. With more direct flights we are all burning ourselves trying to get to the farthest point on the globe in the shortest possible time and get back.

4.6   Summary

Customers, who are they?

- A 'customer' is the recipient and often also a provider (co-producer) in a service process. The word 'customer' refers to all the individuals, units or even organisations to whom, and often with whom, an individual, unit or organisation provides service.
- Customers may be external, internal, intermediaries, end users, stakeholders, payers, beneficiaries, participants, and valuable or non-valuable.
- Operations managers need to develop an understanding of the nature of individual customers and the customers' likely attitude and behaviour.
- Operational categories of customers include the Ally, the Hostage, the Anarchist, the Patient, the Tolerant, the Intolerant, the Victim, the Terrorist, the Incompetent and the Champion.

What are the benefits of retaining good customers?

- A key task for operations managers is retaining valuable customers.
- The benefits of retaining valuable customers, for those organisations that wish to do so, include increased revenues, reduced costs, positive word-of-mouth recommendations and long-term revenue streams.
- Retention can be measured in various ways including the number of active accounts, willingness to recommend (such as the Net Promoter Score) or by calculating lifetime values.

How can managers develop good customer relationships (B2C services)?

- Managing customer relationships is about establishing, maintaining and enhancing relationships with customers for mutual benefit.
- There are three main forms of customer relationship:
  - relationships based on a portfolio of services, frequently found in higher-volume operations
  - personal relationships created between an individual customer and an employee, particularly prevalent in low-volume professional organisations
  - temporary relationships, which recognise the transactional, one-off nature of many services.
- There is often a link between customers' perceived risk in purchasing or using the service and their desire for a type of relationship with the provider.
- Customer relationship management (CRM) is used by some high-volume consumer services to try to grow more profitable business by better understanding the needs of individual customers.
- CRM attempts to integrate the many communication channels between an organisation's units and its customers.

How can managers develop good business relationships (B2B services)?

- Building business relationships can be different to building many consumer relationships.
- Business markets often comprise a small number of powerful customers who are seeking solutions to problems. Many business relationships are close, complex and long-term and

each relationship is part of a network of relationships; others are short-term and adversarial in nature.

- There are many types of business enterprise, such as contracts, partnerships, alliances, strategic/global alliances, partnering, joint ventures, and networks; each of these encompasses slightly differing forms of relationships.
- Measuring business relationships is the key to improvement.
- Service level agreements (SLAs) are often used in contractual transactional relationships.
- Strategic relationships require jointly developed metrics.
- Key account management is helpful for organisations with a small number of strategic partners.
- Building personal relationships underpins many business relationships.

4.7 Discussion questions

1 How would you classify yourself and your colleagues/friends in terms of your customer attitude to a particular service? Could everyone be converted into Allies and if so, how?

2 Calculate your lifetime value for three service organisations which you use, for example supermarket, clothing retailer, music download website, bar or bank. What are the problems in assessing lifetime values?

3 Assess the personal relationship you have with a professional service provider, such as university lecturer, doctor, counsellor, financial advisor. How well is the relationship managed?

4.8 Questions for managers

1 Is your organisation pursuing a relationship approach? Is this what your customers desire?

2 Have you considered the resources required for developing customer relationships? How have you justified any additional resources?

3 To what extent do your processes take into account the differing needs of your target customer segments?

4 Do you understand the value of a customer? Can you calculate a Net Promoter Score and/or the average lifetime value of customers?

5 How important is customer retention to your business? If so, what is your retention rate and how could it be improved?

6 How do you go about jointly developing your key strategic relationships?

Robert Johnston and Rhian Silvestro, Warwick Business School

The National Brewery has over 5,000 public houses (bars) in the UK. All of its public houses (pubs) used to be 'tenanted', i.e. a manager (tenant) was appointed to run the pub and was overseen by an area manager. The area managers would pay regular visits to assess the pub's financial position, the success of recent activities and the pub manager's plans for the future. Because the big brewers, of which National is one, owned the majority of pubs in the UK, they were able to tie their pubs to sell just their own products thus squeezing smaller real-ale brewers out of the market. Following a review by the Monopolies and Mergers Commission (MMC), legislation was introduced to force them either to sell a proportion of their pubs or to release them from their tie to the brewery's products.

Some of the big brewers took their pubs back into management and therefore outside the jurisdiction of the legislation, while others sold off their chains of public houses to other companies. Unfortunately, both of these strategies had the effect of reducing the likelihood of the introduction of guest beers. National decided to change over 2,000 of its tenanted pubs to leased pubs and give the tenants the opportunity to purchase (usually) a 20-year lease. This was seen by many tenants as a golden opportunity to have not only security and control over their futures but also something of value that they could either pass on or sell in the years to come. Under the new lease the lessees (the lease holders) were required to sell National's beers and lagers but were permitted to sell one other guest beer or lager; there was no tie on other beverages. The lessee also paid National Brewery rent which was calculated on the basis of 50% of net profit.

National recognised that with each of these pubs becoming an independent business in its own right, away from the direct control of the parent company, it needed to create a new body to help and support these pubs in their growth and development. Thus a partnership approach was born through a specially created subsidiary, National Support Services (NSS).

To provide the new, extensive and comprehensive range of support and developmental services, National got rid of the area managers and appointed NSS managers (NSSMs) to work with lessees to help them develop their businesses. Many of them previously worked as area managers but over 50 per cent were new to the business. The services included sales promotions packages and beer discounts, which were delivered directly by the NSSM, together with advice on catering, property, security, financial matters, legal problems and quality standards. Training, on any aspect of the business, was provided by NSS consultants. All these services were provided free to lessees. Information about the products was provided in glossy brochures available from the NSSMs.

One NSSM, Richard Jenkins, explained how things have changed:

In the days before the lease agreements the then area managers had the right to require meetings with their pub managers and to demand financial and promotional plans. Now, in the new spirit of partnership, the relationship is much more supportive. It is up to the NSSM to prove to the lessee the need for his or her support. This is achieved in all but a very few instances. However, it's OK for those who are doing well and using our services but what do I do if they then turn round and say that, apart from our beer and lager (which they are required to sell under the terms of the lease), they don't want to sell other National products? Should I continue to offer all the services or should I withdraw them? Also, what do I do for the lessee who is running a pub in a poor location? These lessees have not been overly receptive to many of the new possibilities – indeed, many of them just want us to reduce their rents, which we don't have the authority to do, or offer unlimited quantities of discounted or free beer for promotional purposes.

You must realise that delivering the Support Services is not cheap. The payback for these costs comes from the enhanced rental income from our properties. This is achieved by having better-performing businesses because of the support provided by NSS. Some lessees have claimed that their rents have about doubled since the change in agreement. This increase in rents reflects, in part, the increased value that the lessees can now obtain from the premium on the assignment of their business, and their entitlement to take on guest beers.

National has three types of pub – the community pub, the tavern and the food pub – and it has put out to lease about equal numbers of each type. Examples of each of these types of pub are as follows:

- *The White Lion,* a 'community pub', is a male-dominated, traditional pub in a run-down area of Nottingham, where unemployment has been high for the past twenty years. There are several pubs of similar style in the area. The pub does not have a restaurant but offers bar snacks and sandwiches. The bar offers a limited product range and sells mainly beer. The pub was last refurbished fifteen years ago and the décor is now somewhat the worse for wear.

- *The Oak,* a 'tavern', is located in a prosperous working-class suburb in Nottingham. It is a popular family pub, although there are a number of similar offerings in the area. The pub was refurbished at moderate cost five years ago. It remains in good condition and has a friendly atmosphere. The Oak has one restaurant offering a standard menu, and the typical spend on food is around £12 per head. Pub lunches may be ordered from the bar. There is an indoor family area and an outdoor play area for children.

- *The Castle,* a 'food pub', is a new pub located in an affluent, suburban location in a residential area in Nottingham. The pub is well differentiated in its locality, having a smart, fashionable, 'designer' feel to it, with bright, well co-ordinated furnishings and fittings. The pub targets the business community at lunchtimes. It is popular with 'yuppies' and 'dinkies' (double income, no kids) in the evenings. There is a 'wayside-inn'-style restaurant, which offers an extensive menu including traditional and ethnic dishes, where the typical spend on food is around £20–£25 per head. Light meals can be ordered at the bar. Wine and cocktails are popular.

A summary of the financial position of each pub is given in Table 4.5.

Table 4.5 End-of-year financial summaries

	The White Lion	The Oak	The Castle
Trading square footage (front of house)	1,000	1,500	2,000
Mix of income (ex. Accomm.)			
Liquor sales	90%	83%	35.5%
Food sales	6%	14%	63%
Machine income net	3%	2%	0.5%
Other income	1%	1%	1%
Total annual income	£270,000	£480,000	£675,000
Margin			
Liquor margin	45%	53%	58%
Food margin	40%	54%	67%
Gross margin	43%	52%	63%
Cost ratios to total income			
Wages	11%	14%	17.7%
Fuel	2.8%	2.6%	2.9%
Trade expenses	1.8%	2.1%	3.4%
Equipment repairs	1.2%	1.3%	1.5%
Promotions	3.3%	2.8%	2%
Depreciation	2%	2.3%	3%
Rates, water, insurance	3.6%	3.4%	3.5%
Building repairs	2.3%	1.5%	1%
Overall costs	28%	30%	35%
House net profit	15%	22%	28%
Cumulative profit growth over three years (*not* adjusted for inflation)	5%	10%	19%

Lessees have the option to assign (sell) the lease on the open market after the first three years. If the lease were assigned after five years lessees could expect equity growth in the lease ranging between £120,000 and £300,000 depending on the type and size of pub.

Questions

1 How has the lease changed the relationship between the area manager/NSSM and the tenant/lessee?

2 Evaluate National Support Services from the point of view of their customers, i.e. the lessees.

3 How should the National Brewery go about developing its Support Services to meet the needs of all its lessees?

Suggested further reading

Anderson, Erin and Sandy D. Jap (2005), 'The Dark Side of Close Relationships', *MIT Sloan Management Review* 46 (3) 75–82

Buttle, Francis (2008), *Customer Relationship Management*, 2nd edition, Butterworth-Heinemann

Edvardsson, Bo and Tore Strandvik (2008), 'Critical Times in Business Relationships', *European Business Review* 21 (4) 326–343

Fruchter, Gila E. and Simon P. Sigue (2005), 'Transactions vs. Relationships: What should the Company Emphasize?', *Journal of Service Research* 8 (1) 18–36

Johnston, Robert and Roy Staughton (2009), 'Establishing and Developing Strategic Relationships – The Role for Operations Managers', *International Journal of Production and Operations Management* 29 (6) 564–590

Karten, Naomi (2004), 'With Service Level Agreements, Less Is More', *Information Systems Management* 21 (4) 43–45

Maister, David H. (2003), *Managing the Professional Service Firm*, Simon and Schuster, London

Reichheld, Frederick F. (2006), 'The Microeconomics of Customer Relationships', *MIT Sloan Management Review* 47 (2) 73–78

Shaw, Colin (2007), *The DNA of Customer Experience*, Palgrave Macmillan, Basingstoke

Staughton, Roy and Robert Johnston (2005), 'Operational Performance Gaps in Business Relationships', *International Journal of Operations and Production Management* 25 (4) 320–332

Useful web links

Many CRM system software providers publish case studies of successful implementations on their websites: see, for example:
www.oracle.com/applications/crm/siebel

Wikipedia has a good piece on customer lifetime value:
http://en.wikipedia.org/wiki/Customer_lifetime_value

More on lifetime value at
http://chiefmarketer.com/crm_loop/roi/sense_customer_value/

Some information on building business relationships from Leading Insight:
http://www.leadinginsight.com/business_relationships.htm

The Chartered Institute of Marketing (CIM) provides an overview of CRM theories in its knowledge hub:
www.cim.co.uk

Notes

1 See Johnston, Robert (2008), 'Internal Service – Barriers, Flows and Assessment', *International Journal of Service Industry Management* 19 (2) 210–231

2 See for example Christopher, Martin, Adrian Payne and David Ballantyne (2001), *Relationship Marketing: Creating Stakeholder Value*, 2nd edition, Butterworth-Heinemann; Gummesson, Evert (2002), *Total Relationship Marketing: Rethinking Marketing Management*, 2nd edition, Butterworth-Heinemann

3 Reinartz, Werner and V. Kumar (2002), 'The Mismanagement of Customer Loyalty', *Harvard Business Review* 80 (7) 86–94

4 Gremler and Brown use the term 'loyalty ripple effect' to recognise the value of positive word-of-mouth encouragement: Gremler, Dwayne D. and Stephen W. Brown (1999), 'The Loyalty Ripple Effect: Appreciating the Full Value of Customers', *International Journal of Service Industry Management* 10 (3) 271–291

5 Reichheld, Frederick F. and W. Earl Sasser (1990), 'Zero Defections: Quality Comes to Services', *Harvard Business Review* 68 (5) 105–111

6 See for example Knox, Simon D. and Timothy J. Denison (1992), *Profiling the Promiscuous Shopper: A Report Examining Shopper Loyalty in Modern Shopping Centres*, Air Miles Travel Promotions Ltd, Sussex; Keiningham, Timothy, Bruce Cooil, Lerzan Aksoy, Tor Andreassen and Jay Wiener (2007), 'The Value of Different Customer Satisfaction and Loyalty Metrics in Predicting Customer Retention, Recommendation, and Share of Wallet', *Managing Service Quality* 17 (4) 361–384

7 Keiningham, Timothy L., Bruce Cooil, Tor Wallin Andreassen and Lerzan Askoy (2007), 'A Longitudinal Examination of Net Promoter and Firm Revenue Growth', *Journal of Marketing* 71 (3) 39–51; Keiningham, Timothy L., Bruce Cooil, Lerzan Askoy, Tor Wallin Andreassen and Jay Weiner (2007), 'The Value of Different Customer Satisfaction and Loyalty Metrics in Predicting Customer Retention, Recommendation and Share-of-Wallet', *Managing Service Quality* 17 (4) 361–384

8 Reichheld, Frederick F. (2003), 'The One Number You Need to Grow', *Harvard Business Review* 81 (12) 46–54; Reichheld, Frederick F. (2006), *The Ultimate Question*, Harvard Business School Press, Cambridge, Massachusetts

9 See for example Mohr, Jakki and Robert Spekman (1994), 'Characteristics of Partnership Success: Partnership Attributes, Communication Behavior, and Conflict Resolution Techniques', *Strategic Management Journal* 15 (2) 135–152; Morgan, Robert M. and Shelby D. Hunt (1994), 'The Commitment-Trust Theory of Relationship Marketing', *Journal of Marketing* 58 (2) 20–38

10 Adolf, Ruediger, Stacey Grant-Thompson, Wendy Harrington and Marc Singer (1997), 'What Leading Banks Are Learning about Big Databases and Marketing', *McKinsey Quarterly* (3) 187–192

11 Payne, Adrian and Pennie Frow (2006), 'Customer Relationship Management: From Strategy to Implementation', *Journal of Marketing Management* 22 (1/2) 135–168

12 See for example Ford, David, Lars-Erik Gadde, Håkan Håkansson and Ivan Snehota (2011), *Managing Business Relationships*, 3rd edition, Wiley, Chichester

13 Johnston, Robert and Roy Staughton (2009), 'Establishing and Developing Strategic Relationships – The Role for Operations Managers', *International Journal of Production and Operations Management* 29 (6) 564–590

14 Johnston, Robert and Roy Staughton (2009), 'Establishing and Developing Strategic Relationships – The Role for Operations Managers', *International Journal of Production and Operations Management* 29 (6) 564–590

15 Stafford, Edwin R. (1994), 'Using Co-operative Strategies to Make Alliances Work', *Long Range Planning* 27 (3) 64–74

16 Kanter, Rosabeth Moss (1994), 'Collaborative Advantage', *Harvard Business Review* 72 (4) 96–108

17 Gulati, Ranjay (1998), 'Alliances and Networks', *Strategic Management Journal* (19) 293–317

18 Stafford, Edwin R. (1994), 'Using Co-operative Strategies to Make Alliances Work', *Long Range Planning* 27 (3) 64–74

19 See Johnston, Robert and Roy Staughton (2009), 'Establishing and Developing Strategic Relationships – The Role for Operations Managers', *International Journal of Production and Operations Management* 29 (6) 564–590; Ford, David, Lars-Erik Gadde, Håkan Håkansson and Ivan Snehota (2011), *Managing Business Relationships*, 3rd edition, Wiley, Chichester

20 See also Ford, David, Lars-Erik Gadde, Håkan Håkansson and Ivan Snehota (2011), *Managing Business Relationships*, 3rd edition, Wiley, Chichester; Henderson, J.C. (1990), 'Plugging into Strategic Partnerships: The Critical IS Connection', *Sloan Management Review* 31 (3) 7–18

21 Ford, David, Lars-Erik Gadde, Håkan Håkansson and Ivan Snehota (2011), *Managing Business Relationships*, 3rd edition, Wiley, Chichester

22 Staughton, Roy and Robert Johnston (2005), 'Operational Performance Gaps in Business Relationships', *International Journal of Operations and Production Management* 25 (4) 320–332

23 Ford, David, Lars-Erik Gadde, Håkan Håkansson and Ivan Snehota (2011), *Managing Business Relationships*, 3rd edition, Wiley, Chichester

24 Carroll, Steven R., William M. Petrusic and Craig Leth-Steensen (2009), 'Anchoring Effects in the Judgment of Confidence: Semantic or Numeric Priming?', *Attention, Perception, & Psychophysics* 71 (2) 297–307

25 For more information on this process visit http://www.shape-international.com/

26 Payne, Adrian, Martin Christopher, Moira Clark and Helen Peck (1995), *Relationship Marketing for Competitive Advantage*, Butterworth Heinemann, Oxford; Maister, David H. (2003), *Managing the Professional Service Firm*, Simon and Schuster, London

Chapter 5
Managing customer expectations and perceptions

Chapter objectives

This chapter is about how to gain insight into customers' expectations and perceptions to create satisfied customers.

- What is customer satisfaction?
- What influences expectations and perceptions?
- How can expectations and perceptions be 'managed'?
- How can service quality be operationalised?
- How can managers capture customers' expectations?
- How can a service be specified?

5.1 Introduction

Just as service can be seen from two perspectives, service provided and service received (see Chapter 1), the quality of the service (service quality) can also be defined from these two perspectives, as operational service quality and customer perceived quality. Operational service quality is the operation's assessment of how well the service was delivered to its specification. Customer perceived quality is the customer's judgement of (satisfaction with) the quality of the service: their experience, the quality of the 'products' and the perceived benefits, compared to their needs and expectations.

In terms of customer perceived quality, operations managers need to understand, and influence, their customers' expectations to ensure they provide a service that meets or possibly exceeds those expectations. If, as a result, customers are satisfied, or indeed delighted, they are more likely to become valuable customers who not only use the service again but are positively disposed towards it and may even recommend it to others (we sometimes refer to this as their post-purchase intentions). Indeed, customers are the ultimate arbiters of the quality of the service.

Although the need to satisfy customers is something that almost 'goes without saying', this is precisely the problem with many organisations. Assumptions are made about what customers really want and, even if customers have been consulted, it may have been such a long time ago that the information is at best irrelevant, and often positively dangerous. Professional services, in particular, frequently suffer from an attitude of thinking that they know best, because they are the experts. This might be true, but this attitude can create blind spots when dealing with customers.

Understanding what satisfies and delights customers is something that must be continually addressed, using a variety of means to ensure that the answers do not fall into well-established patterns because the way the questions are asked does not vary sufficiently. Customer satisfaction is something that can be managed to some extent by influencing customers' perceptions and expectations of service delivery. This demands in-depth understanding of this subject.

It is no accident that many of those companies that have a reputation for excellent service spend time and money listening to customers. Disney, for example, invented a new term for the activity of collecting information from customers. It is called 'guestology' – reflecting Disney's approach to treating its visitors as guests rather than mere 'customers'.

We also need to consider operational service quality. Operations managers need to create a specification for their service which reflects customer needs and expectations. In service organisations this is not straightforward. But let's start with perceived service quality – the customer's perspective.

5.2 What is customer satisfaction?

In simple terms, satisfaction is the result of customers' overall assessment of their perceptions of the service (the service process, their experiences and outcomes such as the quality of the 'products', the benefits obtained and perceived value for money), compared to their prior expectations (see Figure 5.1).[1]

If customers' perceptions of the service match their expectations (P=E) then they should be satisfied (or at least satisficed). If their perception of the service exceeds their expectations (P>E) then they will be more than satisfied, even delighted. If their perceptions of the service do not meet their expectations (P<E) then they may be dissatisfied, even disgusted or outraged.[2] Importantly satisfaction is a continuum, from extreme delight to extreme dissatisfaction. Here we will use a +5 to −5 scale to represent this continuum (see Figure 5.2).

As well as satisfaction being the customer's overall assessment of the service, the customer may also feel delighted, satisfied, or dissatisfied with the individual steps (transactions or touch points) in the service process. This is sometimes referred to as transaction satisfaction. We will develop this point in Section 5.4.2 and Chapter 7.

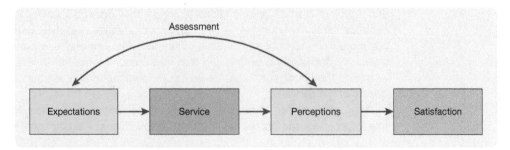

Figure 5.1 Customer satisfaction

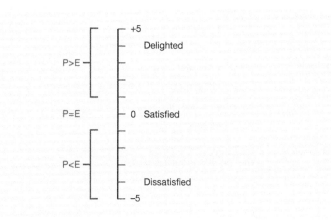

Figure 5.2 The satisfaction continuum

5.2.1 Perceptions–expectations gap

If there is a mismatch between perceptions and expectations, this, in simple terms, is usually caused by either a mismatch between expectations and the service (Gap 1 in Figure 5.3) and/or a mismatch between the service and customers' perceptions of it (Gap 2 in Figure 5.3).[3]

There are several reasons why Gap 1 might exist. The service may have been inappropriately specified, designed or enacted, or there may be insufficient resources to meet expectations. It is also possible that the customer may have inappropriate expectations. An inappropriate specification or design of the service may be the result of a poor understanding of customer expectations by managers. Managers may have not put enough time and effort into either specifying the service or getting feedback from customers about what they feel to be an appropriate type or level of service. Insufficient resources may be the result of a poor understanding of market requirements or demand profiles.

These 'internal' reasons often stem from a lack of determination to deliver consistent standards. Managers frequently report that their organisation does not take time and trouble to understand what its customers require and therefore the service design process is flawed from the outset. This flows into poor or inappropriate service design and results in poor resource utilisation.

Inappropriate expectations may be the result of inappropriate marketing, promises made by the organisation that cannot be delivered, or inappropriate word-of-mouth referrals or organisational image, which may be a result of poor service experiences in the past. Also, there

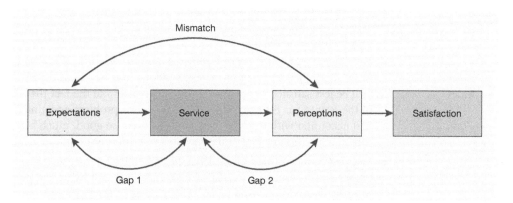

Figure 5.3 Simplified gap model

Table 5.1 Reasons for gaps

	Gap 1	Gap 2
Internal causes	Lack of understanding of customer expectations Inappropriate specification and/or provision Poor service design Insufficient resources	Incorrect or inappropriate service provision
External causes	Inappropriate expectations of the service experience and/or outcomes	Inappropriate perceptions of the service experience and/or outcomes

are some customers who have quite unrealistic expectations of some service organisations and can cause a great deal of aggravation and nuisance as a result. These individuals either need their expectations reshaping before or during service delivery, or removing from the operation, if this is feasible (see Chapter 10).

Gap 2 may be the result of either incorrect provision of a service or customers inappropriately perceiving the service. Incorrect provision is not unusual in many service organisations. Service operations are often complex, human-based activities and things do go wrong. A mismatch as a result of poor service provision can be removed or at least reduced through service recovery (see Chapter 13). Table 5.1 summarises the reasons for the existence of the gaps and therefore dissatisfied customers.

Additionally, customers' perceptions of the quality of the service provided (operational service quality) may not be the same as the quality of the service received (customer perceived quality), because customer perceived quality is a matter of personal perception (see Section 5.3).

5.2.2 Downsides of the expectation–perception approach to customer perceived service quality

While the expectation–perception approach to understanding perceived service quality is extremely useful in focusing on the outcome of customer satisfaction and helps identify mismatches between operational and customer views of quality, it does have some downsides:[4]

- *Service could be perceived to be 'good' when it is 'bad'.* If customer expectations are particularly low (and indeed may have been deliberately created that way), poor operational service quality may be perceived as highly satisfying because expectations have been exceeded. This may look like a reasonable state, but it is clearly one that makes for-profit organisations vulnerable to competitive threat from higher-quality providers, or may lead to government 'interference' in public sector organisations.

- *Service could be perceived to be 'bad' when it is 'good'.* Likewise, it is also possible that if expectations are high, due to over-promising, for example, then a good operational service may be seen as inadequate.

- *Service that was 'good' last time may only be 'OK' this time.* If a service was perceived to have been 'good' then the customers' expectations may be raised for next time; thus they may well be less satisfied on subsequent occasions, despite the fact that the operational quality of the service has remained unchanged. This is a problem encountered by Disney. Visitors' first encounter with the Magic Kingdom is often so good, much better than expected, that subsequent visits are sometimes reported to be poorer in quality, i.e. less satisfactory.

- *Satisfied customers may switch.* Even though a particular service may meet customers' expectations and customers are satisfied, customers may still switch suppliers, if there is a choice. Alternative service providers may offer a superior level of service or additional service features, or customers may be naturally disloyal or inquisitive. When it comes to measuring satisfaction, we need to remember to also measure the customers' post-purchase intentions; in particular, will they return? (See Chapter 4 on the Net Promoter Score and Chapter 9). Conversely, it is also important to remember that some dissatisfied customers will not (or cannot) switch; they remain as customers often creating particular problems for service employees!

Nortel, the telecommunications company, surveyed its customers and discovered that those who scored up to 4 on a scale from 1 to 5 (1 = very dissatisfied, 5 = very satisfied) were vulnerable to switching. Only those scoring above 4.5 could be thought of as reasonably loyal. Avis Rent A Car tracks likelihood to repurchase alongside customer satisfaction. The company has developed a 'customer satisfaction balance sheet', estimating the cost to the company in lost sales as a result of poor service.

These issues reinforce the need to link closely the creation of expectations in the minds of customers with the capabilities of the service process i.e. to communicate messages to set appropriate expectations and design and deliver service to meet them and manage them during the service process.

5.2.3 Confidence

Before we spend time developing the notion of customer satisfaction through a better understanding of customer expectations and the formation of perceptions, we would like to introduce the related but distinct notion of customer confidence.

Whereas satisfaction is an assessment by the customer following a service experience, confidence, or the lack of it, does not require previous experience or contact with the organisation.[5] This is an important notion for all organisations, and especially those with which people may have no or little contact, for example, social services, police, fire services, coroners' courts, hospitals, local schools and legal services.

Confidence is about having belief, trust or faith in an organisation, its staff and services. Our feeling of confidence in organisations such as the police will not only affect our feeling of well-being and our quality of life but importantly it may well influence how we interact with that organisation, i.e. our predisposition towards it. If we feel confident in the local police service, for example, we may, when caught for a minor offence, be more willing to co-operate with the police. Furthermore, if we feel confident in the police we may be more willing to provide assistance as a witness at an incident, or provide information about suspicious events, or even support officers attending incidents (or at least not make their jobs more difficult). All of this helps to improve the performance of the police service itself. Confidence may also affect our willingness to fund the police through local taxation.

For some organisations, understanding and measuring customer confidence may be more appropriate than customer satisfaction. Indeed some people might argue that customer satisfaction is a wholly inappropriate measure to be applied to some of the police service's customers (i.e. criminals).

Research has shown that our confidence pre-service, i.e. before we receive any service, is influenced primarily by three things over which the organisation may have very limited control or influence:[6]

- *personal beliefs* (beliefs held by the individual about that organisation)
- *media* (for example television (news or even drama) coverage of the organisation)
- *word-of-mouth* (the communicated experiences of others)

and three things that organisations have control and influence over:

- *visibility* of the organisation, its services and its employees
- *familiarity* with the organisation's employees, services or abilities
- *communication* (knowledge of the service and its abilities).

By managing these factors, organisations can have an important impact on their potential customers and the efficiency and effectiveness of the service they deliver.

5.3 What influences expectations and perceptions?

Since the degree of satisfaction, or dissatisfaction, is the result of customers' perceptions compared to their expectations, it is appropriate to spend a little time defining expectations and perceptions and explaining how they come about.

5.3.1 Perceptions

Our perceptions are our own personal impression and interpretation of the service provided and so customers will perceive each service in their own personal, emotional and sometimes irrational way. We use our senses, vision, smell, touch, taste and hearing, to experience the world around us and the services we receive. How we perceive a service (and all other events) depends upon the experiences each of us have had in our past, our culture, language, beliefs, values, interests and assumptions.[7] The artist David Hockney said about art, 'We see with memory, which is why none of us sees the same thing, even if we're looking at the same thing.' 'Reality' is not always real. For example, much has been written about the placebo effect, where reassurances, or incantations, from a doctor (or other 'professional'), with or without a pill with no medicinal properties (or a professional's report), has a significant effect on most people's psychological and also physical well-being.[8]

A service received is what we each, individually, perceive it to be. For example, if a customer has had a privileged background and is used to being looked after, their experience of a high-class restaurant may well be quite different to someone from a more humble background (or a different country). While the privileged person may experience and perceive attentive staff and appreciate well-laid tables, the other person may find the staff obsequious and overbearing, and the number of knives and forks confusing, even anxiety-making.

In service (and indeed in business and life situations) we may filter our experiences even more:

- *Selective filtering.* We tend to only notice what is relevant to current needs and 'ignore' other parts of the experience. The 'privileged' person may notice a mark on the tablecloth and complain, the other person may not even notice it.

- *Selective distortion.* We tend to modify and seek information that supports personal beliefs and prejudices. The European visiting an American restaurant may well notice the size of the portions being served, confirming their personal prejudices about Americans.

- *Selective retention.* We tend to remember only those things that are relevant to our needs and beliefs. After a restaurant meal, some diners may remember and talk about the quality of the food, others the state of the toilets and others the attentive, or good looking, staff.

5.3.2 Expectations

Our expectations of a service will lie somewhere on a range, or continuum, between ideal and intolerable (see Figure 5.4). An intolerable train journey may be one that arrives very late, or even not at all, where the carriages are filthy and the staff abusive. An ideal train journey might be clean, on time, very fast, and include chauffeur-driven transport at either end.

Some points on this continuum could be defined as follows:[9]

- *Ideal.* The best possible.
- *Ideal feasible.* The level of service that a customer believes should be provided given the price or the industry standard.
- *Desirable.* The standard that the customer wants to receive.
- *Deserved.* The level of performance that the customer ought to receive, given the perceived costs.

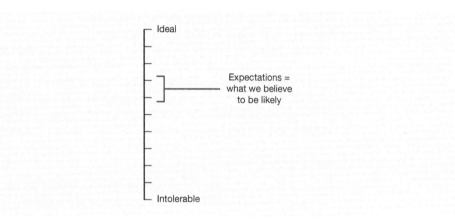

Figure 5.4 Range of expectations

- *Minimum tolerable.* The minimum tolerable standards – those that must be achieved.
- *Intolerable.* The standards the customers should not receive.

An important point here is that we should be careful when asking customers about their 'expectations'. The following questions, for example, would each provoke a different response as they refer to different points on the scale:

- What would you like?
- What should be provided?
- What would be acceptable?

Our expectations, defined as what we believe to be likely, i.e. what we believe will happen, rather than should happen, may not be a single point on this scale but a range (see Figure 5.4). This range, or zone, of expectations, as shown in Figure 5.4, is sometimes referred to as the zone of tolerance. This zone of what could be considered to be an 'acceptable' level of service by a customer is shown in Figure 5.5. The importance of this zone of tolerance is that customers may accept variation within a range of performance and any increase or decrease in performance within this area will only have a marginal effect on perceptions.[10] Only when performance moves outside of this range will it have any real effect on perceived service quality.

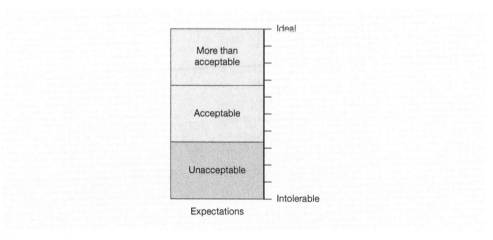

Figure 5.5 Range of expectations and the zone of tolerance or acceptable outcomes

It has been suggested that the width of this zone of tolerance is inversely proportional to the customer's level of involvement and commitment.[11] This involvement refers to a customer's level of interest in a service, the importance they attach to it, and their emotional commitment to the service.[12] For example, students who are highly engaged, committed to, and paying for, a particular programme of study may well be sensitive towards the level of tuition provided, the quality of the materials delivered, the support provided for additional work and the quality of marking for example, and raise issues and concerns when things are not felt to be right. Less committed and involved students may be willing to accept almost whatever happens.

Fuzzy expectations

In some instances customers' expectations may be somewhat unclear and they may not be certain what they expect from a service provider, although they may have quite clear views about what is unacceptable. Such vague ideas about what is required have been called 'fuzzy' expectations.[13] Expectations, as a whole, are seldom fuzzy but they usually include elements which are more or less fuzzy. In some cases these expectations may be implicit and are not actively or consciously thought about by customers, but they may become explicit when expectations are either not met or exceeded.

Whether customers' expectations are fuzzy or crystal clear, operations managers have to be certain about the expectations they are trying to meet. They need to understand them, define them and then specify them to ensure that what they deliver meets that specification (operational service quality – see Section 5.7). In many cases this will require providing guidance to customer-facing staff to encourage them to ask questions to clarify the real needs of the customer, rather than to assume that what they are being asked for is actually what is required. Customers are often afraid of looking silly in front of other people (both customers and staff), and may ask for something quite inappropriate, leading to eventual dissatisfaction and defection.

In effect, service operations managers need to revisit the service concept (Chapter 3) to identify possible gaps between what is in the mind of the customer and what is in the mind of the service provider.

Influencing expectations

The positioning of our expectations on the continuum between intolerable and ideal will be influenced by many things (see Figure 5.6). Our expectations about a train journey might be influenced by our previous experiences and the price we are paying, for example.

- *Price* often has a large influence on expectations. The higher the price, the higher up the continuum towards ideal are customers' expectations. Expectations of a customer flying

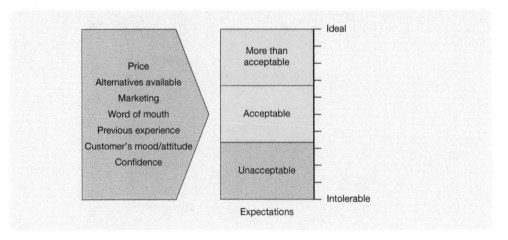

Figure 5.6 Expectations – key influences

tourist class from Paris to Chicago will be at a different level to customers flying business or first class. All three customers will have similar expectations about safety and timeliness, but expectations about legroom, quality of food, attentiveness of the service and ease of check-in may vary considerably. Price is perhaps one of the most important influences as customers are concerned not just about the service and their experiences and outcomes but also its value (see Chapter 3).

- *Alternative services available* will also help define and set expectations. If you know that one airline provides a limo service when flying business class, you may expect other carriers to do the same.

- *Marketing* can have a considerable influence on expectations. Marketing, image, branding and advertising campaigns help set expectations, often at great cost to the organisation.

- *Word-of-mouth* marketing, which is less controllable, can have a profound effect on a customer's expectations. Indeed, in some situations, word-of-mouth may have a stronger influence than organisational marketing.

- *Previous experience* will help shape expectations, as prior knowledge not only makes them clearer and sharper but allows customers more accurately to position them on the scale. Previous experience also acts as a moderator on marketing information either from the organisation or from word-of-mouth. It is important to note that previous experience may not be of the service provider in question but may be of other service providers. Our expectations for how we will be treated when we ring up our electricity supplier with a query will be influenced by our experiences with other contact centres, such as other utilities, retailers or financial services. This aspect is often forgotten by service organisations that continue to think that because they are as good as any other organisation in their sector, this is good enough. This is clearly not true.

- *Customers' mood and attitude* can affect their expectations. Someone in a bad mood or with a poor attitude to an organisation may have heightened expectations; someone less concerned and more tolerant may have a wider zone of tolerance and thus a wider range of expectations.

- *Confidence* about an organisation, even before we have used an organisation, will also influence our expectations. If we have confidence in our child's new school because of its reputation, for example, we may have a higher set of expectations as to how we and our child will be treated.

Expectations are dynamic. They are not fixed on a continuum between intolerable and ideal. They will change over time and indeed during the service itself. Customers are continually experiencing many service situations and consuming services. Their expectations are under continual review and change. So what a customer may have felt to have been acceptable last time may well be different next time, as influenced by some of the factors above.

Expectations of a service never used

Because our expectations can be based on what we believe to be likely, we therefore do not need to have experienced a service to have expectations about it. People who have not experienced a funeral may have some clear expectations about the nature, mood and style of the event, and more fuzzy expectations about the actual series of events. These may be quite clear and explicit if they have, for example, witnessed such events second-hand, perhaps on television or in novels.

5.4 How can expectations and perceptions be 'managed'?

Two key roles for operations managers that we will cover in this section are, firstly, how they can manage and influence customer expectations and, secondly, how they can manage (manipulate) customers' perceptions during the service process.

5.4.1 Managing expectations

While one might argue that managing expectations is predominantly the role of marketers, operations do have two important roles to play here. Firstly it is the duty of operations managers to ensure that the marketing and strategy functions within an organisation know the capabilities of the operation, the nature and quality of service that it can actually deliver and indeed what it can't. This enables the marketing function to try to influence customers' expectations so that there is a good chance those expectations will be met. Secondly, the operation has an opportunity to influence and shape customer expectations during the early stages of a service process. Careful attention to the design of the first few steps of the service and the clues and messages (see Chapter 7) is required to help set the right expectations. For example, the customer entering a restaurant sees the way that it is set out and will draw conclusions about the level of service provided. If the tables and chairs are functional and there are no tablecloths or decorations, customers will be more prepared to expect simpler service than if they go into one with comfortable seats, tablecloths and ornate decorations.

5.4.2 Managing perceptions

Managing customer perceived quality during the service process is a dynamic activity.[14] Figure 5.7 combines Figures 5.2, 5.4 and 5.5 earlier (the levels of expectations and zone of tolerance, and one of the outcomes of a service – the level of satisfaction and dissatisfaction), and shows how expectations give way to a perception of satisfaction during the service process and the customer's experience of it.[15] The figure shows the zone of tolerance extending from expectations through the process/experience to the level of satisfaction.

Peak, beginning and end experiences

It is important to note that overall satisfaction may not be the average of the customer's perception of satisfaction with the various stages of the service process. Research has shown that satisfaction is heavily influenced by how the experiences felt when they were at their peak (best or worst) and how they felt when they ended, sometimes referred to as the peak-end rule.[16] While a very good or very bad transactional experience will override other experiences, customers are also likely to be heavily influenced by the final stage (transaction) of their

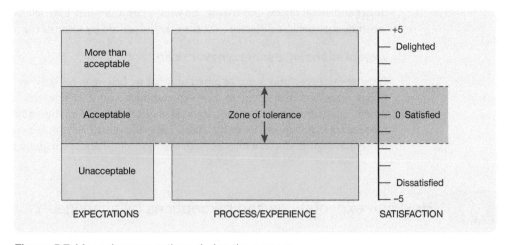

Figure 5.7 Managing perceptions during the process

Source: Adapted from Johnston, Robert (1995), 'The Zone of Tolerance: Exploring the Relationship between Service Transactions and Satisfaction with the Overall Service', *International Journal of Service Industry Management* 6 (2) 46–61.

experience. By designing a good end to an experience we can manipulate customers' overall feeling of satisfaction (providing there have been no particularly bad experiences). We would also argue that the early stages in the process can also be important. These can set customers' expectations and create a good initial impression. Arriving at a hotel's reception where the customer is dealt with quickly and pleasantly, the forms are prefilled, only needing a signature, and a glass of champagne is offered, can lower the zone of tolerance so that following satisfactory stages may be perceived as excellent. We can use the zone of tolerance to illustrate some of these impacts.

Figure 5.7 depicts something similar to a control chart (see also Chapter 9), which managers can use first to identify customer expectations – what is acceptable, less than acceptable and more than acceptable (see Sections 5.5 and 5.6) – and then to assess the impact of each stage (touch point) or transaction during the service process/experience. This helps managers understand how they can design their service to include the appropriate interventions at appropriate times to achieve the desired level of satisfaction.

A number of suggestions have been made about the use of this model.[17] Take, for example, a patient with an appointment to see a doctor for a routine medical examination. We might consider there to be seven stages (touch points) in the customer's journey:

1 Arrival at the clinic

2 Reception

3 Waiting for the doctor

4 Introduction to the examination by the doctor

5 Examination

6 Discussion of findings

7 Departure.

Expectations may have been managed (influenced) by the medical practice through its code of conduct, for example, which informs patients that they should have to wait no longer than ten minutes to see the doctor, that they will be treated with care and consideration, and that all medical facts will be explained to them in a meaningful way (see Figure 5.8).

A number of outcomes are possible:

● Performance within the zone of tolerance results in satisfaction. Providing the customer's perceptions of the transactions are not greater or less than acceptable, the

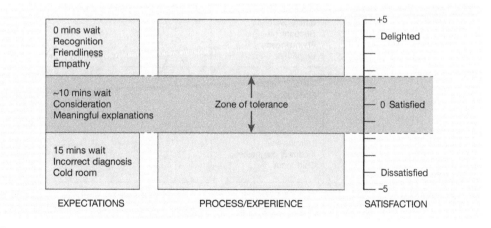

Figure 5.8 Managing perceptions at a clinic

Source: Adapted from Johnston, Robert (1995), 'The Zone of Tolerance: Exploring the Relationship between Service Transactions and Satisfaction with the Overall Service', *International Journal of Service Industry Management* 6 (2) 46–61.

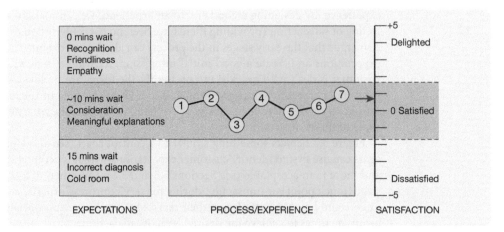

Figure 5.9 Adequate performance satisfies the customer

Source: Adapted from Johnston, Robert (1995), 'The Zone of Tolerance: Exploring the Relationship between Service Transactions and Satisfaction with the Overall Service', *International Journal of Service Industry Management* 6 (2) 46–61.

outcome will be a 'satisfied' customer with a 'score' somewhere within their zone of tolerance (see Figure 5.9). It has been suggested that the quality of a performance within the customer's zone of tolerance may not be consciously noticed, so for an organisation wishing to make an impact it will need to build in positive (or maybe even negative) interventions.

● Sufficient incursions above the zone of tolerance threshold, particularly at the start or end of the process, will result in a highly satisfying outcome (delight). By doing something that delights the customer (enhancing factors, see Section 5.5.2), the doctor's surgery may be able to delight the patient. For example, the receptionist greeting the patient by name and inviting them to take a seat and bringing them a coffee might be quite unexpected (at least on the first occasion) and delight the customer (see Figure 5.10). The satisfaction 'score' may not be the mean score, but delighting (and indeed dissatisfying) incidents may have the effect of skewing the resulting level of satisfaction.

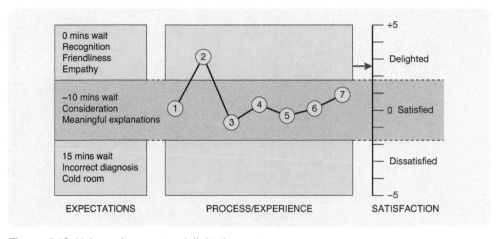

Figure 5.10 Using enhancers to delight the customer

Source: Adapted from Johnston, Robert (1995), 'The Zone of Tolerance: Exploring the Relationship between Service Transactions and Satisfaction with the Overall Service', *International Journal of Service Industry Management* 6 (2) 46–61.

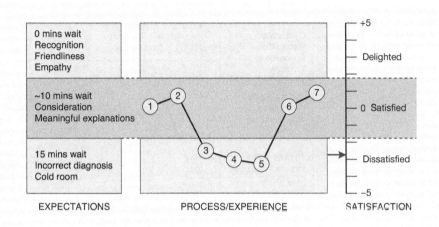

Figure 5.11 A dissatisfying outcome

Source: Adapted from Johnston, Robert (1995), 'The Zone of Tolerance: Exploring the Relationship between Service Transactions and Satisfaction with the Overall Service', *International Journal of Service Industry Management* 6 (2) 46–61.

- Sufficient incursions below the zone of tolerance threshold will result in a dissatisfying outcome. A delay of 12 minutes (a hygiene factor – see Section 5.5.2) may be forgiven, but this coupled with a brusque treatment and a cursory examination may well lead to dissatisfaction (see Figure 5.11).

- Some dissatisfying and satisfying transactions may be compensatory. Lack of spaces in the car park, resulting in a walk of 500 metres in the rain to the surgery, will count as a dissatisfying transaction, but a profuse apology from the receptionist coupled with particularly caring treatment by the doctor may compensate for the initial problems (see Figure 5.12).

- Several satisfying transactions will be needed to compensate for a single dissatisfying transaction. It could be that one dissatisfying transaction will require compensation by more than one delighting transaction (as above).

- A failure in one transaction may raise the dissatisfaction threshold. A dissatisfying experience may also have the effect of shifting the zone of tolerance upwards, and/or maybe

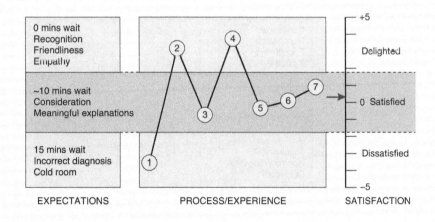

Figure 5.12 Enhancers compensate for failure

Source: Adapted from Johnston, Robert (1995), 'The Zone of Tolerance: Exploring the Relationship between Service Transactions and Satisfaction with the Overall Service', *International Journal of Service Industry Management* 6 (2) 46–61.

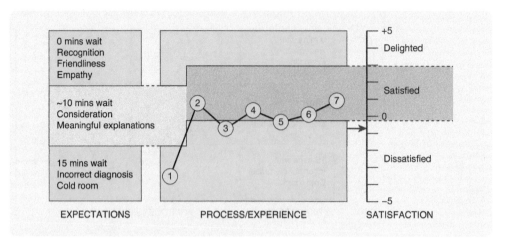

Figure 5.13 Dissatisfaction shifts the zone of tolerance

Source: Adapted from Johnston, Robert (1995), 'The Zone of Tolerance: Exploring the Relationship between Service Transactions and Satisfaction with the Overall Service', *International Journal of Service Industry Management* 6 (2) 46–61.

reducing its width. For example, if patients have had to walk 500 metres in the rain their dissatisfaction with this transaction may be such as to negatively dispose them towards the rest of the service. This could mean that future transactions that might previously have been within their zone of tolerance are now felt to be dissatisfying (see Figure 5.13). This shifting of the zone increases the likelihood of the outcome being a feeling of dissatisfaction.

- A delighting transaction, especially effective if located at the start of the process, may lower the zone of tolerance. An enhancing transaction may lower the zone of tolerance (and/or widen it) so that further transactions that might before have been within the acceptable range are now felt to be delighting. This has also been referred to as the 'halo effect'.[18] Prompt treatment by the receptionist, a feeling of being expected and welcome, and all the forms ready to be signed, for example, may not only delight but positively dispose the patient to the rest of the service, increasing the likelihood of a delighting outcome (see Figure 5.14).

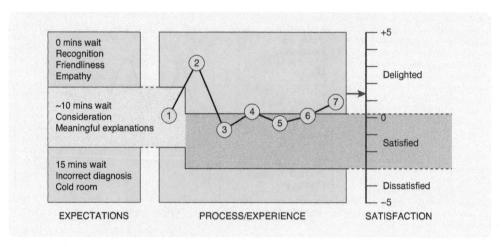

Figure 5.14 Delight shifts the zone of tolerance

Source: Adapted from Johnston, Robert (1995), 'The Zone of Tolerance: Exploring the Relationship between Service Transactions and Satisfaction with the Overall Service', *International Journal of Service Industry Management* 6 (2) 46–61.

Manipulating the width of the zone of tolerance

It would seem sensible for organisations wishing simply to satisfy their customers to ensure that there are no problems during the service process (i.e. failures on hygiene factors – see Section 5.5.2). Delighting transactions are unnecessary; the organisation is more likely to satisfy customers if their zone of tolerance can be made as wide as possible by appropriate marketing of the service.

For organisations seeking to delight their customers, a narrower zone of tolerance will increase the likelihood of delighting (and also risk dissatisfying) the customer. Some delighting transactions are needed – ideally early in the process – to affect the level and possibly the width of the zone of tolerance. A delighting transaction at the end may also serve to put the icing on the cake. Although a delighting early transaction can have considerable impact, it has been shown that a build-up to a strong end-of-process experience results in higher perceived service quality.[19]

Making the intangible tangible

A final method of manipulating service perceptions is by making the intangible tangible.

In section 5.4.1 on expectations we explained how an organisation needs to ensure that early clues in the service process can help set the right expectations for the customer. Such clues can also be used to manipulate perceptions (see also Chapter 7). For example, the managers at the RAC (see Chapter 9) recognise the importance of their patrols looking clean and tidy and having clean vans. Customers may associate these clues with professionalism and capability and thus perceive a more competent repair having been made to their car.

Such intangible factors are vital to many service experiences, and customer perceptions of them can be strengthened simply by trying to make them tangible at appropriate places in the service process/experience. The toilet paper folded into a point in the hotel bathroom is a tangible representation of less tangible cleanliness and care. A management consultant's cufflinks/jewellery or well-cut suit/dress and expensive car are tangible representations of reliability and professionalism.

5.5 How can service quality be operationalised?

Both operational service quality (see Section 5.7) and perceived service quality can be defined in terms of the quality factors or dimensions of service quality. These factors enable operations managers to capture and operationalise expectations to help understand the nature of expectations and perceptions, create instruments to measure customer satisfaction (see Section 5.6) and create service specifications (see Section 5.7).

5.5.1 Service quality factors

The service quality factors are those attributes of service about which customers may have expectations and which need to be delivered at some specified level.

Figure 5.15 provides eighteen quality factors which attempt to capture the totality of service quality.[20] These eighteen may be consolidated into broader dimensions[21] and indeed may not capture every aspect of service quality for every organisation. However, they are at least a starting point to help us define, deliver and measure service quality. These factors have been defined as follows:

- *Access.* The physical approachability of the service location, including the ease of finding one's way around the service process or route through the process.
- *Aesthetics.* The extent to which the components of the service and their experience of it are agreeable or pleasing to the customer, including both the appearance and the ambience of

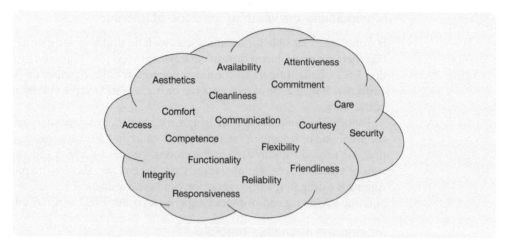

Figure 5.15 Eighteen service quality factors

the service environment, the appearance and presentation of service facilities, 'products' and staff.

- *Attentiveness/helpfulness.* The extent to which the service, particularly contact staff, either provide help to the customer or give the impression of being interested in the customer and show a willingness to serve.

- *Availability.* The availability of service process, facilities, staff and 'products' to the customer. In the case of contact staff this means both the staff/customer ratio and the amount of time each staff member has available to spend with each customer. It also includes both the quantity and range of services (and 'products') available to the customer.

- *Care.* The concern, consideration, sympathy and patience shown to the customer. This includes the extent to which the customer is put at ease by the service and made to feel emotionally (rather than physically) comfortable.

- *Cleanliness/tidiness.* The cleanliness, neat and tidy appearance of the inputs to the service process, including the service environment, facilities, equipment, the contact staff and even other customers.

- *Comfort.* The physical comfort of the service environment and facilities.

- *Commitment.* The staff's apparent commitment to their work, including the pride and satisfaction they apparently take in their job, their diligence and thoroughness.

- *Communication.* The ability of service staff to communicate with customers in a way they will understand. This includes the clarity, completeness and accuracy of both verbal and written information communicated to the customer and the ability to listen to and understand the customer.

- *Competence.* The skill, expertise and professionalism with which the service is executed. This includes the carrying out of correct procedures, correct execution of customer instructions, the degree of 'product' or service knowledge exhibited by contact staff, the provision of good, sound advice and the general ability to do a good job.

- *Courtesy.* The politeness, respect and propriety shown by the service, usually contact staff, in dealing with customers and their property. This includes the ability of staff to be unobtrusive and uninterfering when appropriate.

- *Flexibility.* A willingness on the part of the service worker to amend or alter the nature of the service to meet the needs of the customer.

- *Friendliness.* The warmth and personal approachability (rather than physical approachability) of the service, particularly of contact staff, including a cheerful attitude and the ability to make the customer feel welcome.

- *Functionality.* The serviceability and fitness for purpose of service.
- *Integrity.* The honesty, justice, fairness and trustworthiness with which customers are treated by the service organisation.
- *Reliability.* The reliability and consistency of performance of the service and its staff. This includes punctual service delivery and the ability to keep to agreements made with the customer.
- *Responsiveness.* The speed and timeliness of service delivery. This includes the speed of throughput and the ability of the service to respond promptly to customer service requests, with minimal waiting and queuing time.
- *Security.* The personal safety of customers and their possessions while participating in or benefiting from the service process. This includes the maintenance of confidentiality.

These factors cover many aspects of a service, which we defined in Chapter 1, including:

- *Inputs:* for example, staff availability, appearance, and competence; the appearance, aesthetics, accessibility and comfort of the facilities.
- *The service process:* for example, process reliability, staff responsiveness and communication skills, the functionality and reliability of the technology.
- *The service experience:* for example; staff friendliness and courtesy, and a feeling of security.
- *Outcomes:* for example, the functionality and reliability of the service received.

5.5.2 Hygiene and enhancing factors

Although they will vary from organisation to organisation and also from customer to customer, the service quality factors can be divided into four groups. These groupings are defined in terms of a factor's ability to dissatisfy and/or delight: see Figure 5.16.[22]

- *Hygiene factors* are those that need to be in place: if they are they will satisfy, if not they will be a source of dissatisfaction. They are not likely to be a source of delight. For a bank, security, integrity and functionality, for example, are expected to be acceptable; if they are not acceptable they will dissatisfy. On the other hand, if these factors are over-specified they will not delight. A very large number of security checks will not delight customers; indeed they could dissatisfy them. Having all cash machines in perfect working order all of the time will not delight them either.
- *Enhancing factors* have the potential to delight if they are present, but if they are not there they are not likely to dissatisfy the customer. Customers of a bank may be delighted with a warm, caring approach by a member of staff or their flexibility in dealing with a problem;

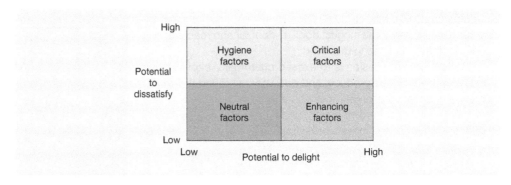

Figure 5.16 Delighting and dissatisfying factors

Source: Adapted from Lockwood, Andrew (1994), 'Using Service Incidents to Identify Quality Improvement Points', *International Journal of Contemporary Hospitality Management* 6 (1/2) 75–80.

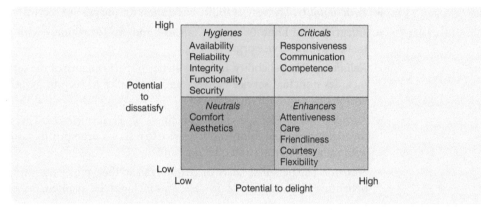

Figure 5.17 Four types of factors for a bank

however, these things are not necessarily expected so, if they are not provided, their absence may not lead to dissatisfaction.

- *Critical factors* have the potential to both delight and dissatisfy. Responsiveness, communication and competence of bank staff and systems must be at least acceptable so as not to dissatisfy the customer, but if more than acceptable they have the potential to delight.

- *Neutral factors* have little effect on satisfaction. The comfort or aesthetics of a banking hall may play no part in customers' satisfaction or dissatisfaction (see Figure 5.17).

We believe that managers should not only be aware of the expectations of their customers but should also realise the importance and potential effect of the various factors (see Case Example 5.1). We need to know which factors will delight and which will dissatisfy in order to manage the perception of satisfaction during the service process (see earlier). How we can find these factors and identify the enhancers, hygienes and criticals is explained in the next Section 5.6.

Case Example 5.1	TNT Express Dubai

TNT Express, a division of the Dutch company TNT NV, is an international market leader in global express services ensuring its business customers' parcels and freight are delivered safely and on time. TNT delivers over 4.4 million items a week to over 200 countries using its network of over 2,300 company-owned depots, hubs and sortation centres. It employs around 160,000 staff worldwide, and operates 30,000 road vehicles and 48 freighter aircraft. It has one of the biggest door-to-door air and road express delivery infrastructures in the world.

The company's mission is to exceed customers' expectations in the transfer of their products and documents around the world. It aims to satisfy customers every time, by providing reliable and efficient solutions in distribution and logistics. The company prides itself in being honest, being passionate about its people, and striving to continually improve what it does.

Mark Pell was the Managing Director of the Gulf Office situated in Dubai. He was responsible for operations in the Gulf Corporation Council countries: Bahrain, Kuwait, Qatar, Oman, Saudi Arabia, and the United Arab Emirates. He explained his role:

Source: TNT Dubai

As MD I spend most of my time working with my management team trying to provide the direction and ensuring that everyone understands our strategy. We have been very successful in this region over the last few years. This is of course due in no small measure to the booming economic environment but also due to our success in ensuring that people at all levels in the organisation understand what we need to achieve and what their role is in trying to achieve our goals. It's still a tough competitive environment in the sectors where we work; automotive, high tech, telecoms, banking and oil, for example. Customers want to get something from A to B, usually quickly and generally as cheaply as possible. But things have changed recently, customers now simply assume that we will deliver on time and to the right place and that the service will be good. These are just prerequisites. They now expect much more. Though price is obviously important, it's now very much about how our employees treat our customers. Our business customers expect us to treat them like an important customer, to value their business, and to make them feel special. They also expect everyone in the business who has contact with them, whether it's a customer service advisor, the person who picks up their parcel or their contact in our payments office, to be affable, pleasant and personable, even charming!

The factors do not always neatly fall into one category or another. Figure 5.18 shows the relative frequency of mentions made of the factors in a study of UK banks. What is striking is that the factors with the tendency to dissatisfy (hygienes and criticals) are systemic and concern the organisation's ability to deliver its core services: functionality, reliability, competence etc., whereas the factors with a tendency to delight tend to be the more interpersonal factors, such as attentiveness, friendliness, courtesy etc.

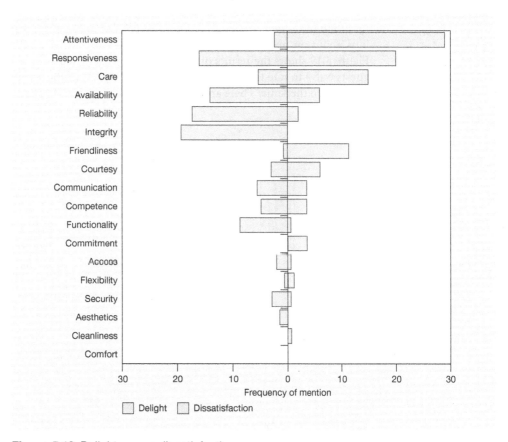

Figure 5.18 Delight versus dissatisfaction

Source: Adapted from Johnston, Robert (1995), 'The Determinants of Service Quality: Satisfiers and Dissatisfiers', *International Journal of Service Industry Management* 6 (5) 53–71.

Care should be exercised in trying to identify neutral factors: in the research cited above the fact that few people mentioned security does not mean it is a neutral factor. It simply indicates that there were no instances of security having been the source of dissatisfaction or delight.

5.6 How can managers capture customers' expectations?

The eighteen quality factors provide a base to help us understand and define customer expectations (whether for internal or external customers) and define appropriate levels, i.e. create the internal operational quality specification. They also help us to measure customer satisfaction, which we will cover in Chapter 9.

5.6.1 Methods to capture customer expectations

There are many different methods available to gather information about customers' expectations of a service.[23] Some quantitative methods, such as questionnaires and surveys using a quantitative approach, can be structured around all or some of the eighteen quality factors and analysed by each factor. Other, more qualitative, approaches tend to collect descriptive data and provide the interpretation of events by customers in their own words. This creates more difficulties in analysis and interpretation in order to extract meaningful summaries. Such approaches do, however, have the benefit of providing ideas and examples that managers and employees can use and discuss to better understand and improve their services.

- *Questionnaires and surveys*, written or verbal, can be a good means of soliciting opinions about an organisation's services and to identify what customers find important. Figure 5.19 shows the results of a questionnaire asking customers of a hotel (mid-week guests only) to rate the importance of various aspects of the service. The staff were also asked to do the same. There are several interesting mismatches between the views of staff and guests.

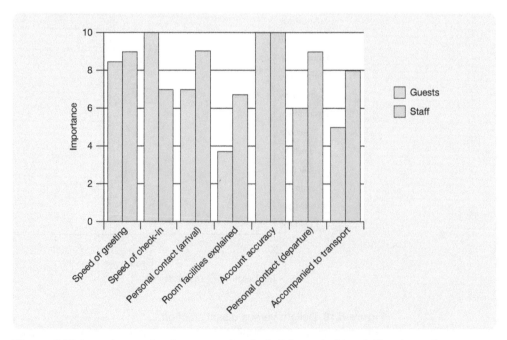

Figure 5.19 Importance of various aspects of a hotel as rated by staff and guests

- *Focus groups* usually comprise groups of about fifteen customers with a trained facilitator, brought together to discuss one or a few aspects of a particular existing or planned service.

- *Customer advisory panels* are similar to focus groups but are likely to meet regularly with a more structured agenda.

- *New/lost customer surveys* are very useful ways of finding out what attracts customers to the organisation and indeed why they left. While many organisations are now conducting exit interviews, the most successful rely heavily upon the direct involvement of senior managers to ensure appropriate access, information and action.

- *Complaint/compliment analysis* can be undertaken upon customers' voluntary contributions, although they tend to be more negative than positive. They do provide information about the extremes of delight and dissatisfaction. Case Example 5.2 explains how Singapore Airlines makes use of its complaints and compliments.

- *Critical incident technique* (CIT) attempts to identify the things that delight and dissatisfy customers. Critical incidents are events that contribute to, or detract from, perceived service or product performance in a significant way. The CIT instrument usually comprises two questions. The first question asks customers to think of a time when they felt very pleased and satisfied with the service/product received and to describe, in a few sentences, the situation and why they felt so happy. The second question requires customers to think of a time when they were unhappy and dissatisfied with the service/product they received and to describe, in a few sentences, why they felt this way.

- *Sequential incident analysis* combines CIT, walk-through audits and process mapping (see Chapters 7 and 8).[24] Customers are 'walked through' a pre-prepared process map of the service they have recently encountered and asked for their experiences of each stage or transaction in the process. This technique identifies not only critical situations but also potentially critical ones.

Case Example 5.2 **Singapore Airlines (SIA)**

SIA employs varied and systematic methods to obtain information from its passengers, including quarterly passenger surveys and focused group work with its frequent flyers. The company also uses its magazine for frequent flyers, to ask for passengers' reactions to proposed new ideas. It also checks out the service for itself by conducting on-site audits with test calls to reservations, for example, to see how service is being delivered. Also when any members of staff fly in its aircraft they are asked to submit reports of their travel experiences. Senior staff members must submit a comment sheet on each flight with their expense account. SIA staff also monitor their competitors and often go and check out their services.

Source: Singapore Airlines

SIA takes both compliments and complaints seriously; indeed there is a vice-president with responsibility for complaints and compliments. Every letter has to be acknowledged, investigated and followed up, even letters of compliment. In 2004, Lam Seet Mui, the senior manager for human resource development, explained:

> We investigate all complaints. Then not only do we try to recover the customer or the situation, we will also use it as a learning lesson. If we don't learn something from a complaint then we've failed. We also take compliments seriously. Not only do we disseminate them so that people can share in the success, but we try to learn things from them too. They can help us understand what we need to do to excel.

Sim Kay Wee, the senior vice-president responsible for cabin crew, added:

> We do try to deal with problems at the time they arise. If a problem occurs on board the crew will try to recover immediately. Any follow-up or written complaint is overseen by the customer affairs department. However we do the investigation, we find out precisely what happened and report to them. We try to do it personally and quickly.

SIA also produces newsletters for particular groups of staff. *Highpoint*, for example, is aimed at keeping its 8,000 in-flight personnel informed about the airline's latest offerings and its commitments to passengers. The newsletter has a regular feature page with about eight or nine extracts from letters – half compliments and half complaints. An example of each follows.

An example compliment:

> I noticed the service, although in economy class, was professional and better than any flights I have ever been on. Miss Iris lee was the most hardworking amongst all the crew. She came round distributing newspapers, drinks, postcards, playing cards, amenities etc. As a director of travel and tours, I fly often and I have never come across such an outstanding cabin hostess . . . She loves to fly and it shows.

An example complaint:

> We were sitting close by the galleys and were able to observe the cabin crew at work throughout the flight, and the impression we gained was that they were unable to cope with a full load of passengers. There seemed also to be a lack of leadership and organisation – the cabin crew were rushing back and forth getting in each other's way – not the smooth activity which we have come to expect from Singapore Airlines.

Higher Ground is a bi-monthly newsletter aimed at the ground services staff, including ticketing, reservations and check-in, as well as baggage handling, logistics and transportation. *Higher Ground* also contains extracts from letters, usually two complaints and one compliment.

An example compliment:

> I would like to pen a note of appreciation for the extra help your staff gave my aged parents when they took your SQ860 from Singapore to Hong Kong. They were told at the check-in counter to come back to see your staff. My brother accordingly brought them to the counter near the check-in time. Then one of your staff very kindly brought them into the restricted area, through immigration and right to the departure room. This was of great help to them as they do not understand the signs in English and may have had to look around or ask around for the direction to the departure room. Walking extra would also be troublesome for my mother who is recovering from a stroke. Thank you once again to your staff for going out of their way to assist my parents. I am indeed proud of our national airline.

An example complaint:

> On 26 July we flew Singapore Airlines. Prior to the arrangement being made and also a few days before the actual flight, I reiterated the comment that my mother would require a wheelchair for both embarkation and disembarkation . . . She had travelled last year by Singapore Airlines and had no trouble whatsoever. At [embarkation] a wheelchair was provided and we boarded the plane with no problems . . . On arrival . . . we were not docked at a bridge, but parked in the middle of the airfield. I was then asked if my mother could manage to get down two external steep flights of stairs and to walk to a bus that would

then take her to the terminal. As she had come on by wheelchair I would have thought it was patently obvious that this was totally impossible for her. We were told that it was our fault that [the airport] had not been informed. I explained that I had done as much as I could in informing [the station at departure], and they certainly knew she required a wheelchair to get on the plane and therefore, obviously, to get off the plane. It took an hour to get some means of transport to take her off the plane and into the airport terminal.

Source: This illustration is based on a case study written by Robert Johnston, Warwick Business School, and Jochen Wirtz, National University of Singapore, 2004. The case was commissioned by the Institute of Customer Service as part of a study into service excellence. The authors gratefully acknowledge the sponsorship provided by Britannic Assurance, FirstGroup, Lloyds TSB, RAC Motoring Services and Vodafone. The authors would like to thank the interviewees for their participation in this project and also Jasmine Ow, National University of Singapore, for her valuable assistance.

5.7 How can a service be specified?

Operational service quality is the operation's assessment of how well the service was delivered to its specification, i.e. its conformance to specification (see Figure 5.20). There are a few key questions we want to cover here, including where the specification comes from, what it looks like and how we ensure conformance to it.[25]

5.7.1 Where does a specification come from?

A service specification is an extension of the service concept. The service concept provides a broad description about the service provided, the customer experience and its outcomes (see Chapter 3). This in turn should either be based on the needs, requirements and expectations of customers, or alternatively have been devised by the organisation because it believes that there will be a need or desire for it. The specification then takes the elements of the concept and identifies the quality factors associated with each, details the standards to be achieved in each and the organisation's procedures to ensure conformance to the standard (operational control).

5.7.2 What does a specification look like?

There will be several quality factors associated with each element of a service (see Table 5.2). An airline, for example, will have several quality factors associated with each flight, such as

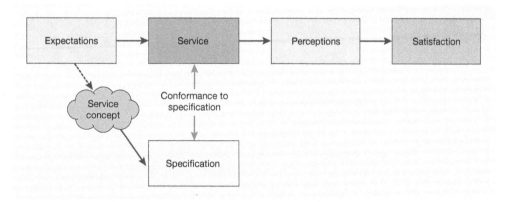

Figure 5.20 Operational service quality – conformance to specification

Table 5.2 A simplified service specification

Service elements	Quality factors	Standard	Procedures for conformance
Flights	On time	±15 mins	Pre-flight clearance with ATC and weather checks
	Safe flight	Zero critical mechanical failures	Pre- and post-flight checks plus routine maintenance
Cabin service	Attentive staff	Friendly and frequent interactions	Customer surveys and supervisor checks
	Safety aware	Correct briefing and security checks	Supervisor checks
Catering	Quality meal	Correct temperature	Adherence to cooking instructions
	Choice of meal	2 choices in economy, 3 in business	Feedback to caterers

being on time, safe, professional delay handling, disabled access to flight etc. There will be other quality factors associated with the cabin staff and service, such as attentive staff, safety aware staff, competent staff etc. The catering will also have its quality factors, such as quality of the meal, passengers having a choice of meal, staff competence in serving the meal etc. There will be standards associated with each factor, some of them explicit and others tacit. For example, the airline's standard for 'on time' might be plus or minus five minutes. Its standard for attentive staff might be their level of friendliness and having two or three interactions with each passenger. Some of these standards may be set down in operating manuals or in regulations. Others may be more tacit and shared through oral instructions, pictures, or shared understandings through role-play during training.

5.7.3 How do we ensure conformance to the specification?

Service organisations will have a variety of means of ensuring conformance for each of these factors (see Table 5.2 and also Chapters 9 and 11). Ensuring on-time departure will require co-ordination with ground staff to ensure all passengers' bags are loaded promptly, discussions with air traffic control to establish clearance on time and checks for weather problems to allow for changes in route and increasing average speed to ensure an on-time arrival. The airline's desire for attentive staff will be checked by supervisors on board providing coaching to members of staff where necessary. Appropriate recruitment and training procedures will also have a role to play in ensuring that staff look after their passengers well.

5.8	Summary

What is customer satisfaction?

- Satisfaction is the result of customers' overall assessment of their perceptions of the service (the service process, their experiences and outcomes such as the benefits obtained), compared to their prior expectations.
- If there is a mismatch between perceptions and expectations it is usually caused by either a mismatch between expectations and the service and/or a mismatch between the service and customer perceptions.
- A related notion is customer confidence. Confidence is about having belief, trust or faith in an organisation, its staff and services. Unlike satisfaction which is one outcome of a service, confidence does not require previous experience or contact with the organisation.

What influences expectations and perceptions?

- Perceptions are our own personal impression and interpretation of a service.
- How we perceive a service depends upon our past experiences, our past, our culture, language, beliefs, values, interests and assumptions.
- Expectations are what a customer believes to be likely, lying on a continuum, between ideal and intolerable.
- Expectations are dynamic and are influenced by price, the alternative services available, marketing, word-of-mouth, previous experience, customers' mood and attitude and their confidence.

How can expectations and perceptions be 'managed'?

- Operations need to ensure the marketing and strategy functions understand the nature and quality of service that it can actually deliver and indeed what it can't.
- The design of the operation can influence and shape customer expectations during the early stages of a service process.
- Customer perceived quality is a dynamic process and can be influenced through the appropriate interventions during the service process/customer experience.

How can service quality be operationalised?

- The service quality factors are those attributes of service about which customers may have expectations and which need to be delivered at some specified level.
- Neutral factors have little effect on satisfaction; hygiene factors will dissatisfy but not delight; enhancing factors will delight but not dissatisfy; and critical factors both dissatisfy and delight.

How can managers capture customer expectations?

- The eighteen quality factors provide a base to help understand and define customer expectations.
- The methods available include questionnaires and surveys, focus groups, customer advisory panels, new/lost customer surveys, complaint/compliment analysis, critical incident technique and sequential incident analysis.

How can a service be specified?

- A service specification takes the elements of the service concept and identifies the quality factors associated with each, then details the standards to be achieved in each and the organisation's procedures to ensure conformance to the standard.

5.9 Discussion questions

1 What methods are most effective in identifying the influencers of customer satisfaction, given that some aspects of service may be unconsciously experienced by customers?

2 For a high-volume/low-variety service (business-to-consumer) and for a low-volume/high-variety service (business-to-business or professional service) identify potential gaps between customer expectation and customer perception of service delivery. What strategies would you suggest these organisations utilise to close these gaps?

3 Collect a few customer survey forms, from a range of service providers, and evaluate them.

5.10 Questions for managers

1 When was the last time your organisation carried out a detailed study of customer satisfaction? Assess the methods used and, more importantly, the impact of the exercise.

2 Who compiled your customer satisfaction survey questionnaire? Have you checked with customers as to how relevant it is? What are the drivers of satisfaction for your customers (internal or external)?

3 What are the reasons for gaps between customer perceptions of service and their expectations? How can they be closed?

4 Do you understand the zone of tolerance for your service delivery? Are customer expectations sometimes fuzzy? What guidance and/or resource is required to clarify these expectations?

5 What is the most effective method of assessing customer satisfaction? How widely have you communicated the findings of customer research?

Case Exercise The Northern Breast Screening Unit

Rhian Silvestro, Warwick Business School, and Marilyn Merriam

Breast cancer is the most common cause of death from cancer in women. England and Wales have the highest mortality rates for breast cancer in the world, making it a major public health problem which is a national target area in the government's Strategy for the Health of the Nation. The National Health Service (NHS) Breast Screening Programme aims to reduce mortality from breast cancer through early identification of the symptoms, by screening women aged between 47 and 70 every three years.

The Northern Breast Screening Unit (NBSU) serves some half a million residents, with an uptake on invitations for screening of 77 per cent (compared to the national target of 70 per cent and an 'achievable quality standard' of 75 per cent). The NBSU is part of a major hospital whose mission statement is as follows:

We aim to provide high quality acute and specialist services which:

- *are responsive to customer needs*
- *use leading edge and effective medical technologies*
- *are at a cost that compares favourably with the rest of the NHS*
- *have motivated and properly trained staff.*

To this end the hospital supports a number of quality audit and improvement initiatives including ISO 9000 and Investors in People. The NBSU employs 32 members of staff including part-timers. There are four radiologists, seven full-time radiographers, two breast care nurses, and a number of receptionists and office staff. The unit is also supported by several part-time radiographers and visiting surgeons.

Last year a small patient satisfaction survey was conducted to obtain information about patient expectations and perceptions of the service and to identify areas for improvement. Staff from the different functional areas were also interviewed in order to identify any gaps between patient expectations and perceptions and staff perceptions of the quality of service provided.

Thirty-two patients were interviewed. These included sixteen patients who had come to the NBSU for screening and sixteen patients who had been screened and had been called back to the NBSU because they were diagnosed with breast cancer. Each patient was asked to assign the relative importance, on a 5-point scale, of a series of quality factors (importance was used as a surrogate for expectations). They were then asked to rate, again on a 1–5 scale, their perception of the service levels delivered with regard to each factor. Table 5.3 lists the statements which were used to capture each quality factor and Table 5.4 shows the mean values assigned for each factor by the staff and patients.

Staff were provided with the same list of factors and asked to rate on a scale of 1–5 how important they believed the factor to be to the patients, and what service level they believed the patients perceived

Table 5.3 The statements used to capture each quality factor

Quality factor	Statements used
Access	Was the NBSU easy to find?
	Were there transport problems in getting here?
Availability	Were you given as much time as you wanted with staff?
Care	Were you shown concern, consideration and sympathy? Were you treated with patience?
Communication	Were you provided with enough information in a way you could understand?
Competence	Were you impressed by the skill, expertise and professionalism of the staff?
Courtesy	Were staff polite and respectful?
	Were staff discreet and unobtrusive when necessary?
Functionality	Did the equipment seem adequate in delivering the service?
Reliability	Was the NBSU reliable and consistent in performance?
Privacy	Were you given enough privacy?
Responsiveness	Was there much waiting and queuing?
Comfort	Was the unit comfortable?

Table 5.4 Mean values assigned for each factor by the staff and patients

	Access	Availability	Care	Communication	Competence	Courtesy	Functionality	Reliability	Privacy	Responsiveness	Comfort
Importance											
Nurse	4	4	5	5	5	5	4	5	5	4	4
Radiographer	4	4	5	5	5	4	4	4	4	4	4
Manager	4.5	4.2	3.8	4.2	4.5	4.2	3.8	3.8	4.2	3.45	3.75
Screened patients	4.01	4.12	4.12	4.84	4.8	4.71	4.41	4.59	4.74	4.16	4.06
Diagnosed patients	4.12	4.72	4.92	4.88	4.91	4.61	4.98	4.99	4.91	4.86	4.98
Perceptions											
Nurse	3	4	4	4	4	4	3	4	4	3	4
Radiographer	3	2	4	4	4	3	3	3	3	4	3
Manager	4.5	3.2	3.8	4.2	4.6	4.2	4.8	3.8	4.2	2.8	3.75
Screened patients	3.51	4.68	4.68	4.85	4.88	4.91	4.19	4.63	4.35	4.63	4.35
Diagnosed patients	3.62	4.67	4.32	4.51	4.53	4.71	4.55	4.75	4.07	4.21	4.37

themselves to be receiving. This would facilitate identification of any mismatches between staff and patient perceptions.

Questions

1 Evaluate the quality of service provided by the NCBSU.

2 What recommendations would you make for improvement?

Suggested further reading

Andreassen, Tor Wallin (2001), 'From Disgust to Delight: Do Customers Hold a Grudge?', *Journal of Service Research* 4 (1) 39–50

Ding, David Xin, Paul Jen-Hwa Hu, Rohit Verma and Don G. Wardell (2010), 'The Impact of Service System Design and Flow Experience on Customer Satisfaction in Online Financial Services', *Journal of Service Research* 13 (1) 96–110

Dixon, Matthew, Karen Freeman and Nicholas Toman (2010), 'Stop Trying to Delight Your Customers', *Harvard Business Review* (July–August) 2–7

John, Joby, Stephen J. Grove and Raymond P. Fisk (2006), 'Improvisation in Service Performances: Lessons from Jazz,' *Managing Service Quality* 16 (3) 247–268

Johnston, Robert (2004), 'Towards a Better Understanding of Service Excellence', *Managing Service Quality* 14 (2/3) 129–133

Nadiri, Halil and Kashif Hussain (2005), 'Diagnosing the Zone of Tolerance for Hotel Services', *Managing Service Quality* 15 (3) 259–277

Ojasalo, Jukka (2006), 'Quality for the Individual and for the Company in the Business-to-Business Market: Concepts and Empirical Findings on Trade-offs', *The International Journal of Quality and Reliability Management* 23 (2/3) 162–178

Olsen, Line Lervik and Michael D. Johnson (2003), 'Service Equity, Satisfaction, and Loyalty: From Transaction-specific to Cumulative Evaluations', *Journal of Service Research* 5 (3) 184–195

Pollack, Birgit Leisen (2008), 'The Nature of Service Quality and Satisfaction: Empirical Evidence for the Existence of Satisfiers and Dissatisfiers', *Managing Service Quality* 18 (6) 537–558

Verhoef, Peter C., Gerrit Antonides and Arnoud N. de Hoog (2004), 'Service Encounters as a Sequence of Events: The Importance of Peak Experiences', *Journal of Service Research* 7 (1) 53–64

White, Lesley and Venkata Yanamandram (2007), 'A Model of Customer Retention of Dissatisfied Business Services Customers', *Managing Service Quality* 17 (3) 298–316

Wittel, Lars and Löfgren, M. (2007), 'Classification of Quality Attributes', *Managing Service Quality* 17 (1) 54–73

Useful web links

For some views about customer satisfaction take a look at:
http://www.marketvaluesolutions.com/customer-satisfaction-article.htm

For some more information about SERVQUAL go to:
http://www.12manage.com/methods_zeithaml_servqual.html

A discussion about perception versus reality:
http://www.internet-of-the-mind.com/perception-vs-reality.html

Notes

1 See for example Bitner, Mary-Jo and Amy R. Hubbert (1994), 'Encounter Satisfaction versus Overall Satisfaction versus Service Quality: The Consumer's Voice' in Rust, Roland T. and Richard L. Oliver (eds), *Service Quality: New Directions in Theory and Practice*, Sage Publications, Thousand Oaks, USA, pp. 72–94

2 This is sometimes referred to in the consumer behaviour literature as the disconfirmation theory; see, for example, Oliver, Richard L. and Wayne S. DeSarbo (1988), 'Response Determinants in Satisfaction Judgements', *Journal of Consumer Research* 14 (4) 495–507

3 This is a simplified version of the gap model developed by Parasuraman, A., Valerie A. Zeithaml and Leonard L. Berry (1985), 'A Conceptual Model of Service Quality and Implications for Future Research', *Journal of Marketing* 49 (Fall) 41–50

4 See for example Grönroos, Christian (2003), *Service Management and Marketing*, 2nd edition, Wiley, Chichester, England

5 Flanagan, Paul, Robert Johnston and Derek Talbot (2005), 'Customer Confidence – The Development of a "Pre-experience" Concept', *International Journal of Service Industry Management* 16 (4) 373–384

6 Flanagan, Paul, Robert Johnston and Derek Talbot (2005), 'Customer Confidence – The Development of a "Pre-experience' Concept", *International Journal of Service Industry Management* 16 (4) 373–384

7 O'Connor, Joseph and John Seymour (2002), *Introducing NLP*, Element, London

8 Brooks, Michael (2010), *13 Things that Don't Make Sense*, Profile Books, London

9 See for example Zeithaml, Valerie A., Leonard L. Berry and A. Parasuraman (1993), 'The Nature and Determinants of Customer Expectations of Service', *Journal of the Academy of Marketing Science* 21 (1) 1–12

10 Strandvik, Tore (1994), *Tolerance Zones in Perceived Service Quality*, Swedish School of Economics and Business Administration, Helsingfors, Finland

11 Johnston, Robert (1995), 'The Zone of Tolerance: Exploring the Relationship between Service Transactions and Satisfaction with the Overall Service', *International Journal of Service Industry Management* 6 (2) 46–61

12 See for example Dibb, Sally, Lyndon Simkin, William M. Pride and O.C. Ferrel (2005), *Marketing Concepts and Strategies*, 5th European edition, Houghton Mifflin, Boston

13 Ojasalo, Jukka (2001), 'Managing Customer Expectations in Professional Services', *Managing Service Quality* 11 (3) 200–212

14 Ojasalo, Jukka (2001), 'Managing Customer Expectations in Professional Services', *Managing Service Quality* 11 (3) 200–212

15 Johnston, Robert (1995), 'The Zone of Tolerance: Exploring the Relationship between Service Transactions and Satisfaction with the Overall Service', *International Journal of Service Industry Management* 6 (2) 46–61

16 Verhoef, Peter C., Gerrit Antonides and Arnoud N. de Hoog (2004), 'Service Encounters as a Sequence of Events: The Importance of Peak Experiences', *Journal of Service Research* 7 (1) 53–64; Schwartz, Barry (2005), *The Paradox of Choice: Why More Is Less*, Harper Collins

17 Johnston, Robert (1995), 'The Zone of Tolerance: Exploring the Relationship between Service Transactions and Satisfaction with the Overall Service', *International Journal of Service Industry Management* 6 (2) 46–61

18 Wirtz, Jochen and John E.G. Bateson (1995), 'An Experimental Investigation of Halo Effects in Satisfaction Measures and Service Attributes', *International Journal of Service Industry Management* 6 (3) 84–102

19 Hansen, David E. and Peter J. Danaher (1999), 'Inconsistent Performance during the Service Encounter', *Journal of Service Research* 1 (3) 227–235

20 Johnston, Robert (1995), 'The Determinants of Service Quality: Satisfiers and Dissatis-fiers', *International Journal of Service Industry Management* 6 (5) 53–71

21 See for example Parasuraman, A., Valerie A. Zeithaml and Leonard L. Berry (1985), 'A Conceptual Model of Service Quality and Implications for Future Research', *Journal of Marketing* 49 (Fall) 41–50

22 Johnston, Robert (1995), 'The Determinants of Service Quality: Satisfiers and Dissatis-fiers', *International Journal of Service Industry Management* 6 (5) 53–71

23 For an evaluation of several methods see Berry, Leonard L. and A. Parasuraman (1997), 'Listening to the Customer – The Concept of a Service-Quality Information System', *Sloan Management Review* (Spring) 65–76

24 Stauss, Bernd (1993), 'Service Problem Deployment: Transformation of Problem In-formation into Problem Prevention Activities', *International Journal of Service Industry Management* 4 (2) 41–62

25 Pinto, Sofia Salgado and Robert Johnston (2004), 'The Object and Nature of Service Specifications' in Edvardsson, B., A. Gustafsson, S.W. Brown and R. Johnston (eds), *Service Excellence in Management: Interdisciplinary Contributions*, Karlstad University, pp. 487–496

Chapter 6
Managing supply networks and supplier relationships

Chapter objectives

This chapter is about how to manage supplier relationships and harness the potential of supply networks.

- What are supply chains and networks?
- What is the role of information and inventory?
- How can service supply networks be managed?
- How can managers develop a global network strategy?

6.1 Introduction

The delivery of all services relies on exchanges of information, products and services between an organisation and its customers and suppliers. The purchase of a book from Amazon by a customer requires the customer to use Amazon's website to search for information and then to send the request for the book with payment information back to Amazon which then, via the postal service, sends the book to the customer. Amazon, in turn, has relationships, information and financial, with its suppliers of books and providers of web-based payments services, for example, and also internal relationships with its internal service providers, HR, IT development, web management, invoicing etc.

The management of these complex webs of relationships is usually referred to, rather simplistically, as supply chain management (SCM). SCM involves managing information, materials, products and service flows through networks of organisations to individual business customers and end consumers. Well-managed networks provide many benefits, such as major cost reductions, improved speed and flexibility, faster response to changes in markets, and higher levels of service to the customer.

In this chapter we will explore some of the issues in managing supply networks and the relationships between their various elements or nodes. We will first look at the various structures of supply networks, then describe the various ways in which organisations manage these often complex networks of flows and relationships. We conclude by discussing global supply networks.

What are supply chains and networks?

In this section we start by defining supply chains and then describe several types of supply chains or networks.

6.2.1 Supply chains

A supply chain is the set of links, or network, which joins together internal and external suppliers with internal and external consumers. Supply chain management (SCM) is concerned with managing the network and the flow of information, materials, services and even customers (as in Case Example 6.1) through the network.[1] SCM is usually looked at from the perspective of one of the major organisations within the network; however we will also be looking at supply networks from the customer's, outside-in, perspective.

6.2.2 Supply networks

Let's consider the example of a book retailer. In essence they will buy books from book publishers (suppliers) and make them available in their shops or on their websites to their customers (see Figure 6.1). Although the arrows in the figure show the movement of the books it is important to realise that there is an opposite flow of information from right to left to order the books and again from left to right to invoice for the books and then money flow from right to left to pay for the books. These channels may be paper or electronic, or in the case of the movement of the books may involve other organisations like the postal service and express mail companies.

Most supply networks are much more complex, and will involve second-tier suppliers; in this case they will include authors who write the books, the printers, and subcontracted proofreaders, for example. There are likely to be third-tier suppliers such as the paper mills that supply the printers, and the case study organisations that provide material and permissions for the authors. There will also be 'second-tier' customers. The 'customer' may not be the user of the books. They may be one of many university programme administrators who are purchasing the books for students ('second-tier' customers) who will buy the books from them or have them provided as part of their course pack. The first-tier customer might also be a library, which enables customers (second-tier) to borrow the books (see Figure 6.2). Supply

S = Supplier   P = Service provider   C = Customer

Figure 6.1 A simple supply chain

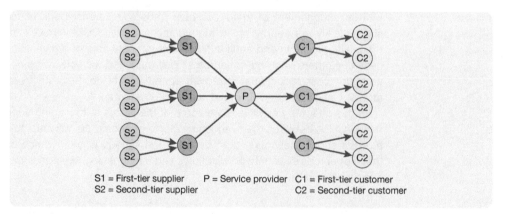

S1 = First-tier supplier   P = Service provider   C1 = First-tier customer
S2 = Second-tier supplier   C2 = Second-tier customer

Figure 6.2 Multi-tiered supply chain

networks may have many more tiers and come in many shapes and sizes. The point is, from an operations management point of view, that even relatively simple supply chains can be complex and difficult to manage, as shown in Case Example 6.1.

Case Example 6.1   Sharnbrook Upper School

Sharnbrook Upper School is located to the north of Bedford, some 70 miles north of London. The school has approximately 1,700 students between the ages of 13 and 18. The majority of the students come to the school through the three middle schools in the area, which teach children between the ages of 8 and 12 years. These 'feeder' schools are situated in the villages of Clapham, Harrold and Riseley. The combined annual intake for Sharnbrook Upper School is just less than 400 students, each of the feeder schools sending about 100 students each, with others joining from 'out of catchment' schools. The three feeder schools are each in turn served by a cluster of lower schools for children from 4 to 7 years old.

There have been a number of attempts in the past to manage this 'pyramid' of schools, but without much tangible success. There has been a perception that Sharnbrook is the big school with all the resources and power, with the smaller schools not wanting to be controlled by their larger counterpart. One of the consequences of this three-tier system is that students moving from middle to upper school have little time to adjust to new subjects and a new school environment before they embark on coursework that contributes to the final marks for the national examinations (GCSE) held at age 16.

Source: Pearson Education Ltd/Jon Barlow

The group of four schools (upper and three middle) recognised the value of working together rather than as four independent units. They call this collaboration 'managing the pyramid', although it is in effect a service supply chain, with raw material being students rather than materials and products. Following supply chain principles, the pyramid has recognised that it may be beneficial for the teaching (value-adding activity) currently carried out in one part of the pyramid to be reallocated to another. An example of this redistribution is language teaching. Some students who show particular talent for languages can be identified during their years in the feeder school, and these students might be able to study more languages if they started earlier. A fairly radical proposal is that language teachers from the upper school might spend time teaching in the feeder schools. This has the advantage of providing specialist skills not always available in the feeder school, and also developing a consistent approach across the feeder system that will facilitate more rapid progress once the students arrive at the upper school.

Other opportunities for managing the total pyramid more effectively include:

- collaboration in developing students' talents in a wider range of sports activities
- achieving greater utilisation of expensive media equipment at Sharnbrook.

This latest attempt to work together has been met with enthusiasm from the headteachers and governing bodies of the schools involved. A significant amount of time has been spent in building relationships and it is encouraging to report that as well as 'top down' pressure from the upper school, there is now significant momentum from the three middle schools and each associated cluster of lower schools to manage the pyramid more effectively.

Source: This illustration was developed with the assistance of Peter Barnard, headteacher of Sharnbrook Upper School, Bedfordshire, UK.

Internal service supply networks will also be found within organisations. The book retailer may have many internal departments (internal service operations), such as purchasing, customer services, operations (retailing) and finance, providing each other with internal services. The purchasing function, for example, will be responsible for handling the orders made by operations and providing pricing guidelines, and the finance team will be responsible for providing purchase orders, and cross-checking them with delivery notes from operations and providing financial control data.

Indeed each organisation within the network will have its own internal supply chain which will interact with different parts of other organisations' internal supply chains. For example the purchasing function in the book retailer may deal with the supplies department of the book publisher, operations may deal with the shipping department, finance with the finance department. All these interrelated activities create a complex web of interrelated relationships within the supply network. One of the major opportunities for these organisations is to develop more effective methods of collaboration across traditional (functional) boundaries (see Case Examples 6.1 and 6.6).

6.2.3 Supply networks – the customer's perspective

Traditionally SCM looks at supply networks from the point of view of an organisation in the middle of the supply network. However, here we would like to take the customer's perspective and look at the supply network from the customer's perspective, outside-in.

A customer, whether a business, a consumer or a user of public services, will not simply be involved in a single supply network but several; they will be the customer/user of multiple supply chains/networks, and they may have to work hard to co-ordinate the activities of all of them to achieve the total service they require. And, to make the situation more complex, those individual networks may have many interconnections (see Figure 6.3 and also the discussion of booking a holiday in Section 4.2).

Take the example of a person wanting to buy a house. They will have to interact with several service supply networks (see Figure 6.3) including:

- the estate agent, whose network includes many people trying to sell their houses
- the sellers with their own lawyer (solicitor), and network of organisations to arrange their next house purchase
- the mortgage (house loan) provider, with their access to funds, and property surveyors
- the buyer's lawyer, who is responsible for checking title deeds with the land registry, for ensuring funds are in place, and for drawing up the contracts, checking them, and getting agreement
- the house removals company which moves the customer's furniture on the right day
- the Post Office which arranges for redirection of mail at the right point in time to the right new address

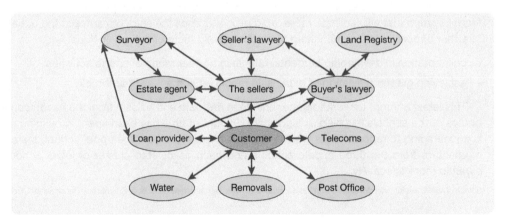

Figure 6.3 A simplified house-moving network from a customer's point of view

- the telecommunications company which transfers the old phone number to the new house at the right time, and provides a final bill
- the water company which needs to produce a final bill at the point of moving and set up a new account at the new address.

The customer will also be reliant upon many of those organisations not only managing their own chains but co-ordinating with the other networks. For example, the mortgage provider will have to instruct a surveyor to check out the property, and this will require them to contact the customer's estate agent to contact the seller to arrange for access to the property. The buyer's solicitor will have to liaise with the land registry to check the title to the property and also check that the customer's mortgage provider has agreed to lend money on the property (which in turn depends on the surveyor). The simple notion of buying a house, as many people will know, can quickly turn into a nightmare of poor connections between the various elements in the network.

The role for the 'customer' (whether an individual or a business) is in trying to co-ordinate the set of activities and interrelationships although often having very little power or leverage to do so, despite being the one usually responsible for paying for the services. Sometimes the customer at the centre of a network is unable to take this co-ordination role. This is the case, for example, with an at-risk child (see Case Example 6.3). Effectiveness is then dependent upon the co-ordination between the various organisations in the network. The key requirement for organisations involved in such networks is collaboration with each other and the customer, which few networks seem to achieve.

6.3 What is the role of information and inventory?

The essential exchange mechanism in service supply networks is information (requests for service, payment instructions etc.). These result in the flow and delivery of products and services. In the case of the Tiffin delivery service (Case Example 6.2) the all-important information is contained in codes painted on the lunch boxes which are transported by the couriers (dabbawallahs) from workers' homes to their places of work. In the book retailer example given earlier, the company will rely on efficient information exchange about costs, quantities, delivery times and locations.

Case Example 6.2 — Lunch delivery in Mumbai

For around 150–350 rupees a month (£2–£5), depending on location, workers in Mumbai can have their hot, home-cooked lunch delivered to their place of work every day. This service is used by factory workers, office workers, managers, students, even schoolchildren. Around 8.00 in the morning they join the crowded trains, buses and roads to go to work or school in the city. Later that morning their wife, mother or maid prepares a hot meal of, for example, rice, dahl, naan bread, vegetable curry and maybe a sweet item. This is then carefully packed in a tiffin,[2] or tiffin box, a tubular-shaped tin with a handle, though many families now use modern colourful insulated lunch bags and boxes. The tiffin is then collected by a dabbawallah (tiffin worker) at around 10.30–11.00, and delivered to the hungry recipient by 12.30–1.00.

This door-to-door service is provided by the Mumbai Tiffin Box Suppliers Association (MTBSA). Within just two hours this network of around 5,000 dabbawallahs picks up and delivers 400,000 tiffins

every working day. Many of the dabbawallahs, recognisable in their Ghandi topis (small white caps), are uneducated and illiterate yet they form part of a vast complex delivery system that makes few errors. To aid correct delivery and return, each tiffin has a unique identifier painted on it, a series of coloured letters and numbers that identifies its home and destination.

In something resembling a relay race, a single tiffin is passed along a chain of up to ten different dabbawallahs as it makes its way from the apartment pick-up where one dabbawallah might be responsible for a whole block, to another who collects from a series of streets, to another who is responsible for a suburb, to another who takes them on the train or bus to the city centre. There are around four hubs in the city next to the train and bus stations, such as the area outside Churchgate Station, where dabbawallahs gather around midday to receive and sort thousands of tiffins, a process that only takes around 10–15 minutes. Each dabbawallah is responsible for locating, sorting and packing their tiffins into crates or onto their bike. They then move them swiftly through the crowded streets by foot, bike or cart to deliver them to their final destinations. Each dabbawallah can carry around 30 tiffins; they weigh around 2 kg each, though several sets or crates of tiffins may be loaded onto carts for the first leg of the journey from the hub. After lunch the dabbawallahs pick up the empty containers and return them through the hub to the dabbawallah who first picked up the tin for return the next morning when the next day's tiffin is collected. (Each customer needs two tiffins.)

All the 5,000 or so dabbawallahs are partners in the MTBSA. They each own a share in the business and have good pay and perks. All the dabbawallahs consider themselves to be shareholders and entrepreneurs. As one tiffin worker explained, 'It's our own business, we are partners; this is a high-status job. We earn more than many educated graduates!' Prospective dabbawallahs have to bring in capital if they wish to join the business. The minimum investment includes a bike, a crate for their tiffins and the topi.

MTBSA is a flat organisation with just three tiers. The top tier is the governing council (president, vice-president, general secretary, treasurer and nine directors), the second tier comprises the supervisors, or mukadams, and the third tier is the dabbawallahs. The dabbawallahs are organised into sub-groups of 15–25, each supervised by a mukadam. The mukadams are also responsible for dealing with disputes, maintaining records of receipts and payments, acquiring new customers and training the junior dabbawallahs. Money is collected from customers during the first week of the month and distributed evenly between the groups of dabbawallahs by the mukadam. Every month there are meetings to discuss customer service, and investigate and resolve any problems.[3]

Despite the large number of tiffins moved each day, the distances travelled, the multiple transfer points, the many handovers, zero documentation and the very short period of time in which it is all accomplished, there are rarely any mistakes. It has been estimated that there is only around one mistake per eight million deliveries.

Effective supply chains, like the one described in Case Example 6.2, are those that work in close collaboration. Having the right information (timely and accurate, for example) and in the appropriate format to be used and understood by all the nodes in the supply chain allows each organisation to better manage their operations and minimise costs. In theory the benefits of good information exchange will be shared equitably with the 'partners' in the supply chain. In practice this does not always happen when the organisations with 'muscle' or buying power may dominate.

For networks that are supplying products, such as a supermarket or a bookstore, inventory (the storage of materials or products) may be required to allow the network to operate effectively for the following reasons:

- Processes require work-in-progress to run. A supermarket company will need to have supplies of food in lorries on the roads delivering the products to the various individual stores.

- Inventory is also put in place because the chain does not operate perfectly. For example, supermarkets require stock on the shelves because they cannot forecast demand with

100 per cent accuracy. The supermarket will invest in more 'safety stock' if it wishes to reduce the possibility of customer dissatisfaction because of empty shelves.

SCM is concerned with reducing inventory through the provision of better information and the management of the flows of materials (logistics) through the supply network. The difficulty is that inventory is often used to enable high service levels. For example:

- Retailers need to combine high levels of product availability with being competitive and responsive to changes in market demand or fashion.
- Equipment service and repair companies need to manage the logistics of spare part availability, often across a geographically dispersed network, while trying to minimise investment in spares inventories.
- An airline wants to ensure that customers receive the choice of meal they require without holding too many extra meals in the limited space available on board.

Organisations need to manage their inventories very carefully because there are significant cost savings to be made. For example, airlines will watch the price of fuel carefully because marginal savings here will have a significant impact on profits. On a smaller scale, a local seafood restaurant will want to develop reliable and frequent sources of supply of fresh fish to serve to its customers, but keeping stocks too long will affect either wastage costs or customers' health!

6.4 How can supply networks be managed?

As we can see, the nature of supply chains can be very messy and complex. The key issues for operations managers are:

- ensuring co-ordination and collaboration between and within supply networks
- ensuring the timely flow of information, products and services
- minimising inventory while maximising service levels and/or minimising costs.

In Chapter 4 we dealt with the relationships between businesses and consumers. In the remainder of this chapter we will explore some the approaches to SCM that help in the better management of supply networks. These include:

- managing through intermediaries
- disintermediation
- outsourcing and off-shoring
- developing supply partnerships
- the purchasing or procurement function
- supplier selection
- measuring performance – service level agreements
- understanding the barriers to supply chain management.

Case Example 6.3 illustrates the complexities of the child protection 'supply chain' in Torfaen County Borough Council in Wales. It highlights the importance of clear procedures, appropriate and achievable supply chain measures, and the need for the development of a shared vision for the supply chain as a whole. It is critical to see the supply chain as more than simply a set of processes or organisational relationships. No matter how well processes are designed and managed, the importance of the commitment of key individuals and their relationships across organisational boundaries should not be ignored.

Case Example 6.3   Child protection – Torfaen County Borough Council, Wales

Everyone wants children to be safe, for society to identify those who are 'at risk', and for those 'in authority' to put processes in place to ensure that no child 'slips through the net'. The key challenge is that a large number of individuals and agencies are involved in this activity, each with a significant contribution to make.

Keith Rutherford, Head of Children's Services, explains that the responsibility for ensuring that the various processes and procedures are adhered to is held by the Local Safeguarding Children's Board. The members of the Board are senior officers from social services, education, housing, the police, probation and youth

Source: iStockphoto/Sheryl Griffen

offending services, the lead officer for children and young people from the local health board, and the named nurse and doctor for child protection within the area. Keith Rutherford says, though, that the key to success is the 'buy in' from all the agencies involved and their commitment to providing a high-quality and effective child protection system. This commitment is delivered through a clear process which sets out the stages and target times for the creation of a child protection plan for each case referred to Children's Services.

Referrals can come from a number of sources, including schools, social services, the police and anonymous reports. If the referral raises significant concerns the Team Manager for Referral and Assessment convenes a Strategy Meeting within eight days to determine if there are child protection issues. Depending on the nature of the concerns immediate protective action may be considered. The police must be in attendance at this meeting and Torfaen Social Services have pre-booked eight slots a week with the police to facilitate attendance. Other professionals to be invited to this meeting would include health professionals, teachers and social workers.

The Strategy Meeting will determine whether a deeper investigation should be carried out by the police and/or by social services. If so, a conference with all concerned must be held within fifteen days of the Strategy Meeting. This includes the professionals involved in the Strategy Meeting and, in all cases, the parents of the children under review. The conference may also include the children where appropriate. In some cases, a solicitor or other advocate for the parents may also be in attendance. If the child's name is to be placed on to the Child Protection Register, a multi-agency core group meeting must be held within ten days after the conference to formulate a child protection plan.

Quarterly reports of the process are provided to the Board, providing information about attendance at the meetings and conferences, reasons for activities outside the target times, referrals, and numbers of children on the register. It is apparent that great care is taken to ensure both that procedures are well defined and that they are adhered to. Keith Rutherford comments that Torfaen has an advantage in that it is a relatively small authority. Some larger authorities recognise this and divide their areas into smaller geographical units to ensure that local communication is not compromised.

Source: This example was developed with the assistance of Keith Rutherford, Head of Children's Services, Torfaen, County Borough Council, Wales, UK

6.4.1 Managing through intermediaries

Some supply chains or networks involve 'middlemen': distributors, agents or dealers who take responsibility for managing a section of the supply chain, thus making managing the chain easier for the service provider or customer.

Many financial service companies, for example, have chosen to sell through brokers, not seeing the customer contact as part of their core business. Car producers, likewise, do not see their role as selling cars to the public and often set up owned or franchised dealerships to deal with the consumer. Travel agents act as the intermediary between customers and tour operators and see their role as helping the customers choose an appropriate holiday and providing information about a wide range of holidays and information and access to a range of related services such as transport to the airport and currency services.

Advantages of using intermediaries

There are many good reasons for using intermediaries, for example:[4]

- *Closeness to customer.* Many customers prefer to deal with an organisation that is physically close to them. This might be because they prefer to deal 'face-to-face', or because they have not got access to electronic processes, or because the nature of the service requires the presence of the service provider. For example, one of the major drivers for customer satisfaction in the ownership of cars is the ease of access to a recognised dealer for service and repair.

- *Local knowledge.* The major supplier may have insufficient knowledge of local conditions and culture. In the development of global strategies, much emphasis is placed on 'thinking globally, acting locally'.

- *Focused expertise.* Microsoft (see Case Example 6.4) has chosen to restrict its activities to software development rather than get involved in the creation and administration of a network of distributors and developers. This allows for a high degree of flexibility as service partners close to the market develop new solutions using Microsoft platforms.

- *Poor service margins.* The volume of service revenue may be too small in some geographical regions for the provision of a dedicated service unit. Capital equipment suppliers may sell only one or two units initially into a region, but must provide after-sales support. Rather than recruit and train service engineers for a few service calls per year, the company may use local service agents, who may also service competitors' equipment.

- *Insufficient capacity.* A strategy adopted by many call centres is to have 'subcontract' capacity available through providers set up explicitly for this type of activity. The information systems available to call centre agents enable them to act in such a manner that the customer is unlikely to detect any difference in service delivery.

Case Example 6.4 Microsoft

Microsoft chooses to sell and provide support for its software through a comprehensive worldwide network of partners and associated companies, rather than deal directly with customers. There are a number of channels for Microsoft to manage in order to ensure that its users receive the appropriate level of service.

One of these channels is managed by Microsoft under the Certified Solution Provider Programme. Microsoft providers are able to receive training, sales support and software, as well as priority information about the latest upgrades and software patches, to ensure that they are up to date and able to give their customers good service.

Source: Alamy Images/Chuck Pefley

For the larger solution providers, Microsoft has introduced a Partner Programme. To qualify for this programme, the provider must demonstrate a number of attributes under the headings of commitment, significance, proactivity and effectiveness. To demonstrate their competence the partner must employ a given number of Microsoft certified systems engineers or solution developers. In return, the partner receives an increased level of support and is allocated the assistance of a Microsoft business development manager. Microsoft requires ongoing evidence not only that their partners are technically competent, but that they have viable business plans.

The partners receive significant sales and marketing support. They are linked to the Microsoft.com home page for potential customers looking for solutions providers. In the Partner Network, they can search for potential collaborators. Partners receive priority notification of potential sales leads from Microsoft's telesales operation, and they have access to 'customer-critical' technical support.

Microsoft emphasises the independence of their providers and provider partners. They are able to sell and support solutions from other software developers. However, it is apparent that Microsoft offers every incentive to its partners to sell proactively and support its own solutions.

In some respects, Microsoft might be viewed as being a relationship broker. Partners are given access to the database of tens of thousands of prospective customers who search Microsoft.com every month. Not only this, but Partners are encouraged to network with other Microsoft partners through the Worldwide Partner Conference and through Partner Channel Builder. In order to move up through the levels of partner from Registered Member, to Certified Partner, and then to Gold Certified Partner, organisations must demonstrate increasing levels of competency to deliver Microsoft solutions, and earn 'partnership points' through a combination of passing Microsoft training qualifications, sales performance, and taking part in promotional activities.

Issues in managing intermediaries

The central issue in dealing with intermediaries is that their objectives may not always coincide with those of the main organisation, or indeed the customer. Figure 6.4 illustrates a 'military' model for after-sales customer support in which various service delivery mechanisms are outlined. This model suggests that intermediaries may be aligned to Mercenaries, fighting for the cause, primarily because they are being paid.

The key dimension in Figure 6.4 is that of in-house control. The trade-off that service organisations adopting the intermediary approach are making is between the potential cost of poor quality of service and lost customers, against the cost of forming and maintaining a distributed network of service units.

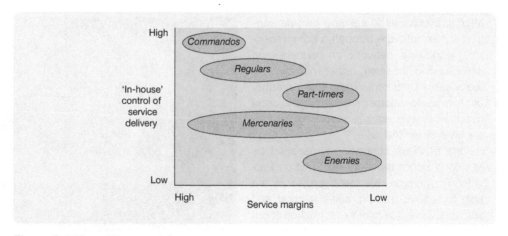

Figure 6.4 The military model

Source: Adapted from Armistead, Colin G. and Graham R. Clark (1992), *Customer Service and Support*, Pitman Publishing, London. Reprinted by permission of Pearson Education Limited.

The reasons for maintaining high in-house control of service include:

- to increase the depth and breadth of a customer relationship
- to ensure that customer complaints are effectively dealt with and that rapid feedback for process improvement is facilitated
- to retain control over innovative products and services for which there is limited resource.

The various service forms are as follows:

- *Commandos.* These are highly trained service personnel, often used as 'hit squads' able to tackle most problems on their own with little or no management direction. They are typically used to support complex products such as process automation or innovative information systems. These service providers are often found in professional services, particularly those that provide support services for software or communication systems.

- *Regulars.* Regulars are less comprehensively skilled than the Commandos and are less able to work without direction. The tasks they carry out tend to be more specialised and, of course, there are more of them. It is important to note that, because they are employed by the parent organisation, there is still a relatively high level of in-house control. This is diminished slightly by the fact that the Regulars are usually geographically dispersed by region or site.

- *Part-timers.* These service providers are the customers themselves, trained by the parent organisation to carry out service tasks for themselves. An example is provided by the photocopier companies that train key operators to change toner cartridges and free paper jams without using expensive service engineers (Regulars).

- *Mercenaries.* Mercenaries are not part of the parent organisation. The prime reason for fighting on the side of the main organisation is that they are being paid to do so. They may switch sides if there is sufficient incentive, and they do not share the culture of the parent organisation.

- *Enemies.* These are not on the same side. It may be that the parent organisation has decided not to provide service in all circumstances, particularly if the profit margins are small.

The challenge is to provide intermediaries with sufficient financial incentive while developing the customer service values required to generate customer loyalty. Strategies include:

- *Financial incentives.* This is particularly relevant when the intermediary is not dedicated to providing service for only one organisation. The parent organisation may provide financial inducements, discounts or credit facilities to encourage the intermediary to favour its services ahead of its rivals.

- *Punishments.* The ultimate sanction for poor performance is for the parent organisation to withdraw its support. This has become more common in recent years in the automobile industry, with manufacturers removing franchises from dealerships. Usually, though, this approach is only used as a last resort, because other dealers, no matter how good they are, wonder if they will be treated in a similar manner.

- *Providing expertise.* One of the most effective ways of motivating intermediaries is to provide support for their business. The parent organisation frequently has considerable resources in areas that are lacking in the intermediary. In Case Example 6.4 we saw Microsoft providing sales support for solution providers who are stronger in technical skills. Caterpillar, likewise, has created high levels of dealer satisfaction through the support given.

- *Training.* McDonald's Hamburger University is occasionally a source of jokes, but there can be little doubt as to its value in creating a consistency of approach throughout the network of outlets, both company-owned and franchised.

- *Information systems and technology.* Provision of process technology will assist in ensuring consistency of delivery. A franchisee generally receives a package of standard equipment and operating procedures to deliver the core service in the manner laid down by the parent organisation. Both Caterpillar and Microsoft provide online technical support to their partners and dealers. This serves the dual purpose of ensuring that high-quality technical support is given to their customers and also training their partners and dealers in the desired approach.

Selection of intermediaries

The recruitment and training of intermediaries are critical, particularly for those organisations choosing to operate through franchises. Franchisees operate under the company brand and any poor performer could seriously damage it. Criteria for selection should be at least as stringent as for the selection of suppliers, but should also include a review of the potential franchisee's commitment to the brand values of the parent organisation.

6.4.2 Disintermediation

A trend in many supply networks has been to circumvent or remove some of these intermediaries, an action referred to as disintermediation. This approach may bring benefits such as reduced costs and greater responsiveness, but may also increase the management task for the person or organisation requiring the service. The holiday industry is a good example (see Figure 6.5). Travel agents traditionally sell holidays to customers through shops in town centres or shopping malls. The customers may be individuals or group travellers. The travel agents sell a range of 'products', or packages, created by a number of tour operators. These tour operators will each negotiate independently with a range of hotels, airlines, restaurants, entertainment activities and venues, and transportation companies, for example, to create a package holiday aimed at a particular market. Given the size of their operations they are often able to achieve substantial discounts and can hold, often on a call-off (or as required) basis, services for many months while the travel agents sell the packages.

Over the last few years, tour operators have been cutting out the travel agents and selling directly to the public, although they have had to incur additional costs of call centres or websites to sell and service their products (see Figure 6.5). Even greater disintermediation is visible as hotels, airlines, car rental companies etc. have made their services available and bookable directly through websites, thus cutting out both tour operators and travel agents (see Figure 6.5). The advantage might be greater control and sometimes lower costs for consumers, but certainly at the expense of considerably greater efforts from them as they have to co-ordinate multiple supply networks (as in Figure 6.3).

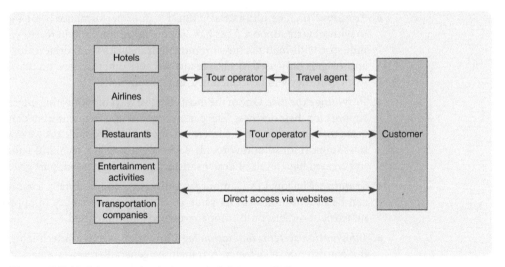

Figure 6.5 Holiday supply chains and disintermediation

Many service organisations continue to use intermediaries for the selling process as well as for service delivery to the end customer or user. These organisations have continued to develop support networks of agents, dealers or franchisees for a variety of reasons. Financial service companies have traditionally dealt through pensions or insurance brokers. This was in part to give the customer confidence that they were being given independent advice, for the same reason that Microsoft uses certified solution providers (see Case Example 6.4). The problem with this approach is that it often leads to confusion as to who is the 'real' customer – the intermediary or the final consumer. Of course, the simple answer is that both groups are customers, but it would be wrong to suggest that satisfying both groups is an easy task.

6.4.3 Outsourcing and off-shoring

Where disintermediation reduces the size of the supply network, outsourcing expands it. Outsourcing, and the related off-shoring, is the splitting out of a part of an operation to a specialist company. Usually it affects a peripheral activity, such as purchasing or accounting functions or call centres, but occasionally a core activity is split off, an example being equipment repairs. Organisations that do this believe that there are financial and strategic benefits to be had from letting a specialist supplier manage what used to be in-house tasks.

In recent years there has been a major increase in organisations outsourcing aspects of their operations that can be managed more effectively (and more efficiently) by specialist companies. Many of these service providers have built upon a particular expertise and have repositioned themselves to provide a package or solution for their customers. Examples include:

- companies which used to maintain building equipment, such as air conditioning or lifts, now providing a total facilities management service, replacing the customer's site maintenance function
- information systems support, including helpdesk functions.

A key reason for the effectiveness of the outsourcers is that they can offer the benefits of economies of scale and investment in information systems that provide opportunities for operational effectiveness.

Outsourcing frequently involves a transfer of employees from the original organisation to the new supplier. This is particularly true in the public sector, and this shift in culture from public service to commercial operation has proved to be a major factor in the success or otherwise of the activity. A report on outsourcing experiences in the public sector in New Zealand suggests four factors that distinguish between success and failure:[5]

- Service centres that build an immediate relationship with their clients based on service were more successful in establishing a viable client base than those which were more interested in maintaining tight controls of transactions.
- Good operational performance builds client loyalty. Poor performance is a major reason for clients to choose new providers.
- Market size is critical to provide the economies of scale required to realise the efficiencies to provide margin.
- A major factor is the ability of senior management to move from a bureaucratic style, somewhat remote from stakeholders, to a more open style and a closer relationship with customers and shareholders.

The manufacturing sector has been able to shift work to low-wage economies for many years. The advent of powerful telecommunications technology has enabled the recent rise of 'off-shoring' of service activities, not just of low-skilled jobs but also of some requiring advanced skills, such as computer programming and medical diagnosis. One commonly off-shored activity is call centre work. India, for example, has become the prime destination for call and contact centres off-shored from the USA and the UK (see Case Example 6.5). As competition and pressures to reduce costs force services abroad, there will be a need to create new jobs in services in their place. However, if both low- and high-skill work is migrating to other countries, there is a question as to what might be left, apart from services requiring personal contact, should the trend continue.

Some organisations are facing a backlash from their customers and shareholders who are questioning the need to off-shore jobs. Other organisations believe there is a benefit to making a point of not off-shoring services. Nationwide Building Society is a case in point. The Society cited 'concern for its customer base' as the reason it decided to invest in its existing UK centres rather than transfer business to India. According to Stuart Bernau, Nationwide's commercial and treasury director,

> We don't have shareholders so our two stakeholders are our employees and our customers, and we wanted to invest in the communities where our business comes from. We'd have to have incredibly good reasons to make the move, and we don't believe the short-term cost-savings of off-shore are proven.

Case Example 6.5   Norwich Union Call Centre, Delhi

EXL runs the Delhi-based call centre for Norwich Union, the UK's largest insurance company. The call centre employs around 900 call executives, and is clean, spacious and air-conditioned. It has a busy but pleasant atmosphere, not unlike some of the better call centres in Europe.

Vikram Talwar, from EXL, explains:

Demand has grown substantially over the last six to nine months. We have about one company a week come and visit us. There are two particular reasons. One obviously is cost. It saves approximately £20,000 per person that they move to India. But there is also the area of quality

Source: Sournik Kar

and productivity. We have only graduates working for us which means that the minimum standard qualification an employee must have to answer a call in India is a university degree.

Although an Indian call centre agent may only earn as much as one-sixth of the salary of their English counterpart, it is double what the average graduate earns in India. The staff also receive many benefits, including free meals in a well-appointed canteen, free healthcare, a gym, and transport to and from work.

The agents, however, are from a different culture to their customers, who may have different expectations, more aggressive attitudes – and strong regional accents. Vikram adds:

Indians understand the UK better than you might think. The relationship India has with the UK has in fact helped us to deliver a quality of service to the UK customer that would not necessarily be true if you were operating out of other places where the UK influence has not been as great as it has been in India.

In addition to customer service training, employees are given additional training in the UK culture, norms and behaviours and in understanding particular regional dialects.

While some customers are surprised and others are annoyed that they are dealing with a call centre in India, EXL believes that providing they deliver the service required, Norwich Union's customers are happy.

Source: This illustration is based on material from the BBC's *Brassed-off Britain* series, first transmitted in June 2004.

6.4.4 Developing supply partnerships

As the pace of competition quickens it has become increasingly common for organisations to enter into partnerships and alliances for a number of strategic reasons:

- to enter a new geographic region, where a partner may have a stronger market presence
- to provide a package of products and services that require the joint expertise of the partners to deliver them
- to develop new expertise in association with others, sharing resources in order to gain joint benefits.

In Chapter 4 we described many types of business relationships, including partnerships, alliances and networks. In this section we want to focus on alliances that have been formed in order to collaborate in the development and/or delivery of a specific set of services.

Alliances

There are three key dimensions of alliances:[6]

- *Focused or complex.* A focused alliance has clearly defined aims, and is set up under particular specific circumstances. Generally, the focused alliance deals with a subset of each of the partners' total activities. An example would be a telecommunications system's provider such as Ericsson or Motorola forming an alliance with a software company in China to market a specific communications solution. It is clear that this agreement does not go beyond these boundaries. A complex alliance would involve a much more substantial part of both partners being involved, perhaps retaining separate brands and marketing identities, but operationally much more interlinked.
- *Joint venture or working agreement.* A major task for a partnership cannot be handled by semi-formal agreements. It is more likely to be dealt with by the formation of a joint venture company. A significant issue here will be the allocation of power between the two partners.
- *Partnership or consortium.* While many strategic alliances take the form of a partnership between two organisations, a complex task requiring a wide range of skills and knowledge may be handled using a consortium. The issues involved in the management of these projects are correspondingly more complex.

Figure 6.6 shows some of the major factors to be considered in assessing the likely success of an alliance. Criteria for assessing the likely success of an alliance include:

- The extent to which the strategic aims of the partners coincide, but do not overlap. If both partners want the same benefits, there is little point in pursuing the partnership.

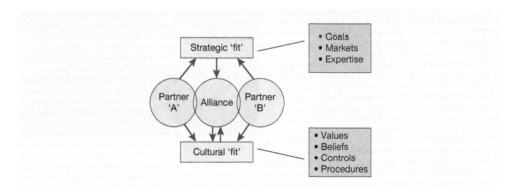

Figure 6.6 Strategic alliances

- The extent to which the two cultures allow for effective working. Are the values, beliefs and general ways of working compatible?

- Are the two partners (A and B in Figure 6.6) able to let the venture work in its own way? The culture of the venture is likely to be different from those of both its 'parents' and may be viewed with suspicion.

- Has there been sufficient discussion and negotiation as to what are the likely benefits for each partner? Is it clear as to which partner is responsible for which activities?

- Is there a dominant partner in the enterprise? Has this been agreed and is the less powerful partner happy with the arrangement?

- Is it clear how long the partnership will last and what are the terms of the dissolution of the partnership?

The experiences of alliances are many and varied. The key issue is the extent to which senior management is truly committed to the process, rather than paying lip-service to the idea. The creation of a co-branded service between a telecommunications company and a financial service organisation was described as a 'clash of corporate egos'.[7] Each partner was used to exerting its muscle since both were powerful in their traditional markets. The initial lack of compromise between the partners at senior level led to a series of disputes at the operational level, including conflicts about what company name would be used by customer service representatives. A study[8] that followed the alliance from inception into its second year found that at the end of the first year the alliance was only moderately profitable, but was showing signs of improvement. Both partners found difficulty in generating mutual trust, having been used to adversarial negotiating stances in the past. The study found that this was a major problem in the early life of the project and staff needed continuing social contact to begin to break down barriers raised on day one. The illustration of Northwards Housing in Case Example 6.6 demonstrates the opportunities to be had when working closely with other, very different, organisations and the importance of building mutual trust.

Case Example 6.6   Northwards Housing

Social housing is provided by local authorities (councils) and not-for-profit organisations such as housing associations and is allocated on the basis of need to people at risk, the homeless or those on low incomes. Northwards Housing is a not-for-profit company created by Manchester City Council, a large metropolitan council in the north-west of England, to manage some of the council's properties. The company provides estate management services, caretaking services, repairs and maintenance services and property improvements to their tenants. Robin Lawler, Northward's chief executive, explained:

> Our area covers the north part of Manchester including some quite tough areas with higher than average

Source: Northwards Housing

unemployment. Our vision is to continue to improve north Manchester by delivering an innovative hous-ing service which involves all customers and stakeholders. Our objectives are to provide warm, safe and affordable homes for all our tenants through advice, support and a multi-million pound investment pro-gramme, which creates jobs for local people and provides excellent value for money. I believe by working with tenants and other agencies and partners we will not only contribute to the regeneration of north Man-chester, but also develop successful communities and help to reduce crime, fear of crime and anti-social behaviour.

We work closely with the private contractors who do the repairs and maintenance on our properties. We are now moving to a more partnering approach with long-term relationships with a small number of contractors to help us design and deliver our major improvements programme. With these partners we will agree what we want to achieve and together agree a process between us; so it's not a case of us giv-ing them a specification and then standing over them while they do it. We also review the work after each phase and we ask the people who have been on the receiving end how satisfied were they, how good were the contractors, how good was the service, and try and learn from that. It all seems to work well. Our levels of satisfaction are about 9.8 out of 10 for repairs.

With our contractors we go for a 'no surprises approach'. We give them lists of properties and infor-mation about layout etc. then also tell them what to expect in terms of the people who live there and any special requirements they have. Then the contractor sends in their people to design the heating system, bathroom or whatever and they come back to talk to us if there is an issue or a problem. We leave them to do a lot of the liaising with the client. They are much more customer focused than they have been in the past when you might have a grumpy builder come in and rip out the kitchen and put one in around you without considering you and your needs.

This is all quite a different way of working for us and it's taken us some time to get our heads around it. But it's a much better arrangement for everyone involved than the more traditional adversarial, single contract for each job approach. It has also been cheaper; we have made major efficiency savings so we can reinvest the savings to do other things even better. For example if we are changing the kitchen and bathroom (which we usually do together) in a retirement flat we will also redecorate the whole flat while we are there. It's been a bit of a challenge for some of our staff where there was a feeling that you just can't trust a contractor, but we have found that contractors actually seem to enjoy working like this, taking responsibility, and then doing a better job!

In terms of our suppliers, we now work with about six other social housing organisations and have cre-ated a procurement consortium, where we pool our experience, share best practice and work together to get a better rate from our suppliers.

We also like to look at things in a much more holistic way, for example we need to do our bit but the police also need to get their bit right, and the council need to do their bit, clean the streets and maintain the play areas for example. We now have structured meetings with an agreed action plan to align all our activities and resources. There are also many informal meetings and phone calls to sort things out. We also have task team meetings when we meet with the police, council officers and others and we might decide to concentrate on a small area, a neighbourhood, identify the issues and the hot spots and decide how, together, we will deal with them. So for example, when we decide to do a blitz in an area we might encourage or help residents tidy up their gardens and make sure their properties are in good condition. The police deal with people with warrants against them for example, and the council will go in and remove untaxed cars and clear up the spare land.

We also work alongside council officers and police community support officers and private sector housing colleagues to consult residents and faith groups about what they see as the priorities for their community. We try to find out what the real problems are – often things like drug dealing, off road biking and rubbish dumping. We also ask them what they would like to see done with bits of spare land etc. and then involve them with the design of things. This co-ordinated approach has a huge impact.

We have also deployed different resources like neighbourhood wardens to go into hot spot areas. It's not just about chasing kids off one street corner to the next, but it's about creating youth engagement projects to give young people worthwhile things to do. The wardens run model car racing, football competitions and so on. We've run a Food and Dance Festival; we've paid for a music project to be done. We have even created junior wardens with all the primary schools who help with picking up litter, making sure that the lights aren't left on, or the taps aren't running in the toilets. We hope this kind of social responsibility spills over into the community as well.

We also work with social services when issues arise. Our contractors sometimes come across cases of domestic abuse and the breakdown of families, so we have developed some processes alongside the police and social services so when our contractors go in and spot problems, they know what to do.

In the past we used to have some big problems in some areas with anti-social behaviour with gangs of people roaming round smashing up cars and houses and you might have the police saying it's a housing problem and the housing saying it's a council problem etc. Now we are all joined up. Now it's a shared problem and we get together to work out what are the real issues and deal with them. It's all about everyone having the right to live safely in an area, looking after themselves, their homes and kids so they can have a peaceful life.

6.4.5 The purchasing or procurement function

The function traditionally responsible for managing the supply chain is the purchasing and supply or procurement department. This is an important activity found in all organisations – public, private, governmental and charitable – and can be responsible for a large amount of spending. Spending by service organisations on, for example, materials, components, facilities, subcontract capacity, IT equipment and supplies, consumables, stationery, travel and insurance, can constitute a significant amount of money, often 30–60 per cent of an organisation's turnover.[9]

Procurement is traditionally an internal service provided by a dedicated team of professionals. It typically operates at the interface between the organisation's external supplier marketplace and the organisation's operational processes. Procurement has many of the characteristics of the marketing function, although it faces the other direction in the supply chain. Procurement is usually responsible for the identification of (internal) customers' needs, translation of those needs into specifications, management of the delivery of products and services and an assessment of the (internal) customer's satisfaction with those products and services. The other elements of the process involve communication with suppliers – sourcing, requests for tenders, price negotiation, ordering, receipt and invoicing.[10]

Unlike marketing, procurement is often seen as a 'Cinderella' activity in many organisations. Despite the economic value of this internal service, managers often see 'promotion' into the purchasing function as a retrograde step into an organisational backwater. It is often held in low regard by its internal customers who see the function as bureaucratic, difficult to deal with, sometimes remote and delivering poor service. Senior managers, too, often see it as a problem area where there is low compliance, with internal customers either abusing or circumventing the systems.[11] It is also regarded as a high-cost activity where there is unnecessary paperwork, material costs and errors.[12] However, good management applied to this area can have a significant impact on costs. A report by consultants PricewaterhouseCoopers suggested that just a 10 per cent reduction in purchase costs could easily lead to a 50 per cent rise in profit margin.[13]

E-procurement

Electronic procurement systems are a form of disintermediation. In essence, e-procurement systems mirror the procurement process through the provision of two distinct, but connected, infrastructures – internal processing (via, for example, corporate intranet) and external communication with the supply base (via, for example, internet-based platforms).[14] The critical difference is that such systems allow individual employees to order products and services directly from their own PCs through the web. Requests and orders are channelled through various forms of 'hub' or database, which act as online catalogues of specifications, prices and, often, authorisation rules. Such systems allow individual employees to search for items, check availability, place and track orders and initiate payment on delivery.

Research found that e-procurement provides three key benefits over traditional procurement:[15]

- *Customer satisfaction.* Internal customers reported greater satisfaction with electronic-based procurement systems. Even though they had to undertake more work (searching, ordering and paying) themselves, they appreciated greater accessibility and availability of purchased products and services, faster fulfilment of requests and much greater control over the process and their own budgets.

- *Process compliance.* E-procurement systems provided greater reliability than traditional systems and, because they were easy for individuals to use, there were less 'maverick' purchases made (for example small purchases that were then reclaimed on expenses). The processes tended also to be more transparent and afforded better control of the purchasing process.

- *Cost reduction.* Not only were there significant savings in the cost of purchasing, but because employees had greater control over the process, less 'emergency' or 'just-in-case' supplies needed to be kept.

An additional and important impact of e-procurement is that the traditional roles of the purchasing department, such as placing and managing orders, can now be done electronically. This leaves the purchasing function in a position where it can either be more easily outsourced or take on a more strategic role, such as evaluating the impact of e-procurement, advising on systems and policies, and driving savings across the whole organisation.

6.4.6 Supplier selection

One of the key decisions for a procurement function is the selection of suppliers, particularly for those who are to undertake critical elements of the supply chain. Some criteria for supplier selection, apart from cost and quality, include:

- financial standing
- people management skills, including training and industrial relations record
- commercial awareness
- productivity
- quality management approach
- focus on continuous improvement activities
- shared values.

For many organisations the cost of the products or services provided may totally determine the choice of supplier, but in some more enlightened companies this is not always the case. Take the example of the restaurants run by Danny Meyer, an American entrepreneur:

> Most businesses ordinarily just go with the best supplier that offers the best price. Of course pricing for us is an important calculation; but for us, excellence, hospitality, and shared values must also be prominent factors in the selection process. It's hard for me to imagine deriving so much pleasure from the restaurant business were it not for the important and enjoyable relationships we've had with our suppliers. And the range of those relationships is broad; greenmarket farmers, wine producers, cheesemongers, printers, graphic designers. The enthusiasm with which we approach each day is infused with a deep respect for how well we represent those people who have supplied us with the tools to succeed.[18]

A major consideration is the extent to which the buyer's requirements comprise a significant amount of the supplier's business. A supplier who is totally dedicated to one buyer may seem like a good idea at first sight, but may lead to complacency in the relationship. Many buying organisations set targets that limit the proportion of business to be transacted with any one supplier. This has a particular benefit in that if the buyer's business should decline in the short term, their supplier base is more likely to remain viable.

However, part of the approach to SCM includes the reduction in the number of suppliers. Concern has been expressed that if the organisation is dependent on a single supplier, that may leave the buyer exposed. Nokia has developed an approach to this issue that is typical of many organisations. Nokia has three types of suppliers:

- *Sole suppliers.* These are used for new technologies where there may be only one supplier capable of delivering to the required specification.
- *Single suppliers.* This is the preferred approach for many components. A supplier will be appointed to provide the organisation's total requirements of a component or family of components for a region or possibly globally. Nokia will have other suppliers who are capable of supplying these components in the event of a problem, but who are currently providing similar products.
- *Multiple suppliers.* These are used only when necessary, perhaps to develop a supplier's capability or to provide locally specific components.

Nokia's approach to SCM has enabled it to develop the flexibility it requires to meet the demands of a market that has the challenges of rapid growth and shortening product life-cycles.

One-stop shops

A consequence of organisations wishing to reduce their administrative overheads is the rise of the opportunity for service providers to sell a comprehensive package to customers. For example, facilities management organisations (FMO) offer full maintenance for organisations that do not wish to employ their own staff to look after their buildings, i.e. they outsource buildings maintenance. So the FMO acts as a one-stop shop for all their needs, from cleaning to maintenance.

6.4.7 Measuring performance – service-level agreements

Service-level agreements (SLAs) are forms of contracts agreed between a service supplier and the service purchaser or user. These are usually found in a business-to-business context and often between internal suppliers and customers where a traditional contract is not felt to be appropriate. They are an important means of managing the relationship between partners in a supply chain.

Whether for internal use or external use, an SLA goes beyond the traditional remit of a contract, i.e. a statement of a service specification and the price that will be paid for it.

While an SLA, like a contract, defines the nature of the products or services and the level of quality to be provided, the idea of an 'agreement' is that it is a mutually agreed view of what can and will be provided, but also, and importantly, it exists for the mutual development of both parties. That is, an SLA is seen to be an integral part of the development of a relationship between a supplier and a customer – indeed the SLA attempts to formalise this relationship.

There are three key features of an SLA: setting a service specification, dealing with day-to-day, routine issues, and the development of the relationship.

Service specification

The core of an SLA is the development and agreement of the service specification. This will include:

- Agreeing the key dimensions of performance, such as response times, availability, accuracy etc. This allows for both customer and supplier to understand what is important about the service from both points of view.
- Agreeing how each dimension will be measured. Discussion and agreement about the measures to be used reduces the likelihood of disagreements at a later date about performance.
- Setting mutually agreed targets for each dimension. It is possible that standards set by one party may be too high for the needs of the other; clarity and agreement over what is needed and what is possible should lead to a feasible and achievable – and indeed low-cost – outcome.
- Defining where the responsibility lies for the measurement of each dimension. Unlike a traditional contract the responsibility for performance measurement may rest with either the supplier or customer, but such information is made openly available to both parties.

Routinised relationship

The routine part of the relationship formalised by the SLA concerns the day-to-day operation of the agreement. This may include:

- Providing a mechanism for reporting performance against standards at agreed intervals. Underpinning an SLA is the sharing of information, the purpose of which should not be unilateral action, as it might be in a traditional contract, but understanding and improvement.
- Setting out the procedures to be invoked if a failure against standard should occur. Routines for dealing with problems should be agreed in advance so that both parties understand their obligations and duties in such event. Failures should not be seen to be negative but as opportunities for supplier and customer to work together to solve each other's problems.

Developmental relationship

A key, though often ignored, element of an SLA is its role in developing a long-term relationship between supplier and customer. This involves providing a mechanism for routine discussion of the measures and targets and to share ideas for all-round improvements. This 'double-loop learning' activity formalises the need to regularly review the agreement, the measures used, the targets applied and the relationship between the parties.

Advantages and disadvantages

Clearly, SLAs require considerably more input of time and effort by both parties than a traditional contract. They have to be tailor-made for each service with each supplier in the supply chain, they can be complex, and they need an investment of time and effort in the long term to secure the potential benefits.

However, they do have the potentially significant benefits of a closer working relationship and therefore better service between supplier and provider. They can reduce risk for the supplier and the purchaser or user, and they create loyalty and reliability by focusing on the development of people and systems rather than on systems of 'punishment'. They also prevent unnecessary and expensive over-provision of quality by defining agreed standards.

Common mistakes in SLAs

Sadly, for many organisations, SLAs degenerate into a traditional contract, missing out on the real benefits that can be obtained. The usual mistakes that are made include:

- too few or inappropriate dimensions of performance
- no mutually agreed targets for each dimension
- responsibility for measures not identified
- no mechanism for reporting and discussion of performance
- no procedures to deal with problems
- mutual benefits not discussed or delivered
- no mechanism for discussion of measures or targets or to share ideas for improvement
- lack of commitment of managers from both parties to derive the benefits from the agreements.

6.4.8 Understanding the barriers to supply chain management

Although SCM makes sense in many ways to organisations, there are a number of barriers to successful implementation, which need to be recognised and overcome:

- *Lack of systems capability.* SCM requires the ability to pass information about changing demand patterns through the chain. Not all companies have invested in the capability to achieve this.
- *Complacency.* Where industry sectors have been reasonably stable, organisations may not see the need for SCM and may ignore it until a new entrant operates in a different mode. A more dangerous form of complacency exists when organisations feel that they have already fully implemented SCM and have lost the drive for continuous improvement.
- *Information used for a variety of conflicting purposes.* This relates particularly to demand forecasts, which may be used on the one hand to create an optimistic picture of the future to manage shareholder expectations, but on the other must be used for detailed planning activities. The former may bear no relation to reality, leading to over-investment in capacity.
- *Mistrust.* Previous, over-inflated estimates of demand may lead to suppliers reducing capacity allocations to levels less than required.
- *Power games.* Reorganisation along supply chain lines may be resisted by individuals whose power base will be diminished as a result. There may also be resistance on the part of suppliers who fear that they will be overwhelmed by a more powerful partner.

Many of the technical problems can be overcome to make the supply chain more effective. As with most significant change programmes, the major resistance comes from the people involved.

6.5 How can managers develop a global network strategy?

Because the combination of supply network design and information technology presents many opportunities for developing competitive advantage, the service operations manager must develop a more considered approach to network design, particularly when wishing to manage in the global context.

Figure 6.7 brings together motivations for extending a global network and the key issues to be addressed in managing it. The major reasons for developing the global network include:

- *Market-seeking motives.* The organisation may have a desire to move into new (geographical) regions. Examples would include the spread of fast-food chains such as McDonald's and Burger King across the globe, and the establishing of national offices for major consultancies such as Accenture or Capgemini.

- *Resource-seeking motives.* More resources may need to be acquired in order to grow more rapidly. This motive is frequently associated with the market-seeking motive as an organisation may take over a competitor in order to move into a new market.

- *Strategic-asset-seeking motives.* In this case, the network expansion might have as one of its goals the acquisition of key assets. This might relate to individuals with particular knowledge, or access to strategic customers.

- *Efficiency-seeking motives.* The transfer of service operations to low-labour-cost economies has become extremely popular as telecommunications technology has enabled processes to be outsourced or 'off-shored' in a way that was only thought possible for manufacturing a few years ago (see above).

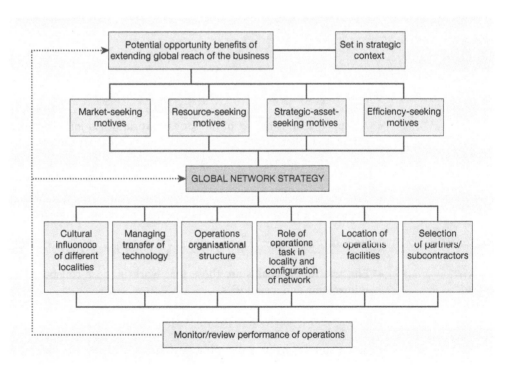

Figure 6.7 Global network strategy

Source: Cranfield SOM paper: *Strategic Global Manufacturing Management*, Professor M.T. Sweeney and Dr M. Szwejczewski (2002).

The operation of the global supply network must take into consideration some of the factors indicated in the lower part of Figure 6.7:

- *Cultural differences.* By this we mean the differences in national culture rather than organisational culture. Even McDonald's, renowned for the consistency of its products, has adapted its service offer, notably in Islamic cultures.

- *Technology transfer.* Technology transfer is frequently thought of as transferring 'hard' processes such as automation or process documentation. It is generally now recognised that the transfer of 'soft' technologies, which influence the organisation's culture, may present a more significant challenge to managing the supply network.

- *Operations organisational structure.* A key decision here is linked to the degree of local autonomy versus central control. Local units frequently feel that the centre exerts too much influence and stifles local responsiveness to customers.

- *The role of each unit in the network.* A global network strategy should bring clarity to each operational unit. In other words, each unit should understand its mission, whether it be to be the lowest cost operation or to provide access to local markets. The key performance indicators (KPIs) should then be developed according to the unit's specific mission.

- *Location decisions.* The unit's location will be decided after its specific role has been clarified.

- *Choice of partners and suppliers.* For many service providers, the choice of key suppliers and partners is a key strategic decision. This is particularly true in services that involve significant amounts of new or emerging technologies. The pace of change is so rapid that it is virtually impossible for one organisation to be able to deliver a total solution.

6.6 Summary

What are supply chains and networks?

- A supply chain is the set of links, or network, which joins together tiers of internal and external suppliers with tiers of internal and external consumers.

- Supply chain management (SCM) is concerned with managing the network and the flow of information, materials, services and customers through the network.

- The role for the 'customer' may involve co-ordinating the set of activities and interrelationships despite often having very little power or leverage to do so.

What is the role of information and inventory?

- Effective supply chains are those that work in close collaboration, carefully managing information and inventories.

How can service supply chains be managed?

- Some supply chains are contracting through disintermediation, others are expanding through outsourcing and off-shoring.

- The main reasons for using intermediaries include closeness to customer, local knowledge, focused expertise, poor service margins and insufficient capacity. The main trade-off to be managed is between in-house control and profit margins.

- It is increasingly common for organisations to enter into partnerships and alliances. There are many forms of partnership, the three main dimensions of which are focused or complex, joint venture or working agreement, and partnership or consortium.

- Procurement tends to be a 'Cinderella' activity and e-procurement is challenging the traditional procurement functions.

- Supplier selection is a key decision area for a procurement function. Several criteria may be used including financial standing, people management and quality management approach. One key issue is the decision to have sole or multiple suppliers.

- Service-level agreements are forms of contracts agreed between a service supplier and the service purchaser or user. The three activities involved in managing SLAs are setting a service specification, dealing with routine issues, and the development of the relationship. Many SLAs do not realise the potential benefits.

How can managers develop a global network strategy?

- Developing a global network strategy requires consideration of:
  - cultural differences
  - technology transfer
  - operations organisational structure
  - the role of each unit in the network
  - location decisions
  - choice of partners and suppliers.

6.7   Discussion questions

1 Select a service organisation and construct what you assume to be its supply chain.

2 Think of the last time you arranged an event or a service, such as a holiday, dinner party, music event . . . What were the issues you faced in co-ordinating the various inputs, including participants, and activities and suppliers?

3 Compare the approaches of two organisations in the same service sector, one choosing to operate through intermediaries, the other preferring to deal with end customers directly. What are the benefits and challenges of each approach?

6.8   Questions for managers

1 How well do you manage your supply network? Who are the parties? How effective are they? What are the mechanisms for review and improvement?

2 Could you be more effective in reaching new markets/providing new services by forming a strategic alliance? What would you require in a partner in such an alliance?

3 If you have service level agreements, how do they benefit both parties?

Case Exercise   The Regional Forensic Science Laboratory

Robert Johnston, Warwick Business School, and Tay Ming Kiong, Department of Scientific Services, Institute of Forensic Science and Forensic Medicine, Singapore.

The Regional Forensic Science Laboratory (RFSL) provides a one-stop service to a range of professionals. These professionals include police officers investigating crimes, narcotics officers who want drugs analysing, fire officers concerned to find the cause of a fire, defence counsels who are trying to strengthen the legal case for their clients, hospitals wishing to identify the cause of cases of poisoning, and private individuals who might be considering taking civil action.

Michael Tay is the head of the RFSL and he explains how his unit operates:

Forensic science is the application of science to the law and our role is to assist our clients in identifying suspects and victims, clearing innocent persons of suspicion and bringing the wrongdoer to justice. Our task is to provide accurate and objective information based on the evidence with which we are provided. We provide both written reports and verbal evidence in legal trials.

We have seven laboratories here, all under one roof, though often exhibits may well be sent from one lab to another for different specialised examinations. The Toxicology Laboratory examines body fluids and organs to determine the presence or absence of drugs and poisons. The Drugs Analysis Laboratory examines exhibits for drug content and body fluids and hair for drug consumption. The Physical Evidence Laboratory applies the principles and techniques of chemistry and physics to identify and compare a wide range of crime-scene evidence: firearms, gunshot residues, tool marks, shoeprints, tyre prints, paints, fibres, explosives etc. The Biology Laboratory examines exhibits for biological material (dried bloodstains, semen, saliva and other body fluids) and identifies the source using conventional serology or DNA typing. The Document Examination Laboratory examines handwriting and typewriting on documents, some of which may be badly charred, for example, to ascertain authenticity and/or source. The Latent Prints Unit processes and examines evidence for latent fingerprints and identifies the source of lifted prints. And the Forensic Pathology Laboratory investigates sudden unnatural, unexplained or violent deaths to determine the cause of death.

I know this sounds quite straightforward and scientific but the reality is rather different – it is fraught with problems and confusion. All the police officers, fire officers and hospitals etc. will send exhibits directly to the appropriate lab. This is fine until that lab sends it to another lab and the client no longer knows who has their blood sample etc.

The sample they give us will have been given to them by someone else. It might have come from a crime scene, from a victim or a suspect or an eyewitness. Because it can take time to get the sample from the origin it means we are under tremendous pressure to undertake the analysis quickly in order to help them complete the investigation. Hospitals, for example, rely on speedy response from the Toxicology Laboratory to ascertain the cause of poisoning so as to be able to administer the right antidote or treatment quickly to save the victim. The other professionals are usually under very tight deadlines imposed by the organisations, such as courts, to which they are responsible.

Yet we have to be very careful to do a thorough and proper job because at the end of the day the real customers are the suspect, either exonerated or convicted, the families and sympathisers of the suspects, the victims and their families who may have suffered terribly, the public, and of course the press and the media. Forensic science carries a heavy weight in the legal system. The judge and jury generally view forensic evidence as objective and impartial when assessing the case against a defendant.

The forensic expert's testimony must be clear and comprehensible to lay persons. Prosecutors, defence lawyers, judges and juries often have little time or inclination to get to grips with highly technical forensic evidence. We have to provide it in an accessible way. Because we have to make the information accessible and understandable, defence lawyers will use it to try to undermine the quality of the forensic science laboratory, our processes and even our staff. Their job is to interpret the evidence in favour of their clients and so they will look for weaknesses in the forensic findings to discredit the evidence or render it inadmissible.

We also have a problem with the evidence that is sent to us. We rely on the people, at the scenes of crime for example, to collect the right type and right amount of evidence. There is also the problem of which evidence to believe – it is possible that it may have been 'planted'.

Furthermore, like many forensic services, our laboratories face significant staff turnover and shortage, which affect capacity, result in loss of expertise and disrupt client relationships. As a result our delivery times can be quite long. The situation is made worse by new technologies that not only are expensive but require a substantial investment in training. Also the people we have are from scientific backgrounds and may be excellent in technical skills but lacking in business sense and customer awareness.

At the end of the day, members of the public want to see justice done, and the criminal punished. They are alarmed when the criminal and judicial processes are unsuccessful in identifying and convicting the criminal. The public expects the correct culprit to be quickly apprehended and dealt with. Mistakes in the criminal justice systems have a wide-ranging impact on the community, victim, victim's family, falsely accused person, investigators, the investigation process, the forensic community and the judicial process. In capital punishment cases, the mistake cannot be corrected because the sentence is irreversible. Justice must not only be done, it must be seen as done, and we have a vital role to play in this. Unfortunately, I sometimes feel that the system is against us and we are not doing all that we should.

Questions

1 Summarise the problems faced by Michael Tay and the other professionals involved in the collection, analysis and use of forensic evidence.

2 How could a supply chain approach overcome some of the problems?

Suggested further reading

Croom, Simon and Robert Johnston (2003), 'E-service: Enhancing Internal Customer Service through E-procurement', *International Journal of Service Industry Management* 14 (5) 539–555

Croom, Simon and Robert Johnston (2006), 'Improving User Compliance of Electronic Procurement Systems: An Examination of the Importance of Internal Customer Service Quality', *International Journal of Value Chain Management* 1 (1) 94–104

Karten, Naomi (2004), 'With Service Level Agreements, Less Is More', *Information Systems Management* 21 (4) 43–45

Sengupta, Kaushik, Daniel R. Heiser and Lori S. Cook (2006), 'Manufacturing and Service Supply Chains: A Comparative Analysis', *Journal of Supply Chain Management* 42 (4) 4–15

Tate, Wendy L., Lisa M. Ellram and Stephen W. Brown (2009), 'Offshore Outsourcing of Services: A Stakeholder Perspective', *Journal of Service Research* 12 (1) 56–72

Womack, James P. and Daniel T. Jones (2005), 'Lean Consumption', *Harvard Business Review* 83 (3) 58–68

Useful web links

A good, but short overview by Daniel Flint in *Supply Chain Management Review*:
www.scmr.com/article/the_service_side_of_supply_chain_management

A hot issue in service management is outsourcing. Here it is discussed by Anna Bawden of the UK *Guardian*:
www.guardian.co.uk—brighton-council-outsource

Another outsourcing piece by Dhanya Ann Thoppil in the *Wall Street Journal*, this time looking at the largest provider or outsourcing services, India's Tata:
blogs.wsj.com—is-tcs-outsourcings-new-poster-child

This piece on outsourcing problems at Stofke on Wheels, and its follow-up comments, typifies the perspective on outsourcing in the non-peer-reviewed literature:
wheels.onebuttonapps.net—poor-customerservice-outsourcing-globalization-and-the-decline-of-the-west

A more considered piece by Alex Noble at finextra.com following Banco Santander's decision to repatriate call-centre operations:
www.finextra.com—fullblog.aspx

A comprehensive piece from the supplier's perspective by Jesscia Twentyman of the *Financial Times*:
www.ft.com/cms/s/0/12a87a7a-a118-11e0-9a07-00144feabdc0.html

A nice summary of financial services offshoring practice by Sukhendu Pal and Lisa Hammond of Centrix Consulting:
www.centrixconsulting.com—LinkClick.aspx

Notes

1 For more details on managing supply chains see also Slack, Nigel, Stuart Chambers and Robert Johnston (2007), *Operations Management*, 5th edition, FT Prentice Hall, Harlow

2 Tiffin is also the word for a light lunch

3 http://www.sixsigmainstitute.com/news/sixsigma/2005/11/mumbais-amazing-dabbawalas.html

4 See for example Armistead, Colin G. and Graham R. Clark (1992), *Customer Service and Support*, Financial Times/Pitman Publishing, London

5 Gill, John (2001), 'Some New Zealand Public Sector Outsourcing Experiences', *Journal of Change Management* 1 (3) 280–291

6 Faulkner, David (1992) 'Strategic Alliances: Cooperation for Competition', in Faulkner, David and Gerry Johnson (eds), *The Challenge of Strategic Management*, Kogan Page, London

7 Hutt, Michael D., Edwin R. Stafford, Beth A. Walker and Peter H. Reingen (2000), 'Defining the Social Network of a Strategic Alliance', *MIT Sloan Management Review* 41 (2) 51–62

8 Hutt, Michael D., Edwin R. Stafford, Beth A. Walker and Peter H. Reingen (2000), 'Defining the Social Network of a Strategic Alliance', *MIT Sloan Management Review* 41 (2) 51–62

9 Croom, Simon and Robert Johnston (2003), 'E-service: Enhancing Internal Customer Service through E-procurement', *International Journal of Service Industry Management* 14 (5) 539–555

10 Croom, Simon and Robert Johnston (2003), 'E-service: Enhancing Internal Customer Service through E-procurement', *International Journal of Service Industry Management* 14 (5) 539–555

11 Croom, Simon (2000), 'The Impact of Web-based Procurement on the Management of Operating Resources Supply', *Journal of Supply Chain Management* 36 (1) 4–13

12 Lamming, Richard C. (1993), *Beyond Partnership: Strategies for Innovation and Lean Supply*, Prentice Hall, London; Hines, Peter (1994), *Creating World Class Suppliers: Unlocking Mutual Competitive Advantage*, Pitman, London

13 Sheng, M.L. (2000), 'The Impact of Internet-based Technologies on the Procurement Strategy', in the proceedings of the 2nd International Conference on Electronic Commerce, Taipei, December 2002

14 Croom, Simon (2000), 'The Impact of Web-based Procurement on the Management of Operating Resources Supply', *Journal of Supply Chain Management* 36 (1) 4–13

15 Croom, Simon and Robert Johnston (2003), 'E-service: Enhancing Internal Customer Service through E-procurement', *International Journal of Service Industry Management* 14 (5) 539–555

16 Meyer, Danny (2007), *Setting the Table*, Harper Collins, New York, p. 267

Part 4 Deliver

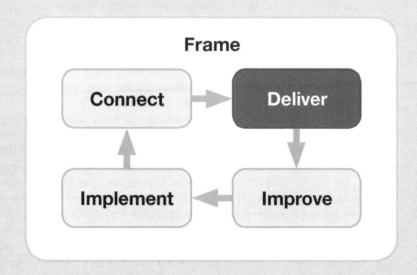

Chapter 7
Designing the customer experience

Chapter objectives

This chapter is about how to design the customer experience.

- What is a customer experience?
- How can the servicescape be designed?
- How can managers design the customer journey?
- What is the role of technology in developing the customer experience?

7.1 Introduction

A holiday consists of many different activities (services): flights, hotel accommodation, meals and tours, for example. Some of the processes to create and provide those services will be highly visible to the customer, such as check-in and a tour to a local landmark. Others may be, at least in part, invisible to the customer. These are back-office operations, such as computerised booking and reservations, or cooking and cleaning at the hotel. Some processes will process customers, an example being the transfer coaches; some processes deal with information, an example being reservations systems; and some processes will process materials, an example being catering services. In Chapter 8 we will cover the design and management of processes from a service provider perspective with a focus more on efficiency. In this chapter we want to focus on effectiveness – the customer perspective. How can we design those processes in which the customer is personally involved to try to ensure that they provide the right experience for the customer?

The idea of the customer experience appears to have resonated with practitioners and academics alike and many managers and service researchers now talk about the customer experience.[1] We need to stress at this point that designing a good customer experience is not just a concern for 'entertainment' type organisations such as theme parks; it is an issue for every service organisation. Whenever an organisation provides a service their customers **will** have an experience, which will be good, bad or indifferent – i.e., a service always comes with an experience however mundane or otherwise the service itself may be.[2]

Indeed, many organisations are now trying to compete on the experience they provide their customers with instead of competing on, for example, the range or price of their services.[3] The customer's experience of a service also has an important impact on the service outcomes – perceived value for money, level of satisfaction and customer loyalty for example (see Chapter 5). Furthermore, really good experiences are said to create close emotional bonds with customers whereas very poor experiences can lead to emotional scarring![4] There is also some evidence that organisations are not particularly good at designing their customer experiences. A survey by Bain & Co. of 362 companies, across several industries and their customers, found that 80 per cent of the senior executives interviewed said they provided a superior customer experience, but just 8 per cent of their customers agreed.[5]

7.2 What is a customer experience?

As we defined in Chapter 1, a customer experience is the customer's direct and personal interpretation of, and response to, their interaction and participation in the service process and its outputs, involving their journey through a series of touch points. In this chapter we will focus on that journey, the customer journey, through the service, the impact it will have on the customer (their emotions) and how it can be 'designed' to deliver the service concept.

And therein lies a problem. Because the experience is a personal interpretation of a service, it exists only in the customer's mind. As we saw in Chapter 5, our perceptions are individual to us and may not reflect the actual situation: they are our own personal view of 'reality'. Thus, no two people can have the same experience.[6] Indeed it has been suggested that we can't actually design an experience, only the mechanisms for creating it.[7] What operations managers can do, however, is to try to build in the right clues and messages into the servicescape (see Section 7.3) and try to design the customer's journey to create the right experience and emotions (see Sections 7.4 and 7.5).

7.2.1 The experience statement

The first critical stage in designing the customer experience is to develop an experience statement.[8] While many organisations define the service they want to provide (see Chapter 5) very few, as yet, have defined the experience they want to their customers to have. Case Example 7.1 provides an example as to how the Britannia Building Society went about defining the experience it wanted to provide its customers with.

Case Example 7.1 Britannia Building Society

Britannia Building Society, now owned by the Co-operative Bank Plc, was one of the largest mutual building societies in the UK. As a mutual company it was owned by, and run for the benefit of, its customers, referred to as members. Before its merger with the Co-operative Bank the company had been working hard to develop the experience it provided to its members. Neville Richardson, Britannia's ex-chief executive, now the chief executive of the merged bank, explained:

We started work on the Customer Experience, not because we thought we

Source: Alamy Images/David Bagnall

had a problem, but because we thought there was an opportunity. Having spent a great deal of time replacing our core systems, undertaking a great deal of work on our culture, values and strategy, we felt these things combined to give us the capability to provide a very different experience based on an emotional level.[9]

Rick Jones was the Development Stream Leader for the Customer Experience Programme and he explained how the company has gone about developing the customer experience:

A year or so ago, we took a paper to our group executive board that suggested they might like to consider the idea of 'customer experience' as a means of developing the business. They seemed to think it was a good idea and asked us to spend the next six months working out firstly what the customer experience should be, and second, what were all the things that we'd have to change to give ourselves the capability to deliver it.

The first thing we did was to set up a high powered steering group to oversee the work of the project team. The steering group was chaired by the chief executive and members included senior people around the business, for example the individuals responsible for the branch network and back office processing. Our remit was to develop an outstanding customer experience as the key strategy for further differentiating Britannia's position in the marketplace.

We then undertook a vast amount of research around what the Britannia experience should be. Our market research department carried out customer forums, telephone interviews, and discussions with customers and we talked to industry experts. We also tried to involve everyone in the organisation. For example, we asked our staff to email us examples of good experiences they'd had with companies, not only so we could better understand what a great customer experience looks like but also so we could go and find out how those organisations were doing it. We went out and visited, mystery shopped, some of them and in some we met and talked to their managers as well. We even took the steering committee out on mystery shopping trips too!

At Britannia we sat in a branch for a whole week and just watched customers coming and going. We looked carefully at their facial expressions, their body language, and listened to their tone of voice. We were trying to identify their emotions and the changes that took place in the branch. We estimated that customers' emotions were changing somewhere between ten and fifteen times in a basic branch interaction. We did the same on the telephone; we sat in our contact centres, listened to phone calls, and evaluated the language, the tone of voice, and the changes in the experience. The team realised very early on that while every customer is different, when you aim to evoke a specific set of emotions, like wanting our customers to feel special and valued, you can tailor the approach for every customer. As a member of staff you are aiming for the same end state each time, but you have the ability to sense and respond differently to each individual customer in achieving the end state. It also means that no matter who the customer speaks to, or which contact/sales channel they use, they come away with a consistent set of feelings about the organisation each and every time. In adopting this approach it has been critical to identify the right feelings we are aiming to evoke.

We also asked each of the customer-facing businesses to nominate 'customer experience all stars': staff who were seen to be good at dealing with customers by their peers. We then invited them to come and spend a week or so with us so we could talk to them about what they did and also test out our thinking on them. They provided a useful reality check for us and the steering committee.

Once the data had been collected the project team set about analysing it. The analysis identified thirteen different feelings. They realised that thirteen was too many to ask staff to concentrate on and set about coming up with a manageable list. One key session involved the members of the project team, the chief executive and all of the steering committee members, and the 'customer experiences all stars'. In an activity resembling a game show, people voted for which of the feelings they were happiest to dispense with. Where conflict resulted, the customer research about the specific feelings being challenged was read out, and the vote was re-run. When five feelings were left, no amount of debate or re-votes could dispense with the remaining feelings – so they became the definition of the customer experience. Rick added:

It was important that we had everyone buy-into whatever the output was, and the best way to do this was for them to create it. By the end of a couple of hours' work we had thirteen groups of learning points to which we could assign an emotion. After some rounds of voting, we whittled them down to five, which we then tested out on a group of customers.

The five key feelings developed by the Britannia team that were to underpin their creation of outstanding customer experiences were: best interests at heart, peace of mind, in control, understood, and special and valued.

We then reported back to the steering group who told us to go away and work out what we had to change to deliver them. We have spent the last six months or so working on brand development, developing our staff and designing training to support the delivery of experience, running hundreds of staff awareness sessions, changing recruitment policies, and redesigning some of our processes and systems. We have done a lot of work and we still have a lot to do, but I reckon we are 60–70 per cent there now. But it's been a massive piece of work, and we're learning more as we go.

A customer experience statement is a description of the customer's experience and the outcomes from the point of view of the customer. It needs to be written in an outside-in way, i.e. from the customer's point of view, including the emotions they should feel as a result of the experience and the benefits they should get from it. This information should already be captured in the organisation's service concept.

Let's take the example of an express parcel company. Their service (service provided) might be to deliver their customers' parcels on time every time. An experience statement, however, is about the service received; how the customer will feel as a result of their experience and the benefits they get from the service. For the parcels company, for example, an experience statement might be 'The customer will have total confidence in us, they will be treated as special and valued customers and can enjoy total piece of mind'.[10]

7.2.2 Emotions

A critical part of the experience statement is the identification of the emotions the organisation wants their customers to feel, or more correctly, the emotions that their customers will want to feel as a result of the service. As we saw in Case Example 7.1, the Britannia team undertook a great deal of market research to understand the emotional needs of customers. They then spent time refining them into a short, clear and agreed list. Having this set of emotions enabled them not only to construct their experience statement but also to redesign their processes and procedures, such as training programmes, recruitment criteria, customer feedback forms etc., to try to ensure that these emotions were actually created in the minds of their customers.

Thinking in emotional terms is not straightforward. Although we constantly feel emotions, we tend not to categorise them. For example, if we are having a 'discussion' with our teenage children, we don't stop and think, OK what emotions am I feeling now, am I proud or compassionate, annoyed or anxious, apprehensive or despairing?

As operations managers and designers it is helpful if we can become more mindful of our emotions. This better enables us to understand how our service may be affecting others. This is also recommended for people wanting to enhance their emotional intelligence. 'Mindfulness' is the practice of comprehending our feelings; becoming aware of them, observing them and then ultimately managing (controlling) them. This is a fundamental element of Buddhist philosophy and also referred to as 'sensory acuity' in Neuro-Linguistic Programming.[11]

There are over 300 distinct emotions, which have been categorised into seven primary emotions; joy, surprise, love, fear, anger, shame and sadness. Joy, for example, includes secondary level emotions including amused, cheerful and euphoric. These primary

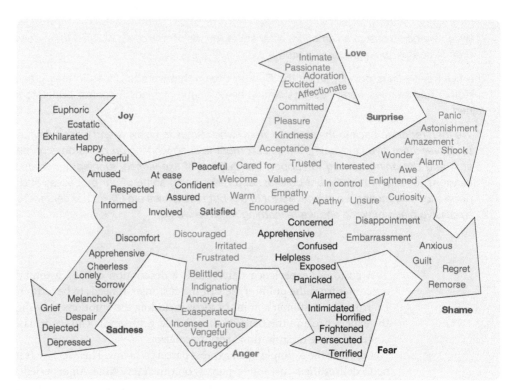

Figure 7.1 Weak to strong emotions

emotions range from weak to strong; love, for example, might range from warm to intimate (see Figure 7.1).[12]

Emotions are the often powerful, subjective feelings with associated physiological states.[13] Emotions are managed by our emotional brain, the limbic system, which floods our neurochemical pathways with hormones in response to real or perceived or imagined stimuli. Our response to emotions can be strong and primitive and this is usually 'regulated' by our pre-frontal cortex, the thinking part of the brain, the rational brain. Positive emotions, like happiness, release endorphins (with similar properties to heroin) which can improve learning, build the immune system, aid memory, reduce illness and stress and even extend life.[14] Slightly stressful situations, threats, fear and feelings of helplessness cause the brain's performance to deteriorate (downshift) resulting in poor muscular co-ordination and muddled thinking.[15] Highly stressful situations can lead to what the psychologists refer to as 'hijacking'. When the heart rate rises to over 175 beats per minute, cognitive skills break down, vision becomes restrictive, the person becomes aggressive, and their muscles contract and become difficult to use. As the emotional brain takes over, reactions become emotional and primal.[16]

There are three important points here. Firstly, although most managers believe they, and their customers, make decisions based on rational argument, most decisions are driven by more emotional responses to situations. Indeed psychologists have repeatedly shown that our ideas about rational decision-making are delusional.[17] Emotions, even at a subconscious level, have a powerful influence on 'rational' decision-making.[18] Secondly, our responses to feelings of emotion are swift and strong (and sometimes wrong) but if positive can create powerful emotional bonds between a customer and an organisation, and if negative can create lasting emotional scars in customers.[19] And thirdly, few organisations (unlike the Britannia) have articulated and agreed the emotions they actually want their customers to feel, despite the fact that all their customers will feel emotions as a result of their experiences with them. Thus service designers need to ensure that their service is designed to try to create the right emotions in customers.

Having defined the experience statement capturing the experience and emotions to be created, we can then set about designing the servicescape and the customer's journey through the service process.

7.3   How can the servicescape be designed?

The customer experience takes place in an environment that will affect the customer's perception of the service provided. The term 'servicescape' is used to describe the physical surroundings of the service.[20] We use it here to include both the physical and informational environment in which a service is both created and provided; it is the environment for both staff and customers. The servicescape of a hospital, for example, comprises the car parks, the buildings, the décor and the arrangement of seats in a waiting room or staff canteen. An internet-based servicescape may include the appearance, user-friendliness and accessibility of an organisation's website.

When operations managers buy or build their facilities they need to ask about more than the size, type, number and location of those facilities; they also need to consider their impact on the customer's experience. Hard chairs without arms, set out in clinical rows in a waiting room, provide one type of experience, whereas clusters of armchairs with coffee tables and magazines provide quite a different one. The choice and style of facilities should therefore be in tune with the desired experience (based on the service concept). That is not to say that all chairs, for example, should be comfortable. Those in fast-food restaurants may be designed to provide adequate support and comfort for leaning forward and eating but are less comfortable for leaning back and relaxing at the end of a meal, thus 'encouraging' customers to leave at the end of the meal.

These features, such as the comfort of a chair, are known as 'clues' (or sometimes 'cues') which create 'messages' for the customer during their experience of the organisation and its service. Clues are indicators, stimuli and signals, indeed anything a customer can hear, taste, touch, see or smell,[21] that have been built (purposely or inadvertently) into the service to provide particular messages. Messages are what customers will infer about the organisation, its services, management or staff. The resultant emotions are how the customer feels, consciously or subconsciously, about the service, the clues it contains and the messages it provides. In designing services and experiences, managers need to be concerned to ensure that all messages emanating from all the clues designed into the service are consistent with the service concept and the desired emotions. In particular there is a need to eliminate those clues which result in messages, or rather mis-messages, inadvertently, or mistakenly, designed into the service that convey the wrong idea about the service and the organisation.

These clues can be designed into the environment (the servicescape), the people or the service process/experience (sometimes referred to as mechanic, humanic and functional clues).[22]

Clues in the servicescape might include location of a building (a prestigious location in the business district or a decaying out-of-town site) and its size (large and imposing or small and run-down) (see Case Example 7.2). The décor and the type of office furniture will provide particular messages about the nature of the service, the likely experience and also its cost. These clues and messages designed into the experience will then lead to feelings such as security, pride, eagerness or amazement. The classic styles of Caesar's Palace or Bellagio's in Las Vegas, the memorabilia of Hard Rock cafés, all seek to create particular experiences, messages and emotions for the customer and in many cases differentiate the service from the competition.

Case Example 7.2 British Airways, Waterside

In 1998 British Airways opened its new head office, Waterside. The aim of the new building was not only to reduce the high costs of managing 14 offices scattered around Heathrow airport and in the centre of London, but also to encourage teamwork and open communication between its employees.

The idea was to create a 'village' atmosphere. A central enclosed 'Street' links all the buildings and makes them feel a part of a whole. The informal atmosphere is created by trees and fountains, coffee shops and restaurants surrounded by glass-walled offices, walkways and lifts. There are no direct lifts linking the underground car park with offices, so employees are compelled to

use the Street and meet each other. Not only is this a place for managers and administrators but it also brings together cabin crew and customer service staff by combining an office block with training rooms (including a mock-up of a Boeing 747), together with staff facilities such as video dispensers, fitness rooms and hairdressers. To facilitate communication Waterside's offices are open plan, with many small 'club' areas where employees can work informally in lounge areas.

BA's chief executive explained:

As a result the atmosphere is informal and transparent. People can see and meet others who work in different departments. In the old building it was different. People worked in their own rooms and had their own space. If you went to visit them it was like going on to someone else's territory. The way we operate here is not only more transparent, it is more efficient.

People clues might include the uniforms, dress and demeanour of the employees which will provide particular messages about their approach, trustworthiness or success. For example the distinctive uniforms of Singapore Airlines flight attendants, the dark well-cut suits worn by consultants, or the casual appearance of a university professor all provide particular messages to, and create particular emotions within, their respective customers.

The process or experience clues are those that are designed into the customers' journey, and we will deal with this in more detail in the next section. Before we do that it is important to recognise that these clues and messages not only signal the nature of the experience and create the experience for the customer but they can also influence their behaviour and that of the staff.

Influencing customer behaviour

Customers' behaviour, and thereby their experience, can be, to some extent, determined by the servicescape – by its ambience, its lighting, its décor or indeed the music.[23] A warm bar may encourage customers to drink more, while the tempo of background music in a shop can influence the pace of shopping and the amount spent by customers.

A number of studies have addressed the issue of environmental design effects (sometimes referred to as aesthetic atmospherics) upon psychological and behavioural responses of consumers in shopping centres, retail outlets and other service encounters.[24] Clean, clear and well-lit food cabinets, for example, lead customers to perceive that the products are fresh.

The servicescape also influences the nature of the interaction between customers and between customers and employees. Seating arrangements or the amount of background noise, for example, may encourage or discourage conversation and/or interaction.

The existence of queues, whether a physical queue or a queue on a telephone for example, provide physical or informational evidence that influences customers' behaviour. The simple existence of a queue, in some countries, encourages customers to modify their behaviour. They will wait in turn, physically position themselves relative to others waiting, and, up to a point, be prepared to accommodate a delay in service. A queue, like other environmental clues such as temperature and lighting for example, may also generate 'approach' or 'avoidance' behaviour. It has been suggested that individuals react to environments in two general and opposite ways: they are either attracted to it or repulsed by it.[25] For some people a queue to enter a restaurant, for example, may signal 'a place to be seen' or a 'popular destination worth trying'; to others it may represent 'crowded and trendy' and may act as a de-selection device (see also Chapter 11).

The design of equipment or information interfaces will also have an effect on customers' behaviour, in particular their ability to interact with and obtain service from remote service providers such as organisations using the internet, remote cash machines or ticketing machines. Fast, easy and user-friendly interfaces will lead to approach behaviour, whereas slow and difficult may well lead to avoidance.

Influencing employees

Just as the physical and informational aspects of a service environment influence customers, they also influence employees and affect their experience of their organisation. It has been suggested that an appropriate environment results in approach rather than avoidance behaviour by employees and as a result they are more committed to the organisation, stay longer, and are more able to carry out their roles effectively.[26] In Case Example 7.2 we saw how the design of the headquarters for British Airways created an informal working environment and encouraged communication between staff.

7.4   How can managers design the customer journey?

The customer's journey is the series of steps they take and the touch points they have as they experience the service process. As Case Example 7.3 shows, a customer's journey involves many interrelated services, some of which predominantly process customers, others information and others materials. Some tasks and activities may be located in the back office, remote from customers, while other tasks or activities take place in the presence of the customer. These front office processes are those that the customers directly experience during their journey. These may be performed in a number of locations: in the organisation's facilities or in the customer's home, for example. Together, these processes – in an appropriate sequence – create the customer experience and deliver the service outcomes. Figure 7.2 shows a simplified diagrammatic representation of some operations processes.[27]

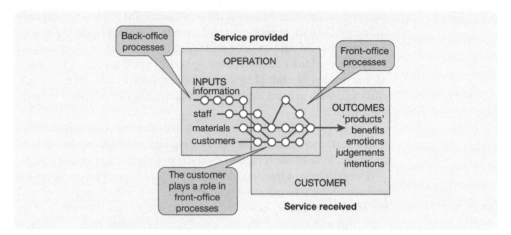

Figure 7.2 A simplified service process

Case Example 7.3   The acute patient's journey

Paul Walley, Warwick Business School

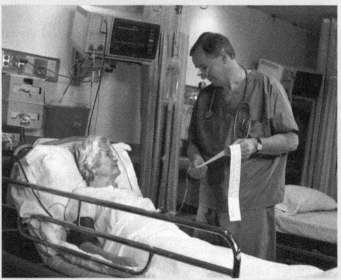

Source: Pearson Education Ltd/Imagestate/John Foxx Collection

When an acutely ill patient needs to be treated urgently, the whole healthcare system has to respond in a co-ordinated manner. For example, if a patient attends a local doctor's (general practitioner's) clinic with abdominal pain and the doctor assesses this as a probable acute appendicitis, the patient needs to be admitted to hospital for surgery immediately. First the local doctor might phone a house officer (doctor) at the local general hospital to agree the probable diagnosis, so that the patient can be 'surgically accepted' by the hospital. An ambulance will be immediately requested, to take the patient to hospital. However, the target response times may be breached if the ambulances in the area are allocated to other emergencies.

When an ambulance arrives to take the patient to hospital, the local doctor usually gives the paramedic a letter of admission to take with the patient. This contains any immediate patient information that the hospital staff may find useful, including drugs that have recently been prescribed for pain relief. Ideally, ambulance paramedics should be given the same information so that they know what treatment has already been given, to avoid duplication. This does not always happen, especially if the doctor is unable to meet the ambulance crew.

When the ambulance arrives at the hospital, it is normal for the patient to be taken to either the accident and emergency (A&E) department or to a specialist 'surgical assessment unit'. First, the patient will have to be booked into the system by a receptionist and the ambulance staff will not be allowed to leave before this is done. This is to ensure that accurate information about the patient's condition is given to the hospital staff receiving the patient. The booking procedure needs to establish the patient's identity accurately, so that the correct patient's notes can be retrieved from the hospital's archives. Other details, such as the patient's next of kin, are also required, so that relatives can be informed, particularly if the patient is extremely ill. The patient's arrival will be cross-referenced with the call to surgically accept the patient.

Once the patient has been booked in, they will be assessed for the urgency of their condition. This 'triage' will usually be performed by a senior nurse. A house officer (doctor), supervised by a senior house officer, will then hopefully provide an accurate diagnosis. The first steps in the diagnosis will usually involve basic blood tests and X-rays. Most hospitals have their own emergency X-ray units attached to A&E, staffed by radiographers. These often become very busy with patients, especially where specialist fracture clinics share the resource. Each X-ray needs to be assessed by a radiologist and a report typed up by a medical secretary. When blood is taken, the most common tests might be analysed using small testing machines located near the A&E department. Most samples are sent to central pathology labs, where they are processed alongside the hundreds of routine samples that each lab has to deal with each day. Skilled pathology technicians operate the equipment and ensure that the results are accurately obtained. Pathologists assess the results, which are usually reported on a computer printout. Urgent results are sometimes telephoned through. Only a few departments have electronic reporting of this type of information.

Often one of the biggest hurdles for the patient is to be found a bed within the hospital. This is the responsibility of a specialist team of bed managers. Wards are divided into medical and surgical units with male- and female-only wards. Given that most hospitals in the UK work with 90 per cent or more occupancy of beds, finding a space for up to 50 acute admissions per day can be a real challenge. Acute admissions typically comprise 30 per cent of all admissions and so emergencies compete with elective cases for bed space. The space available partially depends upon the surgical lists that drive the elective admissions. Commonly, Mondays and Wednesdays see most elective surgery and so these are frequently the most difficult days for unplanned admissions. In many hospitals, medical wards overflow at times. This can result in patient 'medical outliers' being placed on surgical wards, further restricting space. One bed manager highlighted other problems:

> Requests for beds should come through us. This does not always happen, as patients can be admitted via the 'back door' by consultants etc., without telling us. It can be confusing when we think we have free beds but we haven't. We continually monitor where beds are available on the computer and by doing a ward round. We conduct a census on wards to find free beds not recorded on the computer.

When a patient needs urgent surgery, a theatre slot needs to be found. This can be complicated as the theatres usually have particular elective clinical specialisms booked for each half-day session, with just a few slots reserved for emergencies. Theatres are not all equipped in the same way: theatres specialising in orthopaedics, for example, need specialist pieces of equipment. There are also issues to address when assembling the most appropriate surgical team of surgeons, anaesthetists, nurses and support staff, since not all staff are multi-skilled or available. Staff time taken by emergency surgery inhibits other activities such as ward rounds. The theatres also have to ensure that there is a readily available stock of sterilised equipment, and it usually takes 24 hours for used equipment to be cleaned and resterilised.

Patient welfare is also enhanced by the array of support services. The catering services need to provide patients with three meals a day. Cleaning services need to ensure that all areas are kept as clean as possible. This is a difficult task because they must not interfere too much with the daily workload. The traffic of thousands of staff, patients and visitors bring in dirt and waste incessantly. Cross-infection caused by poor hygiene requires a massive co-ordinated preventive programme.

Hospitals also need efficient discharge procedures. If patients are discharged later in the day, they may occupy the bed unnecessarily. Delays can be caused by poor co-ordination with pharmacies, as patients wait for take-home drug prescriptions to be prepared for them. If these are not ready by 5.00 p.m., pharmacies often close for the day, forcing patients to stay an extra night on the ward. Other delays can be caused by waits for porters or transport. Relatives often only pick patients up in the evening, once they have come home from work, causing a bed blockage.

7.4.1 Front-office processes

Front-office processes interact directly with customers and will be visible to them and create the customer's experience. These processes may involve personal contact with service employees (face-to-face or by telephone), or interaction through technology such as the organisation's website.

- *Face-to-face.* Here a customer interacts directly with a service employee, as in a restaurant or in the branch of a retailer in a shopping mall. These encounters may be an essential element of the experience and contribute directly to customer satisfaction. A positive interaction between the customer and the restaurant's serving staff may make a major contribution to the enjoyment of the meal.

- *Telephone.* Telephones are typically employed by contact centres to provide advice, complaint handling or order-taking activities. The advantage of these processes/experiences over face-to-face processes/experiences is that they may be provided by a central resource and may therefore be provided at lower cost. Sometimes such activities are relocated to low-labour-cost economies, providing still further efficiency improvements. As customers become more remote, however, there is a much greater possibility of misunderstandings occurring, and service employees missing clues that would be obvious if the customer were physically present.

- *Internet services and other remote interaction.* Internet-based services enable still further efficiency savings to be made. The internet can provide access for customers at all times and enables them to request information or to order products and services as and when they wish. Other remote service processes include contact through letters or mailings, or through automated service processes such as bank automated teller machines (ATMs).

Whatever the mode of interaction it is important that its impact on the customer experience is recognised. It is all too easy for the process to be designed for the benefit of the service provider and ignore the customer's experience.

The customer often plays an important role in front-office processes and is an operational resource (see Figure 7.2). Customers fulfil many roles, providing themselves and others with service, collecting materials and providing information to staff, for example. The 'selection' and 'training' of these 'customer employees' (see Chapter 10) will be critical for the operation's success. The presence of the customer may have benefits in terms of providing an additional resource and better communication, but also disadvantages because the presence of the customer may inject unpredicted variations into the service process (see Chapter 8).

Examples of front-office processes include:

- a management consultant working with a client to develop a diagnosis of the problem to be solved
- a nurse administering prescribed drugs to a patient
- a contact centre agent answering a customer's query about the progress of a mail order shipment
- a prospective customer navigating the website of an electrical goods retailer in order to select and order a computer.

This demonstrates that there is a wide range of possible front-office processes; some have well-defined routines, as in the contact centre enquiry process, whereas others depend almost entirely on the skill, knowledge and expertise of the service provider. In the case of the management consultant, there may be a preferred approach to problem diagnosis, but this process is likely to be extremely flexible.

The final example in the list illustrates a growing trend for the service designer to shift the activity from provider to customer. Indeed some service organisations are trying to encourage

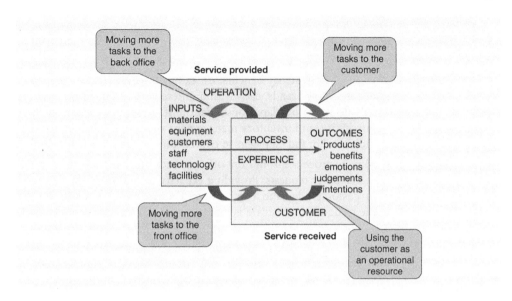

Figure 7.3 Changing front-office and back-office activities

the customer to do more (see Figure 7.3). We are encouraged to use the internet to buy tickets or find out information about holidays and train or plane times, thereby reducing costs for the organisation (and sometimes the costs to ourselves) but usually at the cost of much greater time and effort on the part of the customer. In this case the service designer needs to design a clear customer journey (or route map) to guide the customer through the company's internet site. This demands greater investment in process design and technology, but yields benefits for the provider in lower transaction costs and for the customers in greater access to information and freedom to shop at their own convenience.

All front-office processes have a common problem: the unpredictability of the customer. In the example of the management consultant, the competence and willingness of the client to understand and communicate the true nature of the problem to be studied and solved will have a major impact on the effectiveness of the consultancy process and the customer's experience of it. This variability is also present to some degree in high-volume business-to-consumer services such as fast-food chains. However much the customer is 'trained' to ask for a standard product in a standard manner, there is likely to be a significant percentage of customers who want something different or who disrupt the carefully designed service process by asking for advice or help beyond the expected level.

7.4.2 Back-office processes

Back-office processes (which we will deal with in more detail in the next chapter) operate at a distance from customers and are largely invisible to them. These processes do not have the complication of the customer's presence and are frequently more efficient as a result. Examples of back-office processes include:

- cheque-clearing processes for a retail bank
- computer repair processes
- preparation of food in a restaurant
- most manufacturing processes.

Some organisations are shifting activities from the front office to the back office (see Figure 7.3). Many retail banks, for example, have removed many administration processes from their branches (front-offices) and combine them in high-volume and efficient centralised (back-office) processing centres (such as a cheque-processing centre). There are several reasons why organisations might wish to move activities from the front to back office:

- Common back-office processes serving a variety of customer-facing processes provide cost and consistency benefits. An example would be the company managing a portfolio of restaurant brands, each with a different style, but using food menus with a considerable degree of overlap. Consolidation of common processes such as recipe development, purchasing and inventory management yields major benefit for the company, leaving the individual brand managers to concentrate on the service differentiation issues.

- Moving processes from front office to back office reduces the need for immediate response to customer requests. Providing capacity in the front office to respond to the variations in customer demand (both content and timing) is enormously expensive. Generally, the trade-off in this case is that the customer expects more restricted service and slower response in return for lower prices.

- Expensive technology may require scale to justify its purchase. In this case, the business may operate from a number of locations close to customers, which take orders and deal with other customer service issues, while the bulk of the work is carried out more cheaply at a remote location. In this case longer customer lead times are traded off against lower costs/prices to customers.

Conversely, many organisations are moving some tasks from the back office to the front office (see Figure 7.3). Some organisations recognise that customers need access to technical experts who may, traditionally, be back-office employees, rather than deal through an intermediary such as an account manager or front-line consultant. However, some technical experts have little interest or aptitude in customer service and are best employed at a suitable distance from customer contact!

In some situations, technology has enabled what were back-office processes to be moved to the front office. Not many years ago if you wanted to transfer funds between your bank accounts you had to write a letter to the bank or speak with the bank's contact centre. Now we can do this task, and many more, ourselves via the web, at any time, wherever we are.

7.4.3 Risk and the customer experience

Clearly some experiences/front-office processes are generally more intense in nature for provider and customer alike, as Figure 7.4 illustrates. An aspect of variability in the service encounter is the extent to which the customer perceives some degree of risk or uncertainty. This risk may take a number of forms:

- *Financial risk.* In some situations, it may be difficult for the customer to assess the extent of the risk. The purchaser of a used car does not know how reliable the vehicle will prove

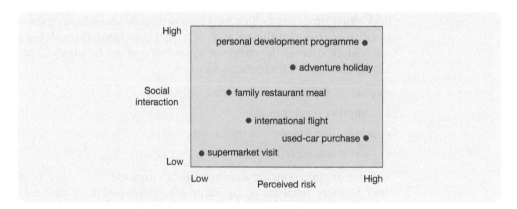

Figure 7.4 Customer-perceived risk and social interaction

to be. In the same way, purchasing a pension plan may feel like an extremely risky activity, particularly for someone who is unfamiliar with financial matters.

- *Physical risk.* Going on an adventure holiday or flying in an aeroplane clearly entails some physical risk. In the former, it could be reasonably expected that customers choosing such a holiday have made some assessment of the risks involved and will see them as part of the expected experience. With an airline flight, although the risk to life and limb is small, it does create a degree of discomfort for many people.

- *Psychological risk.* This type of risk may arise from a number of sources. It may come from the customer's lack of confidence or competence. Anxious customers are likely to prove difficult in the service, not because they are intentionally obstructive, but rather because they channel energies into distracting their thoughts from their concerns. Furthermore nobody likes to feel inferior or incompetent. It is possible that service organisations may make assumptions as to the competence of their customers. If this is combined with a very public display of ignorance, the customer may become either very quiet or very noisy. Finally, a significant number of people find the presence of large numbers of people in close proximity a trial in itself. For some of these 'private' people, any form of social experience can be painful. This may be in stark contrast to the customer-facing employee who may have chosen this role in large part because of its high degree of customer contact.

Figure 7.4 illustrates the extent of social interaction in a routine service experience for a range of service situations. Each of these situations has implications for the extent of desired and possible customer relationships, as discussed in Chapter 4. For example, in the supermarket visit there are limited opportunities for anything more than superficial conversations, whereas a meal in a restaurant where customers and staff know each other reasonably well might lead to interaction that goes beyond the baseline of ordering food.

It should be noted that social interaction is often linked in some way to a mechanism for managing risk. In evaluating the riskiness of the used-car purchase, the customer is frequently judging the trustworthiness of the salesperson. The busyness of the cabin crew on a long-distance flight provides a distraction for those who might be tempted to dwell on the risk of flying, and allows the crew to keep an eye on those who might be suffering from extra anxiety.

There is also a wide range of customer variables that will complicate the customer experience. These include:

- *Customer mindset.* The nature of the service may be reflected in the state of mind of the customer. A customer complaint process will probably not have the customer in the most helpful mindset! On the other hand, customers who are going to a theme park or to a family celebration in a restaurant are more likely to be predisposed to having a good time.

- *Customer mood.* This is somewhat linked to customer mindset, in that people who complain might be expected to be angry, while people going to a celebration might be expected to be in a happier frame of mind. The message here is that it is extremely dangerous to make assumptions about individual customers. Customers who were in a bad mood because they were under pressure or rushed on a previous occasion may turn out to be model customers the next time.

- *Personality clashes.* Some people simply do not get on. They seem to take an instant dislike to each other, or there is something about the other person that reminds them of another difficult or disliked character. Psychologists call this 'transference', which describes the situation when attributes of a previous relationship are transferred to a current relationship. A common example relates to authority figures. If some aspect of the service provider reminds the customer of a hated figure from the past, it is unlikely that this transaction will be successful.

All these factors must be taken into account both in designing the customer experience, and in its day-to-day management.

7.4.4 The need to manage the total chain of processes

Service operations managers need to be able to manage the total chain of processes, which link together to deliver the service to customers or end users (as we saw in Case Example 7.3). Most of us have experienced poor service that results from a lack of co-ordination between activities, a simple example being the person serving you in the restaurant promising you that your meal will arrive in a few minutes without understanding that the kitchen is over-whelmed and the wait will be considerably longer.

Failure to manage end-to-end (e2e) processes leads to inefficiencies across the organisa-tion or chain of organisations that comprise the service supply chain, leading to lack of con-sistency, poor reliability in terms of quality and lead times, and increased cost. We worked with a major technology provider that operated its processes in functional 'silos', with little or no co-ordination between them. The result of this was that some functions were laying off staff one month and rehiring the same staff in the following month. This was clearly damaging to quality, the customers' experience and also efficiency. When this organisation moved to manage and co-ordinate its processes on an e2e basis, the customers' experience as well as operational performance improved dramatically.

In Chapter 6 we described the challenges in managing supply chains which, though sim-ple in concept, prove to be much more complex in application. Service managers must not only deal with the individual issues in managing the back-office and front-office processes, including managing the customers, but also deal with the challenge of integrating activities across the chain. For the technology provider discussed above, many of the individual pro-cess steps required the undivided attention of large numbers of highly qualified engineers. The end result was that artificial barriers were erected between functions, tasks were ill-co-ordinated and activities duplicated. The customers' experience and their satisfaction ranked rather low in the list of operations priorities, with resultant poor performance. On a smaller scale, the conference hotel that does not co-ordinate the activities of room preparation, food service, and greeting and directing course delegates on arrival will not survive in a market that demands both high service standards and competitive pricing.

Managers, including operations managers, have a tendency to draw a boundary around their processes that coincides with the physical or geographic boundary of their responsi-bility. The problem faced by many customers is at the interfaces between the many back-office and front-office processes that together create the total chain of processes. A hospital, for example, comprises many departments: some back-office departments such as cleaning, administration, finance and personnel, and front-office processes such as reception, patient wards, nursing and treatment. While each one may appear to be efficient in its own right, the problems caused by the lack of co-ordination will be felt by customers (not managers or staff) when they attempt to use and experience the service. For example, problems can include:

- There is a desire for prompt treatment, but the doctor's notes have been delayed or are unavailable.
- A request for medicines or equipment is held up because of the paperwork.
- A request is made to turn up on time for an appointment, but there are insufficient car parking spaces outside.

By assessing and designing service processes from the point of view of the 'thing' being pro-cessed, whether it is the customers themselves, something belonging to them such as a file, or information, such as a loan application, we can expose the interface problems. The objective of good service design is to achieve an efficient process from an operations perspective and a seamless experience for the customer. Here are a few 'tests' for seamless experience:[28]

- Customers (or their files, requests, etc.) should
  - flow smoothly through the service
  - experience no discontinuity.

- Staff should
  - ○ take ownership of processes
  - ○ take ownership of individual customers (or their files, requests, etc.).
- Managers should
  - ○ take a process not a functional perspective
  - ○ understand whole processes
  - ○ understand how they fit into the processes
  - ○ work in cross-functional teams to assess and improve the design.

7.4.5 Designing the customer experience

Few service organisations, unlike their manufacturing counterparts, employ specialist 'service engineers' or use 'service laboratories' to help them design, test and evaluate their service and customer experiences. Service design is often an ad hoc or trial and error activity. Most faults and problems are effectively 'designed in', albeit inadvertently, and as a result customers experience poor service and the processes are inefficient.

The keys to good service design are about taking a customer, outside-in, perspective and understanding the whole service process. This may seem obvious, yet in many organisations managers and their staff simply get used to seeing – and therefore ignoring – poor processes, or see them from an internal, inside-out, perspective, thus missing the experience from the customer's perspective.

Several tools and techniques have been developed to help 'engineer' (design and improve) the customer's journey and influence the experience they have:

- customer journey mapping
- walk-through audits
- emotion mapping
- customer experience analysis.

Customer journey mapping

This is a simple, basic but important tool in customer experience design. Journey mapping is the process of capturing the series of touch points that customers encounter during a service or set of services. (This is also sometimes called route mapping for the design of websites, and patient or clinical pathways, care pathways or maps in hospitals, for example.) It can be set out as a simple set of steps. Figure 7.5 shows the first few steps of the customer journey through a hospital. The important point is that it forces staff and managers to look at their processes from the customer perspective, outside-in, and see what the customers have to go through rather than what they see from their inside-out perspective.

Walk-through audits

A walk-through audit undertaken by staff, managers or independent advisors, acting as surrogate customers, can help evaluate and improve the service and the customer's experience.

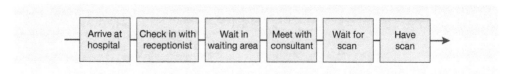

Figure 7.5 Customer journey map of a hospital visit

How easy was it to park the car?	No spaces				Plenty of spaces
	1	2	3	4	5
How did the store look?	Disgraceful				Very clean/tidy
	1	2	3	4	5
How attractive were the displays?	Uninviting				Very attractive
	1	2	3	4	5
How soon were you assisted?	15 mins+		10–15 mins		0–5 mins
	1	2	3	4	5

Figure 7.6 Part of a walk-through audit of an electrical store

The audit should be based on a checklist of questions that guide the 'customer's' assessment of their experience of the service (see, for example, Figure 7.6).[29]

The key requirement for this approach lies in the choice of attributes to assess, and the scales on which the assessment will lie. As the name of the technique implies, it should be developed to identify the critical elements of the customer experience from first contact with the service process through to exit. It is crucial that this audit is not developed solely by people who know the service well, since they are prone to miss detail that they think is irrelevant but customers are affected by. The advantage of this type of approach is that it allows the manager to carry out regular service checks on key aspects of the customer's experience of the service, possibly comparing performance at different times of day between service units.

Emotion mapping

Emotion mapping is a simple but powerful extension of journey mapping and it captures the emotions felt by customers (or managers and staff acting as customers) as they move through the journey. Both negative and positive emotions can be captured (see Figure 7.7),

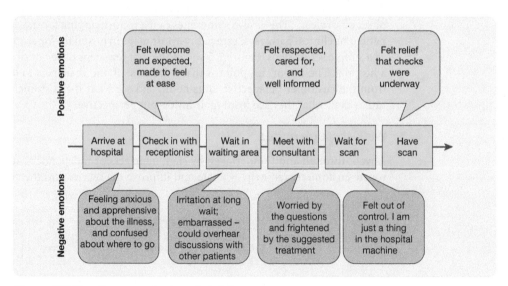

Figure 7.7 Emotion map of a hospital visit

discussed by managers and staff or the customer experience design team, changes made and then re-checked to see the impact of the changes.

Customer experience analysis (CEA)

Customer experience analysis (CEA; sometimes referred to as service transaction analysis or STA)[30] is a development of the walk-through audit and emotion mapping. It incorporates the service concept, the customer experience, the various touch points in the customer's journey and an assessment of each. It also captures the messages and the emotions felt by the customer. This is another simple but powerful tool to assess the customer's experience of a service and help staff and managers improve it. Figure 7.8 provides an example of a CEA applied to a customer of an estate (real estate) agent.

CEA comprises six key stages:

- The service concept needs to be agreed and specified. This alone is often a useful exercise to gain agreement between the employees on the nature of their service and the experience and emotions they want to provide (see Chapter 3).

- Mystery shoppers, independent advisors or preferably managers and their staff walk through the actual customer's journey to assess how customers (might) assess each touch point. Each touch point is briefly described in the left-hand column and an assessment of it in terms of delighting (+), satisfactory (0) or unsatisfactory (−) is noted in the middle columns. (A more detailed 1 to 5, or 1 to 7, scale can be substituted.)

- The interpretation as to why the customer or surrogate customer arrives at this evaluation is entered into the messages column, which describes the deliberate or inadvertent messages provided by the service. For example, an open door may provide an 'inviting' message, while a telephone operator unwilling to deviate from a set script may provide an 'unhelpful and unnecessarily bureaucratic' message to the customer.

- The final column records the emotions felt by the customer during the experience. The top of the column can also be used to record the emotions that customers may feel even before contact is made with the organisation.

Organisation:	Real estate agent	Service concept:		
Process:	Buy a house	Prestige properties with excellent service for the discerning purchaser		
Customer:	Purchaser			
Customer journey	Score			Messages	Emotions
	+	0	−		
Pre-contact					Concerned
Good location	✘			They are accessible/available	Relieved
Good facilities	✘			Expensive but competent	Cared for
Ignored			✘	I am not worth the trouble	Irritated
Introduction		✘		They want to help me	Pleased
Fill in forms			✘	I am just another punter	Annoyed
No pen			✘	They don't really care	Confused
Nothing available			✘	What business are they in?	Frustrated
Go on mailing list			✘	Try somewhere else	Exasperated
Overall evaluation	Poor service design. Little thought for purchasers. Company is not customer orientated. Poor service.				

Figure 7.8 Example of CEA for an estate agent

- The assessments of +, 0 and − are joined to give a very visible profile of the transaction outcomes and an overall evaluation is entered at the foot of the table.
- Working from this sheet, service designers, managers and staff can begin to understand how customers might interpret the service process and then to discuss the improvements that can be made. The exercise can be repeated with a revised process and the profiles readily compared.

CEA attempts to bring a systematic evaluation of a customer's experience of a service. It does not rely upon individual complaints or initiatives but analyses and evaluates the experience, step by step, from the customer's point of view. The main advantages of using CEA are that:

- It requires managers and employees to think about, and express in words, their service concept (including the experience and emotions). This in itself creates an opportunity for healthy debate, and even disagreement, about what the intentions of the organisation actually are.
- It forces managers and employees to see the process from the point of view of the customer (outside-in), increasing their level of customer orientation.
- It asks directly and explicitly what each touch point means to the customer and, importantly, what gives them this impression.
- It assesses the clues designed into the environment (the servicescape), the people and the service process/experience and captures the messages and resulting emotions.

7.5 What is the role of technology in developing the customer experience?

Technology, particularly information technology, plays a key role in many service innovations resulting in often significant changes to the customer experience. The management of innovation, or new service development (NSD), is a key element of the service operation manager's role providing new ways of accessing and interacting with customers. Large service organisations frequently employ formal NSD processes to manage their activities from the creation of ideas, through to successful implementation. These processes usually contain some filtering process, often termed 'stage-gate', to ensure that managers' energies are concentrated on developing innovations consistent with the overall strategy of the organisation.[31]

Innovation ranges from the gradual activity of continuous improvement approaches such as lean thinking and six sigma (see Chapter 12), through to the introduction of new service concepts (see Chapter 3) and the use of technology to radically change the service process (see Chapter 8). In this section we will focus on the role of technology in developing the customer experience.

The vast majority of significant service innovations leading to new customer experiences are linked to information technology, an example being the innovation in the National Library Board of Singapore (Case Example 7.4). We believe that it is a vital aspect of the service operations manager's role to be involved in the innovation process, bringing together an understanding of market opportunity, the development of a culture which encourages innovation, and the ability to understand the impact on, and opportunities to develop, the customer experience, as well as bringing about the desired benefits to the organisation.[32]

7.5.1 Innovation and the role of the internet

Many organisations have restructured their operations to provide electronic-based services for their customers and/or suppliers. Electronic commerce (e-commerce) has challenged

Case Example 7.4	Technology and innovation at the National Library Board of Singapore

The National Library Board of Singapore (NLB) has been making innovative use of a range of technologies to expand its services, to encourage much greater use of the libraries and to reduce costs and increase efficiency dramatically. The NLB was the first public library in the world to prototype radio-frequency identification (RFID) to create its Electronic Library Management System (ELiMS). RFID is an electronic system for automatically identifying items. It uses RFID tags, or transponders, which are contained in smart labels consisting of a silicon chip and coiled antenna. They receive and respond to radio-frequency queries from

Source: Getty Images/AFP

an RFID transceiver, which enables the remote and automatic retrieval, storing and sharing of information. Unlike barcodes, which need to be manually scanned, RFID simply broadcasts its presence and automatically sends data about the item to electronic readers. This technology is already in use in mass transit cashless ticketing systems, ski resort lift passes and security badges for controlled access to buildings.

The National Library Board has installed RFID tags in its 10 million books making it one of the largest users of RFID tags in the world. Customers now have to spend little time queuing; book issuing is automatic, as are book returns. Indeed books can be returned to any book drop at any library where RFID enables fast and easy sorting. Dr Varaprasad, the chief executive, explained:

Customers can drop off books at any time of day or night at the drop off points located on the outside of libraries. Indeed the process is now so well designed that books dropped off one day are on the shelves at the right library by 8.00 the following morning or within minutes if it is from that branch.

From the outside the book drop looks like an ATM machine, but with a large hole covered by a flap. The user places the book in the box below the flap, the book is scanned using RFID and a message on the screen instantly confirms that the book has been deleted from the user's account. In the Jurong Community Library, for example, staff are located right behind the book drop. They take the book and as they pass it by their table it is automatically scanned and they are informed about the required location of the book: the library to which it belongs or, if it belongs to Jurong, the shelf to which it has to be returned. If it belongs to another library it is placed in plastic trays which, when full, are placed in a whooled container which the post office collect and automatically sort and return to the appropriate library using the existing postal system and the Library's RFID technology. If the book belongs to that library it is placed in the appropriate shelf in front of the sorter. Other library staff then take the books from the shelves and return them to the correct shelf in the public part of the library. A returned book can be back on the library shelf within minutes.

Some of the technology is less high-tech. For example, in most libraries books are sorted by staff and located by users using codes typed or written on the bottom of the spine. While this universal system is also used by the NLB, it is supported by colour coding, with each classification, subject, and sub-subject given a different colour. Thus it is easier for users to find the area they are looking for and library staff can easily spot a misplaced book by the break in the colour coding across the shelf.

The NLB has also launched a mobile service via SMS (text messaging). This allows users to manage their library accounts anytime and anywhere through their mobile phones. They can check their loan records, renew their books, pay library payments, and get reminder alerts to return library items before the due-date.

A recent use of its RFID technology coupled with established machine dispenser technology has led to the development of a new concept for the library: book dispensers, aimed at those people who won't or don't come into the library. Mr Chan Ping Wah, NLB's assistant chief executive, explained:

There are, for example, thousands of people working in the CBD (Central Business District) who don't come to the Library. They say, 'I go to work every day. I am very busy. Don't expect me to come to the Library as well'. We could put a book dispenser in the CBD, just like a drinks machine, together with a book drop, and fill it with business books, self-development books, and management magazines. Imagine you are going off for lunch and you work in the CBD. You pass the dispenser, push in your library card, and press the number, out pops the book – 10 seconds – that's all. You go and eat, read the book and drop it in as you go past. It's that easy. Seventy to eighty per cent of these people do not come to the Library, so I have two choices, either build a library in the CBD, which will cost me S$10m, or take a small selection of material to them. These people are only interested in a very small proportion of our stock, so I can select the ones they might want and we can easily and frequently change the selection. This has to be a much better and cheaper alternative. And, I can reproduce this idea at MRT [Mass Rapid Transit] stations for example. You take the MRT, pass a dispenser, get a book and drop it off at another MRT station, that day or another day. We could put lots of these dispensers around the country, targeted on specific groups.

Source: This case example was written by Professors Robert Johnston, Warwick Business School, Chai Kah Hin and Jochen Wirtz, National University of Singapore, and Christopher Lovelock, Yale University. The authors gratefully acknowledge the valuable assistance of Teo Yi Wen, Department of Industrial and Systems Engineering, NUS. The authors would like to thank the interviewees for their participation in this project and Johnson Paul and Sharon Foo for facilitating the research. All Rights Reserved, National Library Board Singapore and the authors, 2007.

traditional business models and has created new ways of accessing customers and providing different customer experiences. It also gives customers much more control as information, such as prices and services offered, are more transparent. Importantly customers can create and then purchase their own customised products and services via the web; intermediaries are no longer required.[33] Examples include holidays, CDs, books and stock trading.[34]

E-commerce is also having a major impact on the cost of doing business, though the costs will vary from organisation to organisation. Thames Water in the UK has identified the costs of various types of transaction for its business (see Table 7.1).

Web-based organisations, either 'brick' (businesses with a physical presence in shopping malls, for example, with additional web channels) or 'click' (internet-only organisations),

Table 7.1 Comparison of transaction costs for letter, telephone and web

Process	Unit cost	% of telephone cost
Letter	£8.30	451
Telephone	£1.84	100
Web		
Query that requires agent response back to customer	£0.92	50
Automated billing query with occasional operator intervention	£0.18	10
Fully automated billing query	£0.09	5

Source: Voss, Christopher (2000), *Trusting the Internet: Developing an Eservice Strategy*, Institute of Customer Service, Colchester. Reprinted by permission of the Institute of Customer Service.

have created multimillion-pound industries in many countries, providing instant, innovative, customer-controlled competition for many traditional service providers. With the availability of the internet in business and homes, email and web-based commerce has become a key way of doing business.

E-service

E-service is the delivery of service using new media such as PCs but also via other technologies such as digital TV, mobile phones and PDAs (personal digital assistants). E-services exist across most of the service sector: for example banks (Egg and FirstE), retailers (Amazon, Nortstar, LastMinute), airlines (Ryanair and easyJet), information (Scoot, Yahoo! and Google) and utilities (Utilities.com). Job hunting, car purchasing, grocery buying, stock trading, community purchasing and auctioning (eBay) can all now be carried out via the web.

For customers this is a very different experience with greater choice and shopping and information gathering available from home or office. For business-to-business customers it means a more transparent market, with transparent pricing, accessibility to more suppliers, the ability to track deliveries and undertake electronic trading such as web-based purchase orders, invoices and payments. The principal advantages for service providers include:

- *Immediate access for customers.* Customers can visit websites at any time of day. The websites do not have to be staffed for 24 hours a day or 365 days a year, but there is the opportunity for customers to make contact at any time.

- *Local business becomes global.* An advertisement for IBM showed an American couple visiting an Italian shop supplying olive oil. The image was of a poor business, struggling to survive, while the couple were running a successful business at home. The couple were amazed to find that, through the internet, this business was supplying customers in the USA, and had a wide range of global customers. Small businesses can now compete globally without the investment in physical sales networks.

- *Opportunities for building brands.* Customers form an impression of an organisation from its website. The messages it conveys, the information it contains, and practical issues such as how easy it is to navigate, all present opportunities to support the brand position.

- *Giving perceived control to customers.* Customers can browse websites at their own discretion. In an online retail operation customers can decide at their leisure what products they wish to purchase, without hassle from sales assistants wanting to boost their commissions, or from other customers in a queue.

- *Making information available to customers.* Websites allow the organisation to make vast amounts of information available for current and potential customers. Again, the advantage is that the customer can choose what to view and what to leave. The organisation does not need to bombard the customer with junk mail, which is frequently seen as both wasteful and intrusive.

- *Linking services.* Opportunities exist to build links between websites of complementary service providers. This creates the ability to form service alliances to increase the range of choice for customers or to create virtual 'one-stop shops'.

Operations implications

The movement to e-service has many important implications for operations management, including how the web can add value, the changing nature of customer relationships, changing service quality factors, and the importance of website design:

- *Value-added service.* For many organisations e-service has led to a reappraisal of what adds value in services and indeed what constitutes a service and customer experience. The support provided by travel agents, for example, is no longer required by some customers, whereas easy access to operators providing a highly customised service may be of significant value. Music shops providing racks of CDs are seen to be of limited value when downloading of preferred tracks to create individualised portfolios is available on customers' phones and computers. Education has also reassessed its teaching role and provides opportunities for web-based learning. From an operation's perspective there has been a shift to front-line activity becoming a predominantly high-value-adding activity focused on the more difficult interactions, with routine and sometimes new services provided more cheaply and directly via the web.

- *The changing nature of customer relationships.* The nature of the relationship with customers has changed as a result of e-service. Instead of the traditional and often specialist outward-facing customer service role providing the interface between the customer and the organisation, web-based services allow the customer to infiltrate right inside the organisation. As a result the nature of customer relationships and the customer experience have been redefined and organisations seek for new ways of dealing directly with the customer. Operations need to consider new ways of tracking customer needs and preferences, and of assessing customer satisfaction and retention. Key questions include:

  o Which customer segments will use web channels?

  o What are the transaction costs?

  o What is the nature of the customer relationships?

  o How will they be maintained?

- *Changing service quality factors.* The attributes of service, the service quality factors, have also changed. New delivery channels have led to new expectations. Research has identified the key quality factors for web-based transactions:[35]

  o *Fast response.* This includes both acknowledgement and service provision, from days or weeks in post-based business to hours and indeed minutes in e-service business.

  o *Automatic response.* Instant acknowledgement of emails to reduce anxiety and uncertainty.

  o *Customer communication.* The provision of information about length of the queue, for example, or how long before a response or delivery is likely.

  o *Choice of phone follow-up.* The option to communicate person-to-person with the company in case of unresolved queries or concerns.

  o *Ability to check status.* The ability to check location of products, or the status of an order, the latest estimated time of arrival of an engineer, or a bank balance.

  o *Links to FAQs.* The ability to see frequently asked questions (FAQs) to deal with obvious queries.

- *Website design.* Design of websites is crucial in attracting customers and keeping hold of them long enough to interact with the site. Good navigability and speed of downloading are vital. Key characteristics of good websites include:[36]

  o *Responsiveness.* This includes both speed of downloading information on to the screen and also the response by the organisation to a customer's request.

  o *Ease of navigation.* This includes limited information on each page, developing a logical and intuitive structure to the pages, and a consistent approach throughout the site. Ease of navigation was found to be a major determinant of customer satisfaction with a website.

  o *Effectiveness.* This includes the time required to perform the tasks on the web and the speed and satisfaction with the service outcome (the delivery of products or the provision of service).

○ *Experience.* Customer satisfaction with the experience of the site may not simply be limited to the above points but may also include the enjoyment of the experience itself, which will encourage customers to return to the site. A range of supportive opportunities and features such as games, music, other links, or additional information, may enhance a customer's experience of a site.

Strategies for change

Professor Chris Voss[37] has identified several key steps in developing an e-service strategy:

- *Upgrade the current service interaction.* Improve existing web-based experience by improving response times, automatic acknowledgements, improving navigation of sites etc.

- *Understand customer segments.* Identify likely users and the services that can be best offered to them via the web.

- *Understand customer service processes and interactions.* Identify service processes, activities, costs and value to help make decisions about the best services or parts of services to make web-based.

- *Define the role of live interaction.* Identify the tasks best suited to live interaction and those best for automation.

- *Make the key technology decisions.* Just because technology is moving rapidly, do not put off purchase decisions since doing so may improve competitive position; however, there may be implementation problems.

- *Deal with the tidal wave.* Be prepared to deal with the significant increase in customer interaction that is associated with web-based services.

- *Customer training.* Develop ways to encourage customers to use the appropriate channels for the appropriate services.

- *Channel choice.* Make decisions about 'brick versus click': a variety of channels of communication or web only, or telephone and web, for example.

- *Web relationships.* Exploit the web experience to build relationships with customers and convert them from browsers into buyers.

Some of the dangers of which internet services must be wary include:

- *Building high expectations.* The immediacy of internet access has many benefits. With online retail operations, customers may place their order in minutes but then wait weeks for delivery.

- *Creating a limited service offer.* Some internet services offer limited choice in order to make the customer process less complex. This may result in compromises, such as the supermarket offering only one brand of a particular category, then only in one size.

- *Focusing on the website at the expense of operational structures.* It can be too easy to focus on the more intriguing and interesting front-end systems for interacting with customers. There is still a need to put in place operational structures to deal with logistics and customer service, for example. The complex problems of moving vast numbers of products to potentially huge numbers of end destinations, or the control and copyright protection of digital information, cannot be ignored. Likewise it is easy to underestimate the high demand for person-to-person interaction to support internet services as individuals wish to make personal contact with the organisation. While new users may need help and reassurance, both old and new users will need to be able to voice their complaints and have them heard.

- *Not managing service recovery.* Internet-based services must develop new strategies for managing customer complaints. As a general principle, service recovery is usually seen to be more effective when there is genuine contact between service provider and customer, often with named people involved from the service organisation. Service organisations must work hard to create that personalisation as a feature of their service recovery mechanisms.

7.6 Summary

What is a customer experience?

- A customer experience is the customer's direct and personal interpretation of their interaction and participation in the service process involving their journey through a series of touch points.
- Because the experience is the customer's personal interpretation of a service, we can't actually design an experience, only the mechanisms for creating it.
- A customer experience statement is a description of the customer's experience and the outcomes from the point of view of the customer, written in an outside-in way.
- A critical part of the experience statement is the identification of the emotions the organisation wants their customers to feel, or more correctly, the emotions that their customers will want to feel as a result of the service.

How can the servicescape be designed?

- The servicescape describes the physical and informational surroundings in which a service is both created and provided.
- Service clues are indicators, stimuli and signals that have been built (purposely or inadvertently) into the service to provide particular messages.
- Messages are what customers will infer about the organisation; its services, management or staff.
- The emotions are how the customer feels, consciously or subconsciously, about those clues and messages.
- The clues and messages not only signal the nature of the experience and create the experience for the customer but they can also influence their behaviour and that of the staff.
- In designing services and experiences, managers need to be concerned to ensure that all messages emanating from all the clues designed into the service are consistent with the service concept and the desired emotions.

How can managers design the customer journey?

- The customer's journey is the series of steps they take and the touch points they have as they experience the service process.
- Front-office processes interact directly with customers and will be visible to them and create the customer's experience.
- Front-office processes may involve personal contact with service employees (face-to-face or by telephone), or interaction through technology such as the organisation's website.
- Some experiences/front-office processes are more intense in nature for provider and customer alike.
- Service operations managers need to be able to manage the total chain of processes (back-office, front-office and external) which link together to deliver the service to customers.

- Several tools and techniques have been developed to help 'engineer' the customer's journey and influence the experience they have, including customer journey mapping, walk-through audits, emotion mapping and customer experience analysis.

What is the role of technology in developing the customer experience?

- Information technology plays a key role in many service innovations resulting in often significant changes to the customer experience.
- Electronic-based services for customers and/or suppliers has created new ways of accessing customers and providing different customer experiences.
- E-service delivers many advantages for service providers though there are many operational implications.
- The key steps in developing an e-service strategy include:
  - o upgrading the current service interaction
  - o understanding customer segments
  - o understanding customer service processes and interactions
  - o defining the role of live interaction
  - o making the key technology decisions
  - o dealing with the tidal wave
  - o customer training
  - o channel choice
  - o web relationships.

7.7 Discussion questions

1 Undertake a customer experience analysis of a service operation, identifying the critical points for management attention.
2 Select a service organisation and identify the key back-office and front-office tasks. What activities have most impact on the customer experience? Could any task move from one area to the other and what would be the implications?
3 Analyse the servicescape of your favourite restaurant/eating place. What aspects encourage the 'right' behaviours in the customers and employees? Are there any aspects of the servicescape that you would change?

7.8 Questions for managers

1 To what extent are the traditional roles of front office and back office in your organisation changing? Has your management approach changed in line with the new task? What are the implications of customers potentially penetrating to the heart of the organisation through mechanisms such as internet-based access?
2 Carry out a walk-through audit and emotion mapping of your service processes, looking at them through the eyes of the customer. What can be improved?
3 What are the opportunities to use technology either to enhance your current customer experience or create a new experience?

Case Exercise   The Southern Provincial Hospice

Kaz Kazeel, Chief Executive of The Southern Provincial Hospice, a registered charity, was considering a report prepared by a brand consultant. She explained the reason for employing the consultant.

Word-of-mouth advertising is really important to ensure that our Hospice has a good reputation in the community. This is not just to attract patients and the funding that comes with them but also to attract donations which form over 80 per cent of our revenue.

Hospices provide end-of-life care for terminally ill patients and their objective is to enable patients to 'die with dignity'. Some patients may stay for lengthy periods; in other cases patients may stay for a week or two to provide a respite for their relatives/carers. All hospices are regulated by the Care Quality Commission (CQC). The essential standards set by the CQC are:

- You can expect to be involved and told what's happening at every stage of your care.
- You can expect care, treatment and support that meets your needs.
- You can expect to be safe.
- You can expect to be cared for by qualified staff.
- You can expect your care provider to constantly check the quality of its services.

Kaz was drawn to one particular paragraph in the consultant's report:

A key element of the Hospice's reputation is the experience you provide. Our evidence suggests that the experience for both patients and their relatives or carers is not as good as some of your competitors. In particular nurses appear to be rushed and procedures executed in an inconsistent manner. Some of the inconsistency is because, like many of your competitors, many of your staff are well-meaning volunteers. Some of them have been involved with the Hospice for several years and, while committed to the Hospice, may be resistant to adopting procedures that might deliver a more consistent service.

Kaz decided that she and her management team would start by focusing on one part of the patient's and their relative's/carer's experience, the admissions process. Admissions were always carried out by a qualified nurse and involved the following main steps:

- Welcome to the Hospice
- Basic information about meals, facilities and visiting periods
- Personal information gathering
- A medical risk assessment.

She asked Tom Zuckerberg (Director of Clinical Services) and Céline du Bois (Head of Volunteers) to prepare an initial review of this process. They firstly looked at the most recent patient survey data. This showed high levels of patient satisfaction with the Hospice care. The overall satisfaction score was 4.7 out of 5. The following was a typical comment from a patient:

They really look after us here and I'm very grateful for all they do. Some things could be better but we don't like to complain or bother them too much.

Tom and Céline then organised a focus group with In-Patient Unit (IPU) nurses to map the patient journey, paying attention to potential patient emotions at each stage. Several issues arose. The negative emotions they captured included feeling stressful, embarrassed, anxious and confused. Also the majority of the attention was focused on the patient and insufficient thought was given to the relatives/carers. The IPU nurses were also concerned that the risk assessments meant that the process was lengthy and involved a lot of box ticking. Furthermore, because this was usually carried out by a senior nurse or the Hospice doctor it sometimes led to the patient having to wait for them to attend.

Questions

1 Develop an experience statement for the Hospice.

2 What issues will Kaz have to deal with to deliver this and how might these issues be overcome?

Suggested further reading

Berry, Leonard L. and Lewis P. Carbone (2007), 'Build Loyalty through Experience Management', *Quality Progress* 40 (9) 26–32

Berry, Leonard L., Lewis P. Carbone and Stephan H. Haeckel (2002), 'Managing the Total Customer Experience', *MIT Sloan Management Review* 43 (3) 85–89

Ding, David Xin, Paul Jen-Hwa Hu, Rohit Verma and Don G. Wardell (2010), 'The Impact of Service System Design and Flow Experience on Customer Satisfaction in Online Financial Services', *Journal of Service Research* 13 (1) 96–110

Edvardsson, Bo, Bo Enquist and Robert Johnston (2005), 'Cocreating Customer Value through Hyperreality in the Prepurchase Service Experience', *Journal of Service Research* 8 (2) 149–161

Edvardsson Bo, Bo Enquist and Robert Johnston (2010), 'Design Dimensions of Experience Rooms for Service Test-drives – Case Studies in Different Service Contexts', *Managing Service Quality* 20 (4) 312–327

Johnston, Robert and Xiangyu Kong (2011), 'The Customer Experience: A Road Map for Improvement', *Managing Service Quality* 21 (1) 5–24

Meyer, Christopher and Andre Schwager (2007), 'Understanding Customer Experience', *Harvard Business Review* 85 (2) 116–126

Morrin, Maureen and Jean-Charles Chebat (2005), 'Person–place Congruency: The Interactive Effects of Shopper Style and Atmospherics on Consumer Expenditures', *Journal of Service Research* 8 (2) 181–191

Pullman, Madeleine E. and Stephani K.A. Robson (2007), 'Visual Methods: Using Photographs to Capture Customers' Experience with Design', *Cornell Hotel and Restaurant Administration Quarterly* 48 (2) 121–144

Shaw, Colin (2005) *Revolutionize Your Customer Experience*, Palgrave Macmillan, Basingstoke

Shaw, Colin (2007), *The DNA of Customer Experience*, Palgrave Macmillan, Basingstoke

Shaw, Colin, Qaalfa Dibeehi and Steven Walden (2010), *Customer Experience: Future Trends and Insights*, Palgrave Macmillan

Silvestro, Rhian and Claudio Silvestro (2003), 'New Service Design in the NHS: An Evaluation of the Strategic Alignment of NHS Direct', *International Journal of Operations and Production Management* 23 (4) 401–417

Verhoef, Peter C., Katherine N. Lemon, A. Parasuraman, Anne Roggeveen, Michael Tsiros and Leonard A. Schlesinger (2009), 'Customer Experience Creation: Determinants, Dynamics and Management Strategies', *Journal of Retailing* 85 (1) 31–41

Zomerdijk, Leonieke G. and Christopher A. Voss (2010), 'Service Design for Experience-Centric Services', *Journal of Service Research* 13 (1) 67–82

Zomerdijk, Leonieke G. and Christopher Voss (2011), 'NSD Processes and Practices in Experiential Services', *Journal of Product Innovation Management* 28 (1) 63–80

Useful web links

For an insight into customer experience design and several more design tools have a look at this excellent site by a leading consulting group:
http://www.beyondphilosophy.com/

For more information on developing customer experiences and journey mapping go to:
http://www.mulberryconsulting.com/

A look at innovation in experiential services from Christopher Voss and Leonieke Zomerdijk:
downloads.experience-economy.com/files/Innovation.pdf

If ever a service sub-sector needed attention to experience design it's the world of car sales. John Reed of the *Financial Times* paints an interesting picture of how BMW is trying to do better:
www.ft.com/cms/s/0/300b6f90-74e6-11e0-a4b7-00144feabdc0.html

A short essay by Tom Neilssen of the BrightSight Group on experience design at jnd.org:
http://jnd.org/dn.mss/words_matter_talk_about_people_not_customers_not_consumers_not_users.html

Notes

1 Johnston, Robert and Xiangyu Kong (2011), 'The Customer Experience: A Road Map for Improvement', *Managing Service Quality* 21 (1) 5–24

2 Berry, Leonard L., Eileen A. Wall and Lewis P. Carbone (2006), 'Service Clues and Customer Assessment of the Service Experience: Lessons from Marketing', *Academy of Management Perspectives* (May) 43–57; Zomerdijk, Leonieke G. and Christopher A. Voss (2010), 'Service Design for Experience-Centric Services', *Journal of Service Research* 13 (1) 67–82

3 Meyer, Christopher and Andre Schwager (2007), 'Understanding Customer Experience', *Harvard Business Review* 85 (2) 116–126

4 Pullman, Madeleine E. and Michael A. Gross (2004), 'Ability of Experience Design Elements to Elicit Emotions and Loyalty Behaviors', *Decision Sciences* 35 (3) 551–578

5 Coffman, J. and D. Stotz (2007), 'How Some Banks Turn Clients into Advocates', *American Banker*

6 Pine, II, B. Joseph and James H. Gilmore (1998), 'Welcome to the Experience Economy', *Harvard Business Review* 76 (4) 97–105

7 Fulton Suri, J. (2003), 'The Experience Evolution: Developments in Design Practice', *The Design Journal* 6 (2) 39–48; Forlizzi, J. and S. Ford (2000), 'The Building Blocks of Experience: An Early Framework for Interaction Designers' in *Designing Interactive Systems 2000*, ACM Press, New York, pp. 419–423

8 Shaw, Colin (2007), *The DNA of Customer Experience*, Palgrave Macmillan, Basingstoke

9 The quote is from Shaw, Colin (2005), *Revolutionize Your Customer Experience*, Palgrave Macmillan, Basingstoke, p. 9

10 Johnston, Robert (2008), 'Internal Service – Barriers, Flows and Assessment', *International Journal of Service Industry Management* 19 (2) 210–231

11 See http://www.wepapers.com/Papers/60205/A_Simple_and_Ordinary_Essay_on_Dhamma and O'Connor, Joseph and John Seymour (2002), *Introducing NLP*, Element, London

12 Parrott, W. Gerrod (ed.) (2000), *Emotions in Social Psychology: Essential Readings*, Psychology Press

13 Purves, Dale, George J. Augustine, David Fitzpatrick, Lawrence C. Katz, Anthony-Samuel LaMantia and S. Mark Williams (2001), *Neuroscience*, 2nd edition, Sinauer Associates, Sunderland, Massachusetts

14 Results of research reported in Pease Allan and Barbara Pease (2006), *Why Men Don't Have A Clue & Women Always Need Shoes*, Orion, London

15 Miller, Suzanne and Kristina Kauffman (2005), *The Brain and Learning*, www.4faculty. org/includes/109r1.jsp

16 Gladwell, Malcolm (2006), *Blink: The Power of Thinking without Thinking*, Penguin Books

17 Brooks, Michael (2010), *13 Things that Don't Make Sense*, Profile Books, London, p. 162

18 Purves, Dale, George J. Augustine, David Fitzpatrick, Lawrence C. Katz, Anthony-Samuel LaMantia and S. Mark Williams (2001), *Neuroscience*, 2nd edition, Sinauer Associates, Sunderland, Massachusetts

19 Pullman, Madeleine E. and Michael A. Gross (2004), 'Ability of Experience Design Elements to Elicit Emotions and Loyalty Behaviors', *Decision Sciences* 35 (3) 551–578

20 See Bitner, Mary-Jo (1992), 'Servicescapes: The Impact of Physical Surroundings on Customers and Employees', *Journal of Marketing* 56 (April) 57–71

21 Berry, Leonard L., Eileen A. Wall and Lewis P. Carbone (2006), 'Service Clues and Customer Assessment of the Service Experience: Lessons from Marketing', *Academy of Management Perspectives* (May) 43–57

22 Berry Leonard L., Eileen A. Wall and Lewis P. Carbone (2006), 'Service Clues and Customer Assessment of the Service Experience: Lessons from Marketing', *Academy of Management Perspectives* (May) 43–57

23 See for example Milliman, Ronald E. (1982), 'Using Background Music to Affect the Behaviour of Supermarket Shoppers', *Journal of Marketing* 46 (3) 86–91

24 See for example Kotler, Philip (1973), 'Atmospherics as a Marketing Tool', *Journal of Retailing* 49 (4) 48–64; Morrin, Maureen and Jean-Charles Chebat (2005), 'Person–place Congruency: The Interactive Effects of Shopper Style and Atmospherics on Consumer Expenditures', *Journal of Service Research* 8 (2) 181–191

25 Mehrabian, Albert and James A. Russell (1980), *An Approach to Environmental Psychology*, Massachusetts Institute of Technology, Cambridge, Massachusetts

26 Bitner, Mary-Jo (1992), 'Servicescapes: The Impact of Physical Surroundings on Customers and Employees', *Journal of Marketing* 56 (April) 57–71

27 See also Armistead, Colin, G. and Graham Clark (1993), 'Resource Activity Mapping: The Value Chain in Service Operations Strategy', *Service Industries Journal* 13 (4) 221–239

28 Developed by Dr Michael Shulver, Warwick Business School

29 Fitzsimmons, James A. and Mona J. Fitzsimmons (2006), *Service Management*, 5th edition, McGraw-Hill, New York

30 For more information see Johnston, Robert (1999), 'Service Transaction Analysis: Assessing and Improving the Customer's Experience', *Managing Service Quality* 9 (2) 102–109

31 Oke, Adegoke (2007), 'Innovation Types and Innovation Management Practices in Service Companies', *International Journal of Operations and Production Management* 27 (6) 564–587

32 Menor, Larry and Aleda Roth (2006), 'New Service Development Competence in Retail Banking: Construct Development and Measurement Validation', *Journal of Operations Management* 25 (4) 825–846

33 Voss, Christopher (2000), *Trusting the Internet: Developing an Eservice Strategy,* Institute of Customer Service, Colchester

34 Gunasekaran, A., H.B. Marri, R.E. McGaughey and M.D. Nebhwani (2002), 'E-commerce and Its Impact on Operations Management', *International Journal of Production Economics* 75 (1–2) 185–197; Zhu, Faye X., Walter Wymer and Injazz Chen (2002), 'IT-based Services and Service Quality in Consumer Banking', *International Journal of Service Industry Management* 13 (1) 69–90

35 Voss, Christopher (2000), *Trusting the Internet: Developing an Eservice Strategy,* Institute of Customer Service, Colchester

36 Voss, Christopher (2000), *Trusting the Internet: Developing an Eservice Strategy,* Institute of Customer Service, Colchester

37 Voss, Christopher (2000), *Trusting the Internet: Developing an Eservice Strategy,* Institute of Customer Service, Colchester

Chapter 8
Designing the service process

Chapter objectives

This chapter is about how to design the service process.

- Why is service process design important?
- What are the main types of service process?
- How can managers 'engineer' service processes?
- How can service processes be repositioned?
- How can managers harness technology in service process design?

8.1 Introduction

In the previous chapter we discussed design from the customer's perspective, designing their experience of the service provided (the service process or service delivery process). In this chapter we want to look at the design of the service process from a provider's perspective with a focus on efficiency. That is not to say one or the other is more important; the process has to be designed both to be efficient and to deliver the right experience, 'products' and benefits as required by the service concept. We will also cover the design of the non-visible, back-office, processes and the role of technology in service process design.

Processes are the lifeblood of the service operation. Rather like DNA providing the pattern for a living organism, a good process ensures that service is delivered consistently, time after time, and creates the desired experience and outcomes for the customer, thus delivering the service concept. Process design, whether for call centres, doctors, social workers, or management consultants, describes and prescribes the procedures to be followed and how staff will use or interact with other resources such as materials or equipment in order to deliver the service concept. Let's take the example of a call centre. Call centre agents in a telephone bank are given clear guidance as to how to speak to the customer, what questions to ask, and what performance standards are expected. The agents also have access to screens on their computers to prompt them to ask particular questions or to help them answer routine enquiries. Finally, the information system will guide the agents through the customer data requirements to be filled in during or immediately after the call.

Moving to a macro level, process managers and designers have to pay attention to how the various activities or sub-processes link together to provide the service concept. In the telephone bank the service is not simply that delivered by the agent but also involves loan application processes, credit card issuing processes, international funds transfer processes and so on. The whole interrelated chain of processes needs to be carefully designed, managed and controlled to deliver value to customers and to the organisation. Unfortunately, many large organisations have such a complex web of processes, both functionally and regionally based, that co-ordination across processes seems to be an almost impossible task.

Designing and then controlling service processes is not easy (we will deal with control in the next chapter). Processes are as varied as the service organisations of which they are a part. Some are extremely flexible, able to meet a wide variety of customer requirements using the same set of resources. Some management consultants, for example, are able to utilise a wide range of approaches in developing customised solutions for their clients. Other processes, such as many call and contact centre operations, are much more closely defined in order to achieve benefits of consistency and efficiency. In a similar manner, some processes depend a great deal on the skill, knowledge and expertise of individual employees, such as medical doctors in general practice, while other processes employ resources such as technology or information systems to reduce the dependence on individual skills, thus enabling the service organisation to deal with greater volumes and to grow geographically.

8.2   Why is service process design important?

Excellent service – which satisfies the customer and meets the strategic intentions of the organisation – is usually the result of careful design and delivery of a whole set of interrelated processes. These processes not only 'process' customers to create the customer experience but also process materials, information and even staff. Many service processes are therefore quite complex, involving many interrelated processes, departments, people, decisions and activities.

Although the service process is only one element of the service operation, it is the 'glue' that holds the rest – the customers, staff, equipment and materials – together. And it is the mechanism that delivers the service concept, creating the customer's experience and delivering the service outcomes.

It is important to note that when we are talking about processes we are not simply referring to the point where the customer receives the service. Service providers that consistently meet both cost and quality targets know that they must manage the chain of processes from start to finish (often designated end-to-end, or e2e, processes) rather than simply the final stage of delivery to customers. It is also crucial to remember that services frequently fail because they have been inadequately designed and executed.

8.3   What are the main types of service process?

As we defined in Chapter 1 a service is a process or activity, and the service received by the customer is their experience of the service provided which results in outcomes such as 'products', benefits, emotions, judgements and intentions. The service process is the set of interrelated activities (processes) that together, in an appropriate sequence, delivers the service concept and creates the customer experience and outcomes. Some processes involve the treatment of the customer (or user) or something belonging to them. The customer often performs some role in the service process or in a part of it (co-production). Most processes require other resources such as staff, equipment and facilities. All processes, whether front-office or back-office, process customers, material and/or information. The back office of a restaurant processes food and turns ingredients into finished dishes. Its front office processes customers during their evening and provides them with a great experience of which the food is only a part. An estate agent processes information about houses and takes customers through the buying or selling process.

There are three key questions operations managers need to ask to understand the nature of their service processes to help them 'engineer' their processes:

- How much service variety does the process have to deal with?
- What type of process is it, in terms of the volume and variety that it can handle?
- Where is the value added for the customer?

8.3.1 Service product variety

In simple terms a car servicing shop might be seen to have one end-to-end process, which includes sub-processes or tasks, such as customer greeting and discussion of the job to be done, initial diagnosis, parts procurement, car service, customer billing and car return. Yet through this one process may flow a variety of types of jobs: some may be routine, such as a 10,000-mile oil change; others may be less routine but still standard activities, such as a gear box repair; others may be non-standard activities that happen infrequently and for which it can be more difficult to predict how long they will take or how many resources they will require, such as dealing with an intermittent electrical fault. The first step in designing and managing service processes is to understand the mix of these 'runners', 'repeaters' and 'strangers'[1] which the process has to deal with.

Runners

Runners are standard activities predominantly found in high-volume operations, such as the request for the balance of a bank account made to a telephone call centre. From an operations point of view, runners

- are often relatively predictable, allowing the operations manager to match resources to forecast demand with reasonable accuracy
- lend themselves to efficient operations through tight process control or automation.

Repeaters

Repeaters are also standard activities, possibly more complex than runners, but which occur less frequently. Repeaters may be created by default rather than by design, when an organisation significantly expands the range of services it offers. This may mean that processes that were designed to handle relatively few standard activities must now deal with much greater variety. Banks have experienced this problem, having moved from providing one or two standard deposit or chequing accounts to offering 'personalised financial packages'. As a result,

- repeaters often absorb more resource than an equivalent runner because lower volumes cannot justify process automation
- there may be some degree of relearning or readjustment of a process required for each reoccurrence of the repeater activity if the previous occurrence was some time in the past.

Strangers

Strangers are non-standard activities, perhaps associated with a one-off project or activity. New service introduction may give rise to stranger activities in the first instance, which usually will migrate to repeaters or runners as service volumes increase. Strangers are the least efficient and indeed the most difficult processes for operations managers to deal with because

- it may be more difficult to forecast demand
- the resources required to deal with demand may be less certain
- they are least well defined in terms of resource requirements.

However, an organisation that is used to dealing with strangers will be much more flexible and adaptable than one that is used to dealing with repeaters or runners.

Managing runners, repeaters and strangers

Table 8.1 gives some examples of these three types of activities in three different organisations. The problem is that all three can and sometimes do exist within the same organisation, such as the car servicing shop described earlier.

Importantly, the relative mix of these activities will suggest the most appropriate type of service process. In addition, the type of service process may limit or restrict the variety of activities that can be carried out. A car service shop that accepts a wide range of jobs will need to have a more flexible process than one that focuses totally on doing oil changes. It will also need more flexible and skilled mechanics and will not have as high a throughput. The oil change specialist may have a high throughput and will need less skilled mechanics but will also need to turn away the potentially higher-margin jobs that are outside its area of competence.

This takes us back to the typology of service processes we introduced in Chapter 2: capability and commodity processes based on the key parameters of volume and variety.

We will also return to the idea of runners, repeaters and strangers in Chapter 11, where we will examine the problems posed for resource management when the mix of service requirements changes faster than the processes. For example, if the mix of surgical procedures in the hospital changed so that there were fewer complex or new operations, and more simple, routine procedures, this might mean that some of the more highly qualified (and paid) surgeons would be surplus to requirements and that there might be insufficient junior doctors to carry out the more mundane activities. A possible short-term solution might be to employ the higher-paid consultant surgeons on routine work. This would dramatically affect the cost base and would no doubt seriously reduce the morale of the surgeons!

Table 8.1 Runners, repeaters and strangers

Service	Runners	Repeaters	Strangers
Car service	Standard oil change and maintenance Gear box repair Replacement of brake pads	Body panel replacement	Intermittent electrical fault Product recall
International airline	Passenger check-in Baggage handling In-flight service Maintenance Scheduling	Aircraft overdue or replacement required 'Serious' customer complaints	Special charter for VIPs
Hospital	Patient records Standard operations Recovery and rehabilitation Domestic services	Surgery with 'complications' Dealing with difficult or distraught patients and relatives	New surgical procedures

8.3.2 Types of process: volume and variety

In this section we start by providing more detail of the key differences between the extremes of high volume/low variety and low volume/high variety, and capability and commodity processes. We then go on to describe processes that do not lie between these extremes, off-diagonal processes. In Section 8.5 we discuss the issues in managing process transitions.

Capability processes

Processes that lie in the top left-hand corner of the volume/variety matrix (Figure 8.1) are typically focused on providing a capability for their customers or users, rather than a 'pre-prepared' service. As such they do not have the clarity of service concept that characterises high-volume consumer services, but they have much more flexibility to change service outcomes, customer experience and service delivery processes. These processes are more suited to managing strangers than runners. Examples of this type of service include:

- traditional professional services, such as lawyers or accountants, particularly those small firms that deal with a wide variety of work for their clients
- companies that sell their creative ability, such as advertising agencies, software developers and engineering design consultants
- organisations that adapt their capabilities to satisfy a wide range of customer needs, such as consultants, counsellors and management development providers.

A key task for all these organisations is to ensure that they maintain their skill base. The firm of lawyers must ensure that it retains its capability to deal with employment or patent law, just as the business school must employ professors of the major management disciplines. A number of attributes generally apply to this type of service operation:

- The service concept is based on the provision of a particular skill set or knowledge base.
- This capability frequently resides with specific individuals, and may be lost to the organisation when the individual leaves.
- Few processes are documented, partly because there is no consistency in types of activity performed, and partly because the individual service providers may resist what appears like an attempt to impose controls on their autonomy.

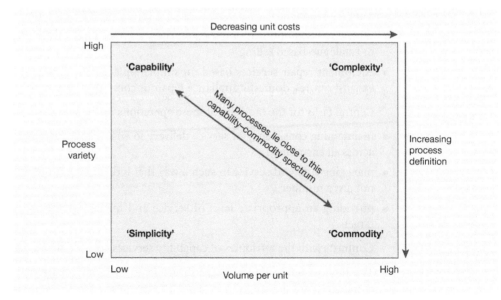

Figure 8.1 Volume–variety matrix

- There is little consistency in approach to tasks. Similar tasks may follow different routes through the organisation, at times dictated by the whims of certain individuals in the organisation.
- Research and development is centred on the individual's capability to deal with a wider range of customer requirements.
- Many professional services are in this category, moving further down the diagonal towards commodity as volume and standardisation increase.
- Such processes tend to be service partnerships or service projects (see the key decision area matrix in Section 8.3.4).
- Strangers and repeaters dominate activities, with few runners except in support functions.

Managers of capability operations must be good at assessing the impact of an additional task on an existing workload. So, for example, a firm of management consultants must be able to negotiate with a new client as to when a new assignment can be carried out without adversely affecting existing assignments. This is a major issue because the firm's real capacity will alter rapidly as assignments call for differing areas of expertise. This is complicated still further by the fact that the level and nature of expertise may not be fully understood at the point where contracts are signed.

Commodity processes

Commodity processes are ideal for runners. These operations are exemplified by high-volume consumer services such as fast-food restaurants, general insurance providers and retailers. The service concept for these organisations is of necessity clear and relatively rigid. This particularly applies when service must be delivered across several service locations, by a wide variety of service employees.

Whereas capability operations offer 'solutions' to their customers, commodity operations are much clearer in their definition and marketing of the service concept. They will tend to compete on their ability to provide consistent operational quality at a competitive price.

One of the most significant service dimensions will frequently relate to the availability of service, through the absence of physical queues or through rapid telephone response.

Examples of these service operations include:

- multi-site services, such as restaurant chains, supermarkets or other retail operations
- centralised communication-based services, such as 'direct' insurance, telephone banking or catalogue-based selling
- equipment repair services based on simple replacement processes, such as car tyre and exhaust centres, domestic appliance repair or computer service.

Central tasks for the majority of these operations include:

- maintaining consistency of service delivery to ensure that customer expectations are met across all encounters
- managing standard service in such a way that individual customers still feel that they are not just a number
- providing an appropriate level of service and managing resource productivity to tight targets.

Contrasts with the attributes of capability services are as follows:

- The service concept is translated into a series of tightly controlled processes, with little opportunity for deviation from standard activities.
- Customer-facing employees are likely to be relatively junior staff and poorly paid.

- The organisation depends on focused training, often of a few days' or weeks' duration, for its customer-facing staff, as compared to several years' professional training for key staff in capability operations.
- Capacity is generally well defined, with an emphasis on developing flexibility to deal with rapid changes in demand.
- The operational focus is typically that of the service factory or DIY service (see KDAM in Section 8.3.4 below).
- The types of service that lie in this area are mass services.
- Activities are typified by runners, with an increasing proportion of repeaters as the organisation seeks to differentiate through mass customisation.

In contrast to capability operations, the central task of managers in commodity operations is to create a planned environment where the various activities of its constituent parts can be carried out as efficiently and consistently as possible. Managing the fast-food restaurant supply chain requires forecasts and schedules to be given to all suppliers in a timely fashion, with as few last-minute changes as possible. Thus capability managers may strive to get better at reacting to changes, whereas commodity managers strive to get better at reducing unforeseen variances to plan. This is important to note as we discuss later in this chapter the challenge of moving along the capability–commodity spectrum. It may be possible to change the process design, but it is certainly harder to change the behaviour of process managers!

Profiling processes

Figure 8.2 summarises key points from the preceding sections in the form of a chart (capability–commodity profile) to assist operations managers to locate their existing processes on the

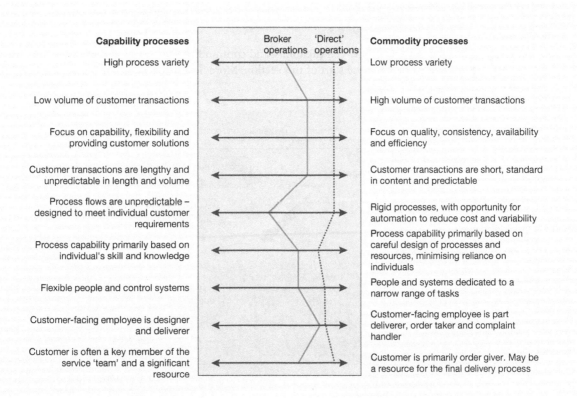

Figure 8.2 Motor insurance process profile

capability–commodity spectrum and to determine whether action needs to be taken to make appropriate adjustments. The figure illustrates the profile for a motor insurance provider, showing the difference between its direct operation, providing policies to individual users, and its support for insurance brokers.

Use of this profiling approach identifies the potential mismatches to be addressed by service managers. These frequently arise because the service task has changed, whereas the delivery processes have not evolved to meet the new requirements adequately. For the insurance company in Figure 8.2, a shift from broker operations to direct operations may well mean that the processes are more flexible than necessary and some staff may be overqualified for their new duties.

This move would almost certainly mean a significant change in management style and, of course, a change in the priorities among the key performance indicators utilised. The direct operation would probably concentrate on fast response and low cost, while broker operations would place more emphasis on flexibility and personal service.

It should be understood that using the volume–variety matrix or the capability–commodity profile to compare and contrast processes in totally different service sectors is of limited value. It is almost meaningless to compare a small firm of corporate lawyers (capability) with a restaurant chain (commodity). It is more helpful to compare different process types within the same sector, as in Figures 8.2 and 8.3.

Hernia operations are now standard procedures, although there was a time when they were in the 'pioneer' category (see Figure 8.3). There are many advantages to being in this commodity area, as the Shouldice Hernia Hospital demonstrates.[2] Hernia operations are carried out there most cost-effectively, with the lowest amounts of 'rework' and with high levels of patient satisfaction. This focused approach has now been replicated across the world and extends to similar surgical procedures. In this case, the move from capability towards commodity does not deskill the surgeon, but it does mean that surgeons may become increasingly specialised and less able to revert to more general surgery.

Off-diagonal processes

The 'line of best fit' between capability and commodity is in reality rather wider than it was portrayed as being at the start of this section. More flexible processes, better support systems

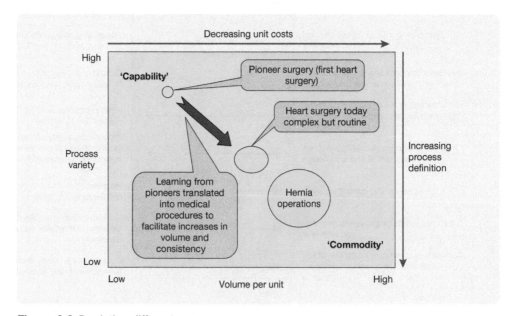

Figure 8.3 Depicting different surgery processes

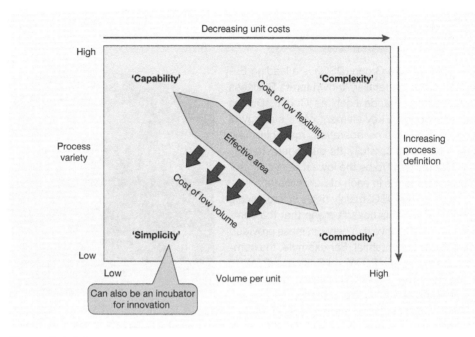

Figure 8.4 Off-diagonal processes

and better training for employees will mean that the 'effective area' can be extended (see Figure 8.4). However, operations may sometimes find that their processes are operating suboptimally because there is not an exact fit between existing processes and market requirements.

Operating in the complexity area

Processes in the top right-hand corner of Figure 8.4 are attempting to provide high-volume services that are capable of great flexibility. Processes in this area, sometimes referred to as 'mass customisation',[3] attempt to provide the customer with whatever they want, however they want it and wherever they want it at an affordable price. One example of this is telephone and internet banking which, although not providing the complete range of banking services, provide a wide range of services, 24 hours a day, every day of the year, accessible from any telephone or computer, and at little cost.

Any operations wishing to push their processes in this direction need to think very carefully about the technology and skills required to operate effectively, and profitably, in this area. We will return to this area at the end of this chapter.

Operating in the simplicity area

The issue here is that the operation is unlikely to be operating as efficiently as it might because it has low volume. This could mean that either resources are underutilised or the organisation is unwilling at this stage to invest in process technology to decrease its unit costs. However, this position could suit a small niche player, such as a microbrewery that produces very small quantities of a single beer for consumption in one or two outlets, or a corporate lawyer with just one or two clients. It is likely that the margins earned by these niche players far outweigh any operational inefficiencies.

However, this position (in the bottom left-hand corner of Figure 8.4) could be employed by large or small organisations as a pilot or as a start-up operation, hence its alternative description as the 'incubator'. PC World Business (Case example 8.1) illustrates the approach taken by the Dixons Store Group to ensure that new businesses move rapidly from the incubator to the 'commodity' position as rapidly as possible.

Case Example 8.1   PC World Business

The Dixons Store Group (DSGi) is a leading European electrical retailer, known for its Business to Consumer Brands such as Currys, Dixons and PC World. A key element of its strategy is to be a high-volume operation, managing unit costs extremely carefully. Its published strategy includes the aim 'To be the lowest cost operator in cost ratio terms in each of our markets'.

It's clear that DSGi mainly deals in large-scale operations but this doesn't mean that the company is afraid to invest in new business provided there is growth potential. For example, the company also includes PC World Business (PCWB), a business-to-business IT retailer, building on the strength of the PC World brand.

As PCWB has grown and developed, more services have been launched to strengthen the service offer. These include finance packages, and the provision of what PCWB terms 'Remote IT Management'. This is the provision of the service traditionally delivered by an in-house IT department.

In order to meet demand, PCWB employs more than 1,000 technical advisors and has established a 500-seat IT helpdesk. Although it has some way to go to meet the scale of PC World, it is now firmly established in the DSGi portfolio. In order to leverage the scale of the Dixons Store Group, technical support is provided by another DSGi business, The Tech Guys. This is a computer technical service provider, employing 3,000 support staff, supplying technical support to both PC World and PC World Business customers.

Source: This case example was developed from material on the PCWB website (www.pcwb.com) and with the assistance of Richard Harrison, Operations Director, PC World Business.

8.3.3 Adding value for the customer

In operations we must be careful to recognise where value is added, or perhaps more accurately where value should be added. We are sometimes guilty of not being sufficiently clear in our definitions and therefore the analysis of added value becomes muddled. The main types of value (benefits of good service) we introduced in Chapter 1 were:

- Customer value, value-in-use: what the customer recognises and pays for (better for the customer)
- Staff value: a better experience for the staff
- Organisational contribution: satisfied customers, improved processes and reduced costs, profitability/financial success, brand value, competitive advantage, and strategic success (better for the organisation).

When we receive a level of service that is beyond our expectations, we sometimes term this added value, though it might more accurately be described as a high perceived level of service. The service process designer must be clear in these definitions in order to avoid solving the wrong problem. Take a bank, for example. We as customers, and even the bank's staff and management, may say that personal interaction between customers and the bank's staff is important, and indeed it is. But from an operations perspective the bank is essentially a big factory that processes millions of financial transactions every day, most of which, such

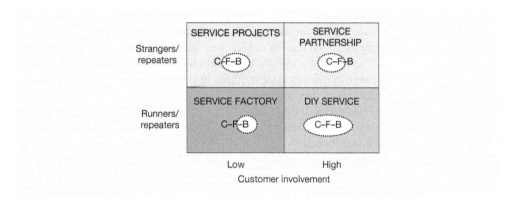

Figure 8.5 Key decision area matrix (KDAM)

Source: Adapted from Larsson, R. and D. Bowen (1989). 'Organisation and Customer: Managing Design and the Coordination of Services', *Academy of Management Review* 14 (2) 213–233 and Clutterbuck, D., G. Clark and C. Arnistead (1993), *Inspired Customer Service*, Kogan Page, London

as maintaining standing orders and direct debits, we do not see or even think about (unless there is a problem!). The bank certainly has to get its customer interaction right but the main value it provides is in handling our accounts and in managing financial movements.

It is therefore important to view service operations in their entirety, i.e. the multiplicity of interrelated processes, both front-office and back-office, and recognise where the bulk of the value-adding activity lies.

8.3.4 Identifying the key decision areas

The key decision area matrix (KDAM) (see Figure 8.5) provides a means of categorising service processes. This matrix helps us understand where the prime value is added and therefore what should be the key focus of attention for operations managers. The figure identifies four types of decision area (the area within the dotted line) in the relationship between C, F and B (customer, front office and back office), for runners/repeaters and strangers/repeaters depending upon the level of customer involvement.

Before exploring this matrix further, it is necessary to define customer involvement. By this we mean the extent to which the customer is an intrinsic part of the service delivery process, and thus can be thought of as a resource for the organisation (see also Chapter 10). There is a difference therefore between customer contact and customer involvement. For example, if you stay in a luxury hotel, the service operation can be described as having high customer contact rather than requiring high customer involvement. Customers directly experience the facilities of the hotel, and there are large numbers of staff to attend to their every need. The hotel would move higher on the customer involvement scale if you were required to make your beds and cook your own meals!

The service factory

A service factory is a high-volume, low-variety operation dealing in runners and occasionally repeaters, with low customer involvement. Examples include high-volume consumer services, such as retail operations, restaurant chains and many financial services. The key decision area for these services is in the back office, where the prime task is efficient and consistent, high-volume operations. For example, if a bank wishes to offer a faster cheque-clearing service to its customers, it will examine the capability of the back office first and foremost. These operations will place as much of the value-adding activities as possible in the back office.

This is not to say that there is not a role for the front-office staff. The front office's role is to make this service factory seem friendly and to give the impression that each customer is valued and special. The front office, however, has no ability to offer significantly different services to individual customers. These organisations may look to provide a degree of personalisation in the front office, but without encouraging customers to make too many special requests, which tend to reduce the efficiency of the operation as a whole.

There is also a role for customers in the service factory. Customers are 'trained' to fit into the service delivery system, filling in the right forms, standing in the correct queues and not making non-standard requests.

The service factory is potentially efficient and consistent (particularly across multi-site operations), but may feel impersonal to customers. There may also be significant problems with low morale in the front office as staff deal with mismatches in customer expectations compared to service delivery.

Do-it-yourself service

DIY services are high-volume, low-variety processes, with runners and repeaters but with high levels of customer involvement. We find examples of this type of service in the leisure industry, in tourism and in sports and fitness clubs. Self-service retailing is also moving from the service factory towards the DIY service quadrant. It could be argued that many internet-based retail services are also found in this quadrant.

We have drawn the key decision area around the total customer, front office and back office chain. This reflects the fact that these services have to balance decisions in all areas. Significant effort lies in the design work for the initial set-up of facilities and networks. Amazon.com has devoted much design time to its internet service and in setting up back-office distribution activities to fulfil customer orders. The capability of the customer must also be included in the design brief to ensure that the service runs smoothly. In the case of Amazon.com, the front-office decisions regarding the design of the website and its ease of access and use by customers are also critical.

Some of these internet-based services rely on significant customer capability in terms of both expertise and equipment. The music sites that allow the customers to download album tracks, creating their own customised collection, currently require a level of sophistication beyond some potential users.

Service projects

Service projects utilise processes that are predominantly repeaters and strangers, with limited customer involvement. A good example of this type of service is provided by a market research company. There is frequently an intensive initial diagnosis/specification phase carried out with the customer by front-office personnel. The second phase consists of research work carried out by staff in the back office without the presence of the customer. There is usually a final stage where results are presented and discussed.

In many small market research firms, of course, the front and back offices are one and the same, although this becomes less common as the organisation grows. The principle remains, however, that service project organisations must have much closer links between front office and back office than is necessary for the service factory, not least because they will be dealing predominantly with strangers and some repeaters, rather than runners, with resultant variability in demand volumes and process type.

The front-office staff must have more skill and flexibility than in a service factory. When face-to-face with a potential customer, front-line employees or service professionals must be able to demonstrate considerable technical as well as interpersonal skill. They must have considerable knowledge as to both capability and capacity of the combined front office/back office, often making commitments on behalf of the organisation based on their diagnosis of the customer's requirements.

Service partnership

Service partnerships involve highly customised service processes with high customer involvement, dealing in either strangers or repeaters. The key decision area is around the customer (or client)–front office partnership. The theme is very much one of co-development, where the service provider is intimately involved with the client. An example is provided by the sort of consultant who works with a management team in the process of strategy development, where there is an expectation that part of the service outcome is that the consultant will mentor management team members as part of their personal development. In this case, the customer is an integral part of the service process.

Because customer and service provider are so directly linked, the effectiveness of this service is often a function of the personal chemistry between the individuals involved. In small consultancies one of the guiding principles is often that consultants will only work with people they like, on the basis that a good working relationship is fundamental in developing a satisfactory outcome.

The challenge for these organisations is to manage the communication link between front office and back office. The back office often provides administrative support and may be perceived to be of lower status than the 'professionals' in the front office.

A mix of decision areas

The challenge for larger, complex service organisations is that all four types of key decision areas may be represented in their operations. To take the example of a bank:

- Service factory: retail banking for consumers – high volume, standard accounts.
- Service projects: business loans for entrepreneurs.
- Service partnership: managing investment portfolios for large corporate clients.
- DIY service: internet and telephone banking.

It is important to recognise and manage this diversity. It is increasingly true that 'one size fits all' is not appropriate. Each operation will require different performance criteria, technology, management style and, ideally, different processes and people.

Task allocation

Operations managers must make the decision as to which tasks are carried out in the front office, which in the back office, and which by the customer. As the service concept extends or changes, it is likely that the positioning of the service, as shown in Figure 8.6, will also change and so too will the allocation of tasks. Figure 8.6 illustrates some examples of task reallocation, which are described below.

- *A reinsurance firm* operating in the City of London has traditionally based its business on cultivating strong personal client relationships, but is under increasing pressure to demonstrate value and to deliver cost reductions, moving from a service partnership approach to a service project environment. The firm realised that the time spent with individual clients

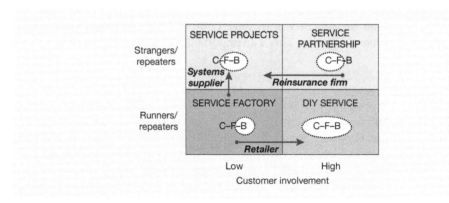

Figure 8.6 Changing task allocation

was becoming less effective and contributed to the retention of an ever-decreasing number of clients. This shift required a major culture change to reduce the time spent with clients, and to develop standard ways of working. It also required a significant investment in information systems to support this change.

- *A retailer* is moving from a physical presence in a shopping mall to also providing internet-based shopping. This represents a move from an organisation largely focused on back-office functions, such as purchasing and logistics, to one that must add to this the ability to design systems that enable the customer to play an increasing role in the delivery system. These systems require a greater sophistication on the part of the customer, perhaps forcing the service provider to give greater thought to the implementation of new technology in terms of initial customer training.

- *The systems supplier* has largely been concerned with the provision of telecommunications and computer 'boxes'. Its operations have been focused on the production of these systems as efficiently as possible in the back office. As product margins have decreased through competition, the company has recognised the need to provide more customised 'solutions' to its customers. The front-office role has moved from being a sales-order-processing activity to providing applications consultancy. The major changes for this organisation involve moving expertise that has traditionally been located in a back office role (remote from customers) to a front-office activity with significant customer interaction. It is also vital for front office and back office to create more integration in their processes to ensure that greater variation in customer requirements can be dealt with effectively.

The key decision area matrix (KDAM) can give an insight into the impact of changes in service concept as they relate to the changing role of the three components of customer, front office and back office. It should be noted that the introduction of new services may mean that traditional distinctions between front and back office may become somewhat blurred. This has been the experience of organisations implementing multimedia contact centres to replace person-to-person service or telephone call centres. The result has been that customers frequently have access to areas within the organisation hitherto 'protected' from customer contact. This clearly poses both a challenge and a significant opportunity for service process design.

8.4   How can managers 'engineer' service processes?

In Chapter 7 we provided several tools that can be used to design the customer experience. These are important because they focus on an outside-in perspective. However, there are several other tools that are very important for designing new service processes and to help assess and improve the design of existing ones, whether back-office or front-office. These include process mapping, lean thinking, kaizen, six sigma, and value stream mapping. Most of these tools we will cover in Chapter 12 on driving continuous improvement. Here we will cover process mapping. This is an important and powerful tool.

8.4.1 Process mapping

Process mapping is the charting of a service process in order to assist in the evaluation, design and development of new or existing processes. There are many types of charting methods in use. However, the essence of mapping is to capture all the activities and their relationships on paper, which normally requires a team of people who understand the various aspects of the process. It is perhaps not surprising that this activity is extremely time-consuming but it can yield some significant results – the first of which is usually the emergence of a shared view and understanding of a process by all those involved in it, and thus a realisation of their role in the end-to-end process.

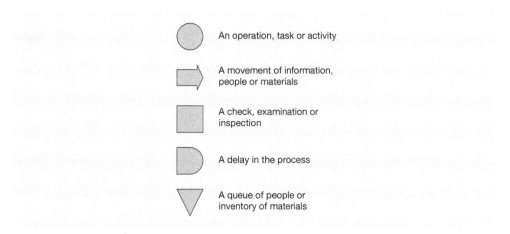

○ An operation, task or activity

⇨ A movement of information, people or materials

▢ A check, examination or inspection

◗ A delay in the process

▽ A queue of people or inventory of materials

Figure 8.7 Traditional operations process mapping symbols

Gaining maximum benefit from process mapping involves two issues, mapping and mapping tools, and turning the map from a descriptive into an analytical tool.

Mapping and mapping tools

The first question to be considered at the start of a mapping activity is the level or degree of detail. Process maps can be used at a macro level, depicting major activities and their relationships, or at a micro level, mapping all the detailed tasks involved in a process or a part of a process, or indeed somewhere in between. The minimum level depends upon the use to which the maps are to be put but is usually that which exposes the overall process and where the main elements are visible. More detailed individual maps can be created if and when required. It is also important to agree mapping symbols and structures. The traditional operations symbols are shown in Figure 8.7.[4]

Different symbols may be appropriate to use in other circumstances and may be more visual and meaningful for the people developing the map, examples being picture of a computer for a computer interface, a queue of people to depict a queue, an in-tray to depict a pile of files in an in-tray. The symbols chosen should be appropriate, but should be common and understandable with a single meaning.

The lines on the chart may be coloured to depict flows of different materials – blue for customers and green for information, for example – or to depict different volumes or routings, such as standard processes versus non-standard processes.

The example in Figure 8.8 shows a simplified process for a loan application, depicting customer activities, front-office activities (the customer service agent – CSA) and back-office activities (the computer). We only identified key information flows in this case to provide an overview of the process. A potential pitfall of process mapping is that too much detail is shown, obscuring the issues and opportunities for improvement.

Analysis of process maps

Process mapping in itself can be a very time-consuming task with little benefit gained. By itself, a process map is of only limited benefit, but it can help communicate the complexity of a process or help individuals agree or realise the steps involved in a process. Process mapping is essentially a descriptive activity: what is required to derive maximum benefit from a process map is to ask key questions that help turn it into an analytical tool:

● *Does the process support the strategic intentions of the operation?* If the operation is expected to provide, for example, high-quality and speedy service to customers, is the process designed in such a way that decisions are made speedily, that end-to-end process performance is minimal and that quality controls are in place at all points in the process?

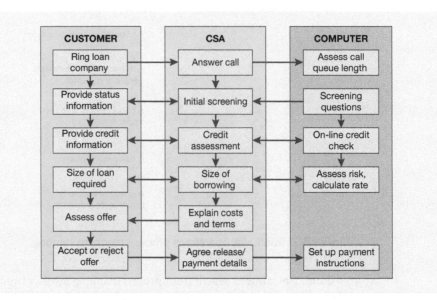

Figure 8.8 Simplified process map for a loan application

- *Does each activity provide added value?* Which elements of the process do not add value? Can they be removed or redesigned?

- *Is the process 'in control'?* For the key elements or maybe every element in the process, what measures and targets are in place to ensure that particular element is performing as expected? Who is responsible for overseeing, controlling and improving that particular element?

- *Who 'owns' and has responsibility for the process?* How many different individuals and/or departments are responsible for parts of the process? Who in particular, or which group of people, is responsible for the design, delivery and improvement of the whole process?

- *Is the level of visibility appropriate?* The process map can be used to identify those activities that involve and/or are visible to the customer, thus differentiating between back office and front office tasks. Should or could any of the activities or tasks be reallocated? Can any of the elements be moved to the back office and away from the customer, which might lead to greater efficiencies? Are there elements that could be made more visible to the customer, which might lead to a greater sense of involvement and ownership and quality?

- *How efficient is the process?* By adding times, distances and resources used, such as numbers of staff, to the various tasks in the process map, the efficiencies of the whole process and various parts of the process can be calculated and bottlenecks identified and removed.

- *How can the process be improved?* What are the likely or main fail-points in the process? What procedures are in place to deal with these? Does everyone who is involved in the process understand their role in the whole process and the effect of their actions upon it?

8.5 How can service processes be repositioned?

Many service processes are under pressure to change. High-variety/low-volume capability operations dealing with strangers may be under pressure to increase volumes and/or drive down the high costs of operating such processes. Low-variety/high-volume commodity-type processes dealing primarily with runners may be under pressure to become more flexible and customise their service for customers (see Figure 8.9).

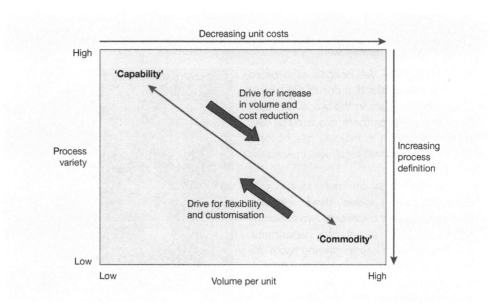

Figure 8.9 Pressures to change

8.5.1 From capability towards commodity

Many innovative organisations have a requirement for growth. The small firm of consultants that has built up a local or national practice may seek to become internationally recognised. Within a global company it may be that an innovative solution developed for an individual customer can be 'packaged' and sold to a much wider range of clients internationally. To do this, a number of issues must be addressed:

- Customers may require greater levels of consistency across service transactions carried out by different providers across locations. For example, a technical consultancy working for a multinational customer must be able to provide the same solution in all locations, probably at the same or similar price.

- Larger organisations tend to be extremely conscious of their image, which may entail setting stricter guidelines for their staff as to the scope and style of work carried out.

- The 'capability' of the organisation, previously reliant on the skills and knowledge of specific individuals, must be replicated through more specialised resources, tighter process management and specific training if the organisation's growth is not to be limited by scarce resources.

- To sustain growth, it is likely that the organisation may have to develop more competitive sales and marketing activities. In some sectors, this might take the organisation into previously non-experienced cost competition.

Perhaps the most significant aspect of this type of transition is the impact on the individual service providers. Many of the individuals in capability organisations will have joined for the professional autonomy that they offer. It is common for these individuals to enjoy the creativity that frequently is part of their role. As the organisation grows, however, these individuals will not be as motivated to turn their creativity into developing consistent and efficient processes. At the same time, the management task will be changing to become rather more positive in providing direction for the organisation as a whole and for its employees. The Ku-Ring-Gai Vet Hospital (see Case Example 8.2) demonstrates the increasing pressure for a move from generalist to specialist that comes with increasing volume.

Case Example 8.2   Ku-Ring-Gai Vet Hospital

The Ku-Ring-Gai Vet Hospital is situated in Sydney, Australia. It is one of the largest veterinary hospitals in the world. Dr Greg Ross, one of the partners, is quoted as saying that their aim in building this hospital was to set a standard for all vets in Australia to follow.

The hospital is on three levels, with seven consulting rooms, three operating theatres, two dental stations, two radiology suites and an intensive care department. The hospital also has a 'grieving room' for distraught owners who wish to be with their pets when they are put to sleep.

This hospital challenges the traditional idea of the local vet dealing infrequently

Source: Pearson Education Ltd/Photodisc/David Buffington

with a wide variety of tasks and yet building strong client relationships with pet owners. The vet specialist is increasingly the model being adopted, as veterinary science follows its human equivalent. Young vets are fast acquiring specialist qualifications, and older vets are being forced back to college to learn new skills.

Despite the 'high-tech' nature of the facilities, the pet owners have not been forgotten in the design process. Glass partitions give visibility for visitors to see what is going on, allaying fears that their pets may not be humanely treated once out of sight of their owners.

The three partners are the veterinarian equivalent of general practitioners. They are able to call on a cluster of specialists, which include small animal practitioners, dermatologists and a behavioural psychologist. Just about every part of a pet that can go wrong now has a specialist attached to it.

Source: This illustration is based on material from Musgrave, A., 'Old Dogs, New Bones', *The Australian Magazine,* 30 November–1 December 1996

8.5.2 From commodity towards capability

Examples of this type of shift may be found in high-volume consumer services. To avoid the trap of becoming a commodity service, competing on price alone, these organisations may extend the range of services on offer, perhaps providing a degree of customisation for individual customers.

Of course, it may be possible to design a service delivery process that delivers a wide range of commodity services without increasing the complexity of the operations task, thus allowing the organisation to move in the direction of the top right-hand corner of Figure 8.9. This is covered in more depth in later sections on flexibility but may frequently be similar to the manufacturing idea of 'mass customisation' incorporating the following two principles:

- *Develop standard 'modules'.* Companies may develop 'menus' of standard services, which may then be arranged in appropriate combinations to provide a degree of customisation for individual customers. The customisation therefore lies in the management of the combination rather than in the development of new services. An example of this type of mass customisation is provided by holiday resorts that allow customers to choose a limited number of activities from a pre-determined list.

- *Postpone customisation until the latest possible stage.* In this approach the delivery process is standardised for all stages until the last. This allows the service operation to gain all the efficiency and consistency benefits of a high-volume/low-variety process. Courier services are adopting this approach by using their basic distribution networks for all customers but using different mechanisms to deliver the package to its final destination.

A major transition occurs when the number of service delivery processes increases significantly. This transition takes the process mix from a few runners to several repeaters. Significant changes in the operations task frequently include the following:

- Shifting the focus of the operation from managing back-office operations consistently and for maximum efficiency towards building front-office flexibility.
- Requiring customer-facing staff to give informed advice as to the best service for an individual customer. Moreover it has become unacceptable for front-line staff in these organisations to act merely as a 'postbox', taking requests from customers for advice but being unable, themselves, to give an immediate response.
- 'Up-skilling' the front line through a combination of greater staff training and the provision of information systems that allow the service provider to act 'as if' an expert.
- Making processes more flexible, often allowing greater discretion on the part of the employee to make choices as to which service commodity will be most appropriate for the customer.

As with the previous case, there are major implications for the service provider and for the role of management. There is far greater onus on front-line staff to possess both technical and interpersonal skills. The service transactions are likely to be longer and more intense in nature. If the customer transaction includes a high degree of diagnosis of customer requirements and the extent to which the various services on offer match these expectations, the front-line employee will require excellent listening and consultative skills.

The second major area for change might be that 'specialist' employees who hitherto had been distanced from the customer, and were able to work in back-office functions, now may have direct contact with customers. This is particularly true in call centre or helpdesk situations where the customer wishes to deal directly with someone who has the expertise and authority to give a decision or advice on complex issues. This may be less of an issue when more transactions take place electronically through the internet or through television-based applications. Of course, not all technical experts have customer-handling skills.

The role of management changes from being the 'enforcer' of the service concept and process to ensuring that the service employees are developed and retained. Many jobs in commodity organisations are low-paid and need very little training, often a few days or weeks. Commodity organisations that are seeking to become more flexible may find that they need to invest several months' training in front-line staff, meaning that employee retention becomes a major focus for management attention.

8.5.3 Strategies for change

The majority of service operations, of course, do not lie at the extremes of the diagonal. For those in the centre of the spectrum, between capability and commodity, there are four basic strategies to deal with transition at whichever point they lie. These are illustrated in Figure 8.10. Few organisations are able to manage these changes without some degree of disruption and the directions for change illustrated in Figure 8.10, therefore, may not be what was planned or desired, but describe what actually occurred.

1 *Building capability through systems and training.* Here the organisation may be wishing to move towards offering solutions for its customers rather than a relatively narrow range of well-defined services. The mechanism for this (preferred) approach is to invest heavily in more powerful information systems, while also expanding the role of the front-office staff. The benefit of this approach is that the organisation is then well placed to deal with the new challenge. The downside is that there may be significant upfront investment, which may not give the desired return.

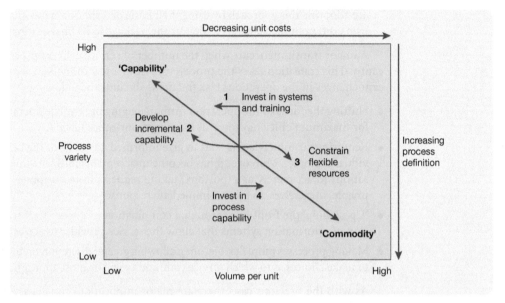

Figure 8.10 Strategies for change

2 *Building capability through incremental development.* In this case the organisation may take what appears to be a less risky approach to building capability. It effectively takes on activities or client assignments that are outside its normal sphere of action, but which it believes can be fulfilled by 'learning' from experience. This process is inherently inefficient and, unless any mistakes are confined to the internal workings of the organisation, potentially damaging to future customer relationships. This is particularly sensitive because capability operations must often work quite closely with customers, in a rather more intimate manner than commodity operations. This clearly means that any deficiencies are not easily hidden.

3 *Moving to a commodity by constraining flexible resources.* An example of this would be a gourmet chef being asked to work in a fast-food, limited-menu restaurant. Although it is possible that the chef would be able to cook burgers and fries, they would be overqualified, too expensive, and after the first meal or two would not be motivated to continue to cook to what will seem a rather repetitive and limiting process. Moving in this direction poses significant challenges for management, employee morale, and in the development and provision of appropriate cost and quality control systems. If these are not in place, the organisation will rapidly become uncompetitive as other organisations manage mass production more effectively.

4 *Moving to a commodity through investment in process capability.* In this case the organisation will have identified a market need for a high-volume version of an existing service or possibly a completely new service. Rather than try to 'muddle through' with inappropriate processes, systems and people, the organisation will invest in a similar way to direction 1. Again, this approach will require initial capital investment, and therefore may appear more risky. However, in some markets there is very clearly a 'first mover' advantage and this approach is becoming more common. In recent years, the investment in a greenfield site for telephone banking has paid significant dividends, not least in allowing these organisations to break away from more traditional banking practices.

Figure 8.11 illustrates the position that many complex service operations may find themselves in after a period of evolution: we refer to this as from start-up to starburst. The operation at start-up is often very focused around a relatively simple task, e.g. the provision of one 'runner' service. The original intent may have been to grow the volume of this one service, perhaps adding a few similar services through time as the business grew. However, the service

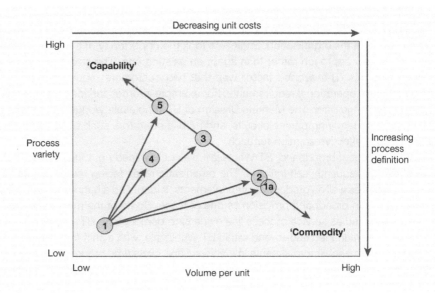

Figure 8.11 Start-up to starburst

range often grows in such a way that operations managers must deliver the full spectrum from capability to commodity.

Case Example 8.3 illustrates how a simple task can grow into quite a complex challenge over a period of time. This is not to say that this is wrong – the point for us to consider is the impact on service operations managers. The network provision and management activity for British Telecom (BT) was conceived as a low-cost, commodity service handling large numbers of standard transactions (position 1 for a very short time during start-up, moving rapidly to positions 1a and 2 in Figure 8.11). However, as BT supported the full range of customers from the domestic household with one telephone line to the major corporate requiring advice as to how to integrate voice and data services (position 5), it can be seen that a major management challenge developed.

Case Example 8.3 BT Wholesale

BT Wholesale is part of the BT (British Telecom) group. Until 2007, its role was to build and manage the central telecommunications network across the UK. BT Wholesale's customers were other telecoms providers and it had a statutory obligation to provide the same level of service to all companies operating in this market, including BT's customer-facing company, BT Retail.

With the proliferation of telecommunications products, what might be thought of as a fairly straightforward activity very soon became extremely complex. BT continued to support older technologies such as telex as well as being committed to an aggressive installation programme for broadband.

Source: BT Image Library

Two factors combined to make a potentially standard activity rather the opposite. The first was the 'engineering culture' of the organisation. Engineers took the opportunity of a new customer requirement to create a completely new approach rather than adapt an existing one. The size and complexity of the organisation contributes to this. The second factor was that two customers requiring a similar service frequently requested different operational requirements. For example internet service providers (ISPs) would not accept a standard broadband offer. The Markets Division of BT Wholesale worked with major customers such as the ISPs, corporates requiring private circuits, and mobile operators such as Vodafone and T-Mobile, in order to engineer a cost-effective solution for each.

With the advent of broadband, BT Wholesale was determined not to fall into the same pattern of too much process variety, frequently self-inflicted. The organisation was facing tough targets in terms of reduced customer lead times as well as productivity improvements. It identified a handful of process families, termed service process lines, with broadband provision as one of these. Some of the most senior managers in the organisation were appointed as service process line owners, to demonstrate BT's commitment to this approach. Each process line was managed end-to-end within BT Wholesale, with a shift from a task focus to a customer focus. Significant performance improvements in efficiency and cycle time reduction were achieved as a result.

The story did not end here as the approach has now moved beyond BT Wholesale to encompass the whole organisation. This has been facilitated to some extent by the merging of telecommunications and information technologies. BT now operates in a global marketplace and must take a wider view. Building on the principles described above, activities across BT have been brought together, further breaking down functional silos. All network and information systems design activities have now been brought together in BT Design, while network and IT operations are now the responsibility of BT Operate. Network repair and maintenance is a standard service delivered by BT Openreach to all its customers.

The customer interface is now owned and managed by three businesses, BT Retail, BT Wholesale, and BT Global Services. This recognises that BT's customers globally have similar requirements and thus can be handled by similar internal processes. The customer-facing divisions now have greater visibility across the value creation activity and are pursuing aggressive quality, response time and efficiency targets.

Source: This case example was prepared with the assistance of Chris Wright, Director of Technology and Transformation, BT Wholesale.

As indicated in Case Example 8.3, the engineering mindset of the organisation has tended to mean that the customised activities appear more interesting and may attract more management attention than the need to create efficient and consistent volume services. This aspect of a dominant company culture can lead to some problems in matching service and process. Frequently, companies consider themselves as operating towards the capability end of the spectrum, whereas they need to operate the majority of their activity towards the commodity end in order to reap quality consistency and efficiency benefits. For example:

- A financial services company considers itself a 'professional' service provider. It thinks of itself as moving towards providing tailored solutions for its customers. The problem with this is that while it promises a great deal to its customers and, at first, contact is very friendly, the company fails to deliver a consistent service, continuing to use labour-intensive, inefficient processes.

- A software company values innovation in its products. However, most of its senior managers have been software developers at some point in their careers and do not understand the processes required to distribute and service its products to a mass market. As a result, these activities are under-resourced and ineffective, jeopardising the future health of the organisation.

8.5.4 Managing the gap between market position and operations

In the previous section we indicated that there may often be a divergence between the market position and the operations approach. In selling the benefits of a particular service

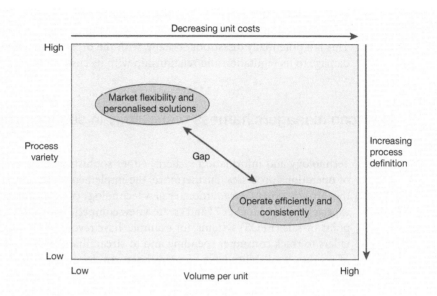

Figure 8.12 The market–operations gap

it is common to find that companies emphasise customer flexibility – providing a personal service – while continuing to operate on a mass-production basis. Figure 8.12 illustrates this effect. This is often a very effective strategy. The main danger is that customer satisfaction will fall if the gap is too great between what is offered and what is delivered. To counteract this, organisations may adopt several strategies to 'manage the gap':

- *Customer service departments.* In many consumer services customer service departments frequently act as 'sweepers' to deal with customer complaints and to provide a relatively cheap human interface between the customer and the service factory of the back office.

- *Named personal contact.* Named contacts provide some personalised attention for the individual. Customers are allocated a specific individual to give confidence that they are not solely numbers in what may feel like a factory-type process. An unusual but appropriate example is in hospitals where nurses, nursing auxiliaries and volunteers provide the individual care valued by patients but not always delivered by a medical system that is focused on maximising utilisation of scarce resource (doctors and consultants).

- *Account or client managers.* Business-to-business services may use account or client managers to provide the point of contact for their customers. In some cases these may operate in a similar manner to the named contact described above. Where there are multiple relationships between individuals or functions/departments in the client and supplier organisations, there is great value in maintaining an overview. Account managers may also play a role in ensuring that the client perceives a level of customisation that is not always as great as it is presented.

- *Change the nature of the service.* Here process is repositioned: from service partnership to DIY, or service factory to service project, for example. The provision of internet-based services, for example, while offering the customers the opportunity to request service at their own convenience, may also become a means whereby customers 'do it themselves' rather than wait for the organisation to respond.

- *Change customer expectations.* All organisations need to try to align customer expectations with the nature of the service. If it is a high-volume, low-touch process it is important to educate customers not to expect personalised service.

Unfortunately, some service organisations adopt the approach of 'hoping for the best', taking no special action to manage the gap between customer expectation and the actual experience. This is a potentially disastrous strategy, with the organisation running the risk of long-term damage to its reputation and relationship with its customers.

8.6 How can managers harness technology in service process design?

Technology and information systems, either sophisticated or simple, are intrinsic elements of operations processes. Furthermore, the implementation of a new information system or the introduction of a revolutionary new technology can transform the process (and customer experience – see Chapter 7) and create a new competitive or working environment. Electronic point-of-sale (EPOS) systems, for example, have revolutionised the retail sector, enabling retailers to track consumer spending and to streamline their supply chains so that high levels of product availability have become the norm. Investment in technology and information systems is likely to be the major expenditure for many service organisations, both at the initial set-up of the operation, and also at frequent intervals as the industry moves forward and adopts similar technologies.

Some services are built around information systems. In terms of the service concept, the outcome of the service is that the user is provided with information as to where to buy particular products or obtain service. Yellow Pages provides a good example of a service built solely on the provision of information for users that has changed its means of operation significantly over the time of its existence. Yellow Pages operations now exist in many countries across the world, providing users with information about how to contact businesses from abattoirs to zoos. In the UK this operation was set up by British Telecom (BT) in 1966, with the aim of increasing the use of telephones. For a number of years it was advertised with the slogan 'Let your fingers do the walking', encouraging users to phone possible suppliers rather than pay them potentially wasted visits.

In 2004 Yellow Pages UK was visited some 38 times a second. There were over 475,000 advertisers who were the paying customers for the service. As the service has grown, so Yellow Pages has adapted its format as new technologies have become available. The original operation was based on the delivery of paper directories to every home in a geographical region. In 1988, the company launched Talking Pages, a telephone-based service, and this was joined in 1996 by yell.com, an internet site.

In common with many services, changing technologies increasingly mean that the organisation deals with customers in many different ways. Behind all this lie two customer requirements, which impact on the design of the service process:

- *Immediate and comprehensive access.* Customers now expect to be able to make contact with the service provider in person, by phone or by internet, 24 hours a day, seven days a week.

- *Control.* Customers want to feel that they are valued and important, rather than simply another piece of material to be processed. Technologies such as the internet allow the customer much more perceived control over what happens. For example, customers can browse through an online retail store, making choices at their own pace. In many cases they feel able to ask more questions than they might have done if they were in a store. Customers are able to compare prices between suppliers before making a purchase. There is no immediate pressure to buy imposed by the presence of a salesperson, or other customers waiting to be served.

8.6.1 The role of technology in service process design

The aim of this section is to discuss the role of technology in service process design, recognising that information systems and the development of facilitating technologies will continue to be areas of key decision-making for the foreseeable future. We will not describe each technological advance in detail, but provide a framework for thinking about implications for the development and delivery of the service concept. Professor Len Berry[5] has provided a helpful set of roles to aid the development of a service process. These roles are:

- multiplying knowledge
- streamlining service
- customising and personalising service
- increasing reliability
- facilitating communications
- augmenting the service

to which we would add

- reducing cost
- increasing customer control.

Reducing cost is often closely linked with the second of Berry's roles, that of streamlining service, but is worthy of separate consideration.

Multiplying knowledge

There are a number of ways that technology can bring both flexibility and an extension to the service concept by leveraging and multiplying knowledge.

- *Leveraging knowledge about customers.* Information systems that ensure that customer-facing employees have all relevant information about the customer available during the service transaction present a more professional image, and allow the core transaction to be conducted more efficiently. When First Direct, the telephone banking service, was conceived, a fundamental requirement was for an information system that allowed any customer to talk to any service employee at any time. Some hotels keep comprehensive records of regular guests regarding their likes and dislikes, which room they prefer, and what their dietary requirements are. At a simple but effective level an airport hotel courtesy bus radios ahead as to which customers are on board so that they can be greeted by name when they arrive. This latter example demonstrates that technology does not need to be complex or expensive to achieve a significant impact.

- *Leveraging knowledge about the service product.* Service organisations that are moving away from offering a standard service may need to up-skill customer-facing staff. A greater choice for customers may require greater knowledge about the product in order to give appropriate advice. Information systems may allow the customer-facing employees to act 'as if' they were experts. Again, these systems vary from extremely complex to very simple. At one end of the scale, an expert system may harness all the knowledge of recognised experts and specialists. At the other extreme, a simple checklist on a computer screen may deal with many customer enquiries without the need to refer to expensive technical help. Many computerised help lines operate on this principle, with on-screen diagnostic routines to aid the customer service agents.

- *Multiplying knowledge about the customers' use of the product.* This is an extension of the previous use of technology, and normally constitutes a change in service concept. Instead of simply selling a product, the service provider seeks to understand how the customer uses it and provides assistance or advice in how to use it more effectively. Truck manufacturers, faced with increased competition, moved the emphasis of their aftermarket operations away from simply selling spares to truck operators. To develop customer loyalty they invested in understanding how truck operators might manage their fleets more profitably. This knowledge was then disseminated through the manufacturers' dealer networks by means of an information system, rather than positioning a fleet profitability expert in each location.

Streamlining service

Technology may be used to eliminate steps in the service process. It is particularly valuable when applied to activities that have a direct bearing on the customer experience. Car rental companies have understood that business customers in particular do not want to spend large amounts of time either filling in paperwork to collect their car or waiting to return it. Smart cards automate the pick-up procedure, and staff with hand-held terminals waiting in the car return lanes speed up the drop-off process. The return process is particularly sensitive as far as the customer experience is concerned because at this stage the customer has effectively obtained all the value they required from the service. The processes from this stage on are perceived to be purely for the benefit of the rental firm, not for the customer, and therefore need to be as efficient as possible.

Many telephone-based operations use a customer database to call up addresses sorted by postal code. Rather than ask the customers to give addresses on the telephone – a lengthy process, prone to error – all that is required is a postcode that locates the street name, and then the house number or name within that locality. This relatively simple information system improves service times and reduces error rates.

Customising and personalising service

Supermarket loyalty cards are an example of the use of technology for customisation. Tesco, through its loyalty card, has built up a database of customer preferences. As a result it is able to target promotions to particular customer groups. Through the information about buying patterns, supermarkets like Tesco's are now able to adapt the mix of products sold in each store to the needs of the area.

Increasing reliability

Technology has a major role in automating routine processes, the 'runner' processes described earlier in this chapter. Customer information can be made immediately available to all parts of the business without the errors that occur when details are transmitted manually.

The performance of some physical products can now be monitored remotely. This is still relatively expensive but is valuable for customer-critical applications. For example, the service provider might monitor the performance of the customer's computer system. Any degradation in performance will trigger a service call to prevent complete failure of the system. In many cases the customer will be unaware that there has been any reduction in performance, or indeed that there has been a service visit.

Facilitating communications

The convergence of voice and data communication systems presents many opportunities for service providers to communicate with customers. A challenge here is to ensure that older technologies are adequately supported. Telephone call centres are being transformed into multimedia customer contact centres, with major opportunities for improvements in communication. However, it is possible that basic operations management principles are not observed in the rush for new technologies. There are many traditional telephone call centres that have insufficient capacity to deal with the increase in demand brought about by greater ease of communication.

Augmenting the service

Technology may allow the service provider to carry out more for the customer. In the 1990s bar-coding and electronic point-of-sale systems allowed some food manufacturers not simply to supply products to retailers, but also to manage the customer's shelf space and inventory for them. Part-time degree courses can be made available globally through the use of electronic conferencing and 'groupware' systems.

Reducing cost

Technology may facilitate the removal of wasteful or repetitive steps in the service process. The resultant reduction in lead time from customer order to fulfilment is in itself likely to yield fewer errors and therefore lower costs. Financial services, traditionally operating through a network of local branches, are able to reduce the cost of their operations by dealing centrally through the telephone or internet.

Increasing customer control

When there is little or no obvious differentiation between service providers in a given sector, the 'feel good' factor is essential to build customer loyalty. A significant ingredient is the sense that a customer has of being valued by the organisation, and of not being merely another account number or statistic. Information systems allow the organisation to respond in ways that build a perception that the customer is important to the organisation. This is enhanced if customers feel that they can influence the service delivery process in some way, rather than being 'processed' in something akin to an assembly line. As was described in Chapter 7, internet systems give this sense of customer control.

Implications of technological advances

Blackboard (Case Example 8.4) offers universities and other institutions many of the opportunities discussed above. In particular students are given more control over their learning through easier access, the transfer of knowledge may be facilitated through careful design of materials and forms of interaction, and the university may be able to provide more courses at lower cost as staff/student ratios may fall. An equally compelling argument may lie in the fact that the current and future generations of students will see e-learning as a core requirement in their choice of programmes of study.

Case Example 8.4   Blackboard.com

Education providers around the world are moving into electronic learning (e-learning). This can mean many different things, and, to some extent, may be resisted by traditional academics who view the classroom as the most effective place for learning. This suspicion as to the value of e-learning is further fuelled by lack of understanding of the opportunities offered by the technologies available.

Blackboard has become one of the preferred suppliers of e-learning solutions, with a wide range of clients drawn from schools, universities and corporate development functions. Professor Penny Boumelha, Deputy Vice-Chancellor of the University of Adelaide, says:

> Our goal is to become adept at taking advantage of the technological changes that will lead to major advancements in teaching and research. Blackboard will enable us to facilitate a flexible approach to distance and multilingual course delivery for remote and overseas students.

Blackboard offers a wide range of applications, which include those directed towards knowledge-sharing, others that facilitate online interaction, and a further group that provide administrative support ranging from assessment recording through to payment systems. Part of Blackboard's appeal is the ease of interaction between systems. Blackboard Learn™ has been adopted by over 2,000 institutions. It enables students and teachers to manage their portfolios, and facilitates content-sharing, assessment management and collaboration through free-form chat, chat lectures, question and answer chats, whiteboarding, class tours and group web-browsing.

It is the experience of the vast majority of Blackboard's clients that they have been taken by surprise by the rapid growth in the use of the system after introduction. The University of Durham, UK, launched Blackboard in September 2000, hoping to have twenty modules and three departments online by December 2000. In the event, more than 300 modules and 21 departments were online by March 2001. This was driven in no small part by student demand, as evidenced by the fact that more than 79 per cent of students enrolled in economics modules signed into their module site during the winter holiday.

Durham seems to be achieving two major objectives in this area: to enhance the student experience and to support new technologies in the learning environment. Dr Barbara Watson, learning technologies team leader, said: 'The University wanted a virtual learning environment (VLE) that was flexible enough for advanced staff to customise and easy enough to make less experienced staff say "Even I can do this."'

As part of the feasibility study, Watson realised that other universities were also investigating VLEs. As a result, four universities in the north-east of England created a joint taskforce to assess the commercial offerings available to educational institutions. This resulted in the purchase of Blackboard applications, key criteria being ease of use and integration with other systems.

For the student, there are many advantages, not simply access to course materials. All students have access through one system to a summary of their own course of study, assessment history, email, and even their social diary.

8.7 Summary

Why is service process design important?

- Excellent service – which satisfies the customer and meets the strategic intentions of the organisation – is usually the result of careful design and delivery of a whole set of inter-related processes.

- The service process is the 'glue' that holds the rest – the customers, staff, equipment and materials – together and is the mechanism that delivers the service concept, creating the customer's experience and delivering the service outcomes.

What are the main types of service process?

- A service process is the set of interrelated activities that together, in an appropriate sequence, delivers the service concept and creates the customer's experience and outcomes.

- Runners, repeaters and strangers help identify the extent of variety to be dealt with by the process.

- Value may be added in the front office or back office or both, with varying degrees of customer involvement.

- The volume–variety matrix helps identify the key attributes of service processes, and the implications of attempting to deal with a wide range of tasks with one process.
- Process profiling can help identify what needs to be changed to reposition a process.

How can managers 'engineer' service processes?

- Process mapping is an important and powerful tool.
- Process mapping is the charting of a service process in order to assist in the evaluation, design and development of new or existing processes.
- Key questions in the analysis of process maps include:
  - Does the process support the strategic intentions of the operation?
  - Does each activity provide added value?
  - Is the process 'in control'?
  - Who 'owns' and has responsibility for the process?
  - Is the level of visibility appropriate?
  - How efficient is the process?
  - How can the process be improved?

How can service processes be repositioned?

- There are pressures on many processes to change their nature.
- Organisations must manage the gap between what is marketed and what is delivered.
- There are four main ways in which service processes can be repositioned:
  - building capability through systems and training
  - building capability through incremental development
  - moving to a commodity by constraining flexible resources
  - moving to a commodity through investment in process capability.

How can managers harness technology in service process design?

- Technology and information systems, either sophisticated or simple, can transform the process (and customer experience) and create a new competitive or working environment.
- Technology has a number of key roles in service process design including:
  - multiplying knowledge
  - streamlining service
  - customising and personalising service
  - increasing reliability
  - facilitating communications
  - augmenting the service
  - reducing cost
  - increasing customer control.

8.8 Discussion questions

1 What examples can you give of capability and commodity service operations? What are the operations management challenges of each type?

2 Select a process, such as cooking a meal for friends or arranging a holiday. Sketch out the service process and evaluate it.

3 Give examples of recent innovation in service processes through the use of technology. What have been the challenges and benefits?

8.9 Questions for managers

1 What is the dominant culture of your service management approach? Is it capability- or commodity-based? Are there any people and activities that do not fit with this culture? How well are they managed?

2 Is there a mismatch between the current performance requirements of your service processes and the task for which they were designed? Have you identified future requirements before attempting to redesign your processes?

3 Identify opportunities to re-engineer some of your processes using technology. How would you manage this innovation?

Case Exercise   Banca San Giovanni

Paola Lustrato, IBM Financial Services Sector Specialist and Dr Rhian Silvestro, Warwick Business School

One key role of banks is to collect money from one party or person and pay (transfer) it to another. These transfers, called payment services, for both individual (retail) and corporate customers, involve transfers using, for example, cheques, credit transfers, banker's orders, and credit/debit cards. As such these payment services are a fundamental part of almost all transactions related to any product in a bank's retail and corporate activities.

Carina Capaldi, the Chief Operating Officer of Banca San Giovanni in Italy, explained the growing importance of these services:

The financial services crisis of the late 2000s has changed the way payment services are perceived by customers. Retail clients are now demanding more transparent, flexible and customised payment services. They also want the funds transferred faster between the parties. Corporate clients also want effective transfer processes but tailored to their needs with easy tracking of movements, and ensuring effective use of their working capital. In essence customers generally are becoming more demanding, requiring increased customisation and higher service levels at lower cost. This gives us an opportunity for developing a competitive advantage. While cost control is obviously important to us, if we can deliver better payment services it will add value to our products and help grow our revenue streams.

To make matters more difficult, these payment services are also facing growing competitive threats from new entrants, such as telecommunication and utility companies, which are offering payment services through their powerful distribution networks. New payment technologies also provide alternatives for consumers; for example 'Obopay', the first mobile payment service allowing consumers and businesses to pay and transfer money through any mobile phone.

Banca San Giovanni (BSG) is one of the leading banking groups in the Euro zone. Due to its network of some 6,000 branches distributed throughout Italy, it has a market share of around 15 per cent and offers its services to over 11 million customers. BSG also has a wider European presence with a network of hundreds of branches and over 8 million customers in retail and commercial banking sectors. In its recent business plan BSG declared that it will 'focus on sustainable growth and creating value by developing stakeholder trust and maintaining strict control over all management decisions'. BSG believes its competitive positioning hinges on operational excellence coupled with intimate customer relationships. The intention is that this should drive service quality, dependability and personalisation, which in turn produces an outstanding experience and inspires customers' confidence and trust. At the same time, BSG is also focused on cost reduction and investment control to ensure its operational efficiency.

BSG's organisation structure is based on the following four business units:

- Retail & Commercial Division: providing traditional lending and deposit collecting activities in Italy for retail and commercial customers
- Corporate & Investment Banking Division: dedicated to corporate clients and financial institutions in Italy and abroad
- Public Finance Division: responsible for government customers, public entities and utilities
- International Subsidiary Banks Division: providing retail activities in foreign markets through subsidiaries and partly-owned commercial banks.

These business units rely on the network of local banks to provide their wide range of products and services. These business units are supported by centralised product- and operations-processing 'factories' (Bank Central Operations) which aim to maximise cost-effectiveness and efficiency. Carina Capaldi is responsible for several support functions, one of which is Payment Operations which handles the traditional back-office transactions that facilitate the provision of payments services across the retail and corporate sectors.

In order to reduce time per transaction and streamline processes BSG consolidated its high-volume payment-processing back-office operations, for both retail and corporate clients, into a few centres called Centralised Territorial Back Offices (CTBOs). However, corporate operations, although using the same branch network to access its customers, requires a detailed technical and legal knowledge about commercial contracts, financial instruments, settlement networks and regulations which govern interbank and supply chain relations. This requires the support of many specialists covering trade, contracts, cash management and factoring (factoring is the service through which a business transfers (or sells) its accounts receivable (i.e. invoices) to a third party (called 'factor') at a discount, in exchange for immediate money). These specialists, and the clients' relationship managers, are available directly to corporate clients via the branch network (this is the current As-Is system as depicted in Figure 8.13).

In order to try to reduce operating costs, duplication and inefficiency in its processes, as well as meet customer requirements for increasing speed and responsiveness, Carina is planning a major reorganisation of Payment Operations. She explained:

While the CTBOs process all the transactions, the specialist staff supporting our corporate clients have varying exposures to different types of clients and different issues so they have inconsistent knowledge and competences. I am proposing to bring these specialists together in what we will call a Middle Office Client Facing (MOCF) as part of the CTBOs to provide a more consistent and knowledgeable service to our clients.

The new structure (see Figure 8.13) will reduce the amount of direct contact with the specialists, with most contact taking place with the Relationship Manager based in the branch, together with new Payment Specialists again based in the main branches. The intention is that the MOCF will improve speed and the quality of support by putting local Relationship Managers (RMs) and Payment Specialists in contact with a centralised and highly competent pool of Product Specialists. Currently there are 24 CTBOs but Carina intends to reduce them to six in the near future. Carina added:

The RMs will be in charge of the overall relationship with clients. They will need to know their customers in terms of financial profile and attitudes, financing needs, investment potential, and business context. They

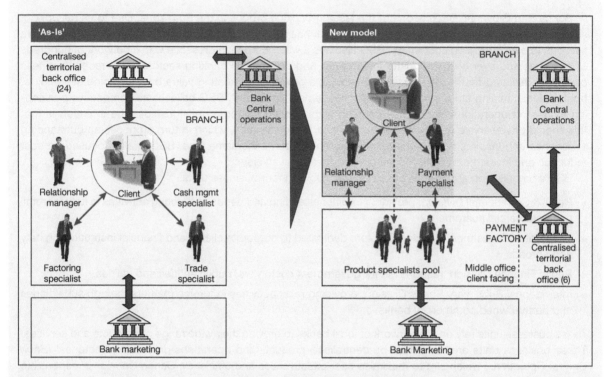

Figure 8.13 The current 'As-Is' model and the new model for Corporate Payment Operations

will be expected to be proactive in proposing solutions to address both their credit needs and investment capacity, based on a deep knowledge of the territorial and industry context. The Payment Specialists will cover a wider territorial region than the RMs and so one Payment Specialist will support several RMs. Payment Specialists will be the experts in transaction banking and should also have some knowledge of the territory within which they operate; however they are not as specialised in the areas of cash management, factoring and trade as were the former branch specialists in the As-Is model. Thus for specialist expertise both RMs and Payment Specialists must interface with Product Specialists in the MOCF.

The Product Specialists will be grouped together to facilitate the exchange and development of a comprehensive range of competences, instead of being associated, as currently, with a specific segment of customers belonging to a limited number of branches. The idea is that the creation of a critical mass of expertise will result in higher levels of competence in dealing with customers, with specialists able to apply greater discretion in tailoring products to client needs and proposing solutions for clients. While currently the branch specialists have limited experience, dealing only with local clients, now the new Product Specialists can acquire more expertise and develop experience in dealing with a wider variety of clients, so they will be more able to customise and respond flexibly to client requirements.

She concluded:

I am sure there will be some teething problems but we are confident that our new model will provide us with lower costs and a higher quality and more customised service for both our retail and corporate clients.

Questions

1 Compare and contrast the existing and new Payment Operations structures.

2 Does the new structure support Payment Operations' objectives?

3 What do you consider to be the benefits and challenges posed by the new structure?

Suggested further reading

Bolton, Ruth N., Amy K. Smith and Janet Wagner (2003), 'Striking the Right Balance: Designing Service to Enhance Business-to-Business Relationships', *Journal of Service Research* 5 (4) 271–291

Cook, Lori S., David E. Bowen, Richard B. Chase, Sriram Dasu, Douglas M. Stewart and David A. Tansik (2002), 'Human Issues in Service Design', *Journal of Operations Management* 20 (2) 159–174

Patrício, Lia, Raymond P. Fisk, João Falcão e Cunha and Larry Constantine (2011), 'Multilevel Service Design: From Customer Value Constellation to Service Experience Blueprinting', *Journal of Service Research* 14 (2) 180–200

Silvestro, Rhian and Claudio Silvestro (2003), 'New Service Design in the NHS: An Evaluation of the Strategic Alignment of NHS Direct', *International Journal of Operations and Production Management* 23 (4) 401–417

Useful web links

For an insight into customer experience design and several more design tools have a look at this excellent site by a leading consulting group:
http://www.beyondphilosophy.com/

For more information on developing customer experiences and journey mapping go to:
http://www.mulberryconsulting.com/

If you want to see SPC applied to a healthcare organisation have a look at:
http://www.isdscotland.org/isd/1123.html

Notes

1   A classification first used by Lucas Industries

2   Heskett, James L. (1983; revised June 2003), 'The Shouldice Hospital', Harvard Business School Case Study (9-683-068)

3   Hart, Christopher W.L. (1995), 'Mass Customization: Conceptual Underpinnings, Opportunities and Limits', *International Journal of Service Industry Management* 6 (2) 36–45; Pine, B. Joseph (1993), *Mass Customization*, Harvard Business School Press, Boston, Massachusetts

4   Slack, Nigel, Stuart Chambers and Robert Johnston (2010), *Operations Management*, 6th edition, FT Prentice Hall, Harlow

5   Berry, Leonard L. (1995), *On Great Service*, The Free Press, New York

Chapter 9
Measuring, controlling and managing

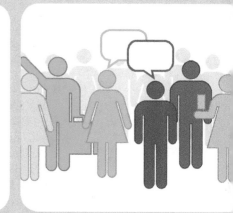

Chapter objectives

This chapter is about how to measure, control and manage service operations.

- Why do managers need to measure things?
- What needs to be measured?
- How can managers measure the customer's perspective?
- How can managers measure, control and manage the operation?

9.1 Introduction

Good performance measurement and management is essential to ensure the operation is doing what it is meant to be doing (control) and that it is improving the efficiency and effectiveness of its activities (improvement). However, performance measurement and management can be costly. Few organisations have calculated just how much time and energy they spend on measuring their performance. Even fewer have calculated if all their systems, procedures and person-hours spent on performance measurement and management provide them with value for money. Indeed some organisations have turned performance measurement into an industry which provides little benefit in terms of controlling or improving their performance. Furthermore, inappropriate measurement can be detrimental to the organisation. By measuring the speed of dealing with applications for a job in a government department, for example, the staff may not give the detailed attention that is needed to identify the best candidates. In universities, focusing on the research output of academics may cause them to spend less time on their teaching quality. Therefore we need to take care to select the right measures and have simple and effective systems to control and improve our operations.

This chapter provides some simple but powerful tools and frameworks, which have been used to great effect in many service organisations, to assess and develop performance measures and systems that help control operations and drive operational and organisational improvement.

Why do managers need to measure things?

Often when we ask managers why they measure things they tell us it's because they need to know where they are, or so they can compare (benchmark) themselves to others. All too often performance measurement is seen as an activity (knowing or comparing) without purpose. We like to hear a second part of the sentence – 'so that we can do something about it'. This is the essential difference between performance measurement and performance management. Performance reporting links the two together.

9.2.1 Performance measurement, reporting and management

Performance measurement is simply about measuring things. Essentially it is the quantification of an input such as staff hours, or an output such as cost, or the level of activity of an event or process such as number of clients dealt with per day. Performance reporting is the way managers, staff or systems, report this information. It usually involves some sort of tabulation or graphic display, with some analysis as to how the measure performs against some agreed target or objective. Performance management, however, is about action. Based on the performance measure and its reporting, performance management is concerned with the actions taken which allow managers to control and improve their operations. Most organisations we have come across spend a lot of time measuring and reporting but precious little on management. There seems little point in doing the first two if the organisation is not going to do the third.

9.2.2 Purpose of measuring and managing performance

Selecting the right measures for an operation is not easy. Indeed, many organisations have too many wrong measures; just because it can be measured doesn't mean it should be measured. If you are going to measure something it should have a clear purpose and it should have systems or processes in place to support or achieve that purpose. These are two useful tests of a performance measure. Table 9.1 provides these two tests plus an additional eight that can be used to audit any performance measure.

There are two main purposes or reasons to measure things in operations; control and improvement. Two secondary reasons which support both of these are communication and motivation.[1]

- *Control.* One key purpose of performance measurement is to provide feedback so that action can be taken to keep a process in control (see Section 9.5). This requires a complete control loop, with measures, targets, a means of checking deviation, feedback mechanisms

Table 9.1   Ten tests of a performance measure

Purpose test	Is there a clear reason for the measure?
System test	Is there a clear system to ensure the results will be acted upon to achieve the purpose?
Truth test	Does it measure what it is meant to measure?
Focus test	Does it measure only what it is meant to measure?
Consistency test	Is it consistent whenever or whoever measures it?
Access test	Are the results available and easily understood?
Clarity test	Is ambiguity possible in the interpretation of the results?
Timeliness test	Can and will the data be analysed quickly enough for appropriate action to be taken?
Cost test	Is it worth the cost of collecting and analysing the data?
Gaming test	Will the measure encourage any undesirable behaviours?

and means to take appropriate action if the process is not meeting the target. This may be used to ensure consistent performance within an organisation, such as costs within budget, and also across organisations, to ensure that government health and safety regulations or discrimination legislation, for example, is being met.

- *Improvement.* Performance measures can provide a powerful means of driving improvement (see Chapter 12). Often simply because something is measured, improvements will follow, as measuring implies it is important, and, as the saying goes, what gets measured, gets done. Further, by linking measures with rewards (such as bonuses) and/or punishments (such as no job), individuals can be motivated to improve their performance – assuming they have control over what is being measured (which is not always the case). Information about what pushes the process on or off target can also help individuals and organisations learn how to manage better the process involved.

- *Communication.* By measuring something the organisation is saying that it is important and needs to be controlled and/or improved. Conversely, by measuring everything (or lots of things) it is implying that nothing is important (amending the saying to what gets measured, just gets measured). A measure, or set of measures, therefore informs employees as to what the organisation requires them to strive for and indeed what they as an individual or a department may be accountable for. It is also an important means of communicating and implementing strategy (see Chapter 15). By measuring speed of response in answering telephone calls, for example, an organisation is saying this is important, and it is implied that employees are expected to strive to meet targets or improve the speed of answering.

- *Motivation.* The measure, or set of measures, used by an organisation creates a particular mindset that influences employees' behaviour. If speed of response is measured but not the quality of the interaction, employees may find themselves, albeit subconsciously, compromising quality for speed. It is important therefore to have the right mix or balance of measures and also a set that supports the strategic intentions of the organisation (see Section 9.3 and Chapter 15).

Some organisations also have to measure some things because it is required, for example by regulators or owners. While clearly this has to be done, managers should not confuse the two, i.e. the things they are required to measure versus the things they need to measure to control and improve their operations.

9.2.3 Systems to achieve the purpose

Having established the purpose for any measure, the second test then is to check that there are systems or procedures in place to support the achievement of that purpose. We often find that although a manager purports that a certain measure is there to help improve the performance of the organisation, there is only a flimsy process, or none, in place to drive improvements. Similarly for the purposes of control, the vital part of the control loop that is frequently missing is action to put the process back on target.

9.3 What needs to be measured?

Just as companies compete on a wide range of dimensions, so organisations need to employ a range of measures, not purely financial or indeed operational. There are four main types of measures (see Figure 9.1), developmental, operational, external and financial (often referred to as the balanced scorecard).[2] The first two are the determinants (or drivers) of success, the second two are the results, the outcomes of success.[3] Developmental measures might include

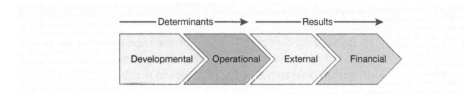

Figure 9.1 Four types of measures

staff satisfaction and staff turnover, the number of service innovations, and level of employee engagement in improvement teams, for example. Operational measures include equipment or staff availability, waiting times, throughput times, the number of customers per day, and number of faults or complaints. External measures include market share, customer satisfaction, and customer repurchase intentions. Financial measures include total costs, cost per customer, revenue per customer, and budget variance.

It is generally accepted that organisations need to have a mix (or balanced scorecard) of these measures. There is little use in driving an organisation only by knowing what the results (financial and external data) are because there is no means of knowing what is determining those results. Conversely, driving an organisation by determinants alone (operational and developmental data) gives no understanding of the results of actions taken. Importantly, both determinants and results are needed to help managers understand the relationships between action and results, i.e. what changes they need to make ('levers to pull') to achieve the desired outcome.

In this chapter we are going to focus primarily on external measures – i.e. how do we measure our success from the customer's perspective – and internal operational measures – how do we measure, control and manage the operation? Before we focus on those two areas we want to cover one important question: what is driving the choice of the set of measures?

9.3.1 Linking measurement to strategy

A key objective of performance measurement and management is that they should provide the link between day-to-day operations and the strategic intention of the organisation. Managers need to ensure that the measures are consistent with the organisation's strategy. Organisations that can translate their strategy into their measurement system are far better to be able to execute their strategy because

- they can communicate their objectives and their targets
- they create a shared understanding of the organisation's strategic intentions
- managers and employees can focus on the critical drivers
- investment, initiatives and actions are aligned with accomplishing strategic goals
- operations managers can communicate with and influence strategic decision makers.

Based on their work with many clients around the world, performance management consultants 2GC (see www.2gc.co.uk) and Kaplan and Norton[4] have found that one of the best ways of linking measurement to strategy is using strategic linkage models (or strategy maps). This approach, sometimes referred to as second generation scorecards, tries to ensure that the objectives of all the different parts of an organisation support higher-level objectives which in turn support the organisation's strategy.

Strategic linkage maps provide operations employees with 'a clear line of sight into how their jobs are linked to the overall objectives of the organization, enabling them to work in a coordinated, collaborative fashion toward the company's desired goals. The maps provide a visual representation of a company's critical objectives and the crucial relationships among them that drive organizational performance'.[5]

In strategic linkage models it is not the measures that cascade down the organisation through linked scorecards (i.e. the same things being measured at all levels in an organisation), but the objectives, leaving managers in the various parts of the organisation to develop their own and appropriate measures and targets to ensure they deliver their objectives. This approach not only helps to align all organisational and operational activities with strategy but also reduces the amount of unnecessary measurement and reporting that other measurement systems tend to encourage.

In Figure 9.2 we provide a simplified example of a strategic linkage diagram for a firm of consultants. The example depicts some of the objectives (or rather shorthand versions of them) at just three levels in the organisation – head office, local office and the individual consultant – for the four main measurement areas associated with the balanced scorecard. The organisation's strategy is contained in the oblong at the top of the diagram, the objectives are contained in the ovals, and the arrows show major linkages. Managers at all levels then need to devise appropriate measures and targets to meet their objectives.

This objective-driven approach to performance measurement has emerged as best practice from years of development around the world, because strategy maps/strategic linkage diagrams

- are more flexible, and easier to develop, communicate, maintain and 'cascade'
- have been proven across a wide range of industries and functions.

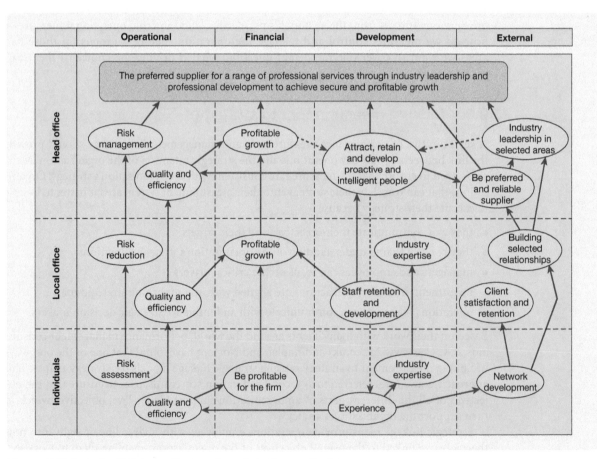

Figure 9.2 A strategic linkage diagram for a firm of consultants

How can managers measure the customer's perspective?

External data is important to allow operations managers to know how effective their actions are, yet often the external and internal measures they use to assess their processes miss out on a customer perspective. An interesting question to ask is: looking at the set of measures used by an operation, would its customers measure its performance in the same way? Operations managers too easily fall prey to inside-out thinking and see their measures from an internal, operations perspective. As a result measuring what is important to customers can easily be overlooked. Although operations managers may well measure customer satisfaction, they may ignore, or overlook, detailed measures of performance that are important to their customers and thus concentrate on the more comfortable and familiar operations measure of performance. Jan Carlzon, for example, when he was chief executive of SAS, noted that its cargo operations were measuring the wrong things:

> We had caught ourselves in one of the most basic mistakes a service-oriented business can make [their cargo customers wanted prompt and precise cargo delivery] . . . yet we were measuring volume and whether the paperwork and packages got separated en route. In fact, a shipment could arrive four days later than promised without being recorded as delayed.[8]

A telecommunications company measured the number of orders (such as requests for new telephone lines from customers) completed within eight working days. This totally ignored the needs of customers who urgently required additional telephone capacity or, at the other extreme, customers who were not in a hurry because they were moving house in three weeks' time. The company's procedure of scheduling jobs on a first come, first served basis managed to upset most of their customers. Changing the measure to the percentage of orders completed within a two-hour timescale agreed with the customer not only greatly increased customer satisfaction, but also reduced the number of calls made by customers to chase up the supply. It also reduced the cost of the operation and increased its efficiency. Indeed the company found that the average time required by customers was two days in excess of their own eight-day target, so the customer advisors had more time available to them to schedule the appointments.

9.4.1 Measuring customer satisfaction

Customer satisfaction is one frequently used external measure in service organisations. It is usually assessed in a structured way using questionnaires and surveys or mystery shoppers.

Questionnaires and surveys can be constructed using the eighteen quality factors discussed in Chapter 5, or factors that customers have identified as being important in focus groups etc. Questions are then constructed for each factor, and customers are asked to rate their answer on a scale, for example 1 to 5. The questions can be used to assess the customer's level of satisfaction with the various touch points in the customer's journey, their overall satisfaction with the service, the level of various emotions they felt such as trust or informed, and their intentions, such as willingness to return or recommend.

One of the best-known instruments for assessing customer perceived service quality is SERVQUAL. SERVQUAL is a concise multiple-item scale questionnaire that organisations can use to assess their customers' expectations and perceptions of their service and obtain a single customer satisfaction score for tracking and comparison. The instrument itself is a skeleton questionnaire that asks questions of customers about their expectations and perceptions of the services of a particular organisation. It uses five consolidated quality factors or dimensions (assurance, empathy, reliability, responsiveness, tangibles) with 22 items for perceptions and 22 for expectations, using a seven-point Likert scale. A gap score (perceptions minus expectations) is then calculated for each pair of perception and expectation statements. The total of the gap scores is the SERVQUAL score. The gap scores can also be weighted by getting customers to add weights to each dimension. Repeated administration allows an understanding as to how customers' perceived service quality with each of the dimensions is changing over time. This instrument provides a direct measure of satisfaction i.e. perceptions minus expectations (see also Chapter 5).

Mystery shoppers are used by many organisations, in particular retailers, to assess the service that their customers experience. The mystery shoppers can be managers acting incognito but are usually provided by external agencies and work to an agreed scoring system. The problem with this method is that the items, or questions, for scoring have often been developed by managers (inside-out) rather than covering things that are important to customers. Performed in this way they are more like an operational audit, checking that staff provide the right information and stick to the correct forms of address and scripts, rather than dealing with issues that are more important to customers such as solving their problems and being helpful. One particular bank, for example, uses mystery shoppers to check that their staff call their customers by their title (such as Mr Johnston) and try to sell them the product of the week (such as a house loan). However, the bank staff may know the customer well and be on first-name terms, and may know he already has a house loan and is coming to the bank to pay in some money quickly. Calling him Bob and not drawing his attention to the offer of the week would mean they would be scored badly by an incognito mystery shopper overhearing the conversation.

Other more qualitative approaches to understanding and assessing, rather than measuring, customer satisfaction were covered in Chapter 5, including

- focus groups
- customer advisory panels
- complaint/compliment analysis
- critical incident technique
- sequential incident analysis.

These provide more anecdotal information about customer satisfaction and importantly provide insights about what the organisation might need to do to improve its service. One additional important benefit of collecting qualitative, anecdotal data is that senior managers are sometimes more driven to action (and providing resources) when they see the verbatim and often colourful and forceful comments of their customers than when given a numeric overall satisfaction score of, say, 4.2 out of 5.

9.4.2 Problems in measuring customer satisfaction

Collecting information about customer satisfaction is something that many organisations now do. However, all too often there are problems with the instrument and, more importantly, problems in the use of the data.[7]

Problems with the instrument

There are several common problems with customer satisfaction instruments:

- *Changing questions.* One of the most important benefits of collecting satisfaction data is to track trends over time. However, frequently changing the questions undermines this benefit.
- *Too many questions.* There is often a tendency by researchers and market analysts to ask every conceivable question. While it might be helpful to know about every aspect of the service, long questionnaires usually result in poor returns.
- *Missing the point.* The reason for measuring satisfaction is often to find out the impact of customer satisfaction, yet this is often missed out of satisfaction instruments; for example, will customers return, will they provide positive word-of-mouth?

- *Qualitative versus quantitative.* While a survey may be able to tell you that a service has scored 4.2, it will not help you understand what to change or how to change it. Likewise, focus groups may give you some ideas about what to do, but it will not be possible to assess the changes without quantitative data. There needs to be a combination of both qualitative and quantitative assessment of customer satisfaction.

- *Survey-weary customers.* Since so many organisations wish to know about our satisfaction, we often feel disinclined to complete questionnaires, especially if we have no confidence that the organisation will make the changes suggested or deal with the issues identified.

- *Analysis fodder.* In cases where respondents are not asked for any personal views but have to tick a lot of boxes about an organisation and its services, customers feel that they are just being used to feed a data engine, either to keep analysts busy or to help the organisation justify doing whatever it wishes.

Problems in the use of the data

- *Resource hunger.* Many organisations consume large amounts of resource in collecting, coding and analysing satisfaction data, and writing reports with lots of graphs and tables.

- *Lack of impact.* Yet, critically, the measures of customer satisfaction, the analysis and other reports may lead to no or little action. If the data is not actively used to control the operational processes that are meant to deliver satisfaction or improve them, there is little point in collecting and analysing the data in the first place.

- *Satisfaction versus success.* High satisfaction scores do not necessarily lead to organisational success. Just because customers say they are very satisfied does not mean that they are valuable customers (for example, that they provide a profitable revenue stream or support for the organisation, or that they use the organisation frequently). Indeed, customers can be highly satisfied with, say, a restaurant, but still go somewhere else next time.

- *Openness to manipulation.* When organisations link the satisfaction measures to employee reward systems, people may manipulate the system to ensure a beneficial result.

In sum, a lot of customer satisfaction assessment is a waste of time and effort; it drives no discernable improvement, consumes valuable organisational resources and wastes customers' time. There are, however, some exceptions. In Case Example 9.1 we describe how the RAC goes about measuring customer satisfaction and what it does with the data.

Case Example 9.1	The RAC – customer satisfaction is king

Nigel Paget was the RAC's operations director. He explained the importance of measuring customer satisfaction:

Customer satisfaction is absolutely the king here. Each patrol hands out a customer satisfaction card at the end of every break-down and every month the patrols get their customer satisfaction index (CSI) for the customers they have dealt with. We not only measure the patrols' satisfaction rating but we also measure their personal response rate as a means of ensuring that they hand out the forms. We also measure all the other

Source: RAC

things that are important to our customers, such as technical ability, their fix rate and also if they solved the problem. For example, if they can't actually fix the fault, did they solve the problem for the customer, such as take the car to the dealer up the road? We want the patrol to take responsibility and go the extra distance to sort out the problem. Again it is all benchmarked and they receive a bonus for excellent performance.

Around 40,000 customer satisfaction cards are returned a month – that's about 400–500 per person. We know exactly what the customers the patrols served in the previous month actually thought of them. We compare this to their previous performance and to an aggregate score for everyone. We reward people as a result, and so if you are average you get your salary. If you perform above average, you get rewarded on top of that. So the incentive is to be better. Around 15–20 per cent will get the top bonus, which equates to about 10 per cent of salary, but it's on a sliding scale.

Despite the central importance of customer satisfaction and the pressure on an individual's performance, the measurement of satisfaction is seen as a positive that is valued by staff. Managers recognise that sometimes there are customers who do not necessarily answer the questions with integrity, and that sometimes not every interaction with a customer is going to be perfect because someone is a trainee or is just having a bad day. So an individual's measures are compared not only with their previous performance but also with the average performance for everyone else. Nigel added:

They understand that one bad customer report out of 400 in a month is not going to have a disproportionate effect, but 30 or 40 out of 400 will. I find it hugely encouraging that when I sit down with people they will just ask me if I have any ideas as to how they might improve their CSI because they simply want to do better.

Source: This illustration is an extract of a case commissioned by the Institute of Customer Service as part of a study into service excellence. The author gratefully acknowledges the sponsorship provided by Britannic Assurance, FirstGroup, Lloyds TSB, RAC Motoring Services and Vodafone.

9.4.3 Qualitative or quantitative?

One interesting question remains. Which is the more appropriate way to assess customer satisfaction, quantitative methods such as questionnaires or qualitative methods such as focus groups? One way to answer this question is to ask how individual customers come to a view about their satisfaction of a service. There are two different answers to this question: a rational approach and an incident-based approach.

- *The rational approach.* The rational approach would suggest that customers consciously or unconsciously use a weighted average, so that a high score on one attribute or factor may offset a low score on another to arrive at a rational evaluation of the quality of a service. Indeed many satisfaction surveys, such as SERVQUAL, are based on the assumption that a reasonable way of calculating overall satisfaction is by allocating weights to the various factors of transactions (according to importance as perceived by the customer), multiplying the weight by the score (on a 1–5 scale for example) for each factor, and then cumulating them into an overall satisfaction rating.

- *The incident approach.* An alternative view is that customers are less rational and react more to individual incidents. So any single incident – delighting or dissatisfying – could, despite the remaining adequate and satisfying transactions, result in a feeling of overall dissatisfaction or delight (see Chapter 5).

The reality is likely to be some combination of these approaches, which means it is important to take care when constructing algorithms to assess customers' overall satisfaction with a service. It is certainly a mistake to assume that customers can identify with precision the reasons why they are satisfied or dissatisfied with a service. For example, on a training programme participants complained about the standard of the accommodation. It was only in discussion with the group that it emerged that the underlying dissatisfaction was with one of the presenters and that the accommodation, if not wonderful, was in fact satisfactory.

The best way to assess customer satisfaction is by both qualitative and quantitative means. A qualitative answer (a number) allows satisfaction to be tracked and compared to other organisations or parts of the same organisation. The qualitative data helps to answer questions about what went wrong and what needs to be changed.

9.5 How can managers measure, control and manage the operation?

There are a wide range of measures that can be used to control and manage an operation, such as cost measures (for example cost per customer, labour cost per day), quality measures (for example number of errors, number of complaints) and time (for example time to serve or process a customer, waiting times and on-time provision of service, for example). Which are the right measures depends upon the strategy of the organisation and the objectives set for the operation (see earlier in this chapter), legal or statutory requirements, and the measures that operations managers need to make sure they are delivering the service, taking a customer's view about what's important.

Once those measures are known and agreed they need to be measured, reported and used to control or improve the operation.

In this section we will focus on reporting measures and controlling operations using the measures. (We will cover improvement in Chapter 12.) But first operations managers also need to understand the impact of one measure on another.

9.5.1 The relationships between measures

Some organisations are now trying to understand the relationship between the various measures, i.e. understand how a change in one area of performance might impact on another. This is sometimes referred to as 'interlinking'.[8] There is often a danger that focusing on one area and one measure may have a detrimental effect on another. For example a contact centre manager who focuses on speed of response as a key measure of the unit's performance may have a detrimental impact on call quality and on customer satisfaction. Such a focus may also lead to an increase in workload if many repeat calls are required by customers to obtain all the information they need.

By using knowledge about the relationships between developmental, operational, external and financial performance measures, organisations can become systematically smarter. Managers will begin to understand, with greater certainty, the likely effect of making resource decisions, which helps them set appropriate targets and better support the strategic intentions of their organisation. Indeed, some leading-edge organisations are beginning to understand and exploit these relationships to create a business case for service (we will develop this point in Chapter 17). In Case Example 9.2 Sean Guilliam, the head of Lombard Direct's call centre, explains how his operation is taking the first steps towards understanding the relationships between operational, external, developmental and financial measures.

Case Example 9.2	Lombard Direct

Lombard Direct must have one of the best-known telephone numbers in the UK, 0800 2 15000, which is based on their slogan 'loans from 800 to 15,000 pounds'. Lombard Direct is a subsidiary of Lombard Bank, part of the National Westminster Bank group. Unsecured loans over the telephone constitute about 90 per cent of the company's business, other products including insurance on loans, house, contents and motor insurance, savings and a credit card.

The main call centre, in Rotherham, South Yorkshire, is a 24-hour operation that operates every day of the year. The centre handles over 2 million calls a year.

£2,000 to £25,000

Lombard *Direct*

0800 2 15000
www.lombarddirect.com

Written quotations on request. Subject to status and conditions. Calls may be monitored/recorded for training purposes. Lombard Direct, Enfield EN11TW.

Source: Advertising Archives

Monday is a typically busy day, when around 6,000–7,000 calls are received. The call centre has around 200 seats (for the customer advisers – CAs) and employs around 250 full-time equivalent staff, with a large contingent of part-timers. Callers are asked a number of questions to rate their creditworthiness and are allocated into a band. This risk assessment, together with the size of the borrowing requested, determines the rate of interest to be charged.

Sean Guilliam is the head of the call centre and he judges the performance of its CAs on six key performance measures. He explains:

We use the following measures:

- *Telephone availability – the time an individual is available to take calls.*

- *Insurance sales – because we want to encourage the people who take out loans with us to take out our insurance cover on the loans.*

- *Media and product code accuracy – it is very important for our marketing people to know where the customers heard of us. However, our systems are a bit lacking in this area and sometimes the CAs have difficulty finding the right code – there are so many!*

- *Call conversion – where we calculate the number of successful loans sold compared to the number of calls taken.*

- *CATS (Customer Adviser Technical Skills) – procedural accuracy, such as giving the right advice and adhering to data protection requirements.*

- *Call analysis – an assessment of the interactions with a customer and compliance with the correct procedure.*

We have four 'spot' levels and CAs are reviewed every three months. Each level has a set of criteria based on the six key measures. If someone attains a higher level for two assessments they go up one spot level; if they perform less well over three periods they will go down. Each level is worth about an extra £1 per hour, so it is quite significant. Also they need to get to Level 2 before we will offer them a permanent contract, though I think we need to remove this barrier and put everyone on permanent from the start to bring us in line with the industry.

At a call centre level I also monitor loan volumes, utilisation, talk time, service levels and abandon rates. Service level refers to the percentage of calls answered within 10 seconds. Utilisation is total talk time divided by total pay time (including training time and maternity, for example). Talk time is the time each operator spends talking to customers. When you compare this to telephone availability you have to be careful. Yes, you want high productivity, i.e. lots of talk time when available, but too much talk time could indicate either we need more staff because operators could be busy and we could be losing calls, or an individual spends too much time talking to customers. Similarly, when I compare loan conversions and insurance sales, although we want a good ratio of insurance sales to loans, too high a ratio might mean that staff could be doing too hard a sell. We don't want customers put off from using us again. The problem is in balancing flexibility with control! Especially when a 1 per cent increase in insurance sales can contribute a quarter of a million to the bottom line.

One of the big problems in staff scheduling is that call volumes are partly dependent upon marketing spend. And, just to make things interesting, volumes are also affected, as you might expect, by weather, holidays and sporting events, for example. We use the volume expectations from marketing spend to create a volume forecast, we then pro-rata this to forecast the volumes of calls we expect individuals to be dealing with: this determines the number of CAs I need and therefore the costs of the operation. I also monitor 'people measures' such as attrition, absenteeism and staff morale. It can be all too easy to trade-off volumes for morale. We have a great atmosphere here and morale is very high.

To help my planning we have created a correlation model that has looked at the relationships between volumes, utilisation, service levels, abandon rates, costs and 'people measures'. I can see the effect of a change in volume on all my key statistics. I want to get high utilisation, high service levels, low abandon rates, low costs and high morale. When we look at our performance data we are now trying to look across the rows and not up and down. It's a new development but it's about how things link together. It helps us understand the relationships between the key variables and also helps us ask the right questions.

9.5.2 Performance reporting

Many organisations have taken performance reporting to an extreme level by producing thick reporting documents with pages of detailed tabulations and colourful charts which are meaningless to all but those who created them. The solution is to know which measures are important (usually around 4 to 6), measure them carefully and report them simply, but report them with a view to making changes, not just for the sake of reporting them.

A good way we have found in some organisations is by using a simple but visual report form for each measure. Figure 9.3 shows a display for a single (important) performance measure – errors in a process – which includes four quadrants. Rather than simply showing the data (in this case percentage errors) for this month (February), the chart (top left) provides a clear view of the trend and the associated target, thus allowing changes over time to be seen. The top right quadrant provides an analysis of February's data to identify the most frequent source of errors. As a result of the analysis, the bottom right quadrant reports on the actions to be taken to try to deal with the most common errors, and on who will be responsible for taking the action and by when they should report. The final quadrant provides an implementation record that checks the impact of previous action plans: who was supposed to do what, by when, and the effect that it had. The chart also, and importantly, displays the purpose or objective of the measure in the centre, with the person responsible for the measure and follow-up actions top right. We also recommend that if there is no one responsible or no clear objective then the measure and its report should be scrapped!

We would suggest that performance measurement reports should include only a small number of key measures and that for each measure there should be a display of

- the purpose/objective
- the person responsible
- trends over time
- performance against target
- supporting data and analysis

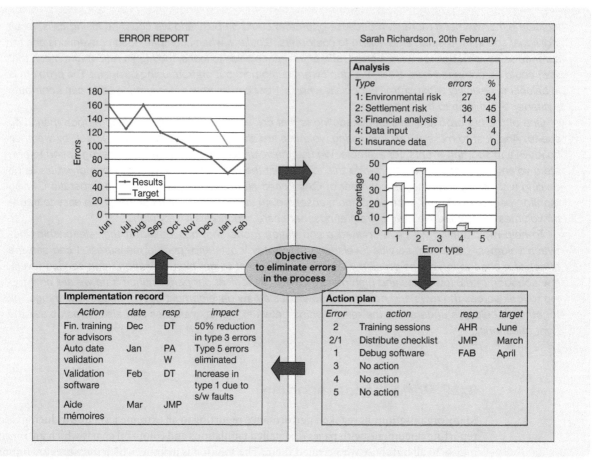

Figure 9.3 Reporting performance

Source: Adapted from work by Neely, Andy D. (1998), *Measuring Business Performance*, The Economist Books, London, and Carole Driver, Plymouth Business School.

- identification of causes/problems
- action to be taken, by whom and by when
- an assessment of action taken.

9.5.3 Controlling performance

A key operational performance objective is to achieve consistency of outcome for customers, i.e. delivering to the specification. Most service organisations report that reliability is one of the most significant factors in influencing customer satisfaction – in other words, 'saying what you do and doing what you say'. This section considers three aspects of control: setting the targets, assessing the capability of a process, and the role of quality systems, such as ISO 9000.

Target setting

While not all measures will have targets associated with them, targets can be a useful means to aid performance management by controlling performance, judging improvements, motivating employees and communicating the speed and size of the change required. Indeed, target setting is a key element of driving performance improvement. There is evidence to suggest that performance improves when clear, defined, quantitative targets are provided.[9] There is, however, an alternative view that suggests that some measures and targets may lead to

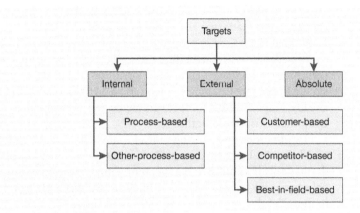

Figure 9.4 Three types of targets

'gaming', that is, playing the system just to meet the target. One museum targeted to increase its number of visitors started counting not only visitors but also delivery personnel just to try and reach its targets. As John Seddon stated, 'Targets drive people to use their ingenuity to meet the target, not improve performance'.[10]

Operations managers need to decide carefully how targets will be set for their measures to control the process, or drive process improvement, and/or motivate the staff. There are essentially three types of target, or benchmarks, against which performance can be compared: internal, external and absolute (see Figure 9.4). (We will cover benchmarking in more detail in Chapter 14.)

- *Internal targets.* Internal targets may be based upon the past performance of the process under consideration (process-based). The target is usually similar to the previous period's target, or slightly greater or lower in order to drive gradual improvements in the process. The key disadvantage of using the process itself as the base for comparison is that, while undoubtedly encouraging improvements in performance, it only provides information as to whether the operation is getting better over time rather than whether performance is satisfactory.[11] The targets may be based upon the performance of other similar internal processes (other-process-based). This encourages comparisons across processes and the sharing of practices between them to try to meet the performance of the best. Comparison with other internal processes has the additional advantage that it provides a relative position for each process within the organisation.

- *External targets.* External targets are based upon comparison with other organisations, using either competitor-based targets and/or 'best-in-field' benchmarks. Competitor-based targets are based on the performance of similar operations in other similar, competing organisations. Best-in-field benchmarks are based upon the performance achieved by organisations that may or may not be in the same industry but where the performance is considered to be outstanding. An important, though often overlooked, external target base for service operations is customer-based targets (just as customer-based measures, too, are easily overlooked), i.e. for a particular activity, what level of service do customers consider to be appropriate?

- *Absolute targets.* Some processes need to be operated with absolutely no defects or 100 per cent adherence to standard. It is unacceptable for life-support machines or stock-market computers or national defence systems to fail; although they do occasionally fail, with serious consequences, their operational targets are absolute.

- *Stretch targets.* A critical question to ask is: by how much should the target be above the current level of performance? Essentially, this depends upon the size of the change in performance required, on the assumption that it is feasible and desirable that such a change can be made (see also Chapter 12).

Internal targets are appropriate for operations wishing to improve their performance continually and incrementally. This would target performance improvements relative to their historical achievements. Often organisations using a continuous improvement strategy, or *kaizen* (see Chapter 12), tend to be both successful and competitive: they may have already outperformed competitors or be the best-practice leader focusing on building upon their existing strengths.

Organisations undertaking radical change of a process should set stretch targets. These are likely to be based on external benchmarks because of the need to improve performance dramatically in relation to that of competitors or external comparators. Reference to external sources for targets, such as competitors, brings both legitimacy and a sense of urgency to those faced with the need for radical change.

- *Employee involvement in target setting.* To motivate employees to try to reach a target level of performance it is essential that they have some control over the variables that affect the performance, and also it helps if they have had a role in negotiating what that target would be, i.e. what they think is achievable. This is what one would expect to find for all processes undergoing continuous, *kaizen*-type, improvement as employee involvement and participation are central to the philosophy of *kaizen*. This approach encourages employees to address questions such as

  o How can you improve what you are doing?

  o How can you improve the process by which you are doing it?

  o How can you improve the way in which you interact with other people?

  This in turn requires the encouragement, support and authority (empowerment) to propose and implement these improvements, backed by a supportive organisational culture and a 'team' approach to problem-solving and improvement.[12] Because of this philosophy of empowerment, participation and involvement, where the responsibility for process improvement rests with employees rather than quality specialists for example, targets should be set through a process involving employees. The employees should decide what might be achievable over a period of time, as it is they who have the responsibility for change and the authority to carry it out.

  For organisations undergoing more radical change targets may be imposed by the senior managers overseeing the change programmes on a command-and-control basis. In radical change programmes, therefore, overall responsibility may rest with senior management champions who devote a substantial amount of their time and effort to both the design and implementation of process change.

- *Linking targets to rewards.* Organisations need to decide what rewards/penalties will be associated with the achievement of their chosen targets. If rewards linked to targets are to work as intended, they must be clearly perceived as sufficient to justify the additional effort to obtain them, directly related to the required performance, and perceived as equitable, and must take into account the complexities of individual versus team-based effort.[13] In addition, the reward structure must also be accompanied by appropriate feedback mechanisms.[14]

  Rewards take a variety of forms, from purely financial to a mixture of financial and non-financial, such as achievement awards and other forms of recognition. To be effective the rewards need to be tailored to the specific requirements of the performance improvement programmes in use within an organisation. While we would expect to find financially based rewards applied in all forms of change programmes, we would suggest that non-financial, and therefore less threatening and more encouraging, forms of reward would be used to promote continuous change. It has been contended that continuous improvement strategies require 'reward systems that place greater emphasis on quality and team-based performance'[15] since they are specifically concerned with the motivation of employees and the elimination of the fear of job losses. Processes undergoing continuous change should therefore base their rewards on a mix of financial and non-financial rewards targeted at encouraging improvements in team-based performance.

In contrast, radical change strategies emphasise individual performance, so the performance measurement system should measure the location of specific results and individual employee performance. Given the higher costs and risks associated with step-change improvements, we would expect rewards associated with such changes to tend to be primarily financial in nature.

Capable processes

The quality management concept of building capable processes is helpful here. This is a fundamental principle of quality management and is at the heart of the Deming philosophy, requiring 'evidence that quality is built in'.[16] Many service operations utilise the statistical process control (SPC) methodology to assess the extent to which a process is capable, or in control.

Figure 9.5 shows the distribution of sample means measuring the performance of two hotels (A and B), which deliver breakfast trays to guests' rooms. In each case, the hotel offers guests a choice of times for delivery of their breakfast tray. Both hotels have chosen 10-minute 'windows' in the belief that this is what customers require. Figure 9.5 shows the distribution of the breakfast tray delivery times for a particular 10-minute window. Hotel A has put in place the processes and capacity to ensure that it consistently keeps its promises, whereas Hotel B appears unable to do so. The former is an example of a capable process whereas the latter is a process out of control. If the promise of meeting this time window is a key element of the 'contract' between provider and customer, the customer satisfaction ratings for Hotel B will be under threat.

Hotel B has two basic strategies that its management might consider:

- to invest in the delivery process to ensure that it can meet its process specification consistently
- to relax the process specification, in this case increasing the duration of the 'time window' offered to guests (perhaps 20 minutes instead of the current 10 minutes).

Of course, the decision as to which to implement can only be made once customer research has indicated how important this issue is and what time window is appropriate.

SPC is based on the production of process control charts. It is normal practice to take a series of measurements and then to plot the mean of the sample readings. This is because

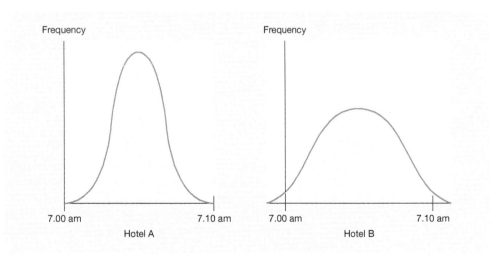

Figure 9.5 A capable process and an out-of-control process

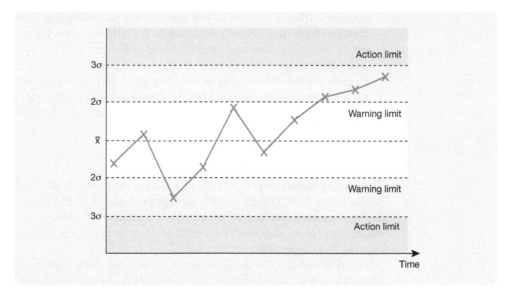

Figure 9.6 Statistical process control chart

under the central limit theorem, the distribution of the sample means tends towards a normal distribution, even if the underlying distribution is not normal.

Processes can be plotted onto a control chart, such as Figure 9.6, to give a visual picture of their state of health. Figure 9.6 shows a plot of sample means taken at random, such as depicting the times breakfast was delivered in the hotel from the previous example. The chart shows the process mean ($\bar{x}$); warning limits set at ± two standard deviations (2σ); and action limits at ± three standard deviations (3σ). The value of process control charts lies in the removal of a temptation to 'meddle' in the process. A number of readings (5 per cent) will be expected to lie between the warning and action limits. The general advice if a reading is taken in this zone is to take another reading before doing anything. Premature adjustments may take the process out of control.

Figure 9.6 shows a process initially in control (the first six readings are a normal pattern), but then showing signs that the process mean has shifted as a run of points are all moving in the same direction as opposed to the normal scattering of readings. As process managers spend time understanding these processes, it is frequently possible to identify causes of variation. These can be divided into those causes that may be avoided, perhaps through automation or better training, and those that are unavoidable. An example of the latter might be the impact of bad weather on a breakdown service.

SPC has been used extensively to control and improve 'runners' in high-volume, standard processes. Examples include:

- accuracy of cheque transactions in a major retail bank
- computer service response times
- sickness and absenteeism in a contact centre
- numbers of customer complaints per thousand transactions.

It would be wrong to give the impression that SPC is easily applied to all service processes. It is clearly applicable to factory-like processes where measures such as response times may be accurately assessed, but it is also valuable to apply the technique to attributes such as the number and intensity of customer complaints. As is often the case, the value may come from the discipline of thinking about the process as much as from the monitoring of the control chart.

Quality systems

Some industries have had a long history of quality assurance, usually for reasons of health, hygiene or safety. Many manufacturing companies have been required to produce evidence of quality plans, schedules of inspection and records of quality checks being carried out. This activity has frequently been viewed somewhat negatively by operations managers, considering it as something that does not add value to the operations activity, and indeed as stifling innovation and change.

It is unfortunate that this quality assurance activity should be viewed as a 'police officer' operating in a somewhat negative way, preventing poor quality but not actively encouraging good quality. The British Quality Standard BS 5750 (now BS EN ISO 9000) and then the International Standard ISO 9000, and their associated standards, aim to correct this biased view of quality assurance.

High-volume commodity-type services whose processes tend towards runners lend themselves most naturally to the quality systems approach. This is because processes can be mapped, and clear, consistent standards can be established and monitored throughout service provision. For example, many hotels have used standard operating procedures (SOPs) for a number of years covering aspects of service delivery such as the way that housekeeping cleans and prepares a room. This activity lends itself to checklists:

- Has the floor been vacuumed?
- Have the complimentary soaps and shampoos been replenished?
- Has the bed been made and turned down?
- Have the waste bins been emptied?

These SOPs translate readily into processes that can be audited for compliance under a quality system. They deal with relatively tangible outcomes rather than less tangible aspects of the customer experience. Retailers, banks and contact centres attempt to measure these aspects of the customer experience by using checklists, which might include statements such as 'Did the member of staff use the appropriate greeting?' or 'Did the member of staff thank the customer for the order?'

The advantages of using quality management systems such as those related to ISO 9000 are as follows:

- Incorporating critical elements of service delivery in a process that has been mapped, described and measured in such a way as can then be audited develops a discipline that may not have existed previously.
- External auditing and recognition of this success in the award of a certificate is good for internal morale and external reputation.
- The better quality management systems include a formal review process, which prompts the organisation to consider what needs to be done differently in order to improve.
- The process of preparing for external accreditation requires the organisation to document its processes and should be used as an opportunity for process redesign before application.

In recent years, the ISO 9000 approach has been totally revised and re-launched as ISO 9000:2000. The emphasis here is on the development of a quality management system that has the objective of creating processes that reflect customer requirements and are sensitive to changing market conditions. The previous criticism of these systems was that they evaluated process adherence rather than looking at whether or not the process was appropriate for the service task. ISO 9000:2000 now concentrates more helpfully on creating the management system to deliver quality targets.

9.6 Summary

Why do managers need to measure things?

- Operations managers measure things to control and/or improve them.
- Performance measurement and management is costly and few organisations have calculated the cost or value of their performance management systems.
- Performance measurement is the quantification of inputs, outputs or activities.
- Performance reporting is the way managers, staff or systems report performance measures.
- Performance management is about the actions taken which result in control or improvement.

What needs to be measured?

- It is generally accepted that organisations need to have a mix (or balanced scorecard) of developmental, operational, external and financial measures. The first two are the determinants (or drivers) of success, the second two are the results, the measure of success.
- The measures should support operational objectives. Those objectives should be part of a systems or cascade (strategy map) of objectives that support the organisation's strategy.

How can managers measure the customer's perspective?

- Customer satisfaction is usually measured in a structured way using questionnaires and surveys or mystery shoppers. Other more qualitative approaches to understanding and assessing customer satisfaction include focus groups, customer advisory panels, complaint/compliment analysis, critical incident technique, and sequential incident analysis.
- There are many problems involved in measuring customer satisfaction including problems with the instrument and problems in the use of the data.

How can managers measure, control and manage the operation?

- Reliability and consistency are important to most service operations and their customers.
- Targets are often used to help control and improve operations. There are three types of target, or benchmarks, against which performance can be compared: internal, external and absolute.
- Capable processes can be created through the implementation of statistical process control.
- Quality systems should not only provide process definition, but should also be the catalyst for quality improvement.

9.7 Discussion questions

1 Key measures used by some call centres are speed of response and call abandonment rate. Assess these measures as drivers of improvement.

2 A tour operator specialising in holidays for young people is concerned about the quality of service provided. Each month the marketing manager reports on the number of complaints received. How could this be better reported to help the firm improve its service?

3 Obtain some customer feedback forms/surveys/internet surveys and assess them in terms of how well they help managers assess and control performance.

9.8   Questions for managers

1   Roughly how much time is spent in your organisation/unit on measuring performance, reporting it, and performance **management**? Are the proportions appropriate and is this money well spent?

2   What are your key performance measures? Assess the purposes, and systems to deliver the purposes, for your key measures. Do they drive the right behaviours? What key elements of service are not reflected in the measurement?

3   Evaluate the mix of measures used at various levels in your organisation. What are the implications of this?

4   Construct a strategy map (strategic linkage diagram) for your organisation. How well do the objectives link and support strategy? How well do the measures you use support your objectives?

Case Exercise   The Squire Hotel Group

The Squire Hotel Group (SHG) runs a chain of 20 hotels, with between 40 and 120 bedrooms, in locations that include Oxford, Warwick and Southport. SHG sees itself in the three-star market, with hotels that have their own personality and style, providing high-quality food and service at an affordable price. The majority of mid-week guests are commercial clients. The normal mid-week occupancy rate is about 80 per cent. Weekend occupancy is about 30 per cent, comprising mainly weekend-break packages. The company does not have any major expansion plans but is trying to strengthen its existing market position.

Squire's managing director, Justin Palmer, believes that it has a high degree of customer loyalty in the commercial sector. He explains:

The hotel managers are expected to integrate with their local community through Chambers of Commerce and Round Tables, primarily to gain visibility but also to demonstrate a local and caring attitude. The image they try to create is a good-quality, small and friendly hotel that local business can rely upon for their visitors. The hotel managers are expected to work hard to develop personal relationships with local firms and may also try to promote other hotels in the chain for any 'away' visits. We get most of our repeat bookings because of the reputation we have developed for the quality of our food and attentive and courteous service.

The Squire Hotel in Oxford has 41 bedrooms and is situated close to Magdalen College. The entrance lobby is small but pleasantly decorated. The room is dominated by a grandfather clock and an elegant mahogany desk. Charles Harper, the hotel's manager, explained:

I do not like the traditional counter arrangement, I like a simple, open and friendly situation with a clear desk to demonstrate our uncluttered and caring attitude. Even our computers are kept in a small room just off the lobby, out of sight. I want my guests to feel that they are important and not just one of the 70 that we are going to deal with that evening.

SHG's hotel managers are totally responsible for their own operations. They set staff levels and wages within clear guidelines set by head office. Although pricing policy is determined centrally, there is scope for adjustment and they can negotiate with local firms or groups in consultation with head office. Charles Harper added:

Every year, each hotel manager agrees the financial targets for his own operation with head office, and if the manager does not reach his target without good reason, he may well find himself out of a job. I believe that it is my job to be constantly improving and developing this business. This is naturally reflected in the yearly profit expectations.

The hotel managers report performance to the group monthly on four criteria: occupancy, profit, staff costs and food costs. The information provided allows senior managers to drill down to the costs of individual people and meals. Charles Harper explained:

My job is to try to get and maintain 100 per cent occupancy rates and keep costs within budget. During the tourist season Oxford has more tourists looking for beds than it has beds, so in the peak season, which is only two months long, we expect to achieve 100 per cent utilisation of rooms. Indeed, I am budgeted for it. This has been a bad year so far. The high value of the pound has kept many American tourists away and our occupancy has sometimes been as low as 90 per cent. In the off-season our occupancy drops to 60 per cent – this is still very good and is due to our excellent location. In the peak season we charge a premium on our rooms. This does not cause any problems, but our guests do expect a high standard of food and service.

We get very few complaints. Usually these are about the food, things like the temperature of the vegetables, though recently we had a complaint from two elderly ladies about the juke-box in the bar. We don't have any formal means of collecting information about quality. Head office may come and check the hotel once or twice a year. We always know when they are coming and try to look after them. We don't use complaints or suggestion forms in the bedrooms because I think it tends to get people to complain or question the service. However, I do try to collect some information myself in order to get an indication from guests about how they feel about the quality or the price. I don't document the results, but we know what is going on. Our aim is to prevent complaints by asking and acting during the service.

I have 40 staff, most of whom are full-time. Ten work mainly on the liquor side, 20 on food and 10 on apartments. There is a restaurant manager and a bar manager. Staff turnover is 70 per cent, which compares very well with most hotels, where turnover can be as high as 300 per cent. In general the staff are very good and seem to enjoy working here.

The restaurant at the Squire Hotel in Oxford has 20 tables with a total seating capacity of 100. The restaurant is well used at lunchtime by tourists and visitors to the local colleges and by local business people. However, there are several excellent and famous restaurants that tend to draw potential customers and even hotel guests away from the hotel restaurant in the evenings.

The restaurant managers have considerable discretion in menu planning, purchasing and staffing, providing they keep to the budgets set by head office. These budgets specify, for example, the food and staff costs for an individual breakfast, lunch and dinner. Overall food costs and staff costs are reported weekly to the hotel manager. The style of restaurants in the hotels varies considerably from carvery to à la carte, with the decisions made on the basis of the type of hotel and the requirements of the local community. Elizabeth Dickens, the restaurant manager, explained:

My job is concerned with keeping to food and staff budgets, and so most of my time is taken up with staffing, purchasing and menu planning. At lunchtime, for example, I provide four items, three traditional and one vegetarian, and these change weekly. We aim to serve a main course within 15 minutes of taking an order. I am constantly looking for new ideas for our menus and better ways of serving but I am constrained by continually tightening budgets from head office. I think we have now reached the point where we are starting to lose many of our established customers. We really do need to respond to the changing demands of our customers in terms of speed of service, particularly at lunchtimes, and changes in diet together with the desire for a greater and more interesting range of meals. I think head office is out of touch with reality.

Questions

1 Evaluate the performance measures in place at the Squire Hotel Group.

2 What improvements would you suggest?

Suggested further reading

Bourne, Mike, Mike Kennerley and Monica Franco (2005), 'Managing through Measures: A Study of the Impact on Performance', *Journal of Manufacturing Technology Management* 16 (4) 373–395

Cobbold, Ian, Gavin Lawrie and Khalil Issa (2004), 'Designing a Strategic Management System Using the Third-generation Balanced Scorecard: A Case Study', *International Journal of Productivity and Performance Management* 53 (7) 624–634

Johnston, Robert and Panupak Pongatichat (2008), 'Managing the Tension between Performance Measurement and Strategy: Coping Strategies', *International Journal of Production and Operations Management* 28 (10) 941–967

Kaplan, Robert S. and David P. Norton (2000), 'Having Trouble with Your Strategy? Then Map It.', *Harvard Business Review* 78 (5) 167–177

Kaplan, Robert S. and David P. Norton (2006), *Alignment: How to Apply the Balanced Scorecard to Corporate Strategy*, Harvard Business School Press, Boston

Neely, Andy D., Chris Adams and Mike Kennerley (2002), *The Performance Prism: The Scorecard for Measuring and Managing Stakeholder Relationships*, Financial Times/Prentice Hall, London

Pongatichat, Panupak and Robert Johnston (2008), 'Exploring Strategy-misaligned Performance Measurement', *International Journal of Productivity and Performance Management* 57 (3) 207–222

Useful web links

For a wealth of information about second and third generation scorecards:
www.2gc.co.uk

The home page of the Performance Management Association, an academic-practitioner association devoted to advancing knowledge and insight into the fields of performance measurement and management:
http://www.performanceportal.org/

Wikipedia has a useful page on measuring customer satisfaction:
http://en.wikipedia.org/wiki/Customer_satisfaction

Notes

1 Neely, Andy D. (1998), *Measuring Business Performance*, The Economist Books, London

2 See for example Kaplan, Robert S. and David P. Norton (1993), 'Putting the Balanced Scorecard to Work', *Harvard Business Review* 71(5) 134–147; Kaplan, Robert S. and David P. Norton (1992), 'The Balanced Scorecard – Measures that Drive Performance', *Harvard Business Review* 70 (1) 71–79; Kaplan, Robert S. and David P. Norton (1996), 'Using the Balanced Scorecard as a Strategic Management System', *Harvard Business Review* 74 (1) 75–85; Kaplan, Robert S. and David P. Norton (1996), *The Balanced Scorecard*, Harvard Business School Press, Boston

3 Fitzgerald, Lin, Robert Johnston, Stan T. J. Brignall, Rhian Silvestro and Christopher Voss (1991), *Performance Measurement in Service Businesses*, CIMA, London

4 See for example Kaplan, Robert S. and David P. Norton (2004), *Strategy Maps: Converting Intangible Assets into Tangible Outcomes*, Harvard Business School Press, Boston; Cobbold, Ian, Gavin Lawrie and Khalil Issa (2004), 'Designing a Strategic Management System Using the Third-generation Balanced Scorecard: A Case Study', *International Journal of Productivity and Performance Management* 53 (7), 624–634

5 Kaplan, Robert S. and David P. Norton (2000), 'Having Trouble with Your Strategy? Then Map It.', *Harvard Business Review* 78 (5) 167–176

6 Carlzon, Jan (1987), *Moments of Truth*, Ballinger, Massachusetts

7 See for example Piercy, Nigel F. (1995), 'Customer Satisfaction and the Internal Market: Marketing Our Customers to Our Employees', *Journal of Marketing Practice: Applied Marketing Science* 1 (1) 22–44

8 Collier, David A. and James R. Evans (2007), *Operations Management*, 2nd edition, Thomson South Western, Mason, Ohio

9 Berry, Anthony J., Jane Broadbent and David T. Otley (2005), *Management Control: Theories, Issues and Practice*, Palgrave Macmillan

10 Seddon, John (2008), *Systems Thinking in the Public Sector*, Triarchy Press, Axminster, UK, p. 45

11 Slack, Nigel, Stuart Chambers and Robert Johnston (2010), *Operations Management*, 6th edition, FT Prentice Hall, Harlow

12 Imai, Masaaki (1986), *Kaizen: The Key to Japan's Competitive Success*, McGraw-Hill, New York

13 Berry, Anthony J., Jane Broadbent and David T. Otley (2005), *Management Control: Theories, Issues and Practice*, Palgrave Macmillan

14 Mullins, Laurie J. (2004), *Management and Organisational Behaviour*, 7th edition, FT Prentice Hall, Harlow

15 Ittner, Christopher D. and David F. Larcker (1995), 'Total Quality Management and the Choice of Information and Reward Systems', *Journal of Accounting Research* 33 (Supplement) 1–34

16 Deming, W. Edwards (1986), *Out of the Crisis*, MIT Center for Advanced Engineering Study, Cambridge, Massachusetts

Chapter 10
Managing people

Chapter objectives

This chapter is about how to motivate people, staff and customers, to deliver great service.

- Why is service delivery a pressurised task?
- How can organisations manage and motivate service providers?
- How can customers be 'managed' and motivated?

10.1 Introduction

If you ask operations managers what is the activity that they spend most time on or that gives them the most problems, almost all of them will tell you that it is managing their staff. Most service organisations employ large numbers of staff, both customer-facing (front-line) employees and back-office employees who support (and thus provide service to) the customer-facing staff. They may be, for example, customer service agents in a bank, computer specialists staffing a help line, or HR professionals providing recruitment and training services to their colleagues.

From a customer perspective, the difference between a mediocre and an excellent experience lies more often than not with the person who serves them – their immediate point of contact. This person represents the organisation and embodies the service. The customer's perception of the service can be influenced to a large extent by the way they view their interaction with them. It is possible for a service organisation to invest in meticulous process design and expensive technology but having failed to invest in its people it will not deliver the right experience and the expected levels of customer satisfaction. This is only the tip of the iceberg because, in such situations, staff will not be motivated to own and improve service processes to deliver required levels of operational quality and productivity.

Managing service providers (front-line staff or customer-facing employees/staff – we use these terms interchangeably) is an important task because:

- These people, individually and collectively, have a crucial role: they are responsible for delivering service to their customers (whether internal or external).
- In most services, the service providers form a significant element in the customer experience.

- Front-line service staff represent the organisation and project its brand values to its customers.
- Employees represent a significant resource for many service businesses, and frequently represent the largest variable cost to the organisation.
- The essence of professional services, in particular, lies in the skill, capability and knowledge of the service providers. Professionals 'are the service', in the sense that it is these people – a blend of their expertise and chemistry with the client – that the customer is buying.

An additional 'service provider' is the customer. In service organisations customers often play an active part in the process of service delivery (co-production) so, just like employees, they are an operational resource that needs to be 'managed': selected, trained and controlled, to do their 'job'.

This chapter deals primarily with the leadership and motivation of service staff and customers as they relate to service delivery, rather than addressing aspects of terms and conditions of employment contracts. But first we need to understand why delivering service tends to be a pressurised task.

10.2 Why is service delivery a pressurised task?

Delivering service minute after minute, day after day, year after year is not easy. For many people this may be a rewarding, fulfilling and enjoyable task; for others it is, at best, a daily struggle and, at worst, a nightmare. All service providers face two distinct but often equally difficult pressures: pressure from their managers (organisational pressures) and pressure from their customers (customer pressure) (see Figure 10.1).

10.2.1 Organisational pressures

The nature of the service task will present challenges for the employee. Some tasks are inherently more stressful than others. There are some challenging tasks faced by the staff in the housing association described in Case Example 10.1, where staff face large numbers of desperate customers and do not have enough resources to keep some of them off the streets. Likewise, the surgeon who performs life-saving surgery may feel more anxiety than a supermarket checkout employee, since the consequences of mistakes are more serious. It has to be

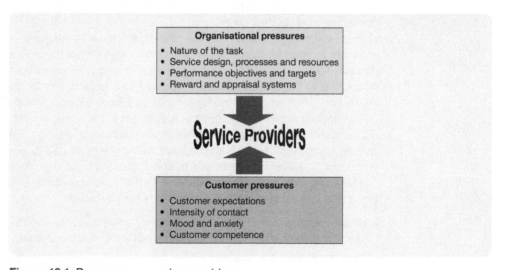

Figure 10.1 Pressures on service providers

noted, though, that reaction to pressure is very much an individual response, which results in some fairly relaxed surgeons and some extremely tense checkout operators! This might seem a trivial point, but organisations that are often under pressure will try to recruit individuals who are better equipped to deal with stress and also try to manage the stressful situations better (see the discussion of the coping zone in Chapter 11).

The service design, the design of processes and the use of operational resources can have a significant impact on staff. For example, service engineers who work from home may well find that their journey times to customers are reduced, but that they miss out on the support of colleagues they might receive if working from a central location. Many organisations have a reception area for visitors staffed by an employee who also operates the telephone switchboard. This creates an inevitable conflict as the employee must make a decision as to who to deal with next; the customer on the telephone or the visitor in front of them.

Almost all organisations set increasingly demanding performance targets. Because these targets are aimed at performance improvement, they frequently conflict. For example, the call centre agent may have to meet a productivity target of average call handling time (ACHT), while maintaining operational service quality targets of accuracy and courtesy. This may not be always possible, particularly when demand outstrips capacity and the service organisation enters the coping zone, as discussed in Chapter 11.

Finally, reward and appraisal systems may be the source of pressure as staff struggle to maintain performance standards that ensure maximum payments.

10.2.2 Customer pressures

Customers bring another set of pressures (see Case Example 10.1). Some of the significant issues for service providers resulting from customer expectations include:

- The constant presence of customers in high-contact services. Serving staff in restaurants are constantly 'on show' and cannot relax.
- Customers like to think that the service transaction they receive is special for them. For the service employee it is likely to be just one of many.
- Customers may have expectations of the service beyond the design specification based on experiences from other service providers.
- Some customers may have totally unrealistic expectations of service delivery.

Case Example 10.1   New Islington and Hackney Housing Association

New Islington and Hackney Housing Association is a registered social landlord and a registered charity that owns and manages 6,500 properties in London and Essex in the UK. Employing around 650 people and with a turnover of around £42 million, it is one of a number of quasi government bodies that provide housing and associated services in areas of significant social deprivation and social exclusion. Fifty per cent of its customers are from black and minority ethnic groups, over 20 per cent have English as a second language and nearly 90 per cent are in receipt

Source: Pearson Education Ltd/Jules Selmes

of some form of government benefit. Many of these people are unemployed and nearly 50 per cent have no qualifications.

These customers have little or no choice. There is a serious undersupply of housing accommodation in London so the alternatives for these customers include the very expensive private rented sector, short-term hostel accommodation or living rough on the streets.

In the main, these people are grateful to the Association for providing them with quality, affordable accommodation, although often they do not directly contribute to the rent unless they find work. There is, however, a minority of customers who are difficult and on occasions abusive and threatening. Bob Heapy, the Association's operations director, explained some of the problems he and his staff face:

I would describe most of our customers as good customers; however, some customers are very difficult to manage. This is sometimes due to their expectation of service levels being in excess of what we are required to provide or indeed can provide for them – often we find that this is because they don't understand what we can or can't do. There are clear service standards expressed in our tenancy agreements (our contracts) with our customers and a key task for us is to assist our customers to understand these standards. This can make our dealings with our customers difficult; customers can be frustrated, anxious, demanding and occasionally aggressive to customer-facing staff. As a result staff require specific skills to manage these customer interactions. We took the view, when we reviewed our customer-contact staffing groups, that we required excellence in 'soft' skills, so we undertook to employ staff from the retail sector, who appeared to demonstrate these competencies, and provided intensive training for 'technical' housing-related skills.

The staff do a fantastic job. They are professional and dedicated and they often choose to work in the not-for-profit sector through a sense of social purpose. We provide our customer-facing staff with good physical conditions of work, and good employment conditions, including rewards and pay all incentivised through a bonus scheme, which is also linked to the individual's performance reviews and appraisals. These appraisals and reviews are undertaken quarterly by line managers, including updating of key personal performance targets. The performance targets are driven by the Operational Plan, which in itself is driven by the overall Organisational Business Plan. In our view this gives a sense of perspective of where an individual fits within the business and how their performance impacts on our business as a whole.

We undertake regular training and development of employees. Another key issue for us is the continuous improvement of the services responding to our customers' needs. Recently we have identified that communication issues were preventing certain groups accessing services, so the provision of community languages became a key requirement. We have been able to include in our recruitment requirements a second language for customer-facing staff. We now have 12 community languages spoken in our customer contact section.

The intensity of the service encounter may contribute to the pressure on service providers. It is likely that the average customer at the supermarket checkout is less demanding than a participant on a management training programme – for two reasons. First, the transaction at the supermarket is completed in a few minutes, whereas the training programme might take place over several days. The extended contact time brings a degree of pressure, but probably more significant is the meaning of this event for the customer. The management training programme may represent a promotion opportunity for the participant/customer and the resulting anxiety may be easily transferred from customer to provider.

The mood of the customer is another major factor in the equation. Many leisure services have a built-in advantage here, because customers are generally in a positive mood and may be more co-operative with service providers as a result. On the other hand, diners at a special celebration meal in a restaurant may be more demanding as they want this occasion to go without any problems. At the other end of the scale, 'customers' of the prison service (inmates) may be less friendly and less co-operative!

Finally, the competence of the customer may have a significant impact on the service provider. Regular airline passengers know the various steps of the check-in process and know where to find flight information. Infrequent fliers slow up the process because they do not know what to do, and they ask more questions for clarification or reassurance. There is also a category of customer that poses yet more challenges for the service provider: the customers who think they know what to do but in reality do not and may cause significant disruption as a result.

Front-line service staff may find themselves playing a wide variety of roles; some of these form part of their formal job description, while others are perhaps unexpected but must be dealt with to some degree. These include:

- *Order taker.* The front-line staff form the interface between customer and organisation.
- *Advice giver.* The customer is often looking for 'inside' knowledge as to what is particularly good or what is not worth purchasing.
- *Image maker.* The brand is delivered by service providers.
- *Service deliverer.* The front-line staff may be the final point of contact for customers.
- *Complaint handler.* The most effective point of service recovery is at the point of delivery. Many informal complaints are dealt with here.
- *Therapist.* For some customers, any human contact is an opportunity to offload problems and to seek support and advice.
- *Trainer.* Front-line staff must be able to deal with both competent and incompetent (possibly new) customers.
- *Coach.* Many customers need confidence building and coaching to ensure a good service experience.

This section has given a very brief introduction to the issues relating to the diversity of customers and their expectations of service providers. Clearly, these pressures are felt most immediately by service staff in customer-facing roles, but are soon transmitted through the system to those in back-office activities, and further on to suppliers and partners in the supply network (Chapter 6).

10.2.3 Resultant issues for service providers

If not managed well, these frequently conflicting forces of organisational and customer pressures result in problems of motivation and stress, for example, causing increased costs, damaged staff and poor service (see Figure 10.2).

- *Motivation.* Many of us have experienced the pressure of continually trying to satisfy groups of people with conflicting demands. For a relatively short period this may give

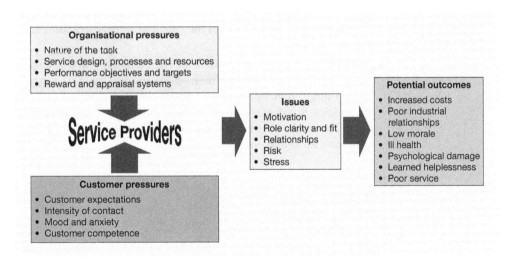

Figure 10.2 Effects of organisational and customer pressure

you an 'adrenaline rush' as you work at superhuman rates, balancing all the various needs. After a while though, enthusiasm may be replaced by apathy, particularly if you feel that you are working harder than others, and that the management does not seem to worry that you are overstretched. In some situations the very nature of the task itself may represent a challenge for employee motivation. Some tasks are rather repetitive, frequently constrained by information systems or other technology requirements to improve productivity and consistency. This relative powerlessness may be a significant factor in poor employee morale.

- *Role clarity and fit.* This issue applies particularly to customer-facing roles and often relates to the situation where the service provider is torn between providing the service that the customer requires or adhering to the level of service laid down, even when there seems to be no logic in so doing. Service organisations frequently report the problem of customer-facing staff becoming more aligned to customer needs than organisational requirements. Although it might seem that it is a good thing for staff to put the customer first, this is not the case when providing extraordinary service effectively costs money!

  Role fit is a particular problem for high-volume services with many employees. The organisation may have the correct headcount but the personalities do not always match the roles. For example, in the call centre on a shift that is difficult to staff, it may be that there are insufficient experienced agents to deal with complex enquiries. Less experienced people must often do their best, attempting to satisfy the customer without the necessary skills or training. Needless to say, customers may not be happy, and the employee may be demotivated as a result – and may not be as willing to help in future.

- *Relationships.* A continuing question for many service organisations is 'do customers have a relationship with the organisation, or are customers more influenced by a particular employee?' The answer, as ever, is 'it depends'. For many professional service firms, the customer is loyal to an individual provider first and to the firm second. In consumer services, however, rapid staff turnover and shift patterns mean that customers rarely encounter the same employee twice. In this case, any 'relationship' between employee and customer is somewhat limited. Despite this, many customers seem to expect a degree of personalisation that they would not experience in their everyday relationships.

- *Risk.* Most activities contain a degree of risk. Some service roles contain obvious elements of risk, such as the risk of violence encountered by officers or health professionals. For others, it may be more subtle, such as the gradual build-up of abuse experienced by some schoolteachers. Risk can be taken to mean that which is encountered directly by the employee, or some aspect of consequence for customers in the event of service failure. Again, some aspects of risk will be obvious, such as the physical risk of a train or plane crash, while others are more hidden, such as the potential damage to a student's future career if they are not well taught.[1]

- *Stress.* Stress is experienced where the requirements and challenges of the situation exceed an individual's perception of their ability to meet them, as a result of their own abilities, the training provided, or the organisation's unhelpful or difficult systems, procedures or policies. Stress may also result from providers being overloaded for long periods of time. The results of stress include robot-like service delivery, becoming overly focused on unimportant details, and ill health.

Potential outcomes

Feelings of frustration, demotivation, lack of control and stress can have serious consequences for the organisation, the service provider and the customer. For the organisation it can mean increased costs of cover for absent staff, high attrition rates and poor industrial relations. For the service provider it can mean low morale, ill health, psychological damage and, of course, poor service delivery. Indeed one common manifestation of stress is organisation-induced and/or customer-induced 'learned helplessness'.[2] A poor working environment induces employees to display passive, maladaptive behaviours, for example to act immaturely, uncreatively and passively, and to be unhelpful to customers and managers. This learned helplessness can be so deeply ingrained that even when changes are made this passive maladaptive behaviour may continue. The outcome from the customer's point of view is poor service and uninterested and unhelpful staff.

10.3   How can organisations manage and motivate service providers?

Service operations managers must employ a range of approaches to help service providers deal with the negative aspects of being between the opposing pressures of organisation and customer (see Figure 10.3). These approaches to managing and motivating service providers include:

- providing inspirational leadership
- harnessing the power of teams and teamwork across the organisation
- clarifying the roles of service providers
- using scripts appropriately
- defining and enabling appropriate levels of employee discretion
- establishing effective communication to employees
- involving employees in performance improvement
- encouraging ownership of customer and process.

Applying these approaches (as discussed below) and protecting employees from some of the pressures can lead to:

- inspired and involved employees
- responsive and responsible employees
- process and customer ownership

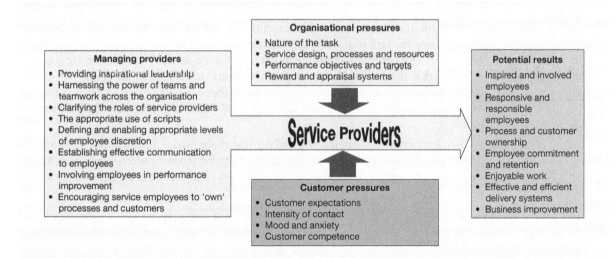

Figure 10.3 Protecting providers from the pressures

- employee commitment and retention
- enjoyable work
- effective and efficient delivery systems
- business improvement.

10.3.1 Providing inspirational leadership

Inspirational leadership in the vast majority of service organisations is not a solo act performed by some charismatic CEO. The UK's Deputy Chief Medical Officer stated:

> It's not a fancy title or a position high up in the hierarchy that makes you a great leader. It's the obstacles you have to overcome and that you overcome every day that make you great. Some of the most inspiring, motivating leaders I know are nurses who aren't high in the pecking order, but who have great influence on the people around them because of the way they lead by example, handling tough situations with grace every day.

When we discuss 'leadership' with managers and executives they usually point to the top of the organisation. We point out that all managers, at varying levels of authority, have a leadership role and need to develop and display leadership qualities. 'Leadership is the privilege to have the responsibility to direct the actions of others in carrying out the purposes of the organisation, at varying levels of authority and with accountability for both successful and failed endeavours.'[3] Today's leading service organisations are good at developing *institutional leadership*, a strategic asset which needs developing and nurturing throughout the organisation.

Leadership can be categorised as transformational or transactional.[4] The essential difference between the two is that transformational leaders develop and project a vision of the future, having energy and influence to encourage others to contribute to this new direction. Transactional leadership, often described as the ability to deal with the day-to-day management of operations, is equally important in the effective running of a service organisation.

Transformational leadership, as is implied by its name, is required at times of significant change. Many of the organisations with a reputation for increasing the quality of service delivery and customer care have done so with the support and leadership of a chief executive who actively demonstrated their personal commitment. Examples of these include:

- Jan Carlzon, the renowned ex-chief executive of the airline SAS who was credited with transforming the airline at a very difficult time during its history. He popularised the notion of service encounters as 'moments of truth' for the service organisation. He is quoted as saying that there were 50,000 'moments of truth' for SAS each day: points of contact between customers and the airline, which will either enhance or detract from the service experience. His 'recipe for success' has been emulated many times since by CEOs across the globe.
- Sir Tom Farmer, ex-CEO of the tyre and exhaust chain Kwik-Fit, who took every opportunity to preach the importance of customer service for business success and who changed the mission statement of the organisation from 'Our aim is 100 per cent customer satisfaction' to 'Our aim is 100 per cent customer delight'.

What is interesting about these and similar leaders is that they are able to communicate a vision in such a way that it motivates the people in their organisations to performance levels significantly greater than might have been expected. Sir Jackie Stewart, a famous racing car driver, said in his autobiography 'Leadership is not about dominating: it is about stimulating people, creating an environment where they can grow, thrive and succeed.'[5]

Different situations and different settings may require differing leadership qualities. These qualities might include the following:[6]

- accountability
- anticipation
- competitiveness
- courage
- credibility
- decisiveness
- dependability
- desire
- empathy
- in touch
- into the detail

- loyalty
- not complacent
- openness
- passionate
- responsibility
- self-confidence
- stamina
- stewardship
- tenacity
- timing
- trusting.

Warren Bennis[7] lists four competencies of great leaders:

- *The management of attention.* The ability of the leader to capture the hearts and minds of people through communicating a focus of commitment and a compelling vision.

- *The management of meaning.* This relates to the importance of bringing substance to the vision in such a way as to make it clear to those following. This is particularly important when dealing with the type of service that contains a high degree of intangibility. It is understandable that the employees in the fast-food restaurant may become overly focused on making and serving burgers or pizzas, but creating the customer experience requires a rather different focus, which can be provided by clear leadership.

- *The management of trust.* One of the key attributes of leaders is reliability. In the same way that customers value reliability of service delivery, employees look to leaders to provide the same degree of security. They do not want messages and programmes that change on what seems like a whim, but want to understand what has to be done well. Clearly, lining up actions with words is part of this attribute.

- *The management of self.* Bennis says that great leaders know their strengths and weaknesses. More specifically, he states that the best leaders do not seem to be easily defeated by mistakes or problems, nor do they start blaming their staff. In a service organisation this is particularly important – enabling staff to listen to customer complaints and institute non-defensive recovery routines.

Each of these attributes has particular application to the leadership of service operations. Of course, not all service organisations are undergoing radical change at all times – although it may frequently feel like it! It is here that transactional leadership is relevant. Some writers have downplayed the importance of this style of leadership, equating it with a mundane form of management that is little more than routine administration of a well-defined concept and its associated processes. This is particularly dangerous in the context of service delivery, which depends to a large degree on the example of front-line leaders.

These first-level managers, supervisors or team leaders have the prime responsibility for providing the day-to-day leadership of a service unit, which may make the essential difference between a robot-like service delivery and one that has life to it. Larkin and Larkin,[8] when discussing the communication of change, state that most staff prefer to hear about change from their immediate supervisor, particularly if senior management is felt to be remote and prone to changing approaches with alarming frequency. There is little doubt that these front-line 'role models' have a major influence in shaping the attitudes and behaviours of those who work with them.

Finally, individual employees may be capable of a form of service leadership as they exercise discretion over the service delivery process, potentially developing new ways of interacting with customers or more productive procedures. This is aligned with developing what psychologists term 'an internal locus of control'. More simply, the aim is to develop a sense of service process ownership in the hearts and minds of the employees. This theme is developed further in a later section on empowerment and employee discretion.

One study which compared manager and employee perceptions of service leader interactions generated definitions of positive and negative leader behaviours.[9] The most significant positive behaviours in this study were:

- formal recognition of service performance through rewards or other recognition programmes
- spontaneous informal recognition, positive praise, and comments to superiors about the employee
- lifting the employee's spirits when under severe work pressure
- helping employees with scheduling requests such as a shift change to deal with a personal issue
- consulting and involvement in change
- problem solving and service recovery effort.

Coaching and employee back-up were thought to be important by managers, but less so by employees.

The research indicated that although there was reasonable consistency between employees and managers regarding the positive attributes, there was less consistency with respect to negative leadership interactions. Employees reported rather more categories of negative behaviours, suggesting a worrying lack of awareness on the part of managers. The most significant negative behaviours were:

- poor styles of criticism or feedback
- poor judgement with people, including failure to support employees, or blaming employees for managerial mistakes
- insensitivity and rudeness.

There are clear links here with the need to see much of service delivery as emotional labour. The extent to which employees feel supported in this emotional labour will clearly impact on the quality of interaction with customers.

10.3.2 Harnessing the power of teams and teamwork

A critical design decision is the extent to which opportunities for teamwork may be built into the service delivery process. Many of the total quality management (TQM) programmes of the 1980s and 1990s evolved into teamwork programmes, as processes were redesigned to reflect the need to become more customer responsive. Several financial services organisations, for example, restructured their customer-facing activities in such a way that a team handles all transactions from sales to service. This frequently led to increases in operational and customer perceived quality and productivity, as team members developed a greater ownership of customers and delivery processes.

However, teams are not appropriate in all situations. For a group of individuals to become a team there must be a real requirement for them to work together because their roles interrelate in some way. In other words, if there is no obvious benefit for the individuals to work together, they remain a group rather than a team. It is important to distinguish here between working in a group and working as a team. Many organisations may claim to be doing the latter, but unless there are real synergies created from the individuals' work together, we would suggest that they are, in fact, simply working as a group of individuals.

That said, we shouldn't dismiss the value of encouraging the formation of social groups within service operations. The benefit of the mutual support of co-workers, particularly in stressful customer-facing roles, cannot be overstated. Most of us recognise the impact of too many demands on our time and energy. Despite our best intentions, the level of energy we devote to yet another request is diminished. There has been a considerable amount of research as to the impact of what is called 'burnout' on the motivation of service employees. In some circumstances, employees may be unable to cope with burnout, leading to unhelpful behaviours with co-workers and with customers.[10] As we've indicated, the impact of burnout can be anticipated and reduced by developing the mutual support mechanisms of a group, providing training to help employees deal with difficult customers, and building in periods away from stressful roles.

There are many benefits of having 'high-performance teams', including:[11]

- Complementary skills and experience exceed those of any one individual. This facilitates a more effective response to demands for innovation and customer service.

- As teams work together to develop clear goals and to improve the processes in which they are involved, they also develop more effective means of communication, which allow them to respond more flexibly to changing customer needs.

- As team members work together and overcome significant challenges, people build trust in others and in others' capabilities. Again, this builds towards a more effective service delivery system.

- Not only does close and collaborative working lead to team success, but high-performing teams often enjoy their work and have more fun than others. A communal sense of humour can be very powerful in dealing with the stress of intensive customer transactions.

A particular point to note for service design is that in some cases the customer is an integral member of the team (see Section 10.4). This is particularly relevant for professional services where the customer's presence and input are essential for service development and delivery. A firm of management consultants must often work alongside their clients in order to carry out their work. Part of the service might be for the consultants to provide mentoring and development for the client's employees.

While there has been a certain amount of research into the formation of management teams,[12] there is relatively little comparable work on the formation and management of teams involved in the day-to-day running of manufacturing processes or service delivery. However, some useful principles for developing successful teams have been identified:[13]

- Setting a demanding performance challenge is more effective in creating a successful team than the use of team-building exercises or appointing team leaders with 'ideal' profiles.

- Organisations need to pay attention to 'team basics'. These include such things as team size, purpose, goals, etc.

- Organisations that emphasise individual performance over team performance erect barriers to team success.

- Teams are a natural unit for integrating performance and learning

Many team initiatives fail because not enough attention is paid to team design and team processes (see Case Example 10.2). In other words, just saying 'let's be a team' is not sufficient to create one. There must be a genuine requirement for a team to operate together if it is to be a success.

One study reported the results of organisations that had redesigned their operations to move towards 'self-directed work teams' which led to increases in productivity and quality.[14] Shenandoah Life was quoted as processing 50 per cent more applications and customer services requests, with 10 per cent fewer people, by using work teams. A powerful example of the impact of teamwork is provided by the Experian consumer service centre in Texas. Some years ago it had all the typical ailments of call centres: low morale, high employee turnover, fragmented service delivery systems and poor quality compliance. A redesign, which included investment in new technology and integrating service functions, combined with a team approach, turned this poor service operation into a benchmark site for call centre operations.

Case Example 10.2 | First Mortgage Direct

A call centre within the First Mortgage Group was organised into a number of teams. Team leaders had a range of objectives:

- to organise and co-ordinate the team
- to update training plans
- to produce weekly performance reports
- to monitor and record holidays
- to deal with queries
- to review sickness.

The issue for Mike Walker, the newly appointed manager, was that there was no consistency or co-ordination across teams. In other words, there was no teamwork at

Source: Pearson Education Ltd/Studio 8

team-leader level. Each team operated independently, creating 'mini call centres' within the unit. This resulted in poor performance, duplication of work and resistance to implementing improvements originating from other teams.

Mike's approach was to clarify the broader vision of the call centre for his team leaders. His objective was to get them to see their role as contributing to the success of the call centre as a whole, rather than simply leading their team. Mike involved his 'team of team leaders' in putting the detail to the vision. This was achieved through brainstorming sessions, benchmarking visits, using advice from the National Society for Quality through Teamwork (NSQT) and focus groups formed from call centre staff.

A number of audits were carried out. A skills audit revealed that there were training and development needs for team leaders to take on more people-focused roles. A task audit showed that team leaders were concentrating on clerical activities to the detriment of less quantifiable tasks such as coaching team members. As a result of this analysis, the team leader role was redefined so that it was expected that 60 per cent of time should be spent in coaching, and only 10 per cent in call handling.

The call centre was reorganised, with an operational support unit dealing with many of the clerical activities previously handled by team leaders. This enabled team leaders to concentrate on performance improvement in line with the vision. Some of the benefits realised by this initiative included:

- more effective team management, despite increases in team size of up to 50 per cent
- 35 per cent increase in productivity
- improved customer service
- increased innovation and proactivity
- fewer ineffective meetings
- a saving in team-leader time of 1.5 days per team leader per week.

Mike Walker reports that the creation of a culture of encouragement and the facilitation of learning has provided a solid platform for future change.

Not all situations are suitable for teams. Here is a helpful checklist for feasibility:[15]

- Are the work processes compatible with self-directed teams?
- Are employees willing and able to make self-direction work?
- Can managers master and apply the hands-off leadership style required by self-directed teams?
- Is the market healthy or promising enough to support improved productivity without reducing the workforce?

- Will the organisation's policies and culture support the transition to teams?
- Will the local community support the transition to teams?

It is important to note that an organisation is unlikely to be able to move from a situation without teams to the autonomy and employee maturity required for self-directed teams in one step. The required change in leadership style and employee discretion is covered in following sections.

The role of team leaders

Research into the role of team leaders has shown that the team leaders play a critical role in the success of teams.[16] And just like all service providers they, too, feel squeezed between the pressure of the organisation pushing for business results and the team members looking for support and care. This feeling is exacerbated in some organisations where the team members see them as managers but managers often see them as part of the team.

The research identified six key attributes of a team leader. They should be:

- approachable
- empathetic
- supportive
- organised
- knowledgeable about the role of the team members
- knowledgeable about the business.

An interesting finding from this research was the importance of building the team of team leaders as well as the teams themselves. Building a strong team can have one disadvantage which is that the relationships within the team can be so strong that the team is reluctant to accept new members or to transfer members to other teams. This will reduce the flexibility to respond to fluctuations in workloads. A way of counteracting this effect is to ensure that the team of team leaders has the understanding to manage resources across the organisation, rather than be solely focused on their individual teams.

10.3.3 Clarifying the roles of service providers

Most people work more effectively when they have a clear understanding of their role, what is expected of them, and how they will be assessed. Research into the effectiveness of service encounters suggests that role conflict and role ambiguity should be minimised if customer-facing employees are to be motivated to provide good service.

- *Role conflict.* In many organisations, service providers may have a number of responsibilities, yet it may be impossible to carry out each role simultaneously. An example is provided by the call centre employee who is charged with reducing queue lengths and also with trying to persuade customers to purchase more services, a task that requires more time to be spent on each transaction. Role conflict may occur when the basic service design is in error, as in the example above, or when the demands of the job are in conflict with the individual's personal view of how much status is conferred on the role. In the UK, for example, service jobs are often seen as rather demeaning, with perhaps some feeling that they are similar in nature to the role of servants to the 'lord of the manor'. This feeling of inequality and lack of value may be detected when employees call customers 'Sir' or 'Madam' in a somewhat sarcastic tone of voice.

- *Role ambiguity.* Role ambiguity occurs when the person is unsure of the requirements of the role.[17] Role ambiguity frequently occurs when service employees perceive that there is a lack of clarity about the guiding philosophy or strategy of the organisation. This may be a result of poor leadership both from senior management and from first-line supervisors.

Both role conflict and role ambiguity may occur as the organisation grows and develops. What was carried out by committed individuals in the early stages of the organisation's existence may be taken over by people who have been recruited more recently. In theory this should be an opportunity to formalise roles and responsibilities, but this may be resisted since it may be felt to be contrary to the entrepreneurial spirit of the original vision.

Service designers must take into account these issues in order to manage all aspects of service delivery, but must pay particular attention to the roles of customer-facing employees. If these people are experiencing role stress of any nature, their ability to create the required service experience is likely to be significantly diminished.

10.3.4 Using scripts appropriately

Many mass service organisations employ the use of scripts as a technique for providing both consistency and efficiency in service delivery. In addition, as we shall discuss later, scripting may also provide a sense of security for customers and employees alike. A familiar script may allow customers to relax because they understand the 'rules' by which the encounter will be played out.

We need to clarify here what we mean by a 'script'. The word 'script' conjures up the idea of a precise set of words to be used in a service encounter. In the service management literature it is used in a much broader way. A script 'is used to denote the precise specification of actions to be taken by service staff in particular situations. Scripts create procedures, which help employees to know what to do, and in what sequence, in specific situations.'[18] Thus, like in the theatre, it may include directions about movement and positioning, mood and tone, the order in which to do things, and the words to be used. The 'words to be used' may range from tightly scripted to improvisational.

Tansik and Smith[19] proposed eleven functions for using scripts in service delivery:

- *To assist the service employee to find out what the customer wants or needs.* The script should be designed to encourage customers to describe their needs in such a way as to allow the employee to diagnose them accurately and offer the appropriate service.

- *To control the customer.* The script should help the employee guide the customer through the system with minimal disruption. This is particularly important where customisation is actively discouraged. 'Can I suggest our special two-course offer?' enables a rapid decision, although there may be a danger of closing off opportunities for selling more profitable services in the cause of an efficient order-taking process.

- *To establish historical routines that may be relevant to the service encounter.* Frequent customers will often become pre-programmed to carry out the necessary actions in the service process without prompting. An example is provided by airline passengers who have packed their luggage in the most appropriate cases, who anticipate the check-in questions, and who have their documents in order before approaching the check-in desk. Tansik and Smith suggest that the service designer should provide the appropriate triggers to what have been termed memory organisation packets (MOPs),[20] which allow the customer to move into what may often be unconscious routines, which may lead to early involvement in the service delivery process. There may be a danger of changing scripts in order to make a differentiation between service providers: this may cause confusion rather than build service quality.

- *To facilitate control of workers.* Scripts may provide the means of increasing consistency across multiple sites and multiple servers. This has the particular benefit of ensuring that the appropriate customer script is activated, and that all the required questions and prompts are given. Scripts have particular value in the process of cross-selling, as for example in a call centre selling direct insurance that encourages the employee to use 'subscripts' such as 'Are you sure you have sufficient cover for your house contents?' or 'Can we help you with any other insurance worries?'

- *To legitimise organisational actions.* Here the script informs the employee as to what behaviours and attitudes the management believes customers expect. The restaurant chain TGI Friday encourages staff to display high energy levels in their interactions with customers, whereas gourmet restaurants might prefer staff to exercise a rather more sedate and relaxed form of delivery.

- *To serve as analogies.* Scripts learned by a worker in a previous employment may be used as the basis for developing new scripts in later, similar situations.

- *To facilitate organised behaviour.* Scripting may allow for the smooth running of a team engaged in interdependent activity. Tansik and Smith provide the example of a surgical team, where the actions of team members are choreographed and rehearsed beforehand. Developing routine medical procedures means that individual team members may change, provided that others can perform their roles. Scripting facilitates this interchangeability.

- *To provide a guide to behaviour.* Scripts set expectations as to what will happen next in a service encounter. Because customers have experienced this or similar service organisations before, there is no need to provide explanation as to why things are done this way or why certain information is requested before the service may be delivered. It is also suggested that scripts may be used to explain service 'fairness'. Most patients in a casualty clinic will tolerate another patient being seen earlier than their turn if the condition is clearly more serious than their own.

- *To buffer or exacerbate role conflict.* A script may deflect difficult questions such as 'Why do I have to give this information?' by the use of scripts such as 'I'm sorry but it's company policy', or 'The financial services regulations require us to gain this information'. Scripts may help when the employee is faced with giving unwelcome or unpopular information to customers.

- *To provide a basis for evaluating behaviour.* Scripts can be used as a checklist for management to evaluate an employee's behaviour. This is commonly used in telephone call centres where supervisors may routinely monitor large numbers of calls. It is particularly relevant where supervisors may be looking for evidence of specific behaviours, such as the generation of sales as well as simple order taking. Scripts such as 'Have you considered . . . ?' may be useful here.

- *To conserve cognitive capacity.* Scripts allow the employee to work on a number of activities simultaneously because the script may be performed as if on 'automatic pilot'.

As can be seen from the list above, scripts can play a valuable part in service design and delivery. Carefully designed scripts can provide opportunities for early involvement of the customer with the organisation and its employees. Scripts can provide both conscious and unconscious means of support for customers and employees alike. They assist in the management of customer expectations, and may facilitate the smooth passage of the customer through the service process because there exists a good understanding of what will happen and what is required of the customer at each stage to enable this to occur.

There are, however, a number of problems with using scripts in the delivery of service:

- *They may become too inflexible.* Customers who do not make the appropriate responses to fit the script may provide inexperienced or poorly trained employees with too great a problem to deal with.

- *They may lead to a customer perception of robot-like behaviour.* The standard restaurant script that prompts the server to ask 'Is everything all right for you?' is frequently greeted with the expected response 'Yes, it's fine, thank you', which is often not a comment about the food, but more a way of getting rid of an intrusion as quickly as possible. Because this script is used too often, without the perceived sincerity that would suggest that there is genuine interest in the response, the possible impression is of someone going through the motions of service with none of the personal attributes of warmth or customer responsiveness required.

- *They may lead to defensive behaviour.* Standard scripts may become a two-edged sword. While they may have a useful role in providing employees with a clear form of words to deal with difficult situations, it may be rather too easy to use a scripted response when the situation requires something rather different.

10.3.5 Defining and enabling appropriate levels of employee discretion

It is neither desirable nor possible to create a script for every service situation, so most service organisations give some degree of discretion to their service providers. This lines up with a general trend in organisations to tap into the brainpower and creativity of all employees, and not exclusively the senior management team. A move to self-directed or semi-autonomous teams and flatter organisations may build on the need to give more people more autonomy in the workplace.

We refer here to discretion rather than empowerment, because most people are 'empowered' – the critical question is how much discretion they have.[21] It is generally accepted that giving clear indications of the limits of an employee's autonomy is more helpful than providing no guidance at all. Empowerment in this context means that these limits are extended for employees. An interesting aspect of empowering employees is, of course, that their managers are to some extent 'disempowered' because they must step back from activities they have previously undertaken.

Kelley[22] summarised the work of earlier writers[23] to develop three types of employee discretion:

- *Routine discretion* means that the employee has discretion regarding how the basic task is performed rather than what task is undertaken. The range of routine discretion may be extended with the complexity of the task. The more complex the task, the less it is possible to describe each step in a rigorously controlled procedure document. Kelley uses the example of an investment advisor who draws on a wide range of information sources in order to make the appropriate recommendation to each client. In the same way, customer-facing employees will make changes in the way that they deal with each service encounter.

- *Creative discretion* is exercised by those who develop both what and how they do things. This may relate to people who do not have a tried and tested formula for doing things, but nonetheless have some training and experience that allows them to make informed judgements as to what to do. At the extreme end of this spectrum might be those creative people who are involved in the innovative activities of the organisation, as in new product design or in the development of strategies that represent a significant shift from what has been the accepted norm.

- *Deviant discretion* differs from routine and creative discretion in that it is generally not approved by the organisation, whereas the other two types are recognised and approved by it. In the service context, Kelley gives the example of the retail salesperson who gives a customer a refund contrary to company policy. This may gain increased customer satisfaction for this individual, but not be approved by senior management. Deviant discretion is potentially disruptive since it usually involves individuals acting on their own authority, rather than on behalf of the organisation. Such people may earn the reputation of being mavericks or 'just plain awkward'. Indeed, an organisation made up of people who operate in this way would be interesting, but rather chaotic! However, an organisation without such people might easily become rather stagnant, without challenge to the status quo.

Figure 10.4 provides a framework for exploring some of the issues around developing or restricting employee discretion.[24] The key dimensions are as follows:

- *Organisational style.* Fluid organisations are those which must change their structure relatively frequently. Project-based organisations, such as consultancies, may organise around expertise. The consultant who is the expert provides the lead, possibly providing direction

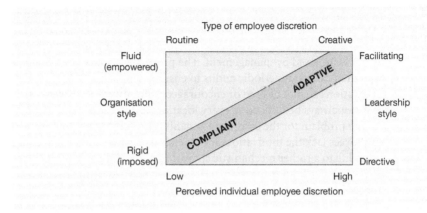

Figure 10.4 Employee discretion

Source: Adapted from Kelley, Scott W. (1993), 'Discretion and the Service Employee', *Journal of Retailing* 69 (1) 104–126

for employees with greater seniority. As the clients' needs shift, so may the requirement for different skills/knowledge sets change, prompting further changes in organisational structure and processes. These organisations will need to adapt processes for each situation so will lie at the 'fluid' end of the scale.

Service operations that have clear operating procedures such as retailers or insurance companies will tend to operate at the rigid end of the scale. For financial services this will enable them to operate efficiently but also to ensure that risk management/compliance procedures are observed.

- *Perceived individual employee discretion.* This will be discussed in more detail below, but it is important to recognise that the issue is frequently how much discretion employees 'feel' that they have, or feel that they are capable of. We will discuss this from the employees' point of view. Some employees may not 'grow into' the discretion they have been given; others may feel that their freedom to act has been curtailed. Clearly this aspect might also be analysed from the manager's perspective, and it is worth considering the issues arising from differences of opinion between managers and employees.

The compliant organisation

The compliant organisation is frequently found in the high-volume/low-variety service operations discussed in Chapter 8. Compliant organisations frequently have the following characteristics:

- Their focus is on consistent service delivery, often across multiple locations and with many servers.
- Such operations have well-developed process documentation, with training for employees as to how they should behave in each situation.
- High volumes and consistent processes lend themselves to automation and/or the employment of relatively low-cost labour.
- The management style employed is frequently somewhat directive, often because employee turnover is such that employees are relatively inexperienced (and with low motivation).
- Performance measurement often relates to short-term indicators such as response times or orders taken.

We need to give a warning here not to assume that all roles in the compliant zone relate to low-paid, low-skilled employees. Airline pilots also fit in this zone. We would like our pilots to operate in a consistent manner and not to exercise too much discretion! However, we will pay our pilots a good deal of money for their skill and responsibility to look after our safety. When things go wrong, we want pilots to follow the procedures they have trained for in the simulator. In effect, to avoid being 'paralysed' by the situation, they become possibly more compliant.

As Figure 10.4 suggests, the problem for these organisations is that the service process feels as if it is imposed by management. The process may have been designed by head-office staff, who then carry out periodic audits to ensure compliance to the pre-determined design. Local innovations are not desired or encouraged, since this might create customer expectations that may not always be fulfilled in every location and will lead to potential increases in unit costs.

The problem for the compliant organisation is therefore that front-line (and often junior) employees lack the motivation or ownership of either the service concept or the customer to bring life to a rather mechanistic style of service delivery. The challenge for service managers is to engender both ownership and a spark of creativity in a workforce that might otherwise appear like robots.

In so doing, the aim is to change the emphasis from compliant to process ownership. The objective here is for the employees to take ownership of service delivery, rather than to feel that it is imposed on them. How this may be achieved is covered more fully in the chapters on service culture and continuous improvement (Chapters 12 and 16), but broadly the approaches utilised are as follows:

- *Communication.* Good communication from management as to how well the organisation is performing and the reason for future strategies. Also, it is useful to open lines of communication from customer-facing employees to senior management in order to facilitate the passage of invaluable customer feedback.

- *Involvement.* Inclusion in process improvement projects is encouraged as and when possible. The aim here is to foster a sense of ownership of both process and customer, because employees have had a hand in process design. Many service organisations have found that continuous improvement activities such as *kaizen* or six sigma have been very beneficial in this area (see Chapter 12).

- *Celebration.* A major problem for the motivation of staff in customer-facing roles is that they are frequently on the receiving end of complaints and abuse and rarely receive praise from customers. Indeed, some customer service functions are set up with the explicit task of dealing exclusively with complaints. Some service organisations counteract both the potential boredom of routine transactions and the deadening effect of dealing with customer complaints by creating rituals of celebration of success.

- *Teamwork.* Organising customer-facing staff into teams may help engender a sense of purpose, and also provide opportunities for job rotation, support and motivation. A major benefit of teams in service delivery is that managers can give the team more 'routine discretion' to make decisions in a range of prescribed areas such as job rotation. This reduces the perception of the organisation as 'big brother' controlling every aspect of employees' work life.

All these approaches have one thing in common: they create a sense that the organisation values the contribution of even the most junior employees. Without this, it is unlikely that service encounters will be anything more than adequate, and they will probably not build customer loyalty.

The adaptive organisation

The adaptive organisation is more often found at the high-variety/low-volume end of the spectrum, which we described as capability organisations in Chapter 8. Many people in professional services, for example management consultants or legal advisors, might fit into this category. The characteristics of adaptive organisations are:

- There are high degrees of creative discretion in developing both product and process.
- There is frequent dependence on key individuals' skill and knowledge.
- There is a resistance to the generation of standard processes, leading to inconsistency in approach.

- There is an emphasis on innovation.
- Research and development activities are often focused on the professional development of the people in the organisation as opposed to the development of service brands and 'products' found in commodity organisations.
- The management style is likely to be 'facilitative', focusing on ensuring that the skilled individuals are able to work to their full potential.
- Performance measures are likely to be rather more long-term in nature than is the case for the compliant organisations. Marketing, for example, may have targets that include the development of a number of new services over a period of months, while an academic may be required to develop new material for teaching next year's course.

The challenge for these organisations is to ensure that a reasonably consistent approach is adopted to service delivery. In many professional service organisations, client relationships are managed by the individual provider, leading to potential inefficiencies. Another weakness here is that individuals are reluctant to share their knowledge with others because this might weaken their position in the organisation. This may cause major problems when key individuals leave, often taking their portfolio of clients with them. Management may need to focus its attention on the following:

- Motivating key individuals, by providing opportunities to extend their skill and knowledge.
- Emphasising situations that require individuals to collaborate in order to carry out their tasks.
- Developing multiple links with clients to ensure that these relationships are not severed when individuals leave the organisation.

Managing transitions

Figure 10.5 illustrates two common conditions that describe what may happen when an organisation decides to increase or decrease the nature and amount of discretion given to individual employees:

- compliant to adaptive: the anxious zone
- adaptive to compliant: the frustrated zone.

Compliant to adaptive: the anxious zone

Service organisations may wish to increase the amount of discretion given to customer-facing employees. This is particularly relevant if the strategy is to increase the range of service options available to customers. In this case, individual service providers may be asked to take more decisions and to carry out a greater proportion of the service process.

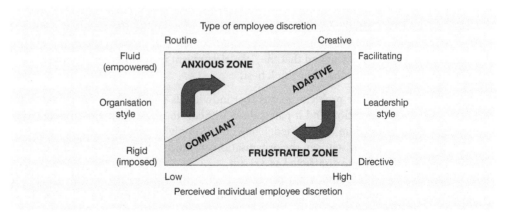

Figure 10.5 Transitions in managing employee discretion

In many cases, of course, the implementation of this change is well planned and executed. Typically, this will involve investment in training and information systems, but no matter how well this is managed, individuals change at different speeds, which are dictated by their individual personality and history. Thus, in this case, the individual employees are being moved from what might feel like a reasonably 'safe' environment where they are provided with a clear structure and process to follow, to one where individual decision-making is required.

This may be summed up as 'being empowered but not feeling it'. The individuals involved want the challenge but either are unsure of their own ability or are uncertain as to how much real discretion the organisation is willing to give them. In this transition, individuals may well not perform immediately to the level of their capability and, indeed, may be written off by the management as not being up to the new task.

In reality, with support and training, large numbers of staff may be able to deal with the added responsibility of increased discretion. There is often a rich vein of talent for continuous improvement activities and the opportunity to build ownership of the service delivery process. It is important to note, though, that customer-facing employees in the anxious zone will probably not always deliver service to the new (usually more demanding) design standards.

Adaptive to compliant: the frustrated zone

Organisations may want to restrict the degree of discretion of some or all of their employees. A common reason for this would be that as a consequence of actual or desired growth, systems and processes are standardised, reducing the opportunity for individuals to develop their own approach to service. This is particularly relevant to professional services seeking to provide consistent services to national or multinational business clients.

For these professional services the implementation of management by process will result in a reduction in autonomy on the part of the individuals in the organisation. A good example is provided by the larger consultancy firms which may seek to develop solutions that may be adapted for a wide range of clients. In this scenario, although consultants may have some discretion to adapt the basic solution to their individual client, the basic design work has been carried out by other people in the firm. This philosophy will clearly change from firm to firm, as will policies regarding brand management and standardisation of approaches to client relationships.

The characteristics of the frustrated zone are as follows:

- Individuals resist the implementation of standard processes (an imposed system), claiming that the system prevents them from operating in the most effective way in delivering solutions to their customers.
- These individuals are frequently extremely vocal about these perceived or real restrictions.
- As can be seen from Figure 10.5, employees in the frustrated zone often perceive that they still have high degrees of discretion, despite the standard processes being implemented. The result is that these employees feel that they are 'above' the system, that it does not apply to them and that they can circumvent its requirements in order to 'get the job done' in the way that they think best.

The problem here is that individuals who have become used to high levels of perceived discretion find it particularly difficult to work in an environment where they feel that their freedom is restricted. They may 'comply' with the system if the alternative is that they lose pay or status in the organisation, but they find the system difficult to accept and are likely to become disaffected as a result.

It is important to recognise the concerns of these individuals because they frequently possess skills that are essential to retain. This may be achieved in some cases by providing them with opportunities for personal development through involvement in activities that do not conflict with the objectives of the more standardised service processes being implemented.

Balancing empowerment and control

The illustration provided by the Open Door Church (Case Example 10.3) demonstrates how organisations in the same service sector may have very different operating philosophies. Individuals who were happy in one organisational culture may struggle in another. It is important to note that when an organisation wishes to make significant changes, individuals must be treated as such, recognising that some will welcome more empowerment or discretion, others will be happiest in more prescribed roles, whereas others will take time and support to grow into a larger role.

Case Example 10.3   Open Door Church, St Neots, UK

The Open Door Church is only a few years old, but is growing rapidly where other, more traditional, faith groups appear to have reached a plateau, or are declining in numbers. There are a number of possible reasons for this success. A fundamental aspect of the Open Door Church is its vision statement of 'Open to God, open to you', which makes the point that church is not supposed to be the exclusive domain of those who are rich and talented. It is for anyone, including those who may be deemed less acceptable by society at large.

The Open Door Church meets on Sundays in a local school, but in reality the organisation is a cluster of small groups or 'cells'. These meet formally on a weekday evening but are encouraged to build relationships internally and with friends and neighbours. The volume of official meetings is much lower than many churches, to give space for life outside, and for members to be a real part of the community. Although the basic format of Sunday services for the whole church, with small groups meeting in homes on weeknights, looks similar to other churches, the underlying emphasis is entirely different. Traditionally, in other churches, the focus is on Sunday services with a small percentage of members meeting in homes during the week. In the Open Door Church, the focus is on the development of cells with their ongoing relationships. These cell groups come together on Sundays, and attendance at the weeknight meetings is frequently higher than that at the Sunday services.

Tony Thompson, the first leader of the church, comments: 'The growth of many churches has been limited by the availability of experienced and talented leaders. We've taken a different approach, encouraging people who are relatively new members to become cell leaders.' This has meant that many more people have the potential to become group leaders, and this in turn has allowed room for growth.

These new cell leaders are given a great deal of support, including training and an 'apprenticeship' as an assistant cell leader. Cell group meetings are quite structured, with a recognised format and detailed notes provided by the church leadership team. John and Janet Lloyd were asked to lead a cell after a short time in the church. 'We were worried that we wouldn't be able to cope with leading the group. We thought we might have to deliver a "second sermon", but the church leaders give us plenty of support and guidance week by week.'

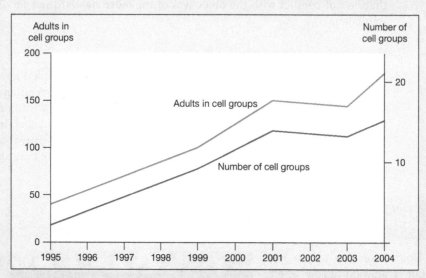

Figure 10.6 Growth in membership

Some people joining the church from more traditional denominations have taken time to adjust to this approach. If they have been group leaders before, it may feel that the role of the cell leader is more defined, possibly lacking freedom. Tony Thompson's response is:

We have made it easier for people to grow quickly into the cell leader role. It used to be so daunting that few people would volunteer for it. As soon as a cell has a stable membership of about 16 members, we're looking for it to become two cells of eight members. This multiplication may happen as quickly as six months and so we need a lot of leaders to sustain our growth.

The statistics shown in Figure 10.6 indicate the speed of growth. Increasing from three cells in 1995 to 15 in 2004 required the identification, training and support of nearly 30 leaders and assistant leaders. This was no mean feat, given that a sizeable proportion of the church's new members were not just new to the church but also new to Christianity.

In 2004 there were nearly 200 adults meeting each week in cell groups. The rate of growth has been more significant than the graph suggests because between 2001 and 2002 50 adults left the Open Door Church to found new ventures in St Ives and Luton. The second group included Tony Thompson, his place being taken by Martin Tibbert, an existing member of the leadership team.

Source: This illustration has been developed from discussions with Tony Thompson, the first leader of the Open Door Church in St Neots, Cambridgeshire, UK, and with his successor, Martin Tibbert.

As we have seen previously, the dilemma is to know how and by how much individual employees can be 'empowered'. Situational leadership theory[25] suggests that a key issue is the maturity of the 'followers': the extent to which they are both willing and able to take more responsibility.

Simons[26] suggests there are four control organisational systems that assist the service manager in moving towards employees taking more ownership of their service processes:

- *Diagnostic control systems.* These are the standard performance measures of the organisation and include indicators such as sales per employee, response times and so forth. Managers may watch these indicators and allow employees to decide how they are to be achieved. Simons maintains that the danger here is that there may be pressure to 'massage' the figures in order to demonstrate ability. Thus, these measures are not sufficient in themselves to give management control.

- *Beliefs systems.* These convey the key values of the organisation. We discuss more of these in Chapter 16 on service culture; Kwik-Fit's mission to provide '100 per cent customer delight' would be a good example. At worst, these statements appear to be simply following the latest trend but, at best, they can inspire employees to look for opportunities to contribute and do things better.

- *Boundary systems.* These are best described as systems that state minimum standards or express the rules that govern acceptable behaviour in terms of what is done or not done.
- *Interactive control systems.* Diagnostic control systems detect when the organisation is failing to meet performance standards. Interactive control systems are focused on detecting in what way the environment and therefore the task of the organisation might be changing. Strategic reviews and customer focus groups might form part of an interactive control system.

Simons asserts that managers need to use all four of these levers together, in order to provide an environment in which employees may operate more effectively.

10.3.6 Establishing effective communication to employees

Many service providers do not appreciate being kept in the dark about the organisation, its current activities and plans for the future; indeed, many service providers appreciate being involved in the process of development and often have important contributions to make. Communication is the key to success and its importance is recognised by some outstanding organisations (see Case Example 10.4).

Organisations use a variety of mechanisms to communicate and listen to their service providers. These include:

- briefings by managers
- annual meetings
- round-table meetings
- question and answer sessions
- intranet-based information and updates
- informal meetings and gatherings
- company newsletters.

Case Example 10.4 describes the variety of mechanisms used by First Direct.

Case Example 10.4 First Direct

First Direct was the first bank in the UK to offer banking services exclusively over the phone. It was launched in 1989 by Midland Bank, which was acquired by HSBC. Peter Simpson was one of the original members of a working group set up to develop a new approach to banking in 1988. He has been First Direct's commercial director since 1991. He explains why First Direct was launched:

We had to find a way to differentiate ourselves from all other banks. Customer satisfaction with banks in general was low and customers felt the banks were all as bad as each other. The existing notion was that a bank required the customer's physical

Source: First Direct

presence. We decided upon the radical idea of a purely telephone operation. Telephone was the obvious channel because just about everybody had a telephone in their house or access to a telephone at work. We went live at midnight on Saturday 1 October 1989. Making a Sunday as our first day of trading made it clear that we were very different and out to provide the customer with a service that they had never experienced before. We took around about 200 calls on the first night and since that day we have never closed.

Matthew Higgins, the manager with responsibility for planning and research, added:

We now take something like 45,000 calls a day but increasingly we are getting more and more web traffic. We launched internet banking back in 1997 and around 400,000 of our customers are now using internet banking in addition to the telephone service.

Although the customer is likely to speak to a different person each time they call, consistency of response is important. This is ensured by each representative having all the caller's details on the screen in front of them, including information about the customer's last call and any issues or problems they may have encountered. Each call is concluded with the operator asking if there is anything else they can do for the customer. However, the bank goes well beyond providing these traditional ingredients of good service. First Direct is a bank with personality. As Matthew explains:

The difference is how people feel when they finish talking to us. They go away with a feeling that they have had a good conversation with a friend. It is taken for granted that what they have asked to be done has been done. If they have asked to pay a bill, it has been paid. If they have asked for a balance, they have got a balance. But it is the extra bit. It is the attitude our people have and their sense of humour. They will also take the initiative. We like our staff to be proactive and to do this they need to feel both competent and confident and be good communicators willing and able to make decisions.

Although staff are incentivised through sales targets they are focused on providing excellent service. They manage the potential conflict between these aims by having good information about their customers. Matthew explains:

The more information we have about specific customers the more we can target better. So we don't, for example, make the mistake of trying to sell somebody a credit card or mortgage if we know they already have one. By talking to our customers we can understand them better and so serve them better and by doing so build up a relationship built on mutual trust.

What is important for us is that a person answers the phone – you don't get a voice that says press one for this and two for that. We want to be there for the customer. We want our staff to use their own style and personality. Obviously we have to ask for security details but, strange as it might seem, our people ask for it in many different ways. It makes it a much more human experience.

There is a balance between giving operators a script and getting them to be themselves. The downside is that mistakes get made, but this is a small price to pay. Mistakes are OK – we don't go around blaming people, otherwise they would want to go back to hiding behind set scripts with no personality or feeling and we don't want that. We accept mistakes and help people learn from them. Mistakes are about support, not blame. If somebody makes a mistake or if someone sees someone else making a mistake we expect them to be very open about it and do something about it straight away. The critical thing is that they tell somebody, their team leader or someone else in their team. We want people to be open and to learn from what they do. The team leaders will happily sit with them and help them sort it out. We don't say 'Don't press that button' or 'Press that button', but we would say 'Is this the one you want?' We try to point them gently in the right direction and even have a bit of a laugh about it as well.

In essence I think we are about 'sorting it with attitude'! We don't just want to sort out paying a bill, for example, but we want to do it with a particular personality and style. It's not written down anywhere – it's just what we do – we all know that. This idea is shared through senior management presentations, team presentations, marketing presentations and in direct discussions one-to-one with team leaders or managers and also through our TV advertising – which is not just aimed at potential or existing customers but also at our staff.

> *We spend a huge amount of time communicating. But that's the very soul of this organisation, so if you don't spend time communicating you might as well pack up and go home. If you can't communicate within the organisation, how can you communicate to customers? Communication has always been our strength.*

Peter Simpson added:

> *First and foremost we are a communications organisation. Second we are a bank selling financial products. The products are of course important, but it's about the way we do it. Without that we are the same as everyone else.*

Matthew explains:

> *A couple of times a year the chief executive does a round of big presentations explaining the goals and plans for the following six and twelve months. This is done in groups of about 200 at a time so it takes a while to get around all 4,000 staff. One of the things that I have always found very refreshing is the amount of often quite confidential information that is shared with absolutely everybody. We trust our staff. The sessions often include question time with a panel of people – we get some very challenging questions!*

First Direct's core values of openness, respect, contribution, responsive, right first time and *kaizen* reflect the way its employees behave to customers – and indeed how they hope and expect customers will behave towards them. The company believes in treating its internal customers in the same way as its external customers. According to Matthew Higgins:

> *Our values are basically commonsense values. They are just there to remind us about how we should operate. We don't ram them down people's throats, otherwise they might lose their meaning. They are just embedded in the way we do things. There is also belief that you would not treat anybody internally any differently from how you would treat a customer. It is about dialogue and information exchange but it is also about treating people as equals.*

The board of directors takes the findings of their customer research very seriously. They are concerned about what their customers think. They are also concerned about what their employees think too. Board members would not hesitate to wander round the floor and talk to people to get their ideas and reactions to new ideas and initiatives or problems. Matthew added:

> *We were talking about service recovery yesterday and the chief operations officer arranged several sessions with a range of people, including people on the phones. Another director, following a particular incident, asked for people's suggestions. Senior managers make a point of listening and responding to the staff. They understand that the people on the phones not only know what is going on but may have many good ideas too because they are talking to customers all day. The directors not only understand the strategic issues but they understand the tactical issues as well.*

Source: This case was commissioned by the Institute of Customer Service as part of a study into service excellence. The author gratefully acknowledges the sponsorship provided by Britannic Assurance, FirstGroup, Lloyds TSB, RAC Motoring Services and Vodafone.

Research has suggested four communication responsibilities for leaders.[27] These have been developed by Synopsis, a consulting firm specialising in communication, and are summarised in the FAME model:

- *Focus.* Leaders must set a clear focus with relatively few priorities, which are repeated and reinforced consistently. Leaders should identify what they want employees to think, feel and do to help.
- *Articulate.* Leaders must be able to turn management-speak into plain language, and to make the messages memorable.
- *Model.* Leaders must champion company/organisational values, lead by example and challenge unacceptable behaviour.

● *Engage.* Leaders must make the connection between the organisation's agenda and the individual's agenda. They must be able to listen, facilitate, ask effective questions and handle any difficulties that may arise when employees speak up.

Many managers believe that they are effective communicators, but Kotter[28] suggests that a significant reason for the failure of many change processes is 'undercommunicating by a power of ten'. The implication is that even when we think we've communicated effectively, we probably haven't! It has been suggested that communication must be carefully planned to avoid contradiction, repetition, overload of trivia and insufficient communication of key issues.[29]

10.3.7 Involving employees in performance improvement

We will discuss this in more detail in Chapter 12, but it is important to emphasise here that actions that build the self-esteem of employees will provide an antidote to the pressure they experience. At the most basic level, it is common sense to involve the people who are closest to any task in its improvement, given that they probably know most about it. Service designers who are remote from routine service delivery may sometimes create processes that are not always 'employee friendly'. Involvement of service employees may create wins for both employee and organisation. This will inevitably mean that the organisation has some investment to make in terms of time, training and management support, but most organisations report benefits from these activities.

10.3.8 Encouraging responsibility for customer and process

This has been discussed in some detail in Section 10.3.5 above. However, it is worth emphasising that in the same way that customers like to feel that they have a degree of control over their own destiny, so also employees like to feel that they too are able to exercise some influence over what happens to the customer they are serving, and the processes they follow.

Encouraging ownership of responsibility for customers largely comes from the example of managers. If the manager/leader is seen to champion the cause of individual customers, following through on problems and questions, employees will follow. Likewise, giving employees responsibility for processes builds the sense of ownership, and of being in control of the process rather than the process controlling them.

10.4 How can customers be 'managed' and motivated?

This chapter has focused so far on employees as service providers. However, in many service organisations the customers also fulfil some provider roles. We would argue that, just like employees, managers need to understand how these 'temporary employees' should be managed so that they fulfil their required roles and display the desired behaviours.[30]

10.4.1 Customer roles

Customers perform a surprising variety of functions in the service process. Their precise role will depend on the nature of the activity and the approach determined by the service designer. These roles include:

● *Service provider.* In many organisations the customer provides themselves – and sometimes other customers – with a service. An obvious example is the task we fulfil in supermarkets, taking items off the shelves, taking them to the cashier, bagging the items and taking them to the car. Less obvious are the roles we play in faith organisations, syndicate or work groups that rely on the involvement of all to create the service (and benefits) for each other. Another role customers provide, to other customers, is that of providing the atmosphere in a restaurant or place of entertainment. By being quiet or joining in the fun customers help set the tone or mood for others to enjoy and/or follow.

- *Service specifier.* In most services the customer must provide clear information about requirements before the appropriate service or product can be selected and delivered. This may be relatively straightforward in consumer services where the service or product is well defined and customers may have wide experience of the scripts (see Section 10.3.4). It may not be as straightforward, however, in customised service, such as many of the professional services, where in many cases the customer has little relevant knowledge or experience.

- *Quality inspector.* Many service organisations will use the customer as a quality control inspector. Organisations may provide formal feedback mechanisms such as focus groups or questionnaires, or may encourage a wide range of comments from customers. Some organisations appear to rely on the customers to bring errors to their attention rather than ensuring zero defects.

- *Trainer/role model.* In some organisations customers are used to help other customers know what to do and how to behave. By being seen to stand in an orderly queue or talk quietly in a restaurant, existing customers define the roles and behaviours for new customers. They may even take it upon themselves to admonish transgressors through a reproachful look or even active intervention.

10.4.2 Benefits of customer involvement

There are many benefits from encouraging the customers to fulfil the desired roles, for example:

- *Inclusion.* Customers who become actively involved in the service process often develop an increased sense of loyalty. Having become involved, these customers are less likely to stop and find another provider in the short term.

- *Resource productivity.* If the customer is carrying out some of the tasks, the service operation requires fewer resources of its own to run. Self-service restaurants and supermarkets provide simple examples.

- *Customer control.* A major advantage for customers who become part of the service process is that they may feel that they have more personal control over what happens to them. This is one of the attractions of internet-based services where customers may access the service at times to suit themselves and also may exit the service at any stage if they so wish.

10.4.3 Customer management issues

Since customers are significant components of service delivery both as recipients and as co-producers of the service experience, it would seem to be sensible to 'manage' customers as if they were 'employees'. However, it can be harder to manage and control customers than employees because (a) they are customers and (b) the organisation may be able to exert only limited control over them. Whereas business-to-business organisations may draw up service-level agreements between them to set standards and use them to monitor and control the service delivered and received, other organisations may have to rely on social mores or 'rewards' and 'punishments'.

Managing customers entails some or all of the following:

- *Defining customer competence.* One of the changes in the service concept that may redefine the way things are done relates to the extent to which the service organisation assumes it is dealing with competent or incompetent customers. For example, telecommunications equipment suppliers formerly dealt exclusively with competent customers – national network operators. The advent of mobile networks and increased competition means that they may now be dealing with entrepreneurs rather than engineers. This opens up possibilities for the development of new services, as well as presenting challenges to accepted ways of working.

● *Customer selection.* It is helpful if organisations have customers who are willing and capable of fulfilling their roles inside the operation. Just as they recruit and select staff to perform particular roles, many service organisations also recruit and select their customers. Organisations, often through their marketing departments, provide information about what services are available, so helping to ensure that the customers with the appropriate (and achievable) needs are attracted to that service. A lack of information can create confusion and lead to unnecessary resources being used. For example if you are at home and feel slightly unwell there are many courses of action open to you. Booking an appointment with the doctor or seeking advice via phone or internet may be sensible options. Some customers turn up at accident and emergency units or phone for emergency ambulances when the situation is not serious, thus absorbing expensive resources that could be better deployed. Organisations need to ensure that they provide customers and potential customers with good information to help them make the right choices not only for themselves but also for the organisation.

Some organisations use high prices or dress codes, for example, to try to ensure that they attract the 'right' type of customer. Others, such as insurance companies or schools/ universities, will screen potential customers to ensure that they are not too high a risk or are academically and socially suitable. Center Parcs, the holiday company, will not take bookings from large single-sex groups, because it does not want its reputation as a family-focused holiday to be damaged by 'inappropriate' behaviour. Lengthy queues to get into a nightclub will not only put off those people who may be less appropriate customers (people like the authors of this book, who might get in and complain about the noise level, for example) but, at the same time, will encourage those who really want to be there; the queue gives the impression that here is a popular and desirable destination.

Whatever the type of service, organisations need to be able to identify the types of customers they want and set up methods of selection (or de-selection) to try to ensure that those people are attracted to the organisations and others are not. Even for organisations that have no freedom in their choice of customers, such as the Inland Revenue or social services, it is helpful if their customers know what services are available, the best way to access them and how to behave when so doing. Such information which helps customers select the right services, locations and access times etc., is also an example of 'customer training'.

● *Customer training.* Customers, like employees, require training. In some organisations this can be provided by other customers. For example, we observe other customers to know what to do and how to behave. We take the supermarket trolley back because we see others do it (or we are motivated by the fact that it has our coin in it). We talk quietly in restaurants because everyone else is doing so.

Sometimes organisations need to allocate time and resources to customer training. Although this may incur set-up costs, it may pay dividends in the long run. A security alarm company discovered that many of the service calls it received were avoidable, but tied up expensive resource in answering them. It embarked on a programme of training key personnel in its customers' organisations. The result was significantly fewer false alarms, which improved productivity and customer satisfaction. At bowling alleys, staff take time to explain to customers that they have to change their shoes, how to operate the equipment, even how to bowl a ball. All this protects their equipment and helps customers have a good time. In some organisations, universities and prisons for example, managers will provide a set of rules and procedures and even ask their customers to sign their agreement to them. Many organisations, including business-to-business ones, use 'scripts' (see earlier) to explain to their customers, usually on the first encounter, what is required of them. Customers who know what to do, and do it well, not only ensure a better service for themselves but also make it more efficient for the organisation.

- *Customer motivation.* Unlike the employee the customer is unlikely to receive any direct financial reward for performing well inside the organisation since they are usually paying, directly or indirectly, for the service. Peer pressure and social mores are usually sufficient to make sure the customer behaves and acts as required. Some organisations provide some small financial incentives, such as slightly cheaper petrol if you pump it yourself, cheaper furniture if you are prepared to assemble it yourself, or 'money off' vouchers for providing information about yourself or the service received. Other organisations use systems of punishments to try to 'motivate' the customer to comply, examples being fines for the late return of library books, expulsion of students or members of particular societies whose behaviour is unacceptable, fines or prison for citizens who break laws and termination of contracts for businesses which fail to do what was required of them.

- *Customer removal.* As a last resort, service organisations will remove customers. This is particularly important in social situations where one group of customers may damage the experience for the majority.

In summary, the customer is not simply a recipient of service but plays an active role in its design and delivery. As such the customer has to be managed within the operation. Just as operations managers have to select, train, motivate and control staff, so do they also have to manage their customers. Importantly, these activities improve the service for the customer, and other customers in the service process, but also make it much more efficient for the operation.

10.5   Summary

Why is service delivery a pressurised task?

- The organisation is a source of pressure for service employees, requiring them to deliver to certain levels of quality and productivity.
- Customers are a source of potential pressure for all service providers: through unrealistic expectations, customer incompetence and anxiety.
- These pressures may lead to issues of motivation, poor customer relationships, anxiety and stress.

How can organisations manage and motivate service providers?

- Clear leadership is essential for counteracting the pressures on service employees.
- Teams and teamworking can provide a powerful mechanism for support and also for building ownership of service processes.
- Well-designed service scripts serve a number of purposes in service design, enabling consistency and providing useful prompts for employees.
- Good service is facilitated by reducing role conflict and ambiguity, and increasing role clarity.
- Defining the degree and type of discretion required for each role is essential, and provides insights for the manager in dealing with operational transitions.
- Internal and external communication is a powerful element in building commitment from customers and employees.

How can customers be 'managed' and motivated?

- Like employees, customers are often service providers.
- The key roles taken by customers include service provider, service specifier, quality inspector and trainer/role model.
- The key issues in managing customers include defining customer competence, customer selection, training, motivation and removal.

10.6 Discussion questions

1 Provide an example of a scripted response. Describe and discuss the advantages and disadvantages in using this script.
2 What are the advantages and disadvantages of using teamwork in student assignments?
3 Evaluate and assess your role as a customer in a supermarket, an internet-based travel agency and a university/college course.
4 From your observation of managers in shops and restaurants, what behaviours assist their staff in dealing more effectively with the pressures they experience, and what actions increase this pressure?

10.7 Questions for managers

1 Are you aware of the pressures on your staff? What should you do about this?
2 How well are you managing staff in transition? Are they anxious or frustrated?
3 Has your organisation realised the full benefit of teamwork? Are the teams progressing towards being self-directed?
4 What is the impact of stress on service delivery? Is there anything you can do to deal with the causes of this stress in the medium term, and alleviate its impact in the short term?
5 What style of leadership is appropriate for the individuals/groups you manage? How much discretion do your staff feel you give them?
6 Make an arrangement to talk to someone whose leadership style you admire. Discover the 'secrets of their success'.
7 What actions can you take to build ownership of customers and processes? How effective is your communications strategy in achieving this?

Case Exercise   The Empress Hotel Group

Robert Johnston and Bridgette Sullivan-Taylor, Warwick Business School

Davina Rullani had just taken over as personnel director at the Empress Hotel Group, a major international five-star hotel chain with its headquarters in Hong Kong. Her task in the previous hotels in which she had worked involved setting up systems and procedures, updating the standard operating procedures, and running customer service training departments that provided and coached scripts, encouraged teamwork and allocated roles and duties. She had personally trained senior hotel managers in leadership and motivation. This hotel chain, she realised, was going to be rather different.

The Empress Hotel Group's chairman and chief executive was Bob Beaver, an evangelical American whose dream was to create 'the most perfect hotel chain in the world'. He felt that the standardised approach to five-star hotels was not appropriate for the discerning international traveller, who wanted a taste of local culture and traditions, not a 'McDonald's experience'. He wanted his hotels to be run by the local management teams, not by head office. He felt the hotels should use local furniture and furnishing and decorations, create local menus and use local produce. He thought the uniforms should be different from hotel to hotel and reflect the local culture and climate, and that the service should be warm and spontaneous.

Davina, like most of the hotel's management, had come from other mainstream chains, which were extremely different. The HR department's role was to create manuals spelling out exactly what should be done, by whom and how. The role of the operations managers was to implement these procedures, and if they were not sure of anything they always knew they could find the answer in one of the manuals that covered one wall in their office.

It surprised Bob, but did not surprise Davina, that the amount of discretion applied by managers in the hotels was, in practice, small. Indeed her predecessor had worked with them to provide systems and procedures, for which he was sacked. Bob was determined to bring about his vision and Davina was instrumental in this.

All the staff were paid slightly above the industry average and Empress Hotels were seen as *the* place to work. As Bob ruefully pointed out, 'It is not necessarily seen as *the* place to stay. We need to put my vision into practice.' Davina's job was to persuade both hotel managers and the staff, from front-of-house to pot washers, to use the discretion they really had to make Empress Hotels the best place in the world to stay.

Davina had to deal with the hotel's facilities, food and service, and she decided to start with the service. On her way out to see her mother in Germany she stopped for a night at the group's highly rated hotel in Dubai, and stayed in the Seychelles on the way back.

She realised she had her work cut out. At check-in both hotels 'processed' her very efficiently but there was no warmth or colour. She asked both receptionists, who were not busy, about local attractions and was told 'See the concierge' (Dubai) and 'There are some leaflets in your room' (Seychelles). Davina also asked the difference between the guestroom she had booked and an executive room and was told '350 dirham' (Dubai) and 'They are on the fifth floor with breakfast included' (Seychelles). At dinner in the hotels' restaurants she was not offered a dessert, although in Dubai she was asked if she would like a coffee.

Back in Hong Kong Davina set herself objectives in three areas:

- Reception – to try to make the service more spontaneous.
- Staff training – to encourage the staff to focus on the needs of the guests and not on the procedures.
- Hotel managers – to help them assess their staff in terms of good service rather than compliance and encourage their staff to do a good job rather than what they have always done.

Davina explained her approach:

It's about mixing discretion with professionalism. We need to get away from standarisation and focus on the customer and let the local colour and culture come out. Training staff is going to be the key, but it's going to be hard when we can't define or specify what they have to do. They will need to have the right skills, be highly motivated and willing to go the extra mile. We just have to bring it about!

Question

1 What would you suggest Davina should do to encourage the staff to exude warmth and spontaneity when their natural instinct is to seek security from procedures and routines?

Suggested further reading

Bateson, John E.G. (2002), 'Are Your Customers Good Enough for Your Service Business?,' *Academy of Management Executive* 16 (4) 110–120

Harris, Richard, Kim Harris and Steve Baron (2003), 'Theatrical Services Experiences: Dramatic Script Development with Employees', *International Journal of Service Industry Management* 14 (2) 184–199

James, Kim and Graham Clark (2002), 'Service Organisations in Transition and Anxiety Containment', *Journal of Managerial Psychology* 17 (5) 394–407

Johnston, Robert and Peter Jones (2004), 'Service Productivity: Towards Understanding the Relationship between Operational and Customer Productivity', *International Journal of Productivity and Performance Management* 53 (3) 201–213

Klidas, Antonis, Peter T. van den Berg and Celeste P.M. Wilderom (2007), 'Managing Employee Empowerment in Luxury Hotels in Europe', *International Journal of Service Industry Management* 18 (1) 70–83

Kong, Mikyoung and Giri Jogaratnam (2007), 'The Influence of Culture on Perceptions of Service Employee Behaviour', *Managing Service Quality* 17 (3) 275–297

Meyer, Danny (2007), *Setting the Table*, Harper Collins, New York

Ottenbacher, Michael, Juergen Gnoth and Peter Jones (2006), 'Identifying Determinants of Success in Development of New High Contact Services: Insights from the Hospitality Industry', *International Journal of Service Industry Management* 17 (4) 344–363

Yagil, Dana (2006), 'The Relationship of Service Provider Power Motivation, Empowerment and Burnout to Customer Satisfaction', *International Journal of Service Industry Management* 17 (3) 258–270

Useful web links

The Centre for Creative Leadership provides publications and research as a valuable resource in this area:
www.ccl.org

This page has links to some interesting pieces on leadership:
http://dspace.dial.pipex.com/town/estate/yg45/leadershipinspirational.html

A helpful site on teams and team motivation:
http://www.innovativeteambuilding.co.uk/pages/articles/motivation.htm

Why not consider the service script like a TV or theatre script? One website gives some pointers which you will need to translate to a service setting:
http://www.screenwriting.info/

Finally, some tips for managing stress . . . :
http://www.stress-counselling.co.uk/management/actionplan.htm

Notes

1 For a more detailed discussion of risk and anxiety in service operations see James, Kim and Graham Clark (2002), 'Service Organisations in Transition and Anxiety Containment', *Journal of Managerial Psychology* 17 (5) 394–407

2 Overmier, James Bruce and Martin E.P. Seligman (1967), 'Effects of Inescapable Shock upon Subsequent Escape and Avoidance Learning', *Journal of Comparative and*

Physiological Psychology 63 28–33; Bowen, David E. and Robert Johnston (1999), 'Internal Service Recovery: Developing a New Construct', *International Journal of Service Industry Management* 10 (2) 118–131

3   Roberts, Wess (1989), *Leadership Secrets of Attila the Hun*, Bantam Press, London

4   Kakabadse, Andrew and Nada Kakabadse (1998), *Essence of Leadership*, Thomson Learning

5   Stewart, Jackie (2007), *Winning Is Not Enough*, Headline Publishing Group

6   Roberts, Wess (1989), *Leadership Secrets of Attila the Hun*, Bantam Press, London; Johnston, Robert (2001) *Service Excellence = Reputation = Profit: Developing and Sustaining a Reputation for Service Excellence*, Institute of Customer Service, Colchester

7   Bennis, Warren, (1999), *Managing People is like herding cats*, Executive Excellence Publishing, South Provo, Utah

8   Larkin, T.J. and Sandar Larkin (1996), 'Reaching and Changing Frontline Employees', *Harvard Business Review* 74 (2) 94–104

9   Testa, Mark R. and Mark G. Ehrhart (2005), 'Service Leader Interaction Behaviours: Comparing Employee and Manager Perspectives', *Group and Organisation Management* 30 (5) 456–486

10 Yagil, Dana (2006), 'The Relationship of Service Provider Power Motivation, Empowerment and Burnout to Customer Satisfaction', *International Journal of Service Industry Management* 17 (3) 258–270

11 Katzenbach, Jon R. (2007), *The Wisdom of Teams*, McGraw-Hill, London

12 Belbin, R. Meredith (2003), *Management Teams: Why They Succeed or Fail*, 2nd edition, Butterworth-Heinemann, Oxford

13 Katzenbach, Jon R. (2007), *The Wisdom of Teams*, McGraw-Hill, London

14 Osburn, Jack D. and Linda Moran (2000), *The New Self-Directed Work Teams*, McGraw-Hill, New York

15 Osburn, Jack D. and Linda Moran (2000), *The New Self-Directed Work Teams*, McGraw-Hill, New York

16 Betts, Alan, Graham R. Clark and Robert Johnston (2004), *Creating the Effective Team Leader*, Research Report

17 Katz, Daniel and Robert L. Kahn (1978), *The Social Psychology of Organisations*, 2nd edition, John Wiley, New York

18 Harris, Richard, Kim Harris and Steve Baron (2003), 'Theatrical Services Experiences: Dramatic Script Development with Employees', *International Journal of Service Industry Management* 14 (2) 186

19 Tansik, David A. and William L. Smith (2000), 'Scripting the Service Encounter' in Fitzsimmons, James and Mona Fitzsimmons (eds), *New Service Design*, Sage Publications, Thousand Oaks, California, pp. 239–263

20 Schank, Roger C. (1980), 'Language and Memory', *Cognitive Science* 4 (3) 243–284; Schank, Roger C. (1982), *Dynamic Memory: A Theory of Reminding and Learning in Computers and People*, Cambridge University Press, Cambridge

21 Bowen, David E. and Edward E. Lawler III (1995), 'Empowering Service Employees', *Sloan Management Review* 36 (4) 73–85

22 Kelley, Scott W. (1993), 'Discretion and the Service Employee', *Journal of Retailing* 69 (1) 104–126

23 See for example March, James G. and Herbert A. Simon (1958), *Organizations*, Wiley, New York

24 Developed from work by Armistead, Colin G. and Graham R. Clark (1993), *Outstanding Customer Service: Implementing the Best Ideas from Around the World,* Irwin Professional, Homewood, Illinois

25 Hersey, Paul, Kenneth H. Blanchard and Dewey E. Johnson (2000), *Management of Organizational Behaviour,* 8th edition, Prentice Hall, Englewood Cliffs, New Jersey

26 Simons, Robert (1995), 'Control in an Age of Empowerment', *Harvard Business Review* 73 (2) 80–88

27 Quirke, William and Dominic Walters (2003), 'What Every Manager Should Know about Communication', *Strategic Communication Management* 7 (5) 26–29

28 Kotter, John P. (1995), 'Leading Change: Why Transformation Efforts Fail', *Harvard Business Review* 73 (2) 59–67

29 Quirke, William and Richard Bloomfield (2004), 'Developing a Consistent Planning Approach', *Strategic Communication Management* 8 (3) 14–17

30 Bowen, David E. (1986), 'Managing Customers as Human Resources in Service Organisations', *Human Resource Management* 25 (3) 371–384; Johnston, Robert (1989), 'The Customer as Employee', *International Journal of Operations and Production Management* 9 (5) 15–23; Mills, Peter K. and James H. Morris (1986), 'Clients as "partial" Employees of Service Organisations: Role Development in Client Participation', *Academy of Management Review* 11 (4) 726–735

Chapter 11
Managing service resources

Chapter objectives

This chapter is about how to manage resources effectively.

- What is capacity management?
- How can managers balance capacity and demand?
- How is day-to-day planning and control carried out?
- How do organisations manage bottlenecks and queues?
- What happens when managers can't cope with demand?
- How can organisations improve their capacity utilisation?

11.1   Introduction

Making the most effective use of operational resources is at the heart of service operations management. Most managers spend a significant proportion of their time and energy in working out how they can serve more customers, improve choice and flexibility, while at the same time cutting costs. Ensuring that resources such as materials, staff, equipment and technology are utilised to the right level has a major impact not only on the efficiency, and therefore the costs, of the operation but also upon customer satisfaction. To add complexity to this challenge, the customer frequently plays a significant part in service delivery and must be thought of and managed in a similar way to internal resources.

For example, the managers of the hub for a large parcel delivery service are responsible for the movement of hundreds of thousands of packages each day, from collection, transportation, sorting, despatching and tracking, to timely and accurate delivery to the customer. The resources they manage on a day-to-day and week-by-week basis include not only the packages but also the hundreds of trucks and drivers, the system of conveyors, and the people and processes employed in sorting out the parcels at the hub, not forgetting the information technology behind it all. In many cases, customers act as a resource for the company, too, when they enter collection details via the website. Like all operations managers, the parcel service managers need to make the best use of their resources while at the same time ensuring they meet customer and organisational requirements.

The previous chapter was concerned with managing people, both staff (or employees – we use the terms interchangeably) and customers. This chapter focuses on all our input resources, materials, equipment, customers, staff and technology and facilities, in particular how we manage, increase or reduce, the operational capacity that they provide us with to try to meet fluctuating levels of demand from customers.

11.2   What is capacity management?

Operations managers are concerned with ensuring that the service process has sufficient resources to deal with the anticipated levels of customer demand in such a way that quality of service meets pre-set targets in the most cost-effective manner. This is a particularly difficult task when managers are faced with very variable demand, not just in terms of volume but the variety of services required, as you can see in the New Zealand water taxi firm described in Case Example 11.1.

Capacity management is a delicate balancing act because both underutilised and overstretched resources can be disadvantageous. Underutilising resources has the potential to damage the long-term success of the organisation in a variety of ways:

- Expensive resources not earning revenue lead to poor financial results. The airline that fails to achieve a high load factor on its planes will struggle to survive.

- In many services, customers are suspicious of services that appear not to be busy. Banks and similar financial institutions find that customers are not happy about using an empty branch, and many diners prefer the 'buzz' of a busy restaurant.

- Service employees may become demotivated if underutilisation persists. Boredom and concern for their long-term employment may lead to poor service attitudes, which again lead to reduced customer satisfaction and lower profitability.

Conversely, resources that are overstretched also lead to problems for the success of the organisation:

- Overloaded resources mean that many aspects of service delivery suffer. A sudden surge of customers into a shop means that waiting times increase and staff cannot devote the amount of attention to customers that is desirable.

- Staff who are continually overloaded make more mistakes and, in the longer term, may decide to leave the organisation in search of less stressful employment.

- To deal with overload, staff may be drafted in to carry out tasks with which they are unfamiliar or for which they are only partially trained. The potential for increased error rate is high and, again, stress levels may be intolerable for some members of staff.

The task of capacity management is to try to achieve a balance between too much and too little resource utilisation, within the financial and operational constraints. Capacity management is concerned with putting a plan in place that makes the best use of resources to deal with the forecasted or expected demand for services.

Case Example 11.1   Pelorus Water Transport

The Marlborough Sounds covers an area of around 4,000 square kilometres at the north end of the South Island of New Zealand. The Sounds are a series of fjord-like water inlets connected to the Cook Strait which separates North and South Islands. The steep, wooded hills and small quiet bays of the Sounds are sparsely populated and access is difficult. Many of the small settlements and isolated houses and holiday homes are only accessible by boat. The main port of Picton sits at the foot of Queen Charlotte Sound. Serving the more isolated Pelorus and Kenepuru Sounds is the small town of Havelock, famous for its green-lipped mussels which are farmed in the Sounds.

John Beavon and Catherine Coates operate one of the few water taxi services from Havelock, Pelorus Water Transport. In what they describe as 'the best job in the world', John and Catherine ferry passengers and their small cargo around the Sounds. Passengers include residents with their shopping, holiday home occupiers and their belongings, backpackers and their rucksacks, builders working on the houses, contract workers, often loggers, and their smaller tools, and government environmental and building officers. They are sometimes involved in medical emergencies evacuating seriously ill people to the road in Havelock. They are also very happy to fill up a few places with tourists and take them along for the ride, doing their utmost to extend the trip for them and show them local features such as gannet and seal colonies and mussel farms or provide guided or unguided walks. They even serve afternoon tea on board!

The work is varied and as with any taxi not particularly predictable and so a degree of flexibility is required not only by the operators but also by their customers. John explained:

We try to get about 10 to 12 people on every trip, and we go out usually two or three times a day. The Sounds are very long and despite having a fast boat (a 24-foot custom-built 25-seater powered by twin 200-horsepower engines capable of cruising at 24 mph, 36 knots, which is pretty fast for water transport) it can take over an hour to reach the furthest point on the Pelorus Sound. Usually the first person to ring up and book the boat on a particular day has the say on what time we depart and where we go to. Then, as others ring or email, we will fit them in around that. We may also have to start making adjustments to the schedule to allow us time to pick the others up and load and unload their equipment. The vast majority are happy when we ring them up and ask them to adjust the times; I guess they realise it might be them we are trying to fit in next time. Obviously some timings are critical and can't change such as when we are bringing people back to Havelock to meet up with other transport.

The helpfulness of customers spills over to create a sense of camaraderie on board. The atmosphere feels more like a convivial bar than a taxi, with John and Catherine on first-name terms with many of their clients.

For exclusive use of the boat for a trip John and Catherine charge around NZ$274 per engine hour. If people are willing to share, as most are, they would aim to charge people 40, 60 or 75 dollars per head depending on distance travelled.

There is one other water taxi based in Havelock, and several other companies offering tours, such as the Mail Boat which covers three set routes three days a week. Access to the Sounds can also be by float plane, based in Picton and travelling between Wellington (in the North Island) and the Marlborough Sounds.

11.2.1 Defining service capacity

Before we discuss the methods available to try to balance capacity and demand we first need to define what capacity is and how it can be measured.

Service capacity is defined as the maximum level of value-added activity over a period of time that a service process can consistently achieve under normal operating conditions.[1] We can define and measure capacity relatively easily at the process level. For example:

- the number of calls a customer service agent can handle in the course of a shift
- the number of meals served by a restaurant during the lunchtime period
- the number of repair calls made by a computer service engineer during an eight-hour day.

It is important to note the words 'under normal operating conditions' and 'consistently'. It may be possible, in some cases, for an individual employee to exceed the throughput rate for a short period. If call centre employees handle 120 calls over 8 hours (15 calls per hour), it may be possible for them to achieve as many as 30 calls in one of these hours, but for this rate not to be sustainable over any length of time.

As we will see later, in Section 11.6, overloading resources may appear to increase output. Indeed, if analysed solely in terms of numbers of customer transactions completed in a given period, this may seem to be the case. However, there may be an impact on the nature of the service, the service concept and also the quality of the service provided. Service organisations must take particular care to ensure that the service concept is not changed in the search for greater productivity. For example, a restaurant may decide to encourage customers to leave their table when they have completed their meal, in order to fit in a second sitting for dinner. On the face of it, the restaurant has doubled its capacity, but customers may feel that the nature of the service has changed and the level of service has deteriorated. Of course there are strategies that the restaurant can adopt to manage this sensitively, but the operations manager must be certain that in increasing productivity the desired service concept is maintained.

11.2.2 Measuring capacity

To manage capacity, we must be able to measure it. A simple measure is the amount of demand in a specified time period. The parcel delivery service may have an overall measure of capacity in terms of the total number of parcels that can be processed overnight; however, this overall measure is not very helpful in managing the day-to-day operation. It is necessary to develop a measure of capacity that is sufficiently detailed to give a 'good enough' estimate of capacity. For the parcel delivery company, some of the key aspects to be considered include:

- The size, weight and value of the parcels to be moved – a package that is small but valuable will provide more revenue per truck movement than something less valuable that takes up a large amount of space.

- The geographical locations served by the company – rural districts have greater travel times, and many inner city areas suffer from traffic congestion.

In determining capacity, a number of factors make the assessment of service capacity difficult:

- *Service mix.* If the service mix (the range of services provided) is made up of high volumes of 'runners' (see Chapter 8), the capacity calculation is relatively straightforward. However, once the service mix incorporates fluctuating volumes of 'repeaters' and 'strangers', the calculation becomes more complex. The customer service agent may be able to handle 120 'normal' calls in a shift; however, if some of the calls are complex enquiries or serious complaints, for example, the number of calls handled will drop significantly.

- *The impact of location.* At first sight, the measure of capacity for a computer service engineer or a telephone engineer would seem to be relatively straightforward. However, if we consider the difference between an engineer operating in a major city and another engineer dealing with rural communities, it can be seen that calculating capacity on the basis of calls completed alone would be inaccurate, since it would take no account of travel times.

- *The extent of intangibility in the service.* Services with low degrees of intangibility are relatively easy to deal with. The number of short transactions per hour in a fast-food restaurant is relatively consistent. However, the customer-facing staff in a gourmet restaurant may have greater discretion as to how to carry out their task. They may perhaps spend time with customers in 'building relationships', with the result that the individual's capacity becomes more difficult to define. This calculation becomes more complex when dealing with knowledge workers, who must combine short-term revenue-generating activities with long-term research and development. Capacity in this case is linked more to the individual service provider. It may be almost impossible for a manager to know when someone is working to capacity when output is so variable.

- *The ease of identification of resource constraints.* The capacity of a process is determined by resource constraints or bottlenecks. In the Karolinska Hospital example (see Case Example 11.3), it was clear that the resource constraint was the operating theatre. Finding ways to increase the effective utilisation of this space was relatively straightforward. For more complex systems, the identification of the key resource constraints may be rather harder. An information systems provider may require a wide range of technical skills relating to different applications and programming languages, but the precise requirements may not be known until part-way into the contract.

11.3 How can managers balance capacity and demand?

Major investments or disinvestments are required to deal with longer-term forecasted or anticipated fluctuations in demand. Alton Towers Resort (see Case Example 11.2) made significant investments every few years to install new or replacement rides to provide the capacity to deal with the increasing numbers of guests it wanted to attract to its theme park. It also invested in hotels and a water park to allow it to enter the year-round short break market. One key issue with such large-scale investments is that this capacity usually comes in large lumps, like a 180-room hotel, and so that capacity may not always be fully utilised when it is first installed/opened. Later in its life that capacity might become stretched and bookings might be turned away. As a result most operations managers spend a great deal of their time dealing with more short- to medium-term capacity management, trying to balance the day-to-day demand for their services with the available capacity. This section begins with a discussion of the longer-term capacity issues then focuses on short- to medium-term capacity management.

Case Example 11.2   Alton Towers Resort

Alton Towers Resort is Britain's answer to Disneyland. It is the UK's leading short break resort with a wide range of family entertainment. The resort, a division of Merlin Entertainments Group Limited, is perhaps best known for its Theme Park's white knuckle rides such as Thirteen, Air, Nemesis, Oblivion, Rita and Ripsaw. Oblivion, for example, is the world's first vertical drop roller coaster. The ride lasts 160 seconds and reaches speeds of up to 100 kph whilst pulling a G-force of 4.5 (astronauts only experience 3G at take-off!). Rita accelerates to 100 kph (62 mph) in 2.2 seconds. The Thirteen ride, opened in 2010, is billed as the scariest in the UK, combining physical and psychological

fear. Some of the other less scary rides include Congo River Rapids, the Runaway Mine Train and Haunted Hollow. Opened in 2009 was Sharkbait Reef by Sea Life. This includes 'touch pools', where guests can interact with various underwater species, and a 10-metre ocean tunnel. In April 2010, a live webcam was installed to allow internet users to watch one of the tanks via the Alton Towers website. Younger guests can enjoy a range of special toddler and child play areas, and those who don't care for the rides or play areas can enjoy the gardens and floral displays, shops, restaurants and daily live shows. To help cope with the British weather about a third of all the rides are either indoors or in covered areas. The range of eating places includes McDonald's, KFC and Pizza Hut as well as Alton Towers' own branded family restaurants. Together they produce the 260 tonnes of chips and four million cans of drinks that the guests consume each year. While the Theme Park is open between March and November, the two hotels, Alton Towers Hotel and the Splash Landings Hotel with its water park, are open all year round.

There is parking for over 6,000 cars and 250 coaches at the Theme Park, which entertains around three million visitors a year. The cost of entry is currently around £30 for adults and £25 for children. Demand peaks at about 50,000 visitors on Easter Bank Holiday Monday and usually runs at about 35,000 throughout the summer. The busiest times are usually during the week. Fridays and Saturdays during the peak season tend to be relatively quiet. The various activities in the Park reach peak demand at different times. The peak time at the gate is 10.30–11.00; for the restaurants it is 12.30–1.00. The major rides are very busy all day with queues reaching their longest in the early afternoon. Fast-track tickets can be obtained for the most popular rides, offering guests an allocated time slot. These tickets can be purchased in advance. The Theme Park employs around 350 full-time and 1,200 seasonal staff. The majority of staff live within a 20-mile radius and to help cope with unexpected fluctuations in demand a pool of staff is available for work at short notice. For flexibility most of the operators are trained to operate several rides.

Each year the company invests in new rides, attractions and infrastructure. For example, in 1994 £12 million was invested in Nemesis. In 1996 the 180-room Alton Towers Hotel was built at a cost of £20 million to allow the company to position itself as a major short break destination. More than 100,000 guests stayed in the hotel in its first year. In 1998 £12 million was invested in Oblivion. Air was built in 2002 at a cost of £12 million. Rita was built in 2005 for £8 million. Thirteen was added in 2010 at a cost of £15 million.

11.3.1 Long-term capacity management

There are four main considerations for making long-term capacity decisions: location, capacity, capability and resilience.

Location decisions

Location is the geographic positioning of a facility or facilities which is providing capacity. Location decisions are often expensive and may have a significant impact not only as an investment cost but also on operations costs, since location may be affected by local wage rates and business rates, for example. Location may also have an impact on revenues, particularly when the operation involves physical contact with customers. For operations that do not require direct physical contact with customers, for example call centres and internet-based service providers such as health or benefits advisory services, location decisions can be made to minimise the physical costs of the buildings and the running costs of the operation. For operations that need direct access to customers, expensive town-centre or out-of-town shopping malls may be essential.

Location decisions are a balancing act between supply-side factors and demand-side factors.[2] Supply-side factors are those that influence the costs and difficulties of a location decision. The demand-side factors are those that influence revenues. Not all the factors below will apply to every location decision but they are an indication of those factors that may need to be taken into account.

Supply-side factors include:

- land costs – the costs of acquiring the land
- labour costs – wage costs, employment taxes, welfare provisions etc.
- energy costs – the cost of energy or the availability or even the consistency of the supply of energy
- transportation costs – the costs of getting resources to the site and of transporting materials to customers
- government factors – local taxes, capital restrictions, financial assistance and political climate, and planning restrictions
- social factors – language and local amenities
- working environment – the history of labour relations and labour supply.

Demand-side factors include:

- convenience to customers – the site's accessibility for customers, including transport network, parking, distance from markets
- labour skills – the availability of particular talents, skills, accents and cultures
- characteristics of the site – the intrinsic and maybe aesthetic appeal of the site
- image – the reputation of the surrounding area and the extent to which there are complementary services in the vicinity.

Capacity decisions

Another key question is: how big should the facility be? For the package distribution operation, some estimate of volumes to be sorted in a relatively short time window each night will be required. Likewise, when deciding the size of a supermarket, call centre, airport, surgery or cinema, the costs need to be weighed against forecast demand – not only short-term demand, but also long-term demand, because the cost of changing facility size can be expensive and sometimes difficult.

The two interrelated issues for operations managers are:

- Facilities can usually only be added in large – and expensive – chunks.
- Capacity needs to match demand.

Adding new facilities usually requires the organisation to commit significant amounts of capital. This can be a risky business because long-term demand can rarely be predicted with any great certainty. If necessary break-even volumes are not met, the facility will not pay for itself. In some cases, such as a theme park where having sufficient customers creates the atmosphere, the service may not be as good as it should be if volume targets are not achieved. If volumes are exceeded, there may be significant localised problems for customers, resulting in customer dissatisfaction and lost business. Given that the majority of forecasts will be wrong (because they are only forecasts), operations managers will invariably suffer from the consequences of over- or under-capacity.

Many airports have suffered from the latter problem; furthermore, owing to the length of time it takes to design a new runway or terminal building, and to go through the planning process and build the facility, volumes may again exceed capacity as soon as the new facility is opened.

As with short- and medium-term capacity management (see Section 11.3.2), there are three main strategies for long-term capacity planning:

- *Plan to exceed demand forecasts.* This strategy is appropriate where there is an expanding market or the cost of building a new facility is inexpensive compared to the cost of, or problems that would be created by, running out, such as electricity or water supply, or air traffic control facilities.
- *Build to forecast.* This approach would balance the likelihood of not having enough and having too much capacity and is appropriate where the costs and consequences of exceeding demand are similar to those for not meeting demand.
- *Plan not to meet forecast demand.* This is an appropriate strategy where it is acceptable not to meet demand or where the cost of capital is very high compared to the costs and consequences of not meeting demand. Football clubs may be able to do this, using price premiums and revenues from television companies to balance the books and even set money aside for future expansion. The problem for some organisations that follow this strategy, such as supermarkets, is that it might give the competition time and income to pursue an aggressive expansionist strategy.

Developing a facility strategy involves steps that are easy to describe but difficult to implement:

- establish a measure of capacity
- develop demand forecasts, ideally several forecasts including optimistic and pessimistic ones, identifying the assumptions on which each is based
- identify alternative means of dealing with the forecasts
- undertake an assessment of the risk involved
- evaluate the alternatives.

Capability

It seems obvious that any new facility should be capable of doing what is required, but this is not as easy as it sounds. There are some airports whose runways are too short to accommodate some of the larger aircraft. A decision taken years ago on the length of a runway when planes were smaller creates constraints on operations now. Doctors' surgeries, too, have changed significantly over the last few years, as doctors form larger practices to share growing administrative costs and ease the burden of 24-hour cover. Surgeries also provide many more facilities than previously, such as well-person clinics and routine surgical operations, for example, putting stresses on facilities designed for a different way of working.

A key problem we face is in forecasting both demand and also the nature of that demand and thus the nature of the services that have to be provided in the future. It is little wonder that many operations management problems stem from the size and nature of the facilities available.

Resilience or flexibility

Although forecasting the size and nature of demand and future services is difficult, if not impossible, the only thing an operations manager can do, apart from keeping their finger on the industry's pulse, is to try to ensure that their facilities have some degree of resilience or flexibility.

Physical resilience can be created through either structural flexibility or developing the potential of the infrastructure. Building flexibility or resilience into a facility can be done in many ways:

- buying extra land to facilitate any possible future expansion
- having a flexible internal structure, with open-plan offices and movable walls
- using flexible equipment, such as cordless telephones or desk-sharing schemes
- adopting different methods of working, such as using more home-based workers
- developing contingencies – railway companies, for example, may plan to use different routes if one route fails.

11.3.2 Short- to medium-term capacity strategies

There are three basic short/medium-term capacity strategies, although, as we will discuss, many organisations employ a mixture of all three (see Case Examples 11.1 and 11.2). These strategies are:

- *Level capacity.* In this case scarce or expensive resources are maintained at a constant level, and the organisation must manage the consequential issues for customer satisfaction and operational service quality.
- *Chase capacity.* The service organisation attempts to match supply to demand as much as possible by building flexibility into the operation. The prime objective is to provide high levels of service availability or fast response, in the most efficient manner.

- *Demand management.* Rather than change the capacity of the service operation, the organisation influences the demand profile to 'smooth' the load on the resources.

Level capacity strategy

The prime objective of this strategy is to maximise utilisation of expensive fixed resources. An airline seeks to fly planes that are as full as possible with passengers paying the highest fares. The key operational measure is the 'load factor', with the airline knowing that if it is exceeding a certain figure (about 80 per cent for an international airline), it will be making profit.

To achieve this level of utilisation, the service organisation may have to make a number of trade-offs, most notably around customer perceived quality of service. Figure 11.1 illustrates the situation in a hospital clinic. Here, the task is to make the most of the medical consultant. The clinic has to solve the problem of always having enough patients for the consultant to work on, with the added difficulty of there being a high percentage of 'no-shows'. The clinic has chosen to overbook appointments, and believes that it is better to upset a few patients rather than lose valuable consultant time.

To deal with the no-shows problem, the clinic has made four appointments at the start of each 15-minute period, estimating that one in four patients do not arrive and that the consultant will require 5 minutes per patient. If all goes to plan, the first patient will be seen immediately, the second within 5 minutes and the third within 10 minutes, but it should be noted that they each have the same 2.00 p.m. appointment. In practice, some of the 2.00 p.m. appointments will still be waiting when the next 'batch' arrives for a (supposed) 2.15 appointment.

Some general principles and issues can be drawn from this example about the level capacity strategy:

- Resource utilisation goals are frequently achieved at the expense of customer satisfaction.
- Customers may receive inconsistent service levels (those with 2.00 p.m. appointments fare better than those with later appointments).
- Customers (patients) accept (or suffer) this poor level of service because the service is valuable to them and there may be no or few alternatives.
- There is a danger that the service provider may become complacent and not make attempts to cut the emotional cost of waiting for the customer, making it potentially vulnerable to competition (in this case private healthcare).

To overcome this problem of variable service levels, the service organisation may use yield management (see Section 11.7) or queue management approaches.

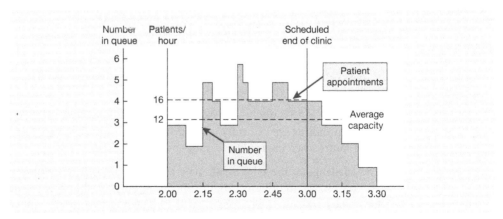

Figure 11.1 Level capacity strategy in an outpatients clinic

Examples of organisations that use the level capacity strategy as their dominant approach include:

- Airlines, which need to maximise the revenue from their most expensive resource (planes). The prime objective is to have planes flying as frequently as possible, preferably full of passengers. This may mean that passengers do not always receive the service they anticipated.

- Professional services, which may have a recognised expert in a specialised field. It is frequently the case that the overall workload will not sustain another professional, leaving clients with a choice as to whether they wait or find an alternative provider.

- Popular restaurants, which may intentionally not expand capacity in order to maintain exclusivity. Having to book days, sometimes months, ahead in order to ensure a table may enhance the service concept.

Examples of approaches adopted under the level capacity strategy include:

- *Promoting off-peak demand.* This is often combined with a pricing strategy to encourage customers to switch. The organisation must be careful that this does not bring about a change in service concept. A restaurant encouraging customers to move to less popular times may institute a 'happy hour' with cheap drinks, which may damage the restaurant's reputation with existing customers.

- *Queue management.* This is dealt with in more depth in Section 11.5, but it is important to point out here that making an assumption that customers will continue to queue can be dangerous. It is, after all, sending the message that their time is relatively worthless, and they are only prepared to wait because they anticipate that the service they receive will be valuable enough to make the wait (lost time) worthwhile.

- *Booking systems.* Making forward bookings is a form of queue management. It allows the organisation to schedule capacity ahead, and for customers to utilise queuing time for themselves. Supermarkets have successfully utilised this system for their delicatessen counters, issuing customers with numbered tickets to ensure that people are served in order, and allowing customers to judge whether they have time to continue shopping before their number is called. As with the physical queue, customers may not want to wait and so may go elsewhere. Indeed, if the organisation has the reputation that customers need to book ahead, it may lose potential sales if customers assume that there is no point in trying.

Chase capacity strategy

This strategy is usually adopted by high-volume consumer services, since a major aspect of their competitive strategy is the provision of ready and rapid access to service. For these services, capital resource utilisation is rarely a prime goal, although cost reduction will be very important. To explain this further, consider the following statements concerning a fast-food restaurant:

- A key objective is to maintain short queue lengths. This is managed by staffing tills and kitchen in line with expected demand.

- If the queues are too long, customers go to another fast-food outlet.

- The premises are not fully utilised: there are only about six hours out of the possible 24 hours when the facilities are 100 per cent utilised.

The challenge of these high-volume standard services is to develop volume flexibility (see Section 11.7.2). In other words, the operation must be able to cope with wide ranges of customer demand, providing consistent service standards at minimum cost. Figure 11.2 shows the demand pattern for a fast-food restaurant, with a crew roster to show how the restaurant manager schedules the staff to deal with the variation in demand.

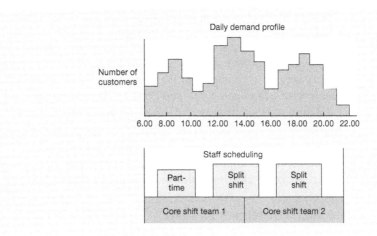

Figure 11.2 Chase capacity strategy for a fast-food restaurant

In this restaurant, the staff are organised into three categories: those on one of the core shift teams, those working split shifts, and those working part-time. The split shifts allow the manager to schedule staff for the forecast demand peaks. There will probably be a weekly rotation between the core shifts and the split-shift personnel. In this example, the early morning peak load is covered by employing part-time labour. In addition, the manager will have a pool of labour to be contacted at short notice to cover absenteeism or an unexpected rise in demand. A common strategy is to extend the length of the split shifts, with some organisations operating a 'compulsory overtime' policy as part of their conditions of employment.

General principles and issues for the chase capacity strategy are:

- Most organisations operating the chase strategy must develop a high degree of volume flexibility. In other words they must be able to respond to changing demand profiles. In most cases this is achieved through employing staff on flexible contracts, allowing the operations manager to decide working hours as required.

- Although a principal objective is to ensure that customer service targets such as availability or response times are achieved, many of these service organisations fall into the commodity category (high volume/low process variety). In contrast to the organisations employing the level capacity strategy, they frequently have relatively little means of differentiation and are therefore rather price sensitive. The challenge in adopting the chase capacity strategy, therefore, is to ensure that costs are strictly controlled and that flexibility is not achieved at any price.

Examples of organisations that employ the chase capacity strategy include:

- Retailers that need to deal with extremely high demand at weekends and after normal office hours.
- Direct insurance companies operating extended hours through call centres.
- Theme parks, which may open up more attractions as demand grows.

Typical approaches to the chase capacity strategy include:

- *Flexible staffing levels.* Some organisations use flexible employment contracts, allowing the operations manager to decide when staff will be working. In some cases staff will work a standard core time, but in many retail organisations staff may not know when they will be working beyond the next few shifts. Another approach is to employ part-time staff who must work 'compulsory' overtime as and when needed. Although this gives flexibility, the operations manager must be aware of the possibility of staff resentment at having to work inconvenient hours, and the knock-on effect of poor customer service.

- *The use of subcontractors or temporary staff.* Organisations may use temporary staff or sub-contractors to deal with short-term overloads. Although these workers may be readily available, they may not be sufficiently trained or motivated to deliver service in the style of the organisation. However, some organisations report that their temporary staff may be more responsive and less complacent than long-service staff. Some call centres use organisations that specialise in what is called 'peak lopping'. Excess calls are automatically routed to the organisation and they are answered in such a manner that customers are unaware of the switch.

- *Making use of customers.* Many service operations may have the option of changing the service process to utilise customers as temporary employees. In effect this is again changing the service concept. Some regular customers may be very happy to be included in the service process – clearing tables, or even serving other customers as well as themselves.

Demand management strategy

Most organisations operate a mixed approach to capacity management. Whether adopting a principally chase or level capacity strategy, most service organisations also operate some degree of demand management. Examples of this approach include:

- *Pricing strategies.* This typically takes the form of offering price incentives to encourage customers to move to off-peak times. The 'happy hour' in the pub or wine bar is a good example.

- *Restricted service at peak times.* The philosophy here is similar, though taking the form of a disincentive. In this case the organisation may provide a limited service at peak times, again encouraging customers to move to less busy times. Some restaurants operate this policy, providing a limited menu at these times.

- *Specialist service channels.* Rather than provide a general service at all times, the provider may choose to segment the demand and to allocate specific times for special needs. Doctors' surgeries are a good example, with advertised times for services such as immunisations, mother and baby clinics, and counselling provision. This allows the surgery to schedule specialist resources to restricted times, often making better use of scarce resources.

- *Advertising and promotion.* Increasing public awareness of the service and informing customers of special offers will stimulate demand. Bookshops not only advertise, but will also stimulate demand by arranging sessions for authors to autograph their works. A particular problem with advertising is that it tends to increase the inaccuracy of any forecasting model used by the business. Although it is possible to track the effectiveness of advertising in stimulating demand, it is often difficult to pre-judge the likely impact of a new campaign.

Putting the strategies together

Most complex service organisations use all three of the capacity strategies in different parts of their operations, depending on the respective underlying cost models. Some examples are shown in Table 11.1.

The prime objective of the airline is to maximise 'load factor' on flights, the utilisation of its most expensive assets. It employs a number of strategies to ensure that it makes the maximum revenue on each flight, using sophisticated yield management techniques (see Section 11.7.1) to help adopt the optimum pricing strategy to sell unsold seats as departure time approaches. The airline may simply oversell seats in the belief that there will be a number of 'no-shows'. Passengers who are then not able to obtain the seat they thought they had booked need to be compensated in some way, although unless managed well that can significantly affect customer satisfaction.

To maximise the opportunity for customers to book seats, the airline employs a chase strategy in its sales department using relatively cheap resource (as compared with planes), scheduling staff to meet forecast demand patterns. It is better to suffer slightly reduced productivity here rather than lose potential seat revenue.

Table 11.1 Capacity strategies

	Level capacity strategy	Chase capacity strategy	Demand management strategy
International airline	Ensure that planes are flying with maximum payload as frequently as possible	Schedule staff reservations department to meet demand to ensure bookings can be made	Promote off-peak demand Try to maximise revenue from each flight (yield management)
Insurance company	Protect back-office experts (actuaries and investment specialists) from variations in customer demand	Schedule direct sales operation (call centre) to provide maximum access for customers	Influence selling cycle so as not to coincide with policy renewal peaks
Restaurant chain	Keep manufacturing of basic food materials as close to 'level' as possible Maintain high utilisation of process plant	Draw up staff rosters to reflect anticipated demand Use part-time staff to manage peaks Call in staff for demand surges	Use promotional activity to stimulate demand in quiet periods Devise special offers to allow for bulk-purchasing discounts

The insurance company uses a level strategy for its actuarial staff (back office), in part because they are relatively expensive, but more because they are often in short supply. The lead time to recruit and train an actuary is measured in years rather than weeks and therefore it makes no sense to attempt to chase demand.

Similarly the restaurant chain will operate a level strategy in its manufacturing function because it has relatively fixed capacity: although it can increase capacity marginally by overtime, significant increases can only be achieved by investing in another kitchen or restaurant.

11.4 How is day-to-day planning and control carried out?

In the previous section we discussed how operation managers decide a capacity strategy, or mix of strategies, thus creating a capacity plan. This sets the broad parameters within which this capacity may be allocated to specific customers and/or tasks in order to meet customer service and productivity targets. This section looks at the mechanisms that may be deployed to micro-manage this plan as effectively as possible. Day-to-day operations planning is concerned with creating a 'schedule' or timetable (often a daily or weekly schedule), based on the capacity plan, which

- allocates staff, customers, equipment and/or facilities to activities (often referred to as loading)
- decides what order things will be done in, e.g. which customers/orders to deal with first (sequencing)
- shows what time each activity will start and finish (scheduling).

Examples of 'schedules' include:

- A table plan for a restaurant – as bookings are received, tables are allocated, giving an instant picture of the loading for any given time period, and the likely start and finishing times. This implies that bookings will be accepted on a first come, first served basis and that customers without reservations may have to be turned away.
- A school timetable that shows where every student, and member of staff, should be at any time of the day, what they should be doing and when things take place.
- An appointment book at a car servicing workshop, providing space for a given number of standard services and more complex jobs, showing who will do which job and roughly how long they are expected to take.

Operations control is concerned with making adjustments to cope with changes as they happen.

11.4.1 Creating a schedule

Most operations have rules or policies regarding the allocation of capacity. Sometimes these rules are relatively informal, developed over time in such a way that most customers are satisfied. Other operations, usually those with more volume and/or complexity, tend to have more formal allocation systems. For example, most leisure centres have one large space or sports hall, which can be used for a number of activities. It might be configured for two five-a-side football pitches, four badminton courts or one tennis court. To create the schedule or timetable, the leisure centre manager must carry out the following tasks:

- Decide the proportion of time that the sports hall will be configured for each of the activities.
- Ascertain the optimal schedule for these activities based on customer preference. For example, badminton clubs may prefer Thursday evenings while five-a-side football may be more popular on Fridays.
- Check the schedule for ease of transition between activities. It may be relatively easy to move from tennis to circuit training because there are relatively few changes to make, but changing from badminton to football might require more staff to move and set up equipment.
- Create a booking schedule for the various slots to allocate capacity (times) to specific customers.

This schedule is required because the leisure centre does not have infinite resources. It is clearly impossible to satisfy all possible customer demands and remain a viable service organisation.

The way that operations deal with this issue is to create sequencing rules in order to manage the prioritisation of allocation. Here are six examples of sequencing rules:

- *First in, first out (FIFO) or first come, first served.* This is the approach used by many consumer services. The leisure centre may allow customers to book up to two weeks ahead for badminton for the Thursday evening time slots of 6.00–7.00 p.m., 7.00–8.00 p.m. and 8.00–9.00 p.m. and will take requests in order until all the courts are full. This scheduling rule is simple and has the advantage of being perceived to be fair to all potential customers.
- *Last in, first out (LIFO).* There are rare occasions when this rule makes sense. The sequence of loading a delivery truck would follow LIFO scheduling so that the first call would be to deliver the products or materials closest to the tailgate of the lorry.
- *Most valuable customer first.* The leisure centre may allow the local football club to have early access to certain parts of the forward schedule and to 'block book' capacity for training. If the club needs to have the use of the hall on every Friday for training, this represents steady income for the leisure centre, though it may be a source of annoyance for other, smaller organisations that are excluded from using the hall for single occasions.
- *Most critical first.* Emergency services adopt variants of this rule, grading the nature of each demand between critical and non-essential. Clearly, life-threatening situations call for immediate action and these demands tend to override all other activities.
- *Least work content first.* In situations where demand far outstrips supply, this rule allows more customers to be satisfied quickly. Airline check-in desks sometimes operate a version of this rule, providing faster service for those passengers with hand baggage only. This means that the total queue is reduced and fewer customers wait. The problem with this rule is that some customers wait far longer than they would under FIFO and are potentially more dissatisfied.
- *Most work content first.* With activities that have long process lead times it might seem prudent to schedule the tasks with the longest time requirement first. This may not always be helpful because, once started, these tasks may become lost in among other 'work-in-progress' and not progress as fast as they could. Using this rule alone does not usually produce the best performance against customer requirement dates.

Different rules may be applied in different circumstances. Where customers arrive together, they generally expect to be treated equally and therefore FIFO will tend to be applied. However, this is not always the case. At the Alton Towers theme park in the UK, it is possible to buy fast-track tickets that enable customers to bypass the queues of customers who pay standard prices. This obvious privilege can cause high degrees of ill feeling among 'standard' customers.

Back-office processes frequently deal with longer lead times than front-office processes, and may apply a number of scheduling rules. In the more complex situations it is possible to use a simple algorithm similar to that used in manufacturing shop floor control, called critical factor calculations. In this approach a comparison of estimated work content against requirement date allows for a calculation of an urgency factor. Each stage in the process is provided with a list of the most urgent jobs, enabling prioritisation. A spin-off from these calculations is a spot check of the performance of the process. If all tasks fall into the 'most urgent' category, clearly significant action is required to avoid major customer dissatisfaction.

11.4.2 Operational control

Systems for control, i.e. to enable the schedule to be adjusted, range from comprehensive, complex and expensive to extremely simple.

At the complex and expensive end of the spectrum are the ERP (enterprise resource planning) systems. These software-based systems, sold by companies such as SAP and Baan, offer the capability to integrate a number of functions across the organisation. For example, sales order processing systems can provide direct input into operations control, and then into supplier management/procurement systems.

At the other extreme, many control systems are basic, but effective nonetheless. Examples are the restaurant table plan, the school timetable and the appointment book, which act as both schedules and control systems. All of these 'systems' can be examined and assessed to see if, and how, changes can be accommodated. If a teacher reports in ill, the 'manager' will have to assess which lessons need to be covered and who might be free to cover them. A restaurant guest who extends the size of their party may be accommodated on a different table; the extra car service for an important client may be added as overtime at the end of the day. In all cases the existence of a detailed schedule/control system is critical to managing the day-to-day planning *and* control of the operation.

Having an effective control system can be a significant source of competitive advantage. The ability of the organisation to provide an immediate response to the question 'When can you do this?' is a major factor in building customer confidence. In recent years, retailers have been able to interrogate logistics systems so that customers can negotiate a delivery slot for their purchase of furniture or electrical products, with some confidence that this promise will be fulfilled.

The Karolinska Hospital operating theatre (see Case Example 11.3) provides a good example of the benefits of a good schedule/control system. Such a system should include:

- *A clear customer flow.* The schedule provides the opportunity for customers to be 'flowed' through the system to arrive at the right time and place. We might compare customers in this way to the work-in-progress (WIP) inventory in a manufacturing process. If WIP is minimised, customer delays are reduced, there is less disruption, and costs are kept to a minimum. An organisation that encourages customers to arrive early because it is unable to manage its schedules may have to invest in larger reception (customer-holding) areas, or suffer a major decline in customer satisfaction.

- *Ensuring supporting resources are available to meet the schedule.* Once the schedule has been established making best use of the availability of scarce resource, all other resources must be scheduled to meet this plan. For the hospital operating theatre this will involve the scheduling of people (operating theatre staff and surgeons), and of course physical inventories such as blood, bandages and surgical instruments. Restaurants, likewise, will match inventories of food to expected customer demand.

- *Creating schedules for interlinking activities.* The schedule allows the operations manager to create a realistic plan for the service as a whole and its many interlinking activities. In some organisations this is termed the master schedule. This then facilitates the production of supporting schedules for all the resources that feed this master schedule, using a variety of scheduling rules matched to each situation.

- *Creating schedules for suppliers.* Good information provides a sound basis for negotiation with key suppliers. This gives rise to the potential for managing day-to-day activity more accurately with less waste (see Chapter 12).

11.4.3 Managing short-term schedules and medium- and long-term capacity plans

The detail of schedules will increase as 'time now' approaches customer requirement dates. To return to the leisure centre example, tomorrow's schedule will tell us exactly which customers have booked a badminton court, and at what time. Moving further forward in time to, say, next month, the manager will be interested only in which evenings are allocated to specific activities which can then be booked by specific individuals as that week approaches. In the much longer term, say a year, the manager will need to know the size of the facility available and any plans to extend the sports hall.

It is essential to know the time period ahead within which it is impossible to change the schedule. A restaurant may be able to deal with changes in customer mix almost up to the last minute, whereas the operating theatre in Case Example 11.3 will require more notice of change in detail schedule. We will return to this topic later in this chapter when we consider resource flexibility, which aims to reduce the period ahead where the schedule must be fixed.

Case Example 11.3   Karolinska Hospital, Stockholm

Karolinska Hospital faced a crisis as the pressure on operating budgets was rising. This prompted an investigation as to how well expensive resources were being utilised. It was soon identified that operating theatres were not being used effectively. In fact, surgeons, operating theatre staff and of course the theatres themselves were idle for more than 50 per cent of the time. It soon became clear that the schedule of patients through the theatre needed to be managed more carefully. The scarce resource was time in the theatre itself, so the management looked at ways to reduce the time that patients spent in the theatre. A significant step forward created a separate patient preparation area allowing this activity to be carried out in parallel rather than in sequence with surgery.

Further investigation revealed that some delays were caused because anaesthetists were called away to other parts of the hospital. Adding anaesthetists formally to the operating room staff team and creating an anaesthesia clinic to evaluate pre-operative patients also improved the efficiency of the system.

Once the throughput through the bottleneck had been increased, more operations could be carried out in the same

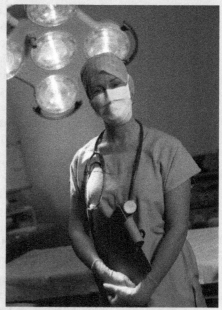

Source: Pearson Education Ltd/Corbis/BrandX

timeframe, and waiting times were dramatically reduced. The unforeseen benefit was that it was now possible to create a much more reliable schedule because the lead time between diagnosis and surgery was dramatically reduced. Patients were happier because they were treated faster and there were fewer 'no-shows' than there had been when lead times were longer. A consistent theatre schedule meant that any tests required prior to surgery could be arranged with more certainty. Previously, these tests had been frequently repeated as surgery dates had been delayed.

For Karolinska, then, this approach to scheduling has paid off in a number of ways. The theatre carries out more operations per day, costs are reduced and patients are seen more quickly. Operating rooms were reduced from 15 to 13, while the number of operations per day was increased by 30 per cent.

Source: This illustration is based on material from the video *Time Based Competition* from Harvard Business School (1993), and from healthcare industry sources.

11.5   How do organisations manage bottlenecks and queues?

Bottlenecks (the parts of a process that constrain or restrict capacity), and the resulting queues of customers or their orders, are features of many service operations. Managing these well can have a significant impact on both capacity utilisation and customer satisfaction.

11.5.1 Bottleneck management

All organisations need to understand their key resource constraints. A clear understanding of these constraints or bottlenecks provides greater clarity as to what is a realistic estimate of capacity. To return to our example in Section 11.4, the key resource constraint of the leisure centre is likely to be the central sports hall. All other resources, such as other facilities and staff, are likely to be linked to the most effective use of this space.

Bottleneck management, or the theory of constraints, is generally well understood in manufacturing organisations. It is seen to be important to manage the bottleneck – the stage in any process with the lowest throughput rate and which therefore determines the effective capacity of the whole operation.[3]

In the same way, it is important for service operations managers to understand where the bottlenecks exist in service processes. For example, a company providing loan finance needed to increase the standard of service provided to its customers, while also increasing productivity of its risk assessment process. The management was given the task of meeting increasing demand without increasing resources. Initially, it was not clear how this could be achieved, but when the process was mapped it became obvious that a problem lay with the actuaries. Figure 11.3a shows a simplified version of the original process flow, with all proposals passing through an actuary's hands for sign-off.

As can be seen from Figure 11.3a, the original capacity was constrained by the throughput of the actuaries at 15 proposals per hour. It was recognised that many proposals did not require actuarial sign-off because the credit scores indicated a clear accept or reject decision, which could be taken by more junior, less expensive staff. The initial processing took slightly longer, but in the revised process (Figure 11.3b) only 50 per cent of the proposals needed to be seen by an actuary. The capacity of the process therefore rose by nearly 50 per cent to 22 proposals per hour.

This improvement was achieved simply by monitoring the activity levels within the process and then deciding whether the current resource constraints were really bottlenecks or not.

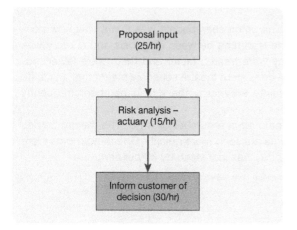

Figure 11.3a Original flow

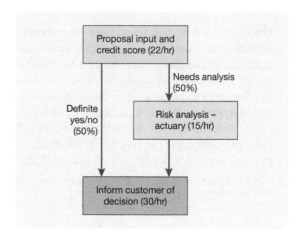

Figure 11.3b Revised flow

Once the assumption that all proposals must be seen by actuaries had been questioned, it became possible to improve response times and productivity simultaneously.

There are some general rules for managing bottlenecks:

- Ensure that only essential work passes through the bottleneck.
- Be ruthless in taking away non-essential activities from the bottleneck.
- Ensure that no substandard work passes through the bottleneck.
- Once you have established where the bottleneck is, devote proportionally more management attention to it to ensure maximum throughput and therefore maximum effectiveness for the process.

And finally, if you have a complex system, the best thing to do is not to try to move the bottleneck. It may be difficult to manage but at least you know where it is![4]

One way to identify a bottleneck is to observe where the queues of work or customers form in the process. In simple processes, this is probably as good a test as any, but it is as well to be wary. Queues may form much earlier in the process because people operating feeder activities may work at a slower rate than is theoretically possible because they believe there is no point in working flat out if the customer or the jobs will have to wait at the subsequent bottleneck. Indeed, service operations might well decide to limit the number of customers accepted into the process because of the potential dissatisfaction caused for customers who have to wait much longer than anticipated.

It is also important to distinguish between long-term and short-term bottlenecks. Long-term or fixed bottlenecks provide the best estimate of the capacity of the operation, and the basic capacity management approach can be determined as a result. However, short-term bottlenecks may frequently occur, giving rise to the need for immediate response. For example, a key member of a call centre may be unexpectedly absent, which may mean that capacity to deal with particular enquiries is dramatically reduced.

11.5.2 Queue management

Queues occur in most service activities. Indeed, for any operation using a level capacity strategy queues are 'designed-in'. Furthermore, no capacity strategy is perfect and queues are almost inevitable. Queues may be lines of people visible to both the customer and employee, or they may be invisible to one and/or the other, as with a queue of callers to a switchboard or a list of customers awaiting a repair engineer.

While queuing theory can be used to calculate the number of servers required to meet forecast demand, resource constraints and forecast inaccuracy invariably mean that operations managers need to look for other ways to minimise the impact of queuing on their customers. It has been shown that not only dissatisfaction with the wait increases with waiting time[5] but also dissatisfaction with the service as a whole.[6]

Given that perceived waiting time is usually greater than actual waiting time,[7] the answer is to try to reduce perceived waiting time, which can also be a great deal cheaper than employing more servers! Ten principles of waiting have been suggested:[8]

1 *Unoccupied time feels longer than occupied time.* It is a good idea to try to provide customers with something to do or forms of distraction so that the time passes more rapidly for them. Some services show promotional videos to people waiting in a physical queue. Waiting areas for lifts often have mirrors to enable customers to check their appearance. Telephone call centres or helpdesks frequently play music while 'on hold', although this is not universally welcomed.

2 *Pre-process waits feel longer than in-process waits.* Once customers feel that they have made a start inside the service process and that something, however trivial, is happening, they tend to feel happier. A simple acknowledgement by a server that they have been noticed can have a significant impact. Also, using pre-process time in some way, such as completing a form or making choices about the service, can reduce the perceived waiting time.

3 *Anxiety makes the wait seem longer.* Sometimes customers do not know whether they have been forgotten or not, which can be allayed by giving them numbered tickets to demonstrate that they are part of the system. Also, the nature of the service will have a significant impact. If the customer is worried about flying or going to the dentist the wait may seem interminable, possibly giving rise to some tense behaviour with service providers. Customer-facing employees should be trained to observe the effects of anxiety and to find ways of giving reassurance.

4 *Uncertain waits feel longer than known, finite waits.* Customers are generally more happy to wait if the expected duration is known, and if there is a good reason for it. If the duration is unknown, research suggests that customers become restless much more quickly. Theme parks frequently position markers at known points in the queue informing customers how long they should expect to wait. Of course, the real wait time is usually a little shorter than this, with customers pleased that they did better than expected!

5 *Unexplained waits seem longer than explained waits.* Being provided with a plausible explanation of a delay reduces uncertainty for the customer. It also gives the impression that the organisation knows it should not take the customer for granted.

6 *Unfair waits seem longer than equitable waits.* Generally, customers expect that those who arrive first should be seen first. Many organisations have replaced the multiple-queue/multiple-server system with a single-queue/multiple-server approach because of the perceived unfairness of being stuck in a slow-moving queue. This approach also eliminates the anxiety as to which queue to join. In some cases, such as a hospital casualty department, there may be a good reason why some customers are seen out of turn, but it still seems to be necessary for there to be an explanation rather than for the provider to assume that other customers will understand.

7 *The more valuable the service, the longer customers will wait.* The more complex the service, and the more it is customised to the needs of the individual, the more likely it is that customers may be prepared to wait. It should be noted, however, that this should not be assumed.

8 *Solo waiting feels longer than group waiting.* The realisation that others are also feeling the pain may reduce the customer's anxiety of thinking that they have made the wrong choice. If others think it is worth waiting, it confirms the customer's decision to wait. Also, people tend to talk to each other, providing a distraction from the length of the wait.

9 *Uncomfortable waits feel longer than comfortable waits.* By making queuing conditions as comfortable and indeed as distracting as possible, the wait time will be perceived to be much shorter. Uncomfortable conditions sensitise customers to the time and poor service.

10 *New or infrequent users experience their wait as longer than frequent users do.* Frequent users of a service may be attuned to a wait and they may be more relaxed because they know what to expect. New or infrequent users are likely to be more anxious and uncertain, so operations should consider trying to identify them and provide them with information and reassurance.

A booking system is a queue, with the advantage to customers that they do not have to physically queue for the service. The advantage for the service provider is that the operations manager is better able to manage resources to meet demand. Alton Towers (Case Example 11.2) has in effect created a 'virtual queue' through its fast-track system. Visitors to the park are given time slots to return to a pre-booked ride which allows them to use their time more effectively. Supermarkets that operate a ticket system at their delicatessen counters are using the same principle. In both cases, the service provider has found a way to ensure equity of treatment for its customers and has enabled customers to make better use of time otherwise spent queuing.

11.5.3 Queuing theory and simulation

Management scientists and mathematicians have studied the behaviour of queues, producing statistical models to predict queue length and so on. Fortunately, few of us need to understand the detail of these models, as there are a number of computer simulations available to help us predict the implications of operational decisions.

Simply put, there are three key parameters to queuing theory: the arrival rate for customers, the server rate, and the number of servers or serving positions available. The arrival rate and server rate must be further understood in terms of their variability. Even if the average server rate and arrival rate are the same, queues will still form if there is variability in these rates. This situation is illustrated in Figure 11.4, which demonstrates the impact of variability in arrival rates and process rates. In this case, the process time is reasonably constant – perhaps because it is a standard process, possibly determined to a large extent by automation or standard scripts – while customers arrive in a more random pattern. In this

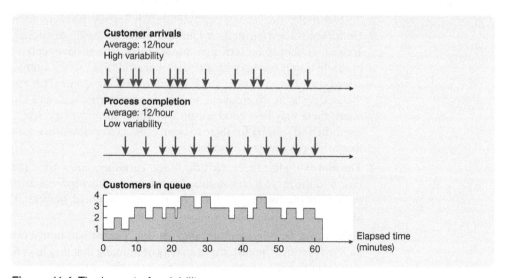

Figure 11.4 The impact of variability on queues

simple system, there may be up to four customers in the queue, the first being served and three waiting. The longest wait time for customers is therefore 20 minutes (4 × 5 minutes), which perhaps is surprising when we know that average process time matches the average arrival rate. The average queue length is about 2.5 customers, implying an average wait time of 12.5 minutes.

Computer simulations now provide invaluable information to the service operations manager. In a more complex situation than that described above, it would be impossible to model the likely outcomes, but a simulation can identify the impact of different queue designs, priority rules and so on. Whether the situation is complex or simple, the key question remains: 'How long is an acceptable waiting time?'

We do not provide a detailed analysis of queuing theory here. Fundamental texts cover this area well.[9] However, useful terminology includes:

- *Calling population.* This describes the customer base. In many cases, the calling population may consist of a variety of groups, each requiring different things. For example, customers contacting the computer company's call centre may enquire about billing, delivery, faults, purchase of service contracts, and so on. A key element of queuing theory is the size of the calling population. Consumer services have so many customers that the calling population is thought of as infinite and the probability of the arrival of a specific customer is unaffected by recent events. If, however, the calling population is relatively small, as exemplified by potential callers to an internal computer helpdesk, the probability of new callers is reduced if significant numbers have already called.

- *Arrival process.* It is clearly essential to understand the arrival pattern for customers. Many arrival patterns follow an exponential distribution. Intervals between customer arrivals in a retail store in a busy period might follow this distribution, with the majority of intervals being rather short, and long intervals being somewhat rare.

- *Queue configuration.* This describes the number of queues and their location. In many retail operations there has been a shift from multiple queues linked to multiple servers, because some queues seem to move faster than others, leading to customers moving between queues and possible ill feeling as customers believe they have been treated unfairly. A single queue leading to multiple servers has the advantage of demonstrating equity of treatment.

- *Queue discipline.* Management will choose the rule to determine who gets served next from the queue. The most common rules were discussed earlier (in Section 11.4.1), though first come, first served is the most popular with physical queues.

- *Balking.* One key measure for service systems is the number of customers who don't join a queue that they perceive as too long. This is referred to as balking.

- *Reneging.* This measures the number who join a queue, wait for a while then leave the service system due to the perceived intolerable delay.

- *Jockeying.* This is the term for customers who switch from one queue to another hoping to receive service more quickly.

11.6 What happens when managers can't cope with demand?

There is usually a point at which service managers find it difficult to cope with increasing demand (the break point: see Figure 11.5). This is when managers and staff enter the 'coping zone'. At these levels of capacity utilisation things are just too busy – staff become stressed, everything becomes a problem and, importantly, perceived quality, i.e. customer satisfaction, declines along with revenues per customer.[10]

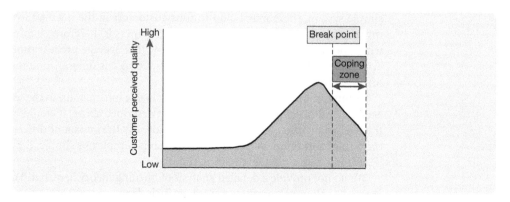

Figure 11.5 The coping zone in a high-quality restaurant

For example, in a restaurant operating at high levels of capacity utilisation, in the coping zone

- Customers have to wait a long time for service.
- There is increasing likelihood of 'stock-outs' (items removed from the menu).
- Customers feel rushed and under pressure not to ask too much from busy serving staff.
- Staff feel under pressure and are less likely to give courteous responses or the personalised service expected.

The break point is usually reached before full or 100 per cent utilisation for two reasons. First, it is often not possible to run any single resource at full capacity for any period of time; staff in a restaurant for example simply cannot work 'flat out' all the time. Second, several resources may be involved and while staff might be working 'flat out', only 80 per cent of the tables might be in use.

Interestingly there may be problems at times of low utilisation, too, which affect both staff and customers. In the case of the restaurant,

- The perception of the overall quality of service experience is low because the restaurant is 'dead'. There is no buzz of conversation; there are often prolonged silences.
- Service may be slow, because although there are not many customers, the kitchen may not be working at maximum effectiveness.
- In the same way, serving staff may be less attentive than might be expected, because again they may not be busy enough to be fully tuned in to customer needs.

Figure 11.5 illustrates the profile of customer perceived quality against capacity utilisation and illustrates how quality may suffer through both too many and too few customers in a high-quality restaurant.

The shape of the profile, the break point and the size of the coping zone will vary between organisations. Figure 11.6 illustrates the relationship between customer perceived quality (satisfaction) and capacity utilisation in a nightclub. Here customers may not enjoy the atmosphere until the place is crammed with bodies! Still, at some point the club's resources will start to struggle with the demand placed upon its resources – door staff, toilets and bar, for example – as it enters the coping zone.

11.6.1 How to manage the coping zone

There are seven steps in building up this profile and managing the coping zone.

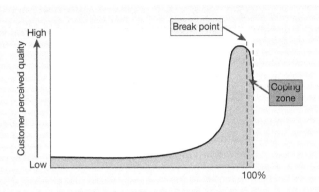

Figure 11.6 The coping zone in a nightclub

Step 1 Identify the service concept

Underpinning the service concept of a high-quality restaurant is the belief that customers may book a table for the whole evening. They will not be rushed to vacate their table since the restaurant has no intention of selling the space twice in an evening. It is intended that the service experience should be relaxed, with staff able to converse with customers and make recommendations about food and wine, where appropriate.

This is a very different concept from a restaurant wishing to create a high-energy situation, often with staff rushing around, and with the customers encouraged to eat up and leave. It is important to be clear as to what the designed or desired service concept is, particularly as the restaurant gets busy.

Step 2 Determine how capacity utilisation is to be measured

For the high-quality restaurant, the best measure of capacity utilisation is the number of tables, and also chairs, that are occupied during the evening. To some extent, other resources such as serving staff or kitchen capacity can be adjusted to the busyness of the restaurant area.

The unit of measure is often best taken at the lowest level that the business analyses or controls performance. A call centre might look at the average loading of a customer service agent on an hourly basis throughout the day, whereas a professional service firm might look at an individual's case load.

Step 3 Draw the outline profile

Figure 11.5 shows the relationship between customer perceived quality and capacity utilisation as it exists for the majority of customers on the majority of occasions. This does not represent all customers at all times. Some customers, for example, prefer the empty restaurant and would rank it as high quality at low utilisation. For others, the occasion and their mood will have a significant influence on where they would place themselves on the profile. This data can be captured from aggregating customer satisfaction indices and comparing it to utilisation at the time.

Step 4 Understand the nature and impact of the coping zone

While we accept that low utilisation is as much of a problem for quality of service as high utilisation is – indeed in some ways it is worse because revenue is also low – here we are focusing on operations working in the coping zone. It is important to recognise the signals that suggest this zone has been reached and be sensitive to them. Tempers flaring, customers looking around or queues appearing may all signal that breaking point has been passed. It is also worth undertaking some financial analysis to try to demonstrate the impact between passing the break point and its effects on costs and revenues, for example.

Step 5 Determine the 'ideal' operating area

In Figure 11.5 we have identified the break point at 80 per cent capacity utilisation. At 100 per cent utilisation, in the case of the restaurant, it would be impossible to seat any more customers. There are two broad approaches that can be adopted:

- Operate at 80 per cent capacity utilisation. Operating at this point would suggest that the restaurant could be losing potential revenue. It is true that it might receive lower short-term revenues, but it may also upset longstanding customers by appearing to be greedy, squeezing as many people as possible into every available space. It is critical to understand the difference between customer satisfaction at 80 per cent and at 100 per cent, and to what extent this significantly reduces the customers' likelihood of returning.

- Operate at 100 per cent capacity utilisation. Generally speaking, this is a short-term cash-generating strategy. It is more appropriate to theme restaurants that are the 'place to be seen' for a period, before those customers that are concerned about fashion move on to the next 'in' place. This strategy might also be appropriate for restaurants in holiday resorts, which do not expect high levels of customer returns.

Our example restaurant depends on long-term customer retention and word-of-mouth advertising. As a result, it targets its operations at the 80 per cent point. To manage this, the owner has removed some of the tables to give a less crowded feel to the area, only replacing them on particularly busy occasions.

As a result, the owner has made the 80 per cent a 100 per cent effective capacity. In other words, at this point, the restaurant is making sufficient revenue to meet its short-term financial goals, and is giving a high level of customer satisfaction to safeguard its future business. It is worth noting that because there is a gap between 100 per cent effective capacity and 100 per cent potential capacity, it is possible for the restaurant to be working at greater than 100 per cent utilisation on some occasions. For many managers this is the norm in their businesses!

Step 6 Understand why coping happens

Clearly it is impossible to maintain the capacity balance on 80 per cent capacity utilisation at all times. Even if the restaurant has a booking policy, there is always the possibility that one of the most valuable customers will book at the last minute and the owner will be reluctant to turn this business away.

In other situations, the launch of a new service or periods of faster than anticipated growth may put parts of the business into 'coping' mode. This has been seen recently in the customer service departments of mobile phone network providers and banks following product launches. In some cases, some of the coping might have been avoided if the company had carried out some forecasting, or had simply communicated internally.

A key point here is to recognise that all but extremely resource-rich organisations will be in the coping zone sometimes. If the coping zone is never entered, the inevitable conclusion is that the organisation has too much resource.

Step 7 Develop coping strategies

Most organisations cope after a fashion. In the restaurant, all the diners are given food, but perhaps not with the greatest customer experience. Likewise, on the crowded flight, all passengers get a meal and a drink, though those that are served last may have limited choice and little time to eat before the aircraft starts its descent.

Left to their own devices, customer-facing staff will find their own ways of coping. Some of these informal coping strategies will be entirely appropriate and innovative, using interpersonal skills and intuition to judge how to handle each customer. Others might be less satisfactory, typified by the following examples:

- Waiters who become overly focused on one task, making it impossible for customers to attract their attention to make yet more demands.
- Doctors' receptionists who, faced with a crowded waiting room, become extremely efficient in their dealings with patients, to the point of rudeness.
- Retail assistants who 'forget' to offer a customer a range of services, knowing that if the customer chooses one of these, their workload will increase.

Operations managers develop coping strategies based on one or more of the following:

- Giving more information to customers alerting them to possible difficulties. An example is an electricity company that after a major storm places a recorded message on its help line to say 'If you're calling about loss of power in this district, we should be able to restore it within two hours.' This reduces the load on overworked telephone lines and operators.
- Intentionally reducing the service on offer, perhaps using a limited menu at peak times in the restaurant.
- Being clear to staff about what really matters most for customers: concentrating on the 'must dos' rather than the 'nice to dos'.
- Building resource flexibility by bringing staff from a lightly loaded area to assist with the overload. Call centres manage this by switching calls to other centres, whereas Disney brings managers from back-office functions to assist with customer-facing operations on busy days. It is important to note that some of this resource may not be as efficient as the normal workforce.

There is a very strong link between prolonged overload and employee stress (see Chapter 10). It is relatively easy for providers to deal with short-term, predictable overloads. If we know we're going to be busy for a week or two, we can prepare for it, and many people get a 'buzz' from working together to cope with a crisis. The real problem with coping comes from protracted periods of overload, without hope of a let-up in the foreseeable future. Management support and appreciation becomes extremely important at this stage.

If the operation is in the coping zone for prolonged periods, it may be necessary for managers to give their staff 'licence to underperform'. For example, nurses in a busy accident and emergency department may not be able to carry out all their duties in the way in which they were trained. If this persists for any length of time, this will lead to stress and possible burnout. Part of the coping strategy, therefore, is to agree which bits of the service are 'must dos' and which bits can be safely left for the time being.

11.6.2 Coping: key questions

We have devoted a lot of space to coping because understanding how the organisation deals with this area may give clues as to where capacity management must be strengthened. The key questions to address are:

- What does the customer perceived quality/capacity utilisation profile look like for your service or services?
- How does this vary by service process and by customer group?

- What measures or early warning signals tell you that you are about to enter the coping zone (as opposed to measures like lost customers or increased complaints which tell you that you *were* in the coping zone)?
- What suffers for customers when you enter the coping zone?
- What suffers for employees when you enter the coping zone?
- How could you manage the coping zone better to reduce the impact on customers and employees?
- How could you avoid being in the coping zone as much?

Of course, coping will affect every part of the organisation, in areas where both chase and level strategies are operating, although coping is perhaps more obvious in operations that are employing a chase strategy. In effect, chase becomes level in the short term because the organisation is not capable of adding another unit of capacity quickly enough to deal with an unexpected surge in demand. Coping is perhaps more sensitive here because, as we have noted, organisations employ this strategy when fast response or high levels of availability to customers are particularly important. In such circumstances, customers are not usually prepared to wait, either because the service is not particularly valuable to them, or because there are alternatives available to them.

11.7 How can organisations improve their capacity utilisation?

There are four important additional ways of trying to improve capacity utilisation:

- yield management
- building flexibility
- reducing capacity leakage
- getting organisational support for capacity utilisation.

11.7.1 Yield management

Yield management is employed extensively by hotels and airlines to deal with the fact that their capacity is perishable (see Case Example 11.4). In other words, if the hotel room is not sold tonight, the contribution from that potential sale is lost for all time.

Yield management is focused on determining the maximum revenue to be obtained from the various segments served by the capacity at hand. Thus the airline estimates how many full-fare-paying (business-class) passengers will book for any given flight, and adjusts the remaining capacity for economy-class passengers and other discount, pre-booked customers. As departure time approaches, the airline may release some capacity to discount travel shops and, as a last resort at the very last minute, to stand-by passengers.

Service managers must be aware, however, of the potential damage to the service concept in using this approach. Full-fare-paying customers may be unhappy to discover that the person in the seat next to them is flying for a fraction of the price. This may give the impression that the airline is merely after every last dollar of revenue, with customer satisfaction of minor importance. The Kowloon Hotel appears to have overcome this particular objection by creating a completely new concept where the charging policy is clear and unambiguous. Customers can therefore make their choice of eating time, knowing that they will be treated equitably.

| Case Example 11.4 | The Kowloon Hotel, Hong Kong |

Sheryl E. Kimes, Cornell University

Yield management, the notion of charging higher prices when demand is high and offering discounts at times of low demand, has traditionally been applied in reservations-based industries such as airlines, hotels and car rental agencies. Managers at the Kowloon Hotel in Hong Kong felt that it might offer them the solution to improving their restaurant revenues.

The Kowloon Hotel on Nathan Road in Hong Kong is well known for its sumptuous all-day buffet. The buffet, which includes a selection of sashimi, oysters, salads and desserts, is open from midday to midnight. As is typical with most restaurants, customers only wanted to dine at particular times of day, and

Source: James Davies

the restaurant was often empty in the late afternoon and late evening. To deal with this problem, the Kowloon Hotel's managers decided to move away from a single price for its buffet and charge different prices depending on when customers arrive.

When guests arrive (check-in) they now receive a 'buffet zone pass'. The cost of the pass varies depending on their arrival time. At noon, the price is HK$118. It increases to $128 at 1.00 p.m., but then drops back to $118 at 2.00 p.m. The 3.00 p.m. price is even lower ($108), but then progressively increases from $128 at 4.00 p.m., to $168 at 5.00 p.m., $208 at 6.00 p.m. and $248 at 7.00 p.m. Following this peak, the price gradually decreases back to $138 at 10.00 p.m. and to only $98 at 11.00 p.m.

Not only has this new pricing system resulted in a 33 per cent increase in revenue – which was attributed to a fuller utilisation of the restaurant space, hence an increase in revenue per available seat hour (RevPASH) – it has also proved to be a hit with customers, with extremely positive customer reaction. As a result, the management has decided to continue the time-of-day pricing for an indefinite period.

11.7.2 Building flexibility

There are four basic forms of operational flexibility:

- *New service flexibility.* This is the requirement of the service operation to introduce new services into an existing mix. It will be necessary to define how frequently this might occur and the extent to which the operation will require new capabilities to achieve it. For example, house loan (mortgage) companies are continually introducing new 'products' with varying interest rates and repayment terms. In this case the frequency of new 'product' introduction is extremely high, but the requirement for new capability is low.

- *Service mix flexibility.* This is the ability of the operation to deliver more than one service. A hotel may provide a number of services simultaneously dealing with business people, holiday travellers, conferences and wedding celebrations.

- *Delivery flexibility.* This is the capability of the operation to change the timing of the activity. Courier organisations are increasing this form of flexibility, offering different speeds of delivery and a range of pick-up and delivery times.

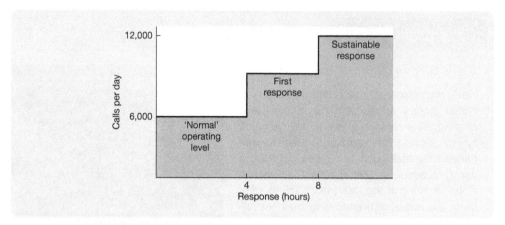

Figure 11.7 Minimum effective lead times for a call centre

- *Volume flexibility.* This form of flexibility is required by many consumer services operating a chase strategy. It refers to the ability of the organisation to change its level of output to cope with fluctuating demand. Thus the call centre may deal with 6,000 telephone transactions on a normal day, but may have to cope with twice that amount following an advertising campaign or a new product or service launch.

It is critical to define carefully the type and extent of flexibility required in order to develop effective capacity management plans.

Figure 11.7 demonstrates the notion of minimum effective lead times – the time it takes to respond to a change in demand. If an unexpected surge of demand occurs, the call centre manager can increase capacity by 50 per cent in four hours. This is accomplished by asking staff to stay on after their normal shift, by calling in off-duty staff, and by bringing in other staff from the organisation to man the phones. It should be noted that this is very much a 'first' or emergency response as some of the staff will not be fully trained and productivity levels will probably suffer as a result. Within eight hours the call centre manager can bring on line more capacity, perhaps from other call centres, if the increase in demand is sustained.

This is a valuable tool in assisting operations managers to plan for foreseeable contingencies. In addition to specifying the type of flexibility required, the service manager must also consider the following:

- *Range.* How much flexibility is required? Does the call centre need to move from 6,000 calls to 12,000 calls or only to 8,000 calls per day? How many new services will be introduced and how frequently?

- *Response.* How quickly must the change be made? Can the call centre change from 6,000 to 12,000 calls in four hours or will eight hours be good enough? Clearly the faster the response, the more expensive it is likely to be.

- *Effectiveness across the range.* Most processes have an optimal range. It is unlikely that they will be equally productive across the potential range; they are likely to strain at the extremes.

- *Cost of providing the flexibility.* What is the premium both for the change in output level itself, and for providing the capability in the first place? For example, providing training so that more staff are multi-skilled represents a significant investment.

There are a number of approaches to building flexibility. These include:

- *Flexible employment contracts.* Employees may be asked to work a given number of hours per week, month or year. In this way, staffing levels may be more easily matched to expected demand. Flexibility in this area may extend to the requirement for staff to move between functions to cover fluctuating workloads. It is important to recognise that these staff may not be as effective when carrying out tasks that are less familiar to them.

- *Overtime.* Asking staff to work longer hours is a common short-term measure for building volume flexibility. However, it is generally accepted that using overtime in the longer term does not give the required increase in output as employees simply expand work to fit the extra time available. In this event, overtime is a poor approach, costing a great deal in extra salary and creating employees who are overtired through being at work for long periods.

- *Short-term outsourcing.* The development of relationships with other service providers who can deal with short-term peaks in demand is a common practice, particularly in call centre activities. This requires some pre-qualification of suppliers, but can provide flexibility at relatively low cost.

- *Menu-driven service (standardisation).* Standardisation of service offers provides opportunities for increased volumes of fewer activities. This creation of 'runner' activities (see Chapter 8) smooths the workload and provides opportunities to provide a degree of customisation or personalisation for customers. This is often referred to as the 'Dell' approach, whereby customers can create their own configuration of computer from a wide range of standard modules on offer. Education providers such as the Open University adopt a similar approach in allowing students to tailor their courses, within pre-determined constraints.

- *Teamwork.* The development of multifunctional teams allows a group of employees to deal with fluctuating workloads rather than simply operate on an individual basis. There are several benefits to this approach, including the support that group members give each other, and the ability to 'flex' capacity very rapidly.

11.7.3 Reducing capacity leakage

Many operations managers carefully plan their capacity in ways we have discussed in this chapter; however, sometimes managers are surprised to find they do not have as much capacity as expected. Here are some possible explanations:

- *Labour sickness and absenteeism.* Prolonged periods of overload and compulsory overtime usually prove counterproductive, with staff taking time off to recover. Alternatively, the organisation may need to look at its management style, placing more emphasis on team building rather than 'command and control' approaches.

- *Labour underperformance.* It is extremely common to find that call centres may have the right number of 'heads' but they may be ineffective because there has been insufficient investment in training. Alternatively, employee churn means that experienced staff leave just at the point when they are becoming effective.

- *Scheduling losses.* There are times when staff are idle with too much capacity for the demand, whereas at other times there is too much demand for the capacity to deal with. This often arises because demand profiles are not understood or are too volatile, or where staff preferences for work patterns do not fit with the business need.

- *Costs of complexity.* The more the organisation deals with a broad range of services, the greater the possibility that staff deal with a greater percentage of tasks that may not be part of daily routine. This potential 'relearning' may give rise to inefficiencies and rework.

- *Quality failures.* The need to deal with quality failures is clearly lost capacity. Of course, part of the role of the call centre may be to deal with poor quality generated elsewhere in the organisation. It is essential that the extent of this rework is understood and charged to the appropriate location.

11.7.4 Organisational support for capacity utilisation

The challenge for operations managers is to understand capacity utilisation in the context of a changing world. Many of the issues need to be resolved by the organisation as a whole, rather than simply confined to the management of service delivery processes. Aspects of this organisational support include:

- *How is the service concept changing?* To what extent do operations managers have 'visibility' in the future strategic direction of the organisation? Without this inclusion in the strategic development process it is unlikely that capacity planning and capacity utilisation and development will be effectively carried out. Often resource managers are left to develop capacity plans that have little relevance because the concept has been changed. For example, many service companies providing repair and maintenance support for information technology have changed the emphasis of their service concept away from servicing equipment towards supporting customers. The nature and length of customer transactions have changed beyond recognition, and a link is required between this change in strategic direction and resource planning for it to be implemented.

- *How well are the internal interfaces managed?* A key role for the operations manager is to manage the internal relationships as well as customer relationships. Co-ordination of marketing promotions and new service introductions is vital, as is getting to the root of quality failures and long-term quality costs. Successful organisations are often those that manage the internal relationships well. This does not necessarily mean that everyone always agrees, but that there is valuable internal debate. In fact, it could be asserted that an organisation without some degree of conflict will not learn and move forward.

- *How important is resource management in the culture of the company?* In some sectors, resource management is seen as a low-level task. The 'stars' of the company are often seen as those who deliver the latest deal or solve the latest crisis. Resource management needs a different type of 'hero' who is able to plan for the longer term and persuade the organisation to think differently about resource management.

11.8   Summary

What is capacity management?

- Capacity management is concerned with putting a plan in place that makes the best use of resources to deal with the forecasted or expected demand for services.
- Service capacity is defined as the maximum level of value-added activity over a period of time that the service process can consistently achieve under normal operating conditions.
- Capacity is influenced by a range of factors including service mix, location, intangibility and resource constraints.

How can managers balance capacity and demand?

- Most organisations adopt a mixture of capacity strategies: level, chase and demand management. The mixture should reflect the strategy of the operation.

How is day-to-day planning and control carried out?

- Day-to-day operations planning is concerned with creating a 'schedule' or timetable based on the capacity plan, which allocates people, customers, equipment or facilities, decides what order things will be done in and shows what time each activity will start and finish.

- Operations control is concerned with using the schedule to make adjustments to cope with changes as they happen.

How do organisations manage bottlenecks and queues?

- Key constraints (bottlenecks) define the capacity of the service process. It is critical to devote management attention to these aspects of operations.
- Queues are inevitable in service operations. Developing 'waiting line' strategies will reduce potential customer dissatisfaction.
- Queuing theory and computer simulations provide valuable means of understanding complex queuing situations.

What happens when managers can't cope with demand?

- Almost all service operations experience a point where demand outstrips supply: customers may perceive a fall in quality, and staff feel under increased pressure. This is known as the coping zone.
- We recommend that organisations develop coping strategies, given that all operations will sometimes be in the coping zone.
- It is important to develop actions to avoid being in the coping zone too much. This usually requires organisation-wide approaches.

How can organisations improve their capacity utilisation?

- Yield management techniques enable services with perishable capacity (e.g. hotel rooms, airline seats) to maximise revenues.
- It is critical to define the nature of flexibility required to meet market demand in terms of range and response. Techniques to build flexibility include flexible employment contracts, overtime, outsourcing, developing menu-driven services, and teamwork.
- Capacity leakage may impact significantly on the ability of the operation to meet its demands.
- Understanding and developing the organisation's support for resource management is an important task for operations managers.

11.9 Discussion questions

1 Select four service organisations and suggest how they might measure capacity, outlining the problems in so doing.
2 What capacity strategies might be used by an insurance broker, an internet retailer and a cruise ship company? Explain why they are appropriate.
3 Describe the last time you were in a queue. Apply the principles of queuing to assess your waiting experience.
4 What is meant by the coping zone? What are the implications for staff and customers of a supermarket when the operation enters this zone?

11.10 Questions for managers

1 How important is capacity utilisation to the success of your organisation? What interest do senior managers take in this aspect of operations?

2 What are your short-, medium- and long-term capacity management strategies? How effective are they?

3 How well is the capacity strategy matched to the financial model of your organisation? Could a significant increase in customer satisfaction be achieved by an increase in relatively inexpensive resource?

4 Do you know where the bottlenecks or scarce resources are in your processes? How effectively are they managed?

5 What is the impact of the coping zone on your staff and customers? What strategies do you have in place to manage this more effectively?

6 What are the major causes of capacity leakage? Are they avoidable?

Case Exercise | Medi-Call Personal Alarm Systems Ltd

Medi-Call provides personal alarm systems to the elderly and infirm. Customers are principally those people who live alone, preferring to stay in their own homes rather than be looked after in some form of institutional care or with family.

The customer has a small transmitter/receiver, which can be worn as a pendant or on the wrist like a watch. If the customer has a problem they press the button on the pendant, which activates a base station located at the customer's telephone. The base station calls Medi-Call's contact centre, which provides 24/7 cover to ensure maximum reassurance for its customers. Medi-Call's agent will attempt to establish contact with the customer. Because the transmitter is so sensitive, it is possible to carry out a conversation up to 50 metres away from the base station. Medi-Call's staff are trained to provide immediate reassurance to the caller, who is likely to be confused and frightened.

Each customer provides a number of contact numbers, including neighbours and immediate family. If there is a problem, as for example an elderly person having fallen and not being able to get up, the normal procedure is for Medi-Call to alert the closest neighbours, asking them to visit and call back. If required, Medi-Call will alert emergency services and also contact family members if appropriate.

The call centre deals with a wide range of demands:

- *Emergency calls.* These result in Medi-Call agents being on the phone for an average of 30 minutes. This time may be spread over a number of calls to the customer, neighbours, family and so on. Each emergency call requires an average of 8 minutes' administration time to ensure records are kept up to date – this normally happens immediately after the call is completed, and definitely before the agent completes their shift.

- *Technical enquiries.* These calls normally come from new customers, unsure about the function of the equipment. The average duration of these calls is 5 minutes, with 1 minute of associated administration time.

- *Reassurance calls.* Medi-Call encourages customers to ring the call centre about once a month to check that the equipment is working properly. Many elderly customers spend long periods by themselves at home and see this as an opportunity to have a rather longer conversation than is strictly necessary. Medi-Call considers this as part of the service it provides. The average reassurance call lasts about 6 minutes, with 1 minute of associated administration time.

A typical morning in the call centre has the profile shown in Table 11.2.

Table 11.2 Call profile

Time	Staff numbers	Emergency calls	Technical calls	Reassurance calls
00.00–01.00	6	4	0	2
01.00–02.00	6	5	0	5
02.00–03.00	6	5	0	7
03.00–04.00	6	4	1	5
04.00–05.00	6	5	0	7
05.00–06.00	6	7	0	5
06.00–07.00	10	12	2	11
07.00–08.00	10	11	4	15
08.00–09.00	10	13	3	15
09.00–10.00	10	9	8	12
10.00–11.00	10	8	8	12
11.00–12.00	10	10	1	13

Medi-Call estimates that its employees are effective for about 80 per cent of the time that they are on shift, and this forms the basis of its staff scheduling system. This figure allows for short comfort breaks, and also recognises that not all staff are fully competent. Medi-Call provides thorough induction training and continuing staff development, but annual turnover of staff is in the order of 20 per cent, and it takes upwards of six months for staff to be fully trained.

The majority of calls are handled by the member of staff who is the first point of contact. In less than 10 per cent of calls, the agent handling the call may ask for assistance from a more experienced colleague or the supervisor.

Questions

1 When does Medi-Call's call centre enter the coping zone? What is the likely impact of this overload on customers and staff?

2 What strategies do you recommend that Medi-Call adopts in busy periods? What actions would you need to take to implement them effectively?

3 Do you agree with Medi-Call's philosophy on reassurance calls? What do you recommend?

Suggested further reading

Johnston, Robert and Peter Jones (2004), 'Service Productivity: Towards Understanding the Relationship between Operational and Customer Productivity', *International Journal of Productivity and Performance Management* 53 (3) 201–213

Kimes, Sheryl E. and Jochen Wirtz (2003), 'Has Revenue Management Become Acceptable?', *Journal of Service Research* 6 (2) 125–135

Klassen, Kenneth J. and Thomas R. Rohleder (2001), 'Combining Operations and Marketing to Manage Capacity and Demand in Services', *Service Industries Journal* 21 (2) 1–30

Kwortnik, Robert J. Jr. and Gary M. Thompson (2009), 'Unifying Service Marketing and Operations with Service Experience Management', *Journal of Service Research* 11 (4) 389–406

Pullman, Madeleine. E. and Gary M. Thompson (2003), 'Strategies for Integrating Capacity with Demand in Service Networks', *Journal of Service Research* 5 (3) 169–183

Thompson, Gary M. (2011), 'Cherry-picking Customers by Party Size in Restaurants', *Journal of Service Research* 14 (2) 201–213

Useful web links

An interesting article on managing demand and supply in health services:
http://www.bmj.com/cgi/content/full/316/7145/1665

Some advice on managing queues and crowds by the Health and Safety Executive:
http://www.hse.gov.uk/pubns/indg142.htm

David Maister's web page provides material on queue management (join a blog!):
http://davidmaister.com/

Some interesting white papers have been published by airport-technology.com about the way they manage and simulate ground control operations at an airport:
http://www.airport-technology.com/downloads/whitepapers/

Notes

1 Slack, Nigel, Stuart Chambers and Robert Johnston (2010), *Operations Management*, 6th edition, FT Prentice Hall, Harlow

2 Slack, Nigel, Stuart Chambers and Robert Johnston (2010), *Operations Management*, 6th edition, FT Prentice Hall, Harlow

3 See, for example, Goldratt, Eliyahu M. and Jeff Cox (2004), *The Goal*, 3rd edition, Gower Publishing, Maidenhead, UK

4 Goldratt, Eliyahu M. and Jeff Cox (2004), *The Goal*, 3rd edition, Gower Publishing, Maidenhead, UK

5 Katz, Karen L., Blaire M. Larson and Richard C. Larson (1991), 'Prescription for the Waiting-in-line Blues: Entertain, Enlighten, and Engage', *Sloan Management Review* 32 (2) 44–53

6 Davis, Mark M. and Thomas E. Vollmann (1990), 'A Framework for Relating Waiting Time and Customer Satisfaction in a Service Operation', *The Journal of Service Marketing* 4 (1) 61–69

7 Katz, Karen L., Blaire M. Larson and Richard C. Larson (1991), 'Prescription for the Waiting-in-line Blues: Entertain, Enlighten, and Engage', *Sloan Management Review* 32 (2) 44–53

8 The ten principles include: Principles 1–8 developed by Maister, David H. (1985), 'The Psychology of Waiting Lines' in Czepiel, John A., Michael R. Soloman and Carol F. Surprenant (eds), *The Service Encounter*, D.C. Heath & Company, pp. 113–123, Principle 9 by Davis, Mark M. and Janelle Heineke (1994), 'Understanding the Roles of the

Customer and the Operation for Better Queue Management', *International Journal of Operations and Production Management* 14 (5) 21–34, and Principle 10 by Jones, P. and Emma Peppiatt (1996), 'Managing Perceptions of Waiting Times in Service Queues', *International Journal of Service Industry Management* 7 (5) 47–61

9   Fitzsimmons and Fitzsimmons (2010) give a useful summary of the key elements of the mathematical theories that underpin this topic: Fitzsimmons, James A. and Mona J. Fitzsimmons (2010), *Service Management*, 7th edition, McGraw-Hill, New York; see also, for example, Slack, Nigel, Stuart Chambers and Robert Johnston (2010), *Operations Management*, 6th edition, FT Prentice Hall, Harlow

10   See for example Armistead, Colin G. and Graham Clark (1994), 'The "Coping" Capacity Management Strategy in Services and the Influence on Quality Performance', *International Journal of Service Industry Management* 5 (2) 5–22; Clark, Graham and Kim James (1997), 'The "Coping" Zone: Stress and Quality', in Jaume Ribera and Julia Prats (eds), *Managing Service Operations: Lessons from the Service and Manufacturing Sectors*, IESE, Barcelona, pp. 385–390

Part 5 Improve

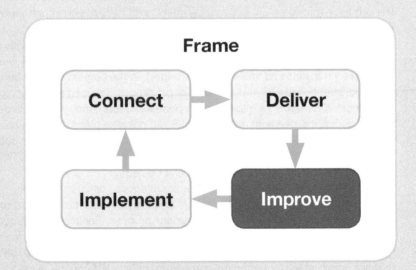

Chapter 12
Driving continuous improvement

Chapter objectives

This chapter is about how to employ a range of tools to improve service operations.

- How can managers use 'value' to drive continuous improvement?
- What are the main approaches to continuous improvement?
- How can managers sustain continuous improvement?

12.1 Introduction

It could be argued that the main reason for studying service operations management is that we learn how to improve our operations. This chapter considers some ways in which improvements to operations are not simply encouraged but are used to drive change through organisations. While processes, people, capacity management and culture (see Chapters 8, 10, 11 and 16) can promote and indeed inhibit operational improvements, there are many ways in which operations managers can make significant improvements to their operations. Performance measurement and management, with its focus on improvement, was dealt with in Chapter 9. This chapter focuses on a range of management tools and approaches that have also been used to great effect in the drive for improvement in service operations.

Continuous improvement (CI) is often referred to as *kaizen*. *Kaizen* is a Japanese word that loosely translates as 'making things better'. In the context of operations, *kaizen* is about continual attention to and improvement of processes. The idea is as much philosophical as it is practical. *Kaizen* has its beginnings in post-war Japan, though more widespread adoption of continuous improvement methodologies did not take place until the early 1990s. Arguably the book that began to popularise approaches such as TQM, lean production, just-in-time etc. was *The Machine that Changed the World* by Womack, Jones and Roos.[1] It was in this book that the term lean production was first coined.

All improvement processes, whether 'continuous' or 'step-change', focus on two key elements: what adds value for customers and the organisation, and how to mobilise service employees to contribute to the improvement process. Ensuring that process improvement is driven by the need to raise the customer's perception of the experience and outcomes might seem self-evident, but examples of organisations improving aspects of operations that are unimportant to customers are commonplace. Of course, we are not just interested in customer satisfaction – improvements in resource utilisation are also valuable in terms of reduced cost and/or increased profitability.

A thread that runs through much of operational improvement is the need to involve all employees. Indeed, this involvement in itself will have an impact on the motivation of employees, frequently bringing about improvements in operational performance, as was implied in the famous Hawthorne studies.[2] However, this involvement in itself is insufficient to sustain improvement unless there are substantive changes in process design, resource allocation, and reward and recognition systems. What cannot be denied is that there is a continual need for organisations to improve operational performance. Customer requirements are continually changing and service providers must guard against becoming complacent. Likewise, stakeholders are looking for confidence that the operation is efficient and well managed and, in the case of shareholders, that their investment has been a good one.

Before we describe some of the main operational improvement tools let us consider the question of what is meant by value.

12.2 How can managers use 'value' to drive continuous improvement?

The various continuous improvement methodologies have several issues in common. One recurring theme is that organisations should pay attention to value, in particular that organisations should move away from internally focused notions of value to customers' ideas of value. We defined value in Chapter 3, but here we want to look at how it can be used to better understand continuous improvement.

A useful first step in understanding value is to deconstruct it. Value can be deconstructed into cost-based value and features-based value. For example, an organisation could remove waste from internal processes and provide essentially the same service at reduced cost, thereby increasing customer value. Alternatively the organisation could enhance the features and benefits of the service. The organisation can make the customer pay for these, but this need not always be the case. When trying to understand value there is also a need to take a 'whole-system' perspective. Consider the local authority that looks in isolation at the costs associated with processing domestic and trade waste. Domestic customers (citizens) could argue that they already pay for waste processing through their council tax. Accordingly, council tax payers receive weekly rubbish collections and have ready access to municipal recycling units. In order to cut the costs of running the waste processing service the council could consider charging commercial/trade customers a premium either for collection of waste or for dealing with it at recycling units.

An unintended consequence of such a decision is that trade customers would have a greater incentive to dump waste inappropriately. At the level of the whole system, then, we can see that this policy in regard to trade waste is itself wasteful and reduces value. This is because the policy provides an incentive for trade customers to dispose of waste inappropriately thus resulting in additional rework (recovery of fly-tipped waste) and pushing up costs overall. This example illustrates the benefits of taking a whole-system view, and of broadening the perspective of waste and, in turn, value.

In his 2011 paper on lean healthcare,[3] Pat Hagan presents a radical re-conceptualisation of value:

> A close examination of the remaining 95 percent of health-care processes reveals that much of what is done is of little or no value to the patient. Therefore, it is unnecessary and can be eliminated without negatively affecting patients. The remainder, although not transformational is, however, necessary. But even here there are opportunities to reduce

waste. A simple example – a blood test – shows how this really works. What really matters to the patient who is having blood drawn? The lab? The technician? The process? In the end, it is 'none of the above'. Patients care about accurate test results, just as they care about having a thoughtful and experienced clinician interpret their test results so that appropriate treatment can be prescribed. That is the crucial 5 percent for the patient. The rest of the blood-test process – from travelling to the lab, to waiting for the technician, to the needle stick, to waiting for the results – is of no value. Some of the process – such as the needle stick – may be necessary, but everything else is arguably unnecessary and should be eliminated. And the necessary work of no value should be reduced to only what is absolutely necessary. When having blood drawn, no one should ever have to be poked twice with a needle; once should be enough.

Hagan is of course correct, but getting organisations to adopt this mind shift can be a huge challenge.

Case Example 12.1	Pirates

Assumptions about what customers value are common-place; organisations and individual service providers 'do what they do'; it is difficult to admit that what is offered is not quite what people want. Sometimes a thorough investigation into value will reveal a 'broken' or redundant business model, and the consequences in terms of service re-design can be painful. Still, re-design is not half as painful as lost relevance, with no customers and no revenue. The recording industry provides a useful illustration of this problem. Until the advent of MP3 compression in the early 1990s, the business model of the recording industry was in essence concerned with selling a good, the vinyl record or CD. MP3 compression enabled illegal file sharing. Illegality aside, the sharing of MP3 files was in its

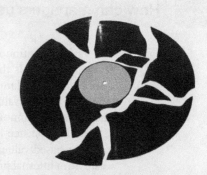

Source: Fotolia.com/Wingnut Designs

earliest days an expression of a constituency's desire for a different service: access to obscure recordings. Pre Napster, most file sharing was done via Usenet newsgroups and the sharers were music 'geeks', the people who just had to have every rare concert bootleg of their favourite band. Because the market for such recordings was small, the large record companies were not interested in serving this demand. In response, a community filled the 'void' with a rudimentary service that provided access to such recordings. Ironically the music geeks were willing to buy rare recordings, but they simply were not available. Still, the MP3 exchange via Usenet groups was small in volume – the process was difficult to set up, and the learning curve was beyond 'normal people'. Napster arrived on the scene in 1999, and made access to such files simple. Their peer-to-peer file-sharing software was easy to install and use, and everyone with a PC and internet connection could access MP3 files. Share they did, in their billions! Naturally enough, the recording industry fought back, and in July 2001 succeeded in shutting down the Napster service. Throughout the Napster saga – and in fact to this day – the record companies maintained that the main issue was one of theft . . . theft of potential revenue from music sales. However, by re-analysing the story from a value perspective, we can see that there was, in the early 1990s, a mismatch between the record companies' offerings and what consumers wanted. Consumers valued access to obscure titles, in small amounts (songs as opposed to whole albums); they wanted music quickly, and at lower costs. The record companies offered titles that would sell in high volume only; they also mainly offered bundle deals only (albums); purchase required the physical purchase of a disk of polycarbonate and a trip to the shops, or a wait for an Amazon delivery. Finally regardless of the cost of production, or of market demand the songs cost roughly £1, for all vendors.

The mismatch described in Case Example 12.1, between the value proposition offered by an organisation (or group in this case) and that wanted by consumers, was clearly unsustainable. It also illustrates the dangers of making assumptions about, or being in denial concerning, what customers value. Legal vendors of MP3s like Amazon's MP3 Store and Apple's iTunes Store have 'eaten the record companies' lunch'. The CD megastores have all but disappeared from the high street and a broken business model is now widely recognised as such, though perhaps not by the record companies!

12.2.1 Find out what customers value

Finding out what customers value is at one level straightforward, but again there are potential pitfalls. The straightforward part is 'asking'. We can ask customers in many ways what they want of our service; surveys and focus groups are examples of some of the approaches we could take (see Chapter 5). The art of surveying customers is relatively mature, and there is no need to review it here. However, one pitfall is worth a mention, and that is the selection of customers to survey. For example, it would be easy to survey current customers of a service to ascertain their notions of value, but these responses would not be half as interesting or valuable to the service organisation as the views of non-customers. Existing customers, by definition, like what is offered currently, and satisfying them slavishly in the long term might take the service organisation up an 'evolutionary dead end'. In many contexts this problem is referred to as the innovator's dilemma[4] wherein organisations become trapped by the guarantee of revenue from current customers and ignore potential future revenues from non-customers.

We could ask non-customers to tell us why they don't use our service and in so doing learn about ways in which we could modify our service concept to accommodate them. Another pitfall here is the 'lack of vision' problem. Sometimes customers cannot internalise and understand a new value proposition until they engage with the 'live' service. The service organisation therefore has to at least pilot a new service to test the customer response, but also take a gamble now and then.

By way of a final note on value. Value is not just a concept relevant at the organisation/customer interface. In order to deliver on a value proposition, all elements of service provision have to understand what it is, and where they can contribute.

12.3   What are the main approaches to continuous improvement?

Improvement strategies are traditionally split into two types which represent different and, to some extent, opposing philosophies.[5] These two philosophies are continuous incremental change and radical step-change.

12.3.1   Continuous incremental and radical change strategies

Continuous improvement (*kaizen*) is an evolutionary approach to operational change and is synonymous with the concept of total quality management. Radical change, in contrast, is a revolutionary approach concerned not with amending processes but totally reinventing them. Table 12.1 summarises the key differences between these approaches.

Continuous change involves modest but continual changes to an existing process, whereas step-change seeks radical changes – indeed the total redesign of existing processes coupled with a significant improvement in performance. The benefits from small, successive continuous improvements are expected to be attained over a long period of time, unlike radical change which aims to create major improvements in the short to medium term. Continuous incremental improvement involves everyone in an organisation and the changes are driven by

Table 12.1 Key differences between continuous and step-change strategies

	Continuous change	Step-change
Existing process	Little change	Redesigned
Improvement expected	Modest	Substantial
Benefits attained	Long-term	Short-term
Change driven by	Employees	Senior management
Senior management time/effort	Small	Substantial
Business risk	Small	High
Capital expenditure	Small	Substantial
Use of information technology	Little	Significant

them, thus requiring little senior management time and effort, unlike radical change which is usually driven by a senior management champion requiring substantial management time and effort. Senior management involvement is required because the risk involved in the total redesign of cross-functional processes is often high, and capital expenditure, often involving the use of IT, can be substantial.[6]

Five of the most common approaches to change, including both continuous and radical, are total quality management, Six Sigma, business process re-engineering, lean thinking and benchmarking. We will cover the first four here, and benchmarking in Chapter 14.

12.3.2 Total quality management (TQM)

Total quality management (TQM) is one of the best-known approaches to continuous improvement and has had a major impact on organisations by putting the customer at the heart of quality decisions and improvements. TQM was developed in the 1950s by Armand Feigenbaum,[7] although it has lost some of its cachet over the last few years as employees and managers have become unhappy about what some people see to be a 'flavour of the month' approach to management thinking. This attitude is unfortunate, as it does not take into account the value – or otherwise – of the approach. As is the case with most management methodologies, there is the potential to cause harm with naive implementation. Those responsible for and those who suffer from such 'tool abuse' rarely blame the implementation!

It should be made clear, however, that TQM is not a 'programme' or an activity with a definitive start and end, but simply good management practice. However, TQM does require a 'thought revolution' in management.[8] The main sources of inspiration for the TQM approaches are the quality gurus, such as Deming, Juran, Ishikawa and Crosby. The two foundation stones of TQM are customer focus and total involvement:

- **Customer focus.** The TQM philosophy is centred on customers, meeting their expectations in order to retain those customers and capture others, thus enhancing profitability and meeting the strategic needs of the organisation. This necessitates identifying which customers the organisation wishes to serve, understanding their expectations and ensuring that all systems, procedures, activities and culture are focused on meeting those needs.

- **Total involvement.** The main difference between the more traditional approaches to quality and TQM is the word 'total'. TQM is based on a culture of continuous improvement, which is shared and enacted by everyone in an organisation, all working with a single purpose of improving what they do.

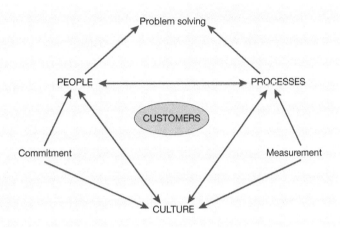

Figure 12.1 Key components of TQM

TQM as a continuous improvement activity has a great deal to offer service organisations; many of its elements are now traditional activities of successful service operations though not necessarily parading under the banner of TQM. The key elements are expressed diagrammatically in Figure 12.1.

The three cornerstones of TQM concern people, processes and culture (covered in more detail in Chapters 8, 9, 10 and 16). People, i.e. employees, are responsible for and capable of driving change in the systems and this is encouraged by an appropriate people-centred, supportive and improvement-based culture. Employees are given the responsibility for improvement, and have an understanding of the processes to which they contribute. To support this there is training in the use of quality tools and techniques, for example process mapping and statistical process control (see Chapters 8 and 9). Measurement systems provide feedback on actions taken and information is provided at the level of the operator (see Chapter 9). Top-management commitment is essential to the successful implementation of TQM because it requires changes organisation-wide and a supportive and appropriate culture (see Chapter 16).

12.3.3 Six Sigma

Motorola Inc. is generally credited with the invention of Six Sigma.[9] Bill Smith, an engineer in Motorola's Communications Division, introduced the concept in order to deal with increasing warranty claims. This continuous improvement approach was then championed by Bob Galvin, the CEO of Motorola, and Six Sigma has become part of the company's culture to the extent that the Motorola University provides training programmes as a major part of its activities. Alongside Motorola, Jack Welch and GE have become major advocates of the Six Sigma philosophy. The GE website proclaims: 'Six Sigma has changed the DNA of GE, it is now the way we work, in everything we do and in every product we design'.[10]

In essence, Six Sigma is focused on reducing variance in processes. The Six Sigma target is 3.4 DPMO (defects per million opportunities). Imagine you are running a call centre with 6,000 customer transactions per day. With what seems like a low problem rate of 1 per cent, you will be upsetting 60 customers a day. At the Six Sigma rate, in theory, you would upset just over one customer a year! The statistical basis for these figures is covered thoroughly in specialist publications, and is summarised in Figure 12.2.

Each process may have a specification. For example, a hotel may promise that a room service breakfast will be delivered between 7.00 a.m. and 7.15 a.m. rather than exactly at 7.10.

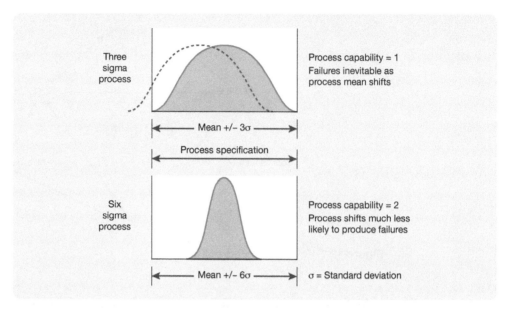

Figure 12.2 Process variation – comparing three sigma and six sigma processes

This allows for variability in the process and fluctuations in supply and demand. A three sigma process (see Figure 12.2) means that the distribution of outcomes only just fits the process specification. In practice, this is not good enough, as the process distribution shifts, perhaps as new items on the breakfast menu are added, or new staff are employed. This explains the move to the six sigma target, because changes in the process are much less likely to impact on customers.

Clearly there are some questions to be answered. It may not be technologically or physically possible to meet the Six Sigma ideal. Critics of Six Sigma suggest that it is not economically viable in many cases. That said, the approach is worth considering for customer-critical processes – those activities that have a significant impact on customer satisfaction. Service operations that have used this approach tend to be those with large volumes of standard transactions, such as back-office functions in financial services.

On the face of it, Six Sigma is a set of tools and techniques aimed at understanding and improving processes. It has become a major industry in its own right, with clearly defined structures and training courses. It claims to be more oriented to business results than TQM, and is facilitated by those who have been through accredited training programmes to become master black belts (expert consultants who have completed a number of Six Sigma projects), black belts (who have completed at least two projects and have leadership and process training), and green belts (who are part-time project members, trained by the black belt).

Six Sigma is clearly more than a statistical process control approach. Motorola now refer to it as a 'four step high performance system to execute business strategy'. The four steps are:

1   *Align.* Six Sigma projects must be aligned to business priorities driven by a balanced scorecard approach, focused on the organisation's bottom line.

2   *Mobilise.* Customer-focused project teams are empowered to take action, sponsored by senior managers acting as process champions.

3   *Accelerate.* Project teams are coached and encouraged to ensure that their projects meet specified milestones, rather than allowing them to drift.

4   *Govern.* Leaders actively sponsor projects and share best practice with other parts of the organisation.

GE's philosophy is somewhat similar, emphasising how customers define quality, the need for customer delight, the need to understand the business from the customers' perspective, and leadership commitment demonstrated through training, employee motivation and investment in project teams.

Whatever one's view on the effectiveness of Six Sigma, most people who have experience of it recommend the DMAIC approach to continuous improvement. This acronym outlines the Six Sigma approach:

- Define the business problem.
- Measure the current state against the desired state.
- Analyse the root causes of the business gap.
- Improve the process using Six Sigma tools.
- Control the long-term sustainability of the solution.

The Legend Hotel in Kuala Lumpur (Case Example 12.2) provides an illustration of the basic approach to Six Sigma deployment. The methodology provides the consistent approach to problem solving much needed in many large organisations. The management of the Legend Hotel observed that many responses to customer feedback were ad hoc and inconsistent. This means that although the immediate problem may be dealt with, there is no confidence that the same problem won't recur.

Case Example 12.2 The Legend Hotel, Kuala Lumpur

Christopher Seow, University of East London Business School, United Kingdom, and K.Y. Tiu, Legend Group of Hotels and Resorts, Kuala Lumpur, Malaysia

The Legend Hotel has 414 rooms and suites and 206 apartments and is situated close to the Putra World Trade Centre (PWTC), a prime trade and convention venue in Kuala Lumpur.

In common with many businesses in Malaysia, the Legend Hotel suffered a downturn in business following the economic crisis of the late 1990s. Realising that the hotel needed to act quickly to improve financial performance, the management

Source: Shutterstock.com/Stuart Jenner

team launched a number of 'Vision and Values Initiatives' to provide direction for the hotel's employees. Unfortunately, many of these initiatives were short-lived. A Customer Service Index Programme launched in 2002 provided focus for department heads to address the issues, but the management team felt that responses tended to be ad hoc and lacking in consistency. Having seen how other businesses had improved their performance through Six Sigma, the management team decided to deploy this methodology in the Legend Hotel.

A leadership jumpstart workshop enabled the team to articulate its mission statement:

The Legend Hotel will achieve leading hotel status by:

- *delivering truly Malaysian standards of service*
- *exceeding all guests' expectations for quality and service*

- *improving continuously*
- *ensuring appropriate in-house, employee personal development.*

An analysis of the hotel's business concluded that 'room accommodation' and 'food and beverage' were the core business for the hotel and the management team focused attention on these two areas.

The Food and Beverage Division consists of seven outlets: Di-Atas Brasserie (Coffee House), Museum Chinese Restaurant, Gen Japanese Restaurant, Berisi Lobby Lounge, Monkey Bar and Restaurant, Room Service, and Banquet and Convention. A SWOT analysis identified lost opportunities and the extreme vulnerability to emerging competition:

Strengths

- Variety of food offered
- Multi-skilled staff
- Knowledgeable chefs
- Panoramic view over city
- Strategic location

Weaknesses

- Lack of customer database
- Lack of publicity
- Expensive car parking
- Poor equipment
- High staff turnover
- Poor air-conditioning
- Old décor

Opportunities

- Market from nearby offices
- Refurbished department store
- Joint promotion with other parties
- Website

Threats

- Freestanding restaurants
- Other hotel restaurants
- New products from competitors

Team leaders were appointed to lead the project teams and they attended workshops on entrepreneurship skills and in the process improvement approach of Six Sigma: Define, Measure, Analyse, Improve, Control (DMAIC). They also received training on an appropriate suite of Six Sigma tools.

An analysis of meal covers and customer spend in the Gen Japanese Restaurant highlighted the fact that numbers and spend were very low when the à la carte menu was being served on Mondays, Tuesdays and Wednesdays. However, performance was much better when buffet dinner was being served on Thursdays, Fridays, Saturdays and Sundays.

The project team of eight service staff and eight kitchen crew conducted brainstorming sessions to identify the root cause of low-value meal covers when the à la carte menu was being served at lunch and dinner. The team identified three main issues: inconsistent service provision, lack of marketing strategy, and insufficient marketing promotion efforts. The team conducted cause-and-effect analysis on these issues and identified areas for improvement. The analysis for the first of these is shown in Figure 12.3. An action plan for Six Sigma improvement was presented to senior management for approval and support. Following implementation, the Gen Japanese Restaurant has since seen a significant increase in customer meal turnover.

The improvement demonstrated in the Gen Japanese Restaurant has encouraged the leaders to deploy the Six Sigma approach in the remaining Food and Beverage outlets in the Legend Hotel.

Vice President (Operations) of the Metroplex Holdings group, Mr K.Y. Tiu, commented:

The deployment of the Six Sigma ethos at The Legend Hotel is bearing fruit. It has led to cross-fertilisation of best practice and accelerated learning amongst the workforce. The inherent discipline within the Six Sigma approach provides structure and a visible road-map for the Legend Hotel workforce to systematically create new knowledge and enhanced customer satisfaction.

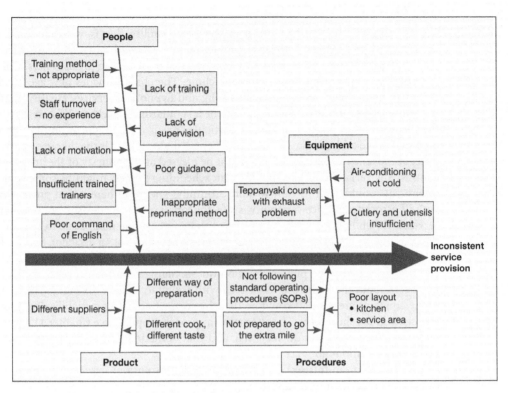

Figure 12.3 Cause and effect for inconsistent product–service quality bundle delivery

One of the challenges faced by all organisations adopting Six Sigma or similar continuous improvement methodologies is to ensure that any training delivered as part of a change initiative is truly embedded in the operation's culture. Some organisations have found the structured approach of Six Sigma – for example the 'belt' system described above, borrowed from the world of martial arts – very helpful in this regard. In order to qualify for a belt, employees must undergo training to the appropriate level, and then deliver financial benefits through an improvement project.

A final quote from GE gives an insight into the value of Six Sigma and similar approaches for service operations:

> Often, our inside-out view of the business is based on average or mean-based measures of our recent past. Customers don't judge us on averages, they feel the variance in each transaction, each product we ship. Six Sigma focuses first on reducing process variation and then on improving the process capability. Customers value consistent, predictable business processes that deliver world-class levels of quality. This is what Six Sigma strives to produce.

12.3.4 Controlling for variability

In Chapter 9 we introduced the concept of process variability and the need for service organisations to control this variability. In the last section we developed these ideas and introduced the notion of Six Sigma levels of process control. We now move on to look at how organisations might respond in practice. Process variability and the uncertainty it can generate will clearly have an impact on the ability of an organisation to reconcile supply and demand.

Service variability

Process variability will in turn result in service variability, that is, variability in the service received. In some contexts, service variability might be a good thing; there are many services where an element of the 'bespoke' and 'random' will be attractive to customers. Consider for example the context of a holistic therapy clinic. The clinic provides new age services such as 'hot stone massage', reiki, NLP counselling and hypnotism services, etc. If you are paying for a therapy session then you might resent a standardised package. You are likely to want the therapist to be responsive to your particular needs. This might mean that the therapist even makes the odd mistake in the 'experimental' dialogue that is the therapy. Far from being upset at the failed 'experiments', you might be pleased at the honesty of the 'investigation'. By contrast any variability in the appointment scheduling process might be something you will resent; you would want therapy to start promptly. The point here is that process variability with its associated service variability is a factor for all services, even 'soft' and human-centric services. Variability is not necessarily a bad thing either. The main issue to take on board is that variability should be the subject of design choice, and not an accident. Service organisations need to look at their processes and make informed decisions about which to control, and to what extent. The previous section on Six Sigma reported concerns by some service managers about the high costs associated with trying to achieve Six Sigma levels of control. These concerns are valid. It could be that the costs of accepting variability are much lower, especially in the short term. The alternative approach, 'coping' (see Chapter 11), is something that operations managers do very well, and they sometimes enjoy it. So which way should service organisations go . . . control, or cope?

The discussion in this section perhaps provides a solution; service organisations need to categorise processes into at least three groups:

1 processes that can operate at high levels of variability
2 processes that need to be controlled, but within broad control limits
3 processes that need to be tightly controlled, where perhaps Six Sigma levels of control are appropriate.

In this way organisations can avoid being overwhelmed, and prioritise their attention. However, a secondary set of questions arise if we try to categorise in this way, and these questions relate to the need for a systematic rationale for the categorisation.

Coping with variability

We can 'rank' our process by considering three factors:

1 the *likelihood of occurrence* of out-of-control processes (failure) resulting in a negative consequence (service failure) for the service organisation
2 the *likelihood of detection* of the failure
3 the *consequences* of the failure.

These factors are derived from the Failure Modes and Effects Analysis (FMEA)[11] methodology. Probabilities are assigned to each factor and are then multiplied together to obtain what is known as a Risk Priority Number or RPN. If such a number is derived for some or all of the processes in our service, we will have a clear ranking of processes that we can then categorise in order to determine a control response. The method can be used as a vehicle for discussion, or can be used to make a clear precedence list for which areas of the organisation should receive attention in terms of attempts at Six Sigma levels of control. In other words, FMEA (and similar methods; there are several variations on the theme) can help answer the categorisation questions raised above.

12.3.5 Business process re-engineering

A well-known radical approach to improvement and change is business process re-engineering (BPR).[12] BPR is about the fundamental rethinking and radical redesign of business processes to achieve dramatic improvements in performance.

The main principles of BPR involve the following:

- *A cross-functional approach.* BPR recognises the need to take a cross-functional approach to improvement, since most processes cut across traditional functional boundaries. It is therefore only through the creation of cross-functional teams working together on their processes that these processes can be radically redesigned.

- *Out-of-the-box thinking.* BPR is meant to be radical and so requires radical thinking. For this to happen, traditional beliefs and views need to be challenged – indeed put aside – to allow total redesign starting with a clean sheet of paper. BPR is about rejecting the conventional wisdom and received assumptions of the past to create something new and very different.

- *Simplification.* BPR attempts to discard wasteful activities and focuses on simplicity and logical ordering. However, the often significant use of IT to enable radical changes can create a source of complexity that can undermine improvements.

Implementing BPR requires the formation of a high-level team with a champion to co-ordinate action.[13] It requires a clear understanding of current processes, facilitated by process mapping (see Chapter 8). Redesign is then a key activity for the team, involving both visioning and detailed concern for measurements and control, to ensure not only the efficacy of the new process but also its improvement.

BPR is clearly a risky activity, both because current processes are rejected and also because of the high capital expenditure required and frequent reliance on IT. It is not surprising, therefore, that many BPR activities – as many as 70 per cent – fail to meet their original objectives.[14] Another key factor in their failure is that, because of their emphasis on business processes, systems and structure, the 'people factor' tends to be overlooked, ignored or underestimated.[15] Indeed, because of the job losses incurred in such radical change, BPR has become synonymous with downsizing.

12.3.6 Lean thinking

Lean thinking, or lean operations (or even lean Six Sigma!), has become another 'banner' under which a cluster of improvement activities can take place.

The essence of lean thinking is to clarify what adds value (as discussed in Section 12.2) for the customer and/or organisation and to strip out all other activities. The objective is to ensure that the customer, or the task being carried out on behalf of the customer, flows through the system as quickly as possible, without non-productive waits, thus reducing cost and improving customer satisfaction.

A home loan provider employed this approach to good effect. The existing end-to-end process was mapped from the time the customer requested a loan to the point that the transaction was completed. It was found that the total elapsed time was nearly eight weeks, compared to the 'value-adding' time of just under two hours. Clearly there were periods where the company could not do anything itself, for example when it was waiting for surveys or for solicitors to act; however, this investigation spurred it into action. The home loan/house buying process also raises many anxieties for customers. The numbers of enquiries about the progress of the loan rise exponentially as time goes on. If the time is reduced, with an equivalent increase in dependability, there will be fewer customer enquiries and fewer employees devoted to this expediting process. By applying the principles of lean thinking (see below) the home loan provider reduced the end-to-end time to four weeks, with a value-adding time of just over an hour.

A broadband service provider could experience similar benefits. For example using the lean philosophy could be applied to managing the process from customer request to installation, dramatically cutting lead times.

The main benefits of lean thinking include:

- reduced process times and/or lead times
- reduced processing costs per item/customer through increased productivity
- increased customer satisfaction, leading to repeat business and word-of-mouth advertising
- reduced costs resulting from a higher completion rate (some customers get part-way through a process and leave because they perceive that the provider is too slow)
- better communication with all the parties in the chain
- reduced customer anxiety
- reduced costs resulting from lower levels of complaints or enquiries.

Removing waste – *muda*

Lean thinking is generally held to have originated through the work of Toyoda and Ohno at the Toyota Motor Company in Japan.[18] The Toyota production system has been studied and copied throughout the world by both manufacturing and service companies which wish to reap the benefits of reduced costs as well as an organisational culture that believes in the possibility of continuous improvement throughout the supply chain. The essence of lean thinking is to drive out *muda*, the Japanese word for waste, which is defined as anything that creates no value for the customer. Ohno identified seven sources of *muda*:

- overproduction ahead of demand
- waiting for the next process step
- unnecessary transport of materials
- over-processing of parts due to poor technology or process design
- excessive inventories
- unnecessary movement of employees
- defective production.

Although developed for manufacturing operations, these all apply to many service operations, particularly those that have factory-like back offices, and those that have the supply of physical product as part of the concept. It is also worth applying Ohno's classification to the service process, considering a customer as the unit of material. This would encourage thinking about the cost to the customer in time or money when dealing with a particular service provider. A reduction in cost for the customer would almost certainly equate to an increase in value, which is the essence of lean thinking (see also the Case Example on lunch delivery in Mumbai in Chapter 6).

The Danish National Injuries Board (Case Example 12.3) demonstrates how lean approaches developed in manufacturing operations like Toyota have been applied to great effect in service situations. The example demonstrates a number of key aspects of lean operations.

One of the major benefits of applying lean approaches, or indeed any of the tools and techniques discussed in this chapter, is the opportunity to engage the employees in the process. Indeed the original philosophy of the Toyota Production System was focused on the efficient use of materials and the humanisation of work. This second aspect was largely forgotten in the original translation into 'just-in-time' in the West, but has fortunately been rediscovered!

| Case Example 12.3 | The National Board of Industrial Injuries, Denmark |

Thomas Christiansen, Implement, Denmark

The National Board of Industrial Injuries (Arbejdsskadestyrelsen (ASK) in Danish) is an agency under the Ministry of Employment. As a neutral authority, it makes decisions in workers' compensation cases. ASK decides whether an injury or a disease qualifies for recognition as an industrial injury, as well as deciding the amount of the compensation. It makes decisions in about 60,000 cases each year.

In addition, insurance companies and injured persons can contact the agency for Private Inquiries of ASK (the P-division) to obtain an impartial statement on the health effects and occupational consequences of a private personal injury, for example injuries sustained in road accidents or in a person's leisure time.

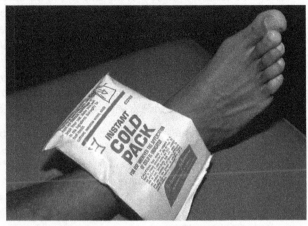

Source: Pearson Education Ltd/David R. Frazier Photolibrary, Inc. Alamy

For some time, ASK has had challenges in the form of long review times and large numbers of current cases. However, it was not the review time itself but the rest of the process which was taking most of the time. This was also the case for the P-division, which handles approximately 6,000 cases per year. This department was also under further pressure from the fact that the customers (such as insurance companies) could de-select a statement from ASK and instead perform the evaluation themselves. More and more customers were drawing attention to the fact that review times were too long with the result that the number of incoming cases was starting to decline.

Long review times had several unfortunate consequences. First of all, they led to many enquiries from customers asking for a status update. This meant that employees had to physically find the case file which took a long time, as there was no electronic tracking process. Secondly, almost all cases required economic and medical information, which could be out of date by the time that the case was finally reviewed. This clearly meant further delays and costs as new data was obtained.

The P-division was therefore under great pressure to improve. Carl Georg Röser, Vice President of the National Board of Industrial Injuries, explained,

We knew that we delivered high quality, but we could also see that the review times were intolerable. As the P-division had to be self-sustaining, we could not solve the problem just by hiring more employees. It took a change in attitude and new processes in order to bring focus on the productivity.

Up to this point, the P-division took the stance that high quality was the most important concern and that things took the required time. Thus, there was an opinion that short review times and high quality were partly conflicting interests and that a decrease in review times would result in reduced quality.

This is where 'lean' was seen as an instrument to achieve both. Röser explained:

The employees had to understand that the value for the P-division's customers lay not just in the quality of the statement itself, but just as much in short review times, so that the customers can also close the cases. Put simply, short review times are also a quality in themselves and they are obtainable through improved work processes. Moreover, we also expect, of course, that improved processes will also lead to decreased resource consumption per case. We will use 'lean' in order to achieve these goals.

It was decided to make employee involvement a key priority from the first kick-off meeting to the following weekly *kaizen* meetings. This approach was chosen because the desired change was to impact not only the process, but also the attitudes and behaviour of the employees.

This approach was a huge success. Röser added:

Before we started, I feared that the employees would be pessimistic, and so it would all come to nothing. There was some turbulence along the way and a few compromises had to be made, but we came through better than expected. I think that the extremely successful kick-off day, where all employees from the youngest student assistant to the top manager were present, resulted in all employees being immensely positive from day one. One of the advantages of 'lean' is the immediate gains which are obtained. It focuses on the employees' participation by them standing by the kaizen boards and adding suggestions. They decide themselves what should be done and, after only a week, things began to change. This immediate impact has meant a great deal to the success of the project.

The first benefit came in increased productivity, with 15 per cent more cases being dealt with by the system. Initially, average review times decreased by only 8 per cent, but this was partly because 'old' cases were included in the statistics. By later in the first year the review times had decreased significantly. A key issue has been that, despite significant productivity gains, the quality of review has not suffered.

Considerable discussion went into creating families of cases. Instead of handling 6,000 individual cases, ASK is dealing with eight families of cases whose processes are consistent enough to consolidate and manage more effectively. Value stream mapping eight families highlighted where processes could be managed more effectively. This activity also revealed where activities previously carried out by highly qualified (and expensive) lawyers could be carried out by administrative staff. This served to cut costs and provide motivation.

The process is continuing to yield benefits and to spread into other parts of the organisation.

The five principles of lean thinking

There are five principles of lean thinking:[17]

1 *Specify value.* As indicated at the start of the chapter, the ultimate customer must define value. It is so easy to revert to a 'producer' (inside-out) mentality that assumes that because the provider thinks that the product is good, it must represent value. Airlines, for example, have not always understood value in these terms, but have provided executive lounges and extra facilities on flights when what passengers really want is rapid, safe travel to their destination without having to wait at airports.

2 *Identify the value stream.* The value stream is the set of actions required to bring the service to the customer. The total supply chain from securing the inputs through to service delivery and use by the customer must be understood in order to identify where activities at particular points in the chain in reality create no value for the customer, but have always been carried out because nobody had an overview of the total chain. When analysing the whole value stream, three types of activities can be identified:

- those that create value for customers
- those that create no value for customers but cannot be eliminated because of current technology or process constraints
- those that create no value and can be removed.

It should be noted that the second of these categories of activities, those that create no value but cannot be removed, must be closely examined to see if this assumption is, in fact, correct. It may be that the activity persists simply 'because we have always done it this way', and so the activity may be eliminated.

Telecom equipment providers such as Ericsson, Motorola and Nortel are working hard to become more involved in their customers' businesses. In order to do this, they must know more about how the customers – the network operators – manage their businesses, and also what the ultimate customers require. This increased customer focus leads to a shortening of the value stream, more focused research and development, lower costs and greater value for customers.

3 *Create flow.* The essence of lean thinking is that work/customers flow continuously and smoothly through a 'pipeline' without stopping. In other words, the tendency to create batches of work/customers that occur when the hand-offs from department to department are not well managed has to be reduced. These discontinuities in the flow of work create the possibility of errors; they slow down the response to customer demand, and create a requirement to manage the workload that could be avoided. Batched work/customers create queues, with the need to manage priorities and to expedite work that, as it gets later, becomes ever more urgent.

This work-flow thinking has been applied with great success to the back offices of many financial services companies, particularly as many have reorganised around customer processes and dismantled the traditional departmental or 'silo' mentality.

4 *Pull not push.* Traditional production systems produce in the hope of selling their wares. This creates *muda* in terms of overproduction and therefore excess cost. The challenge of lean thinking is to have operations schedules governed by demand pull rather than production push. Pull systems are essentially replenishment systems working on the basis of 'sell one, make one'. A good example is provided by McDonald's in the replenishment of burgers as customers buy them. The task for the organisation is to monitor and adjust the replenishment levels as demand patterns vary.

Pull systems require a major shift in operational culture since it means that work-in-progress is significantly reduced and there is not the comfort factor of piles of work-in-progress in the system. The challenge for the service organisation is to find ways to manage the total supply chain in similar ways to the manufacturing examples.

5 *Strive for perfection.* This fifth principle of lean thinking flows from the other four. As partners in the total supply chain apply the lean thinking philosophy, many of the problems are addressed, but, more importantly, a culture of both significant and continuous improvement develops.

Some managers claim that lean principles don't easily transfer into service operations. While this is often used as an excuse, we believe it has little foundation in fact. Most service operations will benefit from building the flexibility in their operations to match customer demand in the short term. A simple example is provided by Japanese Kaiten-Zushi restaurants (Case Example 12.4)

Case Example 12.4 Kaiten-zushi restaurants

The traditional sushi restaurant is a perfect example of demand-driven service delivery. The restaurant is organised around a conveyor belt (see Figure 12.4) which carries individual portions of sushi of the most commonly requested options on plates whose colour indicates the price of the dish. Customers are seated on the outside of the conveyor belt and can take the dishes they require as they pass by on the belt. At the end of the meal, they are charged for the number of dishes they have consumed.

The chefs are situated inside the circular conveyor belt and can immediately see which dishes are popular and which dishes are not selling. They are therefore able to match their

Source: Alamy Images/Portus Imaging

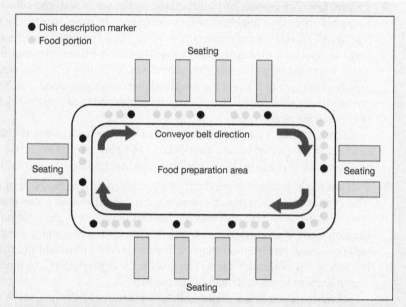

Figure 12.4 Restaurant layout

production directly to customer demand. In some restaurants customers are able to order special dishes, but will of course have to wait longer for these and will pay more for the privilege.

Larger restaurants may have tags or other mechanisms to ensure that an individual dish does not circulate for too long.

Sushi restaurants are a perfect example of lean operations. Production is exactly matched to the customer demand rate as a dish is replaced as it is consumed, with inventory of dishes on the belt kept to a minimum. Because the 'throughput time' from production to consumption is minimised, customer satisfaction is high because the fish is fresh, and costs are reduced because waste is virtually eliminated. The chefs are also able to test the acceptance of new dishes at virtually no cost or risk.

12.3.7 Value stream mapping

Value stream mapping (VSM) is an extremely useful lean thinking tool. Teams map their processes, tracking jobs or customers (or cases in Case Example 12.3) through the system, identifying the total elapsed time in the system and identifying the (few) points where value-adding activity takes place. This tracking of 'as-is' process is a useful starting point to create a leaner 'to-be' process. Value Stream Mapping is usually undertaken at a broader level than process mapping (Chapter 8) and is a helpful starting point in finding waste and identifying its causes in a process.

There are five key stages to VSM:

1 Identify the value stream to map; this might be an operation, a process or a supply network.

2 Map the process showing the information, material and customer flows. Document the times taken at all the various stages to process the job or customer and the total throughput time. This is the 'as-is' process.

3 Identify where value is added (bearing in mind the definition of value in Section 12.2) and the various types of waste, *muda*. (Time taken can be a helpful indicator of waste.)

4 Discuss and create a leaner 'to-be' process.

5 Implement and check that the process/operation/network delivers the required improvements.

12.3.8 Lean Six Sigma

Many large service organisations are putting Six Sigma and lean operations together – 'lean Six Sigma'. The justification is simply to get greater responsiveness through faster throughput (lean operations) combined with the drive for greater quality through reduced variance in service delivery (Six Sigma). As with all initiatives, there is always the risk that this will be just another programme amongst many other approaches and will not receive sufficient attention from senior management. The challenge is not to understand the theories, but to ensure that they are deployed effectively across the organisation.

The experience of the Wells Fargo Home and Consumer Group[18] was that there were some significant stumbling blocks to be overcome:

- *Not budgeting sufficient resources for implementation:* There are major benefits to be realised and significant resources must be released to support deployment.

- *Ensure the measurement system will encourage the right behaviours:* We work with many organisations which will not realise the benefits of a lean Six Sigma implementation because managers are totally focused on short-term goals.

- *Too many meetings:* It is tempting to arrange more and more project meetings, communication events and so forth. The usual result is that there is no time to do anything! The Japanese approach of 'go see', where short meetings are held at the point in the process under review, is a sound principle and deters long meetings isolated from 'real life'.

- *The challenge of standard operating procedures:* A prime aim of lean Six Sigma is to reduce variance. Creating a consistent process, often using standard operating procedures (SOPs), can be helpful but may also evoke resistance which can be anticipated and dealt with. We discussed this further in the challenge of process ownership in Chapter 8.

Our experience is that these problems are replicated in most initiatives of this type.

12.4   How can managers sustain continuous improvement?

Few organisations have nothing to gain from incorporating the continuous improvement approach. However, the extent to which continuous improvement will have a significant and sustained impact upon bottom-line performance will vary from context to context. Many more recent academic research articles on continuous improvement look at this issue of sustainability in some detail. Largely this is due to the scepticism resulting from the failure of many organisations to successfully implement continuous improvement methodologies. Even as far back as the late 1980s and early 1990s managers and academics understood the importance of context, in particular culture, but over the intervening two decades our understanding has been refined.

In the 1990s John Bessant and David Francis at Brighton University[19] looked at the underpinnings of continuous improvement capability. They found that most of the mechanisms used to enable continuous improvement were critically underpinned by a culture of long-term staff development. For example, organisations would need training in basic problem-solving techniques, training in continuous improvement tools and techniques, the setting up of organisational 'vehicles' such as quality circles, the development of idea capture systems and reward systems, and so on. Development in each of these areas is simple in principle, but to develop effective capacity takes time. Certainly it is not the stuff of overnight development at the hands of facilitating consultants. Bessant and Francis also talked about the development of capability for learning or 'double loop learning'.[20] Again, such a capability is partially the result of training (which takes time), but it is also a product of continuity of practice and of learning about, and immersion in, problem solving at the level of individuals and groups within the organisation.

Nicola Bateman, Nick Rich, Peter Hines and Matthias Holweg[21] are amongst many authors who in the last decade or so have written extensively on the sustainability of continuous improvement approaches. Although reported in different ways, the research seems to reinforce the idea that continuous improvement is a long-term and staged development of learning capability. 'Long-term' will obviously be different depending on context, but the rule of thumb seems to be five or six years for the development of continuous improvement capability. This in turn has implications for the nature of an organisational context that would be receptive to continuous improvement ideas. Any organisational context where senior managers are looking for short-term headline-grabbing successes is unlikely to be receptive to continuous improvement ideas.

Another aspect of the organisational setting that is likely to promote sustained development of a continuous improvement capability is stability. Part of the continuous improvement process will be the development of improved operational stability, but it is worth mentioning that the issue here is that stability goes beyond operations. Uncertainties such as impending sale/flotation, change of senior management or large-scale redundancies are obviously likely to have a negative impact on the potential success of the continuous improvement programme. Similarly, operational instability as evidenced by out-of-control processes, queuing, rework etc. would need to be put under tight control before any start can be made on improving the operation.

12.5	Summary

How can 'value' drive continuous improvement?

- Process improvement demands a focus on what adds value for customers and the organisation, and emphasises greater responsiveness as well as cost reduction.
- It is helpful to find out what is valued not only by customers but also by non-customers, i.e. potential customers.
- When defining the value proposition for service, it is important to take a 'whole-systems' perspective on value.

What are the main approaches to continuous improvement?

- Successful improvement approaches involve employees to gain expertise and to promote ownership.
- Continuous improvement ideas from the world of goods manufacturing are relevant to services, but they need to be translated sensitively into the service context.
- Continuous improvement is critically dependent on rigorous use of evidence as a basis for improvement.
- High levels of process control (such as Six Sigma levels of control) might not be necessary for the whole organisation. The organisation has to decide where to apply such control, and where not.

- Radical approaches to improvement such as business process re-engineering are sometimes essential to repair dysfunctional business models; however, they have the potential to cause great harm, and need to be used with care.
- The basis of lean approaches to continuous improvement is the need to drive out waste.
- One of the fundamental tools underpinning lean approaches to improvement is value stream mapping, wherein organisations seek to identify
  - activities that create value
  - activities that create no value for customers but cannot be eliminated
  - activities that create no value and can be removed.

How can managers sustain continuous improvement?

- Sustainability is underpinned by a culture of long-term staff development including training in basic problem-solving techniques and continuous improvement tools and techniques, the setting up of organisational 'vehicles' such as quality circles, and the development of idea capture systems and reward systems.
- Continuous improvement needs to be recognised as a long-term activity.
- Organisational stability also enables the sustainability of continuous improvement.

12.6 Discussion questions

1 What are the significant differences between the various approaches for operational improvement?

2 Think about the last time you used a 'high-touch' service such as a clinic, a hotel, or a restaurant. Sketch the service process, and try to determine which elements were subject to high levels of control. Were there any elements of the service that were not subject to control, but should have been? Why was this so?

3 Think of your experience of service . . . across the whole of the service sector. Can you identify any service providers that appear not to understand what their customers value? Why?

12.7 Questions for managers

1 Have you established an approach for operational review and improvement? Does it matter which approach you use?

2 How would you identify what customers value in your service?

3 Which constituencies would tell you most about how to improve your service?

4 Map the value stream of your major processes. Where is the waste in the process, what activities can you eliminate, and how can you reduce the total time that a 'job' stays in the system?

5 Which aspects of your service would benefit from high levels of process control, and which would benefit from a lighter touch?

| Case Exercise | Cranleigh Metropolitan Council |

Robert Johnston, Warwick Business School, and Zoe Radnor, Cardiff Business School, with the help of Gio Bucci, AtoZ Business Consultancy

Cranleigh Metropolitan Council (CMC) serves a local population of over 350,000 and employs around 14,000 members of staff within seven directorates (departments): Chief Executive's Office, Children's Services, Education & Community Services, Housing, Urban Environment, Law & Property, and Finance. CMC was amongst the top performing local authorities in the country, yet Chief Executive Maeve Andrews was keen to improve the service it provided. She explained the opportunity she saw:

> *CMC provides several hundred services for our customers all of which have many different access points, in different buildings with different opening times and using different systems. For example, Housing Services are in one building, Finance, where you pay your bills, in another and benefit payments (part of Finance) in three others. So anyone wanting, as many people do, to access several services at once have to trail around the city, only then to get referred to another department somewhere else. We also have over 100 different telephone numbers – how is a customer meant to know which is the right one? We have decided we want to create one point of contact, a one-stop-shop, where we can bring all our services together and do as much for the customer at the first point of contact. This will make things much better for the customer and should also create important efficiency savings for CMC.*

The Council seconded Tony Templeton from a firm of transformation consultants to lead an internal team to see if such a concept was feasible, and if it was, to construct an implementation plan. Tony and the small transformation team – four analysts, three technical developers and an implementation support manager – worked well together and quickly established a compelling case for the implementation of a one-stop-shop. The Council gave the go-ahead and provided a large two-storey building right in the heart of the city to become the new one-stop-shop, to be known as Cranleigh Central. The team quickly developed a plan for bringing services together at one point. Senior analyst Sameer Godhwani explained their approach:

> *We try and follow a standard methodology, basically a lean approach, but we have to be flexible to the needs of each area, basically to ensure we keep the Heads of the various directorates on board. The first thing we do is draw up the scoping document, get it agreed and signed off by the directorate involved.*

The scoping document identifies the key members of staff involved, the service areas that need to be covered by the investigation and the resources the directorate would need to commit to the transfer to Cranleigh Central. The team then assesses the existing service to get to know the key players and processes, to understand what will be affected by the change and to identify the current effort that is expended by the directorate delivering the service. They analyse the existing process documentation, look at volumes and observe timings. They then map the process, focusing on inputs, outputs, barriers and enablers. One key objective of this stage is to get the agreement of all those involved. Tony added:

> *We try to agree on where things are not being done efficiently and where they don't add value for the customer. We sometimes hold workshops and focus groups with customers to identify problems and solutions from their point of view too. The scoping document then has to be signed off by the directorate. We then develop a design for the new service to be based in Cranleigh Central. We test the ideas with the key players and prepare a proposal, setting out the processes to be moved to Central, the costs and benefits, and the budget to be transferred from the directorate involved to Central. Once the design document is completed, it is signed off by the head of the directorate and the head of Cranleigh Central. Some existing staff may be selected to move to Central; we entice them with slightly higher pay. Sometimes new staff are hired to run the new processes in the one-stop-shop. We then thoroughly test all the systems to ensure that what has been developed matches the design. Once the analysts are happy, my team arranges for a demonstration to both the directorate's staff and Central's staff to get the project signed off by those involved. We embark on further testing, create any necessary publicity for the public and then we go live with*

that service. The fastest design has been three weeks, the longest took 15 months. Generally the length of the process is dependent upon lots of factors including size of directorate, willingness, commitment and range of services etc.

However, it's not been easy bringing about change. Obviously we have to spend a lot of time with the people who are directly affected by what we come up with and it takes a lot of time and patience to get them on board, especially when their jobs are affected. Even when the transfer is seen as a good idea and the directorate work with us in partnership mode, it can still be quite painful dealing with all the issues. We have to rely on our soft skills. And, it's not becoming easier either. In fact as we start to move into some of the areas which really don't want to be part of this, it will become more difficult. So far we have only worked with areas that have been more receptive.

We started off being careful to work only with directorates that were keen and interested in the one-stop-shop concept. We really wanted to focus on high volume, low complexity and telephone-based services, but in fact we worked with any directorate that was interested. While the main motivations for inclusion into Cranleigh Central were that the service would be better for the customer and it would lead to overall efficiencies, some directors were less willing than others for us to evaluate their services. Some people are a bit precious about their services. It's not always easy getting them to commit to change.

The team has encountered some resistance to get some directorates involved in the transfer of services, in particular through fear of job losses. Indeed the shift in services to Cranleigh Central has resulted in job losses in some areas. And where there has been a reduction in costs it is not seen as an actual saving in the directorate because they have lost part of their budget, and responsibility, to Central.

Two years after the start of implementation Cranleigh Central opened with a blaze of publicity. Employing around fifty people, it quickly became a convenient, friendly and accessible customer contact point for many of the Council's services. It has long opening hours. It has its own call centre (able to deal with a wide range of queries) located on the first floor and accessed by one telephone number. There is a website and email address for queries too. It also has its own walk-in centre on the ground floor. This is a large, spacious, modern-looking building with large glass doors leading towards a reception area. In the area beyond reception are located cash machines for paying Council bills, private rooms for conversations with advisors, and computers providing free internet access. Residents can, for example, pay their tax bills, report faulty street lights or missed bin collections, report abandoned vehicles, pay housing bills and even register births and deaths. It also provides access to other services such as Age Concern and the Citizens Advice Bureau as well as other public sector and community agencies such as local transport and tourist information.

Although some of the front-office operations from three of the directorates, such as reporting faulty street lights, are now centralised at Cranleigh Central, the back-office operations, such as mending the faulty lights, are still delivered by the directorates involved. Central simply passes the information they receive to the appropriate team in the appropriate directorate.

Two years and six months into the implementation phase, Maeve Andrews suddenly announced that no further services would be moved to Central and that a review would be undertaken of the work so far. She even hinted that one possible outcome might include the closure of Cranleigh Central. Tony was furious. He explained:

The satisfaction scores of all the services we have moved have gone through the roof and even with the set-up costs, such as staffing costs, software development, hiring and training costs of Central, we have managed to break even in the first twelve months. We are also projecting a £10 million saving next year and double that in the following year. We feel like we have been stabbed in the back.

Questions

1 Is the approach taken a 'lean approach' as claimed?
2 Why do you think the project is in danger?
3 What could Tony and his team have done differently?

Suggested further reading

Barney, Matt (2002), 'Motorola's Second Generation', *Six Sigma Forum Magazine* 1 (3) 13–16

De Feo, Joseph and William Barnard (2004), *Juran Institute's Six Sigma: Breakthrough and Beyond*, McGraw-Hill, New York

Hammer, Michael and James Champy (2004), *Re-engineering the Corporation: A Manifesto for Business Revolution*, Harper Collins, New York

Harrington, H. James (2007), *Business Process Improvement – The Breakthrough Strategy for Total Quality, Productivity, and Competitiveness*, McGraw-Hill, New York

Imai, Masaaki (2007) *Gemba Kaizen: A Commonsense, Low-cost Approach to Management*, McGraw-Hill, New York

Kelly, William (2007), 'Deployment: 7 Stumbling Blocks to Overcome', *Six Sigma Forum Magazine* (www.asq.org), (August) 16–21

Womack, James P. and Daniel T. Jones (2003), *Lean Thinking*, Free Press, New York

Womack, James P., Daniel T. Jones and Daniel Roos (2007), *The Machine that Changed the World*, Simon & Schuster

Useful web links

Further information about lean thinking is provided by the Lean Enterprise Academy:
www.leanuk.org

For application of lean thinking to public sector organisations, John Seddon of the Vanguard Academy provides some useful insights:
http://www.lean-service.com

Another source of information about lean is:
http://www.lean.org/

Have a look at Ron Kaufman's library:
http://www.upyourservice.com/library/index.html

A really good list of improvement resources from Ronald Pollock at:
http://www.ischool.utexas.edu/~rpollock/tqm.html

A thoughtful article on Six Sigma in services, by Elisabeth Goodman:
elisabethgoodman.wordpress.com—lean-and-six-sigma-in-rd-and-service-delivery—opportunities-and-challenges/

Notes

1 Womack, James P., Daniel T. Jones and Daniel Roos (2007), *The Machine that Changed the World,* Simon & Schuster

2 Roethlisberger, Fritz and William J. Dickson (1939), *Management and the Worker,* Harvard University Press, Boston, Massachusetts

3 Hagan, Pat (2011), 'Waste Not, Want Not: Leading the Lean Health-care Journey at Seattle Children's Hospital', *Global Business and Organizational Excellence* (March/April) 25–31

4 Christensen, Clayton M. (1997) *The Innovator's Dilemma: When New Technologies Cause Great Firms to Fail,* Harvard Business School Press

5 See, for example, Imai, Masaaki (2007), *Gemba Kaizen: A Commonsense, Low-cost Approach to Management*, McGraw-Hill, New York; Slack, Nigel, Stuart Chambers and Robert Johnston (2010), *Operations Management*, 6th edition, FT Prentice Hall, Harlow

6 Hsaio Ruey-Lin and Richard J. Ormerod (1998), 'A New Perspective on the Dynamics of Information Technology-enabled Strategic Change', *Information Systems Journal* 8(1) 21–52

7 Feigenbaum, Armand (1986), *Total Quality Control*, McGraw-Hill, New York

8 Kaoru, Ishikawa (1991), *What Is Total Quality Control? – The Japanese Way*, Prentice Hall, Englewood Cliffs, New Jersey

9 Barney, Matt (2002), 'Motorola's Second Generation', *Six Sigma Forum Magazine* 1 (3) 13–16

10 www.ge.com/sixsigma

11 McDermott, Robin, Raymond J. Mikulak and Michael Beauregard (2008), *The Basics of FMEA*, 2nd edition, Productivity Press, New York

12 Hammer, Michael (1990), 'Re-engineering Work: Don't Automate, Obliterate', *Harvard Business Review*, 68 (4) 104–112

13 Harrington, H. James (2007), *Business Process Improvement – The Breakthrough Strategy for Total Quality, Productivity, and Competitiveness*, McGraw-Hill, New York

14 See, for example, Hammer, Michael and James Champy (2004), *Reengineering the Corporation: A Manifesto for Business Revolution*, Harper Collins, New York; and Tennant, Charles and Yi-Chieh Wu (2005), 'The Application of Business Process Re-engineering in the UK', *The TQM Magazine* 17 (6) 537–545

15 Clark, Jon (1995), *Managing Innovation and Change: People, Technology and Strategy*, Sage Publications, Thousand Oaks, California

16 Ohno, Taiichi (1988) *The Toyota Production System: Beyond Large-scale Production*, Productivity Press, Portland, Oregon

17 Womack, James P. and Daniel T. Jones (2003), *Lean Thinking*, Free Press, New York

18 Kelly, William (2007) 'Deployment: 7 Stumbling Blocks to Overcome', *Six Sigma Forum Magazine* (www.asq.org) (August) 16–21

19 Bessant, John and David Francis (1999), 'Developing Strategic Continuous Improvement Capability', *International Journal of Operations and Production Management* 19 (11) 1106–1119

20 Argyris, Chris (1999), *On Organisational Learning*, 2nd edition, Wiley Blackwell

21 See, for example, Bateman, Nicola and Arthur David (2002), 'Process Improvement Programmes: A Model for Assessing Sustainability', *International Journal of Operations and Production Management* 22 (5) 515–526; Rich, Nick and Nicola Bateman (2003), 'Companies' Perceptions of Inhibitors and Enablers for Process Improvement Activities', *International Journal of Operations and Production Management* 23 (2) 185–199; Bateman, Nicola (2005), 'Sustainability: The Elusive Element of Process Improvement', *International Journal of Operations and Production Management* 25 (3) 261–276; Hines, Peter, Matthias Holweg and Nick Rich (2004), 'Learning to Evolve: A Review of Contemporary Lean Thinking', *International Journal of Operations and Production Management* 24 (10) 994–1011

Chapter 13
Learning from problems

Chapter objectives

This chapter is about how to learn from problems to improve an operation and its services.

- Why do problems occur?
- How can complaining customers be dealt with?
- How can managers use problems to drive improvement?
- How can managers prevent problems occurring?

13.1 Introduction

In the previous chapter we provided a range of tools to help operations managers build a culture of improvement. One area that deserves a chapter in its own right is how we can learn from problems. Indeed some people would say this is the best way that people learn how to improve what they do.

There is a big danger here, in that problems, such as people making mistakes or things going wrong, are seen in a negative light. We want to show that problems (difficult situations needing a solution) are naturally occurring events in service operations and should be welcomed because they give us much needed insight into what we need to improve and how to do it. The critical point is that problems must lead to improvements. Sadly, many organisations don't seem to be able to learn from their problems and have a culture of fear, or at least mistrust, where problems are covered up. In these situations problems will continue to recur with no individual or organisational learning, or improvement, taking place.

Dealing well with problems is important. It exposes issues and drives improvement in the operation. It is the good way of creating delighted customers. (In a study of critical incidents it was found that over half of delighted customers felt so because of something having gone wrong and the organisation dealing well with the situation.[1]) And, as we shall see in Chapter 17, dealing well with problems is one of the key hallmarks of a world-class service organisation.

13.2 Why do problems occur?

Despite our best efforts to design operations well (Chapters 7–11) and to continually improve what we do (Chapter 12), things go wrong. This is not surprising because service operations are usually complex, human-based systems involving the provision of many services. Their process involves a wide range of inputs – staff, technology, facilities – with the additional variable, the customer, whose inputs are not always as predictable or consistent as we might like. Problems such as errors, mistakes and failures are simply inevitable.

Such problems have two types of consequences, operational consequences and customer consequences. The operational consequences of things going wrong can vary from minor delays or costs to major disasters. A member of staff turning up late for work may lead to some short delays in service. A colleague spilling a drink into a computer keyboard will lead to some additional costs. However, a breach of computer security in a bank, or a highly infectious disease being found in a hospital, could lead to much more serious consequences. These operational consequences lead to customer consequences ranging from customers complaining about the delay in service to the death of a patient and legal action from relatives.

Customers' willingness to complain, or to take other forms of action, are increasing. In recent years organisations such as holiday firms, train companies, police services, health services and local government have reported year-on-year increases in complaints of between 8 per cent and 80 per cent.

There are several possible reasons for this growth. Perhaps the quality of some services has declined as organisations have squeezed operating budgets. Or customer perceived quality of service has declined, as customers become increasingly service aware and more intolerant of poor service. This might have been brought about by greater pressures on time and/or on available money, making consumers – and indeed businesses – much more concerned about value for money. Additionally, there has been a growth in consumer movements and government initiatives, which have alerted people to their consumer rights and the obligations of organisations in delivering good service. Whatever the reasons, finding and dealing with problems, what we refer to as service recovery, is becoming an increasingly important task for service organisations.[2]

13.2.1 Types of problems

Problems and failures are not always 'service' failures, i.e. problems with the service process – they could be the result of faults in the products, equipment or facilities, or often they are faults due to the customers themselves (see Figure 13.1).[3]

Service failures include process problems such as a late-running doctor's surgery or an airline losing a passenger's luggage. Other problems with a service might include lack of

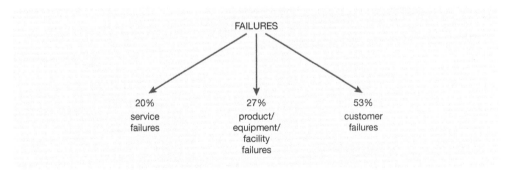

Figure 13.1 Types and proportions of failures in service organisations

Source: Johnston, Robert (1995), 'Service Failure and Recovery: Impact, Attributes and Process', *Advances in Services Marketing and Management: Research and Practice* (4) 211–228

availability of products and services, unresponsive service, and poor or inappropriate treatment being given to customers.

Equipment failures may also cause problems. The failure of computers, automatic doors or air bridges in an airport will disable parts of the process and cause problems for staff and customers.

It is interesting to note that the majority of failures are customer failures. Customer failures can be divided into two types: those caused by 'problem customers' and those caused by customers who make mistakes.[4] Problem customers are those individuals who are involved in serious offences such as staff abuse or drunkenness.[5] Customers who make mistakes, on the other hand, make simple and often inadvertent errors, such as forgetting something or turning up at the wrong time or wrong place.

From a customer's point of view, a failure is any situation where something has gone wrong, irrespective of responsibility. This last part is important. For example, if a courier is late with a parcel the company (the customer) may blame the courier. The courier may have been late because of road works (and blame the local authority) or because there were problems at the originating company's despatch unit (their fault). The despatch unit may have been delayed by the manufacturing process etc. There is usually someone else to blame. Importantly, blame creates denial, and denial gets in the way of learning from the problem. Each and every problem, irrespective of responsibility, provides an organisation with an opportunity to recover, i.e. learn from the problem, solve the problem (if possible) and make things better in the future.

Before we discuss how we can learn from problems, we need to spend a little time explaining how operations managers and their staff can deal with the complaining customer who has been on the receiving end of a problem.

13.3 How can complaining customers be dealt with?

How customers react to problems will depend upon the severity of the problem. It will also depend on the type of person they are and their attitude to complaining, the perceived likelihood of successful redress, and their age and sex.[6]

By scaling consumer dissatisfaction (see also the satisfaction continuum in Chapter 5) from 0 to minus 5, where 0 is not dissatisfied (i.e. satisfied), through extremely dissatisfied, to customers who feel absolutely furious, we can obtain a picture of their likely responses to failures (see Figure 13.2).[7] It should be noted that many other connections are possible. For example an extremely dissatisfied customer may exhibit only a mild reaction and vice versa.

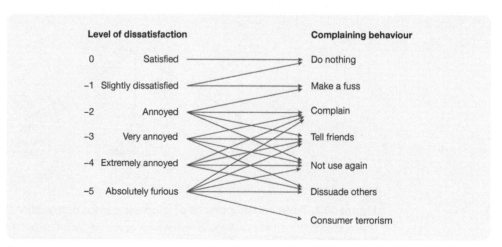

Figure 13.2 Customer complaining behaviour

The more dissatisfied a customer is, the more types of complaint behaviour they will exhibit. For some people a problem or failure may have little effect (level −1) – they may be tolerant or expect poor service. Others, at level −2, may just store up a black mark for future recall when something else goes wrong. Others may make a fuss, not quite a complaint, more of a verbal warning: 'I'm not complaining but . . .'. Complaining formally, verbally or in writing, is the next level which, like all the others, will not necessarily be mutually exclusive (some customers may exhibit several behaviours!). Dissatisfied customers may tell friends and colleagues, indeed may go further and actively dissuade them from using the service again. Others may go to the extreme of becoming a terrorist (level −5)and campaigning against the organisation by putting up signs, putting material on websites, seeking legal redress and sometimes undertaking illegal acts. (One farmer in the UK was so incensed by the treatment he received from his bank that he dumped 10 tons of manure outside its door.)

13.3.1 Word-of-mouth and word-of-mouse

While figures abound about how many people a dissatisfied customer will tell, it has been shown that the number they tell will depend upon their level of dissatisfaction.[8] Slightly dissatisfied customers tell on average three other people, whereas extremely annoyed customers tell over fifteen each, with absolutely furious customers telling sometimes hundreds of people.

A dissatisfied customer telling other people (by word-of-mouth) a bad story about an organisation may have limited reach. Many highly dissatisfied customers now resort to word-of-mouse. Word-of-mouse is much more powerful. Stories put on the internet have global reach and can be shared with hundreds if not millions of people: customers and potential customers. The stories are more lasting as they can be seen and referred to over and over again. The internet also provides opportunities to use other media besides the written word. Customers' stories about an organisation that provided dreadful service can be captured in pictures, songs and videos.

There are now many websites bringing together communities of disaffected customers. Some are general an example being www.complaints.com; other sites focus on particular organisations, an example being http://www.untied.com/ which gathers together people disaffected by United Airlines service. There are also many websites, both official and unofficial, with reviews of books, hotels, restaurants etc. One such report for a four-star hotel one of us was thinking about staying in read:

> Dirty stained carpets. Dripping ceilings. Powdered orange juice in disposable plastic cups for breakfast. The coffee shop looks depressing. In a residential location that's far from the metro or any decent shopping centre. Old TV sets and phones that don't work. Bedsheets that smell weird. Lousy service. I requested for an adaptor that never arrived . . . .

Social networks such as Facebook and video-sharing sites such as YouTube abound with stories from aggrieved customers who have had bad service and/or a poor experience.

13.3.2 Why do customers complain?

An important insight into how to deal with complaining customers comes from asking the question, why do they complain? Yes, something has gone wrong and they have encountered a problem, but complaining was just one route open to them. People tend to complain for a number of reasons:

- to have the problem sorted/corrected
- to prevent it happening to others (have procedures investigated and changed)
- to get an explanation
- to have someone disciplined
- to get financial compensation
- to feel better.

Interestingly, financial compensation, or a payoff, is often well down the list of reasons customers give for complaining. Indeed one study found that the offer of free products or services following poor service was only deemed important by less than 5 per cent of those questioned.[9] The main reason why people complain is to have the problem sorted (for them) and importantly to ensure that it doesn't happen again – i.e. that the organisation learns from the problem. We need to return to this critical point later.

13.3.3 Dealing with complaining customers

An important point is that while problems, mistakes and errors are inevitable, dissatisfied customers are not.[10] It is not usually the problem itself that causes dissatisfaction. Yes, customers are aggrieved, annoyed even, that it has happened. But most, though not all, customers, do accept that problems sometimes occur. (They are much less forgiving if it happens again, of course.) However, it is the way an organisation responds to and deals with the problem that causes dissatisfaction, if handled badly, or delight if handled well. Interestingly, it has been found that those customers who complain and then experience the organisation dealing well with the situation experience higher levels of satisfaction (i.e. delight) than customers who experience a normal, good, day-to-day service. This is called the recovery paradox.[11]

Essentially, good complaint handling consists of three key operational activities: dealing with the customer, solving the problem for the customer, and dealing with, and learning from, the problem within the organisation (this last point we will deal with in Section 13.4).[12]

Dealing with the customer involves five key activities:

- *Acknowledgement.* Acknowledge that the problem has occurred. For some customers, if staff are dismissive of the problem it can create a good deal of dissatisfaction and bad will.

- *Empathy.* Following from acknowledgement, try to understand the problem from a customer's point of view and express some sympathy for their position.

- *Apology.* For some people at dissatisfaction levels –1, –2 or –3, an apology may be enough to satisfy them. Some managers may have difficulty in allowing their staff to say sorry because they may be concerned that it implies fault, opening the way for litigation. In such circumstances, words similar to 'I am sorry this has happened to you' may do the trick. A written apology or a verbal follow-up call from management may delight customers at the lower end of the dissatisfaction scale but may be expected by customers at the highly dissatisfied end.

- *Owning the problem.* A member of staff can give the customer some confidence in the process for dealing with their complaint by getting hold of the problem and assuming clear ownership, and reinforcing this to the customer. The sense of relief felt by a customer may lead to them appreciating the efforts made by the member of staff, increasing both their levels of satisfaction.

- *Involving management.* For more severe cases (customer dissatisfaction levels –3 and less), customers often expect that a more senior person will deal with their problem. This should be part of the process, even if the original employee is perfectly competent to deal with the problem.

Solving the problem for the customer involves two key activities:

- *Fixing the problem for the customer.* The key here is at least to try, or appear to try, to fix it. For customers who are –3 and less on the dissatisfaction scale staff may need to be seen to be putting themselves out to fix a problem and 'jumping through hoops'. At the –5 end of the scale the fixing may need to be seen to be done, or at least overseen by, someone in higher authority.

- *Providing compensation.* Some organisations seem overly keen to dispense compensation or tokens, assuming that this alone will appease customers. Often customers simply want the problem fixed and dealt with so that it does not happen again (see earlier). It is important to note that providing compensation without fixing the problem can lead to greater levels of dissatisfaction. Token compensation may be unnecessary for level –1 and appreciated

Table 13.1 Reasons for not complaining

Reasons for not complaining	Percentage citing those reasons
Did not think anything would change	50
Too much effort	17
Did not want to cause trouble	17
Too busy	8
Too stressful	8

Source: Adapted from Johnston, Robert and Adrian Fern (1999), 'Service Recovery Strategies for Single and Double Deviation Scenarios', *Service Industries Journal* 19 (2) 69–82.

by level −2. Level −3 and −4 customers may require equivalent compensation, a refund and a token gesture whereas level −5 customers may need 'big gesture' compensation – either monetary, products or services, or acts of contrition by management.

13.3.4 Dealing with customers who don't complain

Unfortunately many customers do not complain when something goes wrong, and, as a result, the problem may go unnoticed, and therefore unsolved, by the organisation. The proportion of customers not complaining varies significantly between organisations. It also depends on the nature of the person involved, the seriousness of the complaint and the intensity of dissatisfaction felt. It has been found that 49 per cent of dissatisfied customers in a restaurant will not complain. In stores this is about 44 per cent, whereas for a council with monopoly control over local services only 30 per cent of customers complain when dissatisfied.[13]

Unfortunately, many customers tell others about poor service rather than tell the organisation's staff, who might be able to appease the customer and fix the problem. Research suggests that customers often feel that complaining is just not worth the effort and, more significantly, that if they did, the organisation would not actually change anything (see Table 13.1).[14]

To encourage feedback, complaints and helpful suggestions from customers, organisations need to make it easy for customers to provide feedback; they need to ensure, and to assuring the customers, that things will change, that the organisation takes the feedback seriously and acts on it. The MTR in Hong Kong goes to great lengths to solicit customer feedback (Case Example 13.1).

Case Example 13.1 **MTR Corporation, Hong Kong**

The MTR Corporation operates nine railway lines serving Hong Kong Island, Kowloon and the New Territories. In addition, a Light Rail network serves the local communities of Tuen Mun and Yuen Long in the New Territories while a fleet of buses provide feeder services. The Corporation also operates the Airport Express, a dedicated high-speed rail link providing the fastest connections to Hong Kong International Airport and the city's exhibition and conference centre, AsiaWorld-Expo. The trains carry an average of 3.7 million passengers every weekday, making this one of the most heavily used mass transit systems in the world.

Source: James Davies

Besides running a mass transit system, the Corporation is also actively involved in the development of key residential and commercial projects above existing stations and along new line extensions.

The MTR is regarded as one of the world's leading railways for safety, reliability, customer service and cost efficiency and for continually developing its network and its services to customers. The Corporation's mission is to develop and manage a world-class railway, together with property and other related business, to enhance the quality of life in Hong Kong. Customer service is one of the Corporation's core values. In order to help the company understand how it can better meet the changing needs of passengers it makes enormous efforts to listen to its customers' concerns and needs. Managers undertake annual passenger surveys, home interview surveys, biannual customer service surveys, and focus group discussions. They also run a customer telephone hotline, have station suggestion boxes and even hold station coffee evenings and the occasional radio phone-in. The MTR is obsessed with how customers feel and with developing its services and facilities to meet their needs. 'We listen, we act', said Nancy Pang, marketing and communications manager.

Source: This case is developed from material in http://www.mtr.com.hk and Tocquer, Gerard A. and Chan Cudennec (1998), *Service Asia*, Prentice Hall, Singapore

There are a variety of methods for encouraging feedback. These include:

- *Comment cards.* These should give customers the chance to air their views about the service (What did you like? What went wrong?), ask how the customer thinks the service could be improved (What could we do better?) and ascertain information about whether they will return (Will you use us again? Will you recommend us?). Some organisations also use incentives, such as prizes, to encourage positive and negative feedback.

- *Notices.* Notices are useful in explaining to customers the process for making a comment or complaint. Freephone numbers may help encourage those who would otherwise not provide feedback. A small number of organisations are trying to demonstrate how seriously they take feedback by involving senior managers or sometimes even the chief executive, by providing their contact numbers or email addresses.

- *Websites.* While the number of 'unofficial' websites is increasing (where highly dissatisfied customers 'voice' their opinions about organisations), other organisations are taking the proactive step of capturing feedback via their websites.

- *Staff feedback.* Front-line staff are often the people who pick up the small comments or grumbles and are usually in a position to provide feedback to managers. Sadly, few organisations seem to harness this information stream by having formal or informal feedback and improvement mechanisms, whether unit meetings or paper or web-based systems.

13.4 How can managers use problems to drive improvement?

Given that problems are always going to happen and customers are going to complain, organisations need to be able to use this information in a constructive way to learn from the problems and drive improvements through the organisation. We refer to this activity as service recovery.

13.4.1 Service recovery

Many people use the term 'service recovery' to mean dealing with the customer after something has gone wrong, i.e. apologising to them, fixing the problem for them and maybe providing compensation (as we covered in Section 13.3). We define service recovery as the action of seeking out and dealing with problems and failures in the provision of service in order to improve the service and operational and organisational performance. This definition expands service recovery away from complaint management by another name to the activity of finding failures and potential failures – preferably before the impact of such failures has been felt by the customer – and putting them right, i.e. driving improvements to operational processes and making things better for the customer, the staff and the organisation; the triple bottom line.

The act of recovering from a failure should, of course, lead to satisfied, even delighted, customers. This, in turn, should lead to higher retention rates and therefore all the financial benefits this provides (long-term income streams and reduced costs, etc.) as well as positive word-of-mouth recommendations. The key purpose of service recovery is not necessarily to satisfy the customer per se (i.e. recover the customer), although this may be important, but to use the information gleaned from the failure and its consequences to drive improvements through an organisation by focusing managerial attention on specific problem areas.[15] If the focus of service recovery is solely to satisfy the complaining customer, its potential to prevent the problem recurring – and thus prevent more dissatisfied and lost customers and reduced financial performance – is lost. It is important that dealing with a problem and recovering from a failure should lead to operational improvements. This in turn leads to reduced costs, less waste and fewer problems in the future, which in turn reduces the costs of dealing with problems. Dealing well with problems, satisfying customers and improving processes also makes life easier for staff. So good service recovery should also lead to increased staff satisfaction leading to higher levels of staff retention and then reduced costs.

These are referred to as the main outcomes of service recovery: customer recovery (dealing well with the complaining customer), process recovery (improving operational processes) and staff recovery (making things better for the staff). These three should lead to improvements in the organisation's financial performance (see Figure 13.3). Interestingly, research has shown that the weakest driver of improved financial performance is customer recovery, and the strongest is process recovery.[16] So organisations which focus on recovering the customer and not recovering the processes are not only losing out on preventing problems recurring but also on improved financial performance. Sadly, many organisations do not obtain these benefits and view service recovery simply as a means of trying to pacify a dissatisfied customer.

One critical condition of effective service recovery is having the right service culture (see Figure 13.3).

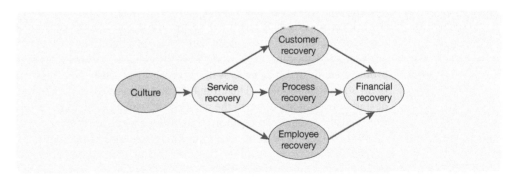

Figure 13.3 Service recovery

Source: Adapted from Michel, S., D. Bowen and R. Johnston (2009), 'Why Service Recovery Fails: Tensions among the Customer, Employee, and Process Perspectives', *Journal of Service Management* 20 (3) 253–273

Creating the right culture

Any organisation that is serious about learning from problems needs to have the right culture. It is often typified by the words 'no blame'. This means that when a problem or a failure occurs, the member of staff is not blamed but the focus of attention is on the problem itself and how it can be resolved for the future. However, should a member of staff make the same mistake twice – well that may be a different matter. This seemingly obvious approach is incredibly hard to achieve. It requires a highly supportive management style, one that stresses learning rather than blaming, where senior managers and indeed managers of all levels model the desired behaviours of support, encouragement and improvement. It also requires a good commitment to the support and training of staff to openly report problems with good mechanisms to deal with the problems and improve processes.

Customer recovery

When things go wrong, organisations have a chance to demonstrate what they can do for their customers. Indeed for some organisations, such as utilities, the occurrence of a failure or a problem is one of the few times that the organisation's staff may come into direct contact with customers. Employee unwillingness to recognise and deal with problems is known to be a key cause of customer dissatisfaction.[17]

Customer recovery involves dealing well with the complaining customer and also being proactive in seeking out feedback from customers about problems rather than waiting for the problem to occur (we dealt with how to do this in Section 13.3).

Managing complaints well should lead to an increase in customer retention but it may also lead to reciprocity. Because the organisation has been seen to go out of its way to sort out a difficult situation for a customer, customers may feel obliged to reciprocate not only by continuing to use its services but also by becoming a champion for the organisation and providing positive word-of-mouth recommendations.

Process recovery

Surprisingly few service organisations, unlike their manufacturing counterparts, are good at taking information about service problems, learning from them and turning them into real improvements.[18] Indeed some organisations make it particularly difficult by setting up remote and disconnected customer service centres, whose role is to pacify customers while not disturbing the rest of the organisation and letting it get on with its 'real' task.

Process recovery involves a number of steps. Firstly the problem needs to be investigated and data collected and analysed. Then the root cause of the problem needs to be identified, and options for improvement considered and costed. It may be that the cost or difficulty of overcoming a problem may be deemed to be greater than the cost and inconvenience caused. In such cases a procedure needs to be put in place to ensure that staff know how to deal with the situation should it occur again. On the assumption that changes are required and deemed necessary and appropriate, whatever was the cause of the problem should be resolved and the problem eradicated. The process then needs to be checked to ensure that the solution has actually solved the problem. Then it may be appropriate to go back to the customer or member of staff who drew attention to the problem, to explain what has been done to fix the problem. This usually delights the customer/member of staff, validates their actions and encourages them to provide more feedback, in a positive way, to the organisation.

Information from customer complaints and from other failure or problem situations should provide organisations with the means (and motivation!) to improve what they do and make things better for the future – not only for their customers but also for their staff, who may experience on a regular basis what might seem one-off failures to customers. TNT, an international market leader in global express services, has achieved some astonishing advances after it used the results of its complaint information (see Case Example 13.2).

Case Example 13.2   TNT Express

TNT Express is the world's leading business-to-business express delivery company. The organisation is serious about complaints and works hard to derive improvements from problems and complaints. It uses a worldwide reporting system to identify all failures in detail, without exception, and then weekly in-depth root-cause analysis is used to identify and solve problems. Indeed, by focusing on complaint data, TNT has improved its performance dramatically, including a 96 per cent improvement in on-time delivery and missed pick-ups down by 78 per cent. This has resulted in less problems and hassle for staff, which has reversed the company's employee

Source: Alamy Images/David Levenson

turnover figures and led to significant reductions in absenteeism. The impact on financial performance has also been evident, with profit before tax up by 81 per cent over two years.

Source: This illustration was developed from material from www.tnt.com and from Barlow, Janelle and Claus Møller (1996), *A Complaint Is a Gift*, Berrett-Koehler, San Francisco.

Employee recovery

Learning from problems, improving operational processes and satisfying customers will of course make things better for the staff. They will be faced with fewer complaining customers, and operational processes will be easier and better.

Problems, however, will still occur and managers need to recognise that some front-line staff may feel a sense of frustration and irritation that a problem has occurred. They may also feel stress caused by having to deal with an unhappy customer, especially where managers are not listening or are not willing to make changes to deal with the cause of the complaints. This leads not only to dissatisfied and disillusioned customers but also to dissatisfied and disillusioned staff, who feel powerless to help or sort out the problems. This helpless feeling, known as learned helplessness,[19] encourages, or rather induces, employees to display passive, maladaptive behaviours, such as being unhelpful, withdrawing or acting uncreatively.[20] The employee alienation associated with this helplessness will be compounded when employees feel that management does not make efforts to recover them from this helpless state. So, just like customers, employees may need to be 'recovered' by their supervisors or managers.[21]

Employee recovery is done in the same way as recovering customers, acknowledgement, empathy, owning the problem, etc., and also investigating and fixing the problem, maybe involving the member of staff in the process.

13.4.2 The acid tests of service recovery

In summary, we suggest that six acid tests can be applied to an organisation to assess its service recovery capability:[22]

1   Is there a culture of learning from problems that drives improvement?

2   Does it lead to increased customer satisfaction (at least for those customers that the organisation wishes to retain)?

3 Does it improve customer retention rates?

4 Does it drive process improvements?

5 Does it lead to a better job for the staff?

6 And, as a result of the above, does it improve financial performance?

On this last point, effective service recovery should lead directly to enhanced financial performance for the organisation. There should be increased revenues from higher levels of retention and from positive word-of-mouth from delighted customers. There should also be reduced costs from continuous operational improvements and lower costs (financial and emotional) in dealing with dissatisfied customers.

Indeed, defined in this way, service recovery should be viewed as a profit centre. Sadly, in many organisations service recovery, or rather complaint management, is seen as a necessary evil and a sunk cost. To understand better these relationships between complaints/recovery and financial performance, organisations need to collect and analyse the data to help them exploit the value of service recovery for the organisation. In Chapter 17 we show how to make the business case for service which can also be applied to service recovery.

13.5   How can managers prevent problems occurring?

We defined service recovery as the action of seeking out and dealing with problems and failures in the provision of service in order to improve service, operational and organisational performance. One key part of this is seeking out problems and stopping them happening in the first place. In Chapter 12 we provided several tools to help organisations continuously improve what they do. There are two additional tools that specifically help uncover and/or reduce problems; failsafing and service guarantees.

13.5.1 Failsafing

Failsafing is one means of trying to reduce the likelihood of failures in service processes.[23] This idea is called *poka yoke* in Japan (from the Japanese *yokeru*, meaning to prevent, and *poka*, inadvertent errors) and was advocated by Shigeo Shingo.[24] *Poka yoke* are simple automatic failsafe devices that can be designed into a service to prevent many inevitable mistakes becoming failures. *Poka yoke* usually have the dual advantages of cheapness and simplicity, and are used to prevent both staff and customers doing the wrong thing.

Poka yoke can be used to reduce customer failures by encouraging customers to do the right thing. Simple but effective examples include airline lavatory doors that need to be locked to have the light come on. Electronic tags on products in a store ensure that they are not inadvertently or intentionally taken out of the store. Mobile phones can be locked to prevent accidental calls being made in your pocket; they can be made so that their batteries only fit one way – the right way – round.

From an operation's perspective *poka yoke* can be used to ensure that staff adhere to procedures in order to reduce or eliminate service failures. Some computerised procedures, for example, will not allow operators to move to the next screen until all the information has been provided on the previous screen. The 'dead-man's handle' on a train will automatically stop the train unless a driver is holding the handle down.

Equipment failures can be prevented, or the consequences minimised, by making them literally failsafe: automatic doors that can only fail when open, traffic lights whose fail mode is amber in all directions. Parallel wiring or having back-up components or systems can dramatically reduce the likelihood of equipment failure.

There are four key steps in failsafing:

1   Identify the potential or actual weak points in a process. This can be done using some of the tools we introduced in Chapters 7 and 8 (such as process mapping, walk-through audits, emotion mapping or customer experience analysis) or from the analysis of complaints data.

2   Brainstorm various ways of reducing or preventing errors.

3   Select, design and implement the most appropriate *poka yoke*. If the failure is not preventable, ensure the staff know how to handle the situation when it arises.

4   Monitor and evaluate the effect of implementation and repeat the above steps if necessary.

13.5.2 Service guarantees

A service guarantee is a built-in form of service recovery. It acknowledges that problems will occur and provides a system to encourage, and reward, customers to report problems so that the organisation is made aware of them and can deal with them. A service guarantee is a promise to recompense a customer for service that fails to meet a defined level. A good guarantee explains what the promise is, what to do if it's not met and what the customer should expect to receive in compensation. For some organisations (see Case Example 13.3), service guarantees are a key part of a customer-focused strategy.

Guarantees require an organisation to formalise the service recovery process. A service guarantee includes the setting up of a clear and inviting mechanism for customers to trigger the guarantee, as well as training and empowering employees to deal with invoked guarantees.[25] It should also specify the compensation for the failure. The guarantee can also be used proactively: for example, a pizza restaurant developed explicit recovery procedures, which included front-line staff invoking the guarantee on behalf of the customer if the pizza was late, apologising and immediately presenting the guest with a voucher for a free pizza (as promised in the guarantee).[26]

Case Example 13.3   **Zane's Cycles**

Zane's Cycles is a bicycle store in Branford, Connecticut, which includes not only a large selection of adult and children's mountain bikes, road bikes and hybrids, and a range of accessories and clothing, but also a large coffee bar (with free coffee) and a children's play area.

Chris Zane is the company president. He described the company's policy:

Source: Zane's Cycles

We provide a lifetime free service guarantee, so we will service the bike for free while ever you own the bike. We also provide a lifetime warranty, covering not only the bike but anything else you might buy in our store – helmets, pumps or clothes – and also a 90-day price protection policy that says if you see the same bike for less elsewhere within 90 days we will refund the difference. We added on the 90-day protection policy after feedback from our customers who told us that if we provided lifetime free service and lifetime warranty we must be expensive. So the 90-day price protection policy gives them confidence that not only do we have the best warranties but that we are also competitive.

Chris Zane founded Zane's Cycles in October 1981 when he was 16 and still at school. He had been running a bike repair business from the age of 12 in the family's garage, and also working in a bike shop in the summer holiday. When the owner of the shop decided to liquidate the inventory because of high operating costs, Chris, after a lot of difficulty convincing his parents to let him run the business and another relative to put up a guaranteed loan, purchased the operating business for the cost of the inventory. His first year's turnover was $56,000. He now has over 40 staff and sells thousands of bikes each year.

Zane's Cycles' guarantees are:

- *Guaranteed for Life. Every bicycle purchased from Zane's Cycles comes with our exclusive 'Zane's Cycles Lifetime Free Service and Lifetime Parts Warranty.' Anytime your bicycle needs service, a full tune-up or just a quick adjustment, we will make those necessary adjustments for free as long as you own your bicycle.*

- *90-Day Price Protection. We guarantee you will never overpay at Zane's Cycles. If you find any item you purchased in stock for less anywhere in Connecticut within 90 days, we'll gladly refund you the difference plus 10%*

- *30 Day Test Ride. To guarantee you have purchased the correct bicycle, ride it for 30 days. If during that time you are not completely satisfied, please return the bicycle for an exchange. We will gladly give you a full credit toward your new selection.*

- *Serious. Fun. Guaranteed. Twenty Five years ago we started with the belief, 'the only difference between us and our competition is the service that we offer.' If you don't feel that we are living up to our mission, let us know and we'll fix it immediately. If you have a concern and would like to discuss it with me directly, please e-mail me. I will personally respond to you.*

Chris explained:

I know a lifetime free service guarantee may sound expensive but it really is not. The products are so well made these days that they actually don't need a great deal of service and a lot of bikes don't get ridden too much anyway. We know most of our customers are going to use their bike for eight to ten years, then want to trade up to a new bike. So we use the guarantee as a tool to help us develop a relationship with the customer.

We don't use lifetime free service to sell the bike. Well, OK it's a sales tool to get the customer through the door for the first time, but then it's a relationship tool to help sell the second and third and fourth bike. And, then that customer will tell their friends that this is the place to buy a bike. For example, someone comes into the store four years after they bought the bike, and they say the gears are slipping, so we service the bike and they come and pick it up and it's actually free. From that point forward they have a completely different relationship with us at a different level and they know we are a trustworthy operation. They become our apostles, promoters of our business. They tell all their friends, 'Hey I went to Zane's, I had the bike four years and they didn't charge me to have the wheels straightened'.

Always with an eye on the long term, Chris's philosophy is to 'give away the first dollar'. He added:

I decided a long time ago to develop programmes that are good for the customers first and then figure out how to make the long-term relationship profitable. I didn't want to 'nickel and dime' my customers. Many companies profit on the small parts and pieces that are hard to find. I, on the other hand, believe a retailer, for pennies, can secure even more profitable long-term customer relationships. At Zane's Cycles, we don't charge for anything under $1. Often a customer comes in for a small part needed to solve a frustrating problem. The master link on his child's bike has broken, and the child is upset because he can't use his bike. Or, while changing a flat tyre, a customer loses an axle nut. We give customers the small parts they need for free. By the way, this programme costs less than $100 a year – the equivalent of one bad print advertisement that no-one ever mentions seeing.

Source: This illustration is based on material from www.zanes.com and from discussions with Chris Zane.

13.5.3 The six acid tests of service guarantees

The acid tests of service recovery can also be applied to a service guarantee:

1 Is there a culture of learning from problems that drives improvement?

2 Does it lead to increased customer satisfaction (at least for those customers that the organisation wishes to retain)?

3 Does it improve customer retention rates?

4 Does it drive process improvements?

5 Does it lead to a better job for the staff?

6 And, as a result of the above, does it improve financial performance?

1 Learning culture

If there is no learning culture, guarantees will not do their job. Indeed this is evident in some organisations where, as soon as somebody invokes the guarantee, i.e. tells the organisation something was wrong, they are immediately given the compensation (vouchers, cash back or whatever). However, the problem is never recorded and nothing is ever done about it.

2 Customer satisfaction

A restaurant that promises to serve a lunch to customers within 10 minutes of order not only focuses the organisation on delivering what is important to customers but also reduces customers' perceived risk (if they need a quick lunch, for example). A service guarantee also reduces the likelihood of a dissatisfied customer walking out of the door without telling anyone what the problem was, thus giving staff a chance to recover the customer and indeed the process.

The key advantages to a customer include:

- *Focusing on satisfying the customer.* A guarantee helps to focus an organisation and its employees on satisfying the needs of a customer. It sharpens them and acts as a constant reminder of the need to satisfy customers.

- *Reducing perceived risk.* For the customer a guarantee may reduce any risk in the purchase, which is important since many services cannot be assessed until experienced. A service guarantee can reduce risk by clarifying the standards of performance the customer can expect, by promising high-quality performance in those service elements that are perceived as important by the consumer, and by the promise of a pay-out and/or rework should the service fail.

- *Creating a positive attitude.* According to the theory of reasoned action, an increased strength of the belief that buying the service will lead to a favourable outcome induces the customer to form a more favourable attitude towards buying, which in turn leads to a stronger behavioural intention towards buying. This strengthening of behavioural intention has a positive impact on customer beliefs, attitude, purchasing intentions and the number of customers actually buying.

- *Dealing with dissatisfaction.* A well-designed guarantee provides customers with clear standards against which to assess a service performance. The guarantee also promises the customer a meaningful compensation if guaranteed standards are not met. This therefore encourages complaining, or feedback, indicating that it is acceptable, indeed encouraged, and provides staff with mechanisms to deal with dissatisfaction. This in turn increases the chance of recovery and therefore customer satisfaction and organisational learning.

3 Customer retention

Customer retention is also increased by resolving complaints as a result of a service guarantee.[27] Also by providing a guarantee organisations may retain customers who might otherwise switch because of a perceived increased risk of purchasing elsewhere. Furthermore, well-designed service guarantees have a high communications quality in themselves and may induce customers to talk about them.[28]

4 Process improvement

Service guarantees, just like service recovery, help identify fail-points in an organisation. Often in the design stage of a guarantee, operations managers are forced to confront the weaknesses of their service processes and support systems to try to ensure that they will meet the required standards.[29] When invoked, service guarantees provide data on poor performance, track errors and thereby help organisations identify and remove fail-points.

5 Staff performance

Guarantees can reduce the stress felt by staff in dealing with problems and complaints. If there is a service guarantee with a clearly laid out procedure for invoking the guarantee, the staff know exactly what to do and indeed their customers know exactly what to expect. Also, service guarantees, by their existence, reinforce the need for employees to provide error-free service by focusing on the things that (hopefully) are of importance to the customer.

6 Financial performance

Service guarantees, well designed and well applied, should therefore lead to customer satisfaction, which drives retention and long-term revenue streams. Reduced perceived risk in the purchase of the service not only helps satisfy existing customers but will help attract new customers to the organisation. Improved process performance should also help retain existing customers as well as attract new ones. Improved performance may also help reduce both the costs of the process and the costs of losing customers or of rework. Significant cost savings can emerge, even though they may not have been the initial motivation for the introduction of a guarantee.[30] Guarantees may also reduce employee costs. After Hampton Inns introduced a service guarantee, employee surveys showed that the guarantee increased employee morale. This was also reflected in a drop of employee turnover from 117 per cent to 50 per cent within three years.[31]

An additional cost, however, is the cost of the compensation specified in the guarantee. This may not be insignificant if the guarantee is to have any meaning for customers, although at least this puts a clear internal cost on failure, which the organisation can seek to reduce. Furthermore, services are real-time performances and cannot be executed 100 per cent failure-free all of the time, i.e. occasional service failures are unavoidable. However, some customers so appreciate the existence of the guarantee and the chance to provide feedback easily that they decline the compensation when it is offered.

13.5.4 Downsides of guarantees

Service guarantees do, however, have their downsides. They imply that the service may well fail – thus the existence of a guarantee will sensitise customers to the performance of the service and maybe even make them look for poor service. Conversely, the standards set in the guarantee may be higher than customers need or even expect, thus unnecessarily increasing the cost of the service.

A frequently quoted concern is that customers may cheat. It has been known for students to order a pizza with a guaranteed delivery time and then to barricade doors and corridors to ensure it is late and therefore free! Research found that despite the reluctance of many organisations to provide them, full money-back guarantees will be abused no more than smaller pay-outs. It is also suggested that guarantees are best targeted at repeat customers because customers intending to use the service again tend not to cheat.[32]

13.5.5 Designing a service guarantee

There are three key aspects to the design of a service guarantee: the design of the promise, the design of the procedure to invoke the guarantee, and the design of the improvement system (see Case Example 13.4).

Case Example 13.4　Datapro Singapore

Jochen Wirtz, National University of Singapore

Datapro Information Services provided IT and telecommunications information and consulting services around the world. It employed over 400 analysts and consultants. Although having sold its pre-packaged information services in Asia for many years, Datapro only started offering consulting services throughout south-east Asia in 1993 via its Singapore office. Being confident about the high quality of its work, but at the same time somewhat lacking the brand equity other providers of similar services enjoyed, Datapro decided to become Asia's first IT consulting firm that explicitly guaranteed its services. Every proposal would contain the following guarantee in the last section just before the acceptance form:

Datapro guarantees to deliver the report on time, to high-quality standards, and to the contents outlined in this proposal. Should we fail to deliver according to this guarantee, or should you be dissatisfied with any aspect of our work, you can deduct any amount from the final payment which it deems as fair, subject to a maximum of 30%.

In the event Datapro should fail to deliver the commissioned report in its entirety at the end of the period, you will

Source: Pearson Education Ltd/Image State/John Foxx Collection

have the option to deduct 10% off the price of the study for each week the said study is overdue, subject to a maximum of 20%. We are able to offer this guarantee as we are confident about the good quality and professionalism of our work. We have secured a large number of blue-chip clients who have been completely satisfied with our services. Our clients in the last 12 months have included: British Telecom, Fujitsu, Sony, Hewlett-Packard, Philips, Intel, etc.

The guarantee was introduced by Datapro in 1994. Datapro had ideally wanted to provide a 100 per cent money-back guarantee, but at the same time wanted to limit the potential financial risks inherent in the introduction of such guarantees. These risks were considerable, with typical projects exceeding a value of well over US $100,000. The guarantee contained a full-satisfaction clause, as well as concrete promises, such as on-time delivery. This mixed design has been shown to be considerably more effective than either full-satisfaction guarantees or other specific guarantees alone.

The marketing impact was dramatic. Clients were delighted that Datapro was willing to stand by its word and guarantee deadlines as well as content quality – especially as deadlines were a thorny issue in Asia's rapidly growing IT markets, and clients were often promised the sky during the proposal stage, only to be confronted with late deliveries subsequently. The guarantee allowed Datapro to promise credible delivery dates, which otherwise might have been discounted by its clients. Datapro's management felt that the guarantee was an effective marketing tool that helped to sell a number of projects, and Datapro's consulting unit was extremely successful, with a revenue and profit growth of around 100 per cent per annum for a number of successive years.

On the operations side, the guarantee pushed Datapro to keep up its quality. For example, it did not have a single late delivery after the introduction of the guarantee, mainly for two reasons. First, case leaders were cautious not to promise delivery dates they knew they could not keep. Second, in the case of unforeseen problems or delays, case leaders would move heaven and earth to bring the case back on track. A similar pressure was on the case teams to keep their clients happy, as a dissatisfied client could mean a significant reduction in revenue and profit for that case, resulting in a steep reduction in staff bonuses.

Datapro was very successful, especially in breaking into the high-growth telecommunications consulting market, and was taken over by the Gartner Group, the world's largest IT consulting firm.

Design of the promise

There are five key elements in the design of the promise:

- *Meaningful.* The promise needs to be based on customers' expectations and to cover what they regard as being the critical determinants of success or failure. If an organisation guarantees something that is of little consequence, the guarantee will have little value. Before embarking on guarantees organisations should conduct market research to understand customer needs.

- *Easy to understand.* A guarantee should be simple to understand and communicated in a clear way. Guarantees that involve pages of fine print will be regarded with scepticism. Indeed guarantees that include constricting conditions which are only revealed on close inspection might be regarded as misleading and lead to dissatisfaction with the service in particular and the organisation in general.

- *Explicit.* The most powerful form of guarantee is one that is explicit – it is quite clear about what is being guaranteed and what the pay-out will be for failure. Federal Express was the first express company to offer a money-back guarantee – its guarantee states 'on time delivery or your money back'.[33] Some organisations, particularly professional service organisations, may use implicit guarantees, where it is implicit that any problems will be dealt with (in an unspecified way).

- *Unconditional.* The most powerful promise is one that guarantees satisfaction without conditions (see Case Example 13.5). Less powerful, though sometimes expedient, are guarantees that offer pay-outs with conditions attached. Airlines providing guarantees of punctuality may not cover instances when the delays are not their fault. The aircraft may be late due to typhoons or air traffic control problems.

- *The pay-out.* The service promise needs to have an appropriate level of pay-out. Too high a level – for example £1,000 for a late delivery of a pizza – may encourage cheating or may even put customers off claiming their rights. Inappropriately small pay-outs (£0.01 for a late pizza) may be deemed to be insulting and customers may not feel it is worth informing the organisation of the problem (which was part of the intention in the first place!).

Case Example 13.5 Radisson Hotels

Radisson is one of the leading full-service global hotel companies with over 420 hotels in 73 countries. The company pursues a strategy of combining global brand strength with local market expertise and service delivery provided by its partners and franchisees. At all levels the company is committed to providing personalised, professional guest service and genuine hospitality at every point of guest contact. The company's vision is centred on quality of facilities and services, 'beginning with the guest in mind'. The company's chief mission is to create loyal, satisfied customers who will return to Radisson.

Radisson has many initiatives in place to try to provide total guest satisfaction,

Source: Corbis/Chris Gasgoinge

including training programmes in marketing, operations, training and public relations, computerised reservations, sales and service, and a sophisticated global reservations system.

Radisson also highlights its hotel employees' 'genuine hospitality' with an advertising campaign – 'The difference is genuine'. The campaign focuses on Radisson hotel employees' proactive efforts to provide high-quality service to the guests, not because of training or operating procedures, but because of the spirit of hospitality, which puts the guest first. This philosophy is underpinned by a guest relations training programme called 'Yes, I can!' This programme tries to instil in staff the need to act positively in all customer interactions, and the company believes that this makes its service distinctive.

Radisson has a guest satisfaction guarantee as part of the brand's worldwide initiative to achieve total guest satisfaction with every guest stay at each hotel, and build long-term guest loyalty. The guarantee, found in every room and on all guest keycard holders, states: '100% Guest Satisfaction Guarantee. Our goal at Radisson is 100% guest satisfaction. If you aren't satisfied with something, please let one of our staff know during your stay and we'll make it right or you won't pay. It's Guaranteed.'

Source: This illustration is based on material from www.radisson.com.

Design of the procedure

The procedure to invoke or use a guarantee needs to be simple and easy. If the customer is expected to fill a set of forms in triplicate and get signatures from all parties involved as well as a written statement from a third party, the guarantee loses all its credibility and all its potential. The system should be easy, non-threatening, clear and known.

Design of the improvement system

A final and critical design aspect, sometimes lost in the marketing hype of service guarantees, is that one of their key purposes – and the most important – is to help the organisation learn from and then drive improvements through the organisation. If the guarantee simply proceduralises a system of pay-outs without providing information to the organisation about failures and encouraging improvement, we believe it is of little value.

13.6 Summary

Why do problems occur?

- Problems occur because service operations are usually complex, human-based systems involving the provision of many services, and with unpredictable input from customers.
- Types of problems include service, equipment or customer failures.
- Dealing well with problems should drive improvements in the operation.

How can complaining customers be dealt with?

- Customers complain in order to have the problem sorted/corrected, prevent it happening to others, get an explanation, have someone disciplined, get financial compensation, and/or feel better.
- Good complaint handling consists of three activities: dealing with the customer, solving the problem for the customer, and dealing with, and learning from, the problem within the organisation.
- Dealing with the customer involves five key activities: acknowledgement, empathy, apology, owning the problem and involving management.
- Solving the problem for the customer involves two key activities: fixing the problem for the customer and providing compensation.
- There are several ways of obtaining feedback from customers who don't complain.
- There are a variety of methods for encouraging feedback. These include comment cards, notices, websites and staff feedback.

How can managers use problems to drive improvement?

- Service recovery is the action of seeking out and dealing with problems and failures in the provision of service in order to improve the service and operational and organisational performance.
- Using problems to drive improvement requires the right culture, customer recovery, process recovery and staff recovery.
- Creating the right culture requires a highly supportive management style, managers who model the desired behaviours and support, encouragement and improvement, with a commitment to staff support and training.
- Customer recovery involves dealing with the customer, solving the problem for the customer, and dealing with, and learning from, the problem within the organisation.
- Process recovery involves investigation of the problem, data collection and analysis, root cause identification, consideration of alternatives and process change.
- Employee recovery requires supervisors or managers to 'recover' them when faced with problem situations.

How can managers prevent problems occurring?

- Failsafing, or using *poka yoke,* can reduce the likelihood of failures in service processes. *Poka yoke* are simple failsafe automatic devices that can be designed into a service to prevent many inevitable mistakes becoming failures.
- Service guarantees are a built-in form of service recovery.

13.7 Discussion questions

1 Think of the last time something went wrong in a service encounter and you complained. Evaluate how well it was handled and whether you think the organisation learned from the problem.

2 Explain why some organisations' complaint processes, though intent on satisfying customers, tend to lead to dissatisfaction.

3 Select a guarantee provided by a service organisation. Discuss its strengths and weaknesses.

13.8 Questions for managers

1 How good is your organisation at capturing information about problems and learning from them.

2 Evaluate your recovery processes. How could they be improved?

3 What would be the impact of offering a guarantee on the service that *you personally* provide?

Case Exercise   Gold Card Protection Service

Executive Bank plc is a bank that attracts premium customers, usually international travellers. As part of its exclusive, and expensive, gold charge card service it offers its customers the opportunity to join, for a small additional annual fee, its card protection scheme, the Gold Card Protection Service.

The card protection scheme simply provides insurance against the theft and misuse of its customers' charge and credit cards (the cards may be issued by any bank, credit company or store). In addition this service also provides a wide range of benefits which are not dissimilar from the card protection schemes run by other companies. These include:

- a 24-hour worldwide freephone number
- a single call to cancel all cards and order replacements
- £2,000 insurance against misuse prior to notification
- unlimited cover after notification
- £2,000 interest-free emergency cash if the customer is stranded abroad
- a lost key and luggage retrieval service
- help in the emergency replacement of driving licence and passport
- payment of emergency hotel bills up to £1,500
- emergency airline or ferry tickets up to £2,000
- emergency car hire assistance.

The Card Protection Service boasts that it provides a 'friendly, efficient and thorough service to all its customers' and that it will 'answer calls within an average of ten seconds, generate loss reports to the card issuers within 20 seconds after the call and always send prompt confirmation of action taken with an email and text message to the customer'.

The following is a letter sent by a customer after having experienced the service.

6 February

Mr Daniel Payne

Customer Services Manager

Gold Card Customer Services

Executive Bank plc

Dear Mr Payne

I am writing to express my profound dissatisfaction with the service provided by your organisation.

At 9.30 a.m. on 17th January I was robbed whilst entering a bus near Warsaw railway station on the way to Warsaw airport. My wallet, containing all my credit and charge cards and a number of personal items, was stolen. I reported this loss to your Card Protection Service at 11.00 a.m. on my arrival at Warsaw airport. I greatly appreciated the opportunity to make a free-phone call.

I was told that all my cards would be stopped immediately and replacements requested. The operator asked if there was any cash in the wallet. I told her that there was about £40 in the wallet. She asked me if I had cash with me and I confirmed that I had. The operator asked for a number where I could be contacted that evening. This was provided.

I was impressed by the arrival of my replacement Executive Gold Card on January 19th.

By Wednesday 24th January all the replacement cards had arrived with the exception of my Standard4 Bank Debit Card. This was an important card as it was my main means of obtaining cash. Having been without the card for a week this was becoming a problem!

On returning home from work at 8.00 p.m. on 25th January I found that the card had still not arrived. I rang the Standard4 Bank's telephone banking service to ask when I should expect to receive my card. I was told that the card had been stopped but no replacement ordered. I was told they would notify my branch but I should ring the branch the following day. I then rang your organisation to try to discover why the replacement card had not been ordered. I spoke to James Creek who informed me that the Standard4 Bank did not accept orders for replacement cards from anyone but the customer and that I should contact my bank directly. I complained that I had not been told this, indeed one week had gone by during which I had assumed it was on its way. James apologised and said the operator should have told me. I then asked James if the small amount of cash that I had in my wallet was also covered. James told me it was and he offered to send me a claim form. I asked why the operator had not checked this with me at the time. James said she should have done so and again apologised and promised to send me a claim form immediately. I felt very dissatisfied with your service at this point. One of my card issuers had sent me, with their replacement card, information about their card protection scheme which I noticed provided free cover for family members. I pointed this out to James and asked him to send me information about your card protection scheme so I could make a comparison. He agreed to do this and also offered me free cover for my spouse for one year to make up for the inconvenience I had suffered. James told me that he would contact my bank to try to sort out the replacement. He sincerely apologised for all the errors.

On January 26th, I rang my bank to check that a card had been ordered. My branch confirmed that a replacement had been ordered by your organisation and it should arrive on the 30th (nearly two weeks after it had been stolen). I complained that it was my main means of getting cash. I was told there was nothing that could be done, though I could call into the bank and they would provide me with some cash from my account. I suggested that might be difficult as I had a full time job.

On January 30th, my debit card arrived telling me I would have to wait for a new PIN number to arrive before I could use it. Further, there was no material from your organisation. I then rang and spoke to you and you apologised for the incidents. You agreed that the material should have arrived by now as stationery orders are processed overnight. I agreed to wait a few more days.

Today is February 6th. I have just received the PIN number for my debit card and have managed to activate it and use it – nearly three weeks after the robbery. I am still without the promised material from your organisation.

I would be grateful if you could answer the following questions.

1 *Why did the operator not tell me that my debit card would not be replaced unless I contacted my bank?*

2 *Why did the operator not tell me that the cash in my wallet was also covered by your scheme and volunteer to send me a claim form?*

3 *Why did the operator not ring/email/text me in the evening to tell me about the problem with the debit card or to confirm that all the instructions had been carried out? I would have very much appreciated this reassurance.*

4 *Why could James order a replacement on the 25th but the initial operator could not do so on the 17th? Did I need to contact the bank or not?*

5 *Why did James not ring me a few days later, on the 27th for example, to check that I had received the material he promised and that everything was now all right?*

6 *Why did I not receive the material?*

7 *Why do you wait till the customer is so fed up and has to ask you to sort something out? I have now made five telephone calls and written this one letter. I have not yet received any call or correspondence from your organisation. I can only conclude that you just don't care.*

8 *Why do you only do what appears to be the minimum possible to deal with an aggrieved customer?*

Please would you tell me why I should continue to pay the large annual fee for the Executive Gold Card and the additional cost for the Card Protection Service for this appalling lack of service?

Yours sincerely

David Smith

David Smith

Question

1 How would you respond to this letter?

Suggested further reading

Cunliffe, Melissa and Robert Johnston (2008), 'Complaint Management and the Role of the Chief Executive', *Service Business: An International Journal* 2 (1) 47–64

DeWitt, Tom and Michael Brady (2003), 'Rethinking Service Recovery Strategies', *Journal of Service Research* 6 (2) 193–205

Holloway, Betsy B. and Sharon E. Beatty (2003), 'Service Failure in Online Retailing: A Recovery Opportunity,' *Journal of Service Research* 6 (1) 92–105

Johnston, Robert and Sandy Mehra (2002), 'Best Practice Complaint Management', *The Academy of Management Executive* 16 (4) 145–155

Johnston, Robert and Stefan Michel (2008), 'Three Outcomes of Service Recovery: Customer Recovery, Process Recovery and Employee Recovery', *International Journal of Operations and Production Management* 28 (1) 79–99

Lidén, Sara Björlin and Per Skålén (2003) 'The Effect of Service Guarantees on Service Recovery', *International Journal of Service Industry Management* 14 (1) 36–58

McColl-Kennedy, Janet R. and Beverley A. Sparks (2003), 'Application of Fairness Theory to Service Failures and Service Recovery,' *Journal of Service Research* 5 (3) 251–266

Michel, Stefan and Matthew L. Meuter (2008), 'The Service Recovery Paradox: True but Overrated?', *International Journal of Service Industry Management* 19 (4) 441–457

Michel, Stefan, Bowen David and Johnston Rober (2009), 'Why Service Recovery Fails: Tensions among the Customer, Employee, and Process Perspectives', *Journal of Service Management* 20 (3) 253–273

Namkung, Young and Soocheong Jang (2010), 'Service Failures in Restaurants: Which Stage of Service Failure is the Most Critical?', *Cornell Hospitality Quarterly* 51 (3) 323–343

Priluck, Randi and Vishal Ashill (2009), 'The Impact of the Recovery Paradox on Retailer-Customer Relationships', *Managing Service Quality* 19 (1) 42–59

Simons, Jacob V. Jr. and Mark E. Kraus (2005), 'Analytical Approach for Allocating Service Recovery Efforts to Reduce Internal Failure', *Journal of Service Research* 7 (3) 277–289

Wirtz, Jochen and Doreen Kum (2004), 'Consumer Cheating on Service Guarantees', *Journal of the Academy of Marketing Science* 32 (2) 159–174

Useful web links

If you want to read lots of complaints or even add your own go to:
http://www.complaints.com/

Have a look at Ron Kaufman's library:
http://www.upyourservice.com/library/index.html

A useful site on service recovery:
http://www.greatbrook.com/service_recovery.htm

Notes

1 Johnston, Robert (1995), 'Service Failure and Recovery: Impact, Attributes and Process', *Advances in Services Marketing and Management: Research and Practice* (4) 211–228

2 Hocutt, Mary Ann, Michael Bowers and Todd Donavan (2006), 'The Art of Service Recovery: Fact or Fiction?', *Journal of Services Marketing* 20 (3) 199–207

3 Johnston, Robert (1995), 'Service Failure and Recovery: Impact, Attributes and Process', *Advances in Services Marketing and Management: Research and Practice* (4) 211–228

4 Johnston, Robert (1998), 'The Effect of Intensity of Dissatisfaction on Complaining Behaviour', *Journal of Consumer Satisfaction, Dissatisfaction and Complaining Behavior* (11) 69–77

5 Bitner, Mary Jo, Bernard H. Booms and Lois Moh (1994), 'Critical Service Encounters: The Employee's Viewpoint', *Journal of Marketing* 58 (10) 95–106

6 See, for example, Blodgett, Jeffery, Donald Granbois and Rockney Walters (1993), 'The Effects of Perceived Justice on Complainants' Negative Word-of-mouth Behavior and Repatronage Intentions', *Journal of Retailing* 69 (4) 399–428; Hedrick, Natalie, Michael Beverland and Stella Minahan (2007), 'An Exploration of Relational Customers' Response to Service Failure', *Journal of Services Marketing* 24 (1) 64–72

7 Prakash, V. (1991), 'Intensity of Dissatisfaction and Consumer Complaint Behaviors', *Journal of Consumer Satisfaction, Dissatisfaction and Complaining Behavior* (4) 110–122

8 Johnston, Robert (1998), 'The Effect of Intensity of Dissatisfaction on Complaining Behaviour', *Journal of Consumer Satisfaction, Dissatisfaction and Complaining Behavior* (11) 69–77

9 TNS Survey 2004, http://www.tnsglobal.com/

10 Heskett, James L., W. Earl Sasser and Christopher W.L. Hart (1990), *Service Breakthroughs: Changing the Rules of the Game*, Free Press, New York

11 Michel, Stefan and Matthew L. Meuter (2008), 'The Service Recovery Paradox: True but Overrated?', *International Journal of Service Industry Management* 19 (4) 441–457

12 See, for example; Johnston, Robert and Adrian Fern (1999), 'Service Recovery Strategies for Single and Double Deviation Scenarios', *Service Industries Journal* 19 (2) 69–82; Johnston, Robert and Sandy Mehra (2002), 'Best Practice Complaint Management', *Academy of Management Executive* 16 (4) 145–155

13 Williams, Tom (1996) *Dealing with Customer Complaints*, Gower, Aldershot

14 Johnston, Robert and Adrian Fern (1999), 'Service Recovery Strategies for Single and Double Deviation Scenarios', *Service Industries Journal* 19 (2) 69–82

15 Van Ossel, Gino and Stefan Stremersch (2003), 'Complaint Management', in Van Looy, Bart, Roland Van Dierdonck and Paul Gemmel, *Services Management: An Integrated Approach*, Financial Times Pitman Publishing, London, pp. 171–196; and Tax, Stephen and Stephen Brown (1998), 'Recovering and Learning from Service Failure', *Sloan Management Review* 40 (1) 75–89

16 Michel, Stefan, David E. Bowen and Robert Johnston (2009), 'Why Service Recovery Fails: Tensions among the Customer, Employee, and Process Perspectives', *Journal of Service Management* 20 (3) 253–273

17 Bitner, Mary Jo, Bernard Booms and Mary Tetreault (1990), 'The Service Encounter: Diagnosing Favorable and Unfavorable Incidents', *Journal of Marketing* 54 (1) 71–84

18 Johnston, Robert (2001), 'Linking Complaint Management to Profit', *International Journal of Service Industry Management* 12 (1) 60–69

19 Martinko, Mark and William Gardner (1982), 'Learned Helplessness: An Alternative Explanation for Performance Deficits', *Academy of Management Review* 7 (2) 195–204

20 Bowen, David E. and Robert Johnston (1999), 'Internal Service Recovery: Developing a New Construct', *International Journal of Service Industry Management* 10 (2) 118–131

21 Bowen, David E. and Robert Johnston (1999), 'Internal Service Recovery: Developing a New Construct', *International Journal of Service Industry Management* 10 (2) 118–131

22 Johnston, Robert (2001), 'Linking Complaint Management to Profit', *International Journal of Service Industry Management* 12 (1) 60–69

23 Chase, Richard and Douglas Stewart (1994), 'Make Your Service Fail-safe', *Sloan Management Review* 35 (3) 35–44

24 Shingo, Shigeo (1986), *Zero Quality Control: Source Inspection and the Poka-Yoke System*, Productivity Press, Stamford, Connecticut

25 Hart, Christopher (1993), *Extraordinary Guarantees – A New Way to Build Quality throughout Your Company and Ensure Satisfaction for Your Customers*, Amacom, New York

26 Wirtz, Jochen (1998), 'Development of a Service Guarantee model', *Asia Pacific Journal of Management* 15 (1) 51–75

27 Gilly, Mary C., William B. Stevenson and Laura J. Yale (1991), 'Dynamics of Complaint Management in the Service Organization', *Journal of Consumer Affairs* 25 (2) 295–322

28 Heskett, James, W. Earl Sasser and Christopher Hart (1990), *Service Breakthroughs: Changing the Rules of the Game*, Free Press, New York

29 Hart, Christopher (1993) 'The Power of Guarantees as a Quality Tool', *CMA Magazine* (5) 28

30 Firnstahl, Timothy (1989), 'My Employees Are My Service Guarantee', *Harvard Business Review* 67 (4) 28–32

31 Greising, David (1994), 'Quality: How to Make It Pay', *Business Week* 8 August

32 Wirtz, Jochen and Doreen Kum (2004), 'Consumer Cheating on Service Guarantees', *Journal of the Academy of Marketing Science* 32 (2) 159–174

33 www.fedex.com

Chapter 14
Learning from other operations

Chapter objectives

This chapter is about how to learn from other operations to improve performance.

- What is benchmarking?
- How can benchmarking help organisations improve their performance?
- What are the different types of benchmarking?
- How do organisations go about benchmarking?
- How can quality awards and academic studies help with benchmarking?

14.1 Introduction

Many managers believe the situations they face are unique. In our experience this is rarely so and there are usually many other people who have faced the same or at least similar situations and challenges. There are always opportunities to learn from others so that mistakes are not repeated and ideas can be borrowed and adapted. There are many ways in which service organisations can learn from what other organisations and their operations are doing, such as reading management magazines or textbooks such as this one. We would also highly recommend going and talking to other managers, seeing what they do and finding out what works, what doesn't and why. This is usually referred to as 'benchmarking'. By benchmarking with other organisations, operations managers can see how well they are doing and, more importantly, obtain some ideas that they can adapt to their own situations to improve their own performance.

In this chapter we will start by defining benchmarking, explain why it is important and identify the various types of benchmarking that can be undertaken. We will then focus on the important part, how to do benchmarking. We will also spend a little time explaining the useful role of quality awards in benchmarking.

14.2   What is benchmarking?

Views differ on the origin of the term benchmarking. Some authors refer to the benchmark used by cobblers. Customers would place their bare foot or shoe on a bench and the cobbler would make a mark at each end as a basis for constructing the shoe. A more common view is of the benchmark as a reference point, originally a surveying term for a mark cut in a building used as a base point for measuring altitude. Whichever is true, a benchmark serves as a reference point that informs activity. In the context of managing service operations, benchmarks are measures or targets against which performance can be compared. Benchmarking is the activity whereby a measure or target of a process or some other aspect of an organisation or operation is compared with a similar aspect of something else in order to learn and to improve performance. The measure or target could be from another operation inside the organisation (internal benchmarking) or from another organisation (external benchmarking). In everyday business usage, the term benchmarking is often taken to mean external, 'best-in-field' benchmarking. Thus benchmarking implies a process of searching for the best practice that will encourage improvements and result in superior performance for the benchmarking organisation. The search is not necessarily limited to the benchmarker's industry, which could be a problem for competitive organisations, but may be for best practice wherever that may be.

The advantage that benchmarking provides over some other methods of learning is that by benchmarking **practices** against other organisations, managers can gain insight into **how** the desired level of performance was achieved, thus suggesting how it can be achieved in their own organisation. Even if the process is invisible, e.g. in the back office, or the situation is different, the very existence of a better process, or better business results, can stimulate learning and improvement.

14.3   How can benchmarking help organisations improve their performance?

Benchmarking can assist organisations in five important areas of performance improvement. It can help:

1   assess how well the benchmarking organisation is performing compared to a benchmark organisation
2   set realistic performance targets
3   search out new ideas and practices
4   stimulate creativity and performance innovation, and
5   drive improvement through an organisation.

The essential purpose – driving improvement (point 5) – can easily be overlooked in an organisation's desire to undertake benchmarking; the benefits realised are often limited to point 1 and sometimes point 2. Some managers skip these important stages and focus their efforts on point 3. While this can be the fun and certainly interesting part of benchmarking, without following through to points 4 and 5 the activity becomes little more than 'industrial tourism' (see below).

14.4 What are the different types of benchmarking?

Another reason for missed potential is that many benchmarking activities become concerned with, and then bogged down with, **metrics.** Organisations become embroiled with the establishment of good comparators of performance between operational processes so that the organisation can (as in point 1) assess how well a process is performing. If these are used as a means of comparison it can be misleading because organisations measure things in different ways and collect different data. Therefore a great deal of time and effort can be spent on trying to establish a base by which performance can be compared. The process of 'metric benchmarking' is shown in Figure 14.1.

14.4.1 Metric versus practice benchmarking

While metric benchmarking fulfils the desire to know whether performance is relatively good or bad, it does not necessarily help managers understand *how* they might go about improving their own processes. In contrast, **practice benchmarking** (which can actually be carried out without knowing how good or bad the respective processes are) is an attempt to search out new ideas and practices and stimulate creativity and performance innovation (points 3 and 4 above) in order to learn and improve performance (point 5). This involves seeking out ideas and practices that might be adapted for the benefit of the organisation (see Figure 14.2). It is important to recognise that practice benchmarking is further removed from the historical definition of benchmarks (creating a reference point) and much more concerned with the purpose of benchmarking: the quest for superior performance.

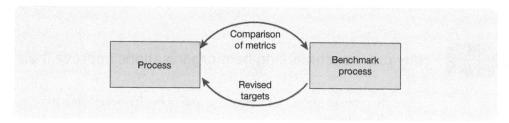

Figure 14.1 Metric benchmarking

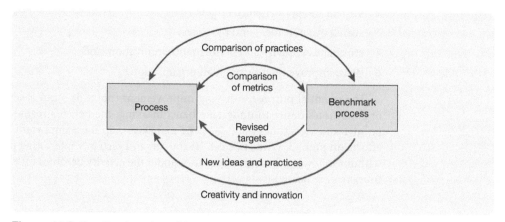

Figure 14.2 Practice benchmarking

14.4.2 Metric benchmarking

Metric benchmarking is the process of collecting some of the measures and targets used by other operations and comparing them to your own performance. It is important to note that metric benchmarking can result in damaging behaviours if used naively. Another operation's benchmark, measure or target will be a function of the other organisation's strategy (see Chapter 9) and will be affected by a unique set of contextual and environmental factors. However, if the benchmark is a measure which is important to your customers then it might be worth considering benchmarking against that measure. On the other hand, if the benchmark is an internal measure, such as speed of delivery, then it might be unwise to use this benchmark to encourage internal process improvement without incorporating, or understanding, the many contextual factors that impact upon it, such as numbers of staff, technology used, equipment and other resources available etc.

In other words, if a customer values a particular measure, the benchmarking organisation may wish to improve to make its own performance match or better the benchmark operation. However, if that measure is invisible to customers, an internal measure, then using it to drive performance improvement effectively means that one is importing elements of the other organisation's strategy with its allocated set of resources. This approach is usually doomed to failure. Bringing another organisation's strategy into one's own context is never a good idea.

These reservations aside, metric benchmarking obviously has its uses. Its primary purpose is to stimulate the question '*why* is performance different?' In turn, this question should stimulate learning.

14.4.3 Practice benchmarking

While metric benchmarking is essential for establishing whether the performance of a particular process is relatively better or worse and therefore by how much a process can be improved, practice benchmarking is important in understanding *how* the process can be improved. There are also dangers with this approach. Practice benchmarking can easily fall into the trap of 'industrial tourism'. Industrial tourism occurs when managers enjoy the activity of finding, going to and looking at other processes and operations but those experiences do not lead to improvements. The simple test of the value of benchmarking is whether it leads to improvement. One of the ways in which organisations can avoid the pitfalls associated with both metric and practice benchmarking is in adopting the correct sequencing of the two activities. We would recommend that organisations first undertake practice benchmarking to obtain an understanding of other processes and to benefit from quick gains, and then follow this with metric benchmarking once a relationship and mutual benefits have been obtained.

Practice benchmarking can take many forms. At its most simple, it involves visits to other organisations providing opportunities to observe practice that might be useful in the home context. Such visits are often mediated via clubs and benchmarking organisations. In some ways the quality award schemes operate as benchmarking clubs (see Section 14.6).

14.4.4 Process benchmarking

Benchmarking can happen at the level of an organisation, function or process. One organisation could compare its sales figures or its return on equity, for example, with another. However, at this level there are so many factors influencing the figures that it can be extremely difficult to learn anything from comparisons, except that you are better or worse than the benchmark organisation. Benchmarking at a lower level, such as the function, or better still an individual process, usually enables more learning to take place. One function might compare its absentee statistics with another and ask the question why is one better? What can be learned? At a process level you might compare your speed of service or customer satisfaction with others' and then visit and test those processes to try to understand why they perform better and what you might need to do to improve.

We would recommend benchmarking at a process level, and part of the interest here is in finding a process with similar characteristics though different in application, technology etc. For example SouthWest Airlines, a low-cost airline in the USA, wanted to improve its turnaround times at the airport, to help keep costs low. Instead of comparing itself against other airlines, among which it was already one of the fastest, it compared its practices to Formula One pit stops. By developing ideas found in Formula One the airline was able to make significant time savings.

14.4.5 Levels of benchmarking

Both metric and practice benchmarking can take place at different levels:

- internal – between processes within the same organisation
- competitor/peer – external organisations in the same or similar markets, or providing similar services
- non-competitor – external organisations that don't compete in the same market, or provide similar services.

Internal benchmarking

In larger organisations there are many opportunities for learning from comparing internal operations. These can be wonderful opportunities to share best practice. Some organisations actually formalise the process whereby high-performance units become exemplars or practice leaders for given areas of activity. The approach can have its disadvantages, however. For example, in the UK National Health Service becoming a practice exemplar can be problematic as it generates a considerable administrative burden associated with visits from other parts of the service who want to learn from you. The additional scrutiny can be stressful for service staff too. This reservation aside, sharing of practice at the level of informal visits and 'practice development clubs' or similar seems, in our experience, to work very well.

Competitor/peer benchmarking

Competitive benchmarking can be carried out with or without the participation of the benchmark organisation. Information about the benchmark organisation can be gathered from public domain sources, academic sources, purchased market research reports etc. We would not recommend it, but some organisations engage the services of specialist investigators to gather benchmarking information. It continues to surprise us, however, how often leading players in an industry are willing to allow competitors access to their processes. Perhaps this confidence is one important aspect of being a leader in any area of human activity. Market-leading service organisations know full well that the process they expose to competitors today will soon be superseded by a better one – theirs! One of the organisations discussed elsewhere in this book is Singapore Airlines. Singapore Airlines famously exposes a great deal of what would be considered proprietary in other organisations. They know that by the time other organisations benchmark, and improve to reach their benchmarks, they themselves will have moved on.

So which peers/competitors should one choose for benchmarking? The question of who is best in the industry is usually straightforward to answer. Customer surveys, the information derived from customer advocacy group reports and so on should reveal the top-scoring service organisations. What is often more interesting in the context of benchmarking is the criteria used to assess organisations. These criteria provide a ready-made suite of outcome benchmarks. One caveat, however: it is dangerous to assume that consumer associations, consumer advocacy groups and so on have designed their assessment criteria after talking to consumers. So it might be useful for the benchmarking organisation to make an independent assessment of what consumers actually value.

Case Example 14.1 — The benchmark that nobody wants!

Consumer groups can help benchmarking organisations identify the best services. However, the downside (or upside, depending on your perspective) is that they also identify the worst! Consumer affairs blog 'The Consumerist' has an annual award for the worst performing services in the USA, the 'Worst Company in America Award' (see http://consumerist.com/2009/05/how-to-deliver-aigs-golden-poo-trophy.html if you want to see the actual award). Past winners of the award and its 'Golden Poo' trophy include BP, Comcast, AIG and the RIAA.

Another issue to consider when looking at public domain league tables is impartiality, or the lack of it. League tables are often sponsored by a 'player' in the industry. So it would be quite easy to respond to a customer league table that is in fact a set of benchmarks established to show a particular sponsoring organisation in a good light.

Non-competitor benchmarking

Finding organisations that don't compete or indeed provide similar services, but employ similar functions, such as HR, or similar processes, such as invoicing, can provide some novel opportunities for learning. Looking at such organisations doesn't limit innovations and ideas to those already in the industry but stimulates creativity and learning from different environments. For example, many services have a great deal to learn from manufacturing organisations. Processes are processes. Manufacturing organisations have been formally engaged in process optimisation for about a century now. If the service organisation can identify processes that have a structural similarity to a process in a manufacturing organisation, then there is no reason why benchmarking and learning cannot take place. Additionally, the service organisation is unlikely to be competing directly with the manufacturing benchmark organisation, so collaborative benchmarking is more likely. There is also much potential to engineer creative connections for learning from organisations engaged in completely unrelated activity, such as the Formula One example discussed earlier.

Case Example 14.2 on the National Basketball Association illustrates examples of each of the three types of benchmarking, as well as metric benchmarking. The study essentially begins with metric benchmarking using public-domain information, but then builds up the analysis to ask questions about practice comparisons.

Case Example 14.2 | Benchmarking the NBA: bouncing accepted wisdom

A few years ago Mahmoud M. Nourayi carried out a benchmarking study of National Basketball Association (NBA) games over three basketball seasons. The study looked at both output metrics (progression to the playoffs) and practice (player and team behaviour on the field) in teams that reached the NBA playoffs and those that did not. A key finding of the study was that the top-performing teams were effective not just because they played better overall, but because at team and individual level they engaged in different practices than teams that performed less well. The utility of the study was that teams wishing to improve could address specific behaviours on the field, and also 'import' appropriate behaviours via different recruiting practices.

The top performing teams in the study had a significantly larger number of field goals made (FGM) in spite of the fact that they took fewer field goal attempts (FGA). This ratio suggested greater efficiency in the use of FGAs, mainly by better shot-selection. Top-performing teams also took advantage of extra free throws awarded to them and made (successfully scored points from) a significantly larger number of free throws than their opponents. However, the free throw percentage (FT%) did not appear to be significantly different. (Conventional wisdom in basketball is that the more a team attacks the basket the larger the number of free throw attempts.) Furthermore, top-performing teams took advantage of their FGAs by attempting and making a larger number of three-point field goals. (A three-point

Source: Getty Images

field goal is a field goal made from beyond the three-point line, a designated arc radiating from the basket.)

A rebound is the act of successfully gaining possession of the basketball after a missed field goal or free throw. Rebounds in basketball are a routine, as possession changes after a shot is successfully made. There are two categories of rebound: 'offensive rebounds', in which the ball is recovered by the offensive side and does not change possession, and 'defensive rebounds', in which the defending team gains possession. One might reasonably expect the team with more *missed* shots to get more opportunities to grab offensive rebounds. Therefore, a larger number of offensive rebounds is not necessarily associated with wins. However, top-performing teams had a definite advantage on *defensive* boards (a turnover that does not result in a dead ball) in that they had a significantly larger number of defensive rebounds.

Shot selection is usually influenced by the team's point guard(s) who may be credited with 'assists' for the field goals made. (An assist is when player A passes the ball to player B and player B makes the shot in a short time, resulting in player A getting an assist.) The study showed that that top-performing teams have a larger number of assists.

A team's point guard is generally the person on the court who moves the ball. Therefore, his ability to maintain possession of the ball and his ball-handling skills seem critical for success of the team. This study demonstrated that the number of assists and turnover (lost possession) are critical variables. Top-performing teams have larger assist to turnover ratio.

Top-performing teams were better in defence too. In addition to the superior defensive rebounding, top-performing teams had a better shot-blocking skill and a larger number of 'steals'. (A steal happens when a defensive player legally causes a turnover.) Winning teams had fewer offensive rebounds. Offensive rebounding did not appear as important for teams that played efficiently and made good shot-selection decisions. The results highlighted the value of a good defensive posture, particularly defensive rebounding that reduces the second shot opportunity (an additional chance after missing the first shot) for the opponent.

The fact that a team has more free-throw opportunity is reflective of the number of personal fouls committed by the players of the other team. It is conventional wisdom that players who are in foul trouble (in danger of fouling out of a game) tend to become more hesitant in defence because they fear reduced playing time. This condition provides the opposing team with a higher percentage shots, hence better field goal percentage (FG%).

This study was interesting in that it made use of public domain data on basketball. The study was detailed, but its logic was not particularly complex. The results suggested in general that, amongst other things, 'calmness', accuracy and precision are critical team characteristics. More to the point, the levers of control that could modify these characteristics were available to teams regardless of their relative wealth. Better performance was not just down to money! Thus is demonstrated the considerable power of a relatively simple tool.

Source: This illustration was compiled using information from an article by Mahmoud M. Nourayi (2006), 'Profitability in Professional Sports and Benchmarking: The Case of NBA Franchises', *Benchmarking: An International Journal* 13 (3) 252–271.

14.5 How do organisations go about benchmarking?

A great deal of the benchmarking literature focuses on the benchmarking process. The models capturing how organisations go about benchmarking vary in complexity. The models involve numbers of stages from 8, through 14, to as many as 33![1] Even a cursory look at these models reveals a great deal of commonality, so we have distilled them into a simple five-step model as shown in Figure 14.3.

14.5.1 Plan

Benchmarking needs to be part of a plan, not just a plan for benchmarking, but a broader plan for improvement. Even before the benchmarking activity begins it is wise to at least sketch out the improvement activity that will result. The alternative is ad hoc and undirected improvement activity.

Define objectives

It is essential to undertake benchmarking with clear objectives. It should be a 'given' that we carry out benchmarking in order to improve; improve particular processes or aspects of the service provided. If benchmarking is to encourage change, then we need to understand the nature of the change.

The nature of required change is in part determined by the organisation's strategy. However, strategy is usually articulated in very 'high-level' or overarching terms. Benchmarking is a specific and detailed improvement instrument, so there needs to be some translation from strategy to short- and medium-term operational priorities. Strategy is about where we are going long-term and in broad terms how. Benchmarking requires that we spell out something of what we are trying to do to meet this long-term objective. So we need to articulate specific short- to medium-term outcomes, and also process objectives that will result in these outcomes. Articulating strategy in this way is not easy, and can take some time. Does the organisation wish to pursue a strategy of lowest price, or highest quality, or speediest delivery, or most able to customise? While all of these might be desirable at once, there is a need to concentrate on specific performance criteria to be improved. This then provides clear objectives for the benchmarking activity and also limits the type of organisations that might be chosen as benchmarking targets.

Rates of change

Given that the organisation needs to change, it should think about the rate of change required. It is useful to think about threshold levels of change; closing some performance gaps might be

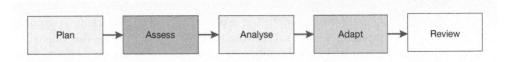

Figure 14.3 Key steps in the benchmarking process

essential in making the service organisation a 'player'. Other changes can take place over longer timescales. Remember that the improvement activity may require considerable resources. Ploughing such resources into rapid change may actually damage some other performance objectives! The rate of change required might also determine the type of benchmarking activity. The desire for continuous and incremental improvements might only require internal benchmarking. For radical step-changes in performance one might expect to use external benchmarks.

Follow through

As is the case with most business research activity, the value of the data derived from benchmarking diminishes over time. This happens for two reasons: firstly the organisation changes, as does its environment and its competition. Secondly, service managers and staff can actually get fired up by the benchmarking activity; they can become excited about very good performance, and also can become determined to close the gaps. If this enthusiasm is not exploited quickly by allocation of resources then managers and staff will see the benchmarking activity as a waste of their time. This aspect of benchmarking is no different from other improvement activity. Maintaining momentum is very important.

The benchmarking team

Much of the data of benchmarking is technical, especially numbers: numbers in spreadsheets, in surveys, customer reports and so on. However, benchmarking is carried out by, analysed by and acted upon by human beings. The benchmarking team needs to consist of experienced managers who can observe without being confused by the complexity and chaos of real-life operational environments. Depending on the nature of the benchmark organisation the team will either need to be such that it has specific expertise about the target, or perhaps more general capabilities. The benchmarking objective defines the team and its structure. Another important aspect of the benchmarking team is continuity. Ultimately the benchmarking team will be creating a set of stretch targets and process interventions. If these are handed to a completely different set of people to implement, then the lack of ownership of both targets and interventions will be a problem. This suggests that the benchmarking team constitutes at least in part the group of managers who will implement process improvements.

Establish roles and responsibilities

Because of the wide variety of processes that could be benchmarked it is impossible to cover every role and responsibility within a benchmarking team. However, it is worth drawing attention to one key position. Benchmarking is a project and therefore needs a project manager. The project manager need not be the benchmarking team leader. Because of the need for inter- and intra-organisational connection, it is probably best to draw the project manager from the senior levels of the organisation. The benchmarking project manager needs to act as a point of contact for all parties involved in benchmarking including the benchmark organisations, and this role implies a high level of interpersonal skills. The project manager needs to manage diaries, schedule the project itself, and facilitate meetings, visits, and so on. Such work requires a considerable amount of managerial time. This time can be resourced internally, but it is also worth considering using an external consultant. The consultant could be expert in the fundamentals of benchmarking but would need to work with local managers for specific context knowledge.

Identify the processes/services for improvement

While benchmarking can take place at an organisational level, i.e. a comparison of key performance measures such as profit, share price and turnover, benchmarking is usually, and most profitably, applied at a process level. Benchmarking at an organisational level has a meaning for external agencies such as investors, groups that might assess the service organisation, and possibly customers. Certainly customers would like to know who's the best in the field at the performance objectives of interest to them. The problem is that customers rarely trust benchmarking carried out by the players in an industry. So organisational benchmarking is best carried out by independent parties such as consumer quality/advocacy groups. While not completely independent, these groups are more likely to be trusted by customers.

In benchmarking processes, the process chosen should be one that will have an impact on the desired objectives. Key activities at this stage include:

- selecting an appropriate process
- defining the process and its objectives
- mapping the process
- assessing the process
- identifying and defining all the measures and targets used
- assessing the measures and targets
- determining current performance and practices
- involving the people who are involved in the process.

The definition of the process for the purposes of benchmarking can sometimes be difficult. For example, consider the case of a forensics laboratory. Clearly the laboratory will provide professional services to the police, the coroner's office and possibly other parties too. However, within this professional service environment there exists a 'factory' process in which a tangible product, the sample, is converted to information. In the competitive environment of forensic services it is the benchmark measures associated with service effectiveness (the outcomes) that are of primary interest to the investors in, and purchasers of, the laboratory service. However, the managers of the forensics laboratory will have little scope for intervention or improvement at the level of these outcomes. Most meaningful intervention will take place at the level of the back-office process. So in this context it would be useful to deconstruct the service and redefine it. For example, if we look at the flows through the forensic service we can identify an 'information product' as the standard unit of 'production' flowing through the service. We can then define performance objectives, measures and benchmarking targets with respect to this process.[2]

14.5.2 Assess

There are several ways of going about benchmarking. Benchmarking may involve a one-to-one relationship between two organisations or possibly two particular departments. Alternatively, benchmarking data and 'round-table' discussions may be facilitated by a third party, such as a benchmarking group. Around the world, various industry bodies have set up a range of service benchmarking surveys, groups and clubs. Benchmarking could be carried out under the umbrella of a large-scale assessment activity using, for example, one of the many nationally-based schemes for improving quality, service or customer satisfaction. Participation in such schemes enables the benchmarking organisation's performance to be compared with many other organisations. Ideally the comparison stimulates questions that will lead to changes in practice.

Define selection criteria for partners

The type of organisations selected for benchmarking will in part be determined by the level of benchmarking selected and the performance objectives for that particular process. For best-in-field benchmarking it is important to think creatively and to move away from traditional sources of comparison to seek out truly different and challenging good performance.

Identify potential win-wins

It should be remembered that benchmarking is not a one-way activity and that both partners can and should gain a great deal from it. Indeed it is through benefits going both ways that a benchmarking activity will stay alive and purposeful. Some key points for dealing with benchmark partners are the following:

- look for mutually beneficial outcomes
- start with practice benchmarking
- discuss objectives with partners to ensure there is comparability, or at least no conflict
- help, or encourage, the partner organisation to develop and maintain a process focus
- set up regular meetings to discuss practice and methods of improvement
- evaluate relative performance through joint definition and agreement of measures and performance levels
- focus on improvement.

14.5.3 Analyse

Compare performance data

The first step within the analysis phase of benchmarking will be that of making comparisons and assessing differences. 'Assessing differences' refers to the need to move from the passive to the active in benchmarking. If there are differences in the level of outcomes, are these explained at the level of process, or perhaps by external factors? In other words, use the benchmarking data to ask **why**?

Compare practices

Does the answer to the question about different levels of performance have an answer in the processes of the benchmark organisation? If so, is there something that the benchmarking organisation could do differently, at the level of process, that would close performance gaps? Process comparisons usually require a high degree of technical familiarity, which is one of the reasons why benchmarking cannot be carried out by consultants alone.

Identify outstanding practices – what do they do?

Like any business activity, benchmarking is time-constrained. Some practices in the benchmark organisation will stand out above others. In prioritising the interventions that should result from benchmarking, and to an extent the data capture and analysis of benchmarking itself, organisations should pay attention to those practices that seem particularly effective in realising exceptional business results. The fact that a practice is 'outstanding' does not mean that it will be transferable, but with experienced managers in the benchmarking team it should be easy to spot quick-win opportunities.

Identify process enablers – how do they do it?

Underlying outstanding practice involves a plethora of enablers at the level of process, staffing, management, culture . . . and so on. Some of these enablers may be transferable, some may not. An important aspect of the analysis task is identifying which of the process enablers has to be transferred along with the practice. In a way, the work of the benchmarking team is much like that of plant chemists who try to extract the suite of active components from complex, naturally occurring sources such as plants and animals. Sometimes it is difficult to isolate a single active chemical. The same is true of organisations.

14.5.4 Adapt

'Adapt not adopt': the phrase is as much a warning as it is an activity. Specific solutions adopted by the benchmark organisation cannot be naively adopted by the benchmarking organisation. Solutions are the product of a multiplicity of factors in the benchmark organisation.

'Copy pasting' a specific solution from one organisation into another is a recipe for disaster. Instead, organisations need to think intelligently about what ideas and innovations to bring from one organisation to another. This is actually quite a tricky thing to do. It usually involves some abstraction from the observation of the specific solution to a set of general principles and then the application of set principles in the benchmarking organisation. In our experience, naive application of solutions as opposed to principles is one of the most common reasons for benchmarking failure.

Set targets for improvement

The existence of a 'gap' between the benchmarking measure or target within the benchmarking organisation and the benchmark organisation does not by itself define a stretch target. Stretch targets have to be actively developed by the benchmarking organisation. The stretch target will be informed by the benchmarking data but also by other factors such as capability, available resources, time pressures, decisions about focus and strategy, and so on.

Identify and challenge current rules/assumptions

While it is sensible to warn potential benchmarking organisations about transferability, it is also worth highlighting the problem of 'not invented here'. This is the resistance to practice that is not rational, but derives from prejudice about the origin of the new practice, process etc. Such resistance is subtle, and can be quite pervasive. Careful selection of the benchmarking team is obviously one counter to the problem. Probably more useful is to ensure that the managers who will drive interventions in response to benchmarking are fully engaged with, and ideally involved in, the benchmarking process itself.

Redesign and implement new processes

The information on processes and process enablers within the benchmark organisation is just a starting point. The information does not, by itself, spell out a blueprint for a new process. The information has to be adapted into a new process within the benchmarking organisation. This means that a core element of 'adapting' is process design, or redesign. Redesign implies a need to respect and accommodate existing routines and processes.

14.5.5 Review

Finally, we come to the 'meta-benchmarking' activity. Benchmarking is not a one-off; if it is working for us we need to do more of it and possibly do it a little better. If the results did not achieve the objectives then we need to know why, and do things differently next time.

The tasks described earlier are often intricate and challenging. It is therefore easy to see how the overall objective of improvement might be missed; so much time and effort is involved in the actual process of benchmarking. This fifth stage of benchmarking is therefore critical: benchmarking of benchmarking! We need to have performance measures in place to assess the benchmarking activity itself, and these measures should clearly track improvement.

When benchmarking is undertaken, success is not guaranteed. Indeed benchmarking can be a very slow and costly activity. It requires a culture that supports learning and improvement, together with the necessary investment and allocation of staff to undertake the work.

The UK school performance or 'league' tables described in Case Example 14.3 highlight some of the problems associated with providing comparative performance data, and bring into question the benefits of this activity. This example also illustrates the trade-off between the cost of developing an ever more complex measurement regime and the need to create a measure that gives a 'good enough' indication of school performance. The league tables are used by a number of different stakeholders with different requirements, and this increases the complexity of the instrument.

Case Example 14.3 | School performance tables

Since 1996 the UK Government's Department for Education has published performance tables for schools. Tables for secondary schools present statistics on such things as examination performance and the extent of unauthorised absence. These tables appear to be very useful for parents wishing to find out which school to send their child to, rather than having to rely on a school's reputation in the area or trying to make a judgement based solely on meeting the headteacher.

Source: Shutterstock.com/Laurence Gough

One of the prime measures for a school teaching 16-year-olds (students who have reached the school leaving age), is the percentage of students achieving good grades in nationally recognised qualifications such as the General Certificate of Secondary Education (GCSE). Performance statistics are produced for each school, showing the trend in its achievement for recent years, its position against other schools in the same local education authority, and comparison with national statistics.

These statistics have great appeal for government ministers, not least because the current tables at national level show a continuing rise in the percentage of students achieving good GCSE grades. It is clear, however, that not everyone is happy with these tables. In an article published on BBC News Online in 1998, Dr Keith Devlin of St Mary's College, California, said that it was very dangerous to take numbers developed to deal with the inanimate world and apply them to the world of people with all of their imprecision and unpredictability.

The need to be aware of the impact of chance is confirmed by others. Professor Ted Wragg of Exeter University, also reported by BBC News, suggested that there were not enough children in the individual schools to make the figures statistically significant, although clearly the national statistics are not a problem. A senior teacher commented that schools that are in prosperous catchment areas perform relatively consistently, but those in poorer areas seem to oscillate, having alternate good and bad years. He said that this 'yo-yo' effect can be very demoralising to staff who feel that they are judged on statistics that, to some extent, may be outside their control.

Some teachers feel that the statistics may be positively dangerous. This may be in part due to the reluctance of professionals to be measured by an external agency, but teachers are also concerned that reducing the performance of a school to a limited set of statistics may mislead parents. The figures, for example, do not demonstrate how well the school has developed the gifted student, the one who would perform well in almost any circumstance, nor do they indicate whether genuine learning has taken place as opposed to good preparation for examinations.

There is also concern that the statistics may be used to remove underperforming teachers, using information which could be flawed. As a result, some teachers spend time ensuring that their figures are presented in the best possible light, knowing that unhelpful conclusions may be drawn if the school is seen to be failing using this set of statistics. There is frustration that so much emphasis is placed upon school performance tables, particularly since they do not appear to present a fair and rounded picture of the school.

Because of the importance placed by the British government on demonstrating increasing levels of student achievement, school league tables have not been abandoned, but the criteria for assessment have been gradually refined in the attempt to provide a fairer measure of success. The value-added measure was introduced some time ago, comparing the success of 16-year-olds with a peer group of those who had similar performance standards at age 11 years.

In 2007 a further refinement was introduced, Contextual Value Added (CVA). This measure incorporates nine coefficients intended to adjust performance based on the circumstances of schools. These include gender, ethnicity, and a range of social factors relating to the deprivation of the school's location. A predicted score is based on prior attainment, adjusted by background. The CVA score is the difference between predicted score and actual performance.

Critics of the CVA suggest that it doesn't remove the temptation to put pressure on individual students and that the new system is so complicated that parents and other interested parties will not understand what the measures mean.

Source: This illustration was compiled from information from www.news.bbc.co.uk and http://www.education.gov.uk/performancetables/ and from interviews with teachers.

14.6 How can quality awards and academic studies help with benchmarking?

14.6.1 Quality awards

Many organisations have been inspired to improve their performance through the use of quality awards. There are awards for quality in many countries, supported by local quality foundations or governments that recognise outstanding organisations, examples being the European EFQM Excellence Award and, in the USA, the Malcolm Baldrige National Quality Award. The European Foundation for Quality Management (EFQM) was founded in 1988 by the presidents of fourteen major European companies, with the endorsement of the European Commission. The EFQM Excellence Awards are presented to organisations that demonstrate excellence in the management of quality as their fundamental process for continuous improvement.

The quality awards are usually based on generic cause–effect models showing some of the key linkages between operations decisions and business performance (see Chapter 17). Most schemes require that the participating organisations provide evidence of a structured and sustainable approach to improvement covering aspects such as leadership, vision and values, customer understanding, people management, systems, practices, procedures and results.

The schemes entail several stages, for example the completion of a self-assessment tool, the comparison of performance against other organisations in the database and then some form of independent assessment and feedback. Some organisations use the self-assessment tool to help drive improvement with no intention of competing for the award. It is the 'comparison' aspect of the schemes that makes them in some ways 'ready-made' benchmarking instruments. However, these instruments should be used with care.

Earlier in this chapter we talked about the dangers of metric benchmarking. In some respects, this danger surfaces again when organisations participate in the various quality award schemes. The generic strategies and the specific advice on process improvements, interventions and so on are derived from large-scale observations of behaviour and business results – in other words, correlation exercises. So we have, in essence, many observations of practice that lead to high levels of performance. These are aggregated into generic relationships. The relationships do not describe actual causal connections, but they are nearly always misinterpreted as such. The 'philosophical' basis of the quality award schemes is that if this practice is imported into the benchmarking organisation it will similarly result in high levels of performance. The reality is that the copying of a particular aspect of practice will result, across a sample of organisations, in quite a large distribution of performance. The reason for this difference is context. Context is everything, and the importance of context is reflected in our exhortation to 'adapt not adopt'.

In some ways, taking the generic advice of a quality award scheme is less damaging than metric benchmarking. This is because of the smoothing effect of statistical aggregation at the level of practice. The benchmarking organisation is less likely to be seduced into adopting extremes of practice. So which organisations should engage with quality award schemes? If levels of performance are very, very low, then the organisation has little to lose and needs all the help it can get. Generic advice and generic benchmarks are probably appropriate for organisations in this domain. However, where performance is already good, organisations can make informed judgements about both what they are trying to do and the benchmark targets they should use as aspirations.

14.6.2 Academic studies

Large-scale academic studies (for example 'Service Competitiveness'[3] and 'Service Probe'[4]) can provide a useful source of benchmarking information. Such studies are not useful for direct benchmarking, as organisations are required to engage with the study from its outset. However, the comparison criteria in the studies are a good source of benchmarking measures. In terms of dynamic benchmarking, large-scale studies can also be a good source of information on trends; in other words a source of the performance criteria that are becoming important to consumers.

Some studies may not be entitled 'benchmarking' or the like. Many industry studies that could usefully inform the contextual basis of a benchmarking study appear in the academic journals relating to service management. Typically there are about three such studies over an average year in the life of the journals. For example, a 2010 paper about servitisation[5] contained a wealth of information on what constituted servitisation. However, in the context of benchmarking, the study provided a wealth of information about what service elements are valued by customers of manufacturing services. In other words the paper provided a ready-made metric for servitisation.

Another study, this time in industrial services, was carried out by Vanumamalai Kannan. In his 2010 paper[6] he ranked 48 performance metrics valued by customers for ocean container shipping services. The study also illustrated the complexity of benchmarking B2B services, where customers' purchase decision-making is the result of a multivariate analysis carried out intuitively by shippers. Both studies derived measures that could have been derived by benchmarking teams. However, what the studies do provide is a feel for the relative importance of benchmarking measures, and they obviously provide a shortcut.

14.7 Summary

What is benchmarking?

- Benchmarking is the activity whereby a measure or target of a process or some other aspect of an organisation or operation is compared with a similar aspect of another organisation or operation in order to learn and improve performance.

How can benchmarking help organisations improve their performance?

- Benchmarking can help managers:
  1 assess how well the benchmarking organisation is performing compared to a benchmark organisation
  2 set realistic performance targets
  3 search out new ideas and practices
  4 stimulate creativity and performance innovation, and
  5 drive improvement through an organisation.

What are the different types of benchmarking?

- Metric benchmarking is the process of collecting some of the measures and targets used by other operations and comparing them to your own performance.
- Practice benchmarking is an attempt to search out new ideas and practices and stimulate creativity and performance innovation in order to learn and improve performance.

- Both metric and practice benchmarking can take place at different levels within the target organisation:
  - o internal – between processes within the same organisation
  - o competitor/peer – external organisations in the same or similar markets, or providing similar services
  - o non-competitor – external organisations that don't compete in the same market or provide similar services.

How do organisations go about benchmarking?

- The key steps in the benchmarking process include:
  - o plan
  - o assess
  - o analyse
  - o adapt, and
  - o review.

How can quality awards and academic studies help with benchmarking?

- Quality awards are usually based on generic cause–effect models and usually require the participating organisations to provide evidence of a structured and sustainable approach to improvement covering aspects such as leadership, vision and values, customer understanding, people management, systems, practices, procedures and results.
- Large-scale academic studies can provide a useful source of information on benchmarking and industry trends.

14.8   Discussion questions

1 Select a process you are involved in, such as being taught, cooking, cleaning etc. What might be the benefits of benchmarking this process and with whom could you compare your performance? How would this lead to the benefits identified?

2 What are the downsides of benchmarking?

3 Obtain information on one of the quality award schemes and assess how effective you think it is.

14.9   Questions for managers

1 Select one of your processes. What might be the benefits of benchmarking this process and with whom could you compare your performance? How would this lead to the benefits identified?

2 Can you identify best practice within your organisation and how could it be shared? And what would be the implications?

3 What would be the advantages and disadvantages of you entering an award scheme?

Mumbai Private Bank

'We are doing well but we cannot afford to be complacent', said Khalid Ahmed, the Chief Operating Officer with Mumbai Private Bank (MPB) in India. 'To keep us on our toes and help us keep improving what we do I think we need to benchmark ourselves against other organisations. Though the problems are which measures do we use and which organisations should we benchmark ourselves against?'

With a head office in Mumbai and 98 branches in most of the larger cities across India, MPB has assets in excess of 900 billion rupees (£13bn) and employs around 3,000 staff. The Bank specialises in providing a top-quality service to higher income earners with a range of savings, investments and loan products. It offers its customers ease of access and convenience and provides specialist sales and service teams who ensure that the highest levels of customer service are provided by phone, post and internet and in person.

Khalid explained how the bank has been trying to develop its performance measurement systems.

We are currently using the balanced scorecard to help us develop our measures and improvement activities. We have found, maybe not surprisingly, that we have quite a lot of financial and market measures, the results, but that we are less good at measuring the enablers, some of the operational and development aspects.

We obviously have a lot of information in terms of volumes about all of our products; mortgages, savings and investments, and details of all money flows on a daily basis – all the day-to-day measures needed for running such a business. We use these performance measures to compare the activities of our various branches. We also have lots of measures of 'competitiveness' and we send monthly returns to the Indian Banks' Association and they provide some broad statistics comparing us to other banks. We do measure customer satisfaction and employee satisfaction but maybe not in a particularly sophisticated way, though we are working on this at the moment.

We want to do some benchmarking to see how we can improve what we are doing and also to try to ensure that what we do is adding value for our customers and other stakeholders. Should we look, for example, at some of the co-operative banks, such as Bombay Mercantile Co-operative Bank, which are often local banks focused on personal service, or the State Bank of India, the largest and oldest bank in India, or Coutts bank in the UK (which also focuses on high earners), or international banks such as HSBC . . . or Oberoi Hotels, or Singapore Airlines? I don't want us to waste our time creating measures for the sake of measuring things. I want us to choose things that will help us improve and know how far in front or behind we are.

Questions

1 What is the purpose of benchmarking?

2 What advice would you give to Khalid Ahmed?

Suggested further reading

Camp, Robert C. (2007), *Business Process Benchmarking: Finding and Implementing Best Practices*, ASQC Quality Press, Milwaukee, Wisconsin

Duffy, Jo Ann M., James Fitzsimmons and Nikhil Jain (2006), 'Identifying and Studying "Best-performing" Services: An Application of DEA to Long-term Care', *Benchmarking: An International Journal* 13 (3) 232–251

Koller, Monika and Thomas Salzberger (2009), 'Benchmarking in Service Marketing: A Longitudinal Analysis of the Customer', *Benchmarking: An International Journal* 16 (3) 401–414

Lambert, Thomas E., Hokey Min and Arun K. Srinivasan (2009), 'Benchmarking and Measuring the Comparative Efficiency of Emergency Medical Services in Major US Cities', *Benchmarking: An International Journal* 16 (4) 543–561

Levenburg, Nancy M. (2006), 'Benchmarking Customer Service on the Internet: Best Practices from Family Businesses', *Benchmarking: An International Journal* 13 (3) 355–373

Meyer, Anton, Richard Chase, Aleda Roth, Chris Voss, Klaus-Ulrich Sperl, Larry Menor and Kate Blackmon (1999), 'Service Competitiveness: An International Benchmarking

Comparison of Service Practice and Performance in Germany, UK and USA', *International Journal of Service Industry Management* 10 (4) 369–379

Mora-Monge, Carlo A., Arash Azadegan and Marvin E. Gonzalez (2010), 'Assessing the Impact of Web-based Electronic Commerce Use on the Organizational Benefits of a Firm: An Empirical Study', *Benchmarking: An International Journal* 17 (6) 773–790

Useful web links

A UK network organisation that undertakes benchmarking for its members:
www.customernet.com

EFQM is an organisation that encourages business leaders to share knowledge, experiences and good practice:
www.efqm.org/

A very thorough guide to online competitor benchmarking by Danyl Bosomworth of smart-insights.com at:
www.smartinsights.com—are-you-benchmarking-against-competitors-effectively

Benchmarking the benchmarkers – no-one escapes comparison! Here is a short essay comparing the comparison sites by Rhian Nicholson of MSN Money:
money.uk.msn.com—articles.aspx

Benchmarking education: the UK government's performance tables for primary and secondary education:
www.education.gov.uk/performancetables

Analysis of benchmarking data in sport: Steven Levitt – of Freakonomics fame – carried out a review of Sumo wrestling performance data to discover major corruption and match fixing. Read the original blog posts here:
www.freakonomics.com/2011/02/02/sumo-more-of-the-same

And another piece by David McNeill of the *Independent* showing that it's still going on:
www.independent.co.uk—thrown-open-the-dark-side-of-sumo-wrestling-2202618.html

Notes

1 See for example Anand, G. and Rambabu Kodali (2008), 'Benchmarking the Benchmarking Models', *Benchmarking: An International Journal* 15 (3) 257–291

2 Rynja, G. and D. Moy (2006), 'Laboratory Service Evaluation: Laboratory Product Model and the Supply Chain', *Benchmarking: An International Journal* 13 (3) 324–336

3 Meyer, Anton, Richard Chase, Aleda Roth, Chris Voss, Klaus-Ulrich Sperl, Larry Menor and Kate Blackmon (1999), 'Service Competitiveness: An International Benchmarking Comparison of Service Practice and Performance in Germany, UK and USA', *International Journal of Service Industry Management* 10 (4) 369–379

4 Search for 'Service Probe' at http://www.cbi.org.uk/

5 Gebauer, Heiko, Bo Edvardsson, Anders Gustafsson and Lars Witell (2010), 'Match or Mismatch: Strategy-Structure Configurations in the Service Business of Manufacturing Companies', *Journal of Service Research* 13 (May) 198–215

6 Kannan, Vanumamalai (2010), 'Benchmarking the Service Quality of Ocean Container Carriers Using AHP', *Benchmarking: An International Journal* 17 (5) 637–656.

Part 6 Implement

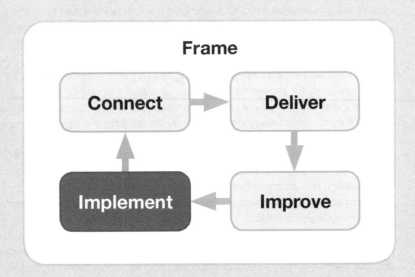

Chapter 15
Creating and implementing the strategy

Chapter objectives

This chapter is about how to create and implement an organisation's service strategy.

- What is a service strategy?
- How can service provide a competitive advantage?
- How can managers turn performance objectives into operations priorities?
- How can strategy be formulated and developed?
- How can a strategy be sustained?

15.1 Introduction

All great service companies have a clear and compelling service strategy. This gives them a 'reason for being' which energises the organisation and defines the service concept and how it will be delivered.[1] If there is a clear strategy, managers know which initiatives to approve and which to reject, customers know what to expect, employees know what to provide and operations knows what it has to deliver and how it has to deliver it. If employees do not know what the organisation's strategy is, or each person has their own view, success is going to be hard to achieve.

A service strategy (or a manufacturing strategy) provides the intellectual frameworks and conceptual models that allow managers to identify opportunities for bringing value to customers[2] and for delivering that value at a profit or within budget. As we discussed in Chapter 2 the role for service operations managers is to help create and deliver that value by contributing to the strategy debate and by developing the operation, its resources, people and processes, to provide for the future success of the organisation.

A strategy is only as good as its implementation. The organisation needs to call on a wide range of abilities in order to create an effective strategy, from the visionary thinker at director level, through the interpretation of this strategy into policies and plans by senior and middle management, to the involvement in and ownership of service delivery by front-line staff. It is not the purpose of this book to describe the strategic process in detail. We are concerned with the creation, communication and implementation of strategy insofar as it has direct relevance to service delivery. In this sense, the three major components of strategy – market and competitive analysis, strategic choice, and implementation – are very important issues for the service operations manager.

What is a service strategy?

Research into strategy development suggests that effective strategies generally are evolutionary rather than revolutionary.[3] Although there is often refined strategic analysis embedded in strategic formulation, the real strategy evolves as internal decisions and external events combine to form a widely shared consensus for action among key members of the management team. Today, we would suggest that key contributors to strategy development must include those in constant contact with market requirements: the customer-facing staff.

These employees, often rather junior and poorly paid in many consumer services, have a key role in strategy development. They often have advance information as to customer likes and dislikes, and about the way that customers' tastes are changing. Crucially, these staff have the task of 'living the strategy'. If they are not committed to the goals and objectives of the organisation, it will be plain for all to see. The old adage that strategy should be 'top down and bottom up' has much to commend it.

15.2.1 Defining service strategy

Service organisations, like all businesses, need to have overarching strategies in place to try to prevent non-aligned and disjointed activities and decisions.[4] A strategy is usually seen in market terms as an organisation's plan to achieve an advantage over its competitors or simply to maintain its position in the marketplace. It is important to note that the language of 'strategy' is often expressed in 'competitive', for-profit, terms; however, many organisations operate in non-competitive situations. Such organisations may wish to ensure that they are able to adapt to their own changing environments, whether economic or political. Service strategy is therefore defined as the set of plans and policies by which a service organisation aims to meet its objectives.

15.2.2 Strategy: harnessing five elements

A strategic plan will harness the various aspects of an organisation and ensure that they support each other and are consistent with the objectives of the organisation. Five critical elements of strategy are the creation of corporate objectives, an understanding of the environment, the development of an appropriate service concept, the identification of appropriate operations performance objectives, and the development of an appropriate operation (see Figure 15.1).[5]

- *Corporate objectives.* These provide the targets or goals for the strategy. If a strategy is a set of plans or policies to meet objectives, there needs to be a statement of those objectives. In part the objectives provide the motivation for change, but they also set out the size and speed of change. Such a statement is an important step in making the change 'public' so that employees are made aware of what is expected of them. In essence the objectives set out the parameters for change.

- *Environment.* All organisations operate in a context and that environment needs to be understood to assess not only the opportunities that it might afford but also the likely response of other organisations and the reaction of customers to change.

- *Service concept.* This identifies the nature of the service (see Chapter 3). The service concept helps the organisation focus on the value that it can provide to customers.

- *Performance objectives.* These provide the means by which a strategy is translated into operations language, setting out the priorities for the operation. Together with the service concept they specify the task for operations (see Section 15.4).

- *Operation.* People, processes, structure, performance measurement systems, supply chains etc. – the operation – may have to be developed and changed to implement the strategy.

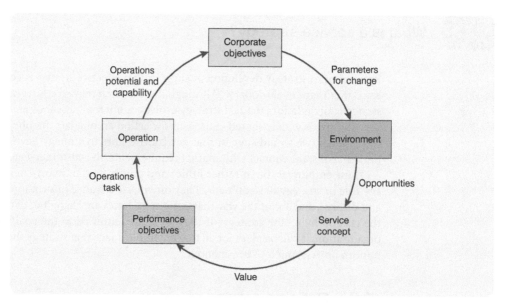

Figure 15.1 Key components of a strategy

(The strategy maps we covered in Chapter 9 are an important means of linking strategy to operations through appropriate performance measurement.) Also the operation may provide the impetus for change through its current, or potential, capability.

15.2.3 An iterative and continuous process

Strategy is an iterative process. The key components, objectives, environment, service concept, performance criteria and operations all need to be aligned in the delivery of service and the achievement of the strategic objectives. This requires a constant checking of all the elements to ensure that objectives can be met. Strategy formulation is therefore not a one-off activity. Organisations need to respond to the two main forces of change that operate upon them: the external and internal environments. As a result, a strategy requires continuous assessment and, if necessary, amendment.

15.2.4 Planned or emergent strategies

Strategies may be intended, formal and planned; alternatively, they may either emerge from an intended strategy that was not realised, or emerge independently of a formal planning process.[6] The creation of intended strategies tends to be a top-down approach, starting with either a statement of corporate objectives or an evaluation of the environment and market opportunities. Emergent strategies tend to be bottom-up processes, often starting with an idea for a new service concept or the emergence of new operational capabilities. Both types of approaches may be at work in successful organisations.

15.3   How can service provide a competitive advantage?

Many for-profit organisations, both manufacturing and service, recognise that by improving the service provided they can make significant and sustainable gains in the marketplace. Service and service delivery can be, and increasingly are, competitive weapons.

For manufacturing and product-oriented organisations, service may be an important means of differentiation, particularly if they are operating in markets where there is little product differentiation or where product development is slow, difficult, expensive or short-lived. The nature of the services available and the way in which services are delivered may provide a means to competitive success.

Service-oriented companies are also recognising that there may be a need to provide high levels of customer service. Increasing competition, declining sales and more service-aware customers are putting pressure on service organisations to rethink and improve the levels of service that they offer. The effects of good service on creating valuable customers, on increasing customer retention and loyalty, and on attracting other customers, as well as on the financial position of an organisation are important (see Chapter 17).

In addition, for organisations that compete on cost (or have an objective to reduce costs), service has a role to play in ensuring right-first-time service provision and low operational costs.

15.3.1 Competing on 'product' or experience

In Chapter 1 we defined service outcomes as the results for the customer of the service process and their experience, including 'products', benefits, emotions, judgements and intentions. The 'products' are the 'functional' output of the service provided, 'products' such as the food and drink provided by a restaurant, or the ability of a delegate on a training course to construct a spreadsheet, or the new heart for the heart operation patient. Some service organisations compete on their 'products' and others on the experience provided, while some manage to compete on both (see Figure 15.2).

As Figure 15.2 suggests, there are a number of positions that the service organisation may take up when compared with the competition. This analysis can also be applied by public sector and not-for-profit organisations, since they, too, are in a form of competition for resources. Civil service departments compete for a larger slice of the country's budget, and charities compete for donor funds.

The five positions suggested by Figure 15.2 are as follows:

- *Failing.* The organisations' 'products' are below industry specification, and their customer experience is poor. Traditional services that have failed to move with market trends find themselves in this position. Some years ago in the fast-food market Wimpy found that it was left behind by McDonald's in terms of higher food standards and faster service.

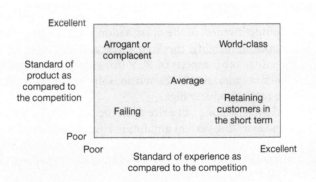

Figure 15.2 Competing on 'product' or experience

- *Arrogant or complacent.* In these organisations the 'product' is excellent, but the way that customers are treated is poor. Professional services sometimes fall into this category, being experienced as arrogant by their clients. They may well know better than their clients, and be the technical experts in their area, but this does not excuse service that can often be offensive. The medical profession often comes in for criticism in this area, dealing with patients not as human beings but rather as another condition to be treated.

- *Retaining customers in the short term.* It is possible to develop customer loyalty through a good experience. However, if the 'product' falls below standard, customers will only tolerate this for a relatively short period. If the service experience is excellent, the emotional switching costs are quite high for customers, but eventually they will leave. Some computer companies have used this strategy to retain customers in the period between phasing out an old product and launching a new one.

- *Average.* This is the position that many high-volume business-to-consumer services believe they occupy. In many of these traditional service sectors there are frequently a number of reasonably established competitors, all conducting business in a similar fashion. The consumer financial service sector in the UK was a good example, with several players and little to choose between them. As the competition has become more fierce, many have chosen to try to differentiate themselves through the way that they deal with their customers.

- *World-class.* These organisations are universally recognised as being the best in all that they do. There are few of these in existence.

Most large organisations will find that they can position their range of services at different points. Some may be world-class, while others are failing. It is important to distinguish between them because each will require a different strategic approach.

15.3.2 Understanding perceived user value

To understand how service or services can be used to create a competitive edge it is essential to understand what is regarded as important by customers. The notion of perceived user value (PUV) can be helpful here.[7] PUVs are the criteria regarded by customers as being important, and on which they will base their assessment of the organisation and its services. The PUVs for a supermarket chain might include stock availability, range of products, store location, etc. Figure 15.3 shows a comparison of PUVs for two supermarket chains.

The scores in brackets on Figure 15.3 denote the relative weighting that customers ascribe to each criterion. Therefore stock availability is weighted at 9/10 whereas checkout speed scores 5/10. This analysis allows the operations manager to determine priorities for action (see also Section 15.4.3) and also to know in what way operations contribute to the overall competitiveness of the organisation. Operations contribute directly to some aspects of PUV (stock availability, checkout speed and customer service advice) and may contribute indirectly to other aspects of PUV (for example, how the service is delivered may have an impact on brand image and the relationship formed with customers, which may facilitate feedback to revise product range).

By separating out price from the other PUVs we have a useful framework for identifying and assessing current and future strategies. This allows the possibility of competing by more than simply being cheaper or differentiated, i.e. competing in both ways (see Figure 15.4). The analysis from Figure 15.4 shows that Supermarket A is of similar size (depicted by the size of the circle) and strategic positioning (weighted average PUV) to Supermarket B. There is a smaller rival, C, which is perceived to be of higher quality but is very expensive. Likewise, D is the low-cost provider in this marketplace and is only slightly smaller than A and B.

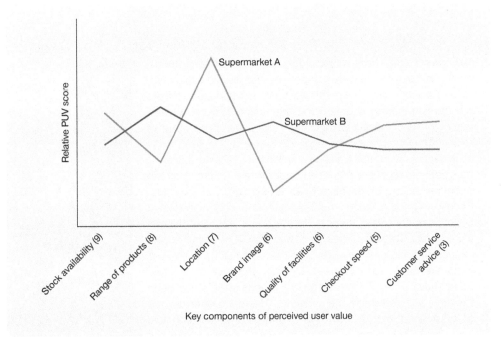

Figure 15.3 PUV criteria for two supermarket chains
Source: Adapted from Bowman, Cliff (1998), *Strategy in Practice*, Prentice Hall, London

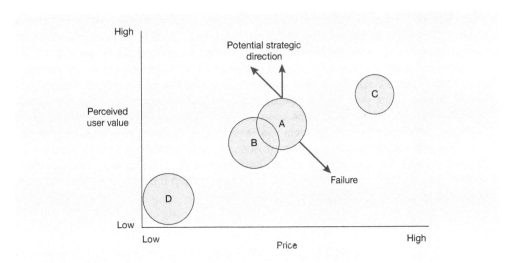

Figure 15.4 Perceived user value and price
Source: Adapted from Bowman, Cliff (1998), *Strategy in Practice*, Prentice Hall, London

The question to be addressed here is to understand which strategic direction to adopt. If A wishes to maintain the price position but wants to increase PUV, inspection of the analysis from Figure 15.3 will be a good starting point. Clearly, high stock availability and product range provide opportunities for enhancing PUV. If this strategy is adopted, operations can determine its contribution in terms of improving service standards without increasing operations cost. If the preferred strategy is to increase PUV and decrease price, then operations has a major task if the reduction in price is not simply to be achieved by reducing margins.

Case Example 15.1 | Telecorp

Telecorp is one of the major global suppliers of telecommunications equipment, with competitors that include Ericsson, Motorola and Nortel. The traditional business of these suppliers has been in the development and production of fixed network equipment – the switches that form the heart of a country's telecommunications structure.

In recent years the traditional business of these telecommunications suppliers has been under threat. Existing stable customer relationships have been broken up. For example, Ericsson, being a Swedish company, has been the preferred supplier to Swedish Telecom, in the same way that Alcatel would relate to France Telecom. In many countries the national telecommunications provider (for example, British Telecom in the UK) has been privatised, with the objective of injecting competitive forces into the industry. Alongside this has been the advent of mobile phone networks. These are often owned by companies that do not have a long history and technical expertise in the telecommunications market, and are operated for profit rather than public service.

Source: iStockphoto/Eimantas Buzas

These forces have combined to threaten Telecorp's profitability in its traditional business. Manufactured product margins have declined significantly, and in some cases have become non-existent. A possible strategy is to remain as a manufacturer in the 'commodity' area, and to become very lean in its operations, but Telecorp has chosen instead to develop services to be sold with its manufactured products and systems to help its new, relatively inexperienced, network customers operate more effectively.

While this general approach is agreed and seen as necessary by the senior management group, the interpretation of the vision to develop significant revenues has caused some discussion. There are two main viewpoints. The first view, largely held by those managers brought up in the fixed network environment, is that Telecorp should continue to be seen as an innovator of telecommunications (physical) products and systems, which also helps customers use Telecorp's products more effectively. The opposing viewpoint is that Telecorp should become a service provider, generating solutions for its customers. In this case, Telecorp should act as systems integrator utilising its own or competitors' products in the most appropriate combination. This second view is largely held by managers from the mobile network side, who have often been recruited from other industry sectors.

The next section develops the strategic positioning analysis from Section 15.3, using additional performance objectives and more detailed scales to identify operations priorities.

15.4 How can managers turn performance objectives into operations priorities?

While the service concept defines the nature of the service to be provided, the performance objectives define the competitive or strategic priorities for the operations. 'Identifying a service strategy boils down to searching for a match between what needs doing and what the firm can do exceedingly well.'[8] The operations performance objectives will (or rather should!) include, or incorporate, customer-based PUVs together with the organisation's view as to how it does or should compete as a whole. Performance objectives are also the basis for the development of performance measurement systems and a key way of linking operations performance measures to strategy. Organisations have to do well, and competitive organisations have to compete, on many different criteria. These might include:

- price
- quality
- availability
- reliability
- speed of service
- flexibility
- range of services
- new service development
- uniqueness.

Two dimensions – importance and performance – can be used to help operations managers prioritise these objectives so that they know where it is appropriate to spend time, effort and money.

15.4.1 Importance

The importance of a factor can be assessed in terms of its importance to customers (internal or external). Three categories of importance are qualifiers, order winners and less important factors.[9]

- *Qualifiers* play an important part in retaining business or sustaining business activity, by which we mean retaining customers or sources of funding or even staff for example. If performance falls below a certain point compared to other organisations, business/customers/funding/staff may be lost. An internet service provider (ISP), for example, may lose customers if access to its network is slower or more difficult than through its competitors. A university that does not perform well in research league tables may lose out on government funds. If a charity does not have sufficient telephone lines and operators available to take donations during an emergency, it may lose out.

- *Order winners* both maintain and attract new business, funds or customers for the organisation. These are special qualifiers that the organisation has chosen as part of its strategy to use as a means of securing an advantage, or a point of differentiation, over other organisations. An ISP may choose price as its order winner, for example. By making its service free to its customers or even providing free phone access to its network, an ISP may gain a significant advantage over its competitors and increase its customer base. A university may attract executive courses by having outstanding facilities, even though its staff may be no better or worse than those in other institutions. A charity can attract new donors through developing new water provision services for victims of droughts or developing a reputation for being first on the ground in war zones.

- *Less important factors* are relatively unimportant but should not be ignored because they may become a source of advantage at some future point. In the case of a bank the comfort of the banking hall may be a less important factor, or the speed of the search routines provided may be less important to an internet service provider.

To help judge the relative importance of individual factors and help identify priorities for improvement, a more discriminating nine-point scale can be used with three points per category (see Table 15.1).

Table 15.1 Judging importance of individual factors

Order winners (attractors)	1	Crucially important to attract business/customers/funds etc.
	2	Important to attract business
	3	Useful for attracting new business
Qualifiers (retainers)	4	Vital for retention of customers/funding etc.
	5	Important for retention
	6	Useful for retention
Less important	7	Not usually important
	8	Rarely considered important
	9	Not at all important

Source: Adapted from Slack, Nigel, Stuart Chambers and Robert Johnston (2010), *Operations Management*, 6th edition, FT Prentice Hall, Harlow.

Table 15.2 Judging performance of individual factors

Better than others	1	Considerably better than others
	2	Clearly better than others
	3	Somewhat better than others
The same as others	4	Marginally better than others
	5	The same as others
	6	Marginally worse than others
Worse than others	7	Somewhat worse than others
	8	Usually worse than others
	9	Considerably worse than others

Source: Adapted from Slack, Nigel, Stuart Chambers and Robert Johnston (2010), *Operations Management*, 6th edition, FT Prentice Hall, Harlow.

15.4.2 Performance

Performance, the second dimension for assessing performance objectives, is concerned with the performance of each objective compared to other similar or competing organisations – whether they are competing in the traditional sense or competing for funds, staff or even kudos! A nine-point scale can again be used to assess relative performance of any of the factors (see Table 15.2).

15.4.3 The importance–performance matrix

By taking its importance score and the performance score, each performance objective can then be plotted on an importance–performance matrix.[10] Figure 15.5 shows the matrix, which is divided into four zones:

- *The appropriate zone* is where performance is better than other organisations for the order winners and at least the same as others for qualifiers and less important criteria. Factors in this area may not require action to improve, but the focus of performance measurement systems may have to be to keep the factor in control. To maintain an edge over other organisations it may be worth considering trying to develop performance in some factors in this zone.

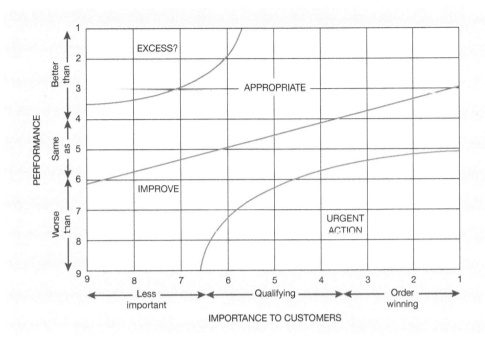

Figure 15.5 Importance–performance matrix

Source: Adapted from Slack, Nigel, Stuart Chambers and Robert Johnston (2010), *Operations Management*, 6th edition, FT Prentice Hall, Harlow.

- *The improve zone* identifies factors that need some attention, such as order winners where performance is similar to others and qualifiers where performance is slightly worse. The focus for performance measurement should be an improvement rather than control and strategies should be developed to improve performance (see Chapter 9).

- *The urgent action zone* identifies factors where urgent attention is required to improve performance (see Chapter 9). It is likely to be an immediate priority to move factors in this area up to at least the improve zone and into the appropriate zone in the medium term.

- *The excess? zone* includes factors that may have higher performance than is necessary. Performance that is significantly better than others may be a waste of resources for qualifiers and certainly for the less important factors. On the other hand, if these factors are considered to be emerging qualifiers or winners, such expenditure may well be appropriate.

By applying the importance–performance matrix, operations managers can translate strategic intentions into clear priorities for the operation, identifying where limited resources may best be spent to support the organisation's strategic intentions.

15.5 How can strategy be formulated and developed?

15.5.1 Strategy drivers

Whether a strategy is planned or emergent, it is usually driven by some force, which may be external or internal. The internal forces or strategy drivers might be existing operational capabilities, or new skills or technologies that have become available or been developed. The changing needs of stakeholders may also act as a force for change – pressure from shareholders, political masters, management or employees for an increased share value, change in direction, reduced costs or improved services, for example. External forces or

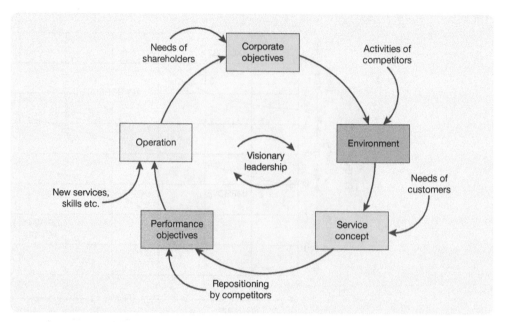

Figure 15.6 Strategy drivers

strategy drivers might include the activities of competitors or changing needs of customers (see Figure 15.6).

Operations-led strategy

Opportunities for change may arise from new developments from within the organisation, such as new services, skills, technologies or processes. The availability of e-commerce technology provides opportunities for new delivery channels for many organisations, requiring a rethinking of strategy, including how to manage, market and finance such developments.

Externally driven strategy

Modifications to strategy may be driven by changes in the organisation's external environment, either actual or anticipated. Such changes might include new competitors entering the marketplace; or the strategic developments of competitors through different positioning or service developments; or the changing needs of customers who require a different service concept, which may be the result of the activities of the competition; or the loss of customers because their needs are not being met.

Corporate-led strategy

The impetus for change may come from the organisation's executive, driven by a desire or need by its stakeholders for a greater return on assets, or expansion, or retrenchment, or diversification, for example.

Visionary leadership

Any one of the above drivers may be sufficient to begin the cycle of strategy formulation and development, though clearly the more drivers that are in evidence, the more pressure there is on the strategy cycle to move. One condition that we believe has a major impact on the strategy formulation process is visionary leadership. This is usually provided by an individual, usually at corporate level, although it is possibly a senior figure within operations, marketing or finance, who takes responsibility for strategy development and acts as the linchpin in the wheel, pulling all the forces together and helping them move in the right direction.

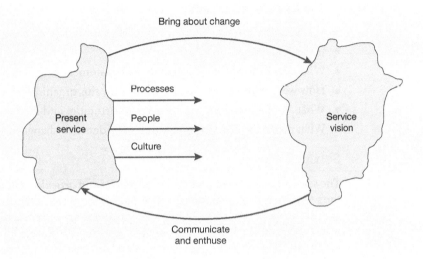

Figure 15.7 Visionary leadership

Visionary leaders understand the current organisation and its service – its processes, people and culture, for example – and are able to create an attractive vision for the future. They are also able to communicate that vision and enthuse others, and thus galvanise the whole organisation to bring about the realisation of that vision (see Figure 15.7).

15.5.2 Key issues in strategy development

Objectives

The development of clear corporate objectives is based on the strategy drivers – the internal or external pressures or opportunities for change. The objectives may well be expressed in financial or competitive terms over a set period of time, for example return on investment, profit, number of new customers or market share. These objectives need to be clearly stated and will provide the means of measuring and monitoring the success or otherwise of the strategy. The key questions that need to be asked are:

- What are the objectives?
- Are they achievable?
- What investment is required?
- What is the timeframe?
- What methods for review are in place?
- What are the contingencies?

Environment

To ensure that those objectives can be achieved, there needs to be a clear understanding of the market and the environment in which the organisation currently operates, or plans to be operating. This will include an understanding of the size and nature of the competition, the nature and size of the market or potential market, existing competing and complementary products and services, the ways the market is currently segmented, and the likely reaction of the competition. One key outcome of this activity is the identification of a potential target market and an assessment of the perceived needs and expectations of the target customers.

The key questions include:

- What are the characteristics of the market or market segment?
- Is the strategy appropriate for them?
- What are the needs and expectations of customers in this market?
- How well are these needs being served – by this organisation, by other organisations?
- What are the strengths, weaknesses, opportunities and threats?
- What might be the reaction of other providers to a change in strategy?

Service concept

The service concept (see Chapter 3) is a *shared* and *articulated* understanding of the nature of the service, which should capture information about the organising idea, the service provided and the service received, including the customer experience and the service outcomes. The service concept is an important way of capturing the nature of a service so that customers know what they are getting and staff understand what they are providing. The service concept can be also be used to help develop new services. The key questions to be asked are:

- What is the concept?
- Is it aimed at a particular market?
- Is it appropriate for that market?
- Can it be understood by customers and providers?
- How will it be communicated to customers and providers?
- Can it be delivered by the operation?

Performance objectives

Having identified a target market and developed a service concept, the operation needs guidance as to how it should manage its resources and activities. This will ensure that the service it provides will meet the corporate objectives and the needs of the target market and will establish how it will differentiate itself from the competition. A clear understanding of the performance objectives and their relative priorities is required (see the discussion of importance and performance above). The key questions include:

- What are the order winners and qualifiers?
- What are the priorities for change?
- What are the measures of performance associated with each objective?
- What are the targets?
- Are they achievable?
- By when have the targets to be achieved?
- What investment is required?

Operation

The design or development of an appropriate operation may be a complex activity requiring a large number of interrelated decisions, connecting processes, employees, customers and infrastructure. New investment may be required or there may be a redeployment of existing resources. The operation plan then needs to be checked against the objectives to ensure that the total strategy is consistent and will achieve the objectives that have been set. Thus the process may have to go through several iterations before a consistent and cohesive strategy is created. The key questions include:

- What changes are required to processes, employees, customer management and infrastructure?
- How will the changes be brought about?

- What resources are required?
- Can the new concept be delivered?
- Will it meet the perceived needs of the target market?
- Can the performance objectives be achieved?

Case Example 15.2   A new strategy for Singapore's libraries

In July 2005, the National Library Board (NLB) in Singapore unveiled its Library 2010 (L2010) Plan, which put forward its new strategic direction for the next five years. Its mission was to provide a trusted, accessible and globally connected library and information service so as to promote a knowledgeable and engaged society. The L2010 Plan recognised that Singapore, with few natural resources, needed to compete on its skills and adaptability and support the development of Singapore as a knowledge-based economy. It also recognised that the use of the Library was inconsistent, with a sharp drop in usage after people leave school and limited use by some minority communities. The L2010 Plan set out a clear aim: to bring the world's knowledge to Singapore to create a positive social and economic impact. The report identified three key ways in which NLB could meet those challenges:

1 Libraries for Life, Knowledge for Success – providing customised services to support Singaporeans' economic and social needs at all stages in their lives.

2 Serving the Whole Community – developing services to support communities that are less well served, ethnic communities, people with disabilities, the unemployed, parents and carers, companies, research communities and professionals.

3 Playing a Vital Role in Singapore's Knowledge Team – working together with other agencies and taking a leadership role to develop a knowledge economy Singapore.

The Library's previous strategic plan, L2000, had been radical and visionary and led to a transformation of the library system in Singapore and by 2004 the library system in Singapore had been reinvented. Libraries had become accessible, attractive, user-friendly and integrated with the communities, which they served. Ms Lim Soo Hoon, Chairman of NLB and a Permanent Secretary in the Prime Minister's Office, explained:

Ten years ago, most people probably saw the Library as serving a purely functional role. If you needed to do research or could not afford to buy books, you would visit the Library. The Library 2000 blueprint helped to change that perception and the Library has moved from being merely a functional space to a welcoming social space as well. Today, we have cafés in our libraries and libraries in shopping centres – essentially, our libraries have integrated with the community and are seen as inviting havens to relax, meet people and share in the company of other book-lovers. It is a great testimony of our success that many libraries in other parts of the world have replicated our efforts in their own countries.

The Library's Chief Executive Officer, Dr Varaprasad, explained his vision for the future and what the Library has to achieve through its new L2010 Plan:

> *This plan marks a new direction for the National Library, and in so doing we will work to create a distinction between the National Library and the public libraries. The first wave was very much concerned with changing the public library function; we must now apply the same vigour to reinventing the National Library. Of course we must continue to develop our public library system and we have many things to do, such as ensure low income groups have access to the Library, encourage young people to use the library, and improve adult literacy.*
>
> *Our National Library function has been somewhat neglected. We need to develop some value-adding or rather knowledge-adding services. For example, we need to develop information useful to businesses to provide them with competitive and market information. Take for example a businessperson about to undertake some new work in Kazakhstan, wanting to know what the business prospects might be like. Our print material might be able to tell him/her its population, its GDP, and provide an overview of its industries and the transport system. On the web s/he will be able to find the cheapest flights and the routes. But, how do you find about the risks of doing business, the future prospects for Kazakhstan, where new investment might come from? Librarians will have to become more specialist and accept they will not be able to answer every query. What they will need to do is to link the customer with knowledge communities. These communities are at the cutting-edge of knowledge and have information that has not yet been written down on websites or in books.*
>
> *Importantly we need to support the development of these knowledge communities and the specialists within them – this is where new knowledge will be created. We need to help create knowledge and create knowledge-based services. NLB should act as an intermediary facilitating the transfer of knowledge between parties and creating new forms of useful knowledge. In order to build knowledge communities we need to understand how they work, how they form, how they operate, how they disband and importantly we need to discover how we capture the knowledge as it is being developed so that we can allow others access to it. We will obviously have to be selective as the number of such communities could be extremely large.*
>
> *This will all require quite different staff skills; at least for those in the National Library, they will need new expertise on knowledge navigation, subject specialism, expertise in content management, information discovery and capture. In sum we need to revolutionise the National Library and do for the National Library what the L2000 Plan did for the public library.*

Source: This illustration was written by Professors Robert Johnston, Warwick Business School, Chai Kah Hin and Jochen Wirtz, National University of Singapore, and Christopher Lovelock, Yale University. The authors gratefully acknowledge the valuable assistance of Teo Yi Wen, Department of Industrial and Systems Engineering, NUS. The authors would like to thank the interviewees for their participation in this project and Johnson Paul and Sharon Foo for facilitating the research. All Rights Reserved, National Library Board Singapore and the Authors, 2007.

15.6 How can a strategy be sustained?

Without constant appraisal of the changes to the internal and external environments and consequent adjustments to strategy, organisations may decay. This has been referred to as 'institutional rusting'.[11] Some of the main operational difficulties faced by organisations in sustaining a strategy are:

- Conflicting objectives, such as the need to provide a customised product using existing processes capable only of delivering a commodity-type service.

- Inappropriate and inflexible operations processes and resources, such as inappropriate equipment and untrained employees.

- Inappropriate investment, including inadequate investment to provide the resources required or develop the existing ones.

- Undetected changes to the service concept as delivered by the operation as opposed to what was originally intended, for example a failure to detect how managers and employees may be reinterpreting the concept in the way with which they are comfortable, as opposed to what is required by customers (concept contamination).
- The addition of multiple (similar) services to a service process originally designed for one service, resulting in potential compromise of service standards across all services.

Strategy therefore involves the process of continually checking the organisation's plans for direction, progress and cohesion in terms of the continually changing environment. The importance–performance matrix can be used to check that operation's priorities are aligned to, and reflect any changes in, strategy. Also, creating, using and updating strategy maps to link strategy through objectives to performance measurement are important means for operations to both implement and sustain a strategy (see Chapter 9).

15.7 Summary

What is a service strategy?

- Service strategy is the set of plans and policies by which a service organisation aims to meet its objectives.
- A strategy involves the creation of corporate objectives, an understanding of the environment, the development of an appropriate service concept, the identification of appropriate operations performance objectives and the development of an appropriate operation.

How can service provide a competitive advantage?

- Organisations may compete on the excellence of their outcomes, the excellence of their experiences, or both.
- Perceived user value provides a means of identifying current and future strategies.

How can managers turn performance objectives into operations priorities?

- The importance–performance matrix helps identify operational priorities.

How can strategy be formulated and developed?

- Strategy drivers include existing operational capabilities, or new skills or technologies that have become available or been developed, the changing needs of stakeholders, the activities of competitors and changing needs of customers.
- Strategy development is an iterative process, which should result in a consistent and cohesive strategy.

How can a strategy be sustained?

- It is necessary continually to check the organisation's plans for direction, progress and cohesion in terms of the changing environment.
- The importance–performance matrix and strategy maps are useful tools to help check the alignment of operational activities with strategy.

15.8 Discussion questions

1 Select four organisations in the same sector, such as four food outlets, pubs or libraries, and assess their relative positions in terms of their outcomes and experiences. How well does this fit with their respective strategies?

2 Identify the PUV criteria for two competing organisations. Score them on each criterion and assess their strategies. What options would they have if they wanted to differentiate themselves from the competition?

15.9 Questions for managers

1 Define and evaluate your service strategy.

2 Do you compete in terms of outcome and/or experience? In what ways could you change?

3 Identify your PUV criteria. How do you score against your key competitors? What are the options for change?

4 Identify all your performance criteria and undertake an importance–performance analysis. Do the priorities identified reflect the organisation's priorities?

5 Evaluate your process for strategy formulation and development.

Case Exercise — Smith and Jones, Solicitors

John Smith and David Jones are lawyers and first met when they had been employed in a large firm of solicitors in London. They both felt that London held few attractions for them and that they would prefer their own small country practice. Six years ago they moved to offices just off the main street in a large market town in the west of England and set up in competition with four other firms of solicitors. It was a slow start but both partners were now very busy and had a secretarial staff of five.

John explained that they have two types of client.

There is the personal client who is the local individual with a small legal problem, like a house purchase or a boundary dispute, and there is the commercial client who is a company, a few of which are local but most are based in nearby cities.

The personal client comes through the door when he or she has a problem. There used to be a lot of loyalty to the solicitors that the client or his or her family had used in the past, but this is declining. We don't do any advertising – indeed, it is only allowed in a very limited form. Most of our clients come either because they want a change from the solicitors they have used before or through recommendations from friends. We have worked hard to build up our local personal clients. I like to try to break down the stuffy image of the law and deal at a simple and straightforward level with the client. This personal approach seems to work very well. You see, many ordinary people in the street are very apprehensive about coming to see a solicitor. To them, I suppose, we are a bit like a dentist, only they extract teeth and we extract money! We always make sure that clients are dealt with promptly and pleasantly by a partner, never by a junior clerk. We see ourselves as a small, local, convenient and friendly firm based on a good, personal and caring image.

When we first came here we obviously had no local work, but we relied upon a few commercial accounts that we brought with us from London. We now work for about ten companies, though no longer for any that are based in London. Some of our commercial work has come about through providing a good service to a personal client. Usually, however, companies have their own favourite firm of solicitors. Sometimes they do give small jobs to other firms just to try them out, so we often get speculative phone calls from potential clients. I reckon sometimes when they ring up they have Yellow Pages in their hands and if you can't help them there and then they will go on to the next firm on the list. Sometimes we get commercial clients through recommendations from other companies or third parties like accountants who have heard that we give a good service. We need to expand our business in this area by giving a good and fast response to our clients.

Now that the firm was well established, John Smith seemed keen not to stand still. He explained:

On local, personal business, solicitors tend to think that if you just sit back, business will just come in and you don't need to make any spectacular effort to keep it. As a result clients are frequently abused. Some solicitors think nothing of telling customers who arrive on the doorstep to go away and come back when they have made an appointment. I think that solicitors have a condescending approach to business. I believe that we have a lot of lessons to learn from the modern age and that we can do a lot more thrusting. I am sure there is a lot of scope. I don't believe that everyone is entirely happy with their solicitor.

John felt that the time was right for his firm to expand, and, although these views were less than enthusiastically shared by his partner, John was determined:

It's time the business grew. We are as established as all the other firms in the area, and although we hold on to a share of clients, it never seems to increase, despite a fair growth in the town's population over the last few years. During that time our costs have been increasing. Our overheads on the property and what we have to pay to keep good staff and lease the equipment is considerably greater than what it was even two years ago. It is not easy just to put up our fees to cover these increases. I know you think we pluck figures out of the air, but most of our clients use us several times and they remember how much we charged them last time. As a result our margins have been getting tighter. However, to expand the business we need another solicitor, but it's going to be difficult to attract someone into the office when they see what their share of the spoils might be. Both David and I would also have to take a cut in our slice of the rapidly declining cake. If we are going to expand and bring someone else in, we will need to put a lot of time and effort into generating more work.

I'm also concerned about the role the building societies and banks may play in the future. The Government seems determined to give away our bread-and-butter business. If we lost conveyancing there wouldn't be enough work for even the two of us.

John explained his ideas for getting more business:

With personal work, I think we need to become more visible. We don't make any efforts to sell our services. We are currently thinking about putting a brochure together listing our services, like one of our competitors has done. We could distribute these to potential clients and also to our current clients to maintain our name in their minds and inform them of our other services.

More personal and commercial work can be brought in by making more contacts. It's surprising what work you can get out of meeting people on trains or at croquet matches. All you have to do is mention that you are a solicitor and you find that they have a problem. We have recently had some business cards printed for occasions like this.

You might think that joining Rotary or a golf club would be a good idea, but I have not joined them for two reasons. First because they are full of solicitors touting for trade, and, second, I can't play golf. You see, you can't afford to run the risk of being a 'bad egg': unless you are a 'good' Rotarian or golf player you may tend to lose credibility. I prefer to play croquet and there is only one other solicitor in the club. I'm also not too bad at it! David Jones has some good ideas for getting business clients. He is making contacts with trade organisations and associations like local chambers of commerce. This could provide a lot of good contacts and also give us a feel for local needs.

The problem is that some of the jobs for personal clients are not very profitable. Indeed, margins in this type of work generally are small. But it is an important part of our business: it accounts for about 85 per cent of our income. The rest of our income comes from a handful of commercial clients. This may at first seem small scale but this work does command high margins. The jobs are sometimes relatively simple, like arranging insurances. Our fees are based on a percentage. It only takes one or two large transactions to generate a substantial amount of income.

Because the commercial jobs command higher margins I want to see us make substantial increases in this area. I think that unless we improve our income from commercial work to around 50 per cent of our total turnover in the next two or three years, we will have done badly. I don't think our location is a bad one. We have some big cities quite close by and we have good connections in Bristol and London.

We have a good location with good staff and the latest equipment – laptops, wireless internet, wireless handheld devices, colour copiers and printers, and we even have our own web site, thanks to David. I must admit that, although I think there are lots of good possibilities, I am not really sure what more I can do.

Question

1 Develop a new service strategy for Smith and Jones.

Suggested further reading

Arbore, Alessandro and Bruno Busacca (2011), 'Rejuvenating Importance-Performance Analysis', *Journal of Service Management* 22 (3) 409–430

Beer, Michael and Russell A. Eisenstat (2000), 'The Silent Killers of Strategy Implementation and Learning', *MIT Sloan Management Review* 41 (4) 29–40

Gebauer, Heiko, Bo Edvardsson, Anders Gustafsson and Lars Witell (2010), 'Match or Mismatch: Strategy-Structure Configurations in the Service Business of Manufacturing Companies', *Journal of Service Research* 13 (2) 198–215

Silvestro, Rhian and Claudio Silvestro (2003), 'New Service Design in the NHS: An Evaluation of the Strategic Alignment of NHS Direct', *International Journal of Operations and Production Management* 23 (4) 401–417

Slack, Nigel and Michael Lewis (2011), *Operations Strategy*, 3rd edition, Financial Times Prentice Hall, Harlow

Useful web links

David Maister's web page provides a wide variety of material on service strategy:
http://davidmaister.com/

A case study on service strategy at TNT at The Times 100:
www.thetimes100.co.uk—case-study--delivering-a-business-strategy--162-416-1.php

A quick overview and 'how to' for the Importance Performance Matrix at Burdett Strategic Consulting:
www.clintburdett.com—research_07_1_ip_matrix.htm

Notes

1 Berry, Leonard L. (1995), *On Great Service: A Framework for Action*, Free Press, New York

2 Normann, Richard and Rafael Ramirez (1993), 'From Value Chain to Value Constellation: Designing Interactive Strategy', *Harvard Business Review* 71 (4) 65–77

3 See, for example, Mintzberg, Henry, Robert M. James and James Brian Quinn (1998), *The Strategy Process*, European edition, Prentice Hall, London; Mintzberg, Henry, Bruce Ahlstrand and Joseph Lampel (1998), *Strategy Safari*, Prentice Hall, Harlow

4 See, for example, Lovelock, Christopher H. (1994), *Product Plus*, McGraw-Hill, New York; Senge, Peter M. (1993), *The Fifth Discipline*, Century Business, London

5 Johnston, Robert (1988), 'Service Industries – Improving Competitive Performance', *The Service Industries Journal* 8 (2) 202–211; Johnston, Robert (1989), 'Developing Competitive Strategies in Service Industries' in Jones, Peter (ed.), *Management in Service Industries*, Pitman, London; Heskett, James L., W. Earl Sasser and Christopher W.L. Hart (1990), *Service Breakthroughs: Changing the Rules of the Game*, Free Press, New York

6 See, for example, Mintzberg, Henry, Robert M. James and James Brian Quinn (1998), *The Strategy Process*, European edition, Prentice Hall, London; Mintzberg, Henry, Bruce Ahlstrand and Joseph Lampel (1998), *Strategy Safari*, Prentice Hall, Harlow

7 Bowman, Cliff (1998), *Strategy in Practice*, Prentice Hall, London

8 Berry, Leonard L. (1995), *On Great Service: A Framework for Action*, Free Press, New York

9 See, for example, Hill, Terry (2000), *Operations Management: Strategic Context and Managerial Analysis*, Macmillan, London; Slack, Nigel, Stuart Chambers and Robert Johnston (2010), *Operations Management*, 6th edition, FT Prentice Hall, Harlow

10 Slack, Nigel, Stuart Chambers and Robert Johnston (2010), *Operations Management*, 6th edition, FT Prentice Hall, Harlow

11 Lovelock, Christopher H. (1994), *Product Plus*, McGraw-Hill, New York

Chapter 16
Understanding and influencing culture

Chapter objectives

This chapter is about how to understand and influence service culture.

- Why is understanding and influencing organisational culture important?
- What is organisational culture?
- What are the main culture types and the implications for service delivery?
- What is the influence of national cultures?
- How can managers influence cultural change?

16.1   Introduction

There is growing understanding amongst service operations managers that the organisation's culture, 'the way things are done around here', has a major impact on service delivery and performance. We were talking to the Chief Executive of a major international consulting and construction company who was reflecting on the inconsistency of service delivery:

> We are absolutely brilliant in a crisis. When things go wrong, we all pull together to make sure that we sort things out as quickly as we can for our customers. The problem is that we don't seem to have the same commitment to service as usual.

Can we explain this? We can identify some of the factors involved such as training, leadership and reward mechanisms. The unique combination of all these factors and more contributes to the organisation's culture. To attempt to implement service improvements without understanding this context is rather naive to say the least. It is tempting to see organisational culture as some sort of mysterious influence on employees' attitudes and actions. We've heard managers blame the lack of success of a service initiative on 'culture' that may or may not exist but which somehow makes the difference between success and failure. Although this is unrealistic, it is useful to reflect on the reasons why some service organisations have been more successful than others despite having similar technologies, processes and skills.

This chapter explores the nature of organisational culture and its impact on the task of the service operations manager. We outline some ways of describing and diagnosing organisational culture and propose some ways that organisational culture can be influenced to assist the operations manager in the task of providing high levels of service experience and outcome, cost-effectively.

16.2   Why is understanding and influencing organisational culture important?

Understanding and influencing organisational culture is central to delivering a consistent service and implementing change.[1] For example, an operations manager may have decided to try to bring about improvements to the operation through team working and providing discretion and autonomy to the workforce. However, if the culture of the organisation is one of fear and distrust created by an individual-based systems of rewards and punishments, with highly centralised decision-making where top-level permission is required for any decision, then success is unlikely. Indeed frustration and upset are the probable outcomes. Managers must understand the current culture, the opportunities and constraints it affords, and how they can influence and bring about changes to it. Furthermore, 'culture' exists at a country level as well as an organisational level. Disneyland Resort Paris (Case Example 16.1) demonstrates the need to understand the impact of national and organisational culture on service delivery. It also indicates the need to understand the impact of national stereotypes on customer expectations.

Case Example 16.1   Disneyland Resort Paris

Disneyland Resort Paris is a holiday and recreation resort 32 kilometres (20 miles) from the centre of Paris. It was the second Disney resort to open outside of the United States (after Tokyo Disney Resort). Entertaining over 12 million visitors a year, it is now one of Europe's leading tourist destinations.

Euro Disney, as it was initially called, opened in April 1992, creating enormous interest as observers wondered whether the magic of Disneyworld would transfer from Florida to France. In particular there was speculation as to whether a European workforce would conform to the strong American Disney culture and whether the national cultures of a European customer base would mean that changes in service delivery would be required.

Source: Getty Images: AFP

Initial performance was rather poorer than hoped for. Attendance in the first year fell significantly short of projections. There has been much speculation as to the reasons for this shortfall including an over-reliance on the American experience of Disney as opposed to being clear about the specific attractions of Euro Disney. Disney's traditional attention to detail seemed to have slipped in making assumptions that the concept would translate directly from Florida to Paris. For example, alcohol was not on sale in the restaurants in the park, something that was expected by European customers. Queue times were longer in Paris than in Florida and the experience was not what Disney customers expected. The choice of location was also criticised – it was cheaper to fly to Florida than to stay in Paris. Also in Florida sunshine was virtually guaranteed.

Disney had followed the tried-and-tested formula, one which had worked in Tokyo. (The Tokyo resort was an exact replica of the resort in Florida and worked well despite the cultural difference.) Some research suggested that Euro Disney would be more successful if it concentrated on being a European resort rather than replicating the American formula.

In order to deal with the challenge of managing the tension between creating strong organisational values and being sensitive to national cultures Disney created its own university for its employees and all cast members attended Disney University in Paris. Salaries were set above the local level in order to attract the best applicants.

Despite this relations with employees were strained in the early days. The 'all-American' workforce aligned to the company's values was certainly not how French labour unions saw the company. Initially cast members were not unionised but in little more than a year, they were represented by one of the toughest unions in France. One trade union member described cast members as slaves, rather than characters. A values programme which creates consistency in the American parks was seen, by some at least, to be focused on creating puppets. French labour unions also protested about the dress code, which they saw as an attack on individual liberty. Relations were further strained when poor financial performance required significant job cuts.

Over time, Disneyland Paris has improved. The company has learned how to adapt the core values of Disney to the European setting. It can be argued that the core offering has not changed but it has needed some local adaptation in marketing and delivery, not least in dealing with the challenge of several languages and national cultures. High turnover of senior managers had a positive impact in that they brought Disney operational practices from other resorts and reinforced the organisation's culture. A name change was also seen as important to overcome the negative publicity that followed its introduction. In addition, while senior managers at Disney associated the word 'Euro' with glamour and excitement, to Europeans it was a term more associated with business, currency and commerce. The park was renamed Disneyland Paris in 1995 and Disneyland Resort Paris in 2002, linking the name with one of the world's most romantic and exciting cities.

Source: This case example was developed from Case Studies: Disneyland Resort Paris: Mickey goes to Europe (IMD Case Ref IMD-4-0280); Euro Disney: Post Script (Richard Ivey School of Business Case Ref 9A95G010); and websites.

16.3 What is organisational culture?

There are two broad schools of thought on organisational culture. The first proposes that culture is something tangible, almost to the point where it can be written down in much the same way that an organisation chart can be included in the organisation's operating manual. In this sense, culture is something that the organisation possesses in much the same way as it might possess a set of resources or products.

The second view is that culture is much less tangible, and only really exists when people in the organisation talk to each other and, by their words and behaviours, act out the culture of the organisation. Writers on organisational culture refer to this view as 'culture as personality'.[2] Described in this way, the culture of the organisation is often hidden below the surface of organisational life, and its impact is not always obvious because there are a number of unspoken and/or unconscious aspects to it. It is this latter view of culture that informs the major part of this chapter.

For service operations managers, the implication is that they must develop an ability to predict, and prepare for, the influence of culture. As we shall see in the next section, the unspoken assumptions about how the organisation operates have a massive influence both on behaviour and on the way that we consider possibilities for service improvements. Insight in this area is fundamental to success.

16.3.1 Basic assumptions and the service concept

In this section we will use Schein's framework for describing organisational culture.[3] This framework, shown in Figure 16.1, suggests that organisational culture has a number of levels or layers to it. It is dangerous to assume that what we might observe on the surface is all that

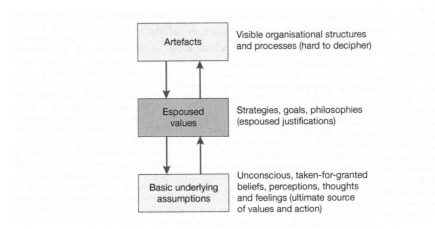

Figure 16.1 Levels of organisational culture

Source: Adapted from Schein, Edgar H. (2004), *Organizational Culture and Leadership*, 3rd edition, Pfeiffer Wiley, San Francisco. This material is used by permission of John Wiley & Sons, Inc.

there is to the organisation. There is much to organisational life that is 'beneath the surface', often exerting powerful influences on the decision-making process. This is one of the reasons why seemingly irrational decisions are frequently made by senior managers who are influenced by unspoken (and often undiscussable) aspects of the way that the organisation thinks about itself, what it is good at, how it assesses success, and what it values.

In the context of this book it is really important to understand the connection between the organisation's underlying basic assumptions and its service concept. If there is a need to make a significant change to the service concept, the underlying culture will tend to revert to the original, preventing successful implementation.

Schein proposed three levels of organisational culture (see Figure 16.1). We will now discuss each in turn.

Artefacts

Artefacts are the visible aspects of the organisation – its structure and processes, and other physical evidence that can be observed or felt by both customers and employees. We all draw conclusions about the organisation from the things we observe.

For the service operation, artefacts might include elements of the servicescape (see Chapter 7) or less intangible issues such as the celebrations of success of good customer service, or in the seniority of the champion of service within the organisation (whether this is at board level or several levels below). Other visible signs of culture of particular relevance to the service operations manager include the measurement and control systems employed (see Chapter 9). Control systems that emphasise the importance of customer satisfaction ratings alongside the financial metrics may be evidence of a customer-focused culture.

Even at this level there may be significant differences between operations within the same broad service sector. The hotel that aspires to be a four- or five-star operation but which does not invest in replacing tired or broken chairs in the lounge is probably not taking the task seriously. Schein, however, makes the important point that it is very dangerous to draw conclusions from the evidence of the artefacts alone, without knowing the deeper levels of culture that may explain them. However, it goes without saying that customers will do just this. Customers will look at the physical evidence and draw their own conclusions.

Espoused values

The second level of culture operates at the cognitive level. It describes the stated strategies and beliefs of the organisation. Thus this level may include aspects of the organisation's mission statement – the general strategy as declared and set down by the leadership team – and statements as to the general values or guiding principles of the organisation. Kwik-Fit's statement that 'Our aim is 100% customer delight' would certainly fall into this category, as would lists of company values that include some of the following:

- We develop teamwork.
- We respect the individual.
- We are committed to outstanding customer service.
- We aim to be the benchmark for the industry.
- We operate with integrity.
- We encourage initiative.

This aspect of culture again refers to a conscious level of human interaction and thought. There is frequently a sense that these espoused values and beliefs are what the organisation might like itself to be, rather than what it is in reality. It is relatively common for organisations to prepare statements that might contain phrases such as 'we work together as a team' or 'we value individuals', which do not necessarily reflect the experience of the members of the organisation. This may not matter if these espoused values can be demonstrated to be 'work-in-progress', with evidence of investment in making them a reality.

A key aspect of espoused values to be taken into account by the service operations manager are those aspects of an organisation's culture which might be interpreted as negative in the eyes of the outside world. An example might be the 'two years up or out' culture of some consultancy firms. This is not usually discussed with their clients, but nonetheless might have an impact on the service provided.

In the same way, the organisation might have stated ambitions in terms of its basic service strategies that are also not borne out in practice. Again, of relevance to service operations managers might be the stated belief of the organisation that delivering 'service excellence' is the key to success. At one level (espoused values) this might be a genuine desire on the part of the organisation's management and employees, while at another, deeper level this may not be as strongly held as one might think at first sight. It is the final level of organisational culture – the basic underlying assumptions – that holds the key to our understanding of why there might be observable differences between what is aspired to and what takes place in practice.

We have found it helpful to encourage organisations to be honest in stating their values and to identify those that genuinely reflect the culture of the organisation and those that might be better described as aspirational or 'work-in-progress'. So, from the list above, we might identify 'we operate with integrity' as broadly true for the organisation, whereas 'we are committed to outstanding customer service' might be a statement of intent rather than reality at this time. This understanding is invaluable for the operations manager seeking to drive service improvement.

Basic underlying assumptions

Basic underlying assumptions refer to those unconsciously held views that are undiscussed and generally unchallenged. Basic assumptions are those beliefs and ways of working that have worked well for the organisation in the past – and are, indeed, its secret of success in the past. These basic assumptions are often expressed in rather more simple, even primitive, terms than many competitive strategies or public sector policies. It is this primitive aspect to the basic assumption that means that it is often deeply held and fiercely defended if anyone (often a newcomer to the organisation) challenges it or suggests it should be changed.

An example of a basic assumption might be the belief that all workers are lazy. A consequence of this belief would be that management would become over-directive, effectively disempowering customer contact employees. The end result would be rather robotic service from demotivated employees, effectively 'living down' to their managers' expectations. Many service organisations operate in this way, although they would probably deny it. The underlying belief or basic assumption would be that keeping a tight control on costs is the right way to increase profit, albeit in the short term. It would be extremely difficult for organisations of this type to implement longer-term customer retention strategies.

Because basic assumptions operate at the unconscious (taken-for-granted) level it is difficult to identify them. Managers and employees may only recognise them when deeply held principles are challenged. A change in service concept, which makes perfect sense at a rational level, may be resisted at an unconscious level, if only because the change moves people out of their comfort zones. An example is provided by medical doctors who agree to a change in surgery procedures so that a patient is seen by the next available doctor. At the rational level they may see the efficiency benefits and agree to the change, but unconsciously they have not changed their basic assumption that the doctor/patient relationship is central to good practice and they will resist the change to the point of ensuring that any pilot scheme is a failure.

We have worked with companies that have a strong track record in producing innovative manufactured products, but realise that they have to develop revenue-earning services to replace declining manufacturing margins, and then find that this is much harder to achieve than they thought. Clearly, this can be explained in part by the need to develop new competencies, but a significant issue is the resistance to change brought about by a reluctance to give up the old, tried-and-tested basic assumption that good manufactured product innovation is the way to success. This is often reinforced by the fact that most, if not all, of the senior management come from the 'good old days' and are also reluctant to move away from areas with which they feel competent to deal. This is why significant change is often only brought about by a change of chief executive.

Ericsson, the telecom equipment provider, found itself in this position in the mid 1990s. It had been extremely successful in bringing innovative products to market. Although the market and profitability trends suggested that this strategy was beginning to fail, Ericsson continued its product-based strategy. Ericsson formulated a strategy based on selling hardware but achieving margin through managing services for their hardware customers. This was an appropriate strategy but very difficult to implement because Ericsson's underlying basic assumption was still success through product innovation, which meant that the company continued to prioritise hardware development and sales over service development. It took a major crisis and a reduction in workforce of nearly 50 per cent for Ericsson to reshape the strategy and to move into 'managed services'.

Organisational culture is only really understood when the 'unconscious' part of the organisation's personality is revealed. One of the most powerful ways of uncovering the key elements of culture is to provide a framework for members of the organisation to discuss these aspects of their world and to begin to understand the various impacts on their behaviour and, therefore, eventually on the service they may provide to customers. The next section describes the cultural web,[4] an instrument which provides a powerful framework for groups to begin to discuss aspects of the organisation. This discussion provides useful clues as to the core elements of its culture.

16.3.2 The cultural web

Figure 16.2 depicts the components of an organisation's cultural web. In this section we first describe the elements of the web and then provide examples of aspects of culture which might help or hinder the generation of a customer-focused organisation or an organisation committed to service excellence.

The paradigm

The word 'paradigm' has been somewhat overworked in recent years, but it is particularly important in understanding organisational culture. The paradigm is essentially the way that we view the world – the sets of values, principles and possibly prejudices that inform our

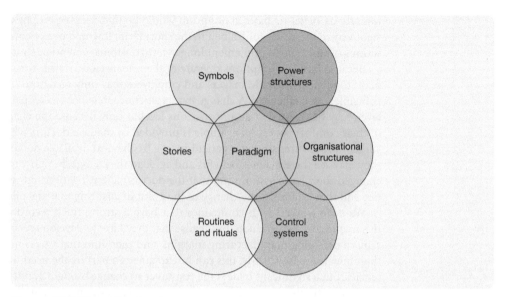

Figure 16.2 The cultural web

Source: Adapted from Johnson, Gerry, Kevan Scholes and Richard Whittington (2009), *Exploring Corporate Strategy: Text and Cases*, 8th edition, FT Prentice Hall.

judgements. Another word used for this is 'worldview', which can be likened to the set of spectacles through which we view the world. A simple illustration is a person's reaction to being offered a sum of money. A person whose belief is that the world is a good place might take the money without suspicion, whereas a person whose belief is that the world is a dangerous place would first ask 'What's the catch?'

The organisation's paradigm may have a number of facets:

- A description of the sector of which the organisation is a part, for example hotels, computer service, government or financial services.

- The principal customer segments that it seeks to serve: global organisations, small businesses or individual consumers.

- In some cases the organisation may express what it does in terms of what the customers are buying rather than what the organisation is providing. For example, the theme park may express its mission as providing magical experiences rather than selling rides; the financial service as providing hope rather than pensions.

- The paradigm may contain some beliefs about what the organisation thinks is good about itself, such as being a risk-taker, innovative, or responsive to customers.

- Finally, it may contain some aspects of the way people think about the organisation that are less positive: it is ruthless, risk-averse or arrogant.

There is overlap between the paradigm as described here, Schein's basic assumptions, and the service concept as designed (see Chapter 3). It is critical to identify any inconsistencies between these three ideas. For example, it may not be obvious to long-serving employees or managers that the organisation is viewed as somewhat arrogant or ruthless by its customers. Clearly if this is the case, the organisation will find it hard to become customer-responsive, having a 'we know best' attitude. A group of managers from a retail service chain carried out a cultural web analysis and were shocked to find that they had not used the words 'service' or 'customer' at any point in their paradigm. They had spoken a great deal about what they thought they were good at, but very little about the need to give the customer what they wanted. (We find it interesting to look at service organisations' annual reports and count how frequently, or often infrequently, the words 'customer' or 'service' are used.)

It is important to identify aspects of the paradigm that are helpful for service delivery as well as those which hinder. Organisations that believe that long-term customer satisfaction is more important than short-term profit will generally find a supportive environment for service delivery.

Organisational structures

This aspect of the cultural web deals with the organisation's structure as it works, at least on paper. It is the structure that may be published in the form of organisational charts, showing who reports to whom. Some questions to ask to understand this aspect of organisational culture are:

- Is the structure hierarchical or flat?
- Is it organised geographically or by product area?
- Is it function- or process-driven?
- Is it bureaucratic or flexible?
- Is it based on teams or individuals?

The form of the organisation will determine to a large extent how responsive to customers it will be. If a customer-facing unit is virtually autonomous, able to satisfy most customer requests from its own resources, it is likely to be more responsive. This of course may be seen as rather inefficient, and the management may prefer to centralise many activities in order to reduce costs. Retail banks have made large investments in creating 'manufacturing' activities to handle back-office transactions more efficiently, but run the risk of being seen to be rather impersonal to individuals wanting to deal with the people they know in the local branch. Moves to offshore these activities to lower labour costs are perceived to increase this potential disconnect.

Much of the value in recent business process re-engineering (BPR) projects has been a greater emphasis on linking together processes and activities that contribute to customer value rather than functional expertise. This may result in the generation of customer focus rather than operational focus. Examples of this may be found in the creation of teams to handle the entirety of a group of customer transactions. This was the case at Cigna in Greenock in Scotland, a company that handles employee benefits for corporate clients. Cigna reorganised its function-based groups (handling sales, service and credit control, into client-focused teams), and discovered that there were quality and productivity improvements as a result.

Some organisations have customer service departments whose role appears to be to protect the organisation and its workings from the customer. Customer complaints are handled efficiently by this group, but the downside is that fewer people meet and deal with customers or hear what really upsets them. The Nationwide Building Society made a practice of handing complaints to the process owners so that these people could also own the process of customer complaint resolution and process improvement.

It is clear that organisational design often contains compromise. Ericsson, the telecommunications company, rightly states that it is a global company. Until recent reorganisations, it was true that Ericsson had global presence, but it did not act globally in any co-ordinated fashion. The view was that each Ericsson country president should have local autonomy. Although this made Ericsson very flexible and responsive to local needs, it was less appropriate when dealing with multinational customers wanting consistency of approach across the world.

Power structures

This aspect of the organisation's culture is particularly important when it comes to changing the way things are done. Power structures may have nothing to do with the way the organisation chart is drawn. Some individuals appear to have far more power than their status would suggest, either because of the force of their personality or because they exert some power based on expertise.

The importance of power structures as they relate to service delivery might be the negative power sometimes wielded by front-line employees. It would appear to delight some employees to withhold information from customers, because this gives them perverse satisfaction. If this is the case, it is quite possible that these employees feel that they are so powerless and undervalued in the organisation that they will employ this negative power tactic as a means of asserting their importance. Managers must be alert to this, partly because customer satisfaction will suffer as a result, but mainly because it may be that there are issues of leadership and motivation to be addressed.

Leaders use a combination of personal charisma, expertise and positional power to bring about change. In bringing about change it is critical to know where the powerful 'pro-change' people are in order to build alliances to see the change through. It is equally important to identify those who are able to block change. It is often necessary to look beyond the ranks of senior management to find individuals who, by reason of their character or past experience, are extremely influential.

For example, in a water company it became clear that a major factor in the delivery of a customer service strategy was the extent to which a group of relatively junior employees would buy into a new customer-focused approach. Rather like non-commissioned officers in the armed forces, this group had the ability to prevent anything occurring that did not fit with their views. The implementation of the service strategy therefore had to include time for getting understanding and commitment from this group.

Of course, power can also be used very positively to engender customer focus. No one can dispute the influence of Lord Marshall at British Airways or Jack Welch at GE in driving through improvements in customer service.

Control systems

Control systems are the guiding infrastructure of the organisation. What is of interest here is the identification of the control systems that have significant impact on the way things are done. For some organisations, everything must follow well-defined procedures which, as we have seen in Chapter 9, may deliver consistent results but leave little room for flexibility. Others have very little in the way of formal controls apart from the need to deliver certain long-term goals. The means by which these are achieved are left to the discretion of the individual.

Performance measurement is at the heart of most control systems (see Chapter 9). Tony Hughes, managing director of Mitchells & Butlers Restaurants, frequently uses the quote 'What gets measured gets managed, but what gets rewarded gets done'. Other examples may be provided by those organisations that reward people for customer satisfaction performance above profit. In the development of IBM's Global Services division which we introduced in Chapter 1 the company developed a principle of putting the customer and customer satisfaction before everything else. While it had a range of key performance measures, customer satisfaction was recognised to be the driver of revenue and profit. Brian Sellwood, general manager of IBM Global Services, said:

> There was always a danger that individual profit targets and business measures of success would come before any other measures of success. We gave out a very strong message that said – the only thing that matters are your customers and if those customers are happy with what you are doing for them. It's customer first, IBM second and individual business and departments third in terms of any decision you make.

Danny Meyer, a famous restaurateur and American entrepreneur, also had strong views about the importance of not only customers but also staff:

> My appreciation of the power of hospitality and my desire to harness it have been the greatest contributors to whatever success my restaurants and businesses have had. I've learned how crucially important it is to put hospitality to work, first for the people who work for me and subsequently for all the other people and stakeholders who are in any way affected by

our business – in descending order, our employees, our guests, our community, our suppliers, and our investors. It stands some traditional business approaches on their head, but it's the foundation of every business decision and every success we've had.[5]

Why do we care for our stakeholders in that particular order? The interests of our own employees must be placed directly ahead of those of our guests because the only way we can consistently earn raves, win repeat business, and develop bonds of loyalty with our guests is first to ensure our own team members feel jazzed about coming to work. Being jazzed is a combination of feeling motivated, enthusiastic, confident, proud and at peace with the choice to work in our team. I place the interests of our investors fifth, but not because I don't want to earn a lot of money. On the contrary, I staunchly believe that standing conventional business priorities on their head ultimately leads to even greater, more enduring financial success.[6]

Kwik-Fit has also focused the efforts of branch managers and staff on customer service by managing inventory and other administrative processes centrally. To avoid losing a business focus, each group of branches has its own 'profit and loss' account to understand how the mission of achieving '100% customer delight' links with business success. A recent service quality initiative in the charity Mencap has been facilitated by providing central support to remove unnecessary 'noise' or bureaucracy from its front-line delivery units.

Organisational control systems often lag behind what is desired to reinforce new behaviours. The manager of a unit responsible for the development of new revenue-earning services for a computer hardware company was frustrated because the regional sales managers were bonused solely on hardware sales. He was on the brink of signing the first major services deal but it was threatened because the hardware content was so small that it would damage the sales manager's bonus. He decided that in order to establish the fact that services were essential for the long-term survival of the company, he would carry the loss-making component on his own budget to maintain the sales manager's support and interest.

Routines and rituals

These are the activities that are not necessarily in the organisation's procedure manual but nevertheless describe the ways that the organisation operates in practice. They have special significance for the organisation. They might range from informal systems, such as ways of getting round bureaucratic or inflexible procedures, through to celebrations of success, such as pub nights or parties.

The managing director of Credit Card Sentinel sent thank-you cards to people who had done well – a relatively inexpensive exercise that brought about tremendous returns in employee satisfaction. Avis and other companies practise 'visible management', where head-office managers spend time each year in the front-line units. Avis found that it was invaluable for head-office staff to understand the issues of the front line, and they frequently discover that renting cars is not as easy as it looks on paper.

Other routines and rituals may be less helpful. The ritual hunt for a scapegoat after each disaster does not contribute greatly to team spirit. Other rituals may become a way of dealing with the difficulties of the job. This is particularly true where staff have to deal with emotionally difficult situations such as in a hospital or at an accident site. Hospitals develop an almost mechanistic approach to their patients to guard against becoming too emotionally involved. This may have an unfortunate impact on patients, who feel they are treated as just another statistic rather than as human beings with feelings.

The analysis of routines is extremely rich as it betrays much of the 'under the surface' life of the organisation. It gives clues about how things really happen as opposed to the sanitised version that appears in the official handbook. When people are able to discuss routines honestly, they may uncover such things as how important decisions are made (corridor conversations and inner cabinets) and how people are promoted (not on merit but on who they know). Recognising this aspect of organisational life is important in order to influence it to support service delivery. Much damage has been done by managers who eliminate informal activities in order to save cost, but then find that team spirit has disappeared.

Symbols

Symbols are the physical evidence of who or what is important in the culture. A couple of decades ago it was relatively easy to see who was important in a large organisation because the managers' status was linked to which floor their office was located on, with directors at the top and junior staff at the bottom. Today, with a move towards flatter organisations and a reduction in overt differences between management and staff, the organisational status symbols have become more subtle. Who has a parking space or a fitted carpet in their office (or who has an office at all) become major talking points. In open-plan offices, the size of a person's desk, or who has a special chair, suddenly become all-important. It is as if these symbols take on a life of their own, as anyone who has been involved with a company car scheme will testify. It may seem on the surface that people have accepted quite major shifts in role during organisational change programmes, but their reaction to the loss of a valued symbol may demonstrate that they are far from happy.

Symbols may also be the human role models of the organisation. Certain charismatic leaders may become symbols of change, as, for example, Richard Branson of Virgin, Herb Kelleher at Southwest Airlines, or Tom Farmer of Kwik-Fit. Their role in modelling customer-focused behaviours cannot be emphasised enough.

The relevance for customer focus may lie in how symbols become linked to service. In a security alarm company, sales staff had cars, while service engineers had vans. This might make rational sense, but sent a clear message that service was very much the poor relation. A compromise was reached by providing service engineers with estate cars, which could, of course, be used for private as well as company use.

Stories

The final aspect of the cultural web is the stories that circulate in the organisation. These are sometimes called the 'war stories' and are generally told to new starters early in their stay in an organisation. In some organisations, these stories are generally positive ('We're ahead of the competition, this is a good place to work'), while in others they tend to be negative ('Welcome to the madhouse, don't take any risks, keep your head down'). In large organisations that have been in existence for several years, and have been through major change, stories relating to the 'good old days' abound.

Part of a process of influencing culture might lie in creating a new set of stories linking heroic acts of customer service to success. The famous stories, such as Federal Express taking initiative to hire a helicopter to get an essential package through, or of Nordstrom refunding a customer for a faulty tyre even though Nordstrom had never sold tyres, do build a culture of customer ownership. On the other hand, stories of staff who have been disciplined for giving relatively small refunds for poor service because they did not follow company red tape are extremely damaging.

Using the cultural web

Table 16.1 shows the cultural web analysis for a financial service company. A typical process for developing this analysis is as follows:

- Develop a common understanding of the key elements of current culture, possibly through the use of facilitated focus groups.
- Examine the current paradigm and decide what aspects would be desirable to change to fit with future strategic direction.
- Identify mismatches between the desired paradigm and current elements of the cultural web.
- Develop action plans to influence or change where possible.

Table 16.1 Cultural web analysis for a financial service company

	Existing cultural web	Desired cultural web
Paradigm	Provider of general insurance and pensions Dealing through brokers, not the general public Profitable because of good investment management Generally risk-averse A 'nice' company	To be seen as providing freedom from worry for customers To be profitable through acting with integrity, providing innovative financial products to meet the changing needs of customers, and delivering them through excellent service
Organisational structures	Regionally organised with branches and sub-branches Hierarchical, with several management grades Insurance and pensions are separate organisations	Organised in teams around customer delivery processes Providing total solutions for customers in 'one-stop-shops' Service delivered direct to consumers
Power structures	Executive management committee Managers who came from Company A prior to the recent merger Actuaries	Executive management committee More influence for those in customer-facing roles
Control systems	Company procedures manual Financial services legislation Risk analysis Sales incentives	Long-term customer retention and profitability Emphasis on developing competence of employees Team incentives
Routines and rituals	Management dinners Senior management visits to branches Promotion on seniority Poor performers 'promoted' to 'special projects'	Recognition of excellent performance in both sales and service Promotion on merit
Symbols	Who has a personal assistant Quality of company car Latest laptop/organiser/IT software	Certificates for achievement
Stories	Amount spent on directors' dining room How good Christmas parties were years ago Senior manager fired for fraud	Celebrations of actions 'beyond the call of duty' Generation of new business through customer referrals

Managers may feel that there is little that they can do to change the organisation's culture. Certainly, to make a major shift in culture is not something that can be accomplished by one individual overnight. However, most managers are part of the power structure, and are able to influence their areas of operation. The value of cultural web analysis as shown in Table 16.1 is that it is possible to identify means of changing aspects of the culture. For example, new reward systems change the emphasis of the control systems relatively quickly. Likewise, it is easy to develop new stories, or to at least ensure that the positive stories are communicated effectively.

In reality, the core culture of an organisation changes extremely slowly. A common pitfall is to claim that a recent initiative has brought about significant cultural change. There may have been a shift in *behaviour* which, if maintained and reinforced, will contribute to culture change. It takes a great deal of time, usually several years, for a shift to be truly embedded in the culture. First Direct (see Case Example 16.2) provides a good example of an organisation that has paid careful attention to all aspects of its culture in order to provide a consistent service.

Case Example 16.2 First Direct

Visitors to First Direct's website will find many words that this bank uses to describe itself. These include personalised, friendly, responsible, innovative and outstanding service.

First Direct, the first 'branchless' telephone bank in the UK, began operations in 1989. Its concept was simple: to provide 24-hour banking for 365 days a year. At the heart of the operation was an information system that allowed the customer to handle any traditional branch transaction in a single telephone call. It would have been tempting to recruit staff for this new operation from First Direct's parent, the then Midland Bank (now HSBC).

The management team took a significant decision to look for people who were fast and efficient, able to work under pressure, but, critically, people with warm personalities. Much of this is due to the vision of a past CEO, Kevin Newman, who is quoted as saying:

Source: First Direct

I believe that in going forward three things need to be developed. We have to be utterly low cost. We must be able to individualise the manufacturing process and recognise that all our customers are individuals. Third, we must build a strong brand as people need to identify with institutions they can trust.

First Direct identified five core values as central to the way it was to operate, and these were incorporated in the training programme for staff, who were to be known as banking representatives (BRs). The core values were responsiveness, openness, right first time, respect and contribution. These values were reinforced by Newman and his management team, who spent a significant amount of their time talking to BRs. Right from day one, Newman wanted First Direct to have a different culture from traditional banks. Everyone ate in the same cafeteria, and managers were on first-name terms with BRs. The only perk that Newman enjoyed was a company car. There was no 'headquarters' – managers and directors sat at desks in the same area as the BRs. There was minimal hierarchy, with managers encouraged to concentrate on leadership and guidance rather than interference and instruction.

BRs undertook a seven-week training course before dealing with customers. The first four weeks were dedicated to understanding the bank's products, while the latter three weeks concentrated on telephone role-playing and relationship building techniques. First Direct made limited use of scripting techniques, and BRs were encouraged to build rapport, using language appropriate to the individual customer. BRs worked in teams, with a team leader acting as a coach. The teams were encouraged to develop their own identities, and to create team names. First Direct invested in facilities for the 24-hour workforce. A security firm guards car parks and reception areas, and hot food is available from 7.00 a.m. until 9.00 p.m. Staff are encouraged to attend lifestyle classes covering subjects as diverse as foreign languages and yoga.

Much of the continued success of First Direct has been attributed to its friendly, responsive culture. First Direct's website proclaims that it 'actively promotes a positive working environment'. This has been achieved without the loss of efficiency or consistency. Clearly, this is due in no small part to the culture created by Newman, his management team, and those who followed them.

Source: This illustration is based on personal experience, from information from First Direct's website (www.firstdirect.co.uk), and Insead case study 597-028-1: *First Direct: Branchless Banking*.

16.4 What are the main culture types and the implications for service delivery?

16.4.1 The 'gods' of management

It is important to know the difference between cultures, recognising too that different cultural environments exist within the same organisation. The culture of the boardroom will be rather different from that in the call centre. Likewise, the culture of the accounts department will be very different from that of the sales team. There are a number of factors that influence this diversity, which include individual personalities, the nature of the role undertaken, and the extent to which people have direct customer contact.

Writers on leadership and culture identify various types of culture.[7] Handy and Kakabadse both identify power, role and task cultures. Handy, however, uses the term 'club culture' for power culture, and introduces a fourth category, existential culture.

Handy aligns each of these cultures to a Greek god, giving a useful insight into the various characteristics of these cultures:

- *Zeus – the club culture.* Zeus was the king of the gods, ruling by patronage combined with fear. This culture is found in entrepreneurial organisations and frequently at the very summit of large organisations. It is excellent for speed of decision-making, where key people are chosen because they think and act like the (central) leader. Such organisations can be very effective when they are based on trust, but can be terrible places when an evil Zeus abuses his power.

- *Apollo – the role culture.* This culture is one of rules and order. It is stable and predictable – excellent when the market is not changing rapidly. The individual's role in the organisation is clear, and little initiative is required. The traditional role culture is safe, because nothing changes and someone else (or the system) takes care of things.

- *Athena – the task culture.* Athena is a warrior-goddess, a problem solver. The basis of this culture is expertise, not experience, age or position. Handy states that this culture works well when the product of the organisation is the solution to a problem. This is an expensive culture, because it is staffed by experts and the outcomes are not predictable, often requiring development time and resource. When Athena cultures get large they require Apollonian cultures to manage the routine activities.

- *Dionysus – the existential culture.* Here the emphasis is that the individual is in charge of their own destiny. Handy suggests that in the other three cultures the individual is there to help the organisation achieve its purpose, but that in this culture the organisation exists to help the individual. Professionals may be grouped together in one building because someone can then organise support systems such as telephones and catering, but there is no interdependence between the individuals.

Table 16.2 provides a summary of some of the ways that these different cultures operate.

The shape of organisational life is changing. The large Apollonian cultures are fast disappearing as they need to adapt more rapidly to changing market demands. More organisations are taking on the form of Athena, the task culture, though frequently with Apollo-like support structures, and with a Zeus at the top.

Recently there has been the emergence of 'virtual' organisations or 'hollow' corporations. These are somewhat Athena-like in concept in that the organisation exists for a particular task and then disbands. Film and television programme-makers operate in this fashion, with a producer being commissioned to gather together a team for the one project. Networks of experts, part Athena, part Dionysus, form loose associations constantly changing shape to meet the current need. However, it would be wrong to believe that Apollo does not exist anymore. There are plenty of Apollo-like organisations in existence still, able to operate consistently and efficiently.

Table 16.2   Summary of different cultures

	Thinking and learning	Influencing and changing	Motivating and rewarding
Zeus (club culture)	Trial and error Watching other Zeuses Learning by sitting with the 'master' Admission of need to learn is a sign of weakness	Change by replacing people, not development Judged by who, not what, you know Credibility is the key	Money is highly valued Reward is to be given responsibility and resource by Zeus Winning is crucial
Apollo (role culture)	Logical and analytical Acquisition of more knowledge and skills through training courses Appraisals and job rotation	Power from position, role or title Rules and procedures Managers implement directors' decisions	Pensions schemes and career planning Increase in formal authority Status symbols
Athena (task culture)	Problem solving Brainstorming Learning as a team Opportunities for development	Persuasion through expertise Debate and consensus Problem definition Need a new problem to solve	Objectives, not role definitions Variety
Dionysus (existential culture)	Learn by total immersion Give up, having mastered a new skill	Difficult to influence Unpredictable, need to negotiate	Opportunity to make a difference in their terms Freedom

There is not necessarily an 'ideal' culture or organisational shape for service delivery. Service operations managers need to recognise the strengths and weaknesses of their organisation and learn to adapt styles to suit their situation.

16.4.2 The 'gods' and service delivery

Inspection of Table 16.2 suggests a number of ways that these different cultures might impact on service delivery:

- *Zeus.* Zeus cultures are very responsive to customers. They are able to react quickly and harness resources to meet the current need. These cultures are particularly effective when a good personal relationship exists between the chief executives of the supplier and the customer organisations. Zeusit types recognise and admire other Zeus personalities. These relationships, if founded on mutual respect and trust, can be very fruitful in developing long-term business. Service delivery to these valued customers is likely to be of high quality, as Zeus will ensure that resources are made available, paying personal attention to this customer. Service delivery to other customers, seen as less interesting to Zeus, may not receive the same attention from the top, and service delivery may suffer as a result. The Zeus culture tends to create repeaters and strangers because Zeus has little or no interest in the routine of runners unless he appoints an Apollo manager to lead 'business as usual' operations.

- *Apollo.* These organisations are extremely consistent in the way that they follow standard operating procedures. Many high-volume services, such as retailers, some public sector organisations, utilities and insurance companies, have much of this culture. The problem is that they may be experienced as rather inflexible by their customers. The attitude of 'that's more than my job's worth' or 'I can't do that' is the downside of the reliability and efficiency that they deliver. This culture thrives on runners, tolerates repeaters and resists strangers.

- *Athena.* This culture is appropriate when the output is a solution for customers, rather than a packaged commodity that an Apollo organisation might deliver. This organisation is therefore flexible, and is good at involving its customers in the process of developing the required solution. Specialist software developers and consultants may fall into this category. The problem with these organisations is that, although they are innovative, they get bored with the continual delivery of the same service solution. At this stage, an Apollo-like organisation form may be appropriate for consistency and cost. This culture seeks the opportunity to develop new capability for strangers, it tolerates repeaters in order to generate sufficient revenue, and it resists runners.

- *Dionysus.* This culture is a nightmare as far as service delivery is concerned. These individuals will only operate if the task is of interest, and no amount of pleading or bribery will change their mind. Customers are liable to be made to feel that they are somewhat inferior to the service provider, only taken on because they are an 'interesting case'. This culture is only interested in strangers, and will not even consider runners.

Finally, an important point to note is that an understanding of the difference in organisational culture is particularly relevant in a business-to-business relationship. Apollo customer cultures are likely to be confused and frustrated by Athena supplier cultures and vice versa.

16.5 What is the influence of national cultures?

A chapter on culture would be incomplete without at least a mention of the influence of national cultures on service delivery. Hofstede conducted a major cross-cultural study of IBM employees to identify characteristics of national cultures. He identified four dimensions that can be used to rate national culture:[8]

- *Power-distance.* A high power-distance rating would suggest that employees are relatively passive, have a liking to be directed, and inhabit a culture that generally expects superiors to wield power. The corollary to this is that superiors frequently exhibit low trust of subordinates. Many Asian cultures have high power-distance ratings. Low power-distance rankings encourage greater mutual trust and an expectation that subordinates will be involved in decision-making. The UK, some of Western Europe and the USA fall into this second group.

- *Uncertainty avoidance.* This dimension evaluates the extent to which the culture encourages risk-taking. Cultures with high uncertainty avoidance adopt strategies such as working long hours and enforcing strict obedience to procedures to deal with difficult conditions. Much of the Japanese work ethic exhibits this tendency. Low uncertainty avoidance encourages a more entrepreneurial spirit, with less concern for following rigid procedures.

- *Individualism–collectivism.* The UK, along with the USA and Canada, places high regard on the achievements of individuals, whereas some cultures value loyalty to extended family or tribe more highly. In the latter case, the emphasis is on belonging, duty and group decision-making.

- *Masculinity–femininity.* The masculinity-dominant cultures place emphasis on acquisition of money and material possessions and on ambition. Managers are encouraged to press for ever-increasing goals and objectives. Where femininity is dominant, the emphasis is on creating a more collaborative environment.

This work is interesting in that it challenges assumptions that all people are the same. It clearly has implications for the implementation of global operations strategies; for example, team-work and empowerment may not translate from one culture to another. It is necessary to point out, though, that the assumption that all people from a national culture rank high on power-distance, low on uncertainty avoidance and so on is clearly inaccurate. One hypothesis is that at an organisational level the company or organisation culture might be more influen-tial, not least because the organisation's recruitment policies will tend to favour 'people like us'. Later studies clearly indicate that company culture has more influence on the behaviour of senior executives in global organisations.

A key issue to be addressed is that of flexibility between the organisational values and the elements of national culture.[9] If the organisational values are perceived to be fundamental to competitive advantage and they clash with national culture, then the service will fail. For example, if McDonald's had been unwilling to compromise over its products, the company would not have been able to succeed in countries with a strong Islamic culture.

The Four Seasons hotel chain has opened hotels across the globe, each reflecting the local culture, yet each adhering to high standards of excellence. Senior managers speak of being cultural chameleons. Antoine Corinthios, president of Europe, Middle East and Africa, em-phasises that there are some global standards such as cleanliness and fast response, but

> What changes is that people do it with their own style, grace and personality; in some cultures you add the strong local temperament. For example, an Italian concierge has his own style and flair. In Turkey and Egypt you experience very different service.

Recognition of this enabled Four Seasons to take over the operation of the legendary George V Hotel in Paris, operating the core standards of the Four Seasons chain but not insisting on the same service and managerial approach that has been applied in other areas.

16.6   How can managers influence cultural change?

16.6.1 Strategies for cultural change

There is not sufficient space here to cover all the aspects of the management of change, so we discuss some of the issues that specifically relate to service delivery. Bate[10] provides a helpful overview of strategies for cultural change. He suggests four basic approaches:

- *Progressive.* This approach is used when there is not time for a consultative approach. Sen-ior managers have to implement change rapidly, frequently upsetting staff in the process. This approach (also termed aggressive) is effective in implementing rapid major change, but is poor in gaining commitment and ownership of the result.

- *Consultative.* This approach is characterised by a great deal of communication and in-volvement. It is excellent for gaining commitment, but poor at implementing a radical solution.

- *Educative.* Here, the organisation provides material and training to explain why the change is necessary. It is based on the view that if people can (rationally) understand the need for change, they will be happy to support it. Education and training have been shown to be effective (we would say that!), but one problem is that people do not react to change ra-tionally. The other common issue with this approach is that the organisational 'road-show' is often seen as playing mind-games with the employees. Hence this is also termed the indoctrinative approach.

- *Corrosive.* This is akin to the organisation's grapevine. Senior management 'lets loose' the key messages at key points throughout the organisation. This approach is much favoured by those who must attempt to manage groups of professionals, who often resist any form of direct control.

Most change processes will contain elements of all four approaches. It is important to note that if, in the early process of change, it has been necessary to employ the progressive/aggressive approach, managers must be alert to the danger of disaffected staff displaying unhelpful customer attitudes.

Bate then outlines five parameters to assess the success of the change process:

- *Expressiveness.* This measures the extent to which the change process communicates a new idea. This is what people call 'hearts and minds'. A new mission statement that captures the imagination of the employees will be invaluable here, particularly if this statement is lived up to by senior management.

- *Commonality.* Culture is produced when people speak to each other. This parameter assesses the extent to which everyone speaks the same language and means the same thing. The question here is 'Is there a sense of solidarity because we know what we are trying to achieve?'

- *Penetration.* To what extent has the change really 'got inside' the organisation? Has it begun to change the way that things are done, particularly at the level of routines and rituals? Has it got to the point where it cannot be ignored?

- *Adaptability.* Is the change process able to deal with the diversity of situations represented in a large, complex organisation? Can those responsible for implementation maintain the essence of the change, making helpful local adaptations? Can it be questioned and rethought in key areas without losing credibility?

- *Durability.* Is it tamper-proof? Will it transcend the departure of the chief executive? Is it clear that this change will not go away?

16.6.2 Actions to ensure success

One of the most helpful summaries of the problems of change management is provided by Kotter,[11] who identified common pitfalls in implementing change, turning them into actions to ensure success.

- *Establish a sense of urgency.* Kotter quotes a key statistic that 75 per cent of managers must accept the need for major and immediate change if it is to be successful. In order to get managers out of their comfort zone, they must be confronted with a compelling case for change. Front-line service employees often require little persuasion as they face the mismatch between customer requirements and delivery on a daily basis.

- *Form a powerful guiding coalition.* For service organisations this is vital to gaining the commitment of customer-facing staff as well as senior management. Kotter suggested that building a team approach is central to success.

- *Create a vision.* Too many organisations implement initiative after initiative without a clear sense of how they fit together. A vision, as with the service concept, should be a unifying factor. Researchers in the area of change management generally agree that creating a picture of the desired destination is a requirement – what will the future look like?

- *Communicate the vision.* Kotter suggests that management generally under-communicates by a factor of ten. Providing opportunities for employees to ask questions, even if management feel that the answers have already been given, is a critical activity. Employees usually trust their immediate manager or team leader more than the senior management team, which is often remote and seen as pursuing its own agendas. The first-line supervisor or team leader is therefore central to the implementation of a new service vision.

- *Empower others to act on the vision.* The objective is to remove obstacles to change. Encouraging employees to attempt new approaches consistent with the vision will build momentum towards the desired change. It is necessary to ensure that job roles and measurement systems are consistent with the change required, rather than hope that they will catch up. Any significant change will meet overt and covert resistance, which must be faced.

- *Plan for and create short-term wins.* Staff need credible evidence of some success within 12 to 24 months. This needs to be managed, and the efforts of employees responsible for these successes should be recognised and rewarded.

- *Consolidate improvements and produce still more change.* It is tempting to slacken off the pressure at the first signs of success. Unless the changes have taken root in the rituals of the organisation, the process is not complete.

- *Institutionalise new approaches.* There must be a conscious attempt to demonstrate how new approaches and behaviours have helped to improve performance. Management should make the links between changes and success as explicit as possible, even though this should seem obvious. Secondly, effort should be applied to ensuring that the next generation of leaders at all levels of the organisation understand and deliver the new culture.

The illustration of Amnesty International in Case Example 16.3 demonstrates the complexity of change in service strategy when those involved have affiliations to more than one group in the organisation. It is insufficient to present a change as 'being the right thing to do', even if this can be supported with rational arguments. In many cases, people's loyalties to local groups may be more powerful than logic.

Case Example 16.3   Amnesty International

Amnesty International was founded in 1961 by Peter Benenson, a British lawyer, and today it has over a million members and supporters spread across over 150 countries. Its objectives are to promote general awareness of human rights and to oppose specific abuses of human rights.

Amnesty has both volunteers and professionals (paid staff). It is organised into two main groups, the International Secretariat in London and over fifty national sections. The International Secretariat is the research headquarters of the organisation, with specialists in many fields sifting and checking information about alleged abuses before initiating action. The national sections contain the 'grass roots' of the volunteer membership, being responsible for activist campaigning, local recruitment, fund raising and so on.

Unfortunately, Amnesty's field of interest is expanding rather than becoming redundant. In many parts of the world there are incidents of human rights abuse. For a number of years Amnesty's work had little co-ordinated international strategy. The approach until the early 1990s was that each of the national sections would be involved to a greater or lesser extent in all aspects of Amnesty's work. This led to a dilution of resources and a somewhat haphazard approach to dealing with abuse of human rights.

Source: Pearson Education Ltd/Corbis

The direction of Amnesty is debated in depth every two years at the International Council Meeting (ICM). It was at the ICM in 1991 that the membership of the national sections understood that, in order to meet the increasing challenges, Amnesty would have to act on a basis of international co-ordination rather than simply be an international organisation comprising many national sections.

The impact on the national sections has been that they are no longer left to develop their own plans in isolation. Under an initiative termed 'specialisation' each section must determine its particular strategic focus, taking into consideration its strengths and opportunities. This development of particular strengths for each national section is linked to an international planning process. The International Secretariat in London has the responsibility for determining priority levels for country research and campaigning projects, in consultation with the national sections.

The national sections were initially nervous that they would lose 'universality' and would lose touch with what was going on across the world. In reality, many sections probably never had the ability or desire to address all the potential issues in every place where Amnesty was involved. Most national sections contain a number of local or regional groups. This same process of specialisation has been applied within national sections to these local groups, each taking on a different emphasis of fund raising, public awareness or specific geographical action.

16.6.3 Capacity for change

Finally, many change initiatives fail because they are under-resourced. This is a concept that should be understood by operations managers. Change fails because managers do not have the capability to manage it. If this is so, the organisation must recruit or buy this ability. Another common problem is that the organisation does not have the capacity to manage the process as well as maintain 'business as usual'. Research has suggested that managers living though change experience something similar to the bereavement process, illustrated in Figure 16.3.[12] The transition curve shows the individual's response to a proposed (enforced) change. From a point of relatively high perceived competence, the individual is initially shocked and then fairly quickly moves to the denial state, which can mean pretending either that the change will go away, or that they can deal with whatever comes their way. This state leads to a downward spiral into reality as they recognise that the new environment

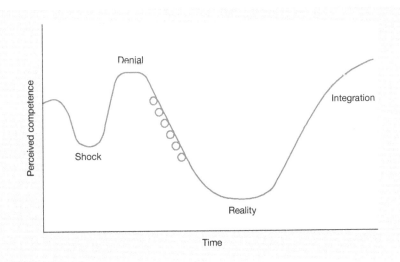

Figure 16.3 The transition curve

will require the acquisition of new skills and new ways of working. Having reached this low point, the individual needs, often by trial and error, to begin to integrate new approaches into their way of working.

Managers going through a change process need time to understand the impact on themselves, let alone those who work for them. The transition curve is generally estimated to require a period of two years to elapse from beginning to end, though this is only an average figure. The implication for operations managers is that they must dedicate resources to managing staff through any period of significant change if 'business as usual' service is to be maintained to an acceptable standard. At each stage of the transition curve managers must respond appropriately.

Shock

In the early stages, when the employees are in shock, it is important to answer questions as honestly as possible, recognising that since the detail has yet to be worked through it is unlikely that definitive answers can be given. Time must be set aside to be available for questioning, even if in the management's eyes nothing is happening. We worked with two companies who were merging. Because of the requirement to harmonise information systems, there was little action apparent to most employees for several weeks. A senior manager told a group of junior managers 'We haven't spoken to you about the merger for some weeks, because we felt there was nothing to say.' You can probably imagine the anger experienced by his audience.

Denial

In the denial stage it is important to continue to reinforce the fact that the change will take place – to reiterate the business or market reasons for the change. It is also important to be careful about how the past is described. There is often a temptation to oversell the future in an effort to gain commitment to the proposed change. In so doing there is a danger of 'rubbishing' the past efforts and achievements, forgetting that the very people you are trying to motivate were very proud of what they achieved. It is sometimes useful to have some form of 'rite of passage', recognising the achievements of the past, and allowing people to mourn before moving on.

Reality

There comes a point when it becomes apparent that the change is going to happen. People may be moved to new roles, new organisational structures are put in place, and some people may leave the organisation. Some people may be unsure as to whether they will be able to cope with new roles and will need a fair amount of mentoring initially. They will need encouragement, since they may not perform as well as they would like. Carrying out pilot studies will help build confidence and reduce resistance to change.

Integration

At this point, the change has become part of the organisation. It is easier to go forward rather than go back, but the manager must be careful not to relax too soon. As we saw in section 16.6.2, one of the common pitfalls is declaring victory too fast. Operations managers must now work through the detail of the organisation's culture, such as reward and recognition schemes, promotion criteria and informal routines, to ensure that the desired behaviours are encouraged.

16.7 Summary

Why is understanding and influencing organisational culture important?

- Understanding and influencing organisational culture is central to delivering a consistent service and implementing change.

What is organisational culture?

- Culture may be considered to be tangible or intangible, and to exist at three levels: as artefacts, as espoused values and as basic underlying assumptions.
- The cultural web is a useful way of understanding organisational culture and can also be used to help managers understand how they can influence culture.

What are the main culture types and the implications for service delivery?

- Culture can be characterised as gods: Zeus – the club culture, Apollo – the role culture, Athena – the task culture, and Dionysus – the existential culture.
- Each type of culture has a different impact on the service delivery system.

What is the influence of national cultures?

- National cultures can be characterised along four dimensions: power-distance, uncertainty avoidance, individualism–collectivism and masculinity–femininity.
- Global businesses must understand potential conflicts between organisational values and cultural norms.

How can managers influence cultural change?

- There are four main strategies for change: progressive, consultative, educative and corrosive.
- The pitfalls to avoid include:
  - not establishing a sense of urgency
  - not creating a powerful guiding coalition
  - lacking a vision
  - under-communicating
  - not removing obstacles to the vision
  - not planning for short-term wins
  - declaring victory too soon
  - not anchoring the change in the organisation's culture
- The transition curve provides insight into the various stages of change, and the manager's role in leading change.

16.8 Discussion questions

1 Construct a cultural web for your university/college course. Which elements of the web help or hinder service delivery? What god of management is at work here?

2 Which elements of the cultural web can operations managers influence? Interview a service operations manager and ask how they can influence the organisation's culture in order to provide better service.

3 Evaluate an organisation's website or annual report and assess the words used, or not used. Describe their paradigm.

16.9 Questions for managers

1 Do you understand what the principal basic assumption of your organisation is? Does it support your service concept, or is the reason for poor performance the fact that your organisational culture is lagging behind your strategy?

2 Can you describe your organisation's/unit's culture in terms of the cultural web? In what way do you think your interpretation differs from other managers in your organisation?

3 What aspects of your organisation's cultural web can you influence? What action is required to support your organisation's competitive strategy?

4 Which of the 'gods of management' fits your organisation? Is this the type of organisation in which you want to work?

5 What lessons can you learn from Kotter's list of reasons for failure in managing change? How do they relate to your experience of change?

Case Exercise North Midlands Fire and Rescue Service

North Midlands Fire and Rescue Service (NMFRS) is one of the largest fire and rescue services in the country serving a population of over 1.5 million people. The service has 55 fire stations and attends around 25,000 emergency incidents per year, mostly fires and road traffic collisions. NMFRS also provides emergency response to hazardous material incidents and maintains a search and rescue team to conduct rescues from collapsed buildings and enclosed spaces. Another primary role of the service is preventative community safety work, such as encouraging people to install smoke detectors.

NMFRS employs 1,868 staff, including 957 full-time firefighters and 420 retained firefighters (those who have other full-time jobs but attend incidents on a call-out basis). The rest are management/support/administrative staff including the Chief Fire Officer's (CFO) team (deputy and assistant CFOs, all of whom worked their way up from being firefighters themselves), a strategy team, HR, finance, procurement, health and safety, communications and training.

Eighteen months ago, after dismissing the previous CFO, the North Midlands Fire Authority (a statutory body comprised of local councillors which oversees the policy and service delivery of NMFRS) appointed Dan Pursell to turn the service around. NMFRS was one of the poorest performing FRSs. It had a higher than average number of fatalities from fires, one of the slowest arrival times to fires, high injury rates and higher than average rates of absenteeism. There was also low morale in its workforce, both support staff and firefighters.

Shortly after his appointment Dan held a series of away days with his team of deputies and assistants, together with the area commanders and the directors of the various administrative departments. Together they created a new vision for their service – 'Making the North Midlands a safer place to live, work and visit'. From this the senior staff developed, over a six-month period of consultation, a set of values for their service:

- *Treating people fairly and with respect*
- *Striving for excellence in everything we do*
- *Being open-minded and learning from experience*
- *Honesty, integrity and mutual trust*
- *Effective and efficient working.*

From this the senior team developed a six-point strategy to guide their work:

- *To meet the needs of local people and make them safer*
- *To continually improve our service to the communities we serve and our engagement with them*
- *To ensure we are open and accountable for our actions*
- *To work in partnership with other service providers (police, local authorities, health services etc.) to improve the quality of life for local people*
- *To have a well-motivated, healthy and safe workforce with the right knowledge, skills and behaviours to provide an excellent service*
- *To manage our buildings and other equipment efficiently and effectively and to minimise our impact on the environment.*

This material was developed into a report called 'Working Together' supported by a set of engaging Power-Point slides. The 'Working Together' report was first presented to the Fire Authority and gained its support. The Fire Authority's Chief Executive commended the Chief Fire Officer and said she looked forward to seeing the results of this work. The Chief Fire Officer then created a road-show, again called 'Working Together', and presented it at several meetings to various groups in the Head Office. He, or one of his deputies, then took the road-show to each of the fire stations (twice because of the different watches – sets of firefighters covering different times of day and night) to inform the staff of the new direction for their Fire Service.

The local firefighters, their watch leaders and local officers were less than impressed. The following is a representative list of comments (collected by an independent researcher) made shortly after the 'Working Together' road-show:

- *This is the first time we have seen a manager for years. They only ever come here to tell us off. We never get any appreciation.*
- *What's this got to do with us and the job we do – how does it help us fight fires and deal with traffic accidents?*
- *HQ is out of touch with the reality. They work on their own projects and agenda but it has no relation to the work we do.*
- *The corporate values are just words: they are not real.*
- *They don't listen to our ideas.*
- *We are not allowed to question anything.*
- *We are not clear what the criteria are for recruitment, probation or my advancement.*
- *No-one has had the courtesy to tell us what the system is or what the success criteria are, and so I can't tell my team.*
- *When we ask questions they are too busy in meetings and away days to tell us.*
- *They don't explain things in fireman's talk.*
- *The presentations are full of management speak.*
- *They do management, we need leadership.*
- *They are good at checking, controlling, creating policies, having meetings – how does that help us?*
- *There is a widening chasm between them and us.*
- *If we need to get something, it always seems to be difficult to get it.*

- *No-one seems to appreciate what we do.*
- *They keep changing things, dropping things and they never follow things through.*
- *They communicate a lot but in the wrong way and only one direction.*
- *We need to introduce training for firefighters not training for leaders.*
- *They forget their grass roots: they are too busy doing their KPIs and politics.*
- *They get a chip implanted when they become management.*
- *It's like dealing with a machine.*
- *We want to do things and have lots of ideas but it's like talking to a blank wall. If it's not their idea they don't want to know.*
- *There is too much emphasis on targets, and they are the wrong targets.*
- *There are too many management initiatives.*

Dan read the list and groaned. He wondered how he could ever make a real difference to his Fire and Rescue Service.

Questions

1 How would you describe the culture of NMFRS?

2 What advice would you give Dan?

Suggested further reading

Edvardsson, Bo and Bo Enquist (2002), 'Service Culture and Service Strategy – The IKEA Saga', *The Service Industries Journal* 22 (4) 153–186

Johnson, Gerry, Kevan Scholes and Richard Whittington (2009), *Exploring Corporate Strategy: Text and Cases*, 8th edition, FT Prentice Hall

Kong, Mikyoung and Giri Jogaratnam (2007), 'The Influence of Culture on Perceptions of Service Employee Behaviour', *Managing Service Quality* 17 (3) 275–297

Prajogo, Daniel I. and Christopher M. McDermott (2005), 'The Relationship between Total Quality Management Practices and Organisational Culture', *International Journal of Operations and Production Management* 25 (11) 1101–1122

Sturdy, Andrew and Peter Fleming (2003), 'Talk as Technique – A Critique of the Words and Deeds Distinction in the Diffusion of Customer Service Cultures in Call Centres', *Journal of Management Studies* 40 (4) 753–773

Useful web links

The Society for Organizational Learning provides some interesting material, including work by Peter Senge and Edgar Schein:
www.solonline.org

An insight into group dynamics and their impact on change is provided by the Tavistock Institute:
www.tavinstitute.org or www.grouprelations.com

The Chartered Institute of Personnel and Development list a number of relevant publications, and provide the viewpoint of HR professionals regarding aspects of change management:
www.cipd.co.uk

Notes

1   De Chernatony, Leslie, Susan Drury and Susan Segal-Horn (2003), 'Building a Services Brand: Stages, People and Orientation', *Service Industries Journal* 23 (3) 1–21; Browning, Victoria (1998), 'Creating Service Excellence through Human Resource Management Practices', *South African Journal of Business Management* 29 (4) 135–142

2   See Hatch, Mary Jo with Ann Cunliffe (2006), *Organizational Theory,* 2nd edition, Oxford University Press, New York; Huczynski, Andrzej and David A. Buchanan (2007), *Organizational Behaviour,* 6th edition, Financial Times Prentice Hall, Harlow; Morgan, Gareth (2006), *Images of Organization,* 4th edition, Sage Publications

3   Schein, Edgar H. (2010), *Organizational Culture and Leadership,* 4th edition, Jossey-Bass

4   Johnson, Gerry, Kevan Scholes and Richard Whittington (2009), *Exploring Corporate Strategy: Text and Cases,* 8th edition, FT Prentice Hall

5   Meyer, Danny (2007), *Setting the Table,* Harper Collins, New York, p. 2

6   Meyer, Danny (2007), *Setting the Table,* Harper Collins, New York, p. 238

7   Kakabadse, Andrew and Nada Kakabadse (1998), *Essence of Leadership,* Thomson Learning; Handy, Charles (2009), *Gods of Management,* Souvenir Press; Hofstede, Geert (1996), *Cultures and Organisations Software of the Mind – Intercultural Cooperation and Its Importance for Survival,* McGraw-Hill, New York

8   Hofstede, Geert (1996), *Cultures and Organisations Software of the Mind – Intercultural Cooperation and Its Importance for Survival,* McGraw-Hill, New York

9   Hallowell, Roger, David Bowen and Carin-Isabel Knoop (2002), 'Four Seasons Go to Paris', *Academy of Management Executive* 16 (4) 7–24

10   Bate, Paul (1995), *Strategies for Cultural Change,* Butterworth-Heinemann, Oxford

11   Kotter, John P. (1995), 'Leading Change: Why Transformation Efforts Fail', *Harvard Business Review* 73 (2) 59–67

12   Bridges, William, (2002) *Managing transitions: Making the most of change,* Nicholas Brearly, London; Kübler-Ross, Elisabeth (1997) *On Death and Dying,* Prentice Hall

Chapter 17
Building a world-class service organisation

Chapter objectives

This chapter is about how to build a world-class organisation and deliver excellent service.

- What is excellent service?
- How do organisations go about becoming and remaining world-class?
- How can managers make the business case for service?

17.1 Introduction

World-class service organisations are those with reputations for providing excellent service (service excellence). This final chapter focuses on excellent service and how organisations can become, and remain, world-class. We hope it will also pull together much of the content of the book so far, because world-class service organisations have superior business performance that is the result of best-practice service operations management, i.e. superior process and experience design, good performance management, excellent staff and customer management, sound resource management and good processes to support continuous improvement and innovation.[1] These practices result from a clear vision, a clearly articulated service concept and strategy and an appropriate culture driven by good leadership. Importantly world-class organisations understand the relationships between their operations decisions and business performance. This enables them to make the business case for investing in service and also make better operational decisions.

The excellent service provided by world-class organisations delivers the 'triple bottom line'. It not only makes things better for the customer, but also better for the staff and better for the organisation, and we would also add, better for the economy.

Excellent service – a good experience, the right outcome with the right 'products' and benefits – will satisfy, indeed delight customers. Any organisation that has a reputation for delivering excellent service is also likely to have good, committed and engaged staff. If staff are constantly having to deal with the impact of poor service – complaining customers, unhelpful or inappropriate internal processes, poor technology, lack of managerial support etc. – they are likely to be unhappy and possibly stressed. Organisations with satisfied customers and good processes tend to have satisfied, even delighted staff, providing they have the right sort of leadership.

Excellent service is better for the organisation; it leads to higher revenues, lower costs (through improved processes), lower customer and staff turnover, thus greater profit in for-profit organisations. It will have excellent operating processes, staff and management (operational excellence) which will deliver the right returns to the organisation and its shareholders in a safe and sustainable way.

Having established its importance, let us explain what service excellence is and then how organisations go about becoming world-class and delivering excellent service.

17.2 What is excellent service?

It is interesting when we ask people what is excellent service. The usual answer is exceeding customer expectations. We need to explain why this is not quite the case.

Excellent service is the provision of a level of operational service quality that results in delight (perceived service quality). As consumers and users of many services, we all know when we have received excellent service and, rather more frequently, we know when we have not. Excellent service has a strong emotional impact upon us as customers, creating intense feelings about the organisation, its staff and its services, and influencing our loyalty to it. Yet many organisations seem to find service excellence elusive, hard to grasp, and also very difficult to deliver. Paradoxically, we, as individuals, instinctively know what it is and how simple it can be.[2]

Research commissioned by the Institute of Customer Service found that, in essence, service excellence is simply about being 'easy to do business with' (not necessarily exceeding expectations).[3] Respondents in the study described excellent service organisations as being 'a pleasure to work with'. The phrases about the nature of excellent service provided by the respondents fell into four categories:

- *Delivering the promise* (statements from focus group members included, for example, 'they do what they say', 'they meet expectations', 'they don't let you down', 'if you ask it just happens', 'it's delivered consistently', 'they are reliable')

- *Providing a personal touch* ('they treat me like an individual', 'they care about you', 'it feels personal', 'they give you the time', 'they know about me, I don't have to keep telling them')

- *Going the extra mile* ('they went out of their way', 'they anticipated my needs', 'they call you back, I didn't have to chase them', 'they fall over themselves to help')

- *Dealing well with problems and queries* ('when it goes wrong *they* sort it out', 'they were happy and willing to sort it out', 'they did not pass me around', 'they phoned me back', 'they know what to do if there is a problem').

The frequency of mention of items within each of these categories (see Figure 17.1) indicates their relative importance. The figures shown in Figure 17.1 demonstrate that the most important thing service operations need to do to be seen to be excellent is to deliver what they promise. The promise can be as simple as what an individual worker, whether a consultant, a housing officer, plumber or engineer, promises to do for their client, such as 'I will come on Thursday at 9.30 and fix your computer'. The promise could be as complex as the service concept – setting out not only the nature of the service to be provided but also what the experience will be like, the 'products' delivered, the emotions felt and benefits obtained. However, it is unusual for a 'promise' to contain so much detail, though it may be inferred.

Delivering the promise is not quite the same as meeting or even exceeding expectations (see Case Example 17.1). A clear promise may well help set expectations, but the point is, providing that promise is delivered (even if it is not quite what you want or expect) customers tend to be delighted. If you book a plumber to repair a leak and they turn up when they

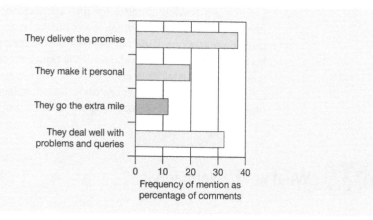

Figure 17.1 Relative importance to customers of service excellence categories

Source: Figures updated from Johnston, Robert (2004), 'Towards a Better Understanding of Service Excellence', *Managing Service Quality* 14 (2/3) 129–133

said they would, do the job, clear up and bill you the agreed amount, i.e. they are reliable and competent and do the job (functionality) (note these are hygiene factors) most customers would be delighted.

Dealing well with problems and queries (service recovery) is the second most important category (see Case Example 17.1). Most people accept that things occasionally go wrong and, as we said in Chapter 13, it's not usually the problem that causes dissatisfaction but the way the organisation deals with it. We also pointed out that dealing well with problems leads to delight (the recovery paradox). In such situations customers expect things to be put right (hygiene factors) and dealt with well (enhancing factors). Indeed it is no surprise that organisations that deal well with problems are world-class; they will have delighted customers, processes that are continually improving, staff who feel well supported and able to deal with the problems, and a culture that encourages staff and managers to find, and fix, problems before they occur.

Case Example 17.1   TNT Express, Thailand

TNT Express is the world's leading business-to-business express delivery company delivering 3.5 million parcels, documents and pieces of freight each week to over 200 countries. Alan Miu is the Country General Manager and runs TNT's operations in Thailand. There are 13 depots across the Kingdom of Thailand, employing 1,000 people and handling around 5,000 consignments a day.

Mr Miu uses a 'hub and spoke' road network to connect the depots in Thailand with his main hub near Bangkok airport. He has also expanded his highly successful international road network,

Source: © 2010 TNT N.V.

called the Asian Road Network, by running several 40-ton-capacity trucks to Malaysia and Singapore in the south and Laos, Vietnam, Cambodia and Southern China in the east. As Alan explained,

This gives us the opportunity to offer three levels of service to our customers, either very speedy international deliveries direct via Bangkok airport using commercial airlines, or I can fly the consignments to Singapore or Hong Kong to connect with our own TNT 747 aircraft from there to Europe, or I can also truck them to other Asian Road Network countries. This gives me several price options and also good contingencies in case of any problems.

TNT is a company committed to delivering excellent service and Alan explained what service excellence means to him.

Service excellence is very simple. It's about just two things. Firstly, don't over commit yourself. You have to understand exactly what it is you can do; then you tell the customer. For example, you say you can do A, B, C. If the customer says they want D and E as well, tell them you can't promise that. OK, if you have a competitor that can, or thinks they can, fine. Often the customer can work out how they can do D and E and you get the job because you are clear, honest and reliable. You must always know, and then say, what you can actually do and not what you can't. We have to set our customers' expectations and then deliver that promise.

Secondly when things go wrong, which thankfully is not too often, such as when there is a flight delay or cancellation, make sure the customer is aware of it. It's essential that we tell them right away when there is a problem – before they find out by themselves. In many cases, by providing the customer the advance information of the problems, they can deal with the consequences of the delay. Last year, for example, we lost a shipment for a very big and important client. I picked up the phone and personally rang their CEO. He asked me if I thought there was any chance we might be able to find it in the next 48 hours. I told him 'no', because that was the likelihood, but I also told him that we were not giving up and we will do our very best to locate it. However, I asked him if there was anything at all we could do to sort it out. Did he have a substitute or a duplicate that we could pick up? Or would he like me to call his contact to explain what has happened? If there was something I could do then to let me know and I would do it. As it happened, he had a substitute so I arranged for it to be picked up and shipped using our special service and it arrived not too late. I find this sort of approach reduces these highly charged and emotional situations and it also actually builds trust and strengthens the relationship between you. People usually accept that problems do happen. What is important is how you deal with them. If we can't deliver the service we promise then we must not be afraid or shy to face up to it, keep the customer informed, and sort it.

Providing the personal touch is an enhancing factor; it doesn't need to be there but when it does it tends to delight. Employees do not need to provide the personal touch, i.e. really care about the customer or take time to explain things etc. But it is appreciated and is a common feature of world-class organisations. It follows that if an organisation can deliver the promise and its staff are comfortable dealing well with problems and queries, they are more able and inclined to provide the personal touch.

Going the extra mile is also an enhancing factor. It is the icing on the service excellence cake (see Figure 17.2). The extra mile is about staff going out of their way to help customers, where nothing is too much trouble, and maybe providing a little something that was not expected. There are two important points here. Firstly, this point is about exceeding expectations, but it is not a necessary condition for excellent service. Second, the 'extra mile' is often only very small things, so organisations can gain enormous leverage by giving a tiny bit extra which their customers often describe as the extra mile.

In summary, service excellence is not about exceeding expectations. It is primarily about delivering what is promised and dealing well with any problems and queries that arise. A personal touch is very pleasing and the provision of a little extra is also not necessary but is much appreciated when it happens (see Figure 17.2).

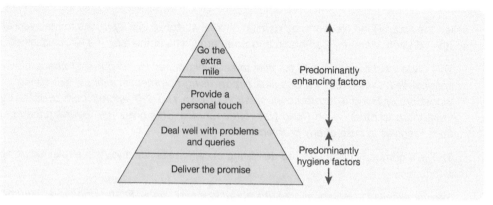

Figure 17.2 Service excellence

It is also important to realise that excellent service can be delivered by a full-service provider, like the Centara Grand Beach Resort Hotel (see Case Example 17.2), or indeed by a no-frills provider (whether an airline, hotel or public sector organisation). Simply put, customers can be delighted by organisations that just do what they say, and, when something does go wrong, it is sorted out well, not just for that customer but for future customers too.

Case Example 17.2   The Centara Grand Beach Resort Hotel, Samui

The Centara Grand Beach Resort Hotel is a de luxe five-star resort hotel on Koh Samui, a tropical island paradise in the Gulf of Thailand. The hotel is located on the palm-fringed Chaweng beach, the longest and most beautiful beach on the island. This 'new colonial' style hotel has 203 sea-facing rooms with private balconies, which overlook the tropical gardens and swimming pools. The hotel has excellent facilities, including swimming pools, tennis courts, a fitness centre, a spa and four restaurants.

David Good was the general manager of the hotel and he explained why guests choose this hotel.

There are three main reasons why our guests come here: location, space and service. Our location is ideal, a beautiful island with a superb all year round climate, but also we are located on Chaweng beach, which is the best beach with the best nightlife. Indeed I reckon we have probably the best piece of property on the best bit of the best beach on the whole island. Space, too, is important. Guests don't like to feel cramped. We have large gardens and common areas so that our guests are able to spread out. They really seem to appreciate that.

Finally there is our service, which is as good as you will find in the best hotels around the world. It is very traditionally Thai. Our staff are very good-natured and friendly and they provide genuine hospitality and warmth. This has a big impact on our guests. We receive many thank-you letters and guests often send us the photographs they have had taken with the staff, asking us to pass them on with thanks. We also have a large number of returning guests, running at around 5 per cent, and growing, which is amazing given the short length of time we have been open.

The hotel provides an outstanding level of service and David went on to explain what this means.

First, we have very few problems or complaints. Indeed, I can honestly say we have no big issues that result in negative feedback. We do, like any hotel, have some minor issues, just small irritations. Right now, for example, we occasionally have problems with water pressure. Some people don't have quite as clear a sea view as they might have hoped, with some trees and bushes in the garden slightly obscuring their view. Some say the curry was a little too spicy.

Second, high quality service is about consistency. Consistency is important. When our guests come back they very much expect the same high level of service that delighted them the first time and that continues to delight them. The issue for us is to provide that same level of service – the smiles, the greeting, the helpfulness – day in, day out.

Thirdly, it's about the little things, personal touches, such as taking time with guests; a few minutes here and there to acknowledge people, or spend a few minutes talking with them. The guest-relations staff, for example, sometimes send small gifts to our guests if it's their birthday or if they are a returning guest or if they're on honeymoon or it's their anniversary. We try and track all these things – little surprises here and there. It's these small things that really stick in people's minds.

17.3 How do organisations go about becoming and remaining world-class?

Many service organisations talk about world-class service; few seem to achieve it. Our work over many years has been with a variety of organisations, from those which are just setting out on their journey to try to become world-class service organisations to those which have made it. These organisations fall into three main types: aspiring, ongoing and embedding, each of which has quite different characteristics and sets of activities that they are usually involved in (see Figure 17.3).

Aspiring

These organisations understand the importance of delivering good service to their internal and external customers. They tend to have detailed, even sophisticated, means of assessing

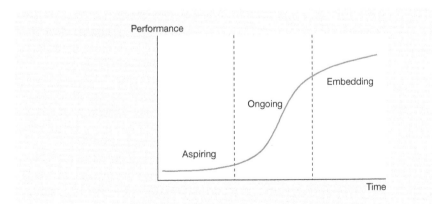

Figure 17.3 The journey to world-class

customer satisfaction through a mix of means, such as customer surveys, feedback sessions and focus groups and often the use of mystery shoppers (though mystery shoppers are often used to perform operational audits rather than gather genuine customer satisfaction data). Senior managers talk about 'excellent service' by which they often mean 'exceeding expectations' – a dangerous notion for many organisations, especially those that can't deliver it. They also use the words 'customer focus' and 'customer orientation' but when asked to define these terms, or indeed their service concept, they struggle. More importantly they rarely have actual plans (plans that are well-thought-out, long-term and consistent with a clear vision) in place to implement changes that they believe will deliver 'excellent service'. Likewise there are no success criteria specified – i.e. what it will look like when they get there and how they will know when they have got there – or even defined staging posts on the journey when partial successes can be celebrated.

Senior management teams spend some time, effort and money undertaking benchmarking tours to 'world-class' organisations to try to see if they can distil the secrets of their success. More often than not they come back empty-handed because they are not clear what they are looking for.

Ongoing

These organisations are well on track in their efforts to become world-class. Some have an agreed top-down plan or road map in place; for others the plan emerges. They have developed, often involving quite some effort, a clear view of what excellent service is. This is usually defined in terms of the promise (what they say they will do to/for their customers), service recovery (what they do on the occasions it goes wrong and, importantly, how they learn from it) and the personal touch (the way they interact with customers; how it feels, including an understanding of the emotions they are trying to create). A senior-level steering group is often appointed to oversee the journey and report back. The group creates a set of work streams covering a range of cross-cutting 'management issues' such as leadership, rewards and recognition, communication, process improvement, etc. Colourful PowerPoint presentations capture and communicate (often to bewildered staff) matrix-style boxes with arrows with no shortage of 'management-speak'.

These work streams are then allocated to senior staff to oversee and implement. The number of work streams usually turns out to be over ambitious and they are reduced to four or five after a year or so. Usually there are agreed milestones and success criteria for each work stream.

The tricky part becomes how to implement these good sounding, motherhood and apple pie, initiatives. The real danger at this point is that they are seen as initiatives that staff can ignore because there will surely be a new and different initiative along in a few months time (sometimes referred to as the BOHICA approach – Bend Over Here It Comes Again).

The work streams usually include one called customer focus, or something similar, but there is usually a great deal of debate as to what goes into this. It may take a few years before management realise that it is acceptable for this to be empty. Most people come to work to do a good job; they want to provide good service to internal and external customers. However, a good job does not always get done. This is not usually the fault of the employees, especially front-line employees since most of them actually want to do a good job. The reason less than excellent service is delivered is because many things get in their way or make it difficult for them to deliver good or even great service; things such as poor systems, difficult or inappropriate processes, poor technology, old working practices, inept management, inappropriate reward systems, inappropriate performance measures etc.[4]

Providing the other work streams start addressing these barriers to excellent service, service will, de facto, improve. Indeed the best way of improving service is not to improve service but to remove the barriers that are preventing great service happening. So, providing the work streams start to address and deal with poor processes (through lean approaches or removing inappropriate metrics, for example), service will improve.

To support the work streams appropriate tool-based training is needed for those charged with overcoming some of the barriers to service. A series of master classes is also often used for session managers to help change their mindsets to better understand what service excellence is and how it can be improved. (One of the biggest barriers to improvement in our research was management mindset.)

At this stage these organisations often get involved in quality award schemes. These help both in identifying some of the issues that need to be dealt with but also in providing external recognition of their success in dealing with them.

Embedding

These organisations have developed, often over a considerable period of time, a reputation for excellent service. They can usually be spotted because they are far from complacent – they rarely accept they are world-class. They recognise that being good means customers have higher than normal expectations and many people are more than willing to try to pull them down. They have a very clear vision to be the best and often renew the detail of their vision every few years. Their definition of what they do is 'outside-in' – it is about what the customer gets from them, often focusing on the customer's experience and the emotions the organisation wishes to evoke, such as 'customers will welcome and appreciate the experience we provide' – unlike 'inside-out' descriptions such as 'we deliver on time'.

The management style is far from paternalistic; it is strong with a great eye for the detail when necessary, but also open and available: not just physically open and 'available' through open-plan offices or walking around, but mentally open through personal engagement with staff and customers with a genuine desire to learn and improve what they do. Internal relationships could be classed, in transactional analysis terms, as adult to adult. The culture, often typified by the words 'no blame', supports and encourages a learning organisation, but frequent mistakes are not tolerated. Issues are shared openly and staff encouraged to learn from the mistakes of others. Service recovery is exceedingly well done. Importantly, service recovery is not defined narrowly as making things better for the customers; it is focused on improving things for the future. Unlike many organisations which spend a deal of time analysing feedback, creating reports and presentations while little actually changes, world-class organisations analyse both positive and negative feedback, so they know what to do more of as well as what to stop doing. This information is used to drive improvements through the organisation. These are not easy organisations to work for; pressure (coupled with passion) is constant.

To maintain their world-class position there are two fundamental approaches that keep them at the top while others chase them. The first is a culture of continuous improvement. There is a structure within the organisation that trains and encourages everyone, whatever their job or position, to continuously challenge what happens and improve what they do. The second is in-built innovation. While very few service organisations have R&D departments like manufacturing companies, world-class service organisations usually do. They take innovation very seriously and have both 'hard' structural approaches (R&D departments) and 'soft' approaches where innovation is built into people's jobs.[5] Time is available and (often) innovative processes are in place to encourage innovation. These two, in turn, create a culture of involvement and ownership.

17.3.1 Characteristics of world-class service organisations

World-class service organisations tend to have impressive business results, both financial and non-financial. The non-financial measures include employee satisfaction, customer satisfaction and market share. Research has shown that excellent for-profit organisations deliver greater profits and larger returns on assets and on equity, with a greater net margin than organisations that deliver poor service.[6] World-class organisations are generally recognised by customers, industry organisations and business commentators. They are often quoted as benchmark organisations, their approaches are imitated by others, and they accumulate a range of accolades and service and quality awards.

There seem to be four main drivers of success: culture and leadership, knowing and delivering the service concept, supportive and committed staff, and excellent systems and processes. Case Example 17.3 describes how Singapore Airlines illustrates many of these world-class characteristics.

Case Example 17.3 Singapore Airlines (SIA)

Singapore Airlines (SIA) is recognised as one of the world's leading carriers. With one of the most modern fleets in the industry, its route network spans 61 cities in 34 countries. Singapore Airlines was the pioneer of in-flight services, including free drinks and complimentary headsets, in-flight telephones and interactive entertainment systems. Today it is still setting industry standards. It has the most advanced in-flight entertainment system, providing a wide range of audio and video programmes 'on demand', enabling passengers to pause, fast-forward and rewind any programme at their convenience. It was the first airline to provide an in-flight email service, and email check-in and text-message flight alerts notifying customers of plane arrivals and delays. For first and business class passengers who want to choose their own menus there is a 'book the cook' service, and on some long-haul routes a cleverly designed flat bed that takes up little more room than a conventional seat. SIA is also, consistently, one of the most profitable airlines in the world.

Source: Singapore Airlines: 002

SIA's mission statement is 'A global company dedicated to providing air transportation services of the highest quality and to earning good returns for shareholders'. This is underpinned by six core values: pursuit of excellence, safety, customer first, concern for staff, integrity and teamwork.

Having an international reputation for service excellence makes delivering excellent service a continuous challenge. Yap Kim Wah, SIA's senior vice president responsible for product and service, explained:

We have a high reputation for service and that means that when someone flies with us they come with high expectations. But still we want them to come away saying 'Wow! That was something out of the ordinary'.

We need to give our customers a great experience and good value. It is important to realise that they are not just comparing SIA with other airlines. They are comparing us against many industries, and on many factors. The new ball game for SIA is not just to be the best of the best in the airline industry but to work at being the best service company.

Dr Goh Ban Eng is the senior manager responsible for cabin crew training. She explained:

Excellent service is really attentive and very personalised service with great attention to the little details. We want the passenger to feel that they don't have to ask for anything. We want to anticipate their needs and at the same time be very warm and caring. And if anything should go wrong they know they will be well taken care of. There is a mutual trust and respect between customers and our staff.

SIA has very elaborate feedback mechanisms to help its staff not only listen to customers but also understand them better. Information is collected from a random sample of customers on about 10 per cent of SIA's flights. SIA also listens to its staff. Yap Kim Wah added:

Our crew are very important people because they are very intimately in contact with our customers. So for every flight that we operate we listen sincerely to our crew. They know that the management takes their feedback very seriously. If they gave us feedback and we didn't do anything about it, they would be disheartened.

Training is central to SIA's goal of continuous improvement. SIA's chief executive officer, Chew Choon Seng, stated,

Training is a necessity, not an option. It is not to be dispensed with when times are bad. Training is for every-body. It embraces everyone from the office assistant and baggage handler to the chief executive officer.

SIA's recent service excellence initiative, called transforming customer service (TCS), involves staff in five key operational areas – cabin crew, engineering, ground services, flight operations and sales support. The programme is about building team spirit among staff in key operational areas to make the whole journey as pleasant and seamless as possible for passengers.

Although SIA is totally focused on the customer and providing continually improving service, managers are well aware of the need for profit. Yap Kim Wah explained how they meet these dual yet potentially con-flicting objectives:

First, it's about what we call 'ownership'. We are very cost conscious; it is drilled into us from the day we start working for SIA that if we don't make money, we'll be closed down. Singapore doesn't need a national airline. Second, the company has made a very important visionary statement that says 'We don't want to be the largest company. We want to be the most profitable.' That's very powerful. And third, we have a rewards system that pays bonuses according to the profitability of the company. It's the same for all of us, the same formula from the top to the bottom. As a result there is a lot of informal pressure from everybody. Everyone is quite open and they will challenge many decisions and actions.

SIA is a visionary company and its senior managers talk about 'globalness' and strategy. However, according to Yap Kim Wah,

You would be surprised that many of our senior people, as well as our departmental heads and managers, go down to detail like a hawk. And, when there is a need, we will hover and if necessary swoop. It can be very painful for the department involved, but the reality is that we are in a very competitive environment and we cannot afford to be soft.

Despite its success, managers at SIA know they cannot afford to be complacent. Every opportunity is taken to develop their staff and systems, to deliver great service – and to reinvent the service by anticipating the potential needs of customers and by benchmarking SIA both inside and outside the industry.

Source: This illustration is based on a case study written by Robert Johnston, Warwick Business School and Jochen Wirtz, National University of Singapore, 2004 and updated 2010. The authors would like to thank the interviewees for their participation in this project and also Jasmine Ow, National University of Singapore, for her valuable assistance.

Culture and leadership

The key to great service is 'genuine service leadership at all levels in an organisation'.[7] Clear and purposeful leadership right from the top of the organisation is needed to develop and sustain a world-class organisation. A willingness to listen encourages communication up and down the organisation. Good leadership is also characterised by a belief in, and investment in, staff, processes, training and the delivery of outstanding service. In world-class service organi-sations senior management is characterised by a lack of complacency; never being satisfied with the status quo and recognising that they, and the organisation, could always do better.

World-class organisations also have a clear service vision. Vision is more than simply hav-ing clarity about where the organisation is going; it is also an ability to communicate enthu-siastically to others. Vision created by great leaders provides employees with something to believe in and something that challenges them; it provides the emotional energy required to deliver outstanding service and it generates commitment to the provision of service.

World-class organisations have clear plans in place that set out how they will achieve their goals and their vision. The vision is not pie-in-the-sky but something concrete that employees feel is both achievable and desirable. The strategy communicates how this will be achieved and defines the employees' part in the activity. An essential attribute of a well-developed strategy is that it has been formulated with ownership and buy-in at all levels in the organisation.

Great service in world-class organisations is delivered by employees who do not need to be defensive in their dealings with customers. A positive attitude is generated by an organisational culture that is consistent with the declared competitive strategy, and that values the contributions of all members. A supportive culture is self-renewing, not looking back to the 'good old days' but encouraging the development of new ways of thinking and acting.

Senior managers in world-class service organisations never lose sight of the 'big picture', keeping strategy, concept and vision at the forefront, while at the same time, however, paying close attention to the detail. David Good, the general manager at the Centara Grand Beach Resort Hotel, said, 'It's about the little things, personal touches, such as taking time with guests; a few minutes here and there to acknowledge people, or spend a few minutes talking with them'. Getting the detail right makes outstanding service providers stand head and shoulders above the rest. It is through the detail that the customer encounters excellence.

Knowing and delivering the service concept

'Excellent service companies define their business in strikingly clear terms.'[8] In world-class organisations the service concept is well defined, communicated and well understood by employees and customers. This brand image is well known in the marketplace and the organisation is known to be a market leader. Other organisations may try to emulate and reproduce the concept but are continually outrun by the organisation that invests in continuous process/service development.

In order to have a well-defined service concept (and provide an appropriate promise to the customer), world-class organisations take great efforts to listen to their customers. They use many methods of listening and take all comments very seriously. Customers' views are used to drive developments, although the need to be financially and commercially viable is never forgotten. The nirvana that world-class service companies seem to have found is in meeting, without compromise, both customer needs and their own criteria for financial success. For world-class service organisations, these two requirements, so often at odds, seem to go hand-in-hand.

Delivering the service concept (and their promises) is about reliability and consistency, a point made by David Good (Case Example 17.2). World-class service organisations do not just deliver outstanding service – they do it routinely and consistently. World-class service providers may surprise their customers with their level of service, their willingness to deal with an issue, their ability to recover the customer after a problem and the speed of their service. World-class service organisations, however, go beyond making the customers say 'wow' about the service, by getting customers to say 'wow' the next time because it was like that again. 'Great service companies . . . couple the basics of service with the art of surprise.'[9]

Customers of world-class service organisations find that not only are they listened to, but the organisation is happy and able to respond to reasonable requests for service. Customers are not greeted with a mechanistic response such as 'I'm sorry, we don't do that', but staff are encouraged to try, within reasonable limits, to satisfy customers. A cliché in hotel receptions is the standard response 'No problem.' For world-class service organisations, this is reality. Another test of a world-class service organisation is to ask yourself, after making a request, 'Do I feel that I have been heard and that the organisation will deal with my request, or do I feel that my request has disappeared into a black hole?'

Supportive and committed staff

Excellent service is delivered either directly or indirectly by employees. World-class service organisations use approaches such as empowerment or self-directed work teams appropriately rather than implement these ideas because they have seen them work elsewhere. Staff are committed to the organisation and to the service concept because they are involved in the process of service development – they are encouraged to own the service processes, to look for ways of improving them, and they are motivated by the right mix of recognition and reward.

World-class service organisations are concerned with the longer-term relationships between customer and provider and try to find ways to deliver the appropriate service to the customer. In many organisations policies, systems and processes exist that often make it difficult to do sensible things. World-class organisations have effective means of both circumventing them (through empowered people) and of allowing employees to challenge and change inappropriate and unhelpful policies, systems and processes.

Excellent systems and processes

World-class organisations have well-designed systems and processes, designed from the outside in. Those processes might include innovation process, recovery systems, reward systems or performance management systems.

Good performance management is an important driver of world-class success. Key drivers are measured, service is carefully quantified and targets set in key areas of the business. Managers understand the links between service and financial results – they can make the business case for service (we want to develop this important point in the next section). Results, both financial and operational, are shared throughout the business. Targets are based not only on what was achieved in the past but also on the activities of competitors and other excellent organisations, perhaps not even in the same field. World-class organisations have a good understanding of the rest of the industry and regularly, and systematically, check out their competitors' services, not just for the sake of comparison but to promote learning and development and growth. Furthermore, world-class organisations celebrate excellence and achievement. Measuring performance and knowing what is excellent is only one step – recognising the people who have achieved excellence and then regarding it through a mixture of financial and non-financial ways validates those achievements, motivates others and sustains excellence.

World-class organisations also continually develop their service. This is not just redesign but requires more fundamental questioning that leads to 'reinvention' of their services. This vigorous search for distinctive service can only be undertaken in an organisation that is confident in its ability to ask and deal with difficult questions. World-class service organisations firmly reject 'me-too' service. Any changes they make are usually based on detailed research, but they also take risks and sometimes 'take a flyer' when it feels right. They are equally willing to drop an idea, despite the investment cost, if an innovation is not seen to be working. They also see service delivery boundaries as flexible and carefully manage overlaps with other service providers.

A total approach to service excellence

There are two important points that need raising now with regard to creating and sustaining world-class status. First, world-class organisations don't just do some of the things above, they do all of them. World-class is about having and taking a total approach to service. If the right culture is not in place, the organisation will be characterised by resistance. If the concept is not clear or not delivered there will be confusion. If the staff are not on board there will be anxiety and if the systems and processes are not right there will be frustration (see Figure 17.4).

Secondly, maintaining world-class status need not be expensive. World-class organisations simply spend their time improving things, but by just a little bit, and in every area. They are a constantly moving target very difficult for others to hit, but, if the culture and systems for continuous improvement are in place it's relatively easy to sustain.

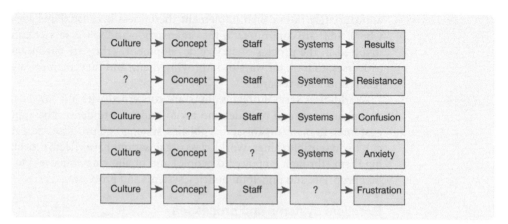

Figure 17.4 The total approach to excellent service

How can managers make the business case for service?

It is important that service operations managers understand the impact of any changes they make to their operation. Although they can usually calculate or estimate the costs associated with any particular change or initiative, they may be much less certain of their impact on the organisation's wider business performance, for example the likely impact on customer satisfaction, retention, revenues, market share and profit.

Many management decisions are simply acts of faith, based upon a well-intentioned belief that actions and decisions will be to the benefit of the business. We believe that most managers have little evidence to support their actions. In this section we want to explore the relationships between operations actions and business performance, in order to help managers create better business cases for investing in improving their operations and providing better service. Understanding these relationships and being able to make the business case for service is a key characteristic of world-class service organisations.

17.4.1 Understanding the relationships between operational decisions and business performance

In most organisations the cause–effect relationships between operational decisions and business performance are extremely complex, involving many factors with inherent lags and delays in their relationships. This complexity is enough to put off many managers, who retrench into 'seat-of-the-pants' management. World-class organisations have moved beyond intuition-based management and are working at understanding the links between their operational drivers and business results. For example if an operations manager knows (and can demonstrate) that an additional spend of £Xm on staff training, or on improving their recovery systems, will yield a £Ym increase in profit, or reduce costs by £Zm, they have a better chance of getting the agreement of the board, and in particular the financial director.

There are three key stages in understanding the relationships between operational decisions and business or financial performance: creating a performance network (or business model) linking drivers to results (such as purpose or requirements), identifying the measures, existing or required, for each of the elements in the network, and exploring the linkages.

Create a performance network (a business model)

The first step is to identify the key operational and business drivers, such as culture, resources or recovery systems, and the organisational results, such as customer satisfaction or profit.

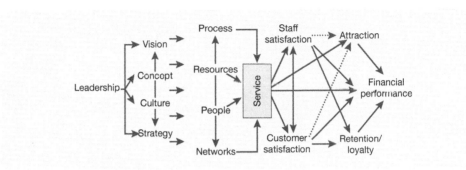

Figure 17.5 A service performance network

Drawing a service performance network (or business model) depicts the likely cause–effect relationships between them, for example that good leadership influences the right culture, or that customer satisfaction improves customer retention and customer retention influences financial performance (see Figure 17.5). These diagrams are often referred to as service profit chains or service value chains.[10] It is unlikely that organisations will be able to capture all the variables in their business model, or indeed all the relationships between them. The main thing is to capture the key ones. Over time the network can be developed and expanded to provide a more compete model of how the business works. These models are equally suitable to not-for-profit organisations – for example, the results may be expressed in terms of adherence to budget and meeting objectives, rather than profit. Figure 17.5 provides an example of a performance network.

Identify the measures

The next step is to identify the measures, existing or required, for each of the variables in the network. For many larger organisations the problem will not be creating the measures but finding the data within the organisation. What we often find is that the variables are measured but the data is kept in different departments. Marketing may have the data on customer satisfaction, HR the staff retention data and Finance the revenue data. In order to start to understand the relationship and how the model works, that data needs to be drawn together. We would recommend that considerable time be put into the planning stages of this because the longitudinal strength of the network created can be undermined by frequently changing the collection instruments. An engineering consultancy company created their business model and found they had plenty of measures available for each of the variables in their model, shown in Figure 17.6.

Explore the linkages

Simple graphical representations of the relationships between each pair of variables may be enough to permit a basic understanding of the relationships between the linkages in the model. Other, more complex methods, such as regression analysis, structural equation modelling and data envelopment analysis, can be employed.[11]

The critical point is that data must be collected over time and the relationships explored at intervals because relationships may not be linear. It may be important to identify optimum points in the relationships between variables so that effort can be moved from one driver, whose power is waning, to one that might have an increasing effect.

Case Example 17.4 shows how one organisation, BUPA, has gone about trying to understand the relationships between some of its drivers and results.

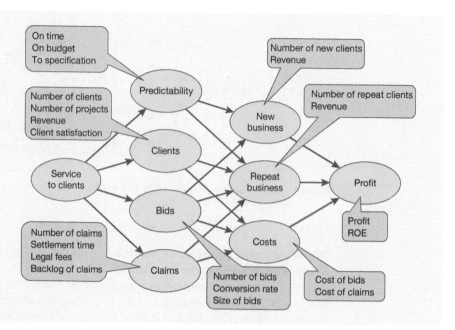

Figure 17.6 A service performance network with measures

Case Example 17.4 | BUPA

BUPA is an international healthcare company with over 10 million customers in 200 countries. BUPA is best known for its private medical insurance. It also runs private hospitals, health screening centres and care homes, and provides travel insurance, health assessments, occupational health and childcare. It has offices in Hong Kong, Ireland, Saudi Arabia, Spain, Thailand and the UK. As a provident association, BUPA has no shareholders to pay. This means that any money it makes is invested back into the business.

Catrin Weston was a senior manager in the Organisation Development Department at BUPA. She has worked closely with

Source: Advertising Archives

Dr Nicholas Georgiades of NGA consultants in attempting to validate aspects of the service value cycle which is based upon the Harvard Business School service profit chain. She describes what happens:

> What we've done so far is to establish significant correlations between the results we get from our annual staff survey, our customer surveys and the profit for each of our 36 hospitals in the UK. We have been tracking the staff satisfaction score, the customer loyalty indicator and the profit for each hospital. We have calculated these correlations twice now and we will be repeating it again this autumn.
>
> Our staff opinion survey, the service organisation profile (SOP), was developed by Dr Georgiades. His company run this for us each year, which is quite a big job because around 12,000 employees and 1,000 managers are currently involved in the survey. The SOP is an empirically developed staff opinion survey based upon the Burke Litwin model of organisation performance. The SOP provides us with a valuable way of mapping the performance of business units, departments and individual managers in the organisation. It

is easy to understand and communicate and not only provides a measure of current performance but also helps managers put together action plans to work on critical issues in their work groups. The questionnaire covers ten key factors: leadership, customer service mission, adaptive culture, management practices, group climate, group tension, job satisfaction, role overload, role ambiguity and career development.

Each year we ask our staff to complete the questionnaire confidentially. NGA undertakes the analysis at an aggregate and individual manager level, so every manager gets their own feedback about how their team sees them as a manager. It also provides information about staff perceptions about BUPA as a whole – its leadership, the organisation's commitment to customer service and its prevailing culture.

When the managers receive their feedback they are charged with sitting down with their team to have an open discussion to explore the key issues. They then agree an action plan to deal with these issues. These plans are then reviewed to check progress at subsequent meetings. Some managers are good at this, others less so!

Some of the issues can't be dealt with at team level because they relate to organisation-level concerns, so every manager sends me a copy of their action plan and I go through them to identify what needs to be done at an organisational level. As a result you get a good idea what influences staff opinions.

Dr Georgiades and I have been working to test the validity of the service value cycle in the 36 BUPA hospitals. The model suggests that employee motivation, loyalty and commitment drive customer loyalty and satisfaction and that in turn customer loyalty and satisfaction drive profitability.

We took the total score on the SOP (averaged for each hospital) as the measure of motivation, loyalty and commitment, and related that score to each hospital's customer loyalty score (taken from consumer opinion surveys) and the profitability measured against target. The evidence was sufficiently strong to suggest that pursuing the goal of improving staff satisfaction, loyalty and commitment was not just a liberal 'good employer – nice thing to do' but had real, tangible results for our customers and for BUPA's profitability.

We are at an early stage in our research at the moment but it is very exciting and has already provided us with some invaluable information.

17.5   A final word

At the end of the day, despite the complexity of the task and the many challenges they face, service operations managers have to do their best to make things work smoothly and efficiently, provide good service to their customers and a great experience for staff, and also meet their organisation's business objectives. Providing excellent service is even more difficult and requires good operational practices to be embedded in the organisation together with a supporting culture and enabling strategy. We hope this chapter has managed to pull together much of the content of the book and will encourage you to build on what you have now and to understand what can be done, and importantly, how it can be done, to make a difference. Enjoy.

17.6   Summary

What is excellent service?

- Excellent service is the provision of a level of operational service quality that results in delight (perceived service quality).
- Service excellence is not about exceeding expectations. It is primarily about delivering what is promised and dealing well with any problems and queries that arise. A personal touch and the provision of a little extra are not necessary but are appreciated.

How do organisations go about becoming and remaining world-class?

- 'Aspiring' organisations measure customer satisfaction, talk about customer focus and exceeding expectations and tend not to have well-thought-out plans for change.
- 'Ongoing' organisations sometimes have a road map in place. They understand what service excellence is and have several work streams in place to deal with some of the barriers to providing excellent service. They employ tool-based training and may be involved in quality award schemes.
- 'Embedding' organisations have a clear vision and an outside-in view of service. The management style is strong, visible and open with a 'no-blame' learning culture. Service recovery is done well and there is a culture of continuous improvement and service innovation.
- There are four main drivers of success: culture and leadership, knowing and delivering the service concept, supportive and committed staff, and excellent systems and processes.
- World-class service organisations tend to have impressive business results, both financial and non-financial.

How can managers make the business case for service?

- A 'business case' enables managers to know and explain the impact of their operations decisions on key results, such as customer satisfaction, retention, costs, revenues, market share and profit, in order to secure investment in the service operation and to provide better service.
- Understanding these relationships is a key characteristic of world-class service organisations.
- The three key stages in understanding the relationships between operational decisions and business or financial performance are: creating a performance network (or business model) linking drivers to results, identifying the measures, existing or required, for each of the elements in the network, and exploring the linkages.

17.7 Discussion questions

1 List a few organisations that deliver world-class service. What is it they do particularly well?
2 Talk to someone whose organisation delivers excellent service. What can you learn from them?
3 How would you make the business case to justify investing more money into your university/college programme?

17.8 Questions for managers

1 How does your organisation stack up against the characteristics of world-class organisations and operations? Where are the opportunities to improve what you do?
2 Are you 'aspiring', 'ongoing' or 'embedding'? What do you have to do to make a change for the better?
3 Sketch out your own performance network incorporating the key drivers and results (outcomes/requirements). List the measures you have for each of the variables. How well do you understand the linkages in the model? What have you learned from doing this?

Case Exercise   Superstore Plc

Rhian Silvestro, Warwick Business School and Stuart Cross, Morgan Cross Consulting

The UK supermarket industry is dominated by four leading chains with all others competing in the second tier. The four main players have all diversified into the non-food sector. While there is price-based competition between the key players, the emphasis has shifted towards competition based on customer loyalty and quality.

Superstore is one of the big four supermarket chains in the UK and operates a chain of hundreds of stores which retail in excess of 40,000 product lines, including food products and non-food items like music, personal care products, clothing and pharmaceutical products. It has positioned itself as a family store offering good value, and, like many of the large superstores, the company has introduced loyalty card technology and a self-scanning service with a view to improving customer loyalty.

In a recent Annual Report the company's chief executive stated that customer satisfaction and loyalty were the real drivers of the company's profit and growth, and that these were influenced by how its people felt about their work, their rewards and their manager. This was also a central theme in the company's management training programme.

To test out this contention Julie Carroll, a senior officer in the personnel department, collected together some existing performance data. The data was a mixture of internal measures, based on the performance of fifteen stores, and a survey of customer and employee perceptions based on six stores. Table 17.1 shows the main areas measured, the measures used, and where appropriate an explanation as to what they mean.

Table 17.1 Performance measures

Area	Performance measures	Explanation
Financial performance	Profit margin	Store profit margin
Productivity	Sales per square metre	
Customer loyalty	*Share of grocery budget*	Customers' estimate of the percentage of grocery budget spent at the store
	Basket size	Average customer spend per visit per store
	Customer referral	Customers' willingness to recommend the store as a place to shop
Customer satisfaction	*Customer satisfaction*	Overall level of customer satisfaction with the store
Service value	*Service value*	Customer perceptions of value of the service delivered by the store
Output quality	Mystery shopper	Aggregate service quality score assigned to the store by mystery shopper
Employee loyalty	*Employee referral*	Employees' willingness to recommend the store as a place of work
	Employee turnover	
	Employee absence	
Employee satisfaction	*Employee satisfaction*	Overall level of staff satisfaction
Service capability	*Ability to affect the customer experience*	Employees' perceptions of their ability to impact on the customer experience
Internal service quality	Operating ratio	Ratio of actual to planned working hours
	Style of supervision	Employee satisfaction with the style of supervision

Note: *Italics* indicate measures based on customer and employee surveys.

Table 17.2 Correlation coefficients between the various data sets

Category	Measure	Sales per sq metre	Share of grocery budget	Basket size	Customer referral	Customer satisfaction	Service value	Mystery shopper	Employee referral	Employee turnover	Employee absence	Employee satisfaction	Ability to affect customer experience	Operating ratio	Style of supervision
Financial performance	Profit margin	0.77	0.91	0.88	0.86	0.70	0.88	0.44	-0.25	0.18	-0.35	-0.87	-0.65	-0.75	-0.63
	Sales per sq metre		0.95	0.60	0.91	0.59	0.92	0.10	0.03	-0.10	-0.04	-0.61	-0.33	-0.65	-0.36
Customer loyalty	Share of grocery budget			0.91	0.99	0.78	0.98	0.71	-0.24	0.02	-0.51	-0.69	-0.46	-0.96	-0.33
	Basket size				0.89	0.72	0.94	0.65	0.05	0.30	-0.58	-0.60	-0.28	-0.80	-0.34
	Customer referral					0.82	0.98	0.68	-0.22	0.06	-0.57	-0.62	-0.39	-0.93	-0.18
Customer satisfaction	Customer satisfaction						0.86	0.66	-0.53	-0.35	0.24	-0.83	-0.47	-0.86	-0.19
Service value	Service value							0.81	-0.21	-0.09	-0.60	-0.64	-0.38	-0.97	-0.26
Output quality	Mystery shopper								0.12	0.07	-0.44	-0.45	-0.12	-0.29	-0.32
Employee loyalty	Employee referral									0.34	-0.44	0.61	0.80	0.36	0.42
	Employee turnover										-0.36	0.10	0.51	-0.27	0.73
	Employee absence											0.13	-0.20	0.25	-0.22
Employee satisfaction	Employee satisfaction												0.93	0.76	0.82
Service capability	Ability to affect customer experience													0.55	0.81
Internal service quality	Operating ratio														0.46

Julie added:

One particular measure calls for some explanation: our store operating ratio is the ratio of actual to planned working hours. This is considered to be a good indicator of the quality of working life at a store because, as the ratio of actual to planned working hours increases, the workplace becomes more stressful and therefore the quality of working life, what we refer to as internal service quality, diminishes.

Julie calculated Pearson's correlation coefficients between the various data sets and her results are shown in Table 17.2. The correlations entered in bold denote significance at the 95% level or higher. (The minimum value of the correlation coefficient necessary for 95% confidence was 0.51 when the sample size was 15 stores and 0.81 where the sample size was 6 stores.)

Julie was not sure what to do next.

Questions

1   What conclusions could Julie draw from the data?

2   What are the issues and implications for the store?

Suggested further reading

Bates, Ken, Hilary Bates and Robert Johnston (2003), 'Linking Service to Profit: The Business Case for Service excellence', *International Journal of Service Industry Management* 14 (2) 173–183

Dixon, Matthew, Karen Freeman and Nicholas Toman (2010), 'Stop Trying to Delight Your Customers', *Harvard Business Review* (July/August) 2–7

Heracleous, Loizos and Robert Johnston (2009), 'Can Business Learn from the Public Sector?', *European Business Review* 4 (4) 373–379

Heracleous, Loizos, Jochen Wirtz and Robert Johnston (2004), 'Cost Effective Service Excellence – Lessons from Singapore Airlines', *Business Strategy Review* 15 (1) 33–38

Heracleous, Loizos, Jochen Wirtz and Robert Johnston (2005), 'Kung-Fu Service Development at Singapore Airlines', *Business Strategy Review* (Winter) 26–31

Heskett, James L., W. Earl Sasser and Joe Wheeler (2008), *Ownership Quotient: Putting the Service Profit Chain to Work for Unbeatable Competitive Advantage*, Harvard Business School Press

Johnston, Robert and Xiangyu Kong (2011), 'The Customer Experience: A Road Map for Improvement', *Managing Service Quality* 21 (1) 5–24

Milligan, Andy and Shaun Smith (eds) (2002), *Uncommon Practice*, FT Prentice Hall, Harlow

Pritchard, Michael and Rhian Silvestro (2005), 'Applying the Service Profit Chain to Analyse Retail Performance: The Case of the Managerial Strait-jacket?', *International Journal of Service Industry Management* 16 (4) 337–356

Reichheld, Frederick F. (2006), 'The Microeconomics of Customer Relationships', *MIT Sloan Management Review* 47 (2) 73–78

Silvestro, Rhian and Stuart Cross (2000), 'Applying the Service Profit Chain in a Retail Environment: Challenging the "Satisfaction Mirror"', *International Journal of Service Industry Management* 11 (3) 244–268

Wirtz, Jochen and Robert Johnston (2003), 'Singapore Airlines: What It Takes to Sustain Service Excellence – A Senior Management Perspective', *Managing Service Quality* 13 (1) 10–19

Wirtz, Jochen, Loizos Heracleous and Nitin Pamgarkar (2008), 'Managing Human Resources for Service Excellence', *Managing Service Quality* 18 (1) 4–19

Useful web links

For more information on the service profit chain and service value chain visit:
http://www.12manage.com/methods_heskett_value_profit_chain.html

For an explanation of the EFQM's excellence model and how to go about developing high performing organisations:
http://www.efqm.org/

A wealth of resources on world-class service at:
www.worldclassservice.co.uk—resources

A story of service excellence, and the importance of staff engagement, by Sarah Cunnane writing in *Times Higher Education*:
www.timeshighereducation.co.uk—story.asp

Notes

1 See for example Heracleous, Loizos, Jochen Wirtz and Nitin Pangarkar (2006), *Flying High in a Competitive Industry: Cost Effective Service Excellence at Singapore Airlines*, McGraw-Hill, Singapore

2 Johnston, Robert (2004), 'Towards a Better Understanding of Service Excellence', *Managing Service Quality* 14 (2/3) 129–133

3 Johnston, Robert (2001), *Service Excellence = Reputation = Profit: Developing and Sustaining a Reputation for Service Excellence*, Institute of Customer Service, Colchester

4 Johnston, Robert (2008), 'Internal Service – Barriers, Flows and Assessment', *International Journal of Service Industry Management* 19 (2) 210–231

5 Heracleous, Loizos, Jochen Wirtz and Robert Johnston (2005), 'Kung-Fu Service Development at Singapore Airlines', *Business Strategy Review* (Winter) 26–31

6 Johnston, Robert (2001) *Service Excellence = Reputation = Profit: Developing and Sustaining a Reputation for Service Excellence*, Institute of Customer Service, Colchester

7 Berry, Leonard L. (1995) *On Great Service: A Framework for Action*, Free Press, New York, p. 7

8 Berry, Leonard L. (1995) *On Great Service: A Framework for Action*, Free Press, New York, p. 238

9 Berry, Leonard L. (1995) *On Great Service: A Framework for Action*, Free Press, New York, p. 78

10 Heskett, James L., W. Earl Sasser and Leonard A. Schlesinger (1997), *The Service Profit Chain*, Free Press, New York; Heskett, James L., W. Earl Sasser and Leonard A. Schlesinger (2003), *The Value Profit Chain*, Free Press, New York

11 See, for example, Hoyle, Rick H. (ed.) (1995), *Structural Equation Modeling*, Sage, Thousand Oaks, California; Thanassoulis, Emmanuel (2001), *Introduction to the Theory and Application of Data Envelopment Analysis*, Kluwer Academic Publishers, Massachusetts

Index